IN PLAIN SIGHT

IN PLAIN SIGHT

SEXUAL VIOLENCE IN ARMED CONFLICT

Editors

GABY ZIPFEL
REGINA MÜHLHÄUSER
KIRSTEN CAMPBELL

zubaan

ZUBAAN
128 B Shahpur Jat, 1st floor
NEW DELHI 110 049
EMAIL: contact@zubaanbooks.com
WEBSITE: www.zubaanbooks.com

First published by Zubaan Publishers Pvt. Ltd 2019

10 9 8 7 6 5 4 3 2 1

ISBN 978 9385932 81 6

Zubaan is an independent feminist publishing house based in New Delhi with
a strong academic and general list. It was set up as an imprint of India's first
feminist publishing house, Kali for Women, and carries forward Kali's tradition
of publishing world quality books to high editorial and production standards.
Zubaan means tongue, voice, language, speech in Hindustani. Zubaan publishes
in the areas of the humanities, social sciences, as well as in fiction, general
non-fiction, and books for children and young adults under its Young Zubaan
imprint.

Typeset in Baskerville by Jojy Philip, New Delhi 110 015
Printed and bound at Thomson Press, Faridabad, India

Contents

Acknowledgments

This book came out of longstanding cooperation in the International Research Group 'Sexual Violence in Armed Conflict' (SVAC; www.warandgender.net). The members engage in ways of thinking together, in sharing reflections and ideas that are characterised by an openness, trust and willingness to learn from each other that has changed our way of thinking about the subject under investigation.

In reference to the 40th anniversary of the publication of Susan Brownmiller's landmark book on *Against Our Will: Men, Women, and Rape*, SVAC organized a conference '*Against Our Will*—Forty Years After: Exploring the Field of Sexual Violence in Armed Conflict' in July 2015 in Hamburg. We were honoured that Susan Brownmiller took part in the intense debate. During those three days, the participants reflected on knowledge gained thus far on the subject and those reflections made their way into this book.

We would like to thank all authors for their trust, and particularly the presenters and participants whose contributions do not figure in this volume: Yonson Ahn, Claire Andrieu, Branka Antic-Stauber, Meira Asher, Kerstin Bischl, Jelke Boesten, Raphaëlle Branche, Janine Natalya Clark, Chris Coulter, Jason Crouthamel, Elma Demir, Verónica Ferreira, Sybille Fezer, Katia Forbert Petersen, Joshua S. Goldstein, Sabine Grenz, Karin Griese, Christa Hämmerle, Carol Harrington, Monika Hauser, Marta Havryshko, Elissa Helms, Smiljana Hesse, Jasmina Husanovic, Tuba Inal, Dobrochna Kałwa, Julie Le Gac, Na-Young Lee, Chiseche Salome Mibenge, Nayanika Mookherjee, Jaimie Morse, Jessica Mosbahi, Alejandra Muñoz, Michiko Nakahara, Alexandra Oberländer, Annette Mari Olsen, Valerie Oosterveld, Maria O'Reilly, Patricia Owens, Donna Pankhurst, Andrea Pető,

Nela Porobić, Mary Louise Roberts, Sofia José Santos, Robin May Schott, Fernando Serrano-Amaya, Sabine Sielke, Silke Studzinsky, Mina Watanabe, Tsukasa Yajima, and Daqing Yang. An international and interdisciplinary encounter of this scope requires the mobilisation of resources and the enthusiasm and support of many. We thank all colleagues who have critically accompanied and supported the production of this volume, in many discussions and with personal commitments.

We particularly thank Gudrun Döllner, Christoph Fuchs, Afra Petersen and Ingwer Schwensen from the library of the Hamburg Institute for Social Research as well as our editorial assistant Jan Kawlath.

Our thanks also go to our friends for their encouragement and patience, in particular to Therese Roth († 2018) who accompanied our work with many inspirations.

Our long standing engagement with the subject of sexual violence in armed conflict would have been impossible without the constant encouraging support of Jan Philipp Reemtsma.

The conference and this volume have been supported by Birkbeck College, University of London (England); the Center for Social Studies at the University of Coimbra (Portugal); Labex, Écrire une histoire nouvelle de l'Europe, Paris (France); Goldsmiths, University of London (England); Hamburg Foundation for the Advancement of Research and Culture (Germany); Hamburg Institute for Social Research (Germany); medica mondiale, Cologne (Germany); promundo (Brasil); Sciences Po, Paris (France); and the Women's International League for Peace and Freedom, Geneva (Switzerland). Financial support was kindly granted by the Hamburg Foundation for the Advancement of Research and Culture and the Gender of Justice Research Project (ERC Grant 313626).

We are very happy that we could win the publisher Urvashi Butalia of Zubaan books. This cooperation opens up promising perspectives of international exchange with Zubaan's project on Sexual Violence and Impunity in South Asia.

Introduction

JOANNA BOURKE, KIRSTEN CAMPBELL, REGINA MÜHLHÄUSER,
FABRICE VIRGILI, GABY ZIPFEL

'Why are you doing this to me?'

Vietnamese woman when she was gang-raped by
US soldiers during the Vietnam War

It is well-known that sexual violence is pervasive in situations
of war and peace. However, this commonly known fact has not
helped to prevent and overcome this form of violence. Rather, it
fosters the idea that sexually-violent behaviour is ahistorical and
that it originates from biological impulses. According to such a
view, it might be possible to limit sexual violence, but it cannot be
overcome or abolished.

In times of war and armed conflict, sexual violence is not only
prevalent and pervasive, but also polymorphic and heterogeneous.
Acts of sexual violence can appear in various forms, including forced
undressing, sexual torture, coerced fellatio, sexual enslavement,
forced prostitution, enforced pregnancy, or vaginal and anal rape
with the penis, fingers, hands and objects. The extent as well as
the intensity to which sexual violence is perpetrated can vary.
In some conflicts, sexual violence is a widespread phenomenon,
while in others its prevalence appears to be comparatively low.
While sexual violence during armed conflict is mostly directed
against women and girls, men and boys can also become victims.
Furthermore, women have sometimes incited, encouraged, or
perpetrated acts of sexual violence.

Attempts to understand and approach these forms of wartime
violence have changed dramatically with growing public awareness

since the 1970s. During this decade, violence in women's everyday lives during times of peace became increasingly visible in public debate and policy. These changes were largely the result of debates within and interventions by women's groups. Women who were victims of this form of violence decided to speak out and publicly relate their experiences. Their accounts of rape in peacetime showed that sexual aggression was not a more or less unavoidable collateral effect of war or a (rare) transgression of accepted limits to wartime violence. Rather, women's narratives exposed the fact that sexual violence was not only part of the lived experience of women in times of peace, but that it was also embedded in the logic of war.

The women's movement of the 1970s developed this insight, and used it to politicise sexual violence perpetrated by men against women in wartime, as well as in times of peace. Feminist analyses of the intersections of power, violence, gender relations and sexuality, increasingly made it clear that sexual violence is a man-made disaster that is structured by cultural, social and historical conditions. In this period, new research focusing on recent history—in particular, colonialism, slavery, World War I and World War II as well as the partition of India, the Bangladesh Liberation War and the Vietnam War—made the phenomenon of sexual violence increasingly visible. The Women's Liberation Movement understood sexual violence primarily as a mechanism and instrument of patriarchal power and hierarchical gender relations, whereas Afro-American feminists insisted on the influence of racist ideologies and politics. Another socio-critical intervention drew due attention to the economic aspects of the gendered division of labour, sexual autonomy and violence. At the same time, the Anti-Vietnam War protests and the international peace movement focused on sexual violence as part of the military conditioning of soldiers in warfare against enemy civilians.

With the growing debate about human rights after 1989, this new awareness also found its way into international policy and law. During the wars in the former Yugoslavia as well as the genocide against the Tutsis and the war in Rwanda and its neighbouring states, the perpetration of sexual violence became central for understanding these conflicts while they were still raging. Non-governmental organizations (NGOs) began devoting resources to supporting the victims of sexual violence and their rights. In the United Nations (UN) system, Special Rapporteurs compiled reports from different theatres of war. Since 1999, the UN Security Council has passed a series of resolutions condemning sexual violence in armed conflict and identifying its widespread or strategic use as a threat to international peace and security. With the jurisprudence of the International Criminal Tribunal for the Former Yugoslavia (ICTY), the International Criminal Tribunal for Rwanda (ICTR), and the International Criminal Court (ICC) as well as other *ad hoc* and mixed tribunals, sexual violence was reasserted as a war crime, and established as an act of genocide (1998) and a crime against humanity (2001), with prosecutions depending on the specific circumstances of each case. This decisive development acknowledged sexual violence in armed conflicts as such, and provided a more appropriate understanding of these acts as crimes.

Interventions from the women's movement, changes in contemporary warfare, and new understandings in international politics and jurisprudence have resulted in sexual violence in conflict becoming the subject of scientific interest and debate. In the past twenty years, a wide variety of research has been published in different disciplines, focusing on sexual violence in various theatres of war and armed conflict throughout various time periods. Today, it is largely acknowledged that sexual violence in armed conflict serves varying functions depending on temporal and spatial contexts. For instance, it has been a component of ethnic or political 'cleansing', a collective punishment or an 'opportunistic' act committed by individual perpetrators. Research has begun to explore different aspects of the subject, including the role of the military as an institution; how the behaviour of individual (male and female) actors in conflict situations is shaped by specific cultural and historical contexts; and the ways in which acts of violence are addressed in the wider society, the media, the politics of memory and in national and international jurisprudence. The emerging body of work on these and other issues indicates a wide range of motives, military rationales and dynamic processes, all of which appear to influence the prevalence, practices and constellations of sexual violence.

Yet despite this increase in public and academic awareness, there is little consensus about the pervasiveness of this violence, its variations and its different forms. There is disagreement about the relationship of sexual violence to pre-war, wartime and post-war circumstances. There are also debates about the cultural and social models of gender that facilitate the perpetration of sexual violence. Recently, Western scholarship has tended to focus on Africa, thereby obscuring sexual violence in other regions, in particular in the Western world. Current debates, such as 'sexual violence as a weapon of war' can be counterproductive in so far as they reduce the phenomenon to a strategically implemented form of excessive violence. In this case, they tend to ignore the complex framework in which this violence occurs, which impedes the analysis of its broader impact and meaning. With the rising influence of large number quantitative studies, methodologies for researching sexual violence are also increasingly debated.

Essential questions such as the practices and politics of gendering, and 'doing gender', or the intertwined nature of violence and sexuality, have increasingly disappeared from public, political and academic discourse about sexual violence in armed conflict. Moreover, even though many insights about the phenomenon have accumulated, the perpetration of sexual violence in armed conflicts still continues unabated.

In order to advance our knowledge and overcome reductive ways of thinking about this complex phenomenon, comparative exploration and international and interdisciplinary exchange is vital. To understand the conditions and factors that affect the occurrence and forms as well as the meanings and consequences of sexual violence, it seems to be helpful to develop conceptual, theoretical and methodological frameworks for investigation and analysis. Following these reflections, the International Research Group 'Sexual Violence in Armed Conflict' (SVAC, www.warandgender.net) was founded in 2010. In meetings and annual workshops SVAC members, interdisciplinary scholars and

NGO experts, compare case studies from different geopolitical, social and cultural spaces, including multifaceted theoretical approaches. Fostering dialogue between scientific, political and judicial practices, and the feminist movement, the research group promotes the systematic development of research questions and methods for comparative and contextual analysis of sexual violence in armed conflict.

This collaboration has led to deeper insights about the histories of practices of sexual violence, which take place in different geographical regions under quite different social and cultural conditions. It has also led to a better understanding of the specific dynamics among perpetrators, victims and bystanders, including variations of these constellations of actors, which are due to different practices of gendering and the organisation of armed violence. It became clear that the politics of generating knowledge fundamentally shape our understanding of this phenomenon. It is crucial to unearth these politics by a critical examination and close reading of sources.

Ultimately, we found that we were left with more questions than satisfying explanations. It became clear that it is now time to reflect on the state of the field: What exactly do we know about the practices of sexual violence in armed conflict? What else do we need to focus our investigations upon? How can we better describe incidences, motivations and responses? What kind of questions do we need to ask, and what theoretical approaches and methods are appropriate to shed light on these blind spots?

In order to open up the debate, and analyse these questions in a broader context, SVAC organised a major international conference 'Against Our Will—Forty Years After: Exploring the Field of Sexual Violence in Armed Conflict' in July 2015 with leading scholars and practitioners. We were very happy to have Susan Brownmiller, the author of Against Our Will (1975), as a keynote speaker. The aim of this interdisciplinary exchange was to explore how wartime sexual violence is understood in the field, to identify gaps in existing knowledge, and to discuss new approaches and move beyond current impasses and understanding. Aiming to organise a dynamic exchange and to catch as many approaches and experiences as possible, we used different formats and forums for discussion. The results of this working together across our disciplines and regions produced important new directions for research, as well as identifying the traps and gaps for researchers and practitioners existing in this field. In the course of this exchange, we developed an approach that insisted on the complex and mutable factors involved, and positioned the occurrence of sexual violence in armed conflicts in the broader historical, social and cultural context of gendered social conditions, cultural imaginations, ideas and attitudes, and political strategies and power relations. To enable this approach, we developed a framework identifying key perspectives for understanding the field.

In this volume, we explore sexual violence in armed conflicts through the following four key perspectives: War/Power; Violence/Sexuality; Gender/Engendering; Visibility/Invisibility. In the course of our collaboration in the SVAC-network, we realised that it is crucial to go beyond conventional ways of working in order to grasp the potential of different disciplinary approaches, new empirical findings and artistic reflections. We thus chose different formats to catch and represent the richness of experiences and methods. 'Intervention' articles introduce and discuss key concepts, debates and problems. These are followed by more open reflections on approaches and case studies. We have furthermore included a continuing self-reflection in the form of a group-conversation on how we generate knowledge on this subject. This conversation represents, on the one hand, conclusions of the discussion of the SVAC-network and demonstrates, on the other hand, how different disciplinary approaches communicate with each other.

The long-term cooperation in the SVAC-network has shown us, among other things, that the scope and breadth of the topic suggests that the work on it should be understood as a work in progress. A critical self-reflection in the research process is necessary in order to minimise traps in the epistemological process. What is it we assume when we deal with this subject, and which gaps do we leave unreflected upon? What are the ideational underpinnings of our knowledge? And what are the political formations that these ideational frameworks structure and support? This volume aims to be a first step in exploring these questions.

REFERENCES

Brownmiller, Susan. 1975. *Against Our Will: Men, Women and Rape.* New York: Simon and Schuster.
Cockburn, Cynthia. 2011. "'Why are You doing this to Me?" Identity, Power and Sexual Violence in War', in Anna G. Jónasdóttir/ Valerie Bryson/Kathleen B. Jones (eds), *Sexuality, Gender and Power: Intersectional and Transnational Perspectives*, pp. 189–204. New York: Routledge.

Gaps and Traps: The Politics of Generating Knowledge on Sexual Violence in Armed Conflict
A conversation with members of the SVAC network

DEBRA BERGOFFEN, PASCALE R. BOS, JOANNA BOURKE, KIRSTEN CAMPBELL,
LOUISE DU TOIT, JÚLIA GARRAIO, ELISSA MAILÄNDER, GABRIELA
MISCHKOWSKI, REGINA MÜHLHÄUSER, FABRICE VIRGILI, GABY ZIPFEL

As a community of researchers and practitioners who participate in the workshops and seminars of the International Research Group 'Sexual Violence in Armed Conflict' (SVAC) we recognise that our work presents unique challenges. Like all scholars we are committed to producing credible accounts of our research. Like all scholars we understand the limitations of our situated positions. In providing analyses of sexual violence, however, we find that the epistemological relationship between us as researchers and the issues we investigate is complicated by the affective horizon of the social and cultural imaginaries that surround sexual violence in general and sexual violence in armed conflict in particular. We also recognise that our work is inherently political in the sense that in seeking to understand this violence we cannot avoid addressing such political questions as: What is the relationship between sexual violence in war times and times of peace? What power structures are served by this violence? How is this violence normalised/excused by social and cultural ideas/ideologies?

The following conversation shows how these issues have arisen in our discussions; how we have struggled with them; how we see our role as scholars and activists who, in exposing the realities of sexual violence, are committed to undoing the politics that enable it.

REGINA MÜHLHÄUSER: The challenge of exploring sexual violence in armed conflict appears to involve more than typical scholarly problems of producing impartial or rigorous knowledge, or of recognising the subjective/situated position of the researcher or practitioner. Instead, it seems that sexual violence both presumes and provokes particular ideas, images and affects. Such imaginations shape the approach of the researcher and practitioner towards conflict-related sexual violence as well as the knowledge she/he produces. Furthermore, this epistemological relationship is not removed from the wider social imaginations of practices of sexual violence in armed conflict. Rather, we confront the complex emergence of this research field in and through such ideas, affects, and images.

In order to unpack these issues and to explore the politics of generating knowledge on sexual violence in armed conflict, it is necessary to reflect on the practices of investigation. How can we approach the subject? What kind of problems arise?

LOUISE DU TOIT: When discussing rape and sexual violence during wartime we are in a sense always too late: we discuss it, not as it is happening, but in hindsight. A clear picture of the extent and duration of wartime criminal violence normally only emerges after the worst excesses have subsided, peace of a sort has been brokered, and space has been cleared for a move beyond the armed conflict. Talk about the meaning of rape in war is thus inevitably tied up with the post-war situation of legal processes of attributing accountability for war crimes, processes of mourning, healing and commemoration, and of nation-building or secession or other such larger political processes. Partial or selective memory is common to all of us, because memory of the past cannot be separated from present imperatives of survival, and so for example we may actively forget things we have lived through because the trauma is too devastating to bear, or because to acknowledge the crimes of the liberators would destroy hope for the future. To forgive or forget what one knows may also be crucial for the survival of one's group—nation or ethnic grouping.

I have thus become intensely aware of how discussions of

wartime rape cannot be separated from either the pre- or the post-conflict situation (is this what we normally call peace?). Looking at rape in the situation of war sheds some light on rape during peace time and vice versa. But in another sense rape also links war and peace: looking at these supposedly straightforwardly distinct categories from the viewpoint of women as (potential) rape victims, there seems to be no clear boundary between war and peace, because so-called post-conflict societies such as South Africa and southern Sudan have extraordinarily high rates of rape. Clearly much more research has to be done on this phenomenon, but it seems as if the very establishment of a new social and political order somehow calls for the high levels of sexual violence against women and perpetrated by men. A state of transition is inherently complex and ambivalent, because one is consciously still recovering from a traumatic past with lingering effects and at the same time trying to invent and establish a new legitimate order on the ruins of the old, illegitimate one. There is thus a strong narrative of 'from' and 'towards', and how sexual violence and the status of women both during and after the war are narrated, constructed and understood within this broader frame, is often a function of political agendas that have very little to do with women (Alcoff 2018). It is thus no wonder that, when women do enter the traditionally male-dominated spaces where transition is discussed, they disrupt the simplistic 'from' and 'to' structure of the narrative, as they talk about 'everyday' sexual violence that they experience in the community and at home at the hands of men in their supposedly 'liberated' or democratic societies. The sexual abuse of women before, during and after war thus complicates and disrupts simplistic grand narratives of oppression, liberation and nationhood—narratives that often more closely reflect the reality of politically powerful men. As Brandon Hamber (2007) has pointed out, women's experiences draw attention to "the multiple layers of power that exist within society and the continuities between past and present" (ibid.: 389) and thus to the need for "a broader view of justice that embraces social and economic justice" (ibid.: 375), and thus to a moral imperative associated with an appreciation of complexity.

GABY ZIPFEL: Sexual violence does not occur without prerequisites from pre-war times and does not falter after a war. Practices in the so-called 'state of emergency' of war are written into the experience and potential for action of a society and are passed on from one generation to the next. This raises the question of the extent to which war and wartime violence affect the way gender characters are shaped, how the sexes relate to each other and how their options for action develop.

Today, for example, the First World War from 1914 to 1918 is generally understood as "one of the formative experiences of the century, perhaps even the decisive factor in shaping it", as Gerd Krumeich (1993: 11) has assessed, as an event that each generation examines anew "in the light of old insights and new experiences, and the theoretical approaches gleaned from their own lifeworld." If this is the case, then it seems high time to ask about the extent to which this war a century ago influenced the gender positions and gender hierarchy in the Western world. Three aspects are elementary in determining the subject status of the sexes in a given social system: firstly, the question of economic independence, that is, the possibility of supporting oneself financially; secondly, the question of citizenship rights and possibilities for participating in the public sphere, and thirdly, the question of sexual self-determination, that is, of control over one's own body and reproductive capacity. Accordingly, it must be asked to what extent the First World War influenced, changed or reorganised and fortified the gender hierarchy based on complementary public and private spheres.

Characteristic for the First World War was, first of all, the integration of the entire society for the purpose of waging war, an integration that made obsolete not only classical conceptions of the spatial segregation of the theatres of war, but also the allocation of tasks according to a gendered division of labour. In lieu of which, the war took on highly complex, manifold meanings for men and women. After the introduction of general compulsory military service in the nineteenth century, the early twentieth century saw, as Karen Hagemann (1998: 17) observed, "the mobilization of expanding sectors of the male population for war, and ever larger parts of the female population on the 'home front'", which "peaked in the first industrialised and technologically highly advanced 'people's war'". In the scenario of the First World War, women can for the first time be identified as the 'home front', where they were assigned positions that lent meaning to the conflict—the hero's mother, the devoted wife, the sweetheart longingly awaiting her lover's return—and where they replaced male workers and provided for their families. As nurses in military hospitals at the front, as auxiliaries in the Women's Army Corps, as farmers to whom prisoners of war were allotted as workers, women were not only close to the field of soldiers' experience and to what soldiers experienced and did in war, they were actually directly involved.

Characterising the First World War as a "so-called people's war legitimated by national interests" implies perceiving it as a state of society, the defining of which, as Ute Daniel (1993: 132) establishes, would first require clarification as to how it was perceived as an event by the various societal groups, classes, and so on, that is "in a sense, how many First World Wars there were and what each of them was like." What needs investigating is this: how the various actors were positioned over the course of the conflict, which options and which impositions the war had in store for them, and how it served to establish, modify or overcome structural orders of society—decisively so in the case of the structural order of a gender hierarchy and a gender-specific division of labour that complemented one another. Further attention should be paid to what sacrifices the war demanded from whom, and what rewards it had in store for them.

REGINA MÜHLHÄUSER: To date, however, it seems as if we still know little about gendered and sexual violence during WWI?

GABY ZIPFEL: In their comprehensive study on the events of World War I in Belgium, John Horne and Alan Kramer (2001: 75) state: "Rapes occurred quite widely, but calculation of the total number is impossible given the difficulty of recording this crime." But what, we have to ask ourselves, exactly is the nature of the difficulty?

For one thing, it is apparently tacitly agreed that, in contrast to other acts of violence, sexual violence is located on the interface between an act of war and an act that is practiced in civilian life. Horne and Kramer (2001: 196) cite the Allied Investigation Commissions that considered that "rape had happened with what the French termed 'unheard-of frequency'" and comment "They were, however, uncertain how to account for it. They felt it had less connection than other types of 'atrocity' to what they saw as the German policy of systematic terror and they placed it at the individualist end of the spectrum of war crimes".

Secondly, Horne and Kramer refer to the role of the victim in the process of keeping such acts secret, or even taboo: "The shame felt by the victims tended to cause understatement of its incidence. [...] As the Belgian Commission commented, cases of rape 'are naturally hidden by the families'" (ibid.). This 'consideration' of the 'shamed' victims of sexual violence makes sense only if the deeds themselves were regarded as self-evident and unavoidable, and the victims were assumed to share the responsibility for their occurrence.

These types of gender stereotypes function to govern social order. They belong to the deep structures of social knowledge, in which what is everyday and presumably natural is stored—unscrutinised circumstances that are 'known' intuitively, but seldom reflected upon, let alone questioned.

JOANNA BOURKE: One problem that we see in research on war and armed conflict is that many scholars do not seem to think that sexual violence is wrong. The historian Kenneth Maddock (1991: 163), for instance, argued that "the rules of war are like the rules of the road: any honest and realistic person will expect them to be broken, but some drivers will commit more frequent and more serious violations than others. [...] Judged by their own standards, however, the covert operators [units which he admitted routinely committed atrocities] were not necessarily exceeding any 'speed limit'."

Maddock is refreshingly blunt. But it is easy to find more insidious ways that atrocity is normalised within mainstream history. I want to give you another example: Peter Schrijvers, a respected military historian, writes about the mass rapes carried out by American troops in Okinawa. He interviewed a corporal who told him of an occasion when he passed a group of ten Marines, who were (in the corporal's words) "quite animated [...] taking turns raping an oriental woman". The corporal reported that "I was furious, but our outfit kept marching by as though nothing unusual was going on" (Schrijvers 2005: 211f). Both the corporal and, by implication, Schrijvers seem to regard the negative emotional response to be the correct ethical response. Moral righteousness existing without any action being necessary.

Schrijvers goes even further, blandly stating that wartime rape "serves to sharpen the aggressiveness of soldiers" and "helps to steel the male bonds between warriors". The clichés are so familiar that it almost seems churlish to ask why gang rapes would, in fact, do either of these things. Why doesn't witnessing atrocities carried out by one's comrades make men 'disillusioned' or 'politicised' rather than keen to kill? What is it about the insecurity of male identity (or, indeed, the shallowness of commitment to the rightness of the cause) that requires the unequal and disproportionate rape of one vulnerable woman by many armed men to facilitate 'bonding'? To repeat these clichés as explanations is precisely to replicate the mantra of senior officers overseeing atrocity. In the words of one: it was important not to "jeopardise the new toughness of spirit". That spirit was "more important than whether or not a few Japanese prisoners got kicked around or killed." All's fair in war.

There is no clear distinction in this history between what the eyewitness thought and Schrijvers critique. Of course, it is the job and duty of historians to trace carefully and accurately the languages used at different times. But it is also the job and duty of the historian to critique those languages, investigating their origins and uncovering the hidden assumptions. As Barbara Johnson (1981: xv) explained, we must read backwards, "from what seems natural, obvious, self-evident, or universal in order to show that these things have their history, their reasons for being the way they are, their effects on what follows from them and that the starting point is not a (natural) given but a (cultural) construct, usually blind to itself."

REGINA MÜHLHÄUSER: What is perceived as sexual violence can change over time and vary from culture to culture. What do we actually recognise as sexual violence? Which forms and constellations do we integrate in our study of the subject?

JOANNA BOURKE: My definition of 'sexual violence' involves the identification of a particular act as sexual, however the term 'sexual' is defined, and a claim that the act is non-consensual, unwanted, or coerced. This opens the way for including acts that were prior not identified as practices of sexual violence, for example military hazing. Hazing rituals in state armies as well as armed groups often involve forced public masturbation and forced imitation or performance of fellatio. In 'sweat parties', naked men are confined in steam-filled shower-rooms; during 'blanket parties', they are stripped naked, wrapped in blankets and beaten. 'Greasings' involve a naked man being smeared in machinery grease and buggered with a plastic tube. Military spokesmen justify such forms of sexualised abuse in functional terms that are *both* gender-negative and gender-positive. The negative is that it gets rid of 'sissies', 'wet tarts' and 'powderpuffs'. The positive function is seen in forging powerful group ties and acting as a rite of passage into manhood. It is taken for granted that pain and distress are necessary in constructing martial masculinities. Furthermore, the warring institution itself is reproduced through instrumental violence against its own members. The appeal to the 'separate culture' of military institutions allows hazing to be justified as a morally relative practice. This belief that elite corpsmen belonged to a culture 'set apart' meant that many victims, too, do not take hazing to be morally wrong. This is why hazing has proved impossible to dislodge.

Military culture (especially of elite units) can assimilate considerable sexualised violence because it defines itself as 'set apart', especially from 'political correctness', feminism and civilian values. Sociologists such as Lionel Tiger—who invented the term 'male bonding'—claimed that the public furore over hazing was due to 'feminisation' or the 'norms of female behavior' being "increasingly and successfully applied to male behavior". It was a fact, he claimed, that women neither enjoy enduring painful ordeals (especially ones that attacked their genitals) nor did they become 'effective contributors' to the "traditional draconian immersion of young men in Marine culture" (Tiger 1999: 215). In other words, they didn't 'enjoy' attacking in return.

Such discussions were particularly vocal in the aftermath of the Tailhook scandal. At the thirtyfifth Annual Tailhook Association Symposium in Las Vegas in September 1991, a two-day debriefing of US Navy and Marine Corps aviation in Operation Desert Storm, 83 women and seven men alleged sexual assault and harassment. Amongst other humiliations, they had been forced to walk down a corridor lined with men who groped them, a form of hazing that is common during 'crossing-the-line' ceremonies, that is, when sailors cross the equator for the first time. In the subsequent public furore, the distinction between hazing and sexual abuse was blurred. For instance, writing in the *Marine Corps Gazette* in November 1992, leading American cultural conservative William S. Lind confessed to being puzzled by the public reaction to the abuse. "After all", he wrote, "no one was raped at Tailhook. From what was in the newspapers, it didn't sound much different from a Dartmouth fraternity on a Friday or Saturday night. Unless the women officers who are protesting their treatment so loudly went directly to flight school from a convent, they surely had some idea what to expect." (Lind 1992: 38)

KIRSTEN CAMPBELL: International criminal law can help us to clarify how we understand sexual violence. In the context of international criminal law, sexual violence is ostensibly a gender-neutral term that refers to violence of a sexual nature against either women or men. The sexual distinguishes violence—such as assault, defined as an unlawful application of force to another—from sexual violence—such as sexual assault, defined as a non-consensual sexual act. For example, there is no intrinsic reason to understand either a person's mouth or an object such as a bottle as sexual, whereas the use of a bottle to simulate fellatio can be a sexual crime, and not simply an assault. As Ann Cahill (2001: 139) points out, "those objects or orifices not always perceived as sexual *become sexualised* in the context of the assault." This model of sexual violence defines the criminality of the act in terms of its sexual nature, and its sexual nature derives from the sexual meaning given to the interaction of particular acts and bodies. For example, the definition of the criminal conduct of 'sexual penetration' generated during the trial against Dragoljub Kunarac at the International Tribunal for the Former Yugoslavia (ICTY) identifies parts of the body that carry sexual meaning, such as penis, vagina, anus or mouth.

However, the difficulty of this notion of the 'sexual' in crimes of sexual violence is that it is always gendered. Judith Butler points out that 'the sexual' is a particular representation of acts and bodies. It represents this act—but not that—as sexual; this body part—but not that—as sexed; this body as female, but that as male. As such, it relies upon 'regulatory ideas' or norms that delineate certain acts as sexual, certain body parts as sexual organs and certain bodies as male and female. These norms give meaning to the otherwise abstract notion of sexual violence because they structure the imaginary content of those harms in relation to masculine and feminine bodies. For example, the definition of sexual violence found during the trial against Jean-Paul Akayesu at the International Tribunal for Rwanda (ICTR) includes acts that do not involve physical contact, such as forced nudity. However, the sexualization of nudity depends upon the classification of particular bodies. In certain social contexts, forcing a female victim to remove her shirt is sexual, whereas forcing a male victim to do the same is not. In Butler's terms (1993: 2), the "regulatory norms of 'sex' […] materialise sexual difference (and consolidate) the heterosexual imperative." As these 'regulatory ideas' constitute bodies as masculine and feminine, they also structure sexuality in terms of a heterosexual norm, since desire for the opposite sex defines normative masculine and feminine sexuality (Butler 1997).

'Sexual violence' can then be understood as materialising ideas of masculinity and femininity, ideas of what it is to be a man or a woman, through its repetition of norms of sexual practices, which acts are appropriate to men or women, that in turn rely upon notions of 'biological' difference, what it 'means' to have a male or female body. If the notion of 'sexual violence' relies upon certain models of sexual acts, organs and bodies, those models in turn draw upon ideas of masculine and feminine acts, organs and bodies. Their construction as masculine and feminine acts structures the 'sexual' as heterosexual. If sexual violence is commonly understood as referring to both women and men, nevertheless, the 'sexual' nature of the offence relies upon ideas of masculinity and femininity, which signify bodies and acts as sexual in specific ways.

GABRIELA MISCHKOWSKI: While international criminal law defines sexual violence in gender-neutral terms, the evidence generated at tribunals does indeed suggest that certain gendered understandings about men and women and their sexuality shape acts of sexual violence, their forms and how they are understood. When we look at sexual violence in the context of attacks committed by various Serb forces against the Muslim population in Bosnia-Herzegovina the dominant narrative is quintessenced in the topos of 'ethnic cleansing rape'. This topos typically refers to the rape of women and girls. This construction rests, among others, on the claim of widespread 'public rape' of women as a means of particular terror, destruction and humiliation of her collective. While the term 'public rape' appears randomly in many newspaper articles and scholarly works, it is hardly ever defined what 'public' means. But since the ascribed function of 'public rape' in cases of 'ethnic cleansing' is to instil a particular terror and humiliation in the victim's community, it can be assumed that the alleged audience belongs to the victim's community which is forced to watch: family members, neighbours or fellow prisoners. This claim of widespread public rape of women and girls, however, is not reflected in the rape accounts that were generated at the ICTY. Just like in domestic rape trials, wartime rape of women tried before the ICTY is a crime without eyewitnesses. Based on my knowledge of ICTY records on sexual violence I would estimate that about 98 per cent of all rape incidents, which are either relevant to the charges or mentioned in testimonies, did not take place in sight of other victims.

Only two situational settings surface in which women or girls were raped in the presence of others than the rapist and the victim. One such setting pertains to the presence of other enemy agents in the context of gang rapes or during interrogations. The other setting pertains to the simultaneous rape of two or, in one case, four women in one room. However, the overwhelming majority of rape accounts before the ICTY describe situations in which women or girls were singled out, separated from their parents, husbands, children, neighbours or fellow detainees, taken to other rooms or buildings and then raped by different men 'in privacy'. This refers to detainment situations, such as camps, as well as situations of attack or occupation, such as house searches. Even in cases of serial rapes, the first man would most often leave before the next came in.

In contrast, demonstrative sexual violence 'in public' did play a major role in cases of sexual violence committed against men. According to the ICTY records, these incidents took place in detention situations either in camps or police stations. Such acts always included a larger audience not only of other soldiers or guards but also, and in the first place, of other detainees. The five or six indictments of the ICTY that pertain explicitly to male-to-male sexual assault focus on one form: Forcing two prisoners to assault each other by committing fellatio, or to mutilate the other by biting off his testicles.

The ICTY mentions no incident of male-to-male rape in the form of penile penetration by a Serb perpetrator of a Muslim victim. If such male-to-male rape took place—as it is often claimed—we must assume that it did so like in the majority of situations of male-to-female penile penetration rape, that is 'in privacy'. As Dubravka Žarkov (2007: 166) noted: "In Balkan norms of sexuality, both men involved in the sexual act are homosexualised." We can thus ask whether this public humiliation of the enemy man through penile penetration would not have fit the self-image of Serb masculinity and was therefore a no-go.

Non-penetrative forms of sexual violence, in contrast, might not even have been considered as sexual. Eric Stener Carlson (2006), who analysed for the ICTY hundreds of cases of sexual assault, draws our attention to the hidden prevalence of, what he calls, 'blunt trauma to male genitals' (BTMG). He distinguishes between two forms of BTMG. One pertains to regular beatings on male genitals with blunt objects without producing any physically observable consequences. He suggests that this is often not recognised as sexual violence, because hitting each other's genitals is normal male behaviour, for example in contact sports like American football, or in street fights. The second form of BTMG pertains to severe genital mutilation effecting male reproductive abilities.

In order to get a better picture of what is actually happening it seems important to me to distinguish between a) enforced fellatio between prisoners, b) beatings on covered and c) naked genitals without physical consequences, and d) severe genital mutilation. Also we need to take into account the positionality between the different actors, that is the detainees who perform these actions to each other and the perpetrators who are initiating, threatening and watching them.

ELISSA MAILÄNDER: In order to better describe and understand such forms of violence, it might be helpful to follow the French anthropologist Véronique Nahoum-Grappe's conception of cruelty (1996). She defines cruelty as a specific form of violence that is distinguished by its intensity and motivation. Violence causes different grades of pain, but cruelty has not only the explicit aim to inflict pain and suffering upon the victim, but also to bring degradation. It can only be implemented in the context of an asymmetrical power relation.

For instance, by humiliating concentration camp prisoners, Nazi camp guards, both female and male, experienced and expressed their *overwhelming* dominance. Considering Elias Canetti's theory of power (1960), the cruel act can be seen to have provided the perpetrator with a vital and lustful exercise of power. Certainly, from the victim's perspective, violence is destructive.

Yet from the perpetrator's perspective, violence is not only attractive and 'creative', violence is—in a Foucauldian sense—also productive. It is a medium or instrument with which to gain prestige, to perform before an audience of colleagues, to realise oneself—and to keep running the system. Especially with regard to cruelty, it is the manner in which such violence is perpetrated that is particularly important, as, both, the body language and the gestures bear meaning.

In my research I examined violent acts by female and male SS-personnel at the concentration and extermination camp Majdanek (1941–44) in German occupied Poland. Interrogating the situational context, the social dynamics and the cultural meanings of the 'everyday culture' and society in the concentration camp, I found three different exemplary forms of concentrational and genocidal violence: extermination, physical ill-treatment and cruelty.

The National Socialist concentration camps were on the one hand sealed-off and tightly regulated, yet at the same time, within these enclosed spaces—so long as violent actors could count on mutual support and secrecy—*everything* was possible. Officially, SS personnel were strictly forbidden from engaging in sexual contact with so-called *Untermenschen* ('subhumans'). Yet the camps were sites of permanent transgression, where the most routine official duties—inspection of the barracks, supervision of prisoners at work, the monitoring of screening, surveillance of prisoners during bathing, the everyday roll call and so forth—constantly provided opportunities for violence and domination, and consequently for sexual violence as well. Carried out by various actors, such acts of violence were largely connected to verbal, gestural and physical violence, which aimed at the sexual integrity of prisoners, humiliated and hurt them.

In the context of the camps that the Nazis established during the war of annihilation in Poland and the Soviet Union, we also find examples of guards who forced prisoners to perform sexual acts with each other. In some cases the camp prisoners were male and female, in others they are both male. In the latter constellation, such acts have typically been perceived as humiliation and violence, not as sexual violence. Currently, this may change. What impact have these perceptions of the historical agents and their respective societies not merely on our understanding of sexual violence, but also on our understanding of men as gendered and sexed beings?

KIRSTEN CAMPBELL: Acts of sexual violence constitute bodies and their sexual difference along axes of identity, ethnicity and power, in context of conflicts in which those persons were often not previously ascribed those identities, and in which those identities are at stake in the conflict itself. Sexual violence in armed conflict works to constitute these identities, making individuals into the social categories of the perpetrator—for example, a 'Jewish man' or a 'Muslim woman'. This reduction to social identities as defined by the violence of the perpetrator, and in particular to one's sex in the case of sexual violence, can be seen as an integral part of the harm.

However, if we take this approach then it is necessary to understand 'masculinity' and 'femininity' as norms that are constituted in relation to each other. For example, male sexual assault involves the feminisation of its victims ('you are not a man'), while female sexual assault involves the reduction of women to their non-masculine role of femininity ('you are a woman'). Moreover, these relational terms are filled with imaginary content in relation to specific social contexts—in this society, this is what it is to be a man, and this is what it is to be a woman—and the content of these is itself subject to contestation in conflict. To identify the specific harms of sexual violence in particular conflicts, it is therefore necessary to identify how notions of 'masculinity' and 'femininity' are given meaning in that social context.

REGINA MÜHLHÄUSER: If we understand sexual violence as a performative act, that is, an action that through its enactment constitutes norms of masculinity and femininity through force or violence, then the question arises: What do we recognise as force or violence?

In my own research on the Second World War I look at the whole spectrum of sexual encounters during war—from violent to non-violent, from forced to consensual, from commercial to non-commercial—and I often find that the boundaries are fluid. On occasion, sexual violence, sexual barter and consensual encounters can merge. And, indeed, 'consensual' does not mean that such encounters in wartime are based on mutual understanding or affection. Women often become involved in such relationships on account of specific needs, pragmatic choices and fears caused by the war. How do we then understand the grey zones between the grey zones between violent and non-violent gendered behaviour?

PASCALE R. BOS: One extremely difficult form of sexual violence to analyse and understand is (forced) prostitution. Under normal circumstances, brothels are imagined as sites of transactional sexual encounters between men (who pay) and women (who get paid), and as such they represent a symbolic space somewhere in between the private (sex in the context of a love relationship) and the public (sex as a business transaction). Moreover, as prostitution is marked by the implied consent of the woman, it is not traditionally associated with sexual violence. In the case of sexual enslavement this dynamic becomes blurred. Because the site of the brothel still suggests that this is a space in which transactional sex occurs which is voluntary on the part of the woman rather than that it represents organised, institutionalised sexual violence, the sexual violence becomes normalised as sex and ceases to be read as violence by the men who participate in it, and by its bystanders. In turn, the women who are forced to perform this labour become implicated in this dynamic. If they 'submit' and 'consent' to sex with the enemy (soldiers) and survive, it will seem as if they participated in a form of transactional sex and 'bought' their survival by participating in a sexual exchange. The entirely non-voluntary nature of this labour becomes erased. Thus imagined, the experience of sexual enslavement in a brothel leaves women both physically and morally (spiritually) compromised. As such, they cease to be victims or martyrs and instead come to epitomise how the moral corruption of the perpetrators also 'pollutes' its victims.

We can find such a reading of forced prostitution/sexual enslavement, for instance, in the case of the 'comfort women' of the Japanese Imperial Army during the Second World War. To date, Japan insinuates that the women volunteered to do this 'job', and thus the survivors are denied the unequivocal status of victims. This constellation becomes even more complicated, however, when the 'customers' of sexual enslavement are not perpetrators, but male detainees, themselves victims, for example in the case of the concentration camp brothels.

Between 1942 and 1945, the Nazis set up brothels in ten concentration camps. They selected non-Jewish women whom, according to the Nazi social hierarchy, were categorised as 'asocial'. Contrary to widespread belief, these brothels were not for the male guard personnel. Rather, sex was intended as an incentive for a certain group of privileged male inmates to enhance their work performance. To analyse this constellation of sexual violence is very difficult, last but not least because in the context of a brothel the sexual contact is usually understood to be about pleasure rather than about violence and as transactional. This particular imaginary—sexual enslavement—thus complicates matters: it does not only make the actual women who worked in actual camp brothels seem less like victims and more complicit in their own victimisation and survival (they 'paid' for it with their bodies), it also makes for a complicated narrative when it is applied to male prisoners. In fact, male prisoners tried to hide and obscure the existence of camp brothels after the end of the war—not so much because they feared to be accused of complicity (which they have been sometimes in recent years), but because they feared to conjure up the picture that life in the concentration camps was easy and enjoyable.

REGINA MÜHLHÄUSER: A problem we face when examining sexual violence in armed conflict in detail seems to be a lack of sufficient data. Still, when one begins to take a closer look, a variety of possible source materials can be uncovered. These include oral and written testimony by civilians as well as combatants, by victims, witnesses and perpetrators of sexual violence; military documents; NGO-reports; judicial material generated during or after an armed conflict; and sources of perception, for instance media reports or cultural productions like literature and film. In order to tap the full potential of existing sources, researchers need to move beyond conventional approaches. Since the use and interpretation of sources varies considerably in different academic disciplines and political fields, it seems helpful to reflect our material and methodological approaches. How do you approach your sources?

ELISSA MAILÄNDER: The experience of violence, and in particular of sexual violence, is challenging to reconstruct, since we have very limited testimonies of personal experience. In my research I examined violent acts by female and male SS-personnel at the concentration and extermination camp Majdanek (1941–44) in German occupied Poland. For the victims, 'experience' in this context must be understood as survival first and foremost, even before we can begin to determine the many forms of suffering, surveillance and dying that characterised their life under the rule of the SS. As for the camp guards, it is very difficult to grasp their everyday experiences of violence. The only moments their narratives about their camp experience was documented was in the context of post-war trials, at which point, whenever it came to the question of violence, they wrapped themselves in silence or engaged an 'exculpatory discourse'.

Since the testimonies on violence from the perpetrator's side are fragmentary, survivor testimony is precious, especially coming from those who worked close to the SS and had so to speak a role as 'participant observers'. With their descriptions we can certainly obtain insight into practices of violence. However, to take into account only the experience of the victims—as Nazi concentration camp research usually does—is problematic, since acts of violence cannot be fully understood exclusively from the victim's perspective. Historians thus get only glimpses of these experiences of the violence, including sexual violence, in the camps by reading carefully between the lines and comparing the perpetrator's statements with other sources and perspectives.

GABRIELA MISCHKOWSKI: I look at court testimonies as historical sources, since they tell us on the one hand about different forms of sexual violence and sexual encounters during a war, but they also give us on the other hand an impression about how sexual violence is interpreted and understood at a specific historical point in time. There are, of course, many limitations as the narratives are guided and restricted by legal rules and requirements to determine the guilt or innocence of the accused, or by exaggerations and omissions by the witnesses, and so on. However, reading the stories against the legal grain can reveal some surprising clues. When you look, for example, at the trials before the ICTY that deal, among other things, with rape and sexual assault in detention camps, you will find that the prosecution strategy typically allows only religious, racial or political discrimination as legally relevant intentions for rape when charging it as part of persecutions. Indeed, legal prosecution tends to negate the differences in the acts by adjusting them and the context in which they take place to pre-defined elements of crimes. The actual testimonies, however, simply do not adhere to this logic and reveal multifaceted ways sexual assaults are staged by the perpetrators which reveal conflicting interests and motives.

Take the example of one witness who testified at the ICTY trial against Zenjil Delalić, Zravko Mucić, Hazim Delić and Esad Landžo. The trial took place in 1997 and was about acts committed against Bosnian Serb men and women in summer 1992 in the so-called Čelebići Camp under the Joined Command of Bosnian Muslim and Croat forces in Konjic municipality, about 50 kilometre south-west of Sarajevo. One witness testified that she was raped six times while she was detained in Čelebići. In addition, there was one attempted rape. Her detailed testimony reveals that the rapes and the attempted rape took place in four different scenarios indicating different functions, intentions and motives on the side of the rapists. However, only the first rape could be termed to be functional for the armed conflict and was integrated into the material for the judgment. A close reading of a court testimony can, in this way, provide us with a new view on different patterns, functions and forms of sexual and gender-based violence as well as the different dynamics that produce, promote and foster it.

When we use court testimonies as sources to analyse acts of sexual violence, however, an ethical problem arises. As a researcher you base your interpretation on witness accounts which were given with the main intention to achieve justice, to hold the perpetrator responsible, to voice the victims' suffering and perception. Your intention, however, is necessarily a different one; you might, for example, filter the court narratives to find patterns and motives or deviations from patterns and motives of sexual violence in a particular war situation. Thus, in a certain way, you use the narrated painful experience of a woman for the purpose of your research. Some women might find the way you make use of their perception or lived experience abusive. But since most witnesses testify anonymously you cannot ask for their permission.

Indeed, the fact that the witnesses often do not testify under their name also poses a problem. To protect their privacy in the public, they receive pseudonyms, usually combinations of letters and numbers. For researchers this poses a challenge, because even if you do not cite someone's name, when you analyse someone's testimony, you place the individual statements made at a trial in a context. This may make it possible to reconstruct the identity of witnesses in spite of the pseudonyms, especially when witnesses come from villages and small towns where everyone knows each other. In situations of on-going conflict or tense post-war negotiations this may put witnesses and their families in danger.

DEBRA BERGOFFEN: I would like to raise another trap that I worry about with increasing concern, that is the voyeur/pornography problem. I provide accounts of victim testimonies, because I think that hearing from survivors in their own words is the best way to touch the horror of their suffering. I know what I want readers to hear. I have no way of controlling what they hear. Gang rape, naked dancing before a crowd of men, sexual humiliation are pornographic tropes. In citing the women's testimonies am I reinforcing these tropes? Can I say that in noting the parallels between pornographic tropes and humiliating sexual violence

I am revealing something about the perpetrators' pleasure, the role of the spectacle in using rape as a military tactic, and the continuity between peace time and war zone images of women, or am I reiterating the spectacle and reinforcing the voyeuristic pleasures of the pornographic gaze?

The discrepancy between the publicity given to sex trafficking and labour trafficking is one manifestation of this trap. The first form of trafficking makes the headlines, the second does not. I do not know how to (re)solve this problem. It may be that seeing the faces of the women who have been subjected to sexual violence will force us to respond to their demand for respect, the principle of the moral demand of the face articulated by Emmanuel Lévinas (1985), but the continued vilification of the so-called 'comfort women', that is, the women and girls who were sexually enslaved by the Japanese army between 1932 and 1945, gives me pause. Having seen their faces and heard their accounts of abuse many people do not respond ethically. The moral demand of the face is destroyed as they are accused of being whores, of being responsible for their plight—of not being 'real' victims. Thus their assailants escape censure. If only 'real' victims have the power to elicit a moral response from us, I cannot avoid asking: what does it take to be a real victim? What assumptions are at work when we distinguish real victims from those who are not really victims? Here it is a case of a trap—the pornographic trap—exposing a gap—the assumptions at work in our definition/concept of victim, the relationship between the ideas of innocence, agency for example, and the perception of a 'real' victim.

REGINA MÜHLHÄUSER: Such ideas also play into the way testimonies are generated. What are women authorised to say, and which parts do they remain silent about? How can we grasp the conditions of speaking?

PASCALE R. BOS: We generally need to reflect more deeply on how testimonies are constructed, be it in court, in interviews, in memoirs, be it by victims-survivors, by perpetrators or by witnesses. In my field, Holocaust scholarship, for example, testimony has often been read or interpreted as if it were a reflection of an easily accessible truth. Toril Moi dubs this tendency 'reflectionism'. A reflectionist reading fails to see the narrative as a reconstruction of a confusing, multi-faceted experienced reality; instead it considers the text "a more or less faithful reproduction of an external reality to which we all have equal and unbiased access." Reservations about reflectionism are central to more recent historical approaches, which rely on poststructuralist notions of language. Language and textuality occupy a pivotal place in this kind of historical analysis, for, as Kathleen Canning (1994: 370) suggests, "Rather than simply reflecting social reality or historical context, language is seen instead as constituting historical events, and human consciousness."

This kind of analysis can be of use to our research as it considers that reality is not only positional and subjective but also constructed in and through language. The process of narrating is embedded in both the cultural understanding and the linguistic capacities of the witnesses, including the victim-survivors. Individuals' experience or consciousness of what happened needs to be seen in relation to their previous experiences as well as in relation to how they conceptualised these experiences and articulated them. Where individuals were positioned in relation to the discourses that determine their reality will affect their narrative. Understanding and analysing experience along these lines means that testimonies (by either women or by men) do not allow us simple access to historical reality. Experience is both uniquely personal and positional, influenced by the different lenses and discourses through which we at different times understand and describe ourselves and the world. As academics, we are engaged in performing historical analyses of these reconstructions, these representations. We need to ask, how is sexual violence constructed—through what kind of language, images, constellations? And what effects does this particular discourse produce in the listener or reader—what affect, and what kind of call for political, cultural or legal mobilisation?

JÚLIA GARRAIO: I think it is also important to look at the strategies of mediating sexual violence, in the way rape stories result from processes of giving meaning to certain forms of violence. Consider, for instance, the use of digital cameras as empirical sources for generating knowledge about sexual violence. The democratisation of access to digital devices has made them increasingly present in contemporary wars. Though they are imbued by expectations of objectiveness and immediacy, their reliability as evidence is often evasive because what is at stake is not necessarily the materiality of the captured images but the credibility of the narratives that are created to signify those images, to make a story out of them.

You probably remember that during the 2011 war in Libya there was much media interest in the videos of rape that the rebels claimed to have found with government soldiers and militiamen and which, so it was often suggested in the media, might indicate the use of rape as a weapon of war by the government. Those videos circulated mostly as an absence: politicians and military commanders affiliated with the rebellion referred willingly to them, but said that they had destroyed them to spare victims from 'shame'. Cultural codes regarding female sexuality (the assumption that the rapes tarnished the 'honour' of the family of the victims) were put forward as explanation both for the recording of rapes and for the destruction of their evidence. There were, nonetheless, at least two videos of sexual violence that reached mainstream media. Both depict someone in a situation of extreme vulnerability and pain. The first video shows a naked woman being held by two men in civilian clothes who insert a broomstick in her anus; the second shows an old bleeding man surrounded by fighters while one of them inserts what seems to be a bayonet in his anus. We don't know the identity of the people in the first video nor their fate, but we know who the old man was and that he was killed shortly after.

Now it is interesting to look at how CNN dealt with both videos. The first is used in the report "Libyan rebels say captured cell phone videos show rape, torture" (Sidner 2011). The journalist, who is with the rebel forces in Misrata, informs that she could not confirm the authenticity of the video. However, a skilled process of editing—blurring of images "to protect the victim" and stressing the audio element—stimulates the public to imagine the

visuality behind the screams of the woman. Despite the wording
that signals insufficient evidence ("it appears", "alleged", "unable
to verify its authenticity"), the framing of the video alongside
the introduction of other elements (for example the testimonies
of a rebellion commander and a psychologist from Benghazi)
encourages an interpretation of the footage as possible proof of a
massive campaign of rape by the government forces.

The second video is one of the many cell-phone videos taken
during the capture and lynching of Gaddafi. When reporting on
the death of Gaddafi, CNN remembered extensively the victims
of Lockerbie as part of a long list of crimes committed by the
dictator. It broadcasted footage of his last moments recorded by
his captors, but not the images suggesting the stabbing with the
bayonet, that is, CNN simply avoided addressing the possible sexual
dimension in the lynching of Gaddafi. How does the constellation
'rebel/sexual offender versus dictator/sexually abused' challenge
dominant conceptions of wartime rape? The first video, the one
with the raped woman, can easily be read according to a familiar
'script': raped in war equals victim, female, vulnerable and civilian;
rapist in war equals aggressor, male, virile and part of the military
(or of a militia, that is, a group in the possession of weapons).
CNN, which had paid so much attention to sexual violence in the
war in Libya (as you can see in its extensive reporting on the case
of al-Obeidi), becomes silent when the dichotomy underlying the
abovementioned script is not upheld.

Indeed, Gaddafi's last moments drastically challenge the
constellation framing that script, especially if we bear in mind the
crimes commonly attributed to Gaddafi's regime, the image of
strength, defiance, military power and virility that he cultivated,
as well as sexual fantasies often projected in his relationship
with women. Male orientalist fantasies of potency had been
pervasive in much of the Western media coverage of his private
life (just think of reports about his female bodyguards, the alleged
relationship with his Ukrainian nurse or rumours surrounding
the inspiration for Berlusconi's 'wild parties'). The Western public
could identify in Gaddafi the attributes that are often associated
with sexual aggressors: male, violent, military, virile, sexually

edacious. Precisely this imaginary makes it harder to imagine him as a victim of wartime sexual violence. Male rape, in general more resistant to public discourse, becomes even harder to address when the target is imagined as a hyper-male and, as it was the case of CNN, as the ultimate incarnation of evil in the conflict, the dictator himself.

This example highlights some of the constraints that frame the mediation of evidence of wartime sexual violence: rape stories become public more easily when they can benefit political agendas and when they corroborate hegemonic gender constructions. What I find so striking with the Western media coverage of the 2011 Libyan war is to see how easily widespread imaginaries of wartime rape were activated right from the beginning of the conflict, thus determining which rape stories were perceived as paradigmatic of the conflict itself. Common strategies of othering sexual violence through a culturalist approach were much present in this process: the effectiveness of rape as a weapon of war was sustained broadly on the assumption that societies dominated by Islam are patriarchal, primitive and prone to stigmatise victims of sexual abuse. But well entrenched processes of gendering were crucial as well: rape victims are imagined as civilian women, while rapists are imagined as men involved in armed violence. In the context of a broad Western support for the rebels who tried to topple the dictatorship, the acts of sexual violence which fell out of the 'script' tended to be sidelined. There was evidence suggesting rapes committed by the rebels, the existence of male victims, the sexual torture of male combatants, as well as the massive sexual abuse of black migrants caught in the civil war, but none of these stories made headlines in Western mainstream media in 2011.

FABRICE VIRGILI: The question how sources on sexual violence are understood, appropriated and mediatised at a particular time in a particular socio-historical context is also crucial when we look at World War II. When I was preparing an exhibition on the topic 'Love, wars and sexuality' in Paris in 2007, I found four photos 'found on a German soldier' in the collection of the Resistance Museum in Champigny. In these photographs we see four soldiers obtaining by force a woman. She is lying on a pile of planks. On the first shot, she struggles when the soldiers undress her. On the following two images, men open her legs, showing her sex/genitals to the photographer. He is the fifth man, did he stay behind the camera or did he also rape the woman? On the last image, one soldier lowers his head looking closer at the victim's vagina. He holds a paper, maybe a picture in his hands.

On all the images, we see the grinning faces of the soldiers. On the contrary, the woman's face is always hidden. We only see her lower body. She is reduced to her sex. What happens before and beyond: penetration, assault, murder? We don't know.

That cameras were widespread in the Third Reich is well known. The most popular picture motifs of soldiers were the landscape in France, monuments in Paris, the civil population in the occupied countries, the POWs, the soldiers' everyday life and also the destruction, 'war scenes'. In spite of the ban to photograph the death of the enemy, many soldiers disobeyed and continued these violent snapshots when the war in Russia started. Why have soldiers taken these photos? What meanings do this kind of photos carry?

During the exhibitions on the crimes of the Wehrmacht by the Hamburger Institut für Sozialforschung (which took place from 1995 to 1999 and 2001 to 2004), these questions have been widely debated. But what about pictures of rape? Are these photos a trophy? Is this a demonstration of militarist and masculine power? But if this would be the case, why is the face of the victim hidden, contrary to many pictures of captives or executed persons? Should we regard these photos as more pornographic, because only the woman's sex is shown? Did one soldier or all soldiers keep the photos secretly or did they show them to their comrades in the 'brotherhood' at the front? And in case of the latter, did the photos present 'good memories'? And did the men boast about it?

Because this kind of source is very scarce it is difficult to know what they mean for their owners. But we know for sure that these photos interested the investigators of the War Crimes Enquiries Commission (Service de recherche des crimes de guerre ennemis—SRCGE). Found during the search of German soldiers, dead or alive, photos become a very important clue for the investigators. The photos moved from memories to proof. Since 1943, a commission investigated at first clandestinely the war crimes committed in France or abroad against French nationals. Then police investigations were organised on all territories after the liberation of France. For the SRCGE, a rape was considered to be a war crime, like the execution of civilians, torture, looting or arson. All these crimes were listed for investigation. Some of them are well known until today like in Oradour-sur-Glane (Destruction of the village and massacre of 642 inhabitants by a Waffen SS company on the 10 June 1944), others remain unknown. However, rape was neither charged at the Nuremberg trials nor in the trials before French military courts.

While these four photos didn't serve as evidence in court, they were used as evidence to the public. Similar to World War I, rape committed by German men became a theme of propaganda. Sexual violence was an effective way to denounce the enemy. In July 1945, the interministerial commission of war crimes chaired by M. Coste-Floret organised an exhibition on 'Hitlerian crimes' at the Grand Palais. Despite the horror of the images shown— the entrance was prohibited under 16 years of age—the visitors were numerous. Two catalogues were published. The hardcover version, the more luxurious one, contained the photos of the rape. But a sheet of tracing paper covered the photos. Behind this, the pictures could only be seen in a blurry way and the title was superimposed in English, French and Russian. At the same time, the organisers chose not to put the photos of the rape in the second catalogue, a cheaper, more easily accessible booklet. Despite these restrictions, rape by German soldiers was no taboo at that time. Still, the forced exhibition of this woman, the smiling men around her suggesting their pleasure could (and can) cause suspicion of voyeurism against him who looks at the picture. Yet we must also consider these sources. The images are essential to understanding the event: the conduct of the violence, the imaginary of perpetrators, the political use and the memory of these rapes committed in wartime.

xlvi GAPS AND TRAPS

JÚLIA GARRAIO: The concepts of legitimate/illegitimate violence
are essential to make sense of the public identification of sexual
violence and its perpetrators. Bernd Hüppauf (1997) has pointed
out the constitutive relationship between violence and the
modern condition. He notices how the Enlightenment's faith in
progress and a civilisation increasingly ruled by reason and free
of wars was accompanied by the emergence of a new concept
of legitimate violence (a violence that could be justified by moral
reasoning). The awareness that modernity was not only unable
to ban violence, but was also constructed on violence, led to
'techniques of relegation', essential for that legitimisation. While
the acceptable violence was interiorised as an exception to the rule
of a peaceful reality, the illegitimate violence was banished to the
'other', that is, it was attributed to another space, time, ideology,
political system, social class, etcetera.

Rape stories which go public tend to lend themselves to
strategies of othering, while the ones which are silenced are the
ones that could challenge the process of othering. When we talk
about World War II: How does it come that in the West there
is a widespread assumption that equates rape in WWII with the
Red Army, even though there is solid evidence documenting
widespread sexual violence perpetrated by the German forces and
by the Western allies as well?

It is often claimed that victors write the history of the past. In
the case of sexual violence in Europe during WWII one has to look
further than 1945: one must consider who won in 1989 and look
deeper into the ideological conflict of the precedent decades. And
it was the Western allies and the Federal Republic of Germany
(FRG), in the meantime part of the Western alliance, who won
1989 and who were therefore able to project their perception of
the rapists.

The existence of two rival German states and consequently of
two competing reconstructions of the past enables us to see how
deep ideology and political agendas determined the memory of
the past and the perception of the perpetrators of sexual violence.
Though both states had a common past until the spring of 1945,
when regarding their post-1945 discourses we might be led to

think that two different pasts were at stake. The FRG made no taboo of the widespread sexual violence in WWII, but it was quite selective in the identification of the perpetrators and very keen to integrate that violence in the ideological battlefield of the cold war. The rapes committed by the Red Army were used as an effective tool to discredit Communism, the Soviet Union and ultimately the neighbouring German Democratic Republic (GDR).

To gain a better understanding of this, fictional texts like novels can help us. I read fiction as representations in the sense put forward by Stuart Hall (1997), who, departing from a constructionist approach to language, understands representation as a construction of meanings through language as a representational system. Hence, I assume that fictions cannot be used as data to inform us about the sociological realities. However, I assume that works of fiction can unveil how a member of a given culture/society produced meanings about his/her reality through the use of the language he/she disposed of, that is, I assume that fictions may help us grasp how sectors of society understood their reality and tried to act on it and to form it by coming forward with explanatory narratives for contested social phenomena.

Consider, for example, the American bestseller *The Big Rape* (1951) by James Wakefield Burke: the representation of the Russian/Slav as a hard-drinker, barbarian and sexual predator and the representation of the Red Army as being full of 'Asian faces' follows a clear propaganda agenda. The rapes are signified as a feature of a whole group (the Eastern nations) and their explanation is full of racist undertones. This Eastern barbarian masculinity and 'destructive violence' has its counterpart in the American troops, who embody a 'protective violence' and potent and civilised masculinity.

The representation of the soldiers of the Red Army as brutal rapists, which can also be seen in the literature of the 'expulsion of Germans from the East', was favoured both from 'above' and from the 'ground': for the State it was a useful strategy to combat Communism and to justify its adherence to Western military, political and economic institutions; for 'ordinary Germans', many of whom had undergone violent encounters with the Red Army, it enabled them to see themselves as victims of war.

Contrary to a widespread assumption, which claims that the rapes committed by the Red Army were banned from the public sphere of the GDR, there were several attempts to address the subject. But the rapes were clearly among memories of the past, which were uncomfortable for the State, as the 'Djacenko-case' shows.[1] In 1958, the authorities banned the sequel of Boris Djacenko's novel *Herz und Asche* (1954). Carla, the German lover of the Russian hero, is raped in the sequel by three Red Army soldiers. Djacenko was a man of the regime, his aim was not to discredit Communism nor demonise Russians. He tried to address the suffering endured by raped women and at the same time discuss why the sexual violence had taken place, giving the perpetrators a chance to explain their acts. One of them, for example, invokes the wartime crimes committed by Germans in the Soviet Union. How would the perception of the perpetrators have developed in the GDR if the authorities had allowed the subject to be discussed in the terms of Djacenko? Would his text have opened the way for a narrative, which is very common in other contexts: the rapist soldier as a victim of war, who was brutalised in a spiral of violence? This narrative could have led to potentially exculpatory discourses; nonetheless by focusing the ambiguities of the perpetrators it could as well have fostered a deeper scrutiny of the subject.

In that sense, a comparative analysis of post-1945 German practices of remembrance signals the pervasiveness of processes of 'othering' sexual violence. It tends to be attributed to the Other, to social/ethnic/national groups which are perceived as different 'from us'. This segregation of the perpetrator and the act of ascribing him and his deed to certain groups open the way for the demonization of this Other as our absolute counterpart.

NOTE

1. On the cultural memories of the rapes in the GDR and the 'Djacenko case' see Dahlke 2000.

REFERENCES

Alcoff, Linda Martín. 2018. *Rape and Resistance*. Medford/Cambridge: Polity Press.

Butler, Judith. 1997. *The Psychic Life of Power: Theories in Subjection*. Stanford: Stanford University Press.

———. 1993. *Bodies that Matter*. New York/London: Routledge.

Cahill, Ann J. 2001. *Rethinking Rape*. Ithaca: Cornell.

Cannetti, Elias. 1960. *Masse und Macht*. Hamburg: Claassen.

Canning, Kathleen. 1994. 'Feminist History after the Linguistic Turn: Historicizing Discourse and Experiences', *Signs: Journal of Women in Culture and Society*, 19(2):368–404.

Carlson, Eric Stener. 2006. 'The Hidden Prevalence of Male Sexual Assault during War: Observations on Blunt Trauma to the Male Genitals', *The British Journal of Criminology*, 46(1):16–25.

Dahlke, Birgit. 2000. '"Frau komm!" Vergewaltigungen 1945: Zur Geschichte eines Diskurses', in Birgit Dahlke/Martina Langermann/Thomas Taterka (eds), *LiteraturGesellschaft DDR: Kanonkämpfe und ihre Geschichte(n)*, pp. 275–311. Stuttgart: Metzler.

Daniel, Ute. 1993. 'Der Krieg der Frauen 1914–1918: Zur Innenansicht des ersten Weltkriegs in Deutschland', in Gerhard Hirschfeld/Gerd Krumeich/Irina Renz (eds), *"Keiner fühlt sich hier mehr als Mensch ..." Erlebnis und Wirkung des Ersten Weltkriegs*, pp. 131–50. Essen: Klartext.

Hagemann, Karen. 1998. 'Venus und Mars: Reflexionen zu einer Geschlechtergeschichte von Militär und Krieg', in Karen Hagemann/Ralf Pröve (eds), *Landsknechte, Soldatenfrauen und Nationalkrieger: Militär, Krieg und Geschlechterordnung im historischen Wandel*, pp. 13–49. Frankfurt a. M.: Campus.

Hall, Stuart. 1997. 'The Work of Representation', in Stuart Hall (ed), *Representation: Cultural Representation and Signifying Practices*, pp. 13–74. London: Sage.

Hamber, Brandon. 2007. 'Masculinity and Transitional Justice: An Exploratory Essay', *International Journal of Transitional Justice*, 1(3):375–90.

Horne, John/Kramer, Alan. 2001. *German Atrocities, 1914: A History of Denial*. New Haven: Yale University Press.

Hüppauf, Bernd. 1997. 'Introduction: Modernity and Violence: Observations Concerning a Contradictory Relationship', in Bernd Hüppauf (ed), *War, Violence, and the Modern Condition*, pp. 1–29. Berlin/New York: De Gruyter.

Johnson, Barbara. 1981. 'Translator's Introduction', in Jacques Derrida (ed), *Dissemination*, pp. vii–xxxiii. Chicago: University of Chicago Press.

Krumeich, Gerd. 1993. 'Kriegsgeschichte im Wandel', in Gerhard Hirschfeld/Gerd Krumeich/Irina Renz (eds), *"Keiner fühlt sich hier mehr als Mensch …" Erlebnis und Wirkung des Ersten Weltkriegs*, pp. 11–24. Essen: Klartext.

Lévinas, Emmanuel. 1985. *Ethics and Infinity*. Pittsburgh: Duquesne University Press.

Lind, William S. 1992. 'Tailhook: The Larger Issue', *Marine Corps Gazette* (Quantico), November.

Maddock, Kenneth. 1991. 'Going Over the Limit? The Question of Australian Atrocities', in Kenneth Maddock (ed), *Memories of Vietnam*, pp. 162–3. Milsons Point: Random House.

Nahoum-Grappe, Véronique. 1996. 'L'usage politique de la cruauté: L'épuration éthnique (ex-Yougoslavie, 1991–1995)', in Françoise Héritier (ed), *De la violence*, pp. 273–323. Paris: Odile Jacob.

Schrijvers, Peter. 2005. *The GI War against Japan: American Soldiers in Asia and the Pacific During World War II*. New York: New York University Press.

Sidner, Sara. 2011. 'Libyan Rebels say Captured Cell Phone Videos show Rape, Torture', *CNN*, 17 June. http://edition.cnn.com/2011/WORLD/africa/06/14/libya.rape.hfr/index.html (accessed 03 January 2019).

Tiger, Lionel. 1999. *The Decline of Males*. New York: Golden Books.

Žarkov, Dubravka. 2007. *The Body of War: Media, Ethnicity, and Gender in the Break-Up of Yugoslavia*. Durham: Duke University Press.

WAR/POWER

Sexual violence in armed conflict is not just a wartime atrocity, but a violent act that also occurs in peacetime. It exists on the borderline of official military practices and intimate behaviour. It is a practice involving gendered actors who are hierarchically positioned in relation to each other. In current debates, there are a variety of theories and assumptions concerning connections between armed conflict and gendered violence. How do conceptions of 'war', 'armed conflict' and 'peace' shape knowledge, practices, and memories of sexual violence?

The practice of war is based on gendered power positions. Sexual violence can only be understood in terms of these power positions and their underlying effects, such as economic dependency. How can the different constellations of victims and perpetrators be scrutinised? How do normative understandings of sexual violence in armed conflict emerge? What about disruptions to these normative understandings? Are there any grey areas and, if so, how can they be integrated into any model of violence? How do international, as well as national, contexts shape responses to sexual violence?

"You have to Anticipate What Eludes Calculation": Reconceptualising Sexual Violence as Weapon and Strategy of War

REGINA MÜHLHÄUSER

Rape is a classic act of terrorism, which not only serves the political function of intimidating a rebellious population, but also allows the rapist to reassert his manhood. [...] Systematic mass rape was a policy implemented by consistently covering up reported rapes and making it clear to GI's that they had no real need to fear punishment.

— Arlene Eisen Bergman, *Women of Viet Nam*, 1974

Despite being prohibited by international law, sexual violence continues to be employed as a tactic of war in numerous conflicts from Myanmar to Ukraine and Syria to Somalia. It includes mass rape, gang rape, sexual slavery, and rape as a form of torture, ethnic cleansing and terrorism. It accounts in large part for why it is often more dangerous to be a woman in a warzone today than it is to be a soldier.

— Actress Angelina Jolie and NATO Secretary General Jens Stoltenberg, *Guardian*, 10 December 2017

Defense: It is alleged that in 2009 the FDLR [*Forces Démocratiques de Libération du Rwanda*, a Rwandan rebel group in the Congo] has carried out sexual violence against hundreds of women throughout the Kivu provinces, and that this has caused a humanitarian disaster. This was allegedly realised and done as part of a plan. Is such a plan known to you?

Witness: Most soldiers are not angels. I do not dispute that there were soldiers in the FDLR who raped, but they did it on their own. [...]

Defense: Have you ever been presented with such a strategy that you yourself should use such means of warfare, that is rape?

Witness: [...] We did not have instructions on killings, looting and rape at the FDLR.

Former FDLR Sergeant, Higher Regional Court
Stuttgart, 16 April 2012.

These three examples illustrate that 'sexual violence as a weapon of war' is not a terminus technicus with a clear-cut definition, nor is 'sexual violence as a policy, tactic or strategy of armed conflict'. Instead, these terms are argumentative topoi charged with significance. What meaning is conveyed depends on the context, the particular debate in which these terms are used, and the interests they may serve.

Calling sexual violence a weapon, tactic, strategy or policy lends it a particular gravity. Using this terminology emphasises that this form of violence is not just an accidental by-product of war, but an intrinsic and regular element of belligerent action. Indeed, speaking about sexual violence as a weapon marks the resulting harm and injustice in a particular way: it is seen as a crime that needs to be morally, politically and legally condemned, *because* it is an element of warfare.

The emphasis on sexual violence as an element of belligerent action makes it possible to understand and convey the societal relevance of this form of violence in times of armed conflict. At the same time, however, the phenomenon itself is isolated, as it comes to seem as if such acts are limited to warfare against an enemy collective and detached from everyday gendered practices of sexual violence. This carries the risk of downplaying the pervasiveness of wartime sexual violence. Only when rape is viewed as an exceptionally abhorrent act and a vehicle for war and genocide does it seem to be recognised as a crime and a grave breach of international criminal law (Copelon 1994: 246f). Sexual violence is less visible, even obscured, and appears less severe if it is not identified as part of a widespread and systematic or orchestrated attack against a (political, national, ethnic, religious) opponent (for example Mischkowski 2008: 245; Mibenge 2008: 147; Buss 2009: 153ff).

The question of whether acts of sexual violence in a particular conflict are regarded as 'conflict-related' is also shaped by a distinctly Western gaze and selectivity that reinforces gendered and racist stereotypes and prevents a deeper understanding of the origins and workings of sexual violence, as Ngwarsungu Chiwengo (2008) has demonstrated regarding the Democratic Republic of Congo. Who is perceived as victim, and which victims are granted assistance, largely depends on which constellations of sexual violence are recognised and condemned by the international community (Crawford 2013: 511–3). Similarly, the assessment of sexual violence as weapon, tactic or strategy also affects who is identified and held responsible as a perpetrator. In many cases, a picture emerges which suggests that perpetrators of sexual violence are solely enemy combatants while same-side perpetration is largely obscured (Buss 2009: 160). What is more, the 'weapon of war' concept shifts the focus away from the direct perpetrators to the commanders or command structures of an armed group.

When practices of sexual violence were first conceptualised as a 'weapon of terror' and a 'weapon of war' by African-American and Jewish feminists in the US in the 1970s—the time of the Women's Liberation Movement, the Civil Rights Movement and protests against the Vietnam War—one main objective was to show that violence against women is not a by-product, but an intrinsic part of armed conflict. These early discussions were based on the insight that rape is a form of violence that evolves within gendered power structures and is structured by its conditions—in times of war and peace (for example Lerner 1972: 172f; Eisen Bergman 1974: 69, 61; Brownmiller 1975: 5, 24, 36, 44, 49, 63, 229, 424).[1] Twenty years later, during the Yugoslav Wars, the genocide against the Tutsi and the war in Rwanda and its neighbouring states, feminist researchers and women's human rights advocates introduced the concept of sexual violence as weapon, strategy or policy into the broader public debate. Emphasising the widespread use of sexual violence since ancient times, they argued that this has a grave impact not only on the individual victim, but also on her immediate surroundings as well as her ethnic/religious/national collective (for example Seifert 1994; MacKinnon 1994; Card 1996). Their efforts were successful, and terms like 'mass rape' and 'genocidal rape' quickly became common in scholarship and the media. But in the course of this public recognition, the interpretation underwent a far-reaching shift: rape was increasingly understood as a deliberate means of destroying an enemy collective, that is, their identity as a people as well as their physical existence (Skjelsbæk 2010: 16). With this framing, sexual violence has also gained increasing recognition by international human rights bodies and was adopted as an issue of international security and peacekeeping, initially with UN resolution 1820 in 2008 (Baaz/Stern 2013: 43ff; Crawford 2013: 510ff).

The current recognition of sexual violence as a weapon, tactic or strategy offers an allegedly clear image of a wartime atrocity perpetrated against civilians. This image allows states and organisations to act in accordance with guidelines of international law and UN mandates. On an epistemological level, however, these concepts seem to have reached a limit. In recent years, different scholars have therefore suggested that it is time to reconceptualise the debate (for example Baaz/Stern 2013; Boesten 2017).

I would like to contribute to such efforts by exploring the relationship between the acts of individual combatants in the field and the calculations of military leadership. How does the perpetration of sexual violence by individual soldiers become part of military calculations and tactical and strategic planning? When, why and how do military commands tacitly tolerate, accept, instigate or orchestrate the perpetration of sexual violence by their men? To explore these questions, it seems crucial to take the specific character of sexual violence (which differs from other forms of violence) as well as the everyday knowledge of violent sexual practices (in war as well as in non-war times) into account.

My considerations derive primarily from my study of warfare conducted by Western state militaries in the Age of the World Wars, and this article relies in particular on German army sources from WWII. Looking at the current debate, one might easily get the impression that sexual violence is primarily incorporated into warfare in non-Western armed groups and recent wars. A closer look, however, reveals similar mechanisms throughout modern wars and current armed-conflicts.

MILITARY AUTHORITIES MUST "ANTICIPATE WHAT ELUDES CALCULATION"

A 'weapon' is commonly understood as anything used against an opponent to harm or destroy, to attack or defend. Strategy and tactics, in contrast, are connected to rational, planned behaviours. From a military standpoint, strategy is generally defined as the overall planning, coordination and application of military means (and often civilian resources as well) to meet overall or long-term political and military objectives. Tactics, on the other hand, are short-term decisions on the battlefield that are deployed to win a battle. While tactics aim at the successful realisation of operational goals, operational planning (strategy) aims at the successful fulfilment of a campaign (Gray 1999: 17–23).

When such terms are used in connection with sexual violence, it is easy to form the impression that this type of violence is part of a pre-meditated plan that is negotiated in the top-down military decision-making structure. While this may not be entirely wrong, the reality seems much more complicated and requires further exploration.

One central factor in such an exploration is the fact that the hierarchical model of military planning and decision making fails to represent what every man and woman who has participated in a military mission knows: no soldier merely follows orders. In the reality of the battlefield and in zones of occupation, soldiers evaluate their orders with regard to their scope of interpretation and action and make situational decisions accordingly. The soldiers' role as representatives of the military institution, their place in the military hierarchy, and the visual power of their uniforms allow them to enact power in ways that would be unthinkable for a civilian. The military command, on the other hand, is fully aware that when soldiers make decisions (sometimes in split seconds) the overall goal of winning the campaign recedes behind the options available at the moment.

Military sociologists have shown that decisions made by individual soldiers in the field are often not primarily motivated by ideology or military aims, and that the strategies of a command and the actions of the individual are never entirely congruent (Biehl 2010). What is more, tactical decisions by small military units and strategic goals can be opposed to each other. Military commands are aware of this discrepancy, and try to make use of the frictions involved in the decisions of individual soldiers. In fact, a military command must succeed in predicting the actions of its men on the ground—and decide if to tolerate, exploit or try to prevent them— in order to remain in control and fulfil tactical and strategic goals. Ulrich Bröckling's concept of the battlefield as a "contingency space par excellence" is helpful in grasping this complexity:

> The battlefield is [...] a zone of frictions, those unforeseen and often unpredictable adversities and slowing forces that distinguish, according to Clausewitz's words, "the real war from that on paper". At the same time it is a place of fortune, of the unexpected chance, of the sudden turning of luck. Contingency, however, not only designates the inaccessible sphere of chance, but also the tangible one of human action. [...] More than other forms of action, the "extended struggle" (Clausewitz) for life and death requires all actors to make the utmost strategic and tactical calculations [...]. This includes meticulously prepared and coordinated operations as well as spontaneous improvisation, command and obedience, as well as self-initiative and self-responsibility. Ultimately, the battlefield is a place of extreme affects—from the stupor of agony to the furor of battle-frenzy—that inhibit or disinhibit action and change its direction.
> (Bröckling 2003: 189; partly cited in Zipfel 2013)

Those who go to war experience that they cannot be fully in control. Regardless of how hard they try to take the right decision, they know that they might die at any moment. "They can experience emotions such as the fear of injury, pain and death, but also anger or hatred as overpowering. Also contradictory affects and emotions, such as the simultaneousness of anger and anxiety, have an effect on their personality," Jens Warburg observes (2010: 260). Social psychologist Rolf Pohl (2012) has suggested that we need to explore the extent to which this experience of loss of control in male soldiers is connected to unconscious misogynist perceptions and affective attitudes to femininity (and if this is radically different for female soldiers).

A military command needs to manage this "radicalized experience of contingency" (Bröckling 2015: 189). It has to mobilise the soldier's potential for violence while simultaneously keeping it in check, which is why soldiers in state armies are subjected to a broad variety of disciplinary measures (Reemtsma 2004). They are trained to deal with their bodily sensations, emotions and affects. This includes efforts to establish action routines for soldiers that they can fall back on when exposed to great emotional stress. Yet despite all these preparations, soldiers do not achieve complete control over their bodies and minds.

The military is aware that it is impossible to fully control the individual and collective action of men and women in military operations. As a consequence, Bröckling asserts, commanders must take "the unavoidable, but never determinable limit of all planning and organization" into account: "Whoever wants to steer needs not only power, but also knowledge. To deal with the frictions, or to be able to deal with them, you have to know them […]. You have to anticipate what eludes calculation" (Bröckling 2015: 190).

If we follow Bröckling's line of argument, military superiors have to reckon with the fact that recruits in certain situations behave in ways that are not conducive to the war aims, and may even contradict and undermine these aims. Since the occurrence of sexual violence in armed conflict is part of our practical knowledge as civilians, we can safely assume that military commanders expect (or at least suspect) that their soldiers will commit sexual violence and anticipate it in their calculations.

So the question is how military commanders deal with expectations as well as the actual occurrence of sexual violence. How do they assess this form of violence and how does it play into their overall thinking about military strategy and tactics? To explore this question, it is crucial to understand the specific nature of sexual violence compared to other forms of violence.

THE AMBIGUITY OF SEXUAL VIOLENCE

While the military demands subjugation and obedience, it also promises to compensate the individual for this inhibition. As Jan Philipp Reemtsma (2004) has argued, "The order 'You must!' is accompanied by the license 'You may.' Soldiers are not only disciplined more rigorously than other people, they can also—at least during war—take more liberties."

Soldiers are thus allowed, within specific limits, to get intoxicated and perpetrate violence against civilians, often following patterns of gendered, racist or religious othering. This is seen as a means of sublimating the hardships of military service, including the imposition to kill and the possibility of being killed. In this context, sexual violence by men against women[2] seems to occupy a specific position, and is different from other forms of violence like looting or beating. Ultimately, there is no military or societal agreement that sexual violence in armed conflicts constitutes a crime that requires prosecution.

This statement may seem contradictory, as the rape of women and girls has been described as a crime in the military codes and rules of conduct of most states and armed groups throughout history. While this is true, historical studies from different theatres of war and armed conflict in the nineteenth and twentieth centuries have demonstrated that military courts generally only indict and pass sentences on sexual violence with specific dynamics and constellations; it does not necessarily mean that they concede the criminal nature of acts of sexual violence. For example, the 1863 Lieber Code (the military code for the US Union Army) codified rape of women and girls as a crime against property, troop discipline and family honour. The number of cases that ended up in court was limited and they were, at least in part, as Crystal Feimster (2013) observes, "about discipline, and enforcing a code of conduct." In a similar manner, Birgit Beck (2005) found that the German army in WWII only prosecuted sexual assault in cases in which it was considered a grave disciplinary problem or to cause serious harm to the reputation of the armed forces. Her work also clearly reveals that the military handled sexual violence differently in different territories. Rape was only brought before the military courts once the Wehrmacht had begun to establish a more long-term occupation regime that required collaboration with large segments of the local population. The military authorities needed to restrain and discipline their men to ensure this cooperation. Verdicts were delivered accordingly at the Western front and during the beginning of the occupation of Poland in 1939/1940. As the war on the Eastern front grew in brutality, however, and after the invasion of the Soviet Union on 22 June 1941, military jurisdiction over rape was hardly implemented at all anymore.

One might argue that this is not all that different from the way militaries handle other forms of violence, like pillage. Indeed, pillage, like rape, is codified as a crime in military law and codes of conduct, yet soldiers are—in certain time periods and within limits—granted the liberty to pillage. Indeed, for a long time, pillage and rape were both treated as property crimes and 'normal' by-products of warfare. However, an 'international prohibition regime' against pillage was established with relatively little controversy in the late nineteenth century while, as Tuba Inal (2013) observes, similar steps for rape were only taken at the end of the twentieth century. Inal sees two central underlying factors here, firstly that "states did not believe they could prevent rape in war because they believed rape in war was inevitable" (contrary to pillage, that was thought could be effectively prevented by disciplining the troops and providing them with food, clothes and luxury goods), and secondly that the victims were predominantly lower class women and they "were not 'property enough' to be protected" (Inal 2013: 170–3).

Underlying Inal's observation that states did not believe they could prevent wartime rape is the understanding that the frictions of the battlefield and sexual excitement are inextricably linked. In April 1942, Hitler asserted: "If the German man as a soldier is to be ready to die unconditionally he must have the freedom to love unconditionally" (cited in Picker 1997: 332). This comment reveals an understanding of prevalent modern thinking: that combat and sex are *the* existential experiences of human, or more precisely, male existence.

The cultural idea that male virility is an affirmation of male vitality can be found in different regions of the world. According to David Tombs: "One of the most significant ways that a man can define himself as victor not victim is through his sexual identity as an active and powerful man" (Tombs 2002: 28). Affirming non-victim status becomes all the more important in wartime.

This finds expression in a tacit agreement in many military formations that sanctions the male soldier's view of sexual advances towards women as a natural part of warring. To start with, the majority of military men do not seem to perceive acts of sexual violence against women as serious crimes. Moreover, male combatants are sometimes not even aware that their actions constitute violence and thus wrongdoing. In September 1940, for example, two Wehrmacht soldiers forced two Jewish women, ages 17 and 18, from their home at gunpoint to a Polish cemetery. They raped one of the women. The other woman was menstruating, so they let her go, but they 'offered' to pay her five Złoty if she came back the following week to have sex with them (Bergen 2006: 181). While the women must have experienced the encounter as violent, the men could view it as somehow consensual, as something the women could agree to, at least in exchange for money.

Why and how this divergence of perspectives works needs to be explored in future research. Gaby Zipfel has suggested one possible point of departure for such an analysis by highlighting the need to assess the ways in which sexual violence in modern times aims not only to inflict pain, but also to exploit the sexual sensations of the victim. A sexually violent act thus also represents an attack on the libido:

A person beaten up in the street may not reckon with the empathy of those present, may even experience blame for allegedly contributing to the violence through some form of provocation, but she/he can assume that her/his experience of violently inflicted physical pain is unequivocally considered an unwanted, negative experience. Victims of sexual violence, in contrast, are often denied a clear assessment in this sense. This is because this kind of attack targets a body that is not only sensitive to pain, but also able to take pleasure. Sexual violence subjects the body of the victim to pain and at the same time seizes its libidinal sensibility. (Zipfel 2018: 91)

These implicit or explicit insinuations that the victim "reacts ambiguously to the attack" arise because of the possibility of sexual arousal as a condition of the body. Thus "a possible agreement between the perpetrator and the victim" is implied ("she asked for it") and the victim is denied empathy and a clear classification of this form of violence as wrongdoing (ibid.)

Only when an act of sexual violence is accompanied by excessive brutality and/or the perpetrator kills the victim during or after the sexual attack is "the previously questioned unambiguity [...] cynically established as proven", not least because now the sexuality expressed in the act of violence practised by the perpetrator and visited on the victim, "can be marginalized" (ibid).

This ambiguous perception of sexual violence, and rape in particular, in civil life is not nullified in armed conflict. Quite the contrary in fact, as it might be precisely this ambiguity surrounding rape (directed against the body as subject both to pain and to arousal and lust) that makes this form of violence such an effective means of warfare. The alleged complicity of the victim suggests that the responsibility for the attack does not lie solely with the perpetrator, and that the victim contributed to her violation. This, in turn, seems to cause the victim's community to view her with suspicion, distrust and contempt. These negative responses may even rebound on and attach to the community itself, in particular the men in the community, since they allowed the act to happen. As such, the rape victim's collective can be seriously shaken, torn apart and destroyed.

Rape victims often report struggling with feelings of defilement and shame. How such feelings are generated and what they mean has yet to be explored in detail. Bülent Diken and Carsten Bagge Laustsen (2005: 116ff) argue that such feelings are connected to the social construction of rape victims as abject. The abject person, they explain, is seen as a threat to the normal social order, because she is defined as polluted (and feels herself to be polluted) and thus no longer able to be part of the normal order. An abject person symbolises not just the other, a subject outside of one's own community; an abject person also denotes indistinction and formlessness and thus a threat within the community.

If we follow this argument, wartime rape is an attempt to devalue women, thereby harming the whole community (ibid.: 117). This resonates with an earlier feminist observation that wartime rape is ultimately directed at men who patriarchal coding positions as protectors of women and the community. Consequently, sexual violence uses women's bodies to transport a message from men to men, namely that the men in the victim's collective are no longer able to protect 'their' women (Seifert 1994).

It therefore follows that military commanders might assess sexual violence as beneficial to the war effort, as it can have a positive effect on the inner workings of an armed group (affirming victor identity, male bonding, loyalty, cohesion) and a devastating effect on the enemy (establishing terror, threatening the social order and reproductive capacities). In some cases, sexual violence is instigated or purposefully adopted; in others it is tacitly tolerated and overlooked. In either case, I argue that sexual violence is part of a military's strategic and tactical thinking. It might not be explicitly spelled out, but it is part of military knowledge and thus—implicitly or explicitly—included in operational calculations.

To further clarify my line of reasoning, I will now turn to the German army during the war in the Soviet Union from 1941 to 1945 as an empirical example and focus primarily on the ways in which the command of the Wehrmacht, the conscription army, included the expectation and occurrence of sexual violence in their tactical calculations.

THE GERMAN WAR OF ANNIHILATION

From the moment war commenced against the Soviet Union, German warfare could be characterised as excessively violent. On 13 May 1941, six weeks before the invasion, the Wehrmacht High Command (OKW) issued the so-called *Kriegsgerichtsbarkeitserlaß* (Military Jurisdiction Decree), which allowed soldiers to shoot 'suspicious' civilians on the spot merely upon an officer's order. About one month later, on 6 June 1941, the *Kommissarbefehl* (Commissar Order) explicitly ordered the Wehrmacht not to take the Red Army's political functionaries as prisoners of war (in accordance with the Geneva Conventions) and to summarily execute them instead. Both decrees rendered the Soviet Union a more or less extra-legal territory. War diaries and daily division reports reveal that German troops humiliated, plundered, violently attacked and murdered the local population, and Jewish men, women and children in particular. In the first phase of the war, they took very few prisoners, executing people perceived as enemy combatants on the spot. Indeed, the majority of German soldiers saw these executions as an acid test of their abilities to overcome any scruples they might previously have had. On 20 January 1942, during what historians later called the Wannsee Conference, senior German government officials and Nazi party functionaries formalised the 'Final Solution to the Jewish Question'—the Nazis' euphemism for the extermination of all European Jews—"irrespective of geographic borders". In the following weeks, the SS, the police and the Wehrmacht began the liquidation of the Jewish ghettoes in Eastern Europe and the systematic mass murder of their Jewish inhabitants (Pohl 2008).

Until recently, it was widely assumed that sexual violence was not part of the horrendous atrocities Wehrmacht soldiers committed during the war in the Soviet Union, mostly because Nazi racial laws prohibited sexual contact between 'Aryans' and Jews. German soldiers who were committed to Nazi ideology, the reasoning goes, would have exercised 'racially aware' self-restraint and the Wehrmacht would have harshly punished soldiers who violated the Nazi racial laws. Recent research has demonstrated that neither of these assumptions reflects the reality on the ground during the War of Annihilation. Sexual violence by German troops was widespread and included coerced disrobement, sexual torture, sexual assault, sexual blackmail, rape, gang rape and sexual enslavement. Sometimes, dead bodies were mistreated and mutilated in sexual ways. German soldiers also frequently visited local prostitutes and official military brothels, and they exploited women who traded sex for protection, food or other scarce goods. In some cases, German men were also involved in consensual liaisons with local women, which at times led to applications for marriage permits, especially in Estonia and Latvia. Under these circumstances, however, 'consensual' did not mean that these encounters were based on mutual understanding or affection. Women entered into sexual relationships with soldiers due in large part to the specific needs, pragmatic choices and fears that resulted from the war (Beck 2005; Gertjejannsen 2004; Flaschka 2009; Mühlhäuser 2010). While heterosexual encounters have recently become the subject of research, sexual violence, sexual trade and consensual relationships between German soldiers and/or with local men remain largely unexplored (Giles 2005; Flaschka 2009; Herzog 2012; Mühlhäuser 2017b).

UNIT COHESION, LOYALTY, MILITARY DISCIPLINE

Scholars of military sociology have explored how social cohesion helps determine the effectiveness of military operations. Indeed, soldiers' survival largely depends upon trust and teamwork. Creating and maintaining cohesion is thus one of the army leadership's most important tasks. Guy Siebold (2007: 287) distinguishes between primary group cohesion (peer and leader bonding) and secondary group cohesion (organisational and institutional bonding). "Peer or horizontal bonding is among members at the same military hierarchical level (e.g., squad or group members). Leader or vertical bonding is between those at different levels (e.g., between squad or group members and their leaders). Peer and leader bonding within a small group (e.g., a platoon) together compose primary group cohesion." Conforming to this pattern, Wehrmacht training aimed to produce officers who were adept at creating conditions in which their men could bond with each other while remaining loyal to their superiors. Granting subordinates the 'liberty' of sexual violence was useful in negotiating this balance. On 7 October 1941, General Major Jürgen W., an artilleryman with the Twentieth Infantry Division, wrote of his battalion's victory in the Russian territory of Nawlja in his diary:

> The village is cleansed in a sharp attack, as if on the training ground; the 6th company proceeds, takes 120 prisoners and a lot of loot. They also capture a trailer with "ladies" for the brave Russians, the inhabitants are slightly damaged by the [machine gun] fire, mind you; but then, why do they go to war. "Tasty girls" is what the privates have to say when they return.[3]

Jürgen W. clearly regarded the rapes committed by his subordinates as a natural (and foreseeable) part of the military operation. He condoned these acts, depicting himself as a father-like figure who displayed benevolent understanding for the men under his command. Permitting, or at least not forbidding, these rapes can be read as an effort to strengthen the bond between his subordinates while also fostering their trust in him.

Anticipation of sexual violence and sympathetic understanding for offenders was also common in the Wehrmacht Supreme Command. On 6 September 1941, Supreme Commander of the Army Walther von Brauchitsch disseminated rules of action entitled "self-discipline" to the troop leaders on the Eastern Front:

> Since the predispositions of men differ, it is [...] inevitable that tensions and distress in the sexual realm will arise here and there that we cannot and should not close our eyes to.
>
> This problem can by no means be solved with a ban on sexual activity. Besides other negative consequences, such a ban would increase the number of sexual violation crimes and the risk of offenses against §175 [the statute of the German criminal code that punished male-male sexual interactions].[4]

Von Brauchitsch's assumption that sexual "tensions and distress" would build up in many men was compatible with contemporary military teachings about the potential effects of the brutality of war on men's sexuality. After World War I, German military doctors observed that soldiers could suffer impotence as a result of their experiences on the battlefield (Crouthamel 2008). What is more, German, British and American WWI soldiers all described experiencing arousal and orgasm while perpetrating violence or killing (Bourke 2000). Military commanders were aware that they had to take the physical and psychological frictions men experienced during battle into account.

While the Wehrmacht command identified a number of risks soldiers' sexual activity presented for military operations (such as the spread of sexually transmitted diseases, the loss of military discipline, the harm to the Wehrmacht's reputation, the resistance that sexual violence could trigger in local populations, the fear of military espionage, and the birth of 'unwanted, racially mixed bastards') they made no serious attempts to prevent their men from being sexually active and perpetrating sexual violence against women. Quite the contrary actually; von Brauchitsch had already instructed military judges to exempt rapists from serious punishment (unless they were known to be repeat offenders or had carried out the act with extreme brutality) long before the Eastern campaign.[5]

Overall, the Wehrmacht directed most of its attention toward limiting the medical, physical and psychological risks of sexual activity for their men. The army medical corps was instructed, for instance, to educate the men about the dangers of sexual contact and the symptoms of sexual transmitted diseases (STDs). In larger cities, the Wehrmacht established "sanitation facilities" where men could disinfect their genitals after sexual intercourse (Mühlhäuser 2010: 178–206).

The Wehrmacht also established military brothels to channel and control soldiers' sexual activities. On 20 March 1942, the Chief Medical Officer in the Army High Command ordered the establishment of brothels for the exclusive use of Wehrmacht soldiers "in the Occupied Territory of Soviet Russia".[6] The circumstances under which the women were recruited remain largely unknown to this day. Apparently, some women were forced into sexual enslavement while others agreed to work in the brothels to ensure their survival and that of their family members (Mühlhäuser 2010: 214ff). It is important to note, however, that even women who agreed to work in the brothels were not free to reject a customer or quit at their will. Ultimately, all the women who served in these military brothels lived in circumstances characterised by force and violence.

In sum, the fact that Wehrmacht commanders and mid-level officers granted their men the liberty to carry out sexual violence can be understood as a strategy to secure the men's loyalty, compensating them for the demands of military life, binding them to the community of male superiority, and securing the commanders' power positions. In addition, the Wehrmacht took measures to minimise the medical and military risks of sexual intercourse—whether forced or consensual—and to increase the availability of controlled sexual activity. Ultimately, the Wehrmacht even engaged in the institutionalised exploitation of women in brothels in order to provide their men with outlets for their "sexual troubles and distress".

ATTACKING THE ENEMY

In the first few months that followed the attack on the Soviet Union, three million German soldiers made incredibly rapid territorial gains along a front of almost one thousand miles by relying on *Auftragstaktik* (mission tactics), a military doctrine developed before WWI to maximise mobility and flexibility. Under this doctrine, higher commanders only communicated a mission's overall goal, leaving the methods for achieving it at the discretion and initiative of the leaders at the tactical/operational command level. Success depended on field-level leaders' understanding of a mission and the individual actions undertaken to achieve the said mission. The *Auftragstaktik* doctrine encouraged risk taking in ways that threatened previous norms of military engagement, and thus allowed for and even encouraged routine breaches of previously established limitations on decision making in the field.

Sexual violence was pervasive in this context. The victims came from all social, national, ethnic and religious backgrounds, and included non-Jews and Jews. The effects of this form of violence were devastating. Many women and girls went into hiding in order to avoid sexual attacks. Documents and testimonies from victims and bystanders reveal that such acts resulted in feelings of existential loss, insecurity and terror. Some sources suggest that survivors felt so scared and ashamed that they concealed their experiences from their families, friends and communities, and from their husbands or fiancées in particular. Indeed, women sometimes faced suspicion that they had somehow participated in their own violation (Mühlhäuser 2010: 47ff).

Acknowledging that such devastating social consequences were likely not the prime motivator for soldiers to perpetrate acts of sexual violence or for military commanders to condone or encourage them, it is clear that both men in the field and the Supreme Command were well aware of these effects. Still, neither mid-level officers nor the Supreme Command curtailed the perpetration of sexual violence. On 10 August 1941, the Ninth Army High Command reported significant numbers of sexual crimes in the combat zone.[7] Three months later, on 10 November 1941, the OKH issued guidelines urging soldiers to exercise "restraint with respect to the other sex." But the guidelines also noted that "rigorous action" should only be taken in cases where German soldiers were "imbruting [*verwildern*] and lacked discipline."[8]

These guidelines accorded with the above-mentioned Military Jurisdiction Decree, which stipulated:

> The judge should order the prosecution of offenses against civilians through court martial only if it is considered necessary for the maintenance of discipline or the security of the troops. This applies, for instance, to serious offenses, such as those arising from sexual abandon [*geschlechtlicher Hemmungslosigkeit*], those that derive from a criminal tendency, or those that indicate that the troops are threatening to imbrute [*daß die Truppe zu verwildern droht*].[9]

The Military Jurisdiction Decree reveals that the German military regarded criminal offenses against civilians, including rape and other forms of sexual violence, as legitimate and reasonable forms of combatting 'Bolshevism'. Only in cases where soldiers lost sight of the military aims of the campaign, where their efforts to satisfy their personal lusts (for sex or blood) or to enrich themselves displayed a complete lack of self-control were they to be subjected to the punishment of military justice.

This reading of the Military Jurisdiction Decree makes it clear that it was in no way the intention of Hitler or the Wehrmacht Supreme Command to give German soldiers license to pillage and rape indiscriminately and/or solely out of individual personal interest or desire. Rather, the decree was designed to facilitate such acts *if* they were carried out in the context of a battle meant to advance Germany's military interests.

The wording "serious offenses [...] arising from sexual abandon" furthermore reveals the assumption, common among both military and civilian policy makers since the mid-nineteenth century, that men could be victims of their biology or be overpowered by their urges. These underlying assumptions demonstrate that the discussion around the lack of military discipline has long been implicitly entangled with questions of sexuality.

It is difficult to determine how issues around sexual violence were communicated down through the chain of command. Exploring the grey areas of indirect encouragement seems to be a promising avenue of inquiry here. On 16 December 1942, for example, General Wilhelm Keitel, Head of the OKW, stipulated that all German soldiers who participated in *Bandenbekämpfung* (combatting partisans) were exempt from any form of disciplinary or judicial punishment. On the contrary, the troops would

> have the right and the duty to use *any* means in this battle, also against women and children, as long as it leads to success. Forms of consideration [...] are a crime against the German people and the soldiers at the front who have to bear the effects of partisan attacks.[10]

The main message of this decree is unambiguous. Warfare against partisans meant abandoning any scruples, even when it came to women and children. While this is not an explicitly verbalised order to perpetrate sexual violence, the wording certainly concedes that combatants had the discretionary power to be as violent as they pleased without any fear of punishment.

In sum, sexual violence was part of the Wehrmacht's strategic arsenal to demean the enemy, destroy social ties, and break the adversary's morale. We can assume that the direct perpetrators of sexual violence typically had no explicit war-tactical motives when they raped a woman, but took advantage of opportunities that arose at a given moment and acted according to what they assumed was acceptable. The Wehrmacht Command, however, gave their men permission to perpetrate sexual violence by not prosecuting the offenders. In certain situations, the Wehrmacht Command even more or less openly encouraged this behaviour.

FACILITATING GENOCIDE

While the September 1935 "Law for the Protection of German Blood and German Honour", which prohibited sexual contact between 'Aryans' and Jews, was more strictly enforced within the borders of the Reich and within the confined spaces of concentration camps (Shik 2009), conditions in the war zone and the killing fields of Eastern Europe were considerably less restrained. Firstly, the Blood Protection Law, as it was generally referred to, was not in effect in the military operation zone, and Wehrmacht authorities had little interest in prosecuting 'race defilement'. Secondly, changing wartime conditions and policies led to a breakdown in discipline among German troops that allowed for sexual violence such as rape and gang rape.

What is more, acts of sexual violence that did not involve genital intercourse were generally not considered 'race defilement'. Indeed, in the camps or in custody of civilian police enforcement, guards systematically implemented certain techniques—such as enforced disrobement, sexual humiliation, certain forms of genital beatings, sexual torture, rape with fingers or objects, or sexual mutilation—as a means to demean, humiliate and threaten Jewish people. Elisa von Joeden-Forgey (2010: 6) coined the term 'life force atrocities' to refer to ritualised forms of violence that target the family and the reproduction of human life: the bearing of children, and the organisation of social, cultural, emotional and spiritual life.

These forms of sexual violence were also pervasive in the killing fields, such as during the evictions of Jews from their homes. Survivor testimonies report that German men touched women's intimate body parts and conducted particularly crude vaginal and anal searches. Such practices were sometimes accompanied by obscene comments and additional forms of humiliation, such as forcing naked women and girls to sing or dance. Women and girls were also purposely beaten on their genitals, their breasts, or their naked buttocks (Mühlhäuser 2010: 126f). Doris Bergen (2006: 188) has argued that such humiliating acts "were not just about practical exigencies or providing some kind of thrill to the male guards [...]; they also provided one more means of removing prisoners from their torturers' sphere of 'normal' treatment of women and fellow human beings." While that might be true, one could also argue that the normalcy of gendered discrimination and violence against women produced a particularly cruel intimacy between perpetrators and victims.

There is also evidence that soldiers did not necessarily understand rape to be 'race defilement'. When Wehrmacht soldier Frank Rothe was questioned by the 682nd Field Police Section after he and two comrades were accused of raping twenty-one-year-old Hinda Kaufmann in front of her family, he conceded:

> The Nuremberg laws are known to me. I nevertheless attempted to have sex with her because at the moment, I did not think that this act was punishable. We also did not think it was punishable because we forced her to have sex with us at pistol-point. (cited in Rossino 1997: 357)

Rothe argued that the rape was a part of the attack against the Jews, and thus part of the military operation rather than a violation of the law.

Even men who acted on the assumption that they could be accused of 'race defilement' appear to have considered the risk relatively low, in part because they could assume that the victims of and witnesses to this form of racial transgression would ultimately be killed (Mühlhäuser 2017a: 397f).

To sum up, German soldiers, SS- and policemen clearly targeted Jewish women (and sometimes men) for sexual violence, often of an extremely cruel nature. And while the military authorities feared that their men would not remain unchanged by their own deeds, that they would "imbrute", the authorities nonetheless appear to have neither disciplined nor sanctioned the behaviour of the men under their command. Nazi authorities may have condoned sexual violence by their men partly in order to encourage their participation in the killing operations. In general, it was a method of attacking and destroying family structures, norms and values.

CONCLUDING REMARKS

The example of the Wehrmacht's actions during the war and genocide in the Soviet Union demonstrates that while military rules and laws to restrict uncontrolled sexual behaviour existed, the implementation of these regulations was structured such that rape only became a subject of disciplinary action or prosecution if the specific act was regarded as counterproductive to military aims. This lack of prosecution created a culture of impunity in which sexual violence became a privilege and, indeed, a right for the soldiers. Soldiers used this space to interpret events and act in accordance with social values, their personal inclinations, the norms that emerged within their small units, and the opportunities presented in specific situations.

While aware of the potential hygienic and disciplinary dangers of uncontrolled sexual violence, the Wehrmacht did very little to stop it and in fact exploited the behaviour of its men for strategic purposes. Furthermore, the Wehrmacht organised the institutionalised exploitation of women in brothels in order to provide their men with outlets for their "sexual troubles and distress" and minimise the risk of STDs.

Permitting sexual violence served different functions inside the larger campaign of a war of annihilation: (1) it fostered cohesion in the small units and loyalty toward superiors in ways that secured military power; (2) it degraded local women and destroyed social ties in the victims' communities, thus communicating conquest; and (3) it became a means to dehumanise the Jews and create a distancing effect toward them that facilitated the genocidal killings. In conclusion, I would like to suggest that the Wehrmacht leadership fostered an understanding of male sexuality as something that needed an outlet, and that could and should be capitalised on productively during war. High and mid-level commanders anticipated the sexually violent behaviour of their men in the field, and exploited it for military aims.

Similar mechanisms have been observed in other situations of war and armed conflict. The fact that rape is pervasive in many civil societies, and the continuing widespread lack of awareness that this form of violence constitutes a crime, creates conditions in which sexual violence in times of armed conflict is deemed normal and acceptable behaviour. As long as military commanders do not take active and strict measures to curtail this form of violence, they are utilising this knowledge in their tactical and strategic thinking— even if rape is not openly communicated, let alone ordered. In this sense, wartime sexual violence is always a military weapon.

NOTES

1. For a more detailed discussion of the early origins of this terminology see Mühlhäuser 2017a: 368–75.
2. Sexual torture of men and boys has recently begun to be discussed as a weapon of war. Empirical research suggests that the gendered meanings, the harms and the consequences of such sexual torture differ significantly from those of sexual violence against women and girls. Future research will need to examine the similarities and differences in more detail.
3. Jürgen W., Tagebuch in Russland, NS-O 22, box 4, Archives of the Hamburg Institute of Social Research.
4. Von Brauchitsch (OKH), 31 July 1940, RH 53-7/v. 233a/167, Bundesarchiv-Militärarchiv Freiburg (hereafter cited as BA-MA).
5. Memorandum, von Brauchitsch (OKH), "Notzuchtverbrechen", 5 July 1940, RH 14/v. 30, BA-MA.

6. Dr. Hanloser (Chief Medical Officer in the OKH), "Prostitution und Bordellwesen im besetzten Gebiet in Sowjetrußland", 20 March 1942, H 20/825, BA-MA.
7. Directive from AOK 9, "Überwachung der Disziplin", 10 August 1941, RG 242/314/679, 649, National Archives and Record Administration (hereafter cited as NARA).
8. Directive, von Manstein, AOK 11 (Abt. Ic, AO Nr. 2379/41), 10 November 1941, printed in: Trial of the Major War Criminals Before the International Military Tribunal, Nuremberg, 14 November 1945–1 October 1946 (hereafter cited as IMT), Vol. 3/4, Doc. 4064-PS, 129–32.
9. "Erlaß über die Ausübung der Kriegsgerichtsbarkeit im Gebiet 'Barbarossa' und über besondere Maßnahmen der Truppe", 13 May 1941. http://www.1000dokumente.de/index.html?c=dokument_de&dokument=0093_kgs&object=translation&st=&l=de (accessed 29 October 2018).
10. Keitel, "Bandenbekämpfung", 16 December 1942, Dok 066-UK, in IMT, Vol 39, 128f.

REFERENCES

Beck, Birgit. 2005. 'Sexual Violence and Its Prosecution by Courts Martial of the Wehrmacht', in Roger Chickering (ed), *A World at Total War: Global Conflict and the Politics of Destruction, 1937–1945*, pp. 317–31. Cambridge: Cambridge University Press.

Bergen, Doris F. 2006. 'Sexual Violence in the Holocaust: Unique or Typical?' *Lessons and Legacies*, 7(7):179–200.

Biehl, Heiko. 2010. Kampfmoral und Kohäsion als Forschungsgegenstand, militärische Praxis und Organisationsideologie', in Maja Apelt (ed), *Forschungsthema: Militär: Militärische Organisationen im Spannungsfeld von Krieg, Gesellschaft und soldatischen Subjekten*, pp. 139–62. Wiesbaden: Verlag für Sozialwissenschaften.

Boesten, Jelke, 2017. 'Of Exceptions and Continuities: Theory and Methodology in Research on Conflict-Related Sexual Violence', *International Feminist Journal of Politics*, 19(4):506–19.

Bourke, Joanna. 2000. *An Intimate History of Killing: Face to Face Killing in Twentieth Century Warfare*. New York: Basic Books.

Bröckling, Ulrich. 2003. 'Schlachtfeldforschung: Die Soziologie im Krieg', in Steffen Martus/Marina Münkler/Werner Röcke (eds), *Schlachtfelder: Codierung von Gewalt im medialen Wandel*. Berlin: De Gruyter.

Brownmiller, Susan. 1975. *Against Our Will: Men, Women and Rape*. New York: Bantam Books.

Buss, Doris. 2009. 'Rethinking Rape as a Weapon of War', *Feminist Legal Studies*, 17(2):145–63.

Card, Claudia. 1996. 'Rape as a Weapon of War', *Hypatia*, 11(4):5–18.

Chiwengo, Ngwarsungu. 2008. 'When Wounds and Corpses Fail to Speak: Narratives of Violence and Rape in Congo (DRC)', *Comparative Studies of South Asia, Africa and the Middle East*, 28(1):78–92.

Copelon, Rhonda. 1994. 'Surfacing Gender: Re-Engraving Crimes against Women in Humanitarian Law', *Hastings Women's Law Journal*, 5(2):243–66.

Crawford, Kerry F. 2013. 'From Spoils to Weapons: Sexual Violence as a Weapon of War', *Gender & Development*, 21(3):505–15.

Crouthamel, Jason. 2008. 'Male Sexuality and Psychological Trauma: Soldiers and Sexual Disorder in World War I and Weimar Germany', *Journal of the History of Sexuality*, 17(1):60–84.

Diken, Bülent/Laustsen, Carsten. 2005. 'Becoming Abject: Rape as a Weapon of War', *Body* & *Society*, 11(1):111–28.

Eisen Bergman, Arlene. 1974. *Women of Viet Nam*. San Francisco: Peoples Press.

Eriksson Baaz, Maria/Stern, Maria. 2013. *Sexual Violence as a Weapon of War? Perceptions, Prescriptions, Problems in the Congo and Beyond*. London: Zed Books.

Feimster, Crystal N. 2013. 'Rape and Justice in the Civil War', *New York Times*, 25 April. https://opinionator.blogs.nytimes.com/2013/04/25/rape-and-justice-in-the-civil-war/ (accessed 29 October 2018).

Flaschka, Monika. 2009. *Race, Rape and Gender in Nazi Occupied Territories*. Ph.D. thesis, Kent State University.

Gertjejanssen, Wendy Jo. 2004. *Victims, Heroes, Survivors: Sexual Violence on the Eastern Front during World War II*. Ph.D. thesis, University of Minnesota.

Giles, Geoffrey J. 2005. 'A Gray Zone among the Field Gray Men: Confusion in the Discrimination against Homosexuals in the Wehrmacht', in Jonathan Petropoulos/John K. Roth (eds), *Gray Zones: Ambiguity and Compromise in the Holocaust and Its Aftermath*, pp. 127–46. New York: Berghahn Books.

Gray, Colin S. 1999. *Modern Strategy*. Oxford: Oxford University Press.

Herzog, Dagmar. 2012. 'Sexual Violence against Men: Torture at

28   REGINA MÜHLHÄUSER

Flossenbürg', in Carol Rittner/John K. Roth (eds), *Weapon of War and Genocide*, pp. 29–44. St. Paul: Paragon House.

Inal, Tuba. 2013. *Looting and Rape in Wartime: Law and Change in International Relations*. Philadelphia: PENN University of Pennsylvania.

Joeden-Forgey, Elisa von. 2010. 'The Devil in the Details: "Life Force Atrocities" and the Assault on the Family in Times of Conflict', *Genocide Studies and Prevention*, 5(1):1–19.

Lerner, Gerda. 1972. 'The Rape of Black Women as a Weapon of Terror', in Gerda Lerner (ed), *Black Women in White America: A Documentary History*, pp. 172–93. New York: Pantheon Books.

MacKinnon, Catherine. 1994. 'Rape, Genocide, and Women's Human Rights', in Stanley G. French/Wanda Teays/Laura M. Purdy (eds), *Violence Against Women: Philosophical Perspectives*, pp. 43–54. Ithaca: Cornell University Press.

Mibenge, Chiseche. 2008. 'Gender and Ethnicity in Rwanda: On Legal Remedies for Victims of Wartime Sexual Violence', in Dubravka Žarkov (ed), *Gender, Violent Conflict, and Development*, pp. 145–79. New Delhi: Zubaan Books.

Mischkowski, Gabriela. 2008. '"Ob es den Frauen selbst irgendetwas bringt, bleibt eine offene Frage." Ein Gespräch über die Probleme und Zwickmühlen der internationalen Strafgerichtsbarkeit', in Insa Eschebach/Regina Mühlhäuser (eds), *Krieg und Geschlecht: Sexuelle Gewalt im Krieg und Sex-Zwangsarbeit in NS-Konzentrationslagern*, pp. 229–48. Berlin: Metropol.

Mühlhäuser, Regina. 2017a. 'Reframing Sexual Violence as a Weapon and Strategy of War: The Case of the German Wehrmacht during the War and Genocide in the Soviet Union: 1941–1944', *Journal of the History of Sexuality*, 26(3):366–401.

———. 2017b. 'Sex, Race, Violence, Volksgemeinschaft: German Soldiers' Sexual Encounters with Local Women and Men during the War and the Occupation in the Soviet Union: 1941–1945', in Devin O. Pendas/Mark Roseman/Richard F. Wetzell (eds), *Beyond the Racial State: Rethinking Nazi Germany*, pp. 455–81. Cambridge: Cambridge University Press.

———. 2010. *Eroberungen: Sexuelle Gewalttaten und intime Beziehungen deutscher Soldaten in der Sowjetunion*. Hamburg: Hamburger Edition.

Picker, Henry (ed). 1997. *Hitlers Tischgespräche im Führerhauptquartier: Entstehung, Struktur, Folgen des Nationalsozialismus*. Berlin: Propyläen.

Pohl, Dieter. 2008. *Die Herrschaft der Wehrmacht: Deutsche Militärbesatzung und einheimische Bevölkerung in der Sowjetunion 1941–1944*. München: Oldenbourg.

Pohl, Rolf. 2012. 'Die Zerstörung der Frau als Subjekt: Macht und Sexualität als Antriebskräfte männlicher Vergewaltigungsstrategien im Krieg', in Gender Initiativkolleg (eds), *Gewalt und Handlungsmacht: Queer–Feministische Perspektiven*, pp. 113–24. Frankfurt a. M.: Campus.

Reemtsma, Jan Philipp. 2004. 'Gewalt: Monopol, Delegation, Partizipation', in Wilhelm Heitmeyer/Hans Georg Soeffner (eds), *Gewalt: Entwicklungen, Strukturen, Analyseprobleme*, pp. 346–61. Frankfurt a. M.: Suhrkamp.

Rossino, Alexander B. 1997. 'Destructive Impulses: German Soldiers and the Conquest in Poland', *Holocaust and Genocide Studies*, 11(3):351–65.

Seifert, Ruth. 1994. 'War and Rape: A Preliminary Analysis', in Alexandra Stiglmayer (ed), *Mass Rape: The War Against Women in Bosnia-Herzegovina*, pp. 54–73. London: University of Nebraska Press.

Siebold, Guy L. 2007. 'The Essence of Military Group Cohesion', *Armed Forces and Society*, 33(2):286–95.

Shik, Na'ama. 2009. 'Sexual Abuse of Women in Auschwitz-Birkenau', in Dagmar Herzog (ed), *Brutality and Desire: War and Sexuality in Europe's Twentieth Century*, pp. 221–46. London: Palgrave Macmillan.

Skjelsbæk, Inger. 2010. *The Elephant in the Room: An Overview of How Sexual Violence Came to Be Seen as a Weapon of War*. Oslo: Peace Research Institute Oslo.

Tombs, David. 2002. 'Honor, Shame, and Conquest: Male Identity, Sexual Violence, and the Body Politic', *Journal of Hispanic/Latino Theology*, 9(4):21–40.

Warburg, Jens. 2010. 'Paradoxe Anforderungen an soldatische Subjekte avancierter Streitkräfte im (Kriegs-)Einsatz', in Maja Apelt (ed), *Forschungsthema: Militär: Militärische Organisationen im Spannungsfeld von Krieg, Gesellschaft und soldatischen Subjekten*, pp. 245–70. Wiesbaden: Verlag für Sozialwissenschaften.

Zipfel, Gaby. 2018. 'Liberté, Egalité, Sexualité', *Mittelweg 36*, (27)4:87–108.

———. 2013. '"Let us have a Little Fun": The Relationship between Gender, Violence and Sexuality in Armed Conflict Situations', *RCCS Annual Review*, 5(1). https://journals.openedition.org/rccsar/469 (accessed 29 October 2018).

War, Rape and Patriarchy:
The Japanese Experience

YUKI TANAKA

Until the late 1980s in Japan, the term 'war crimes' conjured up images of the inhumane treatment or murder of enemy soldiers, especially prisoners of war. By describing and perceiving women in wartime as civilians who held the 'home front' during the war, commentators seem to have perpetuated the belief that women were not the direct victims of war. However, the eruption of the so-called 'comfort women' issue in the late 1980s created awareness throughout Japan that such an idea is both discriminatory and unrealistic. Despite the existence of many books and articles documenting the ordeal of the comfort women, only in the 1990s did the matter become a subject of nationwide debate. It is therefore necessary for the Japanese people as a whole to question not only why and how these crimes were committed but also why it took so long for knowledge of the crimes to become public.

Incidentally, the term 'comfort women,' the official phrase used by the Japanese Imperial forces, was nothing but a euphemism as the women were in reality 'sex slaves' of the Japanese military. The expression 'comfort women' itself has long been and still is a significant factor hindering many Japanese people from comprehending the true nature of this military violence against women. Yet, the term 'comfort women' is now widely used even by progressive historians, feminist scholars and activists who fervently call for justice for the victims of Japanese military sex slave system. Albeit reluctantly, in this chapter I therefore use this old-fashioned phrase instead of the term 'Japan's military sex slaves.'

Two important ideological structures that are fundamental to the Japanese nationalist mentality underlie the comfort women issue. The first of these is xenophobia, which is closely related to the Japanese emperor ideology. The second is the contempt with which women are held in Japanese society and the exploitation of their sexuality by Japanese men. The comfort women issue did not initially gain the attention of the Japanese public, because the Japanese tend to avoid confronting these two nationwide discriminatory attitudes. The recent change in awareness may be related to the fact that not only is the women's movement in Japan gaining strength, but also that the whole society, through its increased internationalisation, is becoming less insular and more aware of the impact of Japanese actions on other cultures. Yet a phenomenon that can be called 'comfort women bashing,' that is, the backlash from nationalistic right-wing organisations against such civil movements calling for justice for the war victims, has also been increasing, especially over the last several years.[1]

However, to see the comfort women affair as a crime committed uniquely by the Japanese is to risk dismissing such acts as aberrations and not recognising their full significance as part of a larger pattern of how war makes women victims. By analysing how all wars affect women, the Japanese people can provide some scholarly and intellectual foundations for the study of war and thereby contribute to the establishment and maintenance of peace.

RAPE AND THE TOKYO WAR CRIMES TRIBUNAL

The necessary materials for such an exercise can be found among the large number of testimonies and other evidence presented at the Tokyo War Crimes Tribunal held immediately after the Asia-Pacific War. The most significant case among these was the rape and massacre of Chinese women by the Japanese 10th Army and 16th Division in Nanjing (known in English as Nanking) in December 1937. Although in Japan this incident is known as the 'Nanjing Massacre,' it is often referred to by non-Japanese as the 'Rape of Nanjing,' a more accurate description of the rape and massacre of numerous Chinese women. The event was described by American missionary James McCallum in his diary, which was presented in evidence at the Tokyo War Crimes Tribunal:

> Never have I heard or read of such brutality. Rape! Rape! Rape! We estimate at least 1000 cases a night, and many by day. In case of resistance […] there is a bayonet stab or bullet. We could write up hundreds of cases a day. (International Military Tribunal for the Far East 1946: 4467)

Other evidence presented to the tribunal was a report prepared by a British resident in Nanjing, Iver Mackay, which contains the following information:

> On the night of December 15 a number of Japanese soldiers entered the University of Nanking buildings at Tao Yuen and raped 30 women on the spot, some by six men […]. At 4 p.m. on December 16 Japanese soldiers entered the residence at 11 Mokan Road and raped the women there. On December 17 Japanese soldiers went into Lo Kia Lu No. 5, raped four women and took one bicycle, bedding and other things […]. On December 17 near Judicial Yuan a young girl after being raped was stabbed by a bayonet in her abdomen. On December 17 at Sian Fu Wua a woman of 40 was taken away and raped. On December 17 in the neighbourhood of Kyih San Yuin Lu two girls were raped by a number of soldiers. From a primary school at Wu Tai Shan many women were taken away and raped for the whole night and released the next morning, December 17. (ibid.: 4526f)

Numerous concrete examples of horrific rape and massacre in Nanjing were recorded in the proceedings of the tribunal. Evidence that Filipinas and Dutch women presented at the Tokyo War Crimes Tribunal is also valuable documentation.[2]

Overall, the incidents of rape and massacre of civilian women by Japanese soldiers, especially in the Nanjing case, have been substantially investigated in numerous books and articles, and a clear general picture of the event has emerged.[3] Also, Japanese soldiers raped and murdered British nurses in Hong Kong and massacred Australian nurses on Banka Island (ibid.: 13454–76).

To gain a picture of activities of the Japanese military brothels in the Pacific region is still difficult because most of the relevant documents were burned soon after the war. However, it can be presumed that a large number of Asian women were sent far away from their homes and into forced prostitution.

THE ESTABLISHMENT OF 'COMFORT STATIONS'

The comfort houses were first established in Shanghai before World War II, possibly as early as 1932. During the Shanghai incident in January 1932, Japanese soldiers raped many Chinese women, and the deputy chief of staff in Shanghai, Okamura Yasuji, set up a comfort station in order to prevent further rape (Utsumi et al. 1992: 37; Yoshimi 1992: 26). In 1938, after the Nanjing massacre, the Japanese forces adopted the general policy of setting up comfort stations in various places in occupied China and 'recruiting' comfort women to staff them, not because of their concern for the Chinese victims of rape by Japanese soldiers but because of their fear of creating antagonism among the Chinese civilians. Thus, many so-called military leisure houses were established where Japanese forces were stationed (Yoshimi 1992: 28f). The word 'recruit' is, of course, an official euphemism; in reality many women were forcibly pressed into prostitution. It is now widely known from various testimonies that the Japanese military forces were directly involved in procuring large numbers of women for sexual slavery. Many Korean women were also exploited in this way and later spoke of their ordeals. It is also clear from the autobiography of Nogi Harumichi, the captain of the Ambon naval police force, that military police, who were supposed to prevent such military crimes, collaborated to procure women for enforced military prostitution (Yamada 1982: 160–72; Nogi 1975: 137–54).

There were three different types of comfort stations: those run directly by the Japanese Army; those ostensibly privately owned and run but in reality under tight control of the Army and only for the use of military personnel; and those privately owned and frequented by civilians but operating under an agreement with the Army to provide 'special services' for military personnel. The second type was the most common, and these stations were usually located next to military supply bases or in the centre of towns in which soldiers were stationed. Units located in more remote places usually had comfort stations directly attached to the barracks. If the unit moved, its comfort station would move with it. Smaller units, which did not have comfort stations, would often have comfort women sent to them for short periods from the larger comfort stations in the towns. However, in the regions where anti-Japanese guerrilla movements were strong and widespread such as northern China and the Philippines, the Japanese troops directly secured comfort women. Furthermore, their methods were wanton: abduction, rape and continuous confinement for the purpose of sexual exploitation. In these cases, 'sexual slavery hostages' rather than 'comfort women' is a more appropriate term to describe the circumstances endured by the victims (Tanaka 2002: 44–50; 2016).

The buildings for the comfort stations were provided by the Army, which also took charge of such matters as hygienic measures, hourly rates for 'services' and designation of days on which members of particular units were permitted to visit (Centre for Research and Documentation on Japan's War Responsibility 1994: 9).

There seem to be four major reasons the Japanese military decided that comfort stations were necessary. As I have mentioned previously, Japanese military leaders were very concerned about the rape of civilians by members of the Japanese armed forces. But they were not motivated by concern for those civilians. For good strategic reasons, they believed that the antagonism of civilians in occupied territories toward their conquerors was exacerbated by such behaviour. They also believed that a ready supply of women for the armed forces would help to reduce the incidence of rape of civilians.[4] What the military leaders apparently did not consider was the possibility that the highly oppressive culture of their armed forces might be contributing to the problem and that at least part of the solution would thus be to reform the military structure.

The military leaders also believed that the provision of comfort women was a good means of providing their men with some kind of leisure. Unlike Allied soldiers, the rank and file of the Japanese armed forces did not have designated leave periods or limited tours of duty. The military leaders had been advised by senior staff that they should make greater provision for both the health and well-being of their men, including such measures as extended leave back home. However most of those suggested measures were never implemented. The notable exception was the provision of comfort women (Centre for Research and Documentation on Japan's War Responsibility 1994: 9f).

The leaders were also concerned about the incidence of venereal disease among the armed forces. They believed that venereal disease threatened to undermine the strength of their men (and hence their fighting ability) and that it could also potentially create massive public health problems back in Japan once the war was over.[5] The leaders believed that a regulated system, such as the comfort houses, would enable them to take effective preventive health measures. It must be said that the measures they employed were thorough even if not completely effective. Those 'recruited' were mostly young, unmarried women because it was believed they were the least likely to be carrying venereal diseases. Army doctors regularly checked the health of the comfort women to ensure that they had not contracted a venereal disease and also provided condoms for the men to use. According to the Centre for Research and Documentation on Japan's War Responsibility, during the war the Army Accounts Department and the Supply Headquarters were responsible for sending condoms to forces stationed overseas, and officials ensured a ready supply. In 1942, for example, 32.1 million condoms were sent to units stationed outside Japan (Centre for Research and Documentation on Japan's War Responsibility 1994: 17). Records suggest a similar thoroughness with medical examinations of comfort women; most of them were examined for venereal disease every ten days. However, such measures could not prevent venereal disease, even if they went some way toward reducing its incidence. For instance, according to a report by medical officers of the 15th Division in northern China in 1942 and 1943, each month 15 to 20 per cent of comfort women were found to be suffering from venereal disease. Evidence from former comfort women suggests the figure could have been much higher (ibid.: 37f).[6]

The fourth concern the leaders had was security. They believed that private brothels could be infiltrated by spies easily. Alternatively, it was thought that the prostitutes working in them could be recruited as spies by the Allies. Kempeitai (military police of the Imperial Japanese Army) members were frequent visitors to comfort stations and kept close tabs on the women to ensure that no spies were among them (Yoshimi 1992: 354).

Why were comfort women almost invariably from Korea, Taiwan, China or various places in Southeast Asia? This might seem odd at first, given that the Japanese were notoriously racially prejudiced against the peoples of these countries. However, racial prejudice provides part of the answer to the question because that very racism helped make these women suitable for the role of comfort women.[7]

The Japanese military forces did not believe Japanese women should be in that role because they were supposed to be bearing good Japanese children who would grow up to be loyal subjects of the emperor. While there were Japanese prostitutes during the war, most of these were in a different position from the comfort women. They mainly worked in comfort stations that served high-ranking officers, and they experienced much better conditions.

Another reason non-Japanese were used as comfort women can be found in international law. In 1910, following an agreement by a number of European nations, the law suppressing trade in women for the purposes of prostitution was proclaimed in Paris. Japan later became a signatory. In 1921 a similar international law banned trade in women and children. Once again, Japan became a signatory. In February 1938 the Japanese Ministry of Home Affairs issued orders to the governors of each prefecture to ensure that only prostitutes over age 21 were issued with authorisations to ply their trade. However, officials believed these laws were not applicable to Japan's colonies and this, combined with the belief in the superiority of Japanese women and the suitability

of women of other races for prostitution, cemented the decision
to use women from colonies and occupied territories as comfort
women. Young unmarried women in the colonies and occupied
territories were thus treated by the Japanese as a resource for that
purpose (Centre for Research and Documentation on Japan's War
Responsibility 1994: 12).[8]

It is impossible to deny that the Japanese military was directly
involved in organising comfort stations and recruiting women
to work in them. Relevant documents discovered since the late
1980s and the recent testimonies of former comfort women,
who only now feel able to speak freely about their ordeals, have
added details about what happened. The Japanese government,
however, is still withholding pertinent documents that could give
a clearer picture, especially about who in the lines of command
should bear individual responsibility.

However, it appears from the available evidence that orders
to recruit women for comfort stations directly controlled by the
military army came from the headquarters of each dispatched
army—that is, from the chiefs of staff of each army. Those
orders would then have been conveyed to staff officers in various
divisions and carried out by the Kempeitai. The Kempeitai usually
operated by forcing the elders of villages in the occupied territories
to round up all of the young women (Centre for Research and
Documentation on Japan's War Responsibility 1994: 13–5).

As for the putatively private brothels, the owners were assisted
by the Kempeitai in the task of recruiting local women. Most of
these women were forcibly taken to the brothels from their villages.
Some women, however, were led to believe that they were going
to do some other kind of job, such as working in a factory, only to
find out too late that they had been deceived (ibid.: 22–4).

In January 1942 the minister for foreign affairs, Tōgō Shigenori,
instructed his staff that comfort women should be issued with
military travel documents. After that time, comfort women did
not require a passport for overseas travel.[9] This indicates that
involvement in decision-making about comfort women went all
the way to the top levels of government. Other documents reveal
a similar picture about high-level involvement. In March 1942

the headquarters of the South Area Army made plans to set up
comfort stations throughout the Asia-Pacific region. One recovered
document shows that orders were issued to Taiwan headquarters
to recruit 70 comfort women and send them to Borneo. The
commander in Taiwan, Lieutenant General Andō Rikichi and the
chief of staff, Major General Higuchi Keishichirō, instructed the
Kempeitai to select three brothel owners to assist them in the task
of gathering the comfort women. Seventy women were in fact
sent to Borneo from Taiwan; all carried military travel documents
with the seal of the head of general affairs of the Ministry for the
Army, Tanaka Ryūkichi and his junior, Kawara Naoichi. Because
the minister of the army at this time was Prime Minister Tōjō
Hideki, he bore final responsibility for the ordeals of the comfort
women (ibid.: 146).[10]

Comfort women were transported to the front lines in Army
ships or on Army railways or trucks. On a few occasions comfort
women were even flown by Army planes to the front lines. The
head of Army supplies was responsible for controlling transport
and must have been ultimately responsible for decisions made
about the transport of the women (ibid.: 17).

Less evidence is available about the role of the Navy than
about that of the Army in the exploitation of comfort women.
However, according to documents written by Rear Admiral
Nagaoka Takasumi, head of general affairs of the Ministry for
the Navy, on 30 May 1942, the Navy was to dispatch comfort
women to various naval bases throughout Southeast Asia. For
instance, 45 women were to be dispatched to the Celebes, 40 to
Balikpapan in Borneo, 50 to Penan and 30 to Surabaya. This
was the second dispatch of comfort women to these bases. These
documents were sent to Rear Admiral Nakamura Toshihisa,
chief of staff of the Southwest Area Fleet. As with the Army,
Navy involvement went to the very top ranks. Admiral Shimada
Shigetarō, the minister for the Navy, can therefore also be held
responsible for the ordeals of the comfort women (Yoshimi 1992:
365–75; Shigemura 1955: 224f).

The available evidence thus gives a clear picture that the very
top ranks of both the Army and the Navy were directly involved

in decision making concerning the comfort women and that other arms of government, such as the Ministry of Foreign Affairs, collaborated with them, also with high-level involvement. The comfort women case could well be historically unprecedented as an instance of state-controlled criminal activity involving the sexual exploitation of women. The history of 'camp followers' (military prostitutes) in European wars provides a strong contrast because evidence suggests that the relevant decisions were made by those on the ground and not back in the metropolitan corridors of power. We Japanese thus have a special responsibility to acknowledge the crimes of our forebears in subjecting the comfort women to their ordeals and, especially, a responsibility to demand that our government gives adequate compensation to the survivors.

The comfort women were treated as 'military supplies,' but relevant documents were either hidden or destroyed at the end of the war. Therefore, it is impossible to know how many women were exploited; the best estimates range from 80,000 to 100,000. According to the Japanese military plan devised in July 1941, 20,000 comfort women were required for every 700,000 Japanese soldiers (Yoshimi 1992: 83f), or one woman for every 35 soldiers. There were 3.5 million Japanese soldiers sent to China and Southeast Asia, and therefore an estimated 100,000 women were mobilised. Eighty per cent of these women are believed to have been Koreans but newly available evidence shows that many from Taiwan, China, the Philippines and Indonesia were also used. Recent testimony by Malaysians indicates that the Japanese forces set up comfort stations in which local Malaysian women were housed (Hayashi 1993). Thus, it is clear that, under the excuse of preventing rape, the Japanese forces exploited large numbers of Asian women as well as women from Allied nations. Although this was the official justification for the programme, it should not be forgotten that these estimated 100,000 women were themselves victims of rape. The following testimony by a former Korean comfort woman drives home the point:

> I was nearly killed several times during my time as a 'comfort woman.' There were some military men who were drunk and were

> brandishing swords at me while making demands for perverted
> sex. They drove their swords into the tatami, then demanded sex
> from me [...]. Afterwards the tatami was full of holes from them
> driving their swords into it [...]. The threat they were making was
> obvious—if I didn't co-operate they would stab me. (Kankoku
> Teishin-tai Mondai Taisaku Kyōgikai 1993:125)

Following the attack on Pearl Harbor in December 1941, the
comfort women system—that the Japanese Imperial forces
established originally in China in the early 1930s ostensibly for the
purpose of preventing rape—quickly expanded to almost every
corner of the Asia-Pacific region. It became hitherto the largest
and most elaborate system of trafficking women in the history
of mankind, and one of the most brutal. The scale of operation
was unprecedented in several ways, as follows: 1) The number of
women involved—estimated to be between 80,000 and 100,000;
2) the international scope of the operation—Korean, Chinese,
Taiwanese, Filipinas, Indonesian, Dutch, Melanesian women
were exploited; 3) the scale of the military-organised system
required for procuring women—Ministry of Army, Ministry of
Navy, Ministry of Foreign Affairs and other official agencies were
involved; 4) the length of time over which the system operated—
thirteen years between 1932 and 1945—and the degree of
violence inflicted upon women; 5) the geographical breadth of
Japan's wartime empire where the system was administered—the
entire Asia-Pacific region.[11]

Was the exploitation of women in military brothels effective
in preventing widespread random sexual violence by Japanese
soldiers? In June 1939, Hayao Takeo, then a lieutenant in the
Japanese military as well as a professor at the Kanazawa medical
college, submitted to the authorities a secret report about particular
battlefield problems and control measures. In one chapter he
analysed the cases of rape by Japanese soldiers and found that
it was impossible to prevent rape by setting up military brothels
and that many Chinese civilians, whenever they saw Japanese
soldiers, feared being raped by them (Yoshimi 1992: 232). He also
stated that the Japanese soldiers who did not rape women in Japan
suddenly became very violent and considered themselves free

to rape Chinese women. In addition, he said that commanding officers often turned a blind eye to rape, believing that rape was necessary to enhance soldiers' fighting spirits (ibid.: 229). Thus Dr. Hayao clearly recognised the two essential issues regarding rape in war. First, on the battlefield in a foreign country, where soldiers are outside the jurisdiction of their own laws of rape, it is extremely difficult to prevent rape, regardless of the availability of prostitutes at military brothels. Second, many officers deem it necessary for their soldiers to rape women in order to stimulate aggression. This was also clear from the testimonies of former Japanese soldiers who said they were given condoms before embarkation, despite officers' instructions not to rape women.[12] But was this behaviour peculiar to soldiers of the Japanese forces?

SEXUAL VIOLENCE BY ALLIED SOLDIERS IN JAPAN

There is no documentary evidence of mass rape by the Allied soldiers during the Pacific War. However, there are many anecdotal testimonies by Okinawans about rape committed by US soldiers during the Okinawa battle between March and August 1945. For example, according to Ōshiro Masayasu, an eminent Okinawan historian who recorded much information on this battle, almost all the women of a village on Motobu Peninsula on Okinawa were raped by a troop of US marines (Masayasu 1988: 171–3).[13]

This was also the case in the occupation of Japan in 1945. From the day they landed, US soldiers engaged in the mass rape of Japanese women. The first reported case was at 1pm on 30 August 1945. Two marines went into a civilian house in Yokosuka and raped a mother and daughter at gunpoint. The marines had landed three and a half hours earlier. There were four reported cases that day in Yokosuka alone (Yamada 1982: 34–6). On 1 September there were eleven rapes reported in Yokosuka and Yokohama. In one of these cases a woman nearly died after she was gang-raped by 27 US soldiers. After that the incidence of rape spiralled upward throughout the period of the occupation and the standard atrocities began to occur: young girls raped in front of their parents, pregnant women raped in maternity wards and so on. Over a period of ten days (30 August–10 September 1945) there were 1,336 reported cases of rape of Japanese women by US soldiers in Kanagawa prefecture (where Yokosuka and Yokohama are situated) alone. If these figures are extrapolated to cover the whole of Japan—and if it is assumed that many rapes went unreported—then it is clear that the scale of rape by US forces was comparable to that by any other force including the Japanese Imperial Army during the war. Yet according to an official US report, only 247 US soldiers were prosecuted for rape in the latter half of 1945, and these figures include prosecutions for rape in occupied Europe (Brownmiller 1975: 77). Clearly there were many soldier-rapists at large in the occupied areas who were not prosecuted.

US forces occupied the bulk of Japan, but some areas such as Hiroshima were occupied by British Commonwealth Occupation Forces (BCOF) composed of Australian, New Zealand and Indian soldiers under the command of British officers. These forces also participated in the rape of civilians. A Japanese prostitute made the following comment about Australian soldiers who landed at Kure (the port of Hiroshima) in November 1945:

> Most of the people in Kure stayed inside their houses, and pretended they knew nothing about the rape by occupation forces. The Australian soldiers were the worst. They dragged young women into their jeeps, took them to the mountain, and then raped them. I heard them screaming for help nearly every night. A policeman from the Hiroshima police station came to me, and asked me to work as a prostitute for the Australians—he wanted me and other prostitutes to act as a sort of 'firebreak,' so that young women wouldn't get raped. We agreed to do this and contributed greatly. (Yamada 1982: 90f)

The Japanese government had discussed ways of dealing with the anticipated problem of mass rape by occupation forces in the week following surrender and before their arrival. On 21 August 1945, Prime Minister Prince Higashikuni Naruhiko called a meeting of several of his ministers to discuss the issue; attendees included the health, internal affairs and foreign ministers and the

attorney-general. This was dubbed the 'comfort women meeting.'
They decided to set up a Recreation and Amusement Association
(RAA) for the occupation forces. A special government fund of
30 million yen was allocated to the project, and the head of the
Japanese police force was ordered to take all measures necessary
to assist such an organisation (Harada 1989: 136). In fact, the
government had already taken the first steps toward establishing
this organisation four days earlier. Governors and police chiefs of
all prefectures had been instructed to procure women from geisha
houses, brothels and nightclubs in sufficient numbers to staff a
nationwide organisation of brothels. In Tokyo the chief of police
summoned all owners of brothels and nightclubs and requested
their cooperation in such a project (Ōshima 1986: 166; Yamada
1982: 25–7). The Japanese politicians who had procured tens of
thousands of non-Japanese comfort women during the war now
turned to the procurement of their own women for the benefit of
soldiers who had recently been their enemies.

According to an internal report, more than 20,000 Japanese
women were mobilised into the RAA by the end of 1945. At
its peak more than 70,000 women worked for the organisation.
As the demand for women to staff the organisation outstripped
the supply of professional prostitutes, geishas and the like, other
groups of women were drafted, including high school students
(who had been put to work in munitions factories toward the end
of the war) from Saitama, Hiroshima and Kawasaki. These young
women were not allowed to return home after the surrender and
were forced to work in the brothels of the RAA (Yamada 1982:
7, 42f). The case of the girls from Hiroshima was particularly
sad: They had been put to work in Kure and had thus survived
the atomic bombing of Hiroshima, in which their families had
perished and their homes had been destroyed. They had nowhere
to return to and were offered no alternative to service in the RAA.
These young women were also victims of rape.

The first brothel the RAA established, named Komachien
(which loosely translates as 'The Babe Garden'), was in Ōmori,
a suburb of Tokyo, and it opened on 27 August 1945. Hundreds
were established soon after all over Japan. One of these brothels

was managed by the mistress of General Ishii Shirō, who headed the notorious Unit 731, a Manchukuo unit that had developed biological weapons and tested them on more than 3,000 Chinese prisoners. The establishment of comfort women brothels did little to minimise the incidence of mass rape by Japanese forces during the war; the same could be said of the RAA project during the occupation.

It is a harsh irony that while the accounts of mass rape and rape in the form of enforced prostitution committed by Japanese forces during the war were heard in the Tokyo trials—and judgment and sentence being passed on the perpetrators—the same practice was continuing throughout occupied Japan with the active participation of Allied forces and the approval of the high command of the occupying forces.[14]

WAR, RAPE AND PATRIARCHY

Why do soldiers rape?

It is perfectly understandable that soldiers should want to have sex, if only as a temporary escape from the horrors they encounter daily. That such a respite is positive is reflected in the following comment by a Vietnam veteran:

> A man and a woman holding each other tight for one moment, finding in sex some escape from the terrible reality of the war. The intensity that war brings to sex, the 'let us love now because there may be no tomorrow,' is based on death. No matter what our weapons on the battlefield, love is finally our only weapon against death. Sex is the weapon of life, the shooting sperms sent like an army of guerrillas to penetrate the egg's defences—the only victory that really matters. Sex is a grappling hook that pulls you out, ends your isolation, makes you one with life again. (Broyles 1991: 79)

However, it must be remembered that consensual sex and rape are dramatically different undertakings (even if the boundary is blurred in some people's accounts of their actions), and it would be very wide off the mark to account for an act of rape as a distorted outlet for an individual's sex drive. Wartime rape is a collective act on a number of levels. As another returned soldier from Vietnam put it: "They only do it when there are a lot of guys around. You know, it makes them feel good. They show each other what they can do—'I can do it,' you know. They won't do it by themselves" (Brownmiller 1975: 107).

Indeed, rape in war is often gang rape. These acts serve as a sharing of the 'spoils' of war and a strengthening of the exclusively male bonds among soldiers. Fierce combat forms strong and intimate links among soldiers, and gang rape is both a by-product of this and a means by which such bonds are maintained in noncombat situations. There is also strong psychological pressure on soldiers to be brave and to be prepared for immediate physical combat, and this is especially so in the presence of other soldiers. The need to dominate the 'other,' the enemy, is imperative in battle with other men. In a non-combat situation, women readily become the 'other' and the target of the desire for domination by groups of tightly bonded men. The violation of the bodies of women becomes the means by which such a sense of domination is affirmed and reaffirmed. In an extreme situation such as war, in which the killing of the enemy is regarded as an act worthy of praise, the moral basis for the condemnation of crimes such as rape falls away, and the moral codes adhered to by soldiers in peacetime lose their validity (ibid.: 32).

The internal power relations of armies work on a strict class system, and enlisted soldiers are always subject to the orders of officers. This creates a contradiction whereby soldiers whose principal task is to dominate and subjugate the enemy must subordinate themselves to the unquestionable authority of their officers. This contradiction is intensified in the battlefield where, for the individual soldier, the imperative to dominate the enemy is literally a matter of life or death, and the need for the officer class to dominate and have unquestioned authority over groups of soldiers becomes strategically imperative. Such a contradiction creates both a high degree of tension and a context in which violence is the standard mode for the release of tension. Consequently, the rape of women perceived as the 'enemy' or 'belonging to the enemy' becomes a frequently used form of release—a reprehensible behaviour, escaping the disciplinary matrix, that is really the underbelly of the disciplinary system. Incidents in which women are raped in front of their families—especially in front of their fathers, husbands or brothers—are common because the violence enacted on the women also serves to humiliate enemy men and to reinforce their subjection to the occupying force. The more absolute the relation of domination between officers and enlisted men within an army, the more heightened is the contradiction between their relations to the subjugated enemy and their situation within their own force. Consequently, their behaviour toward the enemy—soldiers, male civilians and women—becomes more violent.

Rape in war has a number of different effects. During periods of heavy fighting, it serves to perpetuate and intensify the aggressiveness of soldiers. After victory or in noncombat periods, it serves to maintain the sense of dominance and victory and is often viewed by soldiers as the legitimate spoils of war. The Japanese army is not the only force to have used or condoned rape as a device for maintaining the group aggressiveness of soldiers. In the Falklands War of 1982, British soldiers being transported to the war zone by ship were shown violent pornographic films as a way of stimulating their aggressiveness prior to battle. As seen in the Bosnian conflict, rape can be employed on the front line as one of a range of strategies. War and rape are fundamentally related. It is foolish to imagine that the provision of large numbers of involuntary prostitutes (which is itself a form of rape) could prevent the mass or gang rape that is a general feature of modern war.

Moreover, soldiers in battle cannot avoid a further—and irresolvable—contradiction. War is usually presented as an exclusively male activity, a masculine bonding ritual, an activity in which women have no place (Enloe 1983: 15). Yet this is a fantasy of war. The reality is that war and battles frequently occur in areas occupied by civilians and that women are usually present as civilians near the front line. War is presented as an activity that demands physical strength and toughness and is seen as an occasion for the exclusive celebration of these attributes as singular masculine virtues. Therefore, the very existence of military forces is regarded as a living symbol of masculine dominance over the allegedly 'weaker' sex. In such a patriarchal ideology, it is strongly believed that a woman's place is on the home front and not in battle. This ideology demands that women be absent from battle, but its maintenance also requires that such dominance be repeatedly reinforced, especially when women are in fact present in the male domain of the battlefield, either as implicated civilians or as military nurses. Thus, women must be both present and absent at the same time. War as a masculine activity is a continuing attempt to resolve such a contradiction, and yet its very existence is founded on this contradiction. The final recourse in the face of such a contradiction is to eliminate women altogether—hence the frequency with which women are massacred after rape.

Strongly in evidence is a backlash from many military men against what they perceive as an invasion of their domain by women. Many men want to maintain all-male workplaces, and they often respond to the 'threat' of women being present by sexual harassment of those women. This seems to be a particularly common phenomenon in the military, and the kinds of sexual harassment that occur seem to be more extreme than in other workplaces. There have been many rape cases reported in the armed forces of a number of countries in recent times.[15]

War is an inherently patriarchal activity, and rape is the most extreme expression of the patriarchal drive toward dominance of the 'other'. In peacetime, such tendencies are held in check by the rule of law and internalised moral codes. In war the rule of law is often absent, internalised moral codes disintegrate and these normal checks on such activities are largely replaced by incentives. Rape is unique to human beings; it does not form part of animal behaviour. Despite the fact that it is often characterised as 'animal activity', rape is profoundly cultural and patriarchal. As Virginia Woolf indicated in *Three Guineas* (1938), war is not just a military problem but is a problem created by a male-dominated society, and therefore war is closely related to other traditionally male activities such as law and organised religion (Woolf 1992: 151–414). To prevent war requires first destroying the male-dominated culture that creates war and then creating a new culture that ensures real equality between men and women. The same could be said of rape in war.

The eleven (male) judges at the Tokyo War Crimes Tribunal who heard the cases of mass rapes by Japanese soldiers probably never thought that the crimes they were investigating were closely related to their own status in the pre-eminently patriarchal world of the law. Just as Freud failed to see male sexuality as a weapon against women (Brownmiller 1975: 11), the judges of the tribunal failed to see these crimes committed by Japanese forces as a general characteristic of patriarchy.

This article is based on chapter 3 of the revised edition of Yuki Tanaka, *Hidden Horrors: Japanese War Crimes in World War II*, 2018. Reproduced with permission of Roman & Littlefield.

NOTES

1. For details of Japanese nationalist 'comfort women bashing,' see Tanaka 2017; 2016.
2. International Military Tribunal for the Far East. 1946–1948. *Transcripts of Proceedings and Documents of the Judgment.* https://www.legal-tools.org/doc/a4c38a/pdf/ (accessed 20 August 2019), pp. 3904–43, 4459, 4464–6, 4476, 4479, 4526–36, 13638–52. See also Blackman 1989: 20f.
3. For example, see Dō 1973; Katsuichi 1972; Nankin Jiken Chōsa Kenkyū Kai 1992.
4. This idea is clear from the instructions for dealing with Chinese civilians, which were issued on 27 June 1938, by Okabe Naozaburō, chief of staff of the North China Area Army, to all subordinate units. For details, see Yoshimi 1992: 209f.
5. A report prepared by the medical section of the North China Area Army in February 1940 warned that a soldier suffering from venereal disease required an average of 86 days' hospitalisation; thus the spread of such a disease would weaken the strength of the Army considerably. For details of this report, see Yoshimi 1992:

237. On the concern of the military about the potential effect on Japanese public health of venereal disease brought home by soldiers, see a report prepared by a senior officer of the Ministry of the Army on 18 June 1942, reproduced in ibid.: 171f.

6. The fact that seven of 19 comfort women interviewed by the Centre for Research and Documentation on Japan's War Responsibility had suffered from venereal disease also indicates a high rate of infection among the comfort women.

7. Concerning the reasons for the exploitation of non-Japanese women, in particular Koreans, as military sex slaves, see Chapter 2 in Tanaka 2002.

8. For evidence that some minors from colonies and occupied territories were forced to become comfort women, see Yoshimi 1992: 102f, 135–7, 304.

9. This instruction appears in the telegram sent by Tōgō to the head of foreign affairs in the government-general of Taiwan on 14 January 1942. It is reproduced in Yoshimi 1992: 143.

10. An open question is whether Emperor Hirohito also bore responsibility because of his position as grand marshal, the highest position in the Japanese Imperial Forces, even if he was not informed about this matter.

11. For more details of special characteristics of the comfort women system and its historical background, see Epilogue of Tanaka 2002.

12. Unpublished private memoirs written by a former soldier of the Kantō Army, which I obtained a few years ago, clearly testify to such action. However, the author's name is not disclosed here for the sake of privacy.

13. The Japanese forces brought many Korean comfort women to Okinawa well before the battle started, but accurate numbers of these women are unknown. Research indicates that some of these Korean women were forced to serve Americans after the Japanese forces were defeated. For details, see Yamatani 1992: 169.

14. For more details of sexual violence committed by the Allied occupation soldiers against Japanese women immediately after the war and the RAA's activities, see Tanaka 2002.

15. Recently a number of cases of rape and sexual harassment within the military have been reported in Australia. In the United States, too, there have been reports of this phenomenon, which increased noticeably during and after the Gulf War. For example, at a US Navy convention held at the Hilton Hotel, Las Vegas, in September

1991, which celebrated the Gulf War victory, 90 sexual assaults were reported. The victims in 83 cases were women, either female officers or wives who accompanied their husbands to the convention. About five percent of 4,000 participants were female naval officers. Some male officers were wearing T-shirts that had 'Women Are Property' written on the back and 'He-Man Women Haters' Club' printed on the front. For details of sexual harassment at this convention, see United States. Department of Defense. Office of the Inspector General 1993.

REFERENCES

Blackman, Arnold C. 1989. *The Other Nuremberg: The Untold Story of the Tokyo War Crimes Trials*. Glasgow: Fontana.

Brownmiller, Susan. 1975. *Against Our Will: Men, Women, and Rape*. London: Secker and Warburg.

Broyles, William jr. 1991. 'Why men love war', in Walter H. Capps (ed), *The Vietnam Reader*, pp. 68–81. New York: Routledge.

Centre for Research and Documentation on Japan's War Responsibility. 1994. *Jūgun Ianfu Mondai no Shiteki Narabi ni Hōteki Kenkyū*, unpublished paper.

Dō, Tomio. 1973. *Nitchū Sensō Shiryō*, Vols. 8 and 9. Tokyo: Kawade Shobō.

Enloe, Cynthia.1983. *Does Khaki Becomes You? The Militarization of Women's Lives*. London: Pluto Press.

Harada, Katsumasa. (ed.). 1989. *Shōwa Niman-nichi no Zenkiroku: Dai 7 Kan 'Haikyo kara no Shuppatsu'*. Tokyo: Kodansha.

Hayashi, Hirofumi. 1993. 'Marei Hantō no Nippongun Ianjo', *Sekai*, May.

Honda, Katsuichi. 1972. *Chūgoku e no Tabi*. Tokyo: Asahi Shimbun-sha.

Kankoku Teishin-tai Mondai Taisaku Kyōgikai. 1993. *Shōgen: Kyōsei Renkō Sareta Chōsenjin Gun-ianfutachi*. Tokyo: Akashi Shoten.

Masayasu, Ōshiro. 1988. *Okinawa-sen: Minshū no Me de Toraeta Sensō*. Tokyo: Kobunken.

Nankin Jiken Chōsa Kenkyū Kai. 1992. *Nankin Jiken Shiryō-shū*. Tokyo: Aoki Shoten.

Nogi, Harumichi. 1975. *Kaigun Tokubetsu Keisatsutai: Anbon-tō BC-kyū Senpan no Shuki*. Tokyo: Taihei Shuppan.

Ōshima, Yukio. 1986. *Genshoku no Sengo-shi: Sengo o Nipponjin wa dō Ikita Ka*. Tokyo: Kodansha.

Shigemura, Minoru. 1955. 'Tokuyōin to iu Na no Butai', *Tokushū Bungei Shunjū*, Vol.1.

Tanaka, Yuki. 2018. *Hidden Horrors: Japanese War Crimes in World War II*, 2nd Edition. Lanham: Rowman & Littlefield.

————. 2017. '"Comfort Women Bashing" and Japan's Social Formation of Hegemonic Masculinity', in Michael Lewis (ed), *'History Wars' and Reconciliation in Japan and Korea: The Role of Historians, Artists and Activists*, pp. 163–82. New York: Palgrave Macmillan.

————. 2016. 'Introduction', in Maria R. Henson/Sheila S. Coronel/ Cynthia Enloe/Yuki Tanaka (eds), *Comfort Woman: A Filipina's Story of Prostitution and Slavery Under the Japanese Military*, 2nd Edition, pp. xi–xxxvi. Lanham: Rowman & Littlefied.

————. 2002. *Japan's Comfort Women: Sexual Slavery and Prostitution during World War II and the US Occupation*. London: Routledge.

United States. Department of Defense. Office of the Inspector General. 1993. *The Tailhook Report: The Official Inquiry into the Events of Tailhook 1991*. New York: St. Martin's Press.

Utsumi, Aiko et al. 1992. *Handobukku Sengo Hoshō*. Tokyo: Nashinoki-sha.

Woolf, Virginia. 1992. *A Room of One's Own and Three Guineas*. Oxford: Oxford University Press.

Yamada, Sadashi. 1982. *Kempei Nikki*. Tokyo: Shinjimbutsu Ōrai-sha.

Yamatani, Tetsuo. ed. 1992. *Okinawa no Harumoni*. Tokyo: Bansei-sha.

Yoshimi, Yoshiaki. 1992. *Jūgun Ianfu Shiryōshū*. Tokyo: Ōtsuki Shoten.

Crack Troops: Military Masculinity Isn't Masculine

AARON BELKIN

> He was masculine and protective, even as he was feminine
> and submissive.
>
> — Musician Patti Smith's description of the late
> photographer Robert Mapplethorpe

Carol Burke, a folklorist who taught at the US Naval Academy at Annapolis in the 1990s, recounts the following story about bedtime rituals in Bancroft Hall, the dormitory where all 4,200 midshipmen (students) live:

> Before going to bed at the US Naval Academy, a plebe [freshman] shouts "Good night!" to the senior midshipman in the company, and the company commander answers "Good night!" in reply. A litany of goodnights then passes down the chain of the company's command. At the end of this ritual courtesy, the plebe yells the final goodnight: "Goodnight Jane Fonda!" and the entire company shouts its enthusiastic retort: "Goodnight, bitch!" (Burke 2004: 177)

Fonda, whose protests against American involvement in Vietnam included highly publicised wartime visits to Hanoi, is represented in US military culture as the embodiment of the unmasculine that every Naval Academy student is trained to disavow.

Burke's anecdote is open to multiple interpretations, but one implication is how living up to the ideal of military masculinity seems to depend on situating the practiced annihilation of the feminine as central to what it takes to avert the annihilation of the nation. Femininity is coded as an arbitrary, fictional construction which represents weakness, subordination, emotionalism, dependency and disloyalty, and these traits are framed as dangerous aspects of the unmasculine that warriors must reject at all costs if they are to acquire the strength necessary to defend national security. Michael Kimmel, a sociologist who has written widely about masculinity, suggests that warrior masculinity is not unique in this regard. In almost every context, he finds, "Masculine identity is born in the renunciation of the feminine" (Kimmel 1996). Kimmel's observations echo the conclusions of many other scholars who conclude that its production always depends on a disavowal or flight from femininity. Masculinity is said to consolidate when those who strive to embody it reject all parts of themselves which are imagined to be unmasculine, and any characteristic that could possibly be construed as feminine. From this perspective, the ideal of military masculinity depends on disavowing practices which position masculinity in opposition to its unmasculine foils: weakness, subordination, queerness, and so on. In the minds of US Naval Academy plebes, some of whom may not be familiar with Fonda's actual wartime record, Hanoi Jane symbolises all of these things. That's why they disparage her before going to bed every night.

THE MASCULINE PARADOX

Although this bedtime ritual appears to show how the production of military masculinity depends on the renunciation of the feminine, it may be more complex. Killers sometimes say 'good night' just before murdering their prey, and the words also conjure the image of a domestic, night-time routine involving husbands and wives or parents and children. Hence the misogynist aspect of the story in that the plebes gesture at an idealised, nostalgic imagination of a soft-spoken, caring, self-sacrificing woman— just the kind of woman who would wish them good night—but also recode that wife/mother as the archetypal bitch, a stand-in for women everywhere. However, an infantilizing element to the story lines up with the recollection that 'good night' is something that children say to their parents. And, given the context of the all-male sleeping arrangements in Naval Academy dorms, the exchange also can be understood as a queer moment, an echo of what boyfriends and male lovers might say to one another before retiring for the night. In this sense, the crushing of the feminine can be seen as normalizing a queer and adolescent utterance, albeit in the context of violent hostility.[1] At the level of practice, the plebes engage with their own queerness and adolescence at the same time that they reinforce and stabilise fantasies about their invincibility.

Or, consider how Scott Camil, who served as a Marine in the Vietnam War and then returned to the US and became an anti-war activist, was transformed into a killer. When Camil entered basic training in the mid-1960s, by all reports he did not have a killer instinct. Camil, however, was transformed by boot camp, and by the time he arrived in Vietnam he found that he was shameless about taking life. He says that during his two tours of duty, "It got to be a game to see how many people you could kill," and he boasted of cutting off his victims' ears and exchanging them with other soldiers for beer. "Killing," he added, "didn't bother me at all" (Vietnam Veterans against the War 1972). In Camil's case, the indoctrination process seems to have worked, at least when assessed in terms of what the military was trying to do when it sent him to boot camp. Camil had become a warrior and a real man. But what was it about Camil's training that changed him?

Echoing sociologist Erving Goffman's observation about the intimacy of moments when total institutions compel subjects to embrace non-normativity, one possible answer to this question centres on the effects of contradictory messages that Camil received, including instructions about when, whether, where and how to urinate (Goffman 1966: 23). Camil reports that,

> If I wanted to go to the bathroom I would say [...], "Sir, Private Camil requests permission to make a head call, Sir." And he'd say, "Is it an emergency?" And I'd say, "yes sir." And then [...] he could say, "OK but wait one hour, and if you don't go, then you

lied to me. And then I'm going to kick your ass." So like you had
a choice of either pissing in your pants or getting your ass kicked
your ass kicked. (Vietnam Veterans against the War 1972)

On one hand, Camil's drill sergeant expected him to refrain from
urinating, which would have constituted evidence of dishonesty
and invited a violent beating. Masculinity, if pursued via this path,
required restraint, dishonesty and submission to brutality. At the
same time, Camil's drill sergeant expected him to urinate in his
pants, perhaps the ultimate mark of infancy and lack of self-
control, in order to prove his trustworthiness and avoid a violent
capitulation (Grosz 1994). Via either route, the attainment of
masculine status required both a rejection and an embrace of the
unmasculine: hold it in but become a dishonourable liar and take
a beating, or prove your honour and avoid capitulation by 'pissing
in your pants.' Even the avoidance of capitulation would take
place in the context of having to ask for permission to go to the
bathroom. Such conflicting messages would be confusing in any
context. American military culture, however, has produced and
insisted on a range of contradictory expectations which can be
much more intensified than in civilian society. On many different
levels, Camil's achievement of masculine status was built on a
foundation of mixed messages. He was simultaneously expected
to engage with retentiveness/expulsion, honesty/dishonesty,
filthiness/cleanliness.

Looking at different kind of evidence, we can observe
that these kinds of mixed messages are not incidental to the
ideal of military masculinity but that they are, much on the
contrary, fundamental to the ways in which military masculinity
is produced. Let me give you another example. In US military
culture, warrior masculinity has been about protecting one's body
and nation from penetration, about never allowing one's anus to
be penetrated, about obliteration of feminine penetrability. The
warrior's masculinity has depended on being not-subordinate,
not-feminine, not-on-the-bottom, not-penetrated (anally or
otherwise). Whether referencing the relationship between the
US and other countries, the US military and other armed forces,

or US warriors and female or enemy 'others,' penetration has always been the ideal. Penetrability always has been the terror. Penetration has been something that warriors do, as opposed to something that is done to them.

Looking at practices within the US military, however, a different picture emerges. As I demonstrated elsewhere, there are many military rituals and practices that involve forced penetration (Belkin 2012). Among these, the Navy's 'crossing the line' ceremony has been perhaps the most pervasive. The ceremony, whose origins date back to sixteenth-century European naval rituals that marked a ship's crossing of the equator, has been a regular feature of life at sea on US Navy ships. Carrie Hersh, an anthropologist who authored a remarkable study of the ceremony, describes it as "a vivid and unexpectedly sanctioned Naval event in which uninitiated Naval personnel who have never crossed the equator pass through a series of tests which induct them into the realm of the initiated" (Hersh 2002: 278). Despite relatively minor variations, she found that almost all crossing the line ceremonies shared the same form during the last three decades of the twentieth century. The uninitiated, so-called 'wogs' or 'pollywogs' who have never crossed the equator, were forced to complete a number of degrading and humiliating tasks, after which they were welcomed into the realm of the initiated 'shellbacks.' Upon becoming a 'shellback', each sailor was given a card which had to be produced during future crossings. Sailors who lost their cards had to pass the tests a second time. Officers had to participate along with enlisted personnel as both 'wogs' and 'shellbacks' (Zeeland 1995: 157).

Penetration was a central feature of crossing the line ceremonies in the last decades of the twentieth century. Hersh found that "Garbage, sewage, and rotten food are poured over the wogs and into every orifice of their bodies, including their anuses." She says that, "Pollywogs may have substances such as Crisco (vegetable shortening) placed in their anuses and in some cases must retrieve objects from the anuses of other wogs, simulating anallingus (or 'rimming')." One series of tests forced wogs to use their mouths to retrieve an object from a toilet bowl, while another involved an appointment with a shellback designated as "royal dentist"

who squirted "unpleasant substances down their throats." A
sailor named Sonny confirmed that "You get the 'truth serum'—a
syringe without a needle, full of Kool-Aid and Tabasco sauce.
They squirt it in your mouth [...]. From there you start crawling
across the deck. And that's where they pulled my drawers down
and shoved Crisco up my ass!" Another sailor was in the stocks,
"on my hands, and my head was locked in there, and I was bent
over, and someone was behind me pretending they were having
sex with me. And another guy was pouring three-week-old food
on top of my head, and it was dripping all over my mouth" (Hersh
2002: 287f). In yet another case, a sailor

> was given a "greasing" by three shipmates. A greasing involves
> stripping the individual naked and massaging him with a thick,
> black grease used to lubricate heavy machinery. In some cases,
> a flexible tube is forced through the victim's anus and into his
> rectum. The tube is connected to a cylindrical reservoir filled
> with lubricating grease. The reservoir and tube resemble a large
> hand-driven pump. The contents of the piston-driven reservoir
> are then pumped into the victim. (Goyer/Eddleman 1984)[2]

Folklorist Simon Bronner notes that, "To 'disinfect' or 'sanitize'
selected individuals, senior sailors sometimes forced an initiate to
strip and put tubes and other objects in the initiate's rear end"
(Bronner 2006, 2007).

While penetration has been a regular feature of crossing the line
ceremonies, its meaning has been structured with contradictions.
From one perspective, it seems obvious that the ceremony situated
penetrability as a marker of shame, subordination and weakness,
as something done by the initiated to the uninitiated to humiliate
them. Hersh is not wrong in observing that, "These physical
penetrations emphasize the powerlessness of the pollywogs (the
penetrated) and the control which the shellbacks (the penetrators)
have over them" (Hersh 2002: 296). Other scholars who have
studied crossing the line ceremonies agree that they have
recapitulated a master/slave dynamic intended to underscore
the shamefulness, weakness and subservience of the uninitiated,
and that penetration has served as a powerful marker of these

identifications. Bronner says that during ceremonies, "sailors take on feminine roles on board, female (and the sodomized male) charters are externalized, ejected from the self; they are performed in Wog Queen contests, dog auctions, and homosexual enactments as ridiculous, passive, weak and scared" (Bronner 2006: 46).

At the same time that initiated shellbacks have used penetration to enact their masculinity and their dominant status over wogs, however, penetration has not been linked exclusively to dominance in crossing the line ceremonies, nor has being penetrated been connected solely to subordination. Consider that while uninitiated wogs have been penetrated during the ceremonies, they have also penetrated others. In numerous accounts of simulated anal and oral sex, wogs have been ordered to take passive but also active roles, sometimes while bound by chain or leash. One sailor reports that,

> We'd just be going around on our hands and knees in circles, and they'd be smacking us [...] they would pull you off out of the assembly line, and they would say, "Get up there and fuck him, wog! I wanna see you fuck him! Fuck him *hard*, wog! Fuck him like the bitch he is!" (Zeeland 1995: 191. Italics in original)

And there is perhaps no clearer example of the ways in which wogs have penetrated and been penetrated during crossing the line ceremonies than "elephant walks," when, "a line of men moved while holding the genitals of the person in front of them or having a finger in his anus" (Bronner 2007). If penetration were only an indication of masculinity and dominance, then uninitiated wogs would not have been ordered to penetrate other wogs. Related to this point, uninitiated wogs may not have been the only ones to be penetrated, as initiated shellbacks could be penetrated as well. Typically, a day before a crossing the line ceremony, wogs, "temporarily [...] refute the authority of the shellbacks [...] capture shellbacks for a short period of time and perform the same initiation procedures as will be performed the next day by the shellbacks" (Hersh 2002: 285).[3]

Finally, while it is true that being penetrated during crossing the line ceremonies has marked subordination, feminisation and weakness, it has indicated masculinity as well. Echoing the comments of one Marine who noted that, "Marines view being penetrated not at all as female, but as a *manly* test of endurance," some crossing the line participants confirm that violent humiliation can signify masculinity. As one American sailor who participated in the ceremony in the 1960s said, "Endure the humiliation of the ritual and your mates would be reassured that you were one of them ... Yes, the ritual was very abusive ... It was a matter of showing our mates that we were real males" (Bronner 2006: 44f).

As is the case with all rituals, the form and meaning of military initiation ceremonies has changed over time. As women became more integrated into various sectors of the armed forces, they were sometimes called on to serve as spectators of penetration. At a 1991 Air Force Academy gross-out contest, for example, female cadets were forced to watch males eat bread they had used to swab the toilet "as their way of showing allegiance to the squadron" (Boxwell N.D.: 10). After the women protested to administrators, the Academy banned the contests. David Boxwell, a former literature professor at the Air Force and Naval Academies, observes that, "Understanding that the filthiness of male bonding (no matter how 'gross') actually, ultimately only served to reinforce male power and domination at the Academy (as a prelude to a male-dominated military force as whole), female cadets blew the whistle" (Boxwell N.D.: 13). In the 1990s, public scandals involving violent hazing tarnished the Navy's reputation, and Navy leaders issued guidelines to limit perceived excesses (Bronner 2007: 5–7; Hersh 2002: 321). Since that time, crossing the line ceremonies have become less risqué, and some extreme forms of hazing have become less formally institutionalised. Boxwell (N.D.: 3) says that such rituals are "all the more deliriously 'perverse' because they have the smaller-scale intimacy of men self-selecting the cliquish group in which their 'extracurricular' bonds occur". At the Air Force Academy, male bonding is "continuously being invented and reinvented by male cadets in ways that are more surreptitious, smaller-scale, cabbalistic, in a word, 'underground'" (ibid.: 5).[4] Recent examples include bare-knuckle boxing and group masturbation among small numbers of peers.

Without, then, insisting on any fixed or stable interpretation of penetration's meaning or its relationship to masculinity, it nonetheless seems that penetration has been associated with a range of contradictory associations in American military culture. Penetration has signified manliness and weakness. It has marked excommunication and initiation. It has been constitutive of, but also prohibited by, what might be called official or quasi-official norms and practices. It has been enacted by perpetrators and victims of rape. As English professor Richard Rambuss (1999: 96) observes, "The absolutely impervious Marine stands in alignment with— indeed, he hyperbolizes—enduring cultural prescriptions that predicate the maintenance of a man's virility upon his disavowal of softness, passivity, receptivity. Yet if Marines are rendered hard, their bodies remain surprisingly open and vulnerable."

THE CONFLATION OF THE MASCULINE AND THE UNMASCULINE

The US military has compelled the troops to engage in practices whose meanings have been structured by the masculine and the unmasculine in three different ways: First, and echoing the late anthropologist Mary Douglas's insight about the lack of any genuine distinction between purity and pollution, the meanings of the troops' practices have been structured in terms of binary oppositions even though the distinction between the masculine and unmasculine has been blurred. Social control has depended on the masculine's potential to become conflated with the unmasculine, or the "turning one pole of a binarism relentlessly into its opposite" (Savran 1998: 225). Just as military practices have established masculinity in opposition to the unmasculine, these ostensible oppositions have been conflated at the same time. It is hard to say, for example, whether Marines who cleaned their penises with wire brushes during World War Two combat operations in the South Pacific were emasculating themselves in an act of genital mutilation or fortifying themselves in a hyper-masculine genital purification rite that echoed the cleaning of a weapon (Sledge 1990). Yet it may not be an accident that in many military contexts, the difference between strong and weak, polluted and pure, top and bottom, and gay and straight has been clear, but also difficult if not impossible to discern. My research suggests that ambiguity around what constitutes the symbolic order/meaning of masculinity has been a tool that tightened the screw of military discipline by making it impossible for soldiers to know whether or not they are masculine, whether or not they are on the right side of the line.[5] The differentiation of masculinity from the unmasculine, in other words, has gone hand in hand with their conflation. Service members have become doubly confused by the ambiguous message that they are supposed to reject and embody masculinity even though they cannot distinguish it from the unmasculine. Unable to embody subject positions which are coded as oppositional yet indistinguishable, and unable to ascertain the difference between what they are supposed to idealise and that which they must disavow, they have found that surrender to authority is the most viable option. A penchant for obedience and conformity has emerged from the double confusion.

In contrast to Michel Foucault's emphasis on the differentiation of those marked as normative from others classified as deviant, my first observation emphasises the incitement of the unmasculine in each service member. According to Foucault's account of the production of docile troops in nineteenth century European armed forces, militaries' production of delinquency prompted soldiers to differentiate themselves from those marked as deviant by demonstrating their own normativity. Foucault explains how the system of classification developed at the École Militaire condemned those cadets labelled as 'médiocres' to "all the punishments used in the Hôtel or all those that are thought necessary, even solitary confinement in a dark dungeon." For those cadets relegated to the 'shameful' class, "special regulations were drawn up 'so that those who belonged to it would always be separated from the others and would be dressed in sackcloth'." Foucault says that students at the École Militaire experienced "a constant pressure to conform to the same model." The result was the "docile, useful troop". Referencing a range of institutions including the clinic, prison, and military, he observes that, "[…] the 19th century constructed rigorous channels which, within the system, inculcated docility and produced delinquency by the same mechanisms."[6] My interest in obedient masculinity in the American armed forces parallels Foucault's account of the origins of the compliant service member. That said, I depart from his emphasis on the differentiation of those marked as normative from others classified as deviant. In the modern American armed forces, the differentiation of in-groups from out-groups has long corresponded with ambiguous practices which constituted each service member as both masculine and unmasculine. The effectiveness of social control has depended as much on the conflation of the masculine with the unmasculine as on their differentiation.

My second observation is that practices through which military masculinity is enacted have been structured by oppositions which signified, replaced and slipped into one another. For example, military differentiations of the masculine from the feminine often have been represented in terms of sealed-up versus leaky bodies: men's warrior bodies are supposed to be leak-proof like impenetrable armour, while women's bodies have been coded as leaky and soft. Hence the disproportionate emphasis in military medical literature on menstruation and female fluids, as if women cannot have warrior bodies because of their leakiness.[7] In turn, the distinction between leaky and leak-proof can slip into representations of engulfment/liberation, gay/straight, rotting flesh/muscularity, jungle/countryside, pollution/purity, death/life, danger/security, disease/health, and helplessness/control (Burke 2004: 56f; Cameron 1994: 71–3; Grosz 1994: 206; Higate 2003: 6). Former Representative Robert Dornan illustrated the point in a slippery use of a bodily metaphor to describe the military closet:

> [...] the best of your troops can never respect and thereby follow orders totally from someone who likes taking it up the bum, no matter how secret he keeps it. Once it leaks out, they think this person is abnormal, perverted, and a deviant from the norm. (Military Forces and Personnel Subcommittee of the Committee on Armed Services 1994: 378)

Thus, the distinction between dirty and clean has been coded variously in terms masculine/feminine, coloniser/colonised, civilised/barbaric and white/non-white. The accumulation of substitutable oppositions has meant that discipline has been over-determined and multi-balanced, in that the web of double binds that soldiers are obliged to embody/disavow is so confusing and dense that discipline has been nearly impossible to resist.[8]

A third pattern that has amplified military discipline is that practices through which military masculinity is enacted have etched ambiguity in, on and through service members' bodies as well as their identities. In the case of male-male rape, military practices have coded rape victims as carriers of taboo because they have been imagined to be gay, but also because their bodies have been violated like a woman or gay man, here imagined as the passive partner in sodomy. At the same time, male rape victims have been coded as hyper-masculine because they are tough enough to take it like a man, but also because penetration of the male body has served as a demonstration of male privilege.[9] So the question of what is masculine and what is unmasculine has been played out incoherently in, on and through soldiers' bodies, not just their identities. While Mary Douglas and others long have argued that bodies—not just military bodies, but bodies in general—are symbols for social systems, the body of the soldier has come to signify the nation and national security in particularly intensified ways (Douglas 1966; Kristeva 1982). To take one of many examples, during World War Two, literary scholar Christina Jarvis suggests that, "the American military, government, and other institutions shaped the male body both figuratively and physically in an effort to communicate impressions of national strength to US citizens and to other nations" (Jarvis 2010: 4f; Nye 2007: 438). The body's signification of national strength has raised the stakes of discipline in that any soldier who fails to surrender his or her body to the military's contradictory expectations jeopardises not only the armed forces, but the nation itself.

The military body has been well suited to engage in practices that sustain but also blur institutionally-incited contradictions. Consider the exaggerated ways in which military practices have coded the body as a signifier of both purity and pollution, while collapsing the distinction between them. The purification of the

military body (as national body) has been performed at so many
sites that its operation seems almost axiomatic. Uniformed guides
who escort school children on Pentagon tours, for example, have
sported not only perfectly shined shoes, but white gloves as well.
Yet the military body can become polluted in ways that are almost
unheard of in civilian society. During World War One, "[…] a
young officer became incurably shell-shocked after falling atop
the decomposing corpse of a German soldier and choking on a
mouthful of its entrails" (Leed 1979: 19). And while the military
body can mark the difference between purity/pollution as well
as a host of other oppositions in pronounced ways, it can also
conflate them. As cultural studies scholar David Serlin's studies
of military amputations show, prosthetics and rehabilitation have
marked both the heightened vulnerability of the nation, but also
its capacity for regeneration (Serlin 2003, 2004).

DISCIPLINE-AS-COLLAPSE

My research suggests that service members begin to engage in
ambiguous practices on their first day in uniform and continue
throughout their careers. While service in the military sometimes
has been understood as an ego-consolidating experience, an
occasion for forging an integrated, masculine identity, I suggest
that to be masculine in the US armed forces is to acquire a status
whose penchant for conformity and compliance follows from
an institutionally incited and highly confusing split. As theatre
scholar David Savran notes, "the new man validates himself […]
by turning against himself, by producing himself as the ground
on which irreducibly opposing forces collide and do battle"
(Savran 1998: 176). In the military context, the armed forces
invite and compel each service member to be masculine and
unmasculine at the same time. Asked to explain masculinity, a US
Marine responded: "The opposite of feminine! No. To me, what
is masculine? I don't know [Pause.] And I've worked so hard at
being it" (Zeeland 1996: 90).

Military service is designed to produce compliance by
sustaining similar erasures of self, states of mind which echo a

psychological condition known as 'identity diffusion.'[10] According to psychologists, identity diffusion is marked by uncertainty about one's personality, preferences, ideology, goals and even gender. Individuals characterised by identity diffusion do not know who they are. Often they exhibit contradictory character traits, a lack of authenticity and feelings of emptiness (Akhtar 1984: 1381–5; Taylor/Goritsas 1987). In the psychological literature, identity diffusion typically is understood as a confusion about or absence of self which results from early adolescent experiences in families. Without insisting that the collapse of self that can follow from military service is just the same as identity diffusion, I nonetheless suggest that service in the military can incite confusions that are so fundamental that some troops come to manifest some important characteristics of identity diffusion.

Ego uncertainty is central for understanding social control in the armed forces; for understanding how the military produces troops who tend to comply. A number of experimental studies have found that individuals characterised by identity diffusion are more susceptible to peer pressure and more likely to conform to group norms than individuals with more consolidated egos (Toder/Marcia 1973; Adams et al. 1985: 1102). That said, service members' penchant for compliance is not just the result of the fragmentation of identity, but also of the intensity of the masculine ideal with which all troops are ordered to comply/not-comply. As argued above, the military has incited a confusing split within each service member. Compliant warrior identities have consolidated around those splits to the extent that the troops found themselves unable to embody the masculine and unmasculine at the same time. The military has convinced service members that they could be queer, weak, feminine and the like, while promoting idealised warrior archetypes against which the troops have been compelled to measure themselves, setting up the complicated dynamic that lies at the heart of the masculine military subject. By demanding compliance with masculine myths from those who have been ordered to be unmasculine, the military has fragmented service members' identities and generated a series of confusing double-binds that intensify their desire to become masculine while making it impossible to live up to that standard. Given their confusion as to whether or not they are masculine, service members go to tremendous lengths to demonstrate that they deserve that label. Those lengths, I suggest, are the threads which, when sewn together, can make up the fabric of compliance and conformity. Hence my reference to this form of social control as 'discipline-as-collapse.'

Consider this anecdotal account of a recruit whose non-normativity was constituted in terms of a lack of athleticism. There was,

> a fellow recruit who, while lacking the aggressive tendencies of others, was not particularly effeminate in appearance, although the drill instructor continually called him 'girl' or 'faggot.' Each time the recruit failed to keep up with the group on a strenuous run, his fellow recruits were ordered to run circles around him. Angry that he couldn't keep up, four men from the formation tried to spur him on with kicks. Finally, platoon members had to carry him back to the base. Once back, the drill instructor ordered those who had completed the seven-mile run to perform calisthenics and the one who had failed to laugh at his suffering counterparts. Before leaving, the drill instructor exhorted to his platoon: "As long as there are faggots in this outfit who can't hack it, you're all going to suffer." As he turned to go into the duty hut he sneered, "Unless you women get with the program, straighten out the queers, and grow some balls of your own, you best give your soul to God, because your ass is mine and so is your mother's on visiting day." With a roar sixty to seventy enraged men engulfed Green, knocking him to the ground and kicking and beating him (Eisenhart 1975: 13–23).

Or, to take another example, in 1972 at Fort Jackson, South Carolina, a gay American soldier named Pete Randell heard a noise just beyond his quarters. Stepping outside, Randell realised that a gang rape was taking place. He "found about forty guys lined up eagerly near the latrine. The other recruits had realized there was a faggot in the barracks, and two of the bigger guys had pushed him down on his knees and held him in the shower while the entire platoon lined up for blowjobs. The next day, the soldier was gone" (Shilts 1993: 179).

In both anecdotes, service-members who participated in the gang rape and assault certainly were engaged in a brutal performance of being not-gay and not-feminine. Clearly, they disavowed and distanced themselves from those who embodied any markers of the unmasculine such as weakness, queerness and the inability to fight back. That said—and this is the moment that remains under-theorised in the literature—the military has tried to convince service members that they could be queer, feminine and so on in order to necessitate the intensity of that disavowal. Recall the drill sergeant's warning that, "Unless you women get with the program, straighten out the queers, and grow some balls of your own, you best give your soul to God, because your ass is mine and so is your mother's on visiting day." The sergeant coded his men as women who had no courage, who could be raped at will and whose mothers could be violated sexually. Some American troops have found that the best way to navigate the ongoing requirement to be masculine and unmasculine is to conform, to submit to organisational norms and culture, to go with the flow by jumping in when the gang rape starts. Or when the war starts. They have self-neutralised, or policed themselves into conforming with the military's norms, as a way of compensating for the deficit between the unmasculine that the military has induced them to perform, and the masculine ideal with which they are supposed to identify.

American service members have been subject to many forms of power and discipline. Discipline-as-surveillance, for example, refers to disciplines that depend primarily on a soldier's sense of being watched over, warned, or monitored. Richard Whitney, the author of a 1917 study of waste disposal in military camps, recommended that latrine orderlies "should report at once to the medical officer any undue amount of diarrhoea or bowel disturbances among the men. He should also report the failure of any man to cover his droppings with a sufficient quantity of earth [...]" (Whitney 1917: 34). In partial contrast, discipline-as-punishment refers to the formal and institutional use of sanctions of various intensities to punish violations of rules. Alongside discipline-as-surveillance, discipline-as-punishment and other forms of discipline in American military culture, discipline-as-collapse has been a potent and pervasive form of social control in the US armed forces. A scholar who studied indoctrination in the US Marine Corps hit the nail on the head in noting that the goal of training is to turn new recruits into "a tool, a blind instrument to enforce another's aims and purposes" (Shatan 2001, as cited in Burke 2004: 44, 46).

SEXUAL VIOLENCE

If my argument is correct, and military masculinity, or, to be more precise, military masculinit*ies*, are structured by contradictions, and the experiences of the soldiers are characterised by conflicting expectations and practices, what might then be said about the relationship between military masculinities, armed conflict, and sexual violence? Which conditions and experiences facilitate the perpetration of sexual violence (against women and men, against civilians, enemy combatants, against comrades)?

My interpretation of military masculinity furthermore raises questions about the visibility/invisibility of sexual violence. One of the most powerful and compelling aspects of Susan Brownmiller's *Against Our Will*, whose fortieth anniversary marked the rationale for holding the SVAC conference, was not just the documentation of sexual violence's pervasiveness in law, politics and culture, but also the demonstration that its omnipresence was, in some ways, hidden in plain sight for many men. Do the mechanisms that make military masculinity seem unproblematic also help hide the pervasiveness of rape in plain sight?

This article is based on excerpts from Aaron Belkin, *Bring Me Men. Military Masculinity and the Benign Façade of American Empire: 1898–2001*, 2012. Reproduced with permission of Hurst and Company.

NOTES

1. I am grateful to Professors Jeanne Scheper and Sabine Frühstück for their analyses of the anecdote.

2. For other discussions of military ceremonies which involve penetration, see Zeeland 1995; Hersh 2002. Zeeland includes a photograph of a greasing (figure 14).

3. Hersh says that shellbacks are never penetrated.

4. He depicts a number of situations that got out of control. At the US Air Force Academy in the spring of 2000, cadets organised "informal gatherings of between half a dozen and a dozen male members of their own local 'fight club'." These supposedly included "bare-knuckled punching" and only became public when a senior, known as a goofball, soaked bandages in lighter fluid, wrapped them around his hands, and "set them alight for a supposedly spectacular entry in the dorm room where the fight was to happen."

5. In another context, Janet Halley shows how uncertainty surrounding statutory definitions of a propensity to engage in homosexual conduct makes it difficult for all service members, gay or straight, to know whether or not their behaviour is normative and permissible (Halley 1999).

6. Archives Nationales, MM 658, 30 March 1758 and MM 666, 15 September 1763, as cited by Foucault 1975: 182, 199, 168, 300.

7. The abstract of a manuscript on women in combat, for example, reads as follows: "For adult females, feminine hygiene practices constitute health care practices based on physiological necessities for the management of elimination products, including urine, faeces, and menstrual discharge. This study is designed to investigate and to make recommendations for female health practices carried out in combat and non-combat environments by military women" (Czerwinski 1997).

8. Doty, writing about American representations of the Philippines, observes that, "The individual differences presumed by the various sets of oppositions found in this discourse were cancelled out insofar as all of them were quite mobile and interchangeable. They could stand in for one another. They could refer to one thing one day and to another the next day. Spurr points out that the mobility of a concept increases its practical value and enables it to function consistently in the service of power" (Doty 1996: 47).

9. As McClintock notes in a different though nonetheless relevant context, "The disruption of social norms is not always subversive [...] Indeed, privileged groups can, on occasion, display their privilege precisely by the extravagant display of their right to ambiguity" (McClintock 1991: 68).

10. In a different national context, anthropologist Sabine Frühstück (2011) says that "for Japanese service members, the military experience is closer to what Frederic Jameson called a 'fragmentation of the subject'." She refers to the troops' flattened subjectivity and sense of disorientation. For the argument that military indoctrination is not designed to produce a new self and that service members are not "passive participants in the process," see McGurk et al. 2006: 27f.

REFERENCES

Adams, Gerald/Ryan, John/Hoffman, Joseph/Dobson, William/ Nielsen, Elwin. 1985. 'Ego Identity Status, Conformity and Personality in Late Adolescence', *Journal of Personality and Social Psychology*, 47(5):1091–1104.

Akhtar, Shakeel. 1984. 'The Syndrome of Identity Diffusion', *American Journal of Psychiatry*, 141(11):1381–85.

Belkin, Aaron. 2012. *Bring me Men: Military Masculinity and the Benign Facade of American Empire: 1898–2001*. Columbia University Press.

Boxwell, David A. N.D. *Fight Clubs, Circle Jerks, Gross-Out Contests: Male Bonding Rituals at the United States Air Force Academy*. Unpublished manuscript.

Bronner, Simon J. 2007. 'Sailor Men: Are Navy Rituals, like Kissing the Royal Belly, Homophobic or Momoerotic?' *American Sexuality Magazine*, 19 June.

————. 2006. *Crossing the Line: Violence, Place, and Drama in Naval Equator Traditions*. Amsterdam: Amsterdam University Press.

Burke, Carol. 2004. *Camp All-American, Hanoi Jane, and the High-and-Tight: Gender, Folklore, and Changing Military Culture*. Boston: Beacon Press.

Cameron, Craig M. 1994. *American Samurai: Myth and Imagination in the Conduct of Battle in the First Marine Division 1941–1951*. Cambridge: Cambridge University Press.

Czerwinski, Barbara. 1997. *Combat Readiness: Hygiene Issues Related to Military Women*. Houston: Texas University.

Doty, Roxanne Lynn. 1996. *Imperial encounters: The Politics of Representation in North-South Relations*. Minneapolis: University of Minnesota Press.

Douglas, Mary. 1966. *Purity and Danger: An Analysis of Concepts of Pollution and Taboo*. New York: Praeger.

Eisenhart, Wayne. 1975. 'You Can't Hack it Little Girl. Discussion of Covert Psychological Agenda Of Modern Combat Training', *Journal Of Social Issues*, 31(4):13–23.

Foucault, Michel. 1975. *Discipline & Punish: The Birth of the Prison*. Paris: Editions Gallimard.

Frühstück, Sabine. 2011. 'After Heroism: Must Real Soldiers Die?' in Sabine Frühstück/Anne Walthall (eds), *Recreating Japanese Men*, pp. 91–114. Berkeley: University of California Press.

Goffman, Erving. 1966. *Asylums: Essays on the Social Situation of Mental Patients and Other Inmates*. Garden City: Anchor Books.

Goyer, Peter F./Eddleman, Henry C. 1984. 'Same-Sex Rape of Nonincarcerated Men', *The American Journal of Psychiatry*, 141(4): 576–7.

Grosz, Elizabeth. 1994. *Volatile Bodies: Toward a Corporeal Feminism*. Bloomington: Indiana University Press.

Halley, Janet. 1999. *Don't: A Reader's Guide to the Military's Anti-Gay Policy*. Durham: Duke University Press.

Hersh, Carie Little. 2002. 'Crossing the Line: Sex, Power, Justice and the US Navy at the Equator', *Duke Journal of Gender Law and Policy*, 9(277):277–324.

Higate, Paul R. 2003. *Military Masculinities: Identity and the State*. Westport: Praeger.

Jarvis, Christina S. 2010. *The Male Body at War: American Masculinity during World War II*. DeKalb: Northern Illinois University Press.

Kimmel, Michael. 1996. *Manhood in America: A Cultural History*. New York: Free Press.

Kristeva, Julia. 1982. *Powers of Horror: An Essay on Abjection*. New York: Columbia University Press.

Leed, Eric J. 1979. *No Man's Land: Combat & Identity in World War I*. Cambridge: Cambridge University Press.

McClintock, Anne. 1991. *Imperial Leather: Race, Gender and Sexuality in the Colonial Contest*. London: Routledge.

McGurk, Dennis/Cotting, Dave/Britt, Thomas/Adler, Amy. 2006. 'Joining the Ranks: The Role of Indoctrination in Transforming Civilians to Service Members', in Amy Adler/Carl Castro/Thomas Britt (eds), *Military Life: The Psychology of Serving in Peace and Combat, Operational Stress*, Vol. 2, pp. 13–31. Westport: Praeger.

Military Forces and Personnel Subcomittee of the Committee on Armed Services. 1994. *Assessment of the Plan to Lift the Ban on Homosexuals in the Military*. Washington, DC: Government Printing Office.

Nye, Robert A. 2007. 'Western Masculinities in War and Peace', *American Historical Review*, 112(2):417–38.

Rambuss, Richard. 1999. 'Machinehead', *Camera Obscura*, 14(42):96–123.

Savran, David. 1998. *Taking it like a Man: White Masculinity, Masochism, and Contemporary American Culture*. Princeton: Princeton University Press.

Serlin, David. 2004. *Replaceable You: Engineering the Body in Postwar America*. Chicago: University of Chicago Press.

———. 2003. 'Crippling Masculinity: Queerness and Disability in US Military Culture, 1800–1945', *GLQ: A Journal of Lesbian and Gay Studies*, 9(1–2):149–79.

Shilts, Randy. 1993. *Conduct Unbecoming: Lesbians and Gays in the US Military: Vietnam to the Persian Gulf*. New York: St. Martin's Press.

Sledge, Eugene B. 1990. *With the Old Breed, at Peleliu and Okinawa*. New York: Oxford University Press.

Taylor, Steven/Goritsas, Eleny. 1987. *Dimensions of Identity Diffusion*. New York: Guilford Press.

Toder, Nancy/Marcia, James. 1973. 'Ego Identity Status and Response to Conformity Pressure in College Women', *Journal of Personality and Social Psychology*, 26(2):287–94.

Vietnam Veterans against the War. 1972. *The Winter Soldier Investigation: An Inquiry into American War Crimes*. Boston: Beacon Press.

Whitney, Richard. 1917. *A Study of Methods of Waste Disposal for Military Camps*. Unpublished manuscript.

Zeeland, Steven. 1996. *The Masculine Marine: Homoeroticism in the US Marine Corps*. New York: Harrington Park Press.

———. 1995. *Sailors and Sexual Identity: Crossing the Line Between 'Straight' and 'Gay' in the US Navy*. New York: Harrington Park Press.

Violence against Women in New War Economies

MEREDETH TURSHEN

This essay takes the analysis of wartime violence against women out of the individualised context of interpersonal assault and puts it into the realm of war economies, which are highly criminalised, globalised and exist all over the world. The changed character of this century's 'civil' conflicts—the intervention of international military and humanitarian agencies, the regional character of the conflicts, the involvement of organised crime, the complicity of legitimate global industries—are the subject of intense debates around what are called the 'new wars' (Kaldor 1999, 2013; Duffield 2001). New wars—a contested concept—are those funded by sales of such local assets as gold, diamonds and coltan to transnational corporations, often through international criminal networks (Cockayne 2010: 190). New wars take advantage of financial deregulation to create new economic relations in this era of neoliberal capitalism. When protracted, new wars exacerbate the inability of states already weakened by austerity programmes to ensure human security and protect human rights. Most research on new wars fails to consider gender implications or offer evidence of economic opportunities for women in the informal economies of war zones, women's involvement in financing and arming conflicts and gendered impacts of repeated flight, relocation, capture and coerced labour. This essay shows how new war economies create diverse and different constellations and dynamics of sexual violence in armed conflict.

Wartime rape was for many decades a neglected topic deserving of our attention. Since Susan Brownmiller published *Against Our*

Will: Men, Women and Rape in 1975, feminists have emphasised rape as a tactic in war, framing sexual violence as a deliberate, calculated act meant to humiliate and degrade the victim (Baaz/ Stern 2013). The character of the wars in which sexual violence against women is committed has changed since the American war in Vietnam. Protracted conflicts on many continents have created a 'durable disorder,' wrenching women, children and men from their everyday productive activities, rites and celebrations and pitching them into states of violent turmoil, confused movement, precarious existence and deep grief unrelieved by customary rituals and symbols of mourning. These wars, which include lengthy and intermittent civil strife, ethnic and communal violence, disruptive political discord, internal disturbances, states of emergency and suppression of mass uprisings, occur under global neoliberal regimes in an environment of the so-called war on terror. The challenges today are to analyse rape in this context and to view women, not solely as victims of armed conflict, but also as economic actors, perpetrators, war resisters and peacemakers (Moser/Clarke 2001). The impact of strife on women's security deserves an expanded feminist analysis that reaches beyond interpersonal violence to encompass the political economy of the new wars.

WOMEN AND THE NEW WARS

Research on the new wars raises many interesting questions about varied opportunities for women in the informal economies of war zones, including women's involvement in the financing and arming of conflicts that are, or were, backed by trans-border trade of gems and minerals. Too little research has been done on women's food production and marketing in wartime, about women's relation to warring groups that impose irregular taxes, about women's mobility, their work in artisanal mining and participation in smuggling operations and the effect of the devaluation and dollarization of many currencies on women's petty trade. This essay explores how women's wartime livelihood activities endanger them and expose them to violence and the likelihood of attack. War studies rarely use a gendered framework although the breakdown of male/female binaries is most evident when analysing gender in conflict and its aftermath: changes in production and social reproduction are dramatic, violent, visible, traceable and gendered. My hypothesis is that violence is a factor in production, and armed conflict both unleashes and legitimates violence, contributing in some circumstances to higher productivity and profitability for certain participants and eventual receivers of goods and services produced in this way.

Wars occasionally create a political power vacuum (as in the appearance of failed states), but they do not give rise to an economic vacuum: the formal economy may be ruined but an informal one rises in its place. Civilians (and often combatants) must find ways to survive in the context of a dramatic increase in risk and uncertainty, political instability, violence and economic decline (Korf 2004: 276). In this breach arises the phenomenon of violent economies, which depend on criminal proceeds from kidnapping, trafficking, protection rackets, diverted relief aid, remittances from nationals living abroad and revenues from trade in commodities like drugs, gems, timber and minerals. Violent economies comprise many categories of violent actors—conflict entrepreneurs (looters, organised criminals, military managers, political entrepreneurs); conflict opportunists who use chaos as a cover for their nefarious activities; and conflict dependants whose livelihoods depend on prolonging hostilities (Jackson 2005: 160ff). Their violence now matches that of the state because the new wars ended state monopolies on violence; rebel leaders and the governments they seek to overthrow equally wield force and power, and war profiteers and international criminal networks use violence in parallel trade to link up with legitimate international businesses. The violent economic regimes spawned by these new regionalised wars have opened another phase in gender relations and the use of force in production.[1]

In wartime women enter the civilian labour force in significant numbers. One explanation of women's greater participation in the workforce during armed conflict is the 'added worker effect,' which refers to an increase in the labour supply of married women when their husbands die or are unemployed or absent (World Bank 2011: 61). The particular characteristics of civil wars invalidate most generalisations. In Syria, women are commoditised, seen as valuable assets in warring regions, and are used strategically to negotiate transfers through checkpoints and to secure food and other resources for their families; they may be subject to transactional sex, employed as financial mules and kidnapped for ransom (Alsaba/Kapilashrami 2016). Women also join national and rebel armed forces as fighters or camp followers, sometimes for their own protection or personal gain. National armies, although reputed to expose women to sexual assault, are perceived to offer some security and access to scarce supplies. Rebel brigades, which also abuse women and girls, afford opportunities and an alternative, offering a better material life for many women because looting is a ready means to acquire undreamed-of possessions. In areas where farms are over-run and crops are looted, some women grab the advantages offered by joining armed forces. The disadvantages are well known: in a survey of conflicts between 1987 and 2007 in 20 African countries, sexual violence was found to be widespread, systematic, even epidemic, inflicted on young women including female fighters; mutilation and gang-rape were routine and sexual slavery common (Coulter/Persson/Utas 2008).

In the context of the new wars, the gendered division of labour within and outside fighting forces appears to be less discriminating than in pre-war society. Among civilian populations in war zones, women left on their own must manage households and farmsteads (in effect becoming the boss and doing men's work). In military bush camps, captured youths are forced to do all and any kind of work that is necessary to maintain camp life; even sex work is imposed on captive boys and girls (Mazurana et al. 2002: 109). The observation that the gendered division of labour is less differentiated in war economies appears to contradict the widely held opinion that masculinisation accompanies the militarisation of society. Opinion holds that male/female distinctions become more rigid in these circumstances. Military culture does rely on sexism and notions of femininity to reinforce aggressive ideals of masculinity thought necessary for warfare. Yet, as Cynthia Enloe notes of the high percentage of women in fighting forces, "even a thoroughly patriarchal regime may subvert the orthodox sexual division of military labor in order to maintain itself in power" (Enloe 2000: xi). From the viewpoint of military commanders, strategic objectives outweigh sexism and patriarchy in the hierarchy of concerns (Bock 1998: 94f). At least for the duration of the conflict, women may be accepted in new gender roles. Their post-war lives often do not meet their hopes for carrying forward the transformations they experienced (Turshen 2002).

War also provides opportunities for women that would be considered criminal or unsavoury in other circumstances. Work in the shadow (informal or parallel) economy, particularly trading in rebel zones, occasions real benefits as well as such risks as road accidents and being ambushed or taken for a spy. Armed conflict both sanctions and assists the use of violence as well as the commoditisation of certain goods and services not usually available—for example forced labour, sexual servitude and illegal minerals, wildlife and agricultural products (Cockayne 2010: 189). Women may organise, volunteer or participate in these activities— or they are co-opted, abducted or coerced.

WOMEN'S LIVELIHOODS IN CONFLICT ZONES

Although not all transactions that pass through the shadow economy in conflict zones are illegal,[2] criminal activities may infiltrate at all levels and come to dominate deals in civil wars. The existence of armed conflict encourages certain forms of organised crime to flourish under the guise of political struggle (as in rackets—like demands for cash in exchange for 'protection'— to raise money for 'the cause'). In addition, the exigencies of communities in need open channels for illegal business deals to commingle with legitimate deliveries of relief aid.[3] Women producers who organise and push back against their exploitation in informal economies in conflict zones may be beaten and raped to keep them in line (Nordstrom 2010: 168).

Predatory corruption is pernicious when public officials grab public resources such as land or minerals directly or indirectly through private factions; petty corruption exists when basic public services are sold instead of provided by right (Khan 2006). The extraction of protection money from citizens affects in particular poor women who depend heavily on services like water and electricity to conduct business in towns. Theodore Trefon (2009: 16) gives this example of the creative use of predatory administrative power in Democratic Republic of Congo (DRC): municipal hygiene services are responsible for public health issues, but they overlap with municipal environmental services, which are responsible for the cleanliness of public space; this deliberately designed ambiguity facilitates the harassment of service users. When agents from both services approach a market woman selling chickens, she has no idea whose requirements she should respect, or indeed which agent is real and which false. "Escaping them is impossible. Avoiding a tax, be it official or arbitrarily invented on the spot, is a daunting challenge for some and a daily exercise for others" (ibid.: 10). Most women will do whatever they can to outwit the state agent in front of them.

The operation of illegal markets facilitates corruption, which is used systemically by organised crime. Organised crime groups can work with local criminals, leading to an increase in corruption, extortion, racketeering and violence (United Nations Office on Drugs and Crime N.D.). Inefficient government structures, low salaries, excessive bureaucratic regulations and red tape offer many opportunities of bribery and extortion (Chêne 2010). High-level corruption filters down to daily life when women must make informal payments to access medical care and school services. And, importantly, the currency of corruption is frequently sexualised—women and girls are often asked to pay bribes in the form of sexual favours (United Nations Development Programme/United Nations Development Fund for Women 2010).

CROSS-BORDER TRADE

Internal problems are magnified by opportunities for private gain at border crossings. The decay or wartime disruption of one country's physical infrastructure leads to a pivot of commercial activity from internal markets to external trade with better-served nations on its borders. Trade becomes trans-border, markets are regionalised and, in this century, exchange is inevitably globalised.

Today, for example, cross-border trade is the primary means of subsistence for the majority of Congolese living on the frontiers of Burundi, Rwanda, Tanzania and Uganda. Much of the coffee exported from Rwanda is grown in the eastern Kivu provinces and moved from Goma, the provincial capital of North Kivu, to Kigali, capital of Rwanda, and thence to Kampala (Uganda), the Kenyan capital Nairobi and its port city Mombasa (Weijs/ Hilhorst/Ferf 2012: 14). Eastern Congo is still the site of frequent clashes, despite the truce signed in 2003: on 6 December 2016, a Congolese association reported an alarming rise in sexual violence in the Butembo region of North Kivu Province: September, October and November 2016 were said to be months of intense suffering when at least 99 cases of rape were documented. The reality was said to be even more disturbing as many women failed to come forward out of shame or the fear of stigmatisation (Willame N.D.; Reuters 2016). Whenever North Kivu province is insecure, trade between Goma/Congo and Gisenyi/Rwanda is blocked.

For Congolese traders, 75 per cent of whom are women, small-scale commerce is the main activity (male traders have access to more capital and higher earnings and thus opportunities for more lucrative ventures). In a not always successful effort to avoid paying informal tariffs and enduring physical harassment, as 90 per cent of traders do at the Goma border, many Congolese women resort to smuggling, using unpatrolled tracks (Raeymaekers 2009). At the Goma/Gisenyi crossing between Congo and Rwanda, this small-scale cross-border trade in agricultural goods is the primary source of income and principal means of subsistence for about 22 000 people, the majority of them women (Kimanuka/Lange 2010). Although they have interests in common, women traders from the two cities are in competition and distrust each other. The competition created by the Rwandan women's practice of itinerant trading vexes Congolese women traders. Rwandan women claim that their Congolese competitors chase them from the market, that the Rwandans do not have their own markets in Goma, and that Congolese customs services and other persons in Goma harass them when they cross the border. Of importance for female Rwandan traders is the fight against harassment by police and semi-official actors such as maibobo (street children) and Rasta (a gang of Rwanda Hutu rebels) as well as the population at large.

WOMEN IN WARTIME MINING ECONOMIES

We know that structural adjustment programmes changed women's relation to the state (Bakker 2003) but little about how women seeking public services or state protections have fared in the new wars. These conflicts have brought women into contact with new, networked forms of parallel—that is, illegal or unofficial—trade in regional, trans-border structures of alternative governance. Some women are captives, coerced into working; they lack physical and economic security. Others voluntarily migrate to centres of mining and smuggling out of necessity, curiosity or enterprise; they may also find insecurity and a lack of services. Their choice of mine sites is not surprising as on average 30 per cent of the world's artisanal miners are women; the percentage is highest in Africa, ranging from 40 to 50 per cent. Customarily a family affair, artisanal mining was often the activity African farmers practised in the dry season; artisanal mines were not violent settings in the past. In war zones, however, these activities and networks tie into outright criminal enterprises such as the international drug trade, weapons smuggling, money laundering and human trafficking, all of which threaten women's freedom and autonomy.

One study asked whether artisanal mining increases the risk of sexual violence; by imposing data on women's reports of non-partner violence on maps of mining sites in eastern Congo, the authors were able to demonstrate that women living close to mine sites are more likely to be sexually victimised by both partners and non-partners and that women who live close to sites with armed actor presence were at particular risk of sexual violence by someone other than their partner in the provinces of North and South Kivu and Maniema (Rustad,/Østby/Nordås 2016). However, their hypotheses centred on physical proximity and they did not determine whether the women worked at mine sites. My hypothesis is that women's work in artisanal mining puts them at risk of non-partner violence.

Militaries that take control of mine sites often use existing artisanal labour forces of men and women to work for them, subjecting the miners to brutal, slavery-like working conditions. In these militarised and masculinised settings, payment for the work is arbitrary. Congolese women seeking work in the profitable Angola-Congo diamond trade risked rape, theft, betrayal and capture (De Boeck/Plissart 2014: 212). Women from Congo perceived the need for a protector to be so great that they married Angolan soldiers in temporary unions of convenience. The women didn't regard these marriages as real but as strategies that, when successful, gave them economic power and freedom. Filip De Boeck (2000) compares these women's tactics to those men have used for centuries—cementing marriages and alliances to enlarge their social and resource networks by exchanging products (formerly game, palm wine, rubber and slaves, nowadays diamonds and gold). The world of diamond trafficking is characterised by extreme machismo; nevertheless, it has a considerable number of active women participants (De Boeck 2000). This world of conflict diamonds is yet another example of how war transforms gender assignments, sometimes permanently.

Although trans-border structures of alternative governance operate within social networks that inscribe their own forms of legitimacy and regulatory codes on the shadow economy, international codes of conduct and rules of war may be suspended, affording little protection to women. The nodes within parallel networks that command real influence remain under patriarchal control (Duffield 2001: 156). The suspension of legality is often a necessary precondition of asset realisation (the conversion of minerals into guns or cash) through parallel and trans-border manoeuvres. Mark Duffield notes that "the rule of law and protection of customary rights have been an important casualty of the qualification of nation-state competence" (Duffield 1999: 30).

As the state apparatus weakens, women's likelihood of receiving protection also shrinks. These developments are contradictory: on the one hand, statutory laws are no longer enforced to protect women, and on the other hand, as societies break down, customary rights don't protect them either. This means that women's rights are in jeopardy just as new trade networks are developing in the borderlands.

The dynamics of trans-border trade are likely to encourage and enforce informal protectionism. Circuits of extra-legal activity lend themselves to different forms of socially structured control. With few formal qualifications required for positions of power and control, what prevails are ethnic, local, kinship, religious, political or diaspora connections. Invoking colonial legacies of disruptive designations and regional inequities, new wars manipulate identity, perpetuating and hardening ethnic divisions. These throwbacks are likely to spell trouble for women who marry across lines (for example, inter-ethnic or inter-religious marriages). Ethnic cleansing and forcible transfer of assets between groups may be features of conflict situations, and women with multiple affiliations or loyalties will be caught in the crossfire.

MINES AS SITES OF DANGER, PLACES FOR PROFIT

In Congo some women who sell food at the markets, restaurants and kiosks around mining camps also buy and sell gold. However, most women working at the mine sites fall into the hierarchy of workers extracting gold. Income from mining activities varies according to the location of the mine, the market for the mineral involved and the particular task. Men who extract the rock are at the beginning of the supply chain; they may be individual diggers or groups of diggers who employ women on an ad hoc basis to pulverise the stones to extract the gold. The women work without a contract and are thus at risk of not being paid or accusations of theft (Geneen 2011: 200ff). Some women admit that they hide stones in their underclothes. After the rock is crushed the remaining sand is sifted again and again. Three categories of workers are involved. The first is a team of four to six men to rework the sand to extract gold dust; next is a group of women called *mamans bizalus* who are paid to wash, work and crush a quantity of sand once more to find any remaining gold dust. A third category of mainly women (*mamans toras*) and children gather the leftovers to pound, wash and sift the waste yet again.

The work of pulverising stone is physically demanding and many workers suffer not only from fatigue but also from pulmonary diseases including tuberculosis due to the harsh, dusty conditions. Women's reproductive health is affected by the environmental impact of mining. A process commonly used to extract gold, called amalgamation, uses mercury. Exposure to mercury can result in sterility, breast milk contamination and oestrogenic disruption, which is damaging to pregnant and breastfeeding women. Women, sometimes with infants in their arms or toddlers clinging to their skirts, perform the amalgamation tasks. They combine mercury with gold-laden silt to form a hardened amalgam that picks up most of the gold metal from the silt. The amalgam is then heated over an open flame to evaporate the mercury, leaving small pieces of gold. Women and children inhale this gaseous mercury during the burning process.

Female miners face the double risk of being rural women in a war zone and of working outside any legal framework in precarious social, economic and environmental conditions (Heller/Perks 2013). The Congolese are not effectively protected by health and safety laws in the mines, and the women lack supportive social networks in these mining areas. In the most extreme cases in South Kivu, women are subject to coercion, intimidation and sexual violence.

In summary, mining promises quick riches and this illusion undermines and devalues women's work in farming. Mines may be zones of danger where rape, prostitution and violent assault expose women to mental, emotional and physical harm including increased risk of AIDS and other sexually transmitted infections, but mine sites are also locales of opportunity that draw women for some of the same reasons they attract men.

TRAFFICKING AND SMUGGLING OF WOMEN AND GIRLS

During armed conflict, cross-border trafficking of women is thought to be common because of impunity, lawlessness, dysfunctional state institutions and lax border controls, as well as the generally high level of violence and displacement during wars (Wölte 2004). It is also the case that neoliberal rules of finance and trade have enabled international criminal organisations to gain entry to conflict zones and operate with near-impunity. The trafficking of women and girls through and from war zones controlled by warlords already engaged in war-related dealing in small arms and drugs with criminal organisations represents a profitable expansion of their activities. The global profits from human trafficking in 2005 were an estimated 32 billion US$ (International Labour Office 2014). Women and girls are at risk of being trafficked when their livelihoods are destroyed and they are forced to leave their homes; internally displaced persons and refugees are particularly susceptible to being trafficked. The examples discussed here are taken from the conflicts in Congo and Sierra Leone.

Sierra Leone is a source of trafficked labour and destination country for men, women and children subjected to forced work and sex trafficking (United States of America. Department of State. Office to Monitor and Combat Trafficking in Persons 2014). Victims come mainly from rural provinces and are recruited to urban and mining centres for sex work and prostitution, domestic servitude and forced labour in artisanal diamond and granite mining, petty trading, rock breaking, street crime, begging and portering (head loading of merchandise to be transported over distances sometimes as long as 25–50km) (Dzhambazova/ Bashengezi 2012). Trafficking victims may also be found in fishing and agriculture or subjected to sex trafficking or forced labour through customary practices such as forced or arranged marriages. Brima Acha Kamara (2008) writes that parents are exploiting their own sons and daughters, sending young children out to work instead of to school, allowing girls to be taken out of the country to work as maids in Lebanon where they are sexually abused, or forcing them into early, often polygamous, marriages. This exploitation is directly attributed to the war, to family displacement and the breakup of the extended family network, which was a source of support.

The US Department of State ranked Congo as a Tier 3 country, which means that its government does not fully comply with minimum standards of the US Trafficking Victims Protection Act (United States of America. Department of State. Office to Monitor and Combat Trafficking in Persons 2013). The Department of State alleges that the DRC is a source, destination and possibly a transit country for men, women and children subjected to forced labour and sex trafficking. The majority of this trafficking is internal, and armed groups and rogue elements of government forces outside government control in the country's eastern provinces perpetrate much of it. Some Congolese girls are forcibly prostituted in brothels or informal camps, including in markets and mining areas, by loosely organised networks, gangs and brothel operators. Some girls in Bas-Congo Province are reportedly coerced into prostitution by family members or transported to Angola's sex trade. Congolese women and children have been exploited within the country in conditions of domestic servitude, and some migrate to Angola, South Africa, the Republic of Congo and South Sudan, as well as East Africa, the Middle East and Europe, where they are exploited in sex trafficking, domestic servitude or forced labour in agriculture and diamond mines. Pub owners in Bisie, North Kivu, are said to lure young girls from their families and home villages with false promises of legitimate employment near the mines, and then refuse to pay them for the work they perform (Free the Slaves 2011: 17). Instead, the girls are told that their 'pay' is in the form of being given a venue in which to have sex with men for money. Some pub owners take the money directly, some give a portion of the money back to the girls, but they all use the girls' presence and implied sexual availability to attract customers to their establishments. This situation was dramatically interpreted by Lynn Nottage (2008) in her brilliant, Pulitzer Prize-winning play 'Ruined' about the plight of such women in war-torn Congo.

CONCLUSIONS: LIVELIHOODS UNDER DURESS

It is disturbing that gender is not part of the vocabulary of the literature on the political economy of war. This omission is unfortunate, both because the new war studies break, in thought-provoking ways, with past understandings of civil war and because they offer us new insights with which to revise and broaden our analyses of women's wartime experiences.

Civil wars, protracted over more than a decade in Sierra Leone and over two decades in eastern Congo, profoundly altered livelihoods—not just the ways in which women and men earn their living, not only their occupations and employment, but also the social, community, legal, political, security and economic environments in which people work. Abundant evidence confirms that war transforms gender roles in ways that belie the stereotypes that some work is performed exclusively by women and other work is undertaken solely by men or that characterise women only as victims of war. At the same time the political chaos of armed conflict deprives women of customary and statutory mechanisms of protection and recourse in case of assault or injury. When women assume the tasks normally assigned to men in their society, whether by choice or by force, they seem to exchange shelter that has become unsafe for agency that is uncertain and unpredictable—or they lose all control over their lives. Dispossession—as in loss of control of one's labour power, in forced labour arrangements or in the forfeit of one's assets—is a hallmark of the new wars. Protracted armed conflict appears to create patterns of exploitation that are refined over time, and the practices that prove the most profitable become normalised in the post-conflict period. Examples of these dilemmas are drawn from the mining sector. Because extractive industries were critical to the wars in Congo and Sierra Leone, and because women are prominent in mining in both countries, violence in mineral production is discussed in this essay, both the structural violence of the organisation of work and the personal violence that women endure.

In discussions of the risks and perils of the new wars, questions about the gendered impact of repeated flight and relocation, capture and coerced labour remain unanswered: for example, what are the consequences for marriage, childbirth and caregiving? Vital and health statistics are rarely collected in war zones (and intermittent studies are hotly contested, regarded as propaganda by one side or another). The women's health services literature is reduced to reporting the important but numerically minor issue of maternal mortality.

Analysis of women's war entanglements demands use of theoretical concepts elaborated by feminists, especially intersectionality—the overlapping of sexism, racism and class prejudice. The key to intersectional scrutiny of identity in wartime is an interdisciplinary analytic approach to social categories inflected by relations of power, an approach that needs to embrace changing world attitudes towards certain political and religious affiliations. New insights about women as actors and perpetrators are also of use in detecting women's deliberate exploitation of their multiple identities to deal across battle lines and should give us more information about women's everyday forms of resistance. We need more studies of nuanced compromising situations, of equivocal acts of consent, of subtle exchanges of favours, of desperate turns to collaboration, of all the shaded ambiguities in the lives of women and men trying to survive in war zones.

The violence of armed conflict persists in social relations of production long after the truce is signed by diminishing the value of labour, and by destroying the infrastructure of the economy that was the basis of productivity. What emerges from these pages is a portrait of the cumulative impacts on women of violent production regimes that are compounded by armed conflict, enabled by neoliberalism, enmeshed in international criminal networks, abetted by legitimate corporations, and condoned by complicit governments, both women's own states and those of the international community.

Violent economies depend for their existence on a very long human supply chain that crosses national borders and circles the globe. They ensnare poor men, women and children in remote rural regions and infiltrate urban slums. They co-opt government workers in tax and customs offices and in the police and military.

They attract politicians (including heads of state) and self-styled rebel leaders. They engage pilots and pimps, bank tellers and terrorists, jewellers and judges. They lure small entrepreneurs and large company executives alike. And they even tempt UN peacekeepers sent to patrol armed conflicts. At the very end of this supply chain are the consumers—you and me. We are the buyers of mobile phones, bearers of gold chains and fiancées with diamond rings.

NOTES

1. The best descriptions of the operations of war economies are to be found in reports to the United Nations Security Council, which, in the case of the conflict in the Democratic Republic of the Congo (DRC), established panels of experts on the illegal exploitation of natural resources and other forms of wealth. In a series of reports filed between 2001 and 2015, various panels detailed mass-scale looting, systematic and systemic exploitation, and the structures of illegal exploitation in DRC; they named individual actors, including a number of women, who were directly and crucially involved in providing support, entertaining networks, or facilitating exploitation; the panels also produced samples of companies importing minerals from DRC via Rwanda, giving names, country and merchandise.
2. Shadow economies are composed of informal networks that avoid state infrastructures. Goods may be legal but untaxed—foodstuffs, for example; other commodities, like drugs and arms, may be illegal; and children may be smuggled or trafficked.
3. For a detailed description see, Nordstrom 2004: 87ff.

REFERENCES

Alsaba, Khuloud/Kapilashrami, Anuj. 2016. 'Understanding Women's Experience of Violence and the Political Economy of Gender in Conflict: The Case of Syria', *Reproductive Health Matters*, 24(47):5–7.

Baaz, Maria Eriksson/Stern, Maria. 2013. *Sexual Violence as a Weapon of War? Perceptions, Prescriptions, Problems in the Congo and beyond*. London/New York: Zed Books.

Bakker, Isabella. 2003. 'Neo-liberal Governance and the Reprivatization of Social Reproduction: Social Provisioning and Shifting Gender

Orders', in Isabella Bakker/Stephen Gill (eds), *Power, Production and Social Reproduction: Human In/Security in the Global Political Economy*, pp. 66–82. London: Palgrave.

Bock, Gisela. 1998. 'Ordinary Women in Nazi Germany: Perpetrators, Victims, Followers, and Bystanders', in Dalia Ofer/Lenore J. Weitzman (eds), *Women in the Holocaust*, pp. 85–100. New Haven: Yale University Press.

Chêne, Marie. 2010. 'Overview of Corruption and Anti-Corruption in Sierra Leone', *Transparency International*, 22 September. http://www.u4.no/publications/overview-of-corruption-and-anti-corruption-in-sierra-leone/ (accessed 17 October 2018).

Cockayne, James. 2010. 'Crime, Corruption and Violent Economies', in Mats Berdal/Achim Wennmann (eds), *Ending Wars, Consolidating Peace: Economic Perspectives*, pp. 189–218. Milton Park: Routledge for International Institute for Strategic Studies.

Coulter, Chris/Persson, Mariam/Utas, Mats. 2008. *Young Female Fighters in African Wars: Conflict and its Consequences*. Uppsala: Nordiska Afrikainstitutet.

De Boeck, Filip. 2000. '"Dogs Breaking their Leash": Globalization and Shifting Gender Categories in the Diamond Traffic between Angola and DR Congo (1984–1997)', in Danielle de Lame/Chantal Zabus (eds), *Changements au féminin en Afrique noire*, pp. 87–114. Paris: L'Harmattan.

De Boeck, Filip/Plissart, Marie-Françoise. 2014. *Kinshasa: Tales of the Invisible City*. Leuven: Leuven University Press.

Duffield, Mark R. 2001. *Global Governance and the New Wars: The Merging of Development and Security*. London: Zed Books.

——. 1999. 'Globalization and War Economies: Promoting Order or the Return of History?' *Fletcher Forum of World Affairs*, 23(2):21–36.

Dzhambazova, Boryana/Bashengezi, Paulin. 2012. 'Women as Human Pack Horses in the Democratic Republic of Congo', *New York Times*, 28 June. http://www.nytimes.com/2012/06/29/world/africa/female-bearers-in-the-democratic-republic-of-congo.html?pagewanted=all&_r=0 (accesed 11 August 2018).

Enloe, Cynthia. 2000. *Maneuvers: The International Politics of Militarizing Women's Lives*. Berkeley: University of California Press.

Free the Slaves. 2011. 'The Congo Report: Slavery in Conflict Minerals', June. https://www.freetheslaves.net/wp-content/uploads/2015/03/The-Congo-Report-English.pdf (accessed 17 October 2018).

Geneen, Sara. 2011. 'Constraints, Opportunities and Hope: Artisanal Gold Mining and Trade in South Kivu (DRC)' in An Ansoms/ Stefaan Marysse (eds), *Natural Resources and Local Livelihoods in the Great Lakes Region of Africa: A Political Economy Perspective*, pp. 192–214. London: Palgrave Macmillan.

Heller, Katherine C./Perks, Rachel. 2013. 'Extractive Industries in Fragile Settings present Opportunities and Risks for Women', *The World Bank*, 7 October. http://blogs.worldbank.org/energy/extractive-industries-fragile-settings-present-opportunities-and-risks-women (accessed 10 August 2018).

International Labour Office. 2014. *Profits and Poverty: The Economics of Forced Labour*. Geneva: International Labour Office.

Jackson, Stephen. 2005. 'Protecting Livelihoods in Violent Economies', in Karen Ballentine/Heiko Nitzschke (eds), *Profiting from Peace: Managing the Resource Dimensions of Civil War*, pp. 153–82. London: Lynne Reinner.

Kaldor, Mary. 2013. 'In Defence of New Wars', *Stability: International Journal of Security & Development*, 2(1): 1–16.

———. 1999. *New and Old Wars: Organized Violence in a Global Era*. Cambridge: Polity Press.

Kamara, Brima Acha. 2008. 'The Challenges of Trafficking in Women and Children in Sierra Leone', in Obi N. I. Ebbe/ Dilip K. Das (eds), *Global Trafficking in Women and Children*, pp. 163–74. Boca Raton: CRC press.

Khan, Mushtaq H. 2006. 'Determinants of Corruption in Developing Countries: The Limits of Conventional Economic Analysis', in Susan Rose-Ackerman (ed), *International Handbook on the Economics of Corruption*, pp. 216–44. Cheltenham: Edward Elgar.

Kimanuka, Celestin/Lange, Maria. 2010. *The Crossing: Small-Scale Trade and Improving Cross-Border Relations between Goma (DR Congo) and Gisenyi (Rwanda)*, London: International Alert. http://www.international-alert.org/resources/publications/crossing#sthash.PAHkEF6t.dpbs (accessed 17 October 2018).

Korf, Benedikt. 2004. 'War, Livelihoods and Vulnerability in Sri Lanka', *Development and Change*, 35(2):275–95.

Mazurana, Dyan E./McKay, Susan A./Carlson, Khristopher C./ Kasper, Janel C. 2002. 'Girls in Fighting Forces and Groups: Their Recruitment, Participation, Demobilization, and Reintegration', *Peace and Conflict: Journal of Peace Psychology*, 8(2):97–123.

Moser, Caroline/Clarke, Fiona (eds). 2001. *Victors, Perpetrators or Actors: Gender, Armed Conflict and Political Violence.* London: Zed Books.

Nordstrom, Carolyn. 2010. 'Women, Economy, War', *International Review of the Red Cross*, 92(877):161–76.

———. 2004. *Shadows of War: Violence, Power, and International Profiteering in the Twenty-first Century.* Berkeley: University of California Press.

Nottage, Lynn. 2008. *Ruined.* Kate Whoriskey dir. Goodman Theatre, Chicago: Manhattan Theatre Club. First performance: 08 November 2008.

Raeymaekers, Timothy. 2009. 'The Silent Encroachment of the Frontier: A Politics of Trans-Border Trade in the Semliki Valley (Congo–Uganda)', *Political Geography*, 28(1):55–65.

Reuters. 2016. 'Dozens Die in Democratic Republic of Congo as Violence spreads amid Politcal Instability', *The Guardian*, 25 December. https://www.theguardian.com/world/2016/dec/26/scores-die-in-democratic-republic-of-congo-as-violence-spreads-amid-political-instability (accessed 17 October 2018).

Rustad, Siri Aas/Østby, Gudrun/Nordås, Ragnhild. 2016. 'Does Artisanal Mining Increase the Risk of Sexual Violence?' *Quality in Primary Care*, 24(2):77–80.

Trefon, Theodore. 2009. 'Public Service Provision in a Failed State: Looking beyond Predation in the Democratic Republic of Congo', *Review of African Political Economy*, 36(119):9–21.

Turshen, Meredeth. 2002. 'Algerian Women in the Liberation Struggle and the Civil War: From Active Participants to Passive Victims?' *Social Research*, 69(3):889-911.

United Nations Development Programme/United Nations Development Fund for Women. 2010. *Corruption, Accountability and Gender: Understanding the Connections.* New York: United Nations.

United Nations Office on Drugs and Crime. N.D. *Transnational Organized Crime: The Globalized Illegal Economy.* New York: United Nations Office on Drugs and Crime. http://www.unodc.org/toc/en/crimes/organized-crime.html (accessed 17 October 2018).

United States of America. Department of State. Office to Monitor and Combat Trafficking in Persons. 2014. *Sierra Leone: 2014 Trafficking in Persons Report.* Washington, DC. http://www.state.gov/j/tip/rls/tiprpt/countries/2014/226810.html (accessed 17 October 2018).

———. 2013. *Trafficking in Persons Report.* Washington. http://www.state.gov/j/tip/rls/tiprpt/countries/2013/215442.htm (accessed 17 October 2018).

Weijs, Bart/Hilhorst, Dorothea/Ferf, Adriaan. 2012. *Livelihoods, Social Protection and Basic Services in Democratic Republic of the Congo: Secure Livelihoods Research Consortium Working Paper 2*. London: Overseas Development Institute.

Willame, Jean-Claude. N.D. *Chronologies Afrique Centrale: Semaine du 3 au 9 décembre 2016*. https://docs.google.com/ viewer?a=v&pid= sites&srcid=ZGVmYXVsdGRvbWFpbnxjaHJvbm9sb2dp ZXNhZnJppcXVlY2VudHJhbGV8Z3g6MTczYmYyMjg1Y2Zk YjcwNg (accessed 17 October 2018).

Wölte, Sonja. 2004. *Armed Conflict and Trafficking in Women*. Eschborn: Deutsche Gesellschaft für Technische Zusammenarbeit.

World Bank. 2011. *World Development Report 2011*. Washington.

Reflections on Power:
Discourses, Representations, Trauma

JOANNA BOURKE

The difficulties of analysing 'sexual violence in armed conflicts' are legion. In this chapter, I explore three problematic framings of the concept within Western discourses. These are: definitions demarcating the field, visual representations, and trauma emplotment. Focusing on American and British cultures of violence, I will be arguing that representations of wartime sexual violence are tightly bound to ethnonational narratives in which the sexual violence committed by advanced Western powers can be more easily overlooked and its effects distorted. As we will see, there is nothing obvious, natural, or universal about concepts such as 'sexual violence', 'armed conflict', and 'trauma'. These terms may seem to be embedded in humdrum practices and everyday knowledges, but they each have a history that is fluid and infused with problematic assumptions and power dynamics. The way these concepts are employed in academic, artistic, and humanitarian discourses have been framed by ideological, political, and economic forces that inform the way we think about the cruelties of conflict.

BOUNDARY DRAWING

The central question in any analysis is how to define the core terms. For example, what difference does the choice of the words 'armed conflict' as opposed to 'war' make? They are not synonymous. Narrowly defined, 'war' refers to a state of military conflict between nations or states. In his classic statement in *On the Social Contract* (1762), Jean-Jacques Rousseau decreed that "War is constituted by a relation between things, and not between persons [...] War then is a relation, not between man and man, but between State and State" (Rousseau 2003: 6). There are regulations dictating how 'wars' start and finish, as well as rules about the respective roles of participants (uniformed combatants versus civilians, for example). These regulations and rules change over time and are inconsistently applied, but are nevertheless perceived to be important. Conventions of international law also apply, even if they too are regularly breached.

From the late 1990s, however, this narrow definition of 'war' was clearly no longer tenable, if it ever had been. International scholar Mary Kaldor coined the term 'new wars' to draw attention to the fact that most military conflicts in the modern world were no longer between states. Conflicts that are counter-insurgencies or counter-terrorist have become the norm, as have 'irregular' conflicts involving paramilitary personnel or armed civilians. The distinction between military forces and organised crime is blurred (Kaldor 1999). As a consequence, the term 'armed conflict' has become more common in recent decades in an attempt to encompass both the 'old' and 'new' kinds of military violence.

This is clearly relevant to any discussion of 'sexual violence in armed conflicts' because focusing on 'armed conflicts' skews discussions towards irregular warfare and skirmishes between rival communities internal to the nation state. In such conflicts, participants on each side do not necessarily share similar ideologies, internal discipline is weak, and there is little central control over state bureaucrats, resulting in high levels of financial corruption, for example. These are all characteristics that have been shown to result in high levels of sexual violence (Butler/Gluch/Mitchell 2007; Wood 2006, 2009). Although armed conflicts fought by British and American troops have often been labelled 'counter-insurgencies' (namely Philippines, Malaya, Vietnam, Afghanistan and Iraq), and have led to high levels of sexual violence, their 'home' populations have been relatively protected. For British and American civilians, therefore, rapacious violence happens on foreign territories. Unlike the violence meted out in non-Western territories, where rape and sexual abuse is palpably observable, when the perpetrators are American or British the harm is less visible.

A further problem is that, in 'new wars', there are often no formal declarations of war or peace, making it impossible to know when an 'armed conflict' ends. It is therefore difficult to categorically state when 'sexual violence' becomes peacetime, as opposed to wartime, violence. It is not enough to say that 'armed conflict' ceases when the killing stops since many 'armed conflicts' include periods of respite from violence, followed by sudden spikes of aggression. It is tempting, therefore, for the sexual violence that takes place during armed conflicts in non-Western nations to be seen as pervasive to that conflict and 'regional propensities' (or, even worse, 'cultural/religious tendencies'), as opposed to a continuation of abuse prevalent in civilian life.

Furthermore, the debates about sexual violence in armed conflicts have been fundamentally shaped by scholarship emerging out of atrocities committed against women and men in the former Yugoslavia. Here, influential scholars have argued that sexual violence is a weapon of war, purposefully used for political reasons to terrorise specific populations.[1] The problem here is that it again largely excludes the perpetration of sexual violence carried out by American and British militaries—partly because they continue to operate in more traditional war contexts and because the conflict does not take place on 'their' soil. These are not the 'new wars' that Kaldor writes about. This increases the likelihood that the sexual violence that they mete out is viewed in terms of individual criminality as opposed to structural militarism. Again, this renders it less visible and easier to ignore. The rapes carried out by British and American soldiers are examples of 'individual' misconduct; the ones carried out by other groups are the actions of warmongering factions.

These definitional concerns are exacerbated by another form of blind-sightedness. After all, many populations are 'at war' or 'engaged in armed conflict', yet don't recognise it. Advanced military nations such as the United States employ weapons from a distance. For example, since 7 October 2001, the US has been 'at war' in Afghanistan, where they have been engaged in a brutal armed struggle. However, only the victims of sexual assault and rape that take place on Afghan soil are counted as incidents of 'sexual violence in armed conflict'. The thousands of armed men and women who carry out acts of sexual violence within the borders of the US (where, not counting the millions of guns owned by the military, police and government officials, there are 310 million firearms in private hands, or over 101 guns for every 100 civilians)[2] are not considered to be cases of 'sexual violence in armed conflicts.' In other words, the literature on 'sexual violence in armed conflict' uses a definition of war that ignores sexual aggression occurring in the most advanced and active military force globally. States and regions that cannot afford the technological wizardry available to advanced Western nations (which enable them to conduct military incursions at a distance) can be much more readily castigated for rampant sexual violence. The concept of 'engaged in armed conflict' comes down hard and unremittingly on 'rape by machete' in Rwanda or Sierra Leone. It turns a benign face to sexual violence perpetrated by drone pilots and navigators who take part in military aggression at a height of 25,000 feet in the air and from a base in Nevada (7,500 miles away from the battlefield) and then sexually assault family members and friends when they return home in the evening.

It is not only the definitions of 'war' and 'armed conflict' that are problematic. So, too, is the way 'sexual' is defined. Religio-nationalist assumptions mean that drone operatives who spy on Muslim women in a state of semi-undress in the privacy of their home or enclosed gardens are not generally accused of 'sexual' offences.

Gendered assumptions also mean that many forms of violence against men are not labelled 'sexual', even though they involve coerced genital activity or abusive contact with sexual organs. For instance, within the US army, navy, and airforce, acts of 'hazing' (which may involve mandatory masturbation, beating of the genitals or buttocks, being forced to imitate or perform fellatio and the forcible insertion of objects inside anuses) are called 'rites of passage' rather than 'sexual violence.'[3] Indeed, in US forces, hazing is defended on the grounds that it is essential in the forging of the combat soldier. As the Commanding Officer of the Weapons Company, 5th Marines, argued in 1997, hazing in itself is probably necessary since the Marine Corps is "steeped in tradition, lore, and heritage; and hazing is as much part of that tradition as playing tops at a funeral." He noted that equator-crossing ceremonies as well as more blatantly violent rituals such as 'blanket parties' (which was depicted in Kubrick's film 'Full Metal Jacket') are

> rituals that date back thousands of years—bizarre rites of passage that were meant to import tradition to Sailors and Marines. And our unique culture is comprised of young male who relish the warrior spirit, a macho image, and an ability to withstand pain, all factors conducive to hazing. (Wilcox 1997: 37)

Even the *sexual* aspects of abuse in some hazing rituals is considered essential by many proponents, particularly when it involves women in the armed forces. The most notorious example occurred in response to events at the 35th Annual Tailhook Association Symposium in Las Vegas in September 1991, a two-day debriefing of US Navy and Marine Corps aviation in Operation Desert Storm. At the symposium, 83 women and seven men alleged sexual assault and harassment. Amongst other humiliations, they had been forced to walk down a corridor lined with men who sexually molested them. In the subsequent public furore, the distinction between hazing and sexual abuse was blurred. For instance, writing in the *Marine Corps Gazette* in November 1992, leading American cultural conservative William S. Lind confessed to being puzzled by the public reaction to the abuse. "After all," he wrote,

> no one was raped at Tailhook. From what was in the newspapers, it didn't sound much different from a Dartmouth fraternity on a Friday or Saturday night. Unless the women officers who are protesting their treatment so loudly went directly to flight school from a convent, they surely had some idea what to expect. (Lind 1992: 38)

Lind claimed that the public condemnation of the abuses at Tailhook were a classic example of 'fourth generation warfare'

conducted by feminists against the American officer corps.
Feminists "are well on their way to their operational goal: the
femininization of the Armed Forces," he alleged. If women in
the military wanted to be treated as equals, they had to accept
the "back-slapping, practical-joking, locker room atmosphere that
usually prevails where men do dangerous jobs like flying combat
aircraft" (Lind 1992: 38). In this way, coercive and abusive sexual
practices were legitimated as a way of ensuring the elite status of
the US Navy and Marine Corps.

Gendered assumptions lingering behind the concept 'sexual
abuse' can also be illustrated by exploring the treatment of
torture victims. During armed conflicts, male prisoners are
frequently tortured by having their genitals beaten,[4] but this is
rarely categorised as 'sexual assault.' This remains the case even
when the torturers tell their male victims that the assaults on their
genitals are intended to ensure that "you will never again make
Ustasha/Muslim children," as they also told their female victims
(Medical Center for Human Rights 1995b: 1). In other words,
despite widespread acknowledgement of male sexual abuse, it
remains the case that many human rights and anti-torture activists
assume that the sexual torture of men involves forced penetrative
sex. As Harry van Tienhoven of the Refuge Health Care Centre
in Utrecht observed, physicians and nurses "had become familiar
with sexual violence against women, and because this usually
implies rape, they assumed that sexual violence against men would
take the same form, namely anal rape" (Tienhoven 1993: 133).
Male victims often internalise such assumptions (Carlson 1997:
129; McMullen 1990: 83; Sivakumaran 2007). For two years, Eric
Stener Carlson worked for the International Criminal Tribunal
for the Former Yugoslavia's Sexual Assault Investigation team.
He reported that some of the men who were tortured by being
"beaten on the testicles" did not report the crime, not because they
are afraid of revealing sexual assault, but because what happened
to them does not fit their conception of sexual assault.

Carlson claimed that the refusal to see such violence as sexual
violence was partly because "being hit in the testicles during
peacetime is generally considered a 'normal' occurrence,"

especially in sport (Carlson 2006: 20, 23). As a result, the seriousness of such abuse could be minimised.

The converse is true for female perpetrators of sexual cruelty. When the abuse by Americans at the Abu Ghraib Detention Centre was revealed, the American women participants were regarded as much worse than their male comrades in atrocity: they were not merely inhuman, but sexually monstrous. Even when they were engaging in abuses that were not genital in nature, their very womanliness enabled their actions to be sexualised (Ashley 2016; Bourke 2007; Gronnvoll 2010; Sjoberg/Gentry 2007).

MOVING IMAGES

The boundary-drawing performed by definitions of 'armed conflict' and 'sexual violence' can also be seen in visual images of rape in armed conflicts within art and film. In many cases, such representations have simply been disallowed. Censorship is rife. Francisco Goya's (1863) *Desastres de la Guerra* (Disasters of War) series of 1810–15, which included images of sexual sadism, was not exhibited until 1863; Otto Dix's (1924) *Soldat und Nonne* (Soldier and Nun), depicting the sexual violation of a nun by a rapacious Hun, had to be withdrawn from his *Der Krieg* (War) series of 1924; and Pierre-Georges Jeanniot's (1915) *The Rapists*, created during the First World War, was only discovered in 2014.

Even without explicit censorship, the art of sexual violence in wartime is hindered by conventions about 'authenticity.' For example, some galleries and collectors refuse to purchase or exhibit 'war art' when the artist has portrayed scenes that he or she could not have actually witnessed. This was the fate of Peter Howson's (1994) extraordinary 1994 painting *Croatian and Muslim*, which depicts a vicious rape. Although Howson was a government-sponsored war artist, the Imperial War Museum decided not to include his painting in their permanent collection on the grounds that Howson could not have actually witnessed the rape that he painted on his canvas. It was not sufficiently 'authentic.' As artist and critic Paul Gough explains, the painting polarized two schools of thought: those that felt it necessary to depict the true face of warfare using whatever means available to an artist, and those who argued that an artist must bear witness, ocular not just circumstantial, to a scene of horror before committing it to canvas. (Gough N.D.)

In other words, 'bearing witness' requires a certain kind of fidelity to the 'scene of war' as *seen*. One of the consequences of this emphasis on ocular authenticity is that innumerable acts of war—most notably, as Howson discovered, wartime rape—will rarely, if ever, enter the war canon. By definition, raped women (and men) are rendered invisible. *Croatian and Muslim* was eventually purchased by David Bowie.

Those images of sexual violation that not only survived but also proved popular tended to be propagandist. Thus, at the start of the First World War, Dutch artist Louis Raemaekers (1915) sketched *Seduction* depicting a leering German soldier with a pistol to a kneeling woman's head, clearly with rapacious intent. Raemaekers had a clear political agenda: he hoped that his cartoons would persuade the Netherlands and US to give up their neutrality and side with the Allies in the war effort. By making sexual violation visible, artistic representations of sexual violence in armed conflicts could encourage retaliatory violence both in imagination and against the bodies of others.

Censoring stark representations of rape or using such depictions for propagandist purposes are only two of the problems associated with the art of sexual violence in armed conflicts. Representations of this form of violence could contribute to an empathy deficit; it could silence the victims' pain. These risks have incensed critics throughout the centuries, but Susan Sontag's eloquent reflections on the effect of war photography have been the most influential. In her book *On Photography* (1978), she observed that images of violence not only 'transfix,' they also 'anesthetise.' Although she admitted that "an event known through pictures certainly becomes more real than it would have been if one had never seen the photographs." Nevertheless, "after repeated exposure to images, it also becomes less real" (Sontag 1978: 20). Gruesome war-imagery—including the splayed bodies of rape victims—is so much a part of Western visual culture that audiences risk no longer 'seeing' it. Critique is blunted; compassion fatigue hits in. People get accustomed to barbarian ways.

Other critics have warned about the opposite effect: rather than viewers becoming blasé about bloodshed, such images may be stimulating. An image that is self-evidently abhorrent for an artist may be 'read' by some audiences as thrilling, even arousing. Artists and audiences alike could end up celebrating cruelty and openly fetishizing sexual violence. Art can turn sexual violence into a tempting melodrama or consumable drama; 'war as hell' is a beguiling idea.

These risks can be seen in the context of representations of sexual violence during the Holocaust.[5] But they are also strongly featured in non-Western artistic representations of sexual violence which are exhibited in galleries far from the killing fields. An example of how the war art of sexual violence coalesces with an orientalist gaze can be seen by looking at an exhibition at the University of Wisconsin-Madison of art from the civil war in Sierra Leone. The Sierra Leone conflict resulted in extremely high levels of sexual violence. Between 1991 and 2002, it is estimated that 257,000 women were victims of gender-related violence (Cohen 2013: 397). Breasts were amputated; sexual organs, mutilated. Sierra Leonean artists depicted these atrocities within the traditions of mural art with bright warm colours set amongst lush environments, into which they situated scenes of extraordinary carnage.

The organisers of the Wisconsin-Madison exhibition chose to juxtapose the paintings alongside "comments and explanations from natives and experts contained in the videotape and informational wall." They added that "We believe this approach teaches much more than the images alone could" (Ross 2005: 37). Aside from the bizarre implication that 'natives' were not 'experts,' this didactic approach went hand-in-hand with a tendency to co-opt the works of Sierra Leone art for US domestic political purposes. Mariama Ross, one of the organisers of the exhibition, noted that she wanted to ensure that the art was displayed in a way that would "encourage viewers to turn *toward* the people and universal issues behind the images instead of turning away in response to the graphic nature of the images themselves." Ross claimed that the Sierra Leone art made American viewers feel "disturbed, outraged, and vulnerable,"

> not only because we can see our own humanity displayed in the killings and mutilations [...] but because in these post-September 11 times we are forced to suspect that we may not be quite as far removed from such events as we might have previously liked to believe. (Ross 2005: 8)

In this way, the economic (the mining of diamonds and other precious metals for a largely Western consumption), political, and strategic rationales behind the mass rapes and other atrocities in Sierra Leone were folded into an American story about the 'war on terror.' The graphic images of rape depicted in the art were interpreted by many visitors to the exhibition as simply further evidence of primitive Otherness: "poor African women," "violent tribal groups," "patriarchal African culture;" and so on. In effect, the exhibition became another form of colonialism. Audiences were encouraged to assess the art of violence complacently and from a safe distance. Some may even have harboured the illusion that passively viewing the works of art is itself a political response. Representations of 'bare life' threaten to strip history of the structural factors that made the violence possible, including neo-liberal capitalism.

A similar superficiality can be seen in war films. As in painting, victims of sexual assault in war cinema are typically represented as passive, one-dimensional characters who are relentlessly innocent, never violent themselves and not consumed with vengeance. Their totalising innocence is damning. They are not 'real.'

Film representations of violated women also tend to ignore the fact that, in most military conflicts, women actively spur on 'their' men to atrocity. They are even perpetrators of sexual violence themselves. During the conflicts in the Democratic Republic of the Congo and Rwanda a significant proportion of female and male victims claimed to have been victimised by a woman (Johnson et al. 2010: 553; Zongwe 2012: 44). Women not only initiated sexual violence, but also lured other women into situations where they could be abused and holding them down while they were raped. Most notoriously, Pauline Nyiramasuhuko (ironically, the National Minister of Family and Women's Affairs) ordered militia to round up women in her hometown for slaughter, encouraging them to rape the women first.[6] Sexually violent women in Liberia used objects to rape other women and to slash the genitals of both male and female prisoners (The Advocates of Human Rights 2009; Cohen 2013: 385; Specht 2006). In nearly all of these instances of violence, female perpetrators abused in conjunction with, rather than independent from, their male comrades. They are absent from war cinema, however, and situated solely as victims of armed conflict.

American films focussing on the conflict in Vietnam are equally problematic. It is difficult to find a film about the Vietnam War that does *not* include a violent rape scene. In films such as *Casualties of War* (1989) and *Platoon* (1986), rape is depicted as the result of the need for sex—it was "a bit of R&R" (Rest and Recreation). Men who don't act rapaciously are 'queers' or 'gay', further emphasizing the *sexual* interpretation of rape, as opposed to its basis in regimes of power and domination. This perpetuates the myth that rape is a 'natural' consequence of thwarted male desire. It is victim-precipitated (especially if the female victim is a 'guerrilla'). The emphasis is on the American males, not their 'prey,' who do not really seem to possess lives outside of the rape. Even in those films in which the hero stands in opposition to sexual abuse, the emphasis is on the suffering of the Americans rather than the victims. In films such as *My Old Man's Place* (1972), *The Visitors* (1972) and *Welcome Home, Soldier Boys* (1972), 'rapacious Vietnam' brutalises men, who then bring the violence home to American soil.

In the context of Second World War film, sexual violence was an important plank in the revisionist programme. From the 1990s, filmic portrayals of the mass rapes carried out by Red Army soldiers as they moved through Germany contributed to arguments positioning Germans as *victims* of war rather than its instigators. The mass rape of German women was translated into a story whereby Germans were violated by a brutal Soviet culture. In the 1992 film *Liberators Take Liberties: War, Rapes, Children*, even feminist artists like Helke Sander were accused of transforming German women into victims of the war rather than active participants in the atrocities of Nazism (Bos 2006; Grossmann 1996; Heineman 1996).

In a different context, rape in representations of the Second World War turned pornographic, notoriously in the sensationalist film *Ilsa: She-Wolf of the SS* (1974). That film even begins with a soundtrack of one of Hitler's Nuremberg speeches, while the screen tells audiences that

> The film you are about to see is based on documentary fact. The atrocities shown were conducted as 'medical experiments' in special concentration camps throughout Hitler's Third Reich. Although these crimes against humanity are historically accurate, the characters depicted are composites of notorious Nazi personalities; and the events portrayed have been condensed into one locality for dramatic purposes [...]. We dedicate this film with the hope that these heinous crimes will never occur again. (*Ilsa: She-Wolf of the SS* 1975)

What results, though, is the presentation of Ilsa (based on Ilse Koch) as a cartoonish character. She is a blond, bombshell nymphomaniac. Even more disturbing is the way the Holocaust is sexualised in a *feminine* way: indeed, the evils of the Holocaust are linked to feminism. In a commentary on the DVD release of the film, the actress who played Ilsa—Dyanne Thorne—argues that Ilsa was

> on top [...] we want to make that very clear [...] This is the first one [film] where they had a female villain. She was like the leader of the feminists, if you will [...] because even with this scene [the opening castration scene] the victim was the male and the three females are standing there with total control. (*Ilsa: She-Wolf of the SS* 1975)

Although Ilsa is eventually overpowered by a blue-eyed and blond-haired German-American prisoner named Wolfe whose chief asset is his ability to maintain an erection indefinitely, she is eventually killed not by Wolfe or the other prisoners who revolt, but by a male Nazi who enters the camp to quench the revolt. In other words, as historian Lynn Rapaport argues,

> If Ilsa were killed by the American Wolfe, or by another prisoner, it might represent mythologies of democracy overturning Nazism, or of American superiority. But by portraying Nazi atrocities as eroticised encounters between men and women, and Ilsa as the female monster-villain, does the film hold women responsible for Nazi evil? (Rapaport 2003: 70)

Incredibly, the film was immensely popular. In 1974, it was opened in more than 17 countries and surpassed $10 million at the box office (Rapaport 2003: 70f).

Particularly insightful analyses of the problems encountered in representing rape in war films have been carried out scholars Marzena Sokolowska-Paryz and Sara Projansky. Sokolowska-Paryz, for example, argues that naturalistic rape scenes in cinema exonerates perpetrators and re-victimises the violated women. By foregrounding perpetrators and "metonymically equat[ing] the victims with their nations," Sokolowska-Paryz claims that these films make rape seem universal and inevitable. Compounding this is the fact that filmic rape scenes focus attention not on the victims but on the traumatised perpetrators who are portrayed as struggling to act 'honourably' in brutalizing environments. Examples might include films as diverse as *China* (1943), *Edge of Darkness* (1943) and *Dragon Seed* (1944) in which witnessing rape causes men to become keen militarists or resistance fighters. In Sokolowska-Paryz's words,

> These films create a gender-based hierarchy of suffering where the female victim is relegated to the function of the instigating factor of the man's trauma. The woman is downgraded to a fleeting character [...]. In these cinematic representations of war rapes the violation of the female body is of lesser importance than the violation of the male psyche. (Sokolowska-Paryz 2016: 232)

Violence is fetishized; attention paid to perpetrators rather than victims. Rape is portrayed as being 'about' men communicating with each other. It is an indictment of these women's male associates who had failed to fulfil the unwritten 'gender contract', under which men fight to protect women, who, in turn, provide them with nurturance. As Miranda Alison explains, women are reduced to "biological reproducers of the collectivity" and "transmitters of its culture" (Alison 2007: 80). It may even be asked whether the individual women are being raped at all: the 'true victim' is the symbolic body of the community.

The prevailing message of the inevitability of sexual molestation in armed conflicts also incenses Projansky. She is less troubled by the fact that war films are "sometimes sexist, capitalist, racist, nationalist or colonialist (although, of course, many are)." Rather, she worries that

> violence against women is so central to the films, so key to character transformation and narrative development and resolution, so versatile, that it not only seems to be necessary to the films themselves but concomitantly naturalises the policy and negotiating of the gendered, classed, racialised, and natural boundaries in which these films engage. (Projansky 2001: 82)

As a result, artistic representations of rape in times of armed conflict end up erasing social, ideological, and political specificities, leaving only empty clichés: 'wartime masculinity is rapacious' and 'war is hell'. Viewers are left with a depressing, ahistorical morality tale.

TRAUMA TROPES

The third, and final, concern I have with the way the concept of 'sexual violence in armed conflicts' has been framed in American and British discourses is the employment of trauma tropes drawn from Western psychology and psychiatry. As already mentioned, this problem occurs in representations of rape in war films, but is widespread in a vast array of literatures and policy interventions related to armed conflicts. There is a globalisation of the Western psyche, I will be arguing, with its related assumption that, because people in war respond to sexual violence in similar ways, Western-orientated treatment regimes should be introduced and/or imposed.[7]

The first point to note when discussing victims' responses to sexual violence in armed conflict is that many victims of wartime sexual trauma might *themselves* not register an occurrence as 'traumatic' in the Western sense. The idea that there is a 'post-' (as in *post*-traumatic stress disorder (PTSD)) to abuse is based on an assumption that there is a non-assaultive 'before.' It assumes that violence is an event limited in time and different from everyday life. Indeed, the somatic symptoms that victims present might be interpreted by these victims as 'ordinary,' rather than unique responses to a sexual trauma. Nightmares, excessive sweating, trembling, flashbacks and suchlike may be interpreted as part of everyday experiences. In contexts where 'bad events' are endemic and related to issues such as poverty, patriarchy and racial prejudice, the language of psychological trauma might not make much sense.

The prominence given to the 'sexual' component of violence in Western discourses is also not universal. This was what struck anthropologist Robert M. Hayden during a 1993 conference held in New York and entitled 'The Path Beyond Genocide: Constructing Civil Society in Bosnia Herzegovina and the Former Yugoslavia.' At one point, a woman who was present stood up and declared that, as a Bosnian Muslim, she: "felt that the international emphasis on rape was inappropriate, because all Bosnian women were victims: they lost their homes, their sons, their husbands, their jobs, their lives, and whether they had been sexually assaulted or not was not really the most important problem." Hayden observed that her comments were "met with silence. Who was she, after all, to pronounce on such issues?" (Hayden 2000: 36)

In her ethnographic research on Rwandan rape victims, Jennie E. Burnet has gone even further, arguing that "Western notions of sexual consent" may not be "applicable to a culture in which colonialism, government policies, war, and scarcity of resources have limited women's access to land ownership, economic security, and other means of survival." She observed that Western-derived definitions of rape that are predicated on a notion of consent may be less relevant in Rwanda where "initiating sexual encounters can be a coping strategy in the aftermath of conflict and violence." While recognising the extreme constraints women face, she is concerned to acknowledge female sexual agency. She compares the western view of rape, which is "predicated on a consensual model of sexual relations" with "emic Rwandan models of sexual consent." In other words, the definition of rape as non-consensual sex is problematic in cultures where women "do not give explicit, verbal consent to sexual intercourse" but rely instead on "nonverbal cues and 'situational consent'." As she argues, "How do women and girls refuse sexual intercourse when the means of survival are bound up with implicit signs of consent, such as accepting food, clothing, shelter, and protection?" In Burnet's words, the "focus on sexual violence in the genocide context detaches the question of female sexual coercion from the cultural-historical context and political economy of poverty that structures women's agency and limits their options" (Burnet 2012: 97–100, 105f, 112).

Hayden makes a similar point in relation to women during armed conflicts in Rwanda or the Punjab who married men in exchange for protection against the violence. Human rights activists tended to view these women as victims of rape. Hayden cautions against this assumption, partly on the grounds that it could "lead to the determination that women themselves lack the capacity to make crucial decisions, because they remain the real property (territory) of the group to which they have been classified" (Hayden 2000: 36).

The second important point is that the Western-forged 'trauma model' is an extremely individual, privatised one. It shifts attention from the external wound to the inner one; the political becomes personal. In its PTSD formulation (the most common one applied), it fails to take account of cultural variations. After all, the PTSD diagnosis is a culture-bound syndrome, invented in 1980 in an attempt to understand the reactions of young American men returning from the war in Vietnam. But psychiatrists and other medical personnel have long been aware that clinical presentations are highly influenced by cultural precepts: different cultures report different symptoms and responses to the same event.[8] Indeed, anthropologist Arthur Kleinman has gone so far as to argue that the imposition of Western diagnoses outside of the West is a 'category fallacy.' The "reification of a nosological category developed for a particular cultural group that is then applied to members of another culture for whom it lacks coherence and its validity has not been established," he insists (Kleinman 1987). When faced with war-victims who are not responding according to the 'trauma trope,' it is simply lazy thinking to assume that the universal response *is* present, but has been *culturally* repressed.

Indeed, 'trauma' itself might not be the appropriate framework. It risks stripping victims of any agency. As one commentator working with Bosnia rape survivors noted, victims are not approached as "adult, sexual beings with the power—even when severely limited—to make decisions and act" (Helms 2014: 620). For many victims of extreme violence, it makes more sense to emphasise resilience, as opposed to psychic wounding (Hume/Summerfield 1994). Refugees from Mozambique and Ethiopia, for example, valorised 'active forgetting' as a way of coping with trauma (Summerfield 1999: 1455). Rwandans who had experienced or witnessed mass rape and murder also adhered to a resilience model, describing their experiences using linguistic categories that have no direct counterpart in English: '*Kwihangana*' (withstanding), '*wongera kubaho*' (living again), and '*gukomeza ubuzima*' (continuing life), for example. They laud their close personal connections with other survivors (Zraly/Nyirazinyaye 2010). Particularly in genocidal situations, the emphasis on resilience and 'getting on with life' can be an important way of protecting the survivors' dignity and honour, as well as promoting peaceful future relations between divided communities. Social relationships rather than intra-psychic or egocentric ones are prioritised.

This stands in contrast to the approach of many Western analysts who are wary about emphasizing victims' agency on the grounds that it risks 'blaming the victim.' However, it is no judgment on survivors of violence to observe that trauma is not an inevitable outcome of a 'bad event.' It is simply an admission that victims are embedded in social, interpersonal, cognitive, emotional and other networks of being, all of which impinge on their lived experience in the world. 'Trauma' does not have agency; people do. 'Bad events' don't intrude upon a person independent of context.

There is another way of exploring the lack of a direct and necessary relationship between the 'bad event' and 'trauma.' It is not the case that a person 'experiences' a 'bad event', *after which* affective, cognitive and motivational processes 'kick in,' enabling the person to respond and interpret the event. People perceive what is happening around them through the prism of the entirety of their lived experiences, including their sensual physiologies, emotional states, cognitive beliefs and relational standing in various communities. This is not to deny that surviving a mass rape is painful. But different emotional reactions can adhere to even 'very bad events.' Depending on the presence of other objects and people, 'bad events' can elicit feelings of exhilaration, surprise or even pride for having survived. It makes a difference whether the 'bad event' is anticipated or if it is believed to be 'natural.' It makes a difference if the psychological or physiological 'wound' is inflicted by a spouse, former friend or neighbour. Traumas that are followed by financial or other forms of compensation or recognition 'feel' different to traumas that are rudely shunted aside or stigmatised. In other words, trauma is a way of perceiving an experience. Trauma is not the 'bad event' as such but the way people *evaluate* what has happened.

The third and final problem with the imposition of a 'trauma trope' is that it has politico-medical consequences. As the authors of an article on child soldiers conclude, the 'trauma model' is not universal; it wrongly focuses attention on the individual and individual counselling; and it has the effect of shifting power to Western experts at the expense of local cosmologies and therapies (Bracken/Giller/Ssekiwanuka 1996: 123).

Psychiatrist Derek Summerfield argues this point strongly. Based on his work in Bosnia and Rwanda, he observes that "for the vast majority of survivors, posttraumatic stress is a pseudocondition, a reframing of the understandable suffering of war or a technical problem to which short-term technical solutions like counseling are applicable." He believes that the use of 'trauma theory' simply "aggrandises the Western agencies" and leads to ignoring the victims' "own traditions, meaning systems, and active priorities." He reminds fellow psychiatrists, psychologists and NGOs that "misery or distress per se is surely not psychological disturbance in any meaningful sense" and warns against positioning the victim of war's traumas as 'consumers' of Western psychiatric provisions. Crucially, the PTSD diagnosis arises from a culturally-specific idea of the brain as a machine: it is "the result of incomplete emotional and cognitive processes within that machine." This makes little sense in other cultures in which distress is "commonly understood and expressed in terms of disruption to the social and moral order" (Summerfield 1999: 1449, 1452, 1454f).

Summerfield's critique is the most trenchant one, but he is following in a much longer tradition, particularly within feminist thought. In 'Survivor Discourse: Transgression or Recuperation?' (1993), for example, Linda Alcoff and Laura Gray are also worried that the 'trauma script' as promoted in Western cultures prescribes a form of emotional comportment (a confessional one) that may not be appropriate for all rape survivors. They observe that the requirement that victims of rape 'break the silence,' either as a "route to recovery or as a privileged political tactic," risks becoming "a coercive imperative on survivors to confess, to recount our assaults, to give details, and even to do so publicly." Failing to do so "might then be read as weakness of will or as re-enacted victimisation." They suggest that survival might, in contrast, require "*refusal* to disclose." Silence could be less emotionally, financially and physically damning to victims of atrocity than disclosure (Alcoff/Gray 1993: 281). Alcoff and Gray allude to Foucault's analysis of discourse as power. The coercive requirement to 'speak' is even more problematic when it is an expert, therapist, or 'well-meaning' outsider who makes the demand. In other words, confessional discourse requires the adoption and framing of the traumatic experience along rigid lines shaped by Anglo-American legal doctrines and moralistic codes, which may not be in keeping with an individual's process of self-creation.

PTSD treatment regimes have also been exported and imposed on other contexts. These are problematic because they target individuals rather than communities. It has encouraged, for example, separating out 'child soldiers' from other children, who may equally have been affected by sexual violence during armed conflicts. As three researchers working with children in war zones warned, this has had the effect of making the children themselves think of themselves as 'child soldiers,' setting them apart from other children in their cohort who might even envy, rather than abhor, their violence. The result has been to separate children who had taken up arms from their communities on the grounds that they are especially violent and therefore 'different' (Bracken/Giller/Ssekiwanuka 1996: 119). In Mozambique, for example, where 63 per cent of children interviewed in one study had witnessed rape and/or sexual abuse and 77 per cent had seen murder (often in large numbers), Western psychotherapeutic treatments proved ineffective.[9]

They also are divorced from the communities they are intended to help. J. David Kinzie, for example, warned that Bosnian or Somali refugees regarded "highly specific techniques such as cognitive-behavioral therapy or exposure therapy" as "culturally inappropriate" or even "'tricks' to those who have suffered severe interpersonal losses or existential crises" (Kinzie 2009). Another commentator warned that imposing Western psychiatry onto "societies where cultural traditions are very different from those of the West" has the damaging consequence of suppressing "indigenous, culturally consonant, ways of dealing with emotional problems and 'madness'" (Fernando 1991). It is a conclusion echoed by psychologists Nick Higginbotham and Anthony J. Marsella in their analysis of "the homogenisation of psychiatry in southeast Asia." They warned that: "Modern psychiatry's purely secular discourse [...] forces a kind of epistemological break with traditional formulations embodied in many non-Western cosmologies. Psychiatry's reasoning and classification is intended to replace indigenous conceptions of disorder" (Higginbotham/Marsella 1988).

CONCLUSION

In this chapter, I have examined three framings of the concept of 'sexual violence in armed conflicts' through the lens of power-discourses. Definitions are skewed in ways that deflect attention from the violence of American and British forces; representations of sexual violence in art and film are gendered in problematic ways; and there has been an Americanisation of the global psyche. As we have just seen, though, all three discourses have been critiqued, albeit from the margins. Ethnopsychiatrists and anthropologists have been particularly trenchant in drawing attention to the politico-medical assumptions behind nosological systems related to trauma. In art and film, too, there have been powerful artistic attempts to represent sexual violence in armed conflicts in ways that war's victims would find meaningful. Notable examples include feminist artists such as Judy Chicago in 'Double Jeopardy' (1993: 126) and Nancy Spero in 'Torture of Women' (2010: 106, 123). Radical artists like the Chapman brothers have defaced artistic portrays of violence in order to draw attention to their voyeurism and the photographer Sven Torfinn has comprised dignified portraits of individual women who experienced rape during the war in the Congo in an attempt to portray the women as resilient and disrupt the self-image of Western audiences as 'rescuers.'[10]

Nevertheless, sexual violence in armed conflicts remains under-theorised. Clearly, the concept of 'trauma' does a formidable amount of political and ideological work. Trauma is always practised within inter-personal, historical and environmental contexts. This is yet another way of insisting that there is no decontextual trauma-event: trauma is always infused with politics of power. PTSD diagnosis is a political diagnosis as much as a medical one. Similarly, I have argued that what constitutes 'war' or 'armed conflict' is flexible; they reflect deliberate acts of power. Practices become sexually violent through classification and regulation generated by a vast array of agents. Crucially, these agents include victims as well as perpetrators, witnesses, bystanders and national as well as international authorities. They also involve us.

NOTES

1. For example, Bennet 1994; Card 1996; Copelon 2000; Enloe 1998; Franco 2007; Fritzpatrick 2016; Hirschover 2014; Rittner 2012; Seifert 1994.
2. GunPolicy.org, at http://www.gunpolicy.org/firearms/region (accessed 12 October 2018).
3. For a detailed analysis, see Bourke 2016.
4. For example, see Agger/Jensen 1990: 63f; Daugaard et al. 1983: 245; Medical Center for Human Rights 1995a: 4f.
5. For a discussion, see Young 2009.
6. Landesman 2002. See the case minutes of her trial at http://unictr.unmict.org/en/cases/ictr-98-42 (accessed 12 October 2018). Also see Coomaraswamy 1998; African Rights 1995.
7. This is also the title of a book by Ethan Watters (2010).
8. For a discussion, see Gaines 1992; Kleinman 1987; Kirmayer 2001; Waitzkin/Magaña 1997.
9. Boothby 1992: 107. Also see Summerfield 1999: 1455.
10. For a further study of all these artists, see Bourke 2017.

REFERENCES

The Advocates of Human Rights. 2009. *A House with Two Rooms: Final Report of the Liberian Truth and Reconciliation Commission Diaspora Project.* Saint Paul: DRI Press.

African Rights. 1995. *Rwanda: Not so Innocent: When Women become Killers.* London: African Rights.

Agger, Inger/Jensen, Sören. 1990. 'Tortura Sexual de Presos Políticos de Sexo Masculino', in Horacio Riquelme (ed), *Era de Nieblas: Derechos Humanos, Terrorismo de Estado y Salud Psicosocial en América Latina*, pp. 43–66. Caracas: Nueva Sociedad.

Alcoff, Linda/Gray, Laura. 1993. 'Survivor Discourse: Transgression or Recuperation?' *Signs: Journal of Women in Culture and Society*, 18(2):260–90.

Alison, Miranda. 2007. 'Wartime Sexual Violence: Women's Human Rights and Questions of Masculinity', *Review of International Studies*, 33(1):75–90.

Ashley, Ryan. 2016. *Fallgirls: Gender and the Framing of Torture at Abu Ghraib.* London: Routledge.

BeFreier und Befreite. Krieg, Vergewaltigungen, Kinder. 1991/92. [Film] Helke Sander dir. Germany: Bremer Institut Film & Fernsehen/Helke Sander Filmproduktion/Journal Filmproduktion/Westdeutscher Rundfunk.

Bennett, Linda R. 1994. *A Gendered International Relations Analysis of Rape as an Instrument of War: A Case Study of the Rape of Muslim Women by the Serbian Military in Bosnia-Hercegovina.* Melbourne: Griffith University.

Boothby, Neil. 1992. 'Displaced Children: Psychological Theory and Practice from the Field', *Journal of Refugee Studies,* 5(2):106–22.

Bos, Pascale R. 2006. 'Feminist Interpreting the Politics of Wartime Rape: Berlin, 1945; Yugoslavia, 1992–1993', *Signs: Journal of Women in Culture and Society,* 31(4):995–1025.

Bourke, Joanna. 2017. 'Rape in the Art of War', in Joanna Bourke (ed), *War and Art,* pp. 316–23. London: Reaktion Books.

———. 2016. 'Hazing: Bullying in the Military', *Psychology and Education: An Interdisciplinary Journal,* 53(1–2):56–64.

———. 2007. *Rape: A History from 1860s to the Present.* London/New York: Virago.

Bracken, Patrick J./Giller, Joan E./Ssekiwanuka, James K. 1996. 'The Rehabilitation of Child Soldiers: Defining Needs and Appropriate Responses', *Medicine, Conflict, and Survival,* 12(2):114–25.

Burnet, Jennie E. 2012. 'Situating Sexual Violence in Rwanda (1990–2001): Sexual Agency, Sexual Consent, and the Political Economy of War', *African Studies Review,* 55(2):97–118.

Butler, Christopher K./Gluch, Tali/Mitchell, Neil J. 2007. 'Security Forces and Sexual Violence: A Cross-National Analysis of a Principal Agent Argument', *Journal of Peace Research,* 44(6): 669–87.

Card, Claudia. 1996. 'Rape as a Weapon of War', *Hypatia: A Journal of Feminist Philosophy,* 11:5–18.

Carlson, Eric Stener. 2006. 'The Hidden Prevalence of Male Sexual Assault during War: Observations on Blunt Trauma to the Male Genitals', *The British Journal of Criminology,* 46(1):16–25.

———. 1997. 'Sexual Assault of Men in War', *The Lancet,* 349(9045):129.

Casualties of War. 1989. [Film] Brian De Palma dir. USA: Columbia Pictures.

Chicago, Judy. 1993. *Holocaust Project: From Darkness into Light, with photography by David Woodman.* New York: Viking.

China. 1943. [Film] John Farrow dir. USA: Paramount Pictures.

Cohen, Dara Kay. 2013. 'Female Combatants and the Perpetration of Violence: Wartime Rape in the Sierra Leone Civil War', *World Politics*, 65(3):383–415.

Coomaraswamy, Radhika. 1998. *Report of the Mission to Rwanda on the Issues of Violence against Women in Situations of Armed Conflicts.* Geneva: United Nations.

Copelon, Rhonda. 2000. 'Gender Crimes as War Crimes: Integrating Crimes against Women into International Criminal Law', *McGill Law Journal*, 46(1):217–40.

Daugaard, Gedske/Draminsky Petersen, Hans/Abildgaard, Ulrik/ Marcussen, Henrik/Wallach, Marianne/Jess, Per/Hjort, T./ Johnsen, Stan G. 1983. 'Sequelae to Genital Trauma in Torture Victims', *Archives of Andrology*, 10(3):245–8.

Dix, Otto. 1924. *Soldat und Nonne.*[Etching, aquatint and drypoint] At: Gera: Kunstsammlung Gera, Otto-Dix-Haus, Register-Nr. D/G 134.

Dragon Seed. 1944. [Film] Harold S. Bucquet/ Jack Conway dirs. USA: Metro-Goldwyn-Mayer.

Edge of Darkness. 1943. [Film] Lewis Milestone. dir. USA: Warner Bros.

Enloe, Cynthia. 1998. 'All the Men are in the Militias, All the Women are Victims: The Politics of Masculinity and Femininity in Nationalist Wars', in Lois Ann Lorentzen/Jennifer E. Turpin (eds), *The Women and War Reader.* New York: New York University Press.

Fernando, Suman. 1991. *Mental Health, Race and Culture.* London: MIND Publications.

Fitzpatrick, Brenda. 2016. *Tactical Rape in War and Conflict: International Recognition and Response.* Bristol: Policy Press.

Franco, Jean. 2007. 'Rape: A Weapon of War', *Social Text*, 25(2):23–38.

Gaines, Atwood D. (ed). 1992. *Ethnopsychiatry: The Cultural Construction of Folk and Professional Psychiatry.* Albany: State University of New York Press.

Gough, Paul. N.D. *The Artist at War: A Very Dangerous Type of Spectator.* http://www.academia.edu/412499/The_artist_at_war_A_very_ dangerous_type_of_spectator (accessed 12 October 2018).

Goya, Francisco de. 1863. *Desatres de la Guerra.*[Plates, Etching, aquatint, lavis, drypoint, burin, and burnishing] At: New York: Metropolitan Museum of Art. Acc No 51.530.2.

Gronnvoll, Marita. 2010. *Media Representations of Gender and Torture Post-9/11.* London: Routledge.

Grossmann, Atina. 1996. 'Remarks on Current Trends and Directions in German Women's History', *Women in German Yearbook*, 12:11–25.

Hayden, Robert M. 2000. 'Rape and Rape Avoidance in Ethno-National Conflicts: Sexual Violence in Liminalized States', *American Anthropologist*, 102(1):27–41.

Heineman, Elizabeth. 1996. 'The Hour of the Woman: Memories of German's "Crisis Years" and West German National Identity', *The American Historical Review*, 101(3):354–95.

Helms, Elissa. 2014. 'Rejecting Angelina: Bosnian War Rape Survivors and the Ambiguities of Sex in War', *Slavic Review*, 73(3):612–34.

Higginbotham, Nick/Marsella, Anthony J. 1988. 'International Consultation and the Homogenization of Psychiatry in Southeast Asia', *Social Science and Medicine*, 27(5):553-61.

Hirschover, Sabine. 2014. *The Secularization of Rape: Women, War, and Sexual Violence.* Basingstoke: Palgrave Macmillan.

Howson, Peter. 1994. *Croatian and Muslim.* [Oil on Canvas] At: London: Private Collection.

Hume, Francesca/Summerfield, Derek. 1994. 'After the War in Nicaragua: A Psychosocial Study of War Wounded Combatants', *Medicine and War*, 10(1):4–25.

Ilsa: She-Wolf of the SS. 1975. [Film] Don Edmonds. dir. Canada: Aeteas Filmproduktion.

Jeanniot, Pierre-Georges. 1915. *The Rapist.* [Etching] At: London: Park Hill Antiques and Collectables.

Johnson, Kirstin/Scott, Jennifer/Rughita, Bigy/Kisielewski, Michael/Asher, Jana/Ong, Richado/Lawry, Lynn. 2010. 'Association of Sexual Violence and Human Rights Violations with Physical and Mental Health in Territories of the Eastern Democratic Republic of the Congo', *Journal of the American Medical Association*, 304(5):553–62.

Kaldor, Mary. 1999. *New and Old Wars: Organized Violence in a Global Era.* Cambridge: Polity Press.

Kleinman, Arthur. 1987. 'Anthropology and Psychiatry: The Role of Culture in Cross-Cultural Research on Illness', *British Journal of Psychiatry*, 151(4):447–54.

Kinzie, J. David. 2009. 'A Model for Treating Refugees Traumatized by Violence', *Psychiatric Times*, 26(7):43–5.

Kirmayer, Laurence J. 2001. 'Cultural Variations in the Clinical Presentation of Depression and Anxiety', *Journal of Clinical Psychiatry*, 62:22–30.

Landesmann, Peter K. 2002. 'A Woman's Work', *New York Times*, 15 September.

Lind, William S. 1992. 'Tailhook: The Larger Issue', *Marine Corps Gazette* (Quantico), November.

McMullen, Richie J. 1990. *Male Rape: Breaking the Silence on the Last Taboo.* London: Gay Men Press.

Medical Center for Human Rights. 1995a. *Characteristics of Sexual Abuse of Men during the War in the Republic of Croatia and Bosnia and Herzegovina.* Zagreb: N.D.

———. 1995b. *Report of Male Sexual Torturing as a Specific Way of War Torturing of Males on the Territory of Republic of Croatia and Bosnia and Herzegovina.* Zagreb: N.D.

My Old Man's Place. 1971. [Film] Edwin Sherin. dir. USA: Philip A. Waxman Productions.

Platoon. 1986 [Film] Oliver Stone. dir. USA: Hemdale & Cinema 86.

Projansky, Sara. 2001. 'The Elusive/Ubiquitous Representation of Rape: A Historical Survey of Rape in US Film, 1903–1972', *Cinema Journal*, 41(1):63–90.

Raemaekers, Louis. 1915. *Seduction. Germany to Belgium: 'Aren't I a Loveable Fellow?'* [Print] in Louis Raemakers (ed), *Raemaekers Cartoons.* London: Hodder & Stoughton.

Rapaport, Lynn. 2003. 'Holocaust Pornography: Profaning the Sacred in Ilsa, She-Wolf of the SS', *Shofar: An Interdisciplinary Journal of Jewish Studies*, 22(1):53–79.

Rittner, Carol/Roth, John K. (eds). 2012. *Rape: Weapon of War and Genocide.* St. Paul: Paragon House.

Ross, Mariama. 2005. 'Representations of Violence: Bearing Witness', in Patrick K. Muana/Chris Corcoran/Russell D. Feingold (eds), *Representations of Violence: Art about the Sierra Leone Civil War*, pp. 35–40. Madison: Twenty-First Century African Youth Movement.

Rousseau, Jean-Jacques. 2003. *On the Social Contract.* New York: Dover Publications.

Seifert, Ruth. 1994. 'War and Rape: A Preliminary Analysis', in Alexandra Stiglmayer (ed), *Mass Rape: The War Against Women in Bosnia-Herzegovina*, pp. 54–72. Lincoln: University of Nebraska Press.

Sivakumaran, Sandesh. 2007. 'Sexual Violence Against Men in Armed Conflict', *The European Journal of International Law*, 18(2):253–76.

Sjoberg, Laura/Gentry, Caron E. 2007. *Mothers, Monsters, Whores: Women's Violence in Global Politics.* London: Zed Books.

Sokolowska-Paryz, Marzena. 2016. 'War Rape: Trauma and the Ethics of Representation', in Peter Leese/Jason Crouthamel (eds),

Traumatic Memories of the Second World War and After, pp. 223–44. New York: Palgrave Macmillam.

Sontag, Susan. 1978. *On Photography.* London: Allen Lane.

Specht, Irma. 2006. *Red Shoes: Experiences of Girl Combatants in Liberia.* Geneva: International Labor Office.

Spero, Nancy. 2010. *Torture of Women.* Los Angeles: Siglio Press.

Summerfield, Derek. 1999. 'A Critique of Seven Assumptions Behind Psychological Trauma Programmes in War-Affected Areas', *Social Science and Medicine*, 48:1449–62.

Tienhoven, Harry van. 1993. 'Sexual Torture of Male Victims', *Torture: Quarterly Journal on Rehabilitation of Torture Victims and Prevention of Torture*, 3(4):133–5.

The Visitors. 1972. [Film] Elia Kazan. dir. USA: Home Free.

Waitzkin, Howard/Magaña, Holly. 1997. 'The Black Box in Somatization: Unexplained Physical Symptoms, Culture, and Narratives of Trauma', *Social Science and Medicine*, 45(6):811-25.

Watters, Ethan. 2010. *Crazy Like Us: The Globalization of the American Psyche.* New York: Free Press.

Welcome Home, Soldier Boys. 1972. [Film] Richard Compton. dir. USA: Twentieth Century Fox.

Wilcox, Andrew. 1997. 'Hazing is Not a Rite', *Naval Institute Proceedings*, 123/10/1, 136:35–7.

Wood, Elisabeth J. 2009. 'Armed Groups and Sexual Violence: When is Wartime Rape Rare?' *Politics and Society*, 37(1):131–61.

———. 2006. 'Variation in Sexual Violence during War', *Politics and Society*, 34(3): 307–41.

Young, James E. 2009. 'Regarding the Pain of Woman: Questions of Gender and the Arts of Holocaust Memory', *Publication of the Modern Language Association of America*, 124(5):1778–86.

Zongwe, Dunia Prince. 2012. 'The New Sexual Violence Legislation in the Congo: Dressing Indelible Scars on Human Dignity', *African Studies Review*, 55(2):37–57.

Zraly, Maggie/Nyirazinyaye, Laetitia. 2010. 'Don't Let the Suffering Make You Fade Away: An Ethnographic Study of Resilience Among Survivors of Genocide-Rape in Southern Rwanda', *Social Science and Medicine*, 70:1656–64.

Understanding the Gendered Laws of War: A Historical Approach

FABRICE VIRGILI

In the forty or more years since the publication of Susan Brownmiller's pioneering book about rape, *Against Our Will* (1975), mobilisation against sexual violence has made such crimes more visible. Over this period, more research has been carried out on the topic, there have been important advances in the historiography, and many publications have appeared. But the last four decades have also witnessed instances of sexual violence in the wars occurring in several parts of the world. The year 2015 saw the twentieth anniversaries both of the genocide of Tutsis in Rwanda (with French troops present in the country) and of the massacre in Srebrenica (with Dutch UN soldiers nearby), one among a number of atrocities in the former Yugoslavia. Since then, we have witnessed a number of other conflicts: in Afghanistan, Congo, Iraq, Sierra Leone, Chechnya, more recently Libya and Syria, and in most cases they have been marked by outbreaks of sexual violence. At the same time, in the research into war studies carried out during these years, much attention has been paid to women as participants in these conflicts, and to gender as one of the analytical tools necessary for an understanding of societies in wartime.

As the twentieth century ended, wars between sovereign states appeared to be losing ground to other more widespread forms of conflict, sometimes thought to be of lesser intensity, or to civil wars, internal conflicts with political, social, ethnic or religious dimensions, whether or not there was any foreign intervention.

The years since the turn of the twenty-first century have also witnessed an increase in the professionalisation and feminisation of western armed forces. That change has called for further historical reflection on this topic, which is the more necessary since some armies are today, in peace time, recruiting women as soldiers in identical conditions to those of men. Such moves towards feminisation, although far from widespread, have been criticised by many commentators (Capdevila/Godineau 2005). The recruitment of women into armies has met and is still meeting resistance, not only from military institutions themselves, but perhaps even more from the outside world, including academic milieus (Creveld 2001). Nevertheless, this process, which was long confined to certain paramilitary sectors (medical, communications, secretarial), has been extended to almost all kinds of training. In France, only the Foreign Legion now remains an all-male institution, since the bar on women serving in nuclear submarines was lifted in 2014.

The distance travelled since the end of the twentieth century indicates how the development of research on this topic has been marked by several historiographical debates, for example concerning the possible role of wars in campaigns for women's emancipation, or the role of women as both victims and agents in conflicts and violence. Whether in social history, cultural history or the history of private life, gendered identities have been challenged on all fronts.

WAR ON TRIAL

Susan Brownmiller opened her book with a chapter entitled 'In the Beginning Was the Law'. The question of law is still a conspicuous feature of present-day warfare, reflected in research over the last quarter-century. The law of war, national and international justice systems, war crimes, genocide, crimes against humanity, purges, amnesties, reconciliation—all these terms have become familiar references in current conflicts.

That is because since the collapse of the Communist bloc, and the resolution of several other centres of conflict (South American dictatorships, South Africa) a great deal of research, especially in political science, has been devoted to the question of justice in transitional periods (Dobry 2000; Lefranc 2008). During the same period, the conflict in former Yugoslavia and the genocide of the Tutsis in Rwanda led to the setting up of international tribunals: the International Criminal Tribunal for the former Yugoslavia (ICTY) in 1993 and the International Criminal Tribunal for Rwanda (ICTR) one year later. On 1 July 2002, the International Criminal Court (ICC) was established in The Hague. Alongside these developments, in the wake of the 1995 International Women's Conference in Beijing, crimes of sexual violence have been increasingly stigmatised, with rape being for the first time defined as an element in genocide in 1998, by the ICTR (the Akayesu case), and as a crime against humanity in 2001 by the ICTY (the Kunarac case). One of the major changes reflected in recent research, and in developments in international law over the last twenty years, is the prominence now accorded to violence against women. One aspect of this conjuncture in research is that the subject has been tackled both by international justice and by investigative journalism. The intermingling of these approaches may however produce bias: for example, omitting to study defence witnesses, and a perspective that always casts women exclusively in the role of victims (Delpla 2015).

The present concern with law arises at a time when the kinds of conflict which have led to criminal trials (ex-Yugoslavia, Rwanda, but also Sierra Leone, Cambodia, Ivory Coast) have indeed not been governed by the conventions elaborated almost a hundred years ago for the regulation of warfare. The status of prisoners of war, or of the civilian population, and the guarantees accorded to combatants in regular armies appear to have been completely disregarded in the new conditions of confrontation. These very recent events have therefore masked to some extent the long history of attempts to regulate warfare by treaties, laws or conventions, and the sentences passed on those who did not respect them. Most accounts merely content themselves with a brief reference to the Nuremberg trials (1945–46) as the birthplace of international justice and of the desire to 'criminalise history,' forgetting that this wish to bring regulation to warfare has much earlier origins.

Two points are worth highlighting: first, the extent to which the desire to regulate behaviour in war, and therefore to punish transgressors, is observable throughout different periods of history. These examples may not be the result of international agreements, but whether the instruments were national judicial systems, military codes, canon law or customary law, it was rare for a conflict to take place in the past without some kind of limit being applied by the societies involved. Secondly, the extent to which gender analysis can shed light on the definition of these forms of regulation. The gendered laws of war provide three ways of defining the parameters of the combat zone: are both men and women authorised to take part in it? How are sexual norms imposed in wartime? And does the legitimate use of force extend to sexual violence?

The first of these refers to the Augustinian distinction between the just and the unjust war. For a war to be defined as just, it was important to make a radical distinction between combatants and non-combatants, a dividing line of which differentiation between the civil and the military was only one later form. Discrimination between men and women was often superimposed on it. The assigning of roles to men and women within warlike activities was a way of distinguishing the 'good warrior' from the savage, the disciplined soldier from the brute, one's own army from that of the enemy.

Violence towards the other sex thus appears not as a custom 'true for all time,' but on the contrary a limit which might or might not be overstepped. Whether on a large scale or as an exceptional occurrence, rape is evidence of transgression, moral and sometimes legal. That in turn has entailed the need to cover it up or erase it from memory whenever it has occurred.

And finally, despite the desire to regulate behaviour in wartime, massacres have not necessarily been prevented if carried out with discipline, a way of dictating a sexual norm to soldiers, to wives and to conquered populations. The laws of war are also laws of sexuality.

WAR AS AN ALL-MALE ACTIVITY?

Although there were at first few studies of women as combatants and/or perpetrators of acts of violence, with later authors expressing surprise at the exceptional nature of such transgressions, there are now many more (Cardi/Pruvost 2012; Alison 2009; Dauphin/Farge 1997). Our concern here is not so much the story of women as combatants as the way in which laws have been employed to regulate them. Susan Brownmiller evoked the Code of Hammurabi concerning a time when there was no explicit law of war, and when the victor's power gave him free reign to do whatever he wished to the conquered. Nevertheless, under that Code (circa 1750 BCE, Before the Common Era), as confirmed by later laws, certain rules came into play, governing the situation, for example, of a married couple if the husband became a prisoner of war: the law specified such matters as a formal delay before remarriage was permitted, the ownership of property, and the rights of the children of the first or second marriage. This did not of course provide a moral or ethical code for war: what preoccupied the authorities were the socio-economic consequences of war for families. They were similarly concerned, when victorious, with the precise estimation of the spoils of war, of which human beings were the most valuable: this is demonstrated by the listings of prisoners by age and sex. Dividing prisoners up between men and women was a fundamental issue, when one realises that the deportation of populations in either direction could 'increase the fruitfulness' of these 'spoils of war' over new territories.

Yet alongside the commonplace attribution of separate roles for men and women in wartime, there are often exceptions which deserve more attention over the long term. For the medieval period, Joan of Arc has had such posthumous fame that she has become the icon of the woman combatant. In her case, the glorious exception seems to confirm the absence of women. Yet there are other examples, such as Matilda of Tuscany, a wartime leader who lived some three hundred years earlier (Cassagnes-Brouquet 2016). The military role this important figure played alongside Pope Gregory VII in the eleventh century added another source of dispute to the Investitures Quarrel, then at its height: this concerned the right of women to wage war (taking its inspiration both from Greco-Latin antiquity and from the Bible), viewed as usurping masculine authority by the partisans of the Holy Roman Emperor, Matilda was seen as incarnating the miles Christi, the soldier of Christ, by supporters of the Pope. The latter considered her to be a legitimate military leader in the name of the Just War.

Moving from the Just War to the Holy War, the question also arises of the participation of women in the Crusades, their presence being attested in the Christian army, something which disturbed chroniclers on both sides: yet canon law continued to oscillate between enforcing a ban and allowing exceptions. For contrary to the Roman era, a time when women's non-citizenship barred them irremediably from taking arms, the ordered society which took over in about the year 1000 distinguished oratores from bellatores and laboratores, and did not always coincide with gender barriers.

IMPOSING SEXUAL NORMS

In the sixteenth century, in a juridical transposition of the principle of the Just War, lawyers and writers on the theory of warfare, such as Alberico Gentili, incorporated into their texts and codes a condemnation of sexual violence. The death penalty was applied as a punishment in many armies of the time. But the gendered laws of war do not only concern what happens on the battlefield. The construction of modern armies, that is of a fighting force which would be amenable to control and ready to fight, was only achieved through the strict regulation of masculine sexuality (Muravyeva 2016). The countless military codes and regulations (almost 500) which were drawn up in Europe in the sixteenth and seventeenth centuries were devoted to this end, by imposing a heterosexual and marital norm on the men who made up the armies. This was to be the norm in wartime but also in peacetime, since adultery, bigamy, sodomy, bestiality, pimping and rape were all indiscriminately punishable offences.

FABRICE VIRGILI

Through extreme forms of sanction, such as burning at the stake, beheading or 'severe corporal punishment,' the legal penalties applied to sexual relations between men were a major example of the repression of deviant forms of sexuality. This is the explanation for the presence alongside armies of large numbers of women as camp followers (despite prostitution being forbidden). Canteen and catering women, in the eyes of the general staff, were supposed to limit the temptations of 'unnatural behaviour' as well as the many rapes. By extension, military codes of behaviour created a judicial context for sexual norms throughout the population.

In a very different context, several centuries later, the Nazi occupation of Alsace and the Moselle after July 1940 also enforced heterosexual norms. For contrary to the situation in Germany (where Article 175 of the penal code made homosexual relations a criminal offence) in France at the time, while it was possible to experience police harassment, sometimes considerable, for 'offences against public decency,' homosexuality as such was neither a crime nor a misdemeanour in the eyes of the law. The victory of the Wehrmacht in 1940 meant that Alsace-Moselle was annexed not only militarily but sexually (Schlagdenhauffen 2016). Third Reich norms were imposed, at first in practice, then from 30 January 1942 with the force of law, when the territory was attached to Germany. Here the laws relating to sexual behaviour allow us to outline the contours of conquest: the Nazification of Alsace-Moselle took the form not only of forbidding inhabitants from using the French language, or wearing a Gallic beret, but also of outlawing homosexual practices and any form of non-reproductive sexuality. In the rest of occupied France, which was not annexed, that is, not subject to the *Volksgemeinschaft* (People's Racial Community), the occupier was not particularly concerned to prohibit homosexual relations, since anything that might reduce the French birth rate was seen as beneficial to Germany (Virgili 2009).

HIDING AND REDISCOVERING SEXUAL VIOLENCE

Sexual violence, long more or less hidden from history, has recently been much studied: rape in particular has become an established field of historical enquiry (Branche/Virgili 2012; Heinemann 2011, Mibenge 2013). Such violence was a recurrent marker in wartime practice. Although almost always forbidden by customary or canon law, by military regulations, or by international law, sexual violence was nevertheless often cited as a way of denouncing (that is taking revenge for) crimes committed by the enemy, punishable as a method of disciplining one's own troops, but also tolerated as a way of imposing power over the adversary and sometimes even organised, as a means of forcing the conquered population into submission.

In her book, Susan Brownmiller offers a brief history of rape in wartime from *The Iliad* and the rape of the Sabine Women to the Vietnam War and the 1971 Indo-Pakistani War which had only recently ended when she was writing her book. She did not of course fail to refer to the Second World War and the massive incidence of rape. Such rapes, she wrote, whether committed by the Red Army or by the Japanese Imperial Army, were instances of revenge. Both are well known as constituting massive cases of sexual violence during that conflict. However, the memory of these events, whether personal or collective, is complex. Neither the former USSR nor Japan ever recognised responsibility for the violence. On the contrary, they took steps to silence memories of it, seeking to have them forgotten. But the study of the decades since 1945 shows that this imposed silence does not reflect deep feelings, nor does it indicate forgetfulness. Sexual violence continues to provoke trauma in these countries, depending on the memory of the people involved, the political or diplomatic stakes, and the growing influence of the feminist movement.

Let us consider an example from each country: Lithuania (under Soviet rule until it became an independent state in 1990) and Japan. In the Lithuanian case, a rape committed in wartime had to be erased from the record, so as not to tarnish the image of the rapist—a Soviet partisan who was declared a war hero in

1958—but also subsequently that of his victim, who was declared a martyr and on the way to beatification in 1999. In Japan, on the other hand, the debate has been concerned what lies behind the euphemism of 'comfort women,' *ianfu* in Japanese: was this simply 'traditional' prostitution, in return for money, as the Japanese revisionists have argued? Or a gigantic system of sexual slavery serving the imperial army, as many studies have demonstrated (Tanaka 2001; Yoshimi 2000)? As a war crime inadequately dealt with by the courts in the immediate post-war period, it gave rise to an International Women's Tribunal in 2000. This body, like the central committee of the Lithuanian Communist party forty years earlier, was asked to pronounce on the reality of sexual violence. These two cases are unrelated, but the deliberations of the tribunals underline at once the very imperfect handling of sexual violence by the official bodies set up to process them (whether military tribunal, criminal tribunal or international court) and the impact of such mishandling on the definition of war crimes, as well as the extraordinary persistence of the memory of sexual violence.

These two cases, both based on extensive documentary sources, indicate the importance of archives, the primary material of the historian. The Special Archives of Lithuania (*Lietuvos ypatingajame archyve*) held in Vilnius contain three documents relating to the above case: a letter from the plaintiff whose daughter was raped and killed by the partisan Čeponis; a summary of the deliberations of the bureau of the central committee of the Lithuanian Communist Party; and the report of the commission of inquiry, addressed to Moscow. These three documents (now translated and online[1]) demonstrate how seriously the question was taken by the authorities. There was of course no public debate, but there was a genuine inquiry, in order to make sure that one of the most important distinctions possibly awarded in the USSR should not be dishonoured by the behaviour of one of its War Heroes. In the Japanese case, the judgement passed by the Women's International Tribunal in Tokyo can be downloaded from the internet.[2] Indeed, since 2005 the Women's Active Museum on War and Peace has been taking steps to communicate more widely testimonies and archives concerning the sexual slavery system known as 'comfort women.'

Making archives visible poses an important challenge. For a long time research on the subject of sexual violence has been thwarted by the absence of available archives. The archives are not in fact lacking, whether military, medical, legal or private. The injunction on the women concerned to keep silent, and the closing down of discussion on the topic in so many societies does not mean the non-existence of questions, inquiries, files, testimonies—and therefore of archives. The materials are there to continue further research on sexual violence in history, and, quoting the final sentence of Susan Brownmiller's book, to help 'deny it [rape] a future.'

This article is a revised version of the 'Editorial', *Clio: Femmes, Genre, Histoire,* 39(1), 2014, online since 10 April 2015, https://journals.openedition.org/clio/11830. A warm thanks to Sian Reynolds for translating and reviewing it

NOTES

1. Document 1, 2 and 3, in Regamey 2016.
2. http://vawwrac.org/war_crimes_tribunal (accessed 16 August 2018).

REFERENCES

Alison, Miranda. 2009. *Women and Political Violence.* New York: Routledge.

Branche, Raphaëlle/Virgili, Fabrice (eds). 2012. *Rape in Wartime.* New York/London: Palgrave Macmillan.

Brownmiller, Susan. 1975. *Against Our Will: Men, Women and Rape.* New York: Simon and Schuster.

Capdevila, Luc/Godineau, Dominique. 2005. 'Armées', *Clio: Femmes, Genre, Histoire,* 06 June. https://journals.openedition.org/clio/1333 (accessed 16 August 2018).

Cardi, Coline/Pruvost, Geneviève. 2012. *Penser la violence des femmes.* Paris: La Découverte.

Cassagnes-Brouquet, Sophie. 2016. 'Au service de la guerre juste: Mathilde de Toscane (onze–douze siècle)', *Clio: Femmes, Genre, Histoire*, 01 June. https://journals.openedition.org/clio/11845 (accessed 16 August 2018).

Creveld, Martin Van. 2001. *Men, Women, and War*. London: Cassell & Co.

Dauphin, Cécile/Farge, Arlette (eds). 1997. *De la violence et des femmes*. Paris: Albin Michel.

Delpla, Isabelle. 2015. 'Les femmes et le droit (pénal) international', *Clio: Femmes, Genre, Histoire*, 10 April. https://journals.openedition.org/clio/11918 (accessed 16 August 2018).

Dobry, Michel. 2000. 'Les voies incertaines de la transitologie: choix stratégiques, séquences historiques, bifurcations et processus de path dependence', *Revue française de science politique*, 50(4–5):585–614.

Heinemann, Elizabeth D. 2011. *Sexual Violence in Conflict Zones*. Philadelphia: University of Pennsylvania Press.

Lefranc, Sandrine. 2008. 'La justice transitionnelle n'est pas un concept', *Mouvements*, 1(53):61–9.

Mibenge, Chiseche Salome. 2013. *Sex and International Tribunals: The Erasure of Gender from the War Narrative*. Philadelphia: University of Pennsylvania Press.

Muravyeva, Marianna. 2016. '"Ni pillage ni viol sans ordre préalable": Codifier la guerre dans l'Europe moderne', *Clio: Femmes, Genre, Histoire*, 01 June. https://journals.openedition.org/clio/11856 (accessed 16 August 2018).

Regamey, Amandine. 2016. 'Plainte et enquête d'un viol (Lituanie soviétique, 1959)', *Clio: Femmes, Genre, Histoire*, 01 June. https://journals.openedition.org/clio/11983 (accessed 16 August 2018).

Schlagdenhauffen, Régis. 2016. 'Désirs condamnés: Punir les "homosexuels" en Alsace annexée (1940–1945)', *Clio: Femmes, Genre, Histoire*, 01 June. https://journals.openedition.org/clio/11866 (accessed 16 August 2018).

Tanaka, Yuki. 2001. *Japan's Comfort Women: Sexual Slavery and Prostitution During World War II and the US Occupation*. London: Routledge.

Virgili, Fabrice. 2014. 'Editorial', *Clio: Femmes, Genre, Histoire* (Special Edition: *Les lois genrées de la guerre*), 01 June. https://journals.openedition.org/clio/11830 (accessed 16 August 2018).

———. 2009. *Naître ennemi: Les couples franco-allemands nés pendant la Seconde Guerre mondiale*. Paris: Payot.

Yoshimi, Yoshiaki. 2000. *Comfort Women: Sexual Slavery in the Japanese Military During World War II*. New York: Columbia University Press.

VIOLENCE/SEXUALITY

Armed conflict and wartime sexual violence are based on practices of violence. These 'violences' are not necessarily premised on conscious decisions, but are also an expression of affects and emotions. They involve different practices and objects. Complex constellations of violence and bodies challenge us to understand the enactment of these violences and against whom they are directed. How do belligerents deal with emotional and affective energies? What do we know about the experience of sexual violence from the point of view of its victims? How can the bodily aspect of sexual violence be theorised? How can we capture the relationship between individual lived experiences and collective practices of violence in war?

Cultural ideas about sex and gender, as well as conventions of sexuality, represent social and political interests within specific social formations. Acts of sexual violence in armed conflict are not merely expressions of violence in the 'exceptional situation' of warfare. They are also closely linked to everyday sexual practices within specific social and political frameworks. What is the relationship between sexuality and violence in war? What is 'sexual' about sexual violence? How can we conceptualise interspersonal relations such as love or intimacy in these contexts? How can we disentangle the relationship between consensual relations, commercial sex, bartering and sexual violence?

Resisting the Symbolic Power of (War) Rape

LOUISE DU TOIT

The argument in this chapter unfolds in two main steps. First, claiming that a proper interpretation of the meanings of sexual violence in armed conflict requires an explication of its symbolic significance, I analyse the symbolic power put into play through the sexual violation of the feminine or female principle within armed struggle and war. In the second part of the chapter, I flesh out my concern that by rendering war rape more visible as part of feminist struggle to oppose it, we (feminist scholars and activists) may actually enhance the intended symbolic effects of rape as a key and integral aspect of (theatres of) war and armed conflict. Although sexual violation of the feminine is routinely framed as a marginal aspect of war, I claim in this chapter that it in fact covertly lies at the heart of the logic of war and of the modern state. Thus, by heightening its visibility, feminists do expose its centrality to war, but might fail to go further by also disrupting the symbolic order which positions war rape as ontologically powerful and militarily strategic in the first place. And so, instead of combatting it, we may inadvertently encourage the phenomenon if we fail to take the further step.

TOWARDS UNFOLDING THE SYMBOLIC POWER OF FEMALE SEXUAL VIOLATION

Eva Feder Kittay (1988) ponders the asymmetry of the pervasive proclivity of men to use "women's activities and relations to men [as] persistent metaphors for men's projects," in ways that are not reciprocated by women towards men. Put differently, women seem not to routinely take aspects of men's activities within their (men's) world and use them as metaphoric expressions of typical or exclusive women's activities. Kittay provides numerous examples of how Man[1] pervasively mediates his relation, first, to himself, second, to his material world and third, to his social world, through metaphors in which women and their (typical or exclusive) sexed embodiment and activities are central. For one example of the second type of usage, natural forces to be conquered, such as mountains, forests or the ocean, are often feminised (think of the *Odyssey*), as is nature itself ('Mother Nature').[2] Sometimes these metaphors get symbolically and ritualistically concretised in enactments, such as initiation rites and baptisms (Kittay 1988: 63), emulating physical birth. This latter phenomenon is most typical in the third mode, where Woman metaphorically mediates for Man his relation to his social world.

Kittay (ibid.: 64) explains further that this prevalence of the metaphoric vehicle Woman for shaping Man's conceptualisation of the world is the result of (i) the essential alterity which Man ascribes to, or projects onto Woman; also, (ii) both Woman and metaphor are strongly mediational; as Other to the domain of Man, Woman mediates for him with all forms of alterity; and lastly, (iii) both Woman and metaphor are strongly relational; although Woman is Other, she is also viewed by man as "already schematised by proximate and familiar relations" (ibid.: 65). This schema Man then transfers onto more distant or alien domains to structure his conceptualisation of them.[3] Taking points (i) and (iii) together, we see that Man's relation to Woman is deeply ambivalent, in that she is both absolute Other and yet proximate, in the sense of transparently knowable to him. Still, these three convergences do not yet explain why Woman performs this function for Man, while there is no equivalent linguistic phenomenon on women's side.

For Kittay, this situation can be explained by the trans-historically gendered nature of child care. Firmly rejecting any naturalistic explanations, she argues following Chodorow (1978), that we reproduce gender through the near universal centrality of the mother (and relative absence of the father) in the raising of infants and young children. As a result of these practices, boys are contingently forced to shape and assert their identity primarily, first and foremost, *in opposition* to the all-powerful figure of the mother. Thus, boys must repress their initial identification with the mother, while girls may establish a self "through a continuing identity with the mother" (Kittay 1988: 68). The result of all this is simply that women's identity (formation and maintenance) is far less dependent than men's on the centrality of a simultaneously desired and feared Other who must be disavowed, separated from, and definitively overcome. Note that this necessity faced by boys is the result of specific patriarchal social arrangements. Looking at the first of the three points above, it becomes clear that the essential alterity which Man projects onto Woman in his formative years in order to obtain a Self, is not reciprocated by Woman towards Man, since the girl has no similar developmental need for an opposing and inferior Other. The initial identification with the mother for both boy and girl is based on her remarkable power over their existence, apparently fully justified by the fact of her having given birth to them (ibid.: 68), coupled with her nurturing role in alleviating the unique and prolonged vulnerability of human infants. But in the case of the boy, he gradually realises that he cannot replicate *this,* primordial power, in his own life, and he must thus sever the initial identification. He must establish his sense of self in opposition to female power, in the face of what he experiences as his own fundamental lack. Again, these tensions spring from social organisation: strong paternal involvement in infant care may provide the boy with a positive set of capacities with which he may then identify, reducing the psychological need to establish his selfhood mainly on a set of dis-identifications with the mother.

Kittay (ibid.: 69) concludes: "For better and for worse, the self that women develop may well be more accommodating to otherness," culminating for some in "maternal consciousness," a form of consciousness shaped "to accommodate the otherness of the child." Furthermore, women's is, contingently, a consciousness which "comprehends itself not through an opposition, but through a connectedness, an emphatic bond with an Other" (ibid.). In contrast, men's (or rather, paradigmatic Man's), under current parenting arrangements, is a consciousness fundamentally structured in terms of an ambivalent, repressive, oppositional stance. This crisis of origins seems to translate into an inherently fragile masculine sense of self, overdetermined by its ability to disavow, oppose, control and suppress feminine power, in particular female sexual and maternal power. This is the state of affairs which leads Luce Irigaray to assert that the western symbolic order is founded on the logic of matricide, a kind of originary sacrifice. She (quoted in Whitford 1991: 77) formulates it thus: "[The underpinning of the culture] is woman reproducer of the social order, acting as the infrastructure of that order; all of western culture rests upon the murder of the mother [...]." It becomes clear then that the figure of the feminine in the form of the Mother and in the shape of female procreative and nurturing powers and capacities, remains absolutely central, ironically through its overcoming and marginalisation, in the sense of selfhood established by patriarchal Man. This whole psychological drama must be understood as underlying and informing the dominant role that Woman as metaphor plays in the Empire of Man. The formative dynamic in which boys need to assert their independent existence from the Mother naturally lends itself to becoming a powerful metaphor for grasping all "the activities and domains in which man will redefine himself and establish new associations" (Kittay 1988: 69). Typically, when Woman is mobilised as metaphor, Man simultaneously identifies with women's specific powers or activities, and appropriates them, and then proceeds to negate, erase or devalue them in so far as they (still) pertain to her but exclude him (ibid.: 73).[4]

This cultural undervaluing-and-appropriation of women's capacities is bad enough, yet there is something far more sinister in Kittay's analysis of Woman as metaphor. Insofar as Woman mediates for man between man and himself, and between man and the natural world, it is *representations* of Woman that primarily serve as the metaphorical vehicle. However, and crucially for our purposes, in the third function, "woman herself [...], [her embodied sexuality] becomes the metaphoric vehicle" (ibid.: 74). This is the moment in which, according to the Oedipal drama, the son "gives up the Mother as a [concrete] love object—gives her over to the Father—in exchange for the Father's [abstract] social identity." Through this definitive overcoming of his sense of awe, dependence, gratitude and vulnerability towards the powerful life-giver, as and when he turns her into an objectified *exchange medium* for which he may trade his male honour and standing, the son becomes a patriarchal man amongst men. For Kittay, *possessing* value is fundamentally structurally opposed to the function of *signifying* value, and so the basic gendered division of symbolic labour is created: women who signify value (and thus cannot possess value) are possessed by men, both individually and collectively, (who cannot therefore signify value, but can only possess it), whose value they thereby signify. "Through the exchange of women, men establish circles of social interaction with men" and women are transformed into "signifiers whose value comes from their mediating role in the interaction between men" (ibid.). This is the way in which, according to Kittay, the wider social order reflects, replicates and reinforces the individual male psychic drama.

When Mother is finally stripped of her unique, intrinsic, embodied value and becomes a mere exchange medium, she becomes a strangely proximate and obliquely knowable sign of absolute Alterity. To dare to resurrect her as a fully alive agent, citizen, scholar and subject with specific female powers, would threaten to destroy the whole social order. This matricide translates into the private-public distinction and the associated privatisation and de-politicisation of women, signified, arguably, by the veil in some cultures, by 'family values' and anti-abortion advocacy in others. Whatever precise cultural form it takes, the privatisation of female sexuality as a medium of male social exchange silences women's political voice and turns them into inaudible, yet hyper-visible symbols of male power and male bonds. And this is then also why, according to Kittay, war rape can play such a powerful symbolic role: Woman has a key symbolic function in the most fundamental organisation of the collective male bond. Thus, the rape of women in war "is precisely *the* vehicle for expression of the domination of one group over the other. If the sexual exchange of women marks the bond between men, the victor's sexual 'expropriation' solidifies the conquest" (Ibid.: 75; emphasis added). Sexual attack of women takes aim at the heart of the sacrificial gendered organisation of the enemy, an organisation in which the identity, coherence, honour and health of the collective male bond is always already construed in opposition to, and at the cost of, feminine humanity. To rape the women of a collective, is thus not only to shame the men as inadequate protectors of women or to despoil their most prized goods; it is also to erase the male honour bought at the price of the sacrifice of womanhood, in other words, it undoes that sacrifice and destroys its pay-off.

Laura Sjoberg (2013) implicitly works out the insights of Kittay on Woman as pervasive metaphorical vehicle, focusing more on the national and international levels than on the personal and psychological. She argues that "the story of state/nation/ ethnicity constitutes and is constituted by [the] gender trope" (Sjoberg 2013: 171). In this regard, the covert masculine identity of the modern state is reflective of that masculine identity of the normative subject and citizen which is structurally dependent on its superior opposition to Woman. Although they pretend to be gender neutral and inclusive, the stories and histories of collectives, including state, religious and ethnic identities, are usually strongly gendered. One aspect of this is that political voice and agency, and leadership, are conceptualised overwhelmingly in terms of heroic masculine traits. This heroic masculine identity ideal is construed in dynamic and symbiotic opposition with denigrated maternal symbols. Sjoberg demonstrates that modern states live within gendered relations with other states, and are also internally strongly gendered, with these two gendered spheres interpenetrating and reinforcing each other continuously. The gendered nature of states moreover impacts state decision-making on war and serves as one of the primary justifications for war. Female leadership and female soldiers are not necessarily an antidote here. Rather, it is the feminisation of cultures, in the sense of a greater valorisation of traditional feminine values in comparison with traditional masculine ones (for instance dialogue and risk avoidance over aggression and risk seeking), that may ultimately significantly impact on war decisions and justifications (ibid.: 173).

Such a feminising shift is however unlikely, given the stubbornly gendered nature of collective identities. In a male dominated world, women, and those who value typical feminine values, are unlikely to obtain positions of power, especially when it comes to war decisions. Along similar lines as Kittay above, Sjoberg argues that groups of people who live their lives outside, or on the margins, of the traditional spheres of influence regarding national and international policy-making, with little access to political power, and to the technologies of violence,[5] are more likely to have *constitutive or symbolic influence only* and "less likely to be able to control either how their story is related or who they are in it" (ibid.: 215). Clearly, this key insight echoes Kittay's structural opposition between signifying and possessing value. Those who are marginalised are often either *omitted* from official national histories and traditional accounts of war altogether, or they are symbolically (and materially), *appropriated* by and for masculinised and elitist accounts of war-making (ibid.). I would add that when marginalised groups (signifying rather than possessing value) are moved from invisibility into visibility that they tend to become hyper-visible due to their symbolic value. Such hyper-visibility seems however to work against their having a voice, becoming audible, which would allow them to influence *how* they feature in larger hi/stories.

In the case of war rape research, numerous examples of both these strategies have been brought to light: there has been a long history of simply ignoring and omitting war rape altogether from accounts of war, together with a refusal to count the civilian casualties—a history challenged significantly during the 1990s (Hynes 2004: 431–45; Buss 2007).[6] At the same time, with this recent increased visibility of war rape (notably since the start of the *ad hoc* international criminal tribunals for Rwanda and the former Yugoslavia), the previous strategy of denial is now increasingly being replaced by multiple, explicit strategies for *appropriating* war rape for military and propaganda purposes. Doris Buss (2014) for example refers to research by Séverine Autesserre who found that in the Democratic Republic of Congo (DRC), the heightened international visibility of war rape had turned it into "an effective bargaining tool," with different armed groups having threatened with rape in order to strengthen their position in negotiations (ibid.: 14). Similarly, in the context of the aftermath of the Peruvian civil war of the 1980s and 1990s, Kimberly Theidon (2007) shows how war rape stories were either systematically suppressed, or otherwise moulded (appropriated) in such a way that they would serve communities' reparation claims (ibid.: 460). In this manner, as soon as the invisible is made visible, the meaning of war rape gets stripped away from its primary victims and attached to the political capital of a gendered (that is male controlled) collective entity.

It thus becomes clear that gender subordination within the imagined communal or collective existence is essential to the symbolic function, meaning and nature of warfare. It has been said that capitalism needs wars in order to sustain its momentum; it may well be equally true that patriarchy needs war (or at least its constant threat) and that war needs patriarchal arrangements. The fact that sometimes the presumed cause of war was a woman or women does nothing to change this: from the ancient Greek beauty Helen to the 'covered woman' of the Middle East of today, the metaphorical meanings of women's sexualised bodies are fully appropriated for war and its purposes. Sometimes this happens covertly and more recently it happens through a hyper-visualisation which does little to discourage the phenomenon itself. Women's sexuality is particularly well suited to fulfil this metaphoric and symbolic function, given that women's wombs are the literal place of the powers of gestation and birth and thus the material source of future (collective) existence and regeneration.

Sjoberg explains the link between Woman and war thus:

The very availability of war as an option for decision-makers depends upon the assumed presence of an innocent, interior, feminised other generally—the other of war [and thus its ultimate cause and justification]—and women's needs for the protection provided by states specifically. (Sjoberg 2013: 215)

For Sjoberg then, as for Kittay, it is precisely this creation of the 'other *of* war'—strongly gendered and identified with women's sexuality—as the very reason *for* war, which sets up women and their sexuality as prized targets in the logic of war-making, and thereby yields rape as an important war strategy. Thus, the new understanding that rape is far from incidental collateral damage, but in fact a deliberately employed 'weapon of war', integral to war (Buss 2009: 145), is further reinforced. Central to the justification of war, the marketing of war and the propaganda for war, is the gendered trope of the just and brave soldier who is obliged to fight the just cause, which is closely associated with the protection of the vulnerable and feminised civilian, the pre-political source of politics, that is the voiceless 'innocent'. These war tropes are salient because they dovetail so neatly with gendered peace-time nationalisms (Sjoberg 2013: 248) and with the domestic exclusion of the feminised other from both national and international politics and decision-making.

Feminist critiques of the state have highlighted the domestic impact of these gendered inequalities on *inter alia* the equation of protector-ability, masculinity, military service and full citizenship (ibid.). Jean-François Lyotard (1989) understands that the feminine which is "banished outside the confines of the *corpus socians*" forms the limits or boundaries of the men's Empire; thus "we [men, the dominant sex] have to struggle ceaselessly with their [women's] exteriority" (ibid.: 114f). Being positioned as both before (not yet) and outside of the properly human which possesses value, the feminine occupies the Empire's borders, and thereby constitutes its constant preoccupation, its key concern. For Kittay, this will be because the feminine symbolises the value of the male collective. Lyotard illuminates: "[T]he Voice at the Virile Centre" of "the circle of homosexual warriors," "speaks only of [...] the Empire's limits (which are women)" (ibid.: 115). In her turn, Sjoberg (2013: 248) refers in this regard to the "protection racket" of war discourse which pretends to protect women, "while actually producing gender subordination and threats to women's lives," including the high likelihood of both war and peacetime rape. In short: "the protection of vulnerable citizens is used to justify violence that puts those citizens at more risk" (ibid.: 249).

Masculinity becomes that which defends the nation while femininity keeps the nation together (ibid.: 250), or: the female bodies in their sexuality powerfully symbolise the nation (from which they are structurally excluded), defended or fought for, and over, by different male collectives. It lies in the nature of the exchange value accorded to women's sexuality that it precludes intrinsic value, including the value of sexual integrity to the women themselves. It ignores the high personal stake that women have in sexual autonomy and reduces the value of women's sexual integrity to personal or collective male honour. Women's sexuality is symbolically constructed as the clearest, purest or highest expression of collective identity. Heroic masculine identity reaches its apex in war: there, all women's sexualised bodies are systematically and relentlessly turned into mere exchange value, into mere tokens of collective identity. The violence of war feeds on, and consistently reinforces, the presumed vulnerability of the feminised others of war.[7] The hierarchically gendered construction of the nation, combined with the domestic protection racket which heightens during war, actually incentivises deliberate civilian victimisation in theatres of war, Sjoberg claims (ibid.: 250).[8]

Sjoberg illuminates further, using Carl von Clausewitz's strategic term "centre of gravity" (ibid.: 25). He describes such a centre as "neither a strength nor a source of strength but rather a focal point where physical and psychological forces come together." In war, Clausewitz urges, it is of paramount strategic importance to define/discover both your own and your enemy's centres of gravity, since to have such a centre destroyed is to be dealt a significant psychological and symbolic blow, which could lead to actual surrender. "If belligerents fight for *their* women, (or to the extent that they do, or believe that that is why they fight at all), it follows that a belligerent wins an absolute victory by exterminating the women understood as belonging to the opponent" (ibid.: 251). Many masculine collectives see their own centres of gravity in women and children, and precisely to the extent that they do, they set them up as preferred targets for their enemies. Because of the centrality of women's sexuality as an ultimate symbol for what war is about, in many contexts it makes more strategic sense to rape women instead of simply killing them. Ironically, then, women's metaphorical function in war which generally both presumes and reinforces their passivity may actually also protect them. For instance, in the Srebenica massacre, boys and men between twelve and 77 years old were separated out for killing by Serbian forces, while 23 000 women and children were bussed to safety (Engle 2005: 814). In war as in peace, women's bodies are instrumentalized sexually in service of the nation in which they are subordinated, and precisely by virtue of their exclusion as political subjects and agents of violence, they acquire a particularly powerful symbolic meaning over which they have virtually no control: they are set up as the vulnerable foil to the powerful soldiers of war.[9] And being set up as such, different war scenarios may play out for women in a range of different ways, depending on the desired symbolic effect.

In her analysis of the logic of war, Elaine Scarry (1985) arguably throws more light on what Clausewitz calls military "centres of gravity." She states that there is no reason why an international dispute cannot be settled by a chess game, for instance, other than that "the legitimacy of the outcome" of a war, unlike the outcome of a chess game, "outlives the end of the contest because so many of its participants are frozen in a permanent act of participation," that is they have been killed or maimed (ibid.: 62). War thus has an ontological effect; it changes the world and its rules through mass violence. Thus, while the rules of war are as arbitrary as the rules of chess, "the winning issue or ideology" in a war, or the outcome of the conflict "achieves for a time the force and status of material 'fact' by the sheer material weight of the multitudes of damaged and opened human bodies" (ibid.). This idea speaks to the symbolic force of war rape, as it functions within war as itself a kind of theatre and spectacle.

For Scarry, war is not really about physically defeating the enemy. Instead, war (like torture) is a contest between two or more worlds or world views, represented by the two enemies (or torturer and victim), respectively. The raping of enemy women and killing

of civilians in general is therefore a strategy similar to destroying
the enemy's cultural artefacts—they target not the overt force of
the enemy, but rather their 'centres of gravity.' These forms of
attack tend to bring about the defeat of the enemy much more
quickly and effectively than the dealing of blows to their army
(Seifert 1996: 38). This is because wars end, not when armies
are comprehensively destroyed, but rather when the scale, extent
and nature of the destruction gets to the point where it forces the
defeated group *to change their collective perception and understandings*—
of themselves, their culture, their future, of the world as such and
of the relations of domination controlling that world. Wars are
thus won and lost when a successful 'world deconstruction' has
been wrought. Such a deconstruction happens most likely through
clever, targeted, destruction, of material culture, of symbolically
important persons and of elements of consciousness (Scarry
1985: 92). Seen from this perspective, the suffering of the civilian
population "constitutes a crucial element of warfare," rather than
collateral damage. When we persist in honouring only or mainly
military casualties and leave out rape and other civilian victims
in our official rites and discourses of mourning after war, we feed
this central deception of war (Seifert 1996: 38). As an integral
and maybe the most powerful site of the violent, symbolic,
simultaneous construction and deconstruction of worlds, women's
sexuality takes centre stage in the spectacle that is war; it is the
place *par excellence* where worlds get made and destroyed, that is
where wars get won and lost.

THE DANGERS OF MAKING WAR RAPE MORE VISIBLE, MORE SPECTACULAR

If the argument presented so far is correct, then the question
about the likely effects of rendering war rape more visible through
feminist effort to address it more effectively immediately presents
itself.

If war is indeed waged to a large extent through spectacle and
theatre aimed at deconstructing the world view, social order and
centres of gravity of the enemy and if visibly damaged bodies

(especially sexually damaged female bodies) have a particularly powerful symbolic impact on war effort; in short, if the aim of war is "to make up and make real" (Scarry 1985: 21) certain abstract notions that order and justify the distribution of resources, then by rendering *more visible* the spectacle of war rape may serve to amplify its *intended* effects. Rendering war rapes more visible makes it difficult to sustain the idea that they are incidental to war, but it also does nothing by itself to resist the appropriation of their meaning for decidedly misogynist interpretative projects. With the involvement of new social media in war, we have probably entered the era of the hyper-visibility of war rape and other atrocities. Let us consider the dangers or risks that such much greater visibility may entail, viewed from a feminist perspective which is in the first and last place motivated by the desire to put an end to (war) rape. I suggest the following aspects should be taken into careful consideration when feminists increase the visibility of war rape with the aim to better combat it.

(I) First, there are the dangers attached to an 'epistemology of vulnerability'. Lorraine Code cautions that there is a set of

> risks involved in an epistemology of vulnerability and the politics of knowledge: namely, that *knowing* the structural implications of (an)other('s) vulnerability can be as dangerous as it is affirming. No politics of the vulnerable body can affect social transformation(s) without bringing vulnerabilities in their specificity before the public eye [...]. Somehow, the process requires narrating vulnerability into being [...]. But the negotiations are delicate; not least because vulnerabilities exposed—known—can produce the ironic effect of making the vulnerable more vulnerable still, their weaknesses exposed, their 'soft spots' available for damage. (Lorraine Code 2009: 343f)

Indeed, the negotiations are delicate, as we have already seen with the example from the DRC above, where war rape had become for some a powerful bargaining tool. The more we understand and illuminate the reasons, the extent, the 'texture' and the duration of the damage of rape to women's and girls' embodied subjectivities, the more valuable war rape will become as a symbolic strategy in war. We seem to be caught in a double bind: when feminists emphasise women's own experiences of war (including but not limited to rape), through narrative, film, documentary or testimony, this seldom does anything to disrupt, but instead reinforces, the established and exploited notions of women's outsider and relatively powerless status *vis-à-vis* war—coupled, as we have seen, with their heightened symbolic significance. Code says that we cannot successfully, that is transformatively, engage in "a politics of the vulnerable body" without "bringing vulnerabilities in their specificity before the public eye," which in this context (for example in war rape hearings) would also mean that we explain why, for women, sexual violation even without physical pain or injury, constitutes a fundamental human rights violation (see Bergoffen 2012: 23). The same dilemma plays out in feminist struggles against rape in the everyday: also there, one may plausibly argue, it is the symbolic (ontological) power dynamic rather than sexual lust that mostly motivates rapists. Although feminists have for a long time argued that the trivialisation or public neglect of rape leads to impunity and thus to more rape, we should at least consider the possibility that greater social attention to the phenomenon, and especially detailed descriptions of the multiple damages of rape (see Brison 2002), may further fuel its occurrence.

(II) The second aspect to which feminists must pay close attention, is how the meanings of rape (and particularly of rape in war or armed conflict) get framed, and appropriated, and to what purpose. As explained, greater visibility is likely to enhance the dominant symbolic meanings of the sexual violence, and these are seldom feminist meanings. A central insight of Scarry's book, *The Body in Pain*, is that pain resists its expression in language; most powerfully so in the first-person experience of intense pain, when "the world content [...] disappears in the head of the person suffering" (Scarry 1985: 60). There is something about experienced pain which resists its articulation as a certain thing amongst others in the world, because it is in the nature of pain to obliterate the world. When pain does get expressed somehow, says Scarry, "it makes all further statements and interpretations seem

ludicrous and inappropriate," as even talk of human rights seems
to trivialise the reality of the pain, to miss the point by missing the
pain (ibid.). The nature of pain endured for her means that even
if it gets articulated, "it immediately falls back in", into the body
in pain, since "[n]othing sustains its image in the world," where
'world' is the totality of inter- and mutually constitutive forces
and elements in reality. Pain cannot by itself sustain an objective
existence in the world, in the sense that "its own powerfulness
ensures its isolation" (ibid.: 61).

It is this resistance of pain to language and world (that is, to
symbolisation and communication) which for Scarry lends it so
strongly to its appropriation by others, which "allows real human
pain to be converted into a regime's fiction of power" (ibid.: 18).
In war, which aims at hurting bodies, "what is taking place in
terms of pain [is made to] take place in terms of power, in order
to shift what is occurring exclusively in the mode of sentience
into the mode of self-extension and world" (ibid.: 36). In other
words, the spectacle of extreme physical and psychological pain
does not necessarily translate into moral indignation and justice
for the victims. Instead, when a centre of gravity (such as civilians)
is attacked in war, the victims get reduced to inarticulate bodies
and body parts, while the spectacle of their suffering is translated
by the logic of war into the awesome ontological power of the
aggressor. Put differently, through the visual spectacle of suffering,
witnesses are convinced of the 'truth' or 'world' of the attacker,
even as they see other versions of the world (most notably those
of the victims) destroyed. Hereby, the victim is silenced while the
attacker is elevated to a position of almost pure voice and agency.
For this world deconstruction to happen, as said, the spectacle of
sexual violation might be even more effective than killing alone.
We see here "the conversion of absolute pain into the fiction
[spectacle] of absolute power" (ibid.: 27). The one who inflicts
the pain, denies its characteristics in their absolute subjective
reality for the victim, and in the same gesture converts them
into objectified expressions of elements of *his* world. Thereafter,
the "central attributes of pain" get translated "into the insignia
of the regime" (ibid.: 19). In the very proximity of enduring

and inflicting bodily pain, the truth and reality of the pain as experienced, gets obliterated, denied and erased by its translation into the objective power of the enemy (ibid.: 18). When war rape is used to demoralise a male collective, the silencing of women's voices may be doubled: their suffering and its meanings does not belong to them, but first to their collective, and secondly to the enemy who are despoiling them as symbols of the male honour of their collective.

War rape made visible is thus always more than likely to be appropriated for the dominant stories, and framed for agendas, radically other than exposing and addressing sexual violence against women. In fact, it is in the logic of war rape that it must preferably be spectacular. In the context of war, women's sexuality, even more so than in other contexts, cannot be allowed to stand for itself, but is violently and systematically pressed into metaphorical service of the collective. War rape then becomes a prime example of where the rape weapon—penis, man's body, other weapons including penis substitutes—

> [a]s a perceptual [rather than a physical] fact, [...] lifts the pain out of the body and makes it visible or, more precisely, it acts as a bridge or mechanism across which some of pain's attributes— its incontestable reality, its totality, its ability to eclipse all else, its power of dramatic alteration and world dissolution—can be lifted away from their source, can be separated from the sufferer and referred to the power, broken off from the body and attached instead to the regime. (ibid.: 56)

This performance can only benefit from being rendered more visible, and to ever larger audiences.

(III) This brings us to the third risk factor involved in increasing the visibility of war rape. The visibility of women's sex- and gender-specific precarity in war may also function to reinforce the notion that women constitute 'the other of war' and also 'the other of politics'. By this I mean that such an emphasis in itself does nothing to disrupt or challenge the strongly gendered nature of both war and peace. It does nothing to disrupt the radically unjust gendered situation inside the collective in the first place, which sets the scene for both war and war rape, with all their destructive effects. An overly narrow attention to war rape may also contribute enormously to essentialising women's existence and embodiment in terms of sexual vulnerability—where both elements, sexuality and vulnerability, are highly problematic. The rendering of females as particularly fleshy and sexual is typical of a patriarchal and misogynist symbolic universe (see Battersby 1998: 9) and typical of the alterity that the lost boy needs to inflict on the Mother with whom he can no longer identify. Why, after all, should women alone carry the burden of being sexual creatures, being fleshy, being animal and being sexually specific, and moreover of being vulnerable in sexually specific ways? Male bodies are no less sexual, fleshy, animal, sexually specific and vulnerable in sexually specific ways. Yet, a particular overemphasis on female sexual function as vulnerability, tied closely into narratives of collective identity, as I have explained, underpins every war effort and nation-building project.

Several problems flow from these insights. As has been shown in various contexts, the hyper-visibility of war rape often detracts from women's other forms of suffering in war or armed conflict. They too lose loved ones, get starved, get wounded, lose limbs, must survive through the breakdown of public services, get tortured and interrogated, must try to care for and support other vulnerable persons, get looted, suffer starvation and additionally they suffer from increased sexual trafficking and other sexual attacks due to the chaos of war, often with long-term damage as a consequence. But apart from these dangers, such a strong emphasis on women's sexual vulnerability may also deny women's agency, courage, strength and decisions made during war. In fact, as I have said above, we typically not only portray war in strongly masculine, heroic terms, we also tend to exclusively memorialise war in terms of men's suffering and sacrifice.[10] In her fascinating work on the aftermath of the Peruvian civil war, Theidon shows clearly how the women claimed the title of war heroes, for instance for saving their men from imprisonment by granting sexual favours to their captors (Theidon 2007: 464ff). However, within the masculinised identity of the collectives after the war, and also in terms of the fundamental notion that women are not possessors of value (or agents of war) but only signifiers of value (and the 'other', the victims of war), it is symbolically impossible to publicly recognise these women as heroes who made huge personal sacrifices. The masculine self-image of the nation in the aftermath could not afford such an inclusion.

A further problem with an exclusive and narrow focus on sexual violence in armed conflict, perpetrated against women (and children) as the 'other of war,' is that the sexual violation of men gets either ignored and discounted altogether, or instead, it might get singled out from the background of 'routine,' 'normalised' sexual violation of the women, and get treated as particularly significant, detrimental and uniquely damaging, either to the individual victims or to the collective 'honour.' Knowledge and images of men's sexual violation may be repressed in order to protect the gendered meta-narrative in terms of which women's prized but vulnerable sexuality is the preferred symbol of collective identity which serves as a justification for the war. To acknowledge that men also get raped in war is to disrupt this narrative by highlighting the sexuality and vulnerability (and sexual vulnerability) of *all* bodies (Žarkov 2007). Or, alternatively, men's rape may be singled out as particularly damaging, against the background of the normally much more prevalent violation of female sexuality. Clearly, such a strategy also amounts to an injustice and feeds into the view of sexual violence against women as being somehow natural or routine. In the feminist project to both expose war rape and dismantle the symbolic framework which lends it its particular power and effect, and which makes it so prone to appropriation, we need to challenge a one-sided focus on the supposed sexual vulnerability of women, both in the run-up to, and in the aftermath of, war. Highlighting the plight of men who get raped in war may be an important element in the second important step, namely to challenge and change the symbolic framework in which women's sexual vulnerability plays such a central role. In this regard, the work of Lara Stemple (2009) is particularly insightful.

(IV) In the fourth and final place, I am concerned that the

new focus on, and attention to, war rape within feminist literature may detract from the necessary focus on peace time and domestic rape. In fact, I would contend that interrogating the distinction between war and peace from the perspective of women firstly, and from the perspective of rape victims secondly, what strikes one more than anything else is the remarkable durability of unjust gendered arrangements throughout war, transition and peace. It is the way in which the collective is masculinised and women consequently systematically stripped of political power by being portrayed as marginal, violence-less, voice-less and agency-less, which often leads to the hunger for war in the first place. Also, in the aftermath of armed conflict, sexual violence typically remains very high, as women once again get excluded from the re-constitution of the nation, even if Woman in her sexual (birthing) function is appropriated as metaphor for the male-dominated process of rebirthing the collective. Women as the other of war and framed mainly in terms of their sexual violation, are left out of practices of memorialisation and once again their voices and agency get erased. Viewed from the perspective of women, the sexual violence associated with war is not so much an exception as an intensification, a contraction in time and space, of a continuous theme always humming in the background.

Thus, in conclusion, feminist attempts to render war rape more visible must cautiously and rigorously engage with the following questions: what is the link between war and patriarchy—does masculine domination need war and military culture to sustain itself, does it need a sexually vulnerable-ised feminine other as a crucial aspect of its ideological justification? If yes, how can we render war rapes more visible, and more accurately visible, truer to the experiences of the victims themselves, yet at the same time resist the logic of patriarchal culture? How can we strategically use the international developments around war rape—such as we have seen in the International Criminal Tribunal for the former Yugoslavia (ICTY), and the International Criminal Tribunal for Rwanda (ICTR)—to undermine the very logic of just war itself. Why does rape in war draw so much moral attention while rape in peace time remains a trivial internal, 'merely social' matter for most states? Is it maybe because in war masculine collectives turn 'their' women and girls into a centre of gravity for the collective? In other words, does the world sit up and pay attention to war rape but not peace rape because the former but not the latter is an affront, a devastating blow to the sense of self of a masculine collective, because it so effectively destroys *male and thus collective honour*? Because in war rape it is *really*, in the final instance, the men who get raped symbolically, the masculine identity that is decisively dishonoured by being turned into the despised feminised social position? Is this the *real* harm that was punished in the ICTY and the ICTR? If not, how do we explain why war rape is so cautiously circumscribed within a certain war logic in order for it to be condemned unequivocally as a crime against humanity? Why else is there still an "ecology of incredulity" (Code 2009: 333) surrounding rape complaints in peace time, even as war rape gets severely condemned as a crime against humanity and punished accordingly?

NOTES

1. I use 'Man' to refer to the subject of the western symbolic order, and to the dominant speaking position within most cultural constructs. It is also the 'man' of patriarchy, and thus an idealised, finally impossible construct distorting the lived experiences of individual men.

2. Think of the famous passages in which Francis Bacon describes nature as a female being "forced to yield up her secrets" by the male scientist (Kittay 1988: 64) or where Socrates in *Theaetetus* describes his philosophical work as similar to the midwifery practised by his mother.

3. To clarify the relational aspect: Metaphor illuminates new aspects of reality, by mediating between two distinctive domains, "through a transference of semantic relations," which for Kittay (1988: 65) means that metaphor transfers the structural or logical "relations of contrast and affinity which pertain to the vehicle term on to the domain of the topic." Her example is when we describe a sportsperson's game as 'hot.' The established logical relation between heat and cold taken from the domain of temperature is

    thereby used to structure a less well-expressed or more complex domain, namely performance in sport.

4.   Again, Socrates' 'midwifery' is an excellent example of this. His practice he regards as similar, yet superior to that of his mother and all other mothers, in every respect.

5.   Recall De Beauvoir's idea that women are "the second sex" in large part because they are systematically excluded from taking up weapons, thus excluded from exerting violence.

6.   Hynes (2004) provides an overview of the harms of war to women. Ironically, although women and children and their (private, vulnerable) domain have always been construed as outside of war or only in its margins, by the 1990s, 90 per cent of all war casualties were civilians (Hynes 2004: 431). In both world wars of the twentieth century, more civilians than soldiers were killed, and in the Vietnam War, there was a ratio of 13 civilians for every one soldier killed (Seifert 1996: 38). So much for the heroic image of warfare.

7.   The images of Lynndie England's involvement in the sexual torture of Iraqi soldiers in Abu Ghraib prison are telling in this regard. In them, she enacts the stereotypically vulnerable feminine other of war who flaunts her sexuality in front of the sexually impotent and humiliated male enemy. By playfully and sadistically inverting the stereotypical roles, she reinforces war's gendered logic by staging the inability of the enemy soldier to assert his (proper) gender domination over her. She thus stands as a powerful reminder that the mere presence of women in the military does nothing to disrupt these tropes.

8.   Debra Bergoffen (2012: 12) similarly notes that the infamous Ram plan of the Bosnian-Serb command mentions that women and children should be attacked, not because they were considered the most vulnerable members of the community, but rather because "the community's most vulnerable point was its women," which attests to the symbolic function that women's sexuality fulfils within most collectives.

9.   Karen Engle (2005: 812) argues that we should look more closely at women's presumed passivity in, and exclusion from, war, because by presuming that women are without agency, feminist scholars may actually contribute to stripping women of many powers that they do in fact have, "including the power to resolve or prevent conflict." Elsewhere, Laura Sjoberg (2011: 21ff) focuses on the role

of some women in the genocidal rape of women, also arguing that we should develop better feminist tools of analysis to account for women's sexual and wartime violence. My main point here is not to claim that women are completely powerless in war situations, but to draw attention to how women's bodies come to symbolise nationhood in war, largely due to women's exclusion from war and political power, with various implications for women's experiences of war, in particular war rape.

10. One possibly notable exception is the 'Women's Monument' in Bloemfontein, South Africa, which commemorates the 26,000+ women and children who died in British concentration camps during the Anglo-Boer War in South Africa—which became the prime site of memorialisation of this war in South Africa (Snyman 1999).

REFERENCES

Battersby, Christine. 1998. *The Phenomenal Woman: Feminist Metaphysics and the Patterns of Identity*. Cambridge: Polity Press.

Bergoffen, Debra. 2012. *Contesting the Politics of Genocidal Rape: Affirming the Dignity of the Vulnerable Body*. New York: Routledge.

Brison, Susan J. 2002. *Aftermath: Violence and the Remaking of a Self*. Princeton: Princeton University Press.

Buss, Doris. 2014. 'The Limits of Visibility', in Doris Buss/Joanne Lebert/Blair Rutherford/Donna Sharkey/Obijiofor Aginam (eds), *Sexual Violence in Conflict and Post-Conflict Societies: International Agendas and African Contexts*, pp. 3–27. New York: Routledge.

————. 2009. 'Rethinking "Rape as a Weapon of War"', *Feminist Legal Studies*, 17(2):145–63.

————. 2007. 'The Curious Visibility of Wartime Rape: Gender and Ethnicity in International Criminal Law', *Windsor Year Book of Access to Justice*, 25(1): 3–22.

Chodorow, Nancy. 1978. *The Reproduction of Mothering*. Oakland: University of California Press.

Code, Lorraine. 2009. 'A New Epistemology of Rape?' *Philosophical Papers*, 38(3):327–45.

Engle, Karen. 2005. 'Feminism and Its (Dis)Contents: Criminalizing Wartime Rape in Bosnia and Herzegovina', *The American Journal of International Law*, 99(4):778–816.

Hynes, H. Patricia. 2004. 'On the Battlefield of Women's Bodies: An Overview of the Harm of War to Women', *Women's Studies International Forum*, 27(5–6):431–45.

Kittay, Eva Feder. 1988. 'Woman as Metaphor', *Hypatia: A Journal of Feminist Philosophy*, 3(2):63–86.

Lyotard, Jean-François. 1989. 'One of the Things at Stake in Women's Struggles', in Andrew Benjamin (ed), *The Lyotard Reader*, pp. 111–21. Oxford: Basil Blackwell.

Scarry, Elaine. 1985. *The Body in Pain: The Making and Unmaking of the World*. Oxford: Oxford University Press.

Seifert, Ruth. 1996. 'The Second Front: The Logic of Sexual Violence in Wars', *Women's Studies International Forum*, 19(1–2):35–43.

Sjoberg, Laura. 2013. *Gendering Global Conflict: Toward a Feminist Theory of War*. New York: Columbia University Press.

————. 2011. 'Women and the Genocidal Rape of Women: The Gender Dynamics of Gendered War Crimes', in Debra Bergoffen/ Paula Ruth Gilbert/Tamara Harvey/Connie L. McNeely (eds), *Confronting Global Gender Justice: Women's Lives, Human Rights*, pp. 21–34. New York: Routledge.

Snyman, Johan. 1999. 'Die politiek van herinnering: spore van trauma', *Literator*, 20(3):9–33.

Stemple, Lara. 2009. 'Male Rape and Human Rights', *Hastings Law Journal*, 60(3):605–47.

Theidon, Kimberly. 2007. 'Gender in Transition: Common Sense, Women, and War', *Journal of Human Rights*, 6(4):453–78.

Whitford, Margaret. 1991. *Luce Irigaray: Philosophy in the Feminine*. New York: Routledge.

Žarkov, Dubravka. 2007. *The Body of War: Media, Ethnicity and Gender in the Break-Up of Yugoslavia*. Durham: Duke University Press.

Can Masculinity Survive the End of Sexualised Violence?

RENÉE HEBERLE

Sexual violence is embedded in uneven ways in gender identity and sexuality; it is constitutive of masculine and feminine existence, a part of who we come to be in the world as those particular kinds of gendered subjects. Most importantly, for purposes of my arguments in this essay, it is a common means of constituting, enforcing and defending the boundaries of masculinity and femininity within any given context, whether that context is war, prison, the home, educational institutions, the workplace or everyday life on the street. We know it well. On the surface, we appear to have sexual violence sorted out as we study it, moralise about it and criminalise it. Simultaneously, we do not report it, recognise it or understand it in any consistent or rationalised way; we may well imagine a world free of it, but we have no experience of what that might look like (Alcorn 2014).[1] It is not a rational activity as it happens, but it is highly rationalised in the sense of being a clear and present threat throughout our institutional and collective lives.[2]

What would masculinity (and femininity) look like if sexual violence were eliminated? Or, to flip the question, would sexual violence exist if we abolished masculinity (and femininity)?[3] Either way, gender in this form would, I think, undergo significant transformations; we simply do not know what that world would look like. If we read feminist science fiction, for example, Margaret Atwood's *A Handmaid's Tale* (1986) and Marge Piercy's *Woman on the Edge of Time* (1976) we can imagine what it might look like if gender, with masculinity on top, tightens or loosens its grip, but we cannot really know in advance.

In the context of war fighting, the specific topic of this volume and this essay, an additional question is whether the nation-state, or political sovereignty more generally, founded as it has been on acts of sexual and sexualised violence, can survive the end of sexual violence? Sexual violence is experienced and narrated as part of the mythologies and legends and histories of foundings throughout Western history (Matthes 2000). From the kidnapping of Helen to the Rape of the Sabine women to the fears of all sexual/racialised otherness experienced by European men as European nation-states emerged, sexual violence has launched and sustained wars of sovereign assertion and colonisation. It informs, rhetorically and practically, theories of founding in Machiavelli,[4] and resistance against colonisation and wars of independence in Frantz Fanon. The figure of the feminine, with two sides of her coin, her vulnerability and object status, and her threatening wiles and agentic capacity to manipulate men, haunts sovereignty in its many guises; sexual brutality is a significant aspect, symbolic and real, cultural and physical, of founding and building nations—whether it is significant in building other forms of specifically political communities, is a good question. However, the modern nation-state remains the primary (if waning) form of collective political sovereignty that we live with in modernity. Given the significance of sexual violence in the context of the successful foundings of nation-states, it is ironic that it is only in the context of failed, post-colonial, nation-states in the late twentieth century that sexual violence came to attention as a problem to be solved, identified as an illegitimate weapon of war, rather than assumed as a legitimate means to the ends of asserting masculinist sovereign power. The civil wars in Yugoslavia and Rwanda are the contexts that forced the issue to global attention and the International Criminal Tribunal for the Former Yugoslavia and the International Criminal Tribunal for Rwanda to adjudicate sexual violence as a war crime rather than ignore it as collateral damage.

Post-colonial wars,[5] new forms of war fighting, are organised around identity and the radical redrawing of borders rather than interstate conflict (Kaldor 1999), but sexual violence remains embedded in the logic of sovereignty as such. Sovereign assertions of legitimate forms of power, masculinity and sexual violence are entangled in the context of what Kaldor defines as old and new wars.[6] While the idea of 'new wars' has been contentious, it is nevertheless important for understanding the value of sexual violence to contemporary wars (Meger 2011). Feminists have analysed how sexual violence is weaponised and argued it should be adjudicated specifically as an international war crime in the post-Cold War era; gender violence and rape appear to be less like collateral damage and more like strategies invested in the actual winning of identity-based wars. However, the old dynamics of masculinist defences against and sovereign assertions over the feminine, in its many diverse guises, are perpetuated. Recent work has carefully and critically examined discursive constructions of 'rape as a weapon of war' for how they reduce complexity in the interest of creating workable and measurable policy responses (Baaz/Stern 2013). However, I would argue we should also look at the ways sexual violence is imbricated in political priorities and prerogatives formed through and by masculinist power in these 'new' kinds of wars.

How should feminists best frame the questions faced in advocating for and against various policies and practices with respect to sexual violence in the 'new' armed conflicts? Feminist theory as a global intellectual movement has, over the last twenty years, argued that gender as such is not the effect of essential differences between male and female figures. It has taken up and moved beyond Gayle Rubin's famous argument (1975) about how otherwise polymorphous sexed identities become distinguished as man and woman through systems of kinship and exchange. This sex/gender system is not the same everywhere, but it exists in some form everywhere. Gender formations emerge historically, they are not natural or pre-social self-understandings. Since the 1970s, debates about the historically indeterminate form of the sex/gender system, the deeply problematic demand/search for unity among 'women,' (Mohanty 1991), and theorizing that follows upon Judith Butler's thesis about the performativity of gender as habit rather than identity (1990), have informed feminism more broadly. Radical proposals as to the performative doing and undoing of heteronormative gender criticise liberal arguments to adjust men and women as such to demands for 'equal' treatment within systems already defined by masculinist prerogatives (Lorber 2000).

Empirical research and policy-making about sexual violence has not taken up these important developments in feminist and queer thought and practice, sometimes identified as the 'performative turn' or more generally with poststructuralism (Heberle/Grace 2009). That work remains grounded in the assumption that systems must be put into place to make men stop committing sexual(ized) violence against women and punish men when they do commit such violence. Thus, the problem is defined in terms of what men do, not in terms of how sexual violence informs what masculinity becomes, what it is, and what it does. This essay argues that we must consider insights of three decades of feminist and queer theory that could show us how and when masculinity and sexual violence are mutually constitutive enactments. Not all men commit sexual violence, and some women do commit sexual violence. Hence, we need to address masculinity as a social formation. Our question is not whether men or women as such are more prone or more vulnerable. We know the answer to that. Our question is: what kind of radical transformations are necessary in masculinity and thus in femininity to eliminate sexual violence. What kind of 'sacrifice' does masculinity face if we are to live in a world free of sexual violence?

As every scholar of feminism, human rights and sexual violence will attest, international attention to sexual violence in war has increased exponentially in the last thirty years. The opportunities and challenges presented by shifts in international law are being parsed in terms of policy and legal approaches (Lemaitre/Sandvik 2014; Henry 2014; Meger 2011; Oosterveld 2009; Leatherman 2009), but also in terms of the discursive effects on gender and race identity (Philipose 2009). Scholars are also working out when and where rape might become more or less likely given different conditions of conflict (Cohen 2013). Few explicitly adopt the argument I suggest here as a point of departure, that sexual violence is an effect of identities performed as masculine and feminine that exist in complicated relationships of power and hierarchies of dominance. It does not happen only because wars are being fought, it happens because masculinity, as associated with sovereignty and the prerogatives of personhood, is at stake. As a weapon of war, sexual violence takes on different meanings and significance in different times and places, but remains present and apparently intractable when and where masculinity and femininity are assumed to be necessary to make claims to sovereignty and to legitimate personhood.

As noted above, the contemporary forms of sexual violence in armed conflict to which the international community has been paying attention appear not as originating moments of founding, nor as conquest over racialised others as colonial-settler violence. The international community is paying attention to sexual violence as a weapon of wars organised around the elimination of, rather than the control of, otherness (Cohen 2013). Sexualized violence, understood specifically as a weapon of war, rather than as a reason to start a war or as 'collateral damage,' is more likely when ethnic or racial supremacy is at stake (Chinkin/Kaldor 2013). This means sexual violence in armed conflict is not only enacted as a gendered dynamic, but is embedded in ethnic and racialised nationalist identities that perpetuate fear-based distinctions and mutual hostility among peoples.

As we look at the more particular cases of sexual violence in armed conflict, however, it is important to remember, that it is not discontinuous with the presence of the possibility of sexual violence in everyday life. This is not to discount the important insights offered by Meger (2011), among others, who show how exogenous factors influence breakdowns in institutional and economic orders; the subsequent wars over material resources create conditions for increased sexual cruelty and violence to be enacted in the interest of asserting dominance. The evisceration of institutionalised or traditional political and economic orders creates conditions for an increase in sexualised cruelty and intimate forms of violence as, in some sense, weaponised sources of dominance and control. However, it does not cause sexual violence and is not a necessary condition. Sexual violence should be understood as a gendered and gendering dynamic and a kind of action that is structurally and strategically weaponised in particular ways in war; it should not be naturalised as a result of general disorder. Sexual violence is linked to threat and anxiety over resource control and the defence of identity and dominance, and it is always also, ultimately, about sustaining the 'normal' gendered order of things across those divides.

The feminist theoretical project of deconstructing gender seems tangential and even frivolous when juxtaposed with the sense of emergency surrounding sexual violence in armed conflict and elsewhere in everyday life. It appears, perhaps, as impractical. However, performative theories of gender, juxtaposed against those inquiries that assume the universal and morally undifferentiated meaning of sexual violence, have generated insight into how the very practical 'solutions,' whether channelled through medical or legal routes, reproduce the very gender norms that make sexual violence possible in the first place. We should take seriously the significance of post-colonial and transnational feminist critiques of the tendency specific to the West to constitute 'women and children' as those who must be saved from men, who are primarily black and brown (Philipose 2009; Grewal/Kaplan 1994). Other critics question whether the attention to 'women and children' as those who must be saved as victims of sexualised forms of oppression and harm, and not as impoverished or marginalised, but no less agential, persons, obscures the context in which sexual violence is perpetrated and sets out a kind of hierarchy of the suffering that matters in international discourse (Lemaitre/Sandvik 2014). In paying attention to these critiques, interrogating the possibilities for undoing gender, in the varied traditional forms it adopts across cultures, in relationship to eliminating sexual violence, might seem more to the point.

Further, as Sjoberg (2015) has elaborated, women are capable of horrifying acts of genocidal and war-inspired acts of sexual violence. She tells us that women's violence has been obscured because of the framing of sexual violence as something 'men' do to 'women;' sexual violence is not only being committed by men against women (and children). Some women have themselves been perpetrators and/or been complicit in generating and perpetuating the violence. Sjoberg makes clear that this does not challenge the presumption of the masculine and feminine figuration of violence and victimisation. It appears from her work, that the violence women commit does the work of masculinist dominance; it is emasculating in its enactment and has the effect of feminising victims (whether male or female). Women who commit violence such as this are sensationalised in representation precisely because they are violating the terms on which female/woman and the feminine are supposed to map onto one another. Sjoberg rightly argues that the sensationalist coverage of women who commit sexualised violence in combat or genocidal warfare reproduces essentialist and inadequate understandings of how and why that violence occurs and is perpetuated. Her analysis supports the thesis that constructions of masculinity and femininity are implicated in how and why sexual violence is possible in the first place.

The women described in her book are represented as 'monsters,' as impossible figures, precisely because they do not fit within the essentialist models of that which women and men as such are supposed to be capable. However, she does not argue that they are outside the mould of masculinist framing of how sexual violence, power and dominance are intrinsically linked and mutually reinforcing. Sjoberg argues that the deeply ingrained habit of rendering women who commit political or sexual violence as monstrous, as beyond the pale of humanness, or as threatening in some particularly abhorrent way, reproduces misconceptions about the dynamics that cultivate conditions in which this kind of violence becomes possible. Though organised and inflicted by women, the violence as such is recognisable in its assertion of masculinist forms of prerogative. For Sjoberg, the sexualised nature of the violence committed by these women embeds the significance of their cruelty in the dyadic structure of gendered existence. They are not undoing masculinity in enacting this kind of harm against others. Nor are the juridical and political responses; in asserting the monstrosity of the women perpetrators, they reproduce the normalcy of the male empowered by masculinist forms of violence while the female remains subordinate as the feminine figure.

However, it is the case, in some sense, that these women are 'monstrous' and in their monstrosity, in a vicious manner, do their part in undoing the otherwise presumptive association between biological maleness and violence. Rather than accuse the women as gendered anomalies, as other than human, in adjudicating their actions we might come to see more clearly that biology is not destiny and that it is masculinity and masculinist imperatives that take on many monstrous forms, even in the female body.

Asserting dominant identities other than gender, that is ethnic, racial or class, is often the explicit purpose of war; sexual violence is ubiquitous as a weapon in all these kinds of war, whether between nation-states, between colonisers and the colonised or intra-state civil conflicts over resources. But what kind of weapon is it? In colonial and post-colonial wars, racialised sexual violence becomes a weapon of masculinity that is simultaneously defensive and offensive, unlike any other. Consider, the shield is defensive, the sword is offensive; the bomb is offensive, the shelter is defensive; the gas is offensive, the mask is defensive; the block is defensive, the shot is offensive—never can one be the same for both. Yet acts of sexual violence serve both purposes at once. When Europeans colonised the territories of what is now the United States, the rape and sexual cruelty against the women and men who already lived there was clearly a means by which to assimilate and/or eliminate the otherness of Native Americans. War rape was common in the Mexican-American war, specifically as a weapon of conquest; that war was primarily or first and foremost about gaining the southwest territory, not necessarily about fundamentally changing or eliminating Mexicanness (Smith 2005). Both wars were about Europeans forcing indigenous peoples into more barren and constrained territories; both were also about European masculinist identity and sexual brutality against native women and men as a means to shore up that identity, simultaneously offensive in destroying the other and defensive in shoring up the terms of self-understanding on the part of European masculinity. Furthermore, the fear engendered among European women with myths about rapacious natives served to identify white male masculinity with protective and therefore dominant status.

After slavery was formally ended in the United States as an institutional and legal relationship of production, white supremacists sexually brutalised Black women and men in order to undo the threat freed Black people were presumed to pose. Black males could only be powerful if they were Black 'men' and one cannot be a man in that context if 'your women' are taken by force by others. The so-called Indian wars and the even more one-sided race war after the Civil War were as much wars of identity wherein the racialised masculinity of the European/white man was at stake as they were wars about land. Frantz Fanon (2004) and George Jackson (1970) rhetorically reversed the terms of this kind of colonial domination through deploying images of rape and violence against white and European women in the name of undoing the emasculation implied by European and white male rape of African and Black women. We should note that while Black men have raped white women or expected white women to have sex with them as a form of compensation, accusations of rape have been manifested against Black men primarily as a means of terrorizing all African Americans since the end of the Civil War. (Broussard 2013)

In all of these cases, what we might call racialised masculinity, those identifications that define one's capacity for dominance, is asserted on the bodies of all kinds of women and men. Europeanness and whiteness have and continue to be normative and thereby dominant. But racialised masculinity continues to be at stake across the board and can be defended and defined only through the dominance over and control of the bodies of others rendered feminine by means of sexualised violence.

Why is this the case and how might we think about the kinds of wars now being fought to see whether the connections between sovereign assertion, masculinity and sexual violence are fraying or tightening? What follows are some suggested responses to this question.

The feminine has generally, but not everywhere at all times—

and in uneven ways—been experienced as and perceived to be dangerous to masculinity and maleness. Peggy Reeves Sanday's ground-breaking research showed that where gender identity is more rigid, societies are more rape prone (1981). Masculinity and femininity are always only defined in relationship to one another; where gender identity is more rigid, masculinity has more successfully dominated and controlled the perceived 'otherness' of femininity. When nations, peoples, groups and identities are at war, as Janie Leatherman's (2011) work shows, the relationship between men and their environment breaks down and what appeared as passive sexual dominance (with actual violence being veiled in the 'private' spaces of normal life) becomes active and publicly avowed sexual violence. If the feminine is an essential and existential threat to masculinity, when war begins, destroying the women, girls, boys and any non-combatants identified with the feminine or non-masculine, will be associated with destroying the cultural identity of the enemy. Those figures affirmed the identity of the men who are losing the war and their destruction now serves the purpose of the would-be victors. It is not just about conditions of permissiveness for cruelty, sadism or lust, or about attaining individual dominance, though it is about all of that—it is not specifically or even primarily about the dehumanizing or the suffering of the person harmed. It is a means to the ends of never quite secured racial and sexual dominance. Sexual violence will not end as long as masculinity is defined as it is today. Sexual violence will not be eliminated in wars of identity as long as masculinity and femininity are culturally coded in terms of dominance and submission (Pateman 1988) nor as long as masculinity requires defensive mechanisms to continue to be experienced as 'real' (Heberle/Grace 2009).[7]

Sexual violence in armed conflict is carried out through cruelty and abuse, not always death, because the other must see, live with, tolerate, reject or kill—but never again love or recognise or accept—what has been destroyed, creating the living death desired for them by the aggressor. Elaine Scarry (1985) reminds us that the point of war is to injure and kill; when sexual brutality is a precursor to or a part of that killing, it may be a means to humiliate or weaken the enemy because, again, the identity of the enemy and their fighting strength is linked to the feminised non-combatants. If the feminine figure survives the violence, she is forever a sign of the failure of the conquered masculine figure—to protect, to control or to own.

Emasculation through sexual brutality and cruelty is culturally coded to be as devastating as any other kind of conquering strategy. This is what is happening when sexual brutality is a weapon of war. When women are raped or sexually brutalised, their figurative and cultural femininity is simultaneously affirmed and destroyed. They are left to suffer as women. When men are rendered helpless and see this happen or know it is happening, or are raped or sexually brutalised themselves, their figurative and cultural masculinity is destroyed, they are left to suffer as something other than and less than men. When I say figurative and/or cultural, I am not suggesting these harms, this destruction, are any less personal, physical, individualised, intimate, self-destroying or damaging. The masculine is emasculated, 'men' are undone as men, or feminised, while the feminine is left to suffer as such, to (continue to) suffer as 'women.'

But if we were to do away with, or erode, or weaken, the figurative and cultural presence of masculinity and femininity in general, could we lessen the potential for harm done? If we give the world less to hold onto in masculinity and femininity—taking gender as we know it apart—will that defuse sexual violence in armed conflict? I don't think we can prevent it in identity-centred wars otherwise.

This would take work far beyond the kind of very specific and necessary work done on the ground in battlefields and in the aftermath of new civil and genocidal wars. But I would suggest that work must be critically considered in light of whether it reiterates gender norms that create conditions for sexual brutality. The discourse that centres around the protection and support for victims and what I call the 'litany of suffering' strategy, wherein story after graphic story or description is deployed with the intent of shocking the listener into caring about the issue, may result in making masculinist power appear monolithic and undoable (Heberle 1996). Quantitative approaches may result in similar outcomes. Sexual violence in armed conflict is hard to identify and measure, but success in identifying and measuring it will not necessarily lead to undermining its likelihood. It may result in more proficient management of the problem, to more protectionist policies and punitive responses, none of which should be discounted, but none of which should be assumed to deter or prevent sexualised forms of violence.

Criminalisation focuses us on outcomes. The final paragraph of an incredibly informative and helpful page on the *Women in Media, Women Under Siege* (Bates 2012) project website concludes with a paragraph about impunity. This is important, but criminalizing sexualised cruelty, rape, murder, in conflict zones or in homes, is not going to end sexualised violence. It is too embedded as a way of life and as a means by which identities are formed and sustained; the extent to which law can impact identity formations is questionable. I am making a counter-intuitive claim here. We might take as an example the necessary shift in sovereign strategies that occurred as property was privatised in England in the seventeenth and eighteenth centuries. This may seem a stretch, but I think that the privatisation of property, the fundamental requirement of capitalist development, is no more nor less significant a shift in normative sensibilities about identity than that which would be required to eliminate sexual violence as a possibility. When stealing was criminalised in England, site of the earliest developments in capitalist social relations, the state created extraordinary punishments, mostly capital, for what now seem to be petty acts—of need or of spite, such as hunting on royal property or stealing in the marketplace. This caused a vast change in culture as property was violently privatised. The penalties were not implemented in full force so much as they were symbolically wielded to indicate the importance of privatisation, the enclosure laws and on what side the sovereign would place its use of force (Hay 1975).

As modernity has 'progressed' to the point that private property is considered a natural right and undoable as a normative frame for economic distribution, the number and severity of relevant laws decreased dramatically. While the terms on which sexual violence has been identified, adjudicated and punished vary widely across time and space and circumstance, it is safe to say that sovereign power, linked as it is to masculinist hegemony, has not taken anything like the drastically violent steps taken to assure the introduction of private property to Western, and then colonial, territories. In fact, statutory punishments for rape were more severe, if not consistently applied, when white women were legally identified as property and assumed to be under the protection of men as wives, sisters, daughters or mothers (Pleck 1987). There were rarely statutory or community sanctions for sexual violence against women of colour, whether formally held as property or 'free'. The contemporary legal contexts in which women are assumed to be autonomous and personally responsible for their wellbeing, punishments are even less certain and typically, depending upon the racial and ethnic identity of the accused, less severe (Haag 1999).

What about preventive resolutions and treaties? The Geneva Conventions assume violence in its 'necessary' forms will continue because power struggles for dominance and control over peoples, territory and resources are presumably inevitable. The West has been trying to clean up wars fought on battlefields between nation-states in the seventeenth through the twentieth century by creating rules and norms that identify permissible forms of violence and control the excesses of the victor in claiming the spoils. The international community attempts to clean up war-fighting to mitigate destruction. The inclusion of 'gender crimes' as crimes against humanity in the Rome Statute of 1998 governing the International Criminal Court is understood to be a significant breakthrough. However, the terms of modernity work against these state-centred, juridical efforts. The social, cultural, the economic and the moral increasingly dilute political and juridical spaces. Thinkers such as Carl Schmitt (2007), Hannah Arendt (1969) and, ultimately, Michel Foucault (2003), show why modern conflicts over territory and resources will, therefore, include all kinds of violence that move far beyond the traditional battlefield. The battlefield is less clear now than ever and the resources of sovereign states as such are becoming less significant than the cultural, social and economic resources brought to bear in conflict.

In fact, war could be said to be at its 'cleanest,' in a sense, not because of treaties and agreements among nations, but during the 'Cold War.' In the nuclear age, direct violence between the primary antagonists was threatened, not realised; the doctrine of mutually assured destruction did its work, keeping the war between the United States and the Soviet Union 'cold' or 'clean.'[8] And now, some forms of warfare are 'cleaner' of collateral or extra-legal tactics, at least for the highly developed, wealthy side in conflicts, when fought with drone warfare and 'smart bombs.' In fact, changing technologies of war fighting may do more to undermine the assertions of masculinist prerogatives through war fighting and to undo gendered assumptions about it, than treaties or agreements accomplish through the recognition and/ or punishment of sexual violence as something men do to women. Ending sexual violence as a weapon of war may be facilitated by drone warfare, for example. Practices of war fighting are themselves gendered (as is obvious from the prevalence of sexual violence but also clear from the associations with masculinity of the willingness to risk one's life during the activity of killing). Drones thus constitute a stereotypically feminised form of warfare, acting from a distance and unseen by the target. They do not fulfil any clear mission with respect to traditional ways combatants are masculinised. A Black man (hyper-sexualised and a generalised threat to the sexual identity of white men who persistently emasculated Black men through sexualised torture and lynching) ran the drone programme out of the White House in the United States for eight years and women are deploying drones as weapons from computers in offices as commonly as men. Given these developments we might ask whether masculinity as we know it will survive the end of boots on the ground warfare in the West. New technologies may signify an undoing of the terms on which sexual violence has value as such in the dynamics of winning and losing.

Further, while women and men in state sanctioned armed forces are subjected to heightened sexualised threats by their fellow soldiers and commanders, as the actual material process of war fighting shifts, we may see less sexual violence at all levels. As long as the material practices of war fighting are complicated by identity norms and values associated with hegemonic masculinity, sexual violence will persist. If it is true, or somewhat the case, that historically, sexual violence and cruelty has been a cause of wars of vengeance and a collateral effect of war, while more recently getting notice as a weapon of war, then in some wars, enforcement and defence measures for and of masculinity in everyday life have melded into one with war. In increasingly high-tech wars, the effort to reduce collateral damage (ostensibly), to clean up war, may constitute a feminizing trajectory, shifting the gendered stakes and reducing the likelihood of sexual violence as a weapon of war.

As we assess these shifts, however, we have to keep in mind that sexual violence as a weapon of war and sexual violence and cruelty as a weapon in everyday life are linked in complicated ways. The latter precedes the former as persistent possibility and means by which gender and sexual identity is enforced and defended. In wars of different kinds for different purposes, it will be used to enforce and defend ethnicity, class status (in revolutionary intrastate wars) and hierarchical differences in general. This will be layered on the assumed gendered and sexed predominance of men in everyday life who believe they are entitled to use others' bodies as means to their own ends.

Ending the symbolic value and consequent material gains from sexual cruelty means shifting the discursive framing of sexual violence and cruelty. If the frame remains that women, men and children as non-combatants require particular forms of protection and/or particular forms of justice and reparation in the aftermath of conflict, it sustains the assumption that there is something fundamental won and something lost in deploying sexual cruelty. With the undoing of gender identity as constitutive of who one is, perhaps there would be less at stake and sexual violence would not be wielded as a weapon.

Perpetrators of sexual cruelty in wars of identity want to destroy, not to claim. When sex is used as a weapon of war it is not about conquering to rule the other as they are, it is about destroying the other so it does not exist as it did, as noted above, it is simultaneously offensive and defensive. Everything is up for destruction and if destruction is the goal any heinous means will do. We need not debate whether rape and sexualised torture is the 'worst thing that can happen' to a person to assert that culturally it takes on a significance beyond that of property damage and even loss of life. Because it is different than other kinds of brutality in warfare, because it deploys masculinity in a particular way in relation to whatever, in any given context, is understood as the feminine or holding the potential to be feminised, we must pay attention to the terms on which masculinity asserts itself and enacts its prerogatives if we are to live in a world wherein sexualised violence is no longer possible. Masculinity must become a target of political critique and action, not men or war or victimisation, but masculinity as such. If we do not undo masculinity, and by extension, femininity, we will continue to manage, not eliminate, sexualised violence in armed conflict, in the streets or in the home.

Fighting on identity or moral grounds logically requires total war. Total wars and the genocidal wars that leave no 'other' untouched are what we are seeing when rape is deployed as a weapon of war. Rape as a weapon of war is now recognised anew in that it is now embedded as a strategy of the ongoing project of dominance, not merely as a tactic of conquest. Rape as a weapon of war is a strategy of wars of attrition. It is not only strangers who inflict sexual brutality in armed conflict. Those on whom they inflict sexual cruelty might know the perpetrators, but they do it as a group against a group that has been identified not just as an enemy in the Schmittian sense but, as an evil other who should not continue to live as they did. Sexual brutality as a weapon of war is not a particular individual acting against a particular individual (if sexual violence can ever be said to be that). Sexual violence as a weapon of war is a public act with privatised consequences as it leaves profoundly damaged selves in its wake.

The scholarship on sexual violence in armed conflict focuses our attention on issues of 'seeing' and 'recognizing' sexual violence for what it is in the panoply of conflicts in which it is deployed. Recognition is crucial to rendering the prevention of and adjudication of sexual violence central to rather than a peripheral or 'collateral' issue of war and peace-making. Representation matters, it is not secondary to policy or justice, but intrinsically bound to problems of policy and justice. Masculinity thrives in the context of practices and representation that sustain its prerogative as a perpetrator of violence in relation to that which is feminised and vulnerable. Sexual violence is not caused by being male or by being a man, but it is wrapped tightly in dynamics that constitute masculinity and femininity as identity formations. We should continue to ask whether and how masculinity and femininity depend upon sexual violence as a condition for their intelligibility or existence. There is good reason to bring together feminist theory focused on undoing gender as such with the struggles against sexual violence. Eliminating sexual violence may require the abolition of gender. Practical and discursive political movements to combat sexual violence need to be critically assessed as to whether they ultimately liberate us from gender constraints or reiterate the norms that keep us trapped.

NOTES

1. Ted Alcorn (2014) says we cannot develop policy around that which we cannot measure and goes on to say that identifying and measuring sexual violence in war is among the most difficult of policy tasks. It must be done in very localised ways attuned to very particular contexts wherein definitional issues, cultural difference and fundamental fear combine to render sexualised harms difficult to name, interpret or adjudicate.

2. Definitions of and prohibitions against gendered and sexualised violence, rape and sexual harassment are now commonly present in law and policy apparatuses across national and international institutions. Max Weber's understanding of 'rationalisation', that process that institutionalises and standardises otherwise particularised or unevenly distributed or enacted responses to social issues and problems, can be applied in thinking about sexual violence. This means that while sexual violence is not being eradicated, or even reduced in prevalence, it is being managed and adjudicated at national and international levels of engagement. The discursive constructions of sexual violence with reference to

war, education, cultural habits, crime and familial relations render it a more clearly, publicly defined, threat, warranting heightened securitisation and protectionist discourses.

3. I place femininity as the parenthetical here in relation to masculinity as it is the 'second' or derivative formation in the context of the dualism and in the context of the various forms of sexual violence.

4. Chapters 25 and 26 of Niccolo Machiavelli's *The Prince* (1541) are infamous for their graphic references to 'fortuna' as a feminine figure who must be beaten even while she is respected as otherwise outside of man's control over his destiny as politically sovereign.

5. I use the term post-colonial wars because much of the war fighting that has broken out since the end of the Cold War (and with the reduction in associated proxy wars) are in post-colonial, post-imperial regions. To refer to 'civil wars' in places like Iraq, Syria, the Sudan or Nigeria, to list just a few examples, is to let colonial history off the hook for creating conditions where conflict over sovereignty and resources was more likely. These conflicts are traceable to arbitrary colonial borderlines and not attributable specifically to Cold War ideological spheres of interest or purely civil disorders.

6. See Chinkin/Kaldor 2013 for a helpful descriptive analysis of the distinctions they draw between old and new wars.

7. In 'Rethinking the Social Contract: Masochism and Masculinist Violence' (Heberle/Grace 2009) I argue that if we take seriously that masculinity is a cultural construct, an iterative set of performative habits and not an essential expression of natural attributes, we might see that sexual violence is more like a defence mechanism in the face of feminised threats against an incoherently organised, decentred self, vulnerable like any other self to the fracturing and fragmenting forces of modernity. Masculinity requires sexual violence to assert itself as 'real,' whether that 'real' masculine self is perpetrating or protecting against sexual violence.

8. This, of course, did not mitigate the physical violence carried out through proxy wars. Liberalism, communism, capitalism and, of course, the less ideological imperial demands for resources, were fought over in very dirty wars made possible by the superpowers whose violence against one another was obviously limited by the threat of self-annihilation in taking any offensive measures.

REFERENCES

Alcorn, Ted. 2014. 'Responding to Sexual Violence in Armed Conflict', *Lancet Online*, 9 June. https://www.thelancet.com/journals/lancet/article/PIIS0140-6736(14)60970-3/fulltext (accessed 5 July 2018).

Arendt, Hannah. 1969. *On Violence*. Boston: Harvest Books.

Atwood, Margaret. 1986. *The Handmaid's Tale*. Boston: Houghton Mifflin.

Baaz, Maria Ericson/Stern, Maria. 2013. *Sexual Violence as a Weapon of War? Perceptions, Prescriptions, Problems in the Congo and Beyond*. London: Zed Books.

Bates, Laura. 2012. 'What are the Solutions to Wartime Rape?' *WMC Women Under Siege*, 2 July. http://www.womensmediacenter.com/women-under-siege/what-are-the-solutions-to-wartime-rape (accessed 16 October 2018).

Broussard, Patricia A. 2013. 'Black Women's Post-Slavery Silence Syndrome: A Twenty-First Century Remnant of Slavery, Jim Crow, and Systemic Racism—Who Will Tell Her Stories?' *Gender, Race and Justice*, 16(2):373–421.

Butler, Judith. 1990. *Gender Trouble: Feminism and the Subversion of Identity*. New York: Routledge.

Chinkin, Christine/Kaldor, Mary. 2013. 'Gender and New Wars', *Journal of International Affairs*, 67(1):167–87.

Cohen, Dara Kay. 2013. 'Explaining Rape during Civil War: Cross-National Evidence (1980–2009)', *American Political Science Review*, 107(3):461–77.

Fanon, Frantz. 2004. *The Wretched of the Earth*. New York: Grove Press.

Foucault, Michel. 2003. *Society Must be Defended: Lectures at the College de France 1975–1976*. New York: Picador.

Grewal, Inderpal/Kaplan, Caren 1994. *Scattered Hegemonies: Postmodernity and Transnational Feminist Practices*. Minneapolis: University of Minnesota Press.

Haag, Pamela. 1999. *Consent: Sexual Rights and the Transformation of American Liberalism*. Ithaca: Cornell University Press.

Hay, Douglas. 1975. 'Property, Authority, and the Criminal Law' in Douglas Hay/Peter Linebaugh/John Rule/E. P. Thompson/Calvin Winslow (eds), *Albion's Fatal Tree: Crime and Society in 18th Century England*, pp. 17–49. New York: Pantheon Books.

Heberle, Renée. 1996. 'Deconstructive Strategies and the Movements against Sexual Violence', *Hypatia*, 11(4):63–76.

Heberle, Renée/Grace, Victoria. eds. 2009. *Theorizing Sexual Violence*. New York: Routledge.

Henry, Nicola. 2014. 'The Fixation on Wartime Rape: Feminist Critique and International Law', *Social and Legal Studies*, 23(1):93–111.

Jackson, George. 1970. *Soledad Brother: The Prison Letters of George Jackson*. New York: Coward-McCann.

Kaldor, Mary. 1999. *New and Old Wars: Organized Violence in a Global Era*. Stanford: Stanford University Press.

Leatherman, Janie. 2011. *Sexual Violence and Armed Conflict*. Cambridge: Polity Press.

Lemaitre, Julieta/Sandvik, Kristin B. 2014. 'Beyond Sexual Violence in Transitional Justice: Political Insecurity as a Gendered Harm', *Feminist Legal Studies*, 22(33):243–61.

Lorber, Judith. 2000. 'Using Gender to Undo Gender: A Feminist Degendering Movement', *Feminist Theory*, 1(1):79–95.

Matthes, Melissa. 2000. *The Rape of Lucretia and the Founding of Republics*. University Park: Pennsylvania State University Press.

Meger, Sara. 2011. 'Rape in Contemporary Warfare: The Role of Globalization in Wartime Sexual Violence', *African Conflict and Peace Building Review*, 1(1):100–32.

Mohanty, Chandra T. 1991. 'Under Western Eyes: Feminist Scholarship and Colonialist Discourses', in Chandra T. Mohanty/Ann Russo/Lourdes Torres (eds), *Third World Women and the Politics of Feminism*, pp. 51–80. Bloomington: Indiana University Press.

Oosterveld, Valerie. 2009. 'The Special Court for Sierra Leone's Consideration of Gender-based Violence: Contributing to Transitional Justice?' *Human Rights Review*, 10(1):73–98.

Pateman, Carole. 1988. *The Sexual Contract*. Stanford: Stanford University Press.

Philipose, Elizabeth. 2009. 'Feminism, International Law, and the Spectacular Violence of the "Other": Decolonizing the Laws of War', in Renée J. Heberle/Victoria Grace (eds), *Theorizing Sexual Violence*, pp. 176–204. New York: Routledge.

Piercy, Marge. 1976. *Woman on the Edge of Time*. New York: Ballantine Books.

Pleck, Elizabeth. 1987. *Domestic Tyranny: The Making of Social Policy Against Family Violence from Colonial Times to the Present*. New York: Oxford University Press.

Rubin, Gayle. 1975. 'The Traffic in Women: Notes Toward a Political Economy of Sex', in Rayna R. Reiter (ed), *Toward an Anthropology of Women*, pp. 157–210. New York: Monthly Review Press.

Sanday, Peggy Reeves. 1981. *Female Power and Male Dominance: On the Origins of Sexual Inequality*. New York: Cambridge University Press.

Scarry, Elaine. 1985. *The Body in Pain: The Making and Unmaking of the World*. Oxford: Oxford University Press.

Schmitt, Carl. 2007. *The Concept of the Political*. Chicago: University of Chicago Press.

Sjoberg, Laura. 2015. *Women as Wartime Rapists: Beyond Sensation and Stereotyping*. New York: New York University Press.

Smith, Andrea. 2005. *Conquest: Sexual Violence and American Indian Genocide*. Boston: South End Press.

Using the Stigma of Prostitution to Hide the Crime of Sexual Slavery: The Case of the 'Comfort Women'

DEBRA BERGOFFEN

On 4 December 2001 the International Women's Tribunal for Military Sexual Slavery by Japan, found that Japan's World War II 'comfort stations' were sites of rape and sexual enslavement. It convicted Emperor Hirohito and nine other high-ranking military officers and government officials of crimes against humanity. Having no legal standing, the Tribunal could neither secure an apology nor demand reparations. Seen as an Irigarayan mime, however, the Tribunal's unofficial status emerges as its strength. By providing a space for the women to speak and to challenge the language that distorted and silenced their speech, it contested the state's exclusive right to identify and prosecute criminal behaviour and exposed the patriarchal values that determined what was and was not considered a crime. Speaking to the law through its cracks, the Tribunal put patriarchy in the docket. It tied Japan's escape from censure to the gender bias of the World War II criminal tribunals and the misogyny of Japanese and Allied cultures.

As I read the women's testimonies and the Tribunal's reasoning, I find that the stigmatised figure of the prostitute is a lynchpin of this misogyny. Passing the women off as prostitutes, the 'comfort stations' appeared normal. Silenced by the shame of being called prostitutes, the women secured the immunity of the perpetrators. When they did speak, Japan discounted their speech. Accusing the 'comfort women' of being prostitutes, women who freely degrade themselves, Japan charged them with deliberately perverting their speech. Calling them liars, their right to speak and be heard was effectively foreclosed (Price 2012: 74).

When the 'comfort women' broke their fifty-year silence, they rejected Japan's claim that they were prostitutes. They also decided against using the term 'forced prostitute.' Speaking on the condition that they be identified as sex slaves, the 'comfort women' aimed to secure the legitimacy of their testimonies. As sex slaves who did not choose to be immoral, they could not be accused of misusing their freedom to corrupt their words. Given the realities of patriarchal biases, defending their integrity in this way makes sense. The problem, however, is that it inadvertently leaves the vilification of the prostitute that enabled the 'comfort stations' to flourish untouched.

It is time to change the rules of the game. Time to create a world where calling a woman a prostitute could no longer be used as a 'get out of jail free-card' for those who traffic, enslave, rape or abuse women. Time to insist that no woman should have to distance herself from the prostitute to bring charges of war crimes, rape or sexual abuse. Time to say that prostitutes, like all women, have a right to respect and sexual integrity. Time for a sexual politics where the tag prostitute cannot be used to degrade, shame, silence and police women.

THE TRIBUNAL AS MIME

In mimicking the official legal system, the Tribunal may be seen as engaging in the initial phase of Irigaray's mimetic strategy. Detailing the law's gender biases when it comes to applying the legal definitions of slavery to situations where women were raped and treated as sexual property the Tribunal put the law on trial. Miming the rules established to confirm men in their authority and desire (in the authority of their desire), the Tribunal quoted the law to nullify its claims to objectivity and rationality. It showed that legal principles that are in plain sight and readily applied in cases of labour slavery and torture disappear when it comes to prosecuting rape, sexual violence and sexual slavery.

Like Irigaray who bows to the power of the unconscious as she critiques its current expressions, the Tribunal endorses the rule of the law as it seeks to reorient it. Creating a trial chamber presided over by internationally recognised judges who relied on accepted standards of precedent, testimony and evidence, the Tribunal showed what the law could do, made the case for what the law should do, and held it accountable for what it did not do. Miming the law to jam the legal machinery that keeps everything in its assigned patriarchal place (Irigaray 1985: 76, 78), it contested the power of men to speak for women by transforming silenced victims into authoritative accusers. Doing this it endowed the women with what Hannah Arendt identifies as our fundamental human right—the right to have rights—the right to speak in the public sphere and to have one's words count. In validating their speech, the Tribunal took up Irigaray's call to reorient the One of humanity from the One that, speaking in the masculine, passes itself off as the neutral universal that denies the sexual difference, to the One that recognises the sexual difference and establishes the coexistence of different identities within the horizon of the equality of human rights (Irigaray 2001: 12, 24–25).

SILENCED, SLANDERED AND SHAMED BY A NAME

The Tribunal, like Irigaray, uses mime, a technique associated with silence to confront the matter of women either being literally silenced or being spoken for by men. If they are allowed to speak, women find that their words are trapped in the alienating grammar of a logical order that censures and delegitimises their words (Irigaray 1993a: 17, 20). In this case, being disparaged by Japan as prostitutes first silenced the women and later discredited their testimonies. In asserting their authority to name themselves the 'comfort women' disrupted this grammar. They entered the substance of language and upended its symbolic codes (Irigaray 1993b: 121, 1994: 44). As we shall see, however, these codes are not easily undone.

By refusing to be called prostitutes, the women may be seen as asserting the right to protect their identities. This was not a matter, as is so often the case in rape and sexual assault trials, of protecting the identity of an individual woman by concealing her name, but of protecting the status of a group of women from the slander of a name. They insisted that they were not what the Japanese military called 'comfort women,' that is women who agreed to support the time-honoured tradition of maintaining military morale by sexually rewarding soldiers for their service and bravery. They were forced to serve the soldiers' sexual appetites. The legal framework of Humanitarian Law offered them two ways of accurately identifying their status, 'forced prostitution' and 'sexual slavery.' The women rejected forced prostitution. The adjective forced, would not counter the derogatory connotations of the term prostitute. Only the phrase sex slaves spoke to their experience. Most importantly, sexual slavery captured the 'ownership' reality of their situation. Reviewing sources of international law in order to find ways to criminalise the conduct, the Tribunal found that sexual slavery is a crime under international criminal law and thus endorsed the legitimacy of the identity the women chose for themselves (*Prosecutors v. Showa et al.* 2001 WIWCT 606–8). Going beyond the letter of the law, "it observed that the negative connotations of the term prostitute reflect "profoundly discriminatory attitudes toward women" (*Prosecutors v. Showa et al.* 2001 WIWCT 634–6). Seeing themselves as going to prostitutes, the soldiers saw their abusive behaviour as perfectly normal.

Webster's New Unabridged Universal Dictionary supports the Tribunal's observation. Its definition of prostitute is a striking example of the ways that "vocabulary associated with women often consists of slightly derogatory if not insulting terms" (Irigaray 1993a: 20). Though a prostitute is first defined as "a woman who engages in sexual intercourse for money," this non-judgmental language is immediately undermined when 'whore,' defined as "a person who engages in promiscuous sex," is given as its synonym. A third definition, describing the prostitute as "a person who willingly uses his or her talent or ability in a base or unworthy way, usually for money," compounds the discriminatory connotations. The prostitute, originally described as a woman engaged in a simple commercial transaction, but also identified as promiscuous, base and unworthy, emerges as a morally problematic person. Though selling sex, like other commercial transactions, involves several buyers, here dealing with more than one buyer carries the unsavoury tag, promiscuous. Whatever argument may be made for the fact that promiscuous, base and unworthy are not entailed in the primary definition of prostitute, the lives of the 'comfort women' and the experience of women who work as prostitutes make it clear that the hierarchies of dictionary distinctions are irrelevant in the world in which these definitions flourish—they infect each other. Because the prostitute is seen as choosing an unworthy way of life, she is said to get what she deserves and deserve what she gets. Not exactly a free pass for those who establish slave camps, but close, for if they can identify 'their' women as prostitutes, they can count on being protected from social, political and legal censure.

Under the terms of the first definition, a prostitute is a woman who asserts her agency. She sells sex for profit. Under the terms of the subsequent definitions, this agency is denigrated as depraved. The tension in this account of the prostitute raises the question: Why are women who exercise their agency accused of being immoral?

It seems to only (!) be a matter of sexual agency, but if we focus on the matter of agency we can make sense of the fact that women whose agency is used in non-sexual ways are stigmatised as whores. Gail Pheterson (1996: 11, 23) writes: "The whore stigma can disqualify any woman's claim to legitimacy and throw suspicion on any woman accused of economic or sexual initiative." Meredith Tax (1980: 214) reports that the New York 1909 striking shirtwaist workers were vilified as prostitutes. Thenjiwe Mthinsto (cited in Krog 1999: 178–79) found that South African women who resisted apartheid were called prostitutes and sexually abused. By calling the 'comfort women' prostitutes, Japan recognises their agency to discredit their testimonies. Immoral women lie.

In 1993 Japan's chief cabinet minister Yohei Kono, acknowledged the truth of the women's accounts of their lives in the 'comfort stations.' Though he recognised Japan's role in establishing the stations and trafficking the women, he stopped short of accepting Japan's legal responsibility. In 1995 Japan's nationalist right-wing party, insisting that the women were prostitutes and invoking the grammar of untrustworthy agency, held that Japan was innocent of the charges levelled against it. In 2007, Japan's Prime Minister Shinzo Abe, confronted by the possibility of a US congressional 'comfort women' resolution demanding that Japan apologise and in response to opposition lawmaker Kiyomi Tsujimoto's demand that Abe clarify his position on the 'comfort women,' reaffirmed his acceptance of the Kono document's expression of sympathy for the women but rejected its claim that Japan was responsible for their suffering. He insisted that the women were not procured by the Japanese state or military and were not sex slaves (Dudden/Mizoguchi 2007, Mizoguchi 2007, Onishi 2007). In 2014, *The New York Times* reported that *The Yomiuri Shimbun,* the conservative newspaper with the largest daily circulation in Japan, rejected the Kono pledge to educate future generations regarding the facts of Japan's responsibility for the 'comfort stations.' Apparently agreeing with the Kono statement that how Japan remembered the facts of the 'comfort stations' would affect its future actions, the newspaper erased the facts. It said that it was inappropriate to suggest that 'comfort women' were sex slaves and deleted all references to them as sex slaves in its previous reporting (Ramzy 2014; Soble 2014). In that same year Japan assailed the United Nations report calling on it to apologise and pay compensation to the survivors (Fackler 2014). In 2015, bringing their image cleansing campaign to the United States some Japanese historians and academics, insisting that the 'comfort women' were "simply prostitutes," urged McGraw-Hill to 'correct' its college textbook references to sex slaves used by Japanese soldiers during World War II. McGraw-Hill rejected their request (Fackler 2015; Fifield 2015). Ironically, in that same year Japan and Korea reached a "final and irreversible resolution" of the issue. Japan apologised and set up a fund to attend to the women's medical and economic needs. The surviving women reject this agreement, noting that this is not merely a bilateral diplomatic issue, and that Japan still denies legal responsibility and still refuses to offer formal reparations (Yang 2017).

Japan's inadequate apologies and insistent disclaimers make it clear that though we may feel sorry for the suffering of a prostitute, calling a woman a prostitute excuses her assailant. The Tribunal, calling the women sex slaves counters Japan's strategy. It recognises the women's words as truthful and refuses to dismiss their wounds as self-inflicted. Citing international law, the Tribunal defined slavery as the "status or condition of a person over whom any or all the powers attaching to the right of ownership are attached" (*Prosecutors v. Showa et al.* 2001 WIWCT 588). Finding that sexual slavery is "the epitome of objectification and possession, depriving the sexually enslaved person of even the remnants of intimate space and personal integrity," the Tribunal found that forced sex, "is a form of objectification disproportionately visited upon women and rooted in the fundamental failure to treat women as full persons" (*Prosecutors v. Showa et al.* 2001 WIWCT 646).

The Tribunal does not pursue the distinction between forced sex as a crime of slavery and a crime of forced labour. Saying that forced labour does not necessarily entail ownership over a person, it leaves open the possibility that in some cases forced labour, like forced sex, does entail such ownership. However, in finding that forced sex always entails ownership over a person and that it is a form of objectification rooted in the failure to treat women as full persons the Tribunal suggests that there is a unique relationship between sex and personhood such that using a person for sex entails abusing them as a person. When applied to the case of the prostitute this reasoning can be used/abused to support her stigmatisation. In selling sex for profit she can be accused of wilful self-abuse of her personhood. In this way, tying sex to personhood makes it possible to equate selling sex with self-degradation. By obfuscating the distinction between the first and subsequent definitions of the term prostitute, the alienating grammar of patriarchy remains in play.

The Tribunal's distinction between the use of a body for labour which does not necessarily involve one's status as a person, and the use of a body for sex which does, lives outside the courtroom in the distinction we make between the person who sells labour, the domestic worker, and the person who sells sex, the prostitute. The domestic worker is respected. Selling her labour is not seen as selling herself. It is not seen as compromising her dignity. The

prostitute, however, is shunned. By selling sex she is seen as putting
a price on herself and as wilfully degrading her status as a person.

The Tribunal rendered its judgment nine months after the
International Criminal Tribunal for the former Yugoslavia (ICTY)
found three Bosnian-Serb soldiers who raped and sexually enslaved
Muslim women and girls guilty of crimes against humanity. That
its findings echoed that of the ICTY is no accident. Survivors
of the comfort station system and the Bosnian-Serb genocidal
rapes met at the UN 1993 Human Rights Conference in Vienna.
The Tribunal's Chief Justice, Gabrielle Kirk McDonald, was the
former president of the ICTY. The judge Carmen Mari Argi,
served on the ICTY. The Chief Prosecutor, Patricia Viseur Sellers,
was Legal Advisor for Gender-Related crimes in the Office of the
Prosecutor at the ICTY and International Criminal Tribunal for
Rwanda.

Seeing the ICTY and Tribunal in conversation with each
other, learning that the testimonies at the ICTY encouraged the
'comfort women' to speak, and recognizing that the Tribunal, as
an extra-legal space could cite the cultural forces that enable war
time sexual violence, reminds us that ending this sexual violence
will require Irigarayan extra legal tactics as well legal instruments.
Further, seeing that the ICTY has not nullified the law's failure to
protect women returns us to the cultural forces at work fostering
this failure and compels us to address them.

MIMETIC TRANSVALUATIONS

In her analysis of the history of securing women's rights as human
rights, Laura Stemple details the ways these cultural forces work.
She finds that in the struggle to gain credibility for women's human
rights, the rights of respectable women were bought at the price
of the rights of less respectable women by appealing to a long-
established misogynous scale of victimhood-victim hierarchies.
According to this scale, only innocent victims are recognised as
a 'real' victims. Being labelled a prostitute, in undermining your
status as innocent, put you at the bottom (and sometimes outside
the scope) of the victim scale. As innocent and at the top of the

scale, you deserve sympathy and have a right to be heard. As a prostitute you are denied both (Stemple 2009: 630). The 'comfort women,' boxed in by this victim hierarchy, found that they could only reclaim their dignity at the expense of the dignity of those who are called prostitutes.

Finding that the Tribunal's mime of the official legal system exposed the gender biases of the law without, however, challenging the role the denigration of the prostitute plays in these biases, I read the Tribunal's deconstructive mime of the law as clearing the ground for a mimetic transvaluation where the pejorative discourses of prostitution give way to legitimated defamiliarised versions of femininity that "return the masculine to its own language to leave open the possibility of a different language which means that the masculine would no longer be everything" and that the "elsewhere" of women's pleasure will appear (Irigaray 1985: 76, 80).

Drucilla Cornell (1995: 207), working this ground, finds that the right to express the elsewhere of women's pleasure is a crucial women's human rights issue. She argues that so long as this elsewhere is nowhere, women, as objects of men's fantasies, will be reduced to stereotypes that are antithetical to their status as fully human persons.

Cornell (1995: 4) ties our sense of self-respect and worth to three conditions: bodily integrity, access to symbolic forms that allow us to express our individuation, and protection of the imaginary domain. Asserting that sexuality is formative to our individuation and that existing at the mercy of another's fantasies compromises our access to symbolic forms that allow us to express our individuation, she insists that protecting the sexual imaginary is an essential human right. Bringing this argument to the issue at hand, Cornell (1995: 4, 11, 220) finds that so long as the denigration of the prostitute is used to position all women as the object of men's desire, women's full humanity will be compromised. She urges us to recognise the ways that the fate of the prostitute is intertwined with that of 'respectable' women.

BETWEEN THE 'COMFORT WOMEN' AND US

The 'comfort women' reject Japan's claim that they are prostitutes. They insist on being identified as sex slaves. They are right. There is an important difference between a prostitute, a person who decides to sell sexual pleasure for profit, and a sex slave, a person who, as the property of another, is sexually abused and raped to satisfy the sexual fantasies of the men who buy her. The difference, however, is not between an immoral person and an innocent one. Delineating the difference in this way re-enforces misogynist fantasies that threaten women's agency and legitimates the victim hierarchy that menaces us all.

The 'comfort women's' testimonies at the Tribunal and their accounts of their lives after liberation speak to the ways that being treated as prostitutes in the camps and continuing to be identified as prostitutes today destroyed their ability to experience the sexual pleasures and the pleasures of intimate life that Irigaray and Cornell cite as essential to our status as persons.

Seen as 'spoiled goods' many of the women were abandoned and isolated. Some, by hiding their past, married and had children. Having to live their lives as a lie, however, they speak with sorrow of being unable to be truly intimate with their husbands and children. Others, finding men who were willing to marry them despite their past, speak of the ways that being abused as prostitutes destroyed their ability to experience sexual pleasure and grieve the ways this mars their married lives. The women hoped that by abiding by the rules of the victim hierarchy they could return to the world as respectable women. Their hope was betrayed. The label prostitute continues to stalk them. The elsewhere of their desire remains nowhere.

To ask the women who endured the disgrace of the prostitute to take up the task of mimetic transvaluation by insisting that the prostitute, like the sex slave, has a right to be protected from sexual abuse; to ask them to demand that the human right to bodily integrity be affirmed in the case of the prostitute as well as all other human beings, is asking too much. We need to honour the courage of these women who, refusing to be silenced by shame, exposed the brutality of the comfort stations and destroyed the credibility of their Japanese enslavers.

What may be asking too much of the 'comfort women,' however, is not asking too much of us. If they found that they could only buy their dignity at the expense of the dignity of the prostitute, Irigaray, Cornell and Stemple, ask us to re-examine their bargain. They charge us with creating a world where their declaration, 'I am not a prostitute' would no longer be necessary to validate the demand for justice.

REFERENCES

Cornell, Drucilla. 1995. *The Imaginary Domain: Abortion, Pornography and Sexual Harassment*. New York: Routledge.

Dudden, Alexis/ Mizoguchi, Kozo. 2007. 'Abe's Violent Denial: Japan's Prime Minister and the "Comfort Women"', *The Asia–Pacific Journal: Japan Focus*, 5(3). https://apjjf.org/-Alexis-Dudden/2368/article.html (accessed 02 May 2018).

Fackler, Martin. 2015. 'US Textbook Skews History, Prime Minister of Japan Says', *New York Times*, 29 January. https://www.nytimes.com/2015/01/30/world/asia/japans-premier-disputes-us-textbooks-portrayal-of-comfort-women.html (accessed 12 October 2018).

———. 2014. 'Japan Seeking Revision of Report on Wartime Brothels is Rebuffed', *New York Times*, 16 October. https://www.nytimes.com/2014/10/17/world/asia/japan-rebuffed-over-un-report-on-wartime-brothels.html (accessed 12 October 2018).

Fifield, Anna. 2015. 'Professors in Japan fight book's details of WWII sex slaves', *Washington Post*,17 March.

Irigaray, Luce. 2001. *Democracy begins between two.* New York: Routledge.

———. 1994. *Thinking the difference: For a peaceful revolution.* New York: Routledge.

———. 1993a. *Je, tu, nous: Toward a Culture of Difference.* New York: Routledge.

———. 1993b. *Sexes and Genealogies.* New York: Columbia University Press.

———. 1985. *This Sex Which Is Not One.* Ithaca: Cornell University Press.

Krog, Antjie. 1999. *Country of My Skull: Guilt, Sorrow and the Limits of Forgiveness in the New South Africa.* New York: Times Books.

Mizoguchi, Kozo. 2007. 'Japan's Prime Minister Denies World War II Sex Slaves', *The Asia–Pacific Journal: Japan Focus*, 5(3). https://apjjf.org/-Alexis-Dudden/2368/article.html (accessed 02 May 2018).

Onishi, Norimitsu. 2007. 'Japan Stands by Declaration on "Comfort Women"', *New York Times*, 16 March. https://www.nytimes.com/2007/03/16/world/asia/16cnd-japan.html (accessed 02 May 2018).

Pheterson, Gail. 1996. *The Prostitution Prism.* New York: Amsterdam University Press.

Price, Joshua. 2012. *Structural Violence: Hidden Brutality in the Lives of Women.* Albany: SUNY Press.

Ramzy, Austin. 2014. 'Japanese Newspaper Retracts Fukushima Disaster Report and Fires editor', *New York Times*, 11 September. https://www.nytimes.com/2014/09/12/world/asia/japanese-newspaper-retracts-fukushima-disaster-story-and-fires-editor.html (accessed 12 October 2018).

Soble, Jonathan. 2014. 'Japanese Newspaper Prints Apology for Using the Term "Sex Slaves"', *New York Times*, 28 November. https://www.nytimes.com/2014/11/29/world/asia/japan-yomiuri-shimbun-apology-sex-slaves.html (accessed 12 October 2018).

Stemple, Laura. 2009. 'Male Rape and Human Rights', *Hastings Law Journal*, 60(3):605–47.

Tax, Meridith. 1980. *The Rising of Women: Feminist Solidarity and Class Conflict 1880–1917.* New York: Monthly Review Press.

The Women's International War Crimes Tribunal for the Trial of Japan's Military Sexual Slavery (WIWCT) court case: *The Prosecutors and the Peoples of the Asia-Pacific Region v. Hirohito Emperor Showa, Ando Rikichi, Hata Shunroku, Itagaki Seizo, Matsui Iwame, Imequ Yoshijiro, Terauchi Hisaichi, Tojo Hideki, Yamashita Tomoyuki and The Government of Japan,* Judgement from 4 December 2001, Case PT–2000–1–T. http://www.internationalcrimesdatabase.org/Case/981/The-Prosecutors-and-the-Peoples-of-the-Asia-Pacific-Region/ (accessed 10 May 2018).

Yang, Hyunah. 2017. 'Justice Yet to Come: The Korea-Japan Foreign Ministers' Agreement of 2015 regarding the "Japanese Military Sexual Slavery"', *L'Homme: Zeitschrift für feministische Geschichtswissenschaft*, 28(2):115–25.

What Do Bodies Tell?

GABY ZIPFEL

> Does a little booby cry for any ache? The mother scolds
> him in this fashion: What a coward to cry for a trifling
> pain! What will you do when your arm is cut off in battle?
> What when you are called upon to commit harakiri?
>
> *Nitobé*, 1900

WAR AND THE BODY

In his introduction to 'War and the Body', British sociologist
Kevin McSorley defines the reality of war as:

> not just politics by any other means, but politics incarnate, politics
> written on and experienced through the thinking, feeling bodies
> of men and women. From steeled combatants to abject victims,
> from the grieving relative to the exhausted aid worker, war
> occupies innumerable bodies in a multitude of ways, profoundly
> shaping lives and ways of human being. (McSorley 2015: 1)

McSorley describes war as a social interaction between "thinking,
feeling bodies of men and women" in which all the parties
involved are subjected in the extreme to the irreducible condition
Judith Butler calls "precarity" (Butler 2009).

The enactment of war is marked by extreme bodily reactions,
by killing and dying, suffering and enjoyment, panic and triumph.
Emotions, bodily sensations and affects take centre stage. Not only
are the boundaries between individual autonomous bodies blurred
in theatres of war more obviously than in times of 'peace'; so too
are the meanings of interactions between bodies. The substance
of war, agency to kill and destroy accompanied by endangerment

and the risk of being killed, is realised by targeting bodies. War is a test of an individual's capacity to deal with and respond to situations where the vulnerability of the body and capacity to injure emerge, as in armed conflicts and any other situation in which one person targets another for subjugation.

Passing the test of war requires recourse to bodily knowledge, the skill to deal with bodily sensations so as to promote the survival of the self and the defeat of the enemy while developing the ability to accept the risk of injury or death.

THE DESIRE FOR INVULNERABILITY

Ernst Jünger, who opened his 1934 essay 'On Pain' (Jünger 2017: 145) with the Inazo Nitobé quote above, can be read as a protagonist to proponents of the theory that the body's vulnerability to injury, limitations and mortality represent the thorn in the side of the modern concept of the self as an autonomous, sovereign subject[1] and counter the irreducible state of precarity with a "desire for invulnerability"(Taylor 2007, as cited in Zolkos 2016). Jünger, who lived to the ripe old age of 102, enthusiastically interpreted war as the manly realm of experience to end all others, and defined pain in his introduction as one of the

> great and unalterable dimensions that show a man's stature […]. Whenever one approaches the points where man proves himself to be equal or superior to pain, one gains access to the sources of his power and the secret hidden behind his dominion. Tell me your relation to pain, and I will tell you who you are! (Jünger 2017)

Jünger's proposed corporeal-technical *coming to terms with* the irreducible corporeal conditionality through cognitive domestication[2] is based on an instrumental attitude towards the body: the autonomous (male) subject *has* a body that he can control and whose potential (virility) can be deployed. This construction employs an *empowerment strategy* that displaces his *vulnerability* to harm onto another (the other, woman) through the incorporation of the *power* to harm.[3] As a subject vulnerable to harm, this other does not have a body; it *is* a body (Engelhardt 2004).

IT IS LIKE A RAPE

> The first blow makes the prisoner aware that he is impotent—
> and, in this sense, contains the essence of all that follows. [...]
> The other, against whom I am physically in the world and with
> whom I can only be while he does not touch the boundary that
> is the surface of my skin, imposes his own corporeality upon me
> with that blow. He is on top of me and with this he annihilates
> me. [...] It is like a rape. (Améry 1977: 56)

With this description of experiencing torture in a Nazi prison,
Jean Améry hints at what we might find if we pursue answers to
the question: 'what do bodies tell?' Améry's surprising conclusion,
"it is like a rape",[4] significantly shifts the more familiar 'rape is
torture' topos. The latter highlights the intensity of the violent
act of rape, seeks to declare it 'purely' an act of violence enacted
by a perpetrator against a victim. Améry's description goes much
further. By describing the outcome of a painful threat as a threat
to corporeal autonomy, sexual identity and reproductive potency,
Améry marks the extreme ends of corporeal experience: the
experience of life-threatening violence and the experience of
sexuality, which is transformed from a source of pleasure and
vitality into a source of vulnerability and loss of self-confidence.

By imposing his own corporeality upon his victim, the
perpetrator is acting out the intertwinedness of violence and
sexuality. Not only does he inflict bodily pain and injury; he also
turns a vital, embodied ability acted out in a social interaction,
into an experience of dehumiliation.

THE TRUTH OF THE OTHER

The cloaking of the torturer's body is significant in the practice of
torture. While engaged in the act of torture, the torturer has no
face. Whether he gains pleasure from his bodily activity enacted
on another body or not is a central factor in this interaction. The
torture's true triumph is the nullification of the reality of his own
vulnerability for a moment by forcing the physical surrender of
the victim.

The German word for torturer, *Folterknecht*, literally 'torture servant', indicates that the torturer follows a dictum founded on the abstraction of the sovereign, autonomous subject, a dictum to renounce the irreducible precarity all living creatures are subject to: "The sovereign subject poses as precisely not the one who is impinged upon by others, precisely not the one whose permanent and irreversible injurability forms the condition and horizon of its actions" (Butler 2009: 178). Renouncing one's own injurability, as Judith Butler describes it, is accomplished through the displacement of this injurability onto the other: "Such a sovereign position not only denies its own constitutive injurability but tries to relocate injurability in the other as an effect of doing injury to that other and exposing that other as, by definition, injurable" (ibid.). The act of violence serves to reinforce the invulnerability of the self:

> If the violent act is, among other things, a way of relocating the capacity to be violated (always) elsewhere, it produces the appearance that the subject who enacts violence is impermeable to violence. The accomplishment of this appearance becomes one aim of violence: one locates injurability with the other by injuring the other and then taking the sign of injury as the truth of the other. (ibid.)

The autonomous, sovereign subject has to imagine itself invulnerable, since its logic equates vulnerability with susceptibility to harm, which is viewed as a condition of weakness, dependency, passivity, incapacitation, incapability and powerlessness. It is, as Erinn Cunniff Gilson puts it, "conceived as a condition in which one is liable to be harmed" and

> as a character trait, a property, or a state that has negative value— is bad—and thus is to be avoided. It is reductive in several senses. First, vulnerability is reduced to a homogenous property. In effect, when vulnerability is understood as susceptibility to harm, its meaning is narrowed; the presumption is that vulnerability means the same thing for all those deemed vulnerable. Second, it tends to be conceived as a fixed property that is relatively immutable; certain individuals and groups are deemed vulnerable, whereas

others are not, and this attribution of vulnerability is unlikely to change. Third, it is distributed hierarchically. The attribution of vulnerability as a fixed property entails that it characterises some and does not pertain to others, and this attribution is accompanied by a hierarchical ascription of value in terms of agency and other desirable capacities and traits. (Cunniff Gilson 2016: 74)[5]

HAVING A BODY VERSUS BEING A BODY

In war—the ultimate state of vulnerability for everyone who is involved—it becomes extremely difficult to reconcile this schematic attribution of vulnerability with the experienced reality.

This reality, experienced by the body and which must be overcome, is shaped "by countless affective, sensory and embodied ways through which war lives and breeds" (McSorley 2015: 1) —bodily sensations that cannot be seamlessly integrated into the concept of vulnerability described above. This integration necessitates the use of violence on the personal battlefield between those in possession of a body and those who are a body upon whom the war-triggered desire for blurred boundaries (Zipfel 2014) can be both enforced and enclosed.

A former 'comfort woman', Korean Kim Young Suk, describes how Japanese officer Nakamora celebrated this determination of a body with the power to injure and a body vulnerable to injury through her:

> "You, Korean girl, you are very pretty. Let's have some fun." But I was only twelve years old and had no idea what "let's have some fun" meant. Nakamora pulled out his penis. He took off my clothing and I was terrified. He forced me to lay down on the ground and cut me with his bayonet and I bled. He took off my trousers and raped me until I bled.[6]

A PAPER, WRITTEN IN GERMAN

The sense of injustice manifest in the Japanese government's continuing and determined refusal to recognise the systematic crimes perpetrated against the comfort women during the Second World War as crimes reflects the unexpressed legitimacy of treating war practices such as the regular condoning of rape, pillage and murder like combat operations. "On occasion", describes Ruth Harris (1993: 177) regarding the First World War,

> rape took place amid a more generalised scene of pillage and murder. One woman who took refuge in a nearby chateau in Ferté-Gaucher [...] described how four Germans arrived, stole her money and murdered a Frenchman who tried to defend her. Forced to step over the dead man's body, she was raped, saw another woman raped, and then was raped again and again.

One of the most extraordinary elements in the retelling references the perpetrators' utter lack of any sense of injustice or wrong doing:

> In relating to this tale, she revealed what was in her view one of the most bizarre aspects of the encounter: in the midst of the mayhem, the Germans calmly drunk their coffee, a detail which epitomised their utter callousness to the pain they were inflicting.

It seems the soldiers' behaviour cannot simply be attributed to the pronounced cold bloodedness of a few individuals: "However, this kind of encounter was not frequent as one might imagine." An image of the self is grotesquely expressed here, one that demands the victim to acknowledge and accept the deed as legitimate and legitimated:

> The Germans often sought to make contact and even justify their acts to their victims. One woman was raped in front of her friend after the soldier showed her a paper written in German "to make me believe he had a permission from his superior to rape me, on pain of being shot." The desire to reach out while punishing can be seen when Germans sought to impose a parody of domestic interaction on the victim, with rapes initiated after a request for wine, milk, eggs or a meall. [...]
>
> Another victim had to sleep with her attacker at rifle-point, and was obliged next morning to make coffee [...]. (ibid.)

BOOZE, 'BIRDS' AND BRAWLING

The testimony of Japanese officer Suzuki Yoshio before the Women's International War Crimes Tribunal on Japan's Military Sexual Slavery describes the tactic of seeking release in "blow out periods from pent-up discomfort, frustrations, tensions and fears by pursuit of a particular trinity: booze, 'birds' and brawling—a collective desublimation by celebrating violent and sexual acts" (Hockey 2003: 22) as a normal practice: "As the head of an artillery unit I myself allowed the soldiers after an operation in 1944 to 'do as they pleased.'"[7]

Suzuki describes how he experienced the amalgam of fear, sexual excitement and brutal release in and through his own body:

> In a group of older women I met a woman who was about thirty. I sent the others away—she tried to get away by way of the toilets. Seeing her like that heightened my sexual arousal. I undressed her, she was naked and I raped her brutally, beat her with my rifle. She couldn't defend herself, she was shaking, her face was white, and she was speechless, she obeyed me without contradiction.

AS BODIES, WE ARE EXPOSED TO OTHERS

By initiating a bodily interaction, her fear, her bodily sense of vulnerability, provides him with sexual enjoyment he employs to master feelings of friction and tension. In so doing, he eliminates the ambiguity and ambivalence of vulnerability as a means of a sensitive and responsive capacity of the body:

> As bodies, we are exposed to others, and while this may be the condition of our desire, it also raises the possibility of subjugation and cruelty. This follows from the fact that bodies are bound up with others through material needs, through touch, through language, through a set of relations without which we cannot survive. To have one's survival bound up in such a way is a constant risk of sociality—its promise and its threat. The very fact of being bound up with others establishes the possibility of being subjugated and exploited—though in no way does it determine what political form this will take. But it also establishes the possibility of being relieved of suffering, of knowing justice and even love. (Butler 2009: 61f)

"HE ISN'T COMBAT-EFFECTIVE!"

By eliminating the ambiguity and ambivalence of vulnerability as a means of a sensitive and responsive capacity of the body, Suzuki's actions demonstrate his combat effectiveness. Unlike the behaviour of US soldier Dennis Conti which enrages his commander Calley during the Vietnam War.

> During the My Lai massacre in March 1968, when women were raped and killed in the most cruel fashion, Lieutenant William L. Calley was beside himself, as he came across Dennis Conti forcing a young mother to give him oral sex.
>
> Calley ordered Conti to "Get on your goddam pants!" but admitted he did not know "why I was so damn saintly about it. Rape: In Vietnam it's a very common thing. [...] I guess lots of girls would rather be raped than killed anytime. So why was I being saintly about it? Because: if a GI is getting a blow job, he isn't doing his job. He isn't destroying communism [...]. Our mission in My Lai wasn't perverted, though. It was simply 'Go and destroy it'. [...] No difference now: if a GI is getting gain, he isn't doing what we are paying him for. He isn't combat-effective." (Bourke 1999: 173)

"SO IT IS THAT MEN OFTEN FEAR ..."

The high propensity for violence observed in war veterans after a war together with an inability to experience a sexuality decoupled from violence (Baker 1981; Greiner 2007; Bourke 1999) are indications of how lastingly violence enacted and violence experienced write themselves on the body and condition its affective and emotional abilities.

The relatively high frequency of abuse of women within the military community is an indication that the understanding of the body learned during military training produces the same effects. In her analysis of violence in the military community, Deborah Harrison (2003) describes the central importance assigned to control over one's sensations, a control the body tenaciously resists—as Seidler (2015: 227) puts it: "So it is that men often fear what their bodies might reveal if they are allowed to have their voice, which is why bodies have to be sharply controlled as 'other' and so as sources of threat".

WORSE THAN THE MAN

The male subject constructed in keeping with the above feels subjected to ultimately unrealisable demands, which result in the sensation and experience of an ever-present fear of failure. Coupled with the penchant for self-hatred engendered by an attitude towards the body as a hostile 'other', this fear can turn into misogyny expressed in excessive sexual violence, as in the following scene, which occurred during the Second World War in Poland::

> A German police officer forced two Poles, a twenty-two-year-old woman and a man, to dig their own graves, in preparation for execution [...]. A crowd of people gathered, and some ventured to say that the woman appeared harmless. The police officer responded that she was "worse than the man", and moreover he was curious, "whether she was even wearing underpants." He would soon find out, he announced, "because she still has to be interrogated by me." The German police officer then beat the two Poles with a shovel, first the man, then the woman. He also whipped the woman in the face with his leather glove. She fell down, her legs spread apart, and her skirt rode up. Onlookers could see that her undergarments were soaked with blood. The police officer yelled; "Now she is on the rag, so there won't be any fucking." (Bergen 2006: 181)

The German police officer responds to objections from the crowd with a demonstration of his individual power underpinned by a self-assured sense of racial superiority.

DISGUSTING, FULL OF SPERM

In another case from the former Yugoslavia, a Serbian rapist sees himself as part of a network of male bonding (Pohl 2004: 9), "constituted not only as a community of protection and solidarity, but also as an egalitarianx league of men, which produce cohesion through the devaluation of supposedly feminine characteristics and

exteriorise homoerotic libido by transforming it into aggression"
(Bröckling 2003: 197).

The Serbian soldier describes his victim, who had already
been raped by twenty other men, as "disgusting, full of sperm."
The victim's defiled body evokes disgust, an affect that secretly
encourages the perpetrator to kill the victim "with five bullets in
the belly" in the end (Pohl 2004: 9).

AN OBSCENE LINKAGE OF SEX AND EXCREMENT AND DEATH

Joanna Bourke's descriptions of killing rituals observed on scores
of battlefields, many of which seem unreal and downright
carnivalesque, reveal a process of extreme regression soldiers
experience as exhilarating (Bourke 2006: 123). One GI describes
a grotesque and regressive performance in which the corpse of a
Vietcong fighter is defiled: "They had propped the corpse against
some C-rations, placed sunglasses across his eyes and a cigarette in
his mouth, and balanced a 'large and perfectly formed' piece of shit
on his head." The GI holds up under his superior's look of rebuke,

> but inside I was […] laughing. I laughed—I believe now—in
> part because of some subconscious appreciation of this obscene
> linkage of sex and excrement and death; and in part because of
> the exultant realisation that he—whoever he had been—was dead
> and I—special, unique, me—was alive. (Cit. in Bourke 1999: 15)

The enjoyment experienced through the "obscene linkage of
sex and excrement and death" is extraordinary, and it allows the
soldier to triumph over death, at least temporarily, as the 'other', a
"special, superior being."

SURVIVAL AND THE BOUNDARY OF THE BODY

This isolated triumph quite quickly runs up against inevitable
limitations:

> The boundary of who I am is the boundary of the body, but
> the boundary of the body never fully belongs to me. Survival
> depends less on the established boundary to the self than on

the constitutive sociality of the body. But as much as the body, considered as social in both its surface and depth, is the condition of survival, it is also that which, under certain conditions, imperils our lives and our survivability. (Butler 2009: 54)

These cited scenes of reactions and interactions acted out through the body are intended to confound the classical narrative of the hero who conquers his foe (and defends his womenfolk) and valiantly faces death. It initially blinds one to the individual acting and acted upon in a situation of ultimate extremes so that it misses the target and, in Elaine Scarry's words, "the injury and structure of war", by masking death and pain in favour of a fantasy in which war appears as a fair, honourable competition (Scarry 1985): a fair, honourable competition based on legal frameworks, rationally justifiable goals and convictions.

Yet a closer look reveals that the enactment and reproduction of war is actually fundamentally marked by "affective dispositions, corporeal careers, embodied suffering and somatic memories that endure across time and space" (McSorley 2015: 2).

THE WRONG OF SEXUAL VICTIMISATION

Warfare requires recourse to, and the targeted exercise and influence of a pre-reflective, embodied knowledge, of incorporated bodily know-how and practical sense; "a perspective grasp upon the world from the point of view of the body", which "comes into the social world via the construction of meaning, intention and appropriate action" (Hockey 2009: 480).

In her analysis of the experience of war, Christine Sylvester asks: "So what is war?" Her answer references a dense network of actors who are involved in the practice of "large-scale collective violence" in different ways:

It is much the same old story of large-scale collective violence; but it works with myriad more actors, all of whom experience the collective violence differently depending on their location, level and mode of involvement, gender, moral code, memories, and access to technologies (Sylvester 2011: 125).

The protagonists are positioned in a hierarchy, and either exercise or are subjected to agency and interpretational power. The same, fundamental initial condition, our vulnerability as animate beings, does not assert itself in the same way for everyone. The social potential of the ambiguity of human vulnerability—as the reason for our responsiveness to one another—is open to debate:

> Of course, the fact that one's body is never fully one's own, bounded and self-referential, is the condition of passionate encounter, of desire, of longing, and of those modes of address and addressability upon which the feeling of aliveness depends. But the entire world of unwilled contact also follows from the fact that the body finds it survivability in social space and time; and this exposure or dispossession is precisely what is exploited in the case of unwilled coercion, constraint, physical injury, violence. (Butler 2009: 54)

This is all the more explicit in the case of sexual violence.

Furthermore, as Erinn Cunniff Gilson (2016: 2) points out, "The wrong of sexual victimisation inheres in exploiting and appropriating another's ambiguous vulnerability".

Translated from German by Sarah Smithson-Compton.

NOTES

1. In her essay 'Rethinking the Social Contract: Masochism and Masculinist Violence', Renée Heberle presents a very instructive analysis of the paradoxes of liberal, modern subjectivity and their impact on the practice of sexual violence (Heberle 2009).
2. Cf. Tanner 1994.
3. According to Popitz 1986.
4. Gabriela Mischkowski brought this Améryian shift to my attention.
5. In the case cited above Améry is the injurable other, the Jew—in the symbolic order of the modern era, the woman is the classic other.
6. Kim Young Suk, testimony given before the Women's International War Crimes Tribunal on Japan's Military Sexual Slavery, sound recording.

7. Suzuki Yoshio, testimony given before the Women's International War Crimes Tribunal on Japan's Military Sexual Slavery, sound recording.

REFERENCES

Améry, Jean. 1977. *Jenseits von Schuld und Sühne*. Stuttgart: Klett-Cotta.

Baker, Mark. 1981. *Nam: The Vietnam War in the Words of the Men and Women Who Fought There*. New York: William Morrow and Company.

Bergen, Doris L. 2006. 'Sexual Violence in the Holocaust: Unique and Typical?' in Dagmar Herzog (ed), *Lessons and Legacies VII: The Holocaust in International Perspective*, pp. 179–200. Evanston: Northwestern University Press.

Bourke, Joanna. 2006. 'The Killing Frenzy: Wartime Narratives of Enemy in Action', in Alf Lüdtke/Bernd Weisbrod (eds), *No Man's Land of Violence: Extreme Wars in the 20th Century*, pp. 101–25. Göttingen: Wallstein.

———. 1999. *An Intimate History of Killing: Face-to-Face Killing in Twentieth Century Warfare*. London: Granta.

Bröckling, Ulrich. 2003. 'Schlachtfeldforschung: Die Soziologie im Krieg', in Steffen Martus/Marina Münkler/Werner Röcke (eds), *Schlachtfelder: Codierung von Gewalt im medialen Wandel*, pp. 189–206. Berlin: Akademie Verlag.

Butler, Judith. 2009. *Frames of War: When is Life Grievable?* London/New York: Verso.

Cunniff Gilson, Erinn. 2016. 'Vulnerability and Victimization: Rethinking Key Concepts in Feminst Discourses on Sexual Violence', *Signs: Journal of Women in Culture and Society*, 42(1): 71–98.

Engelhardt, Miriam. 2004. 'Vergewaltigung: Zur ordnungsstiftenden Wirkung der geschlechtlichen Codierung von Verletzungsoffenheit und Verletzungsmacht', in Christoph Leill/Andreas Pettenkoffer (eds), *Kultivierungen von Gewalt: Beiträge zur Soziologie von Gewalt und Ordnung*, pp. 175–207. Würzburg: Ergon.

Greiner, Bernd. 2007. *Krieg ohne Fronten: Die USA in Vietnam*. Hamburg: Hamburger Edition.

Harris, Ruth. 1993. 'The "Child of the Barbarian": Rape, Race and Nationalism in France during the First World War', *Past & Present*, 141(1): 170–206.

Harrison, Deborah. 2003. 'Violence in the Military Community', in

Paul R. Hiagte (ed), *Military Masculinities: Identity and the State*, pp. 71–90. Westport: Praeger.

Heberle, Renée. 2009. 'Rethinking the Social Contract: Masochism and Masculinist Violence', in Renée Heberle/ Victoria Grace (eds), *Theorizing Sexual Violence*, pp. 125–46. New York: Routledge.

Hockey, John. 2009. '"Switch On": Sensory Work in the Infantry', *Work, Employment and Society*, 23(3): 477–93.

———. 2003. 'No More Heroes: Masculinity in the Infantry', in Paul R. Higate (ed), *Military Masculinities, Identity and the State*, pp.15–42. Westport: Praeger.

Jünger, Ernst. 2017. 'Über den Schmerz', in Ernst Jünger (ed), *Essays I: Betrachtungen zur Zeit: Sämtliche Werke*, Vol. 9. Stuttgart: Klett-Cotta.

McSorley, Kevin. 2015. 'War and the Body: Introduction', in Kevin McSorley (ed), *War and the Body: Militarisation, Practice and Experience*, pp. 1–32. London/New York: Routledge.

Nitobé, Inazo. 1900. *Bushido: The Soul of Japan: An Exposition of Japanese Thought*. Tokyo: Shokwabo.

Pohl, Rolf. 2004. *Feindbild Frau: Männliche Sexualität, Gewalt und die Abwehr des Weiblichen*. Hannover: Offizin.

Popitz, Heinrich. 1986. *Phänomene der Macht*. Tübingen: Mohr Siebeck.

Scarry, Elaine. 1985. *The Body in Pain: The Making and Unmaking of the World*. Oxford/New York: Oxford University Press.

Seidler, Victor. 2015. 'Bodies, Masculinities and Complex Inheritances', in Kevin McSorley (ed), *War and the Body: Militarisation, Practice and Experience*, pp. 225–30. London/New York: Routledge.

Shay, Jonathan. 1994. *Achilles in Vietnam: Combat, Trauma and the Undoing of Character*. New York: Simon & Schuster.

Sylvester, Christine. 2011. *Experiencing War*. New York: Routledge.

Tanner, Jakob. 1994. 'Körpererfahrung, Schmerz und die Konstruktion des Kulturellen', *Historische Anthropologie: Kultur–Gesellschaft–Alltag*, 3: 489–502.

Zipfel, Gaby. 2014. '"Beyond Good and Evil for Once!" "Authorized Transgressions" and Women in Wartime', *Eurozine*, 25 April. https://www.eurozine.com/beyond-good-and-evil-for-once/ (accessed 06 November 2018).

Zolkos, Magdalena. 2016. 'Porous Skins and Tactile Bodies: Juxtapositions of the Affective and Sentimental Ideas of the Subject', *Humanities*, 5(3): 77.

What is Sexual About Sexual Violence?
Some Preliminary Remarks

GABY ZIPFEL

In our everyday consciousness, the relationship between violence and sexuality is as implicitly omnipresent as it is explicitly unthematized. Taking a discourse analysis approach, a review of a wide range of text forms (expressions used in everyday conversation, literature, reports in the media) would likely reveal a code of practice involving awareness, obfuscation—what Reemtsma (2008a: 7) calls *Verrätselung*—and suppression.

In contrast, the relationship between sexuality and power and sexuality and domination are standard topics of theoretical debate, though the overall impression is that violence is implied when power and domination are discussed. Yet in principle, power and domination are merely positions from which violence can be, but is not necessarily, enacted. As such, analyses based on theories of power offer little insight into the relationship between sexuality and violence per se, and at best refer to violence as a means for creating certain conditions without actually exploring the significance of the phenomenon itself. Psychoanalytical and lexicological theories are the exceptions, as they examine the link between sexuality and violence for its explanatory power regarding individual sex drives. Beyond their diagnostic significance, these theories also offer insights into the social and cultural environment in which sexual drives emerge (Quindeau/Sigusch 2005), such as when the founder of the German 'critical sexology' school of thought Volkmar Sigusch claims sexuality could potentially also be read as "a source and breeding ground for suppression, inequality and aggression" (Sigusch 1996).

CONGRUENCIES

Sexuality and violence can both be initially described as behavioural and experiential contexts based on the affective expressions of vital life via the body. In turn these affects are structured by experience written into the body and the spirit, and by the adoption of constructions of meaning in a specific historical, social and cultural context (Laqueur 1992; Irigaray 1980). Sexual and violent acts and experience are predicated on certain anatomical, hormonal and physiological conditions on the one hand, and on meaningful agreements on the other (Wrede 2000; Simon/Gagnon 2000).

Behavioural and experiential relationships are communicative, reciprocal interactions.[1] Violence and sexuality both produce states of arousal accompanied by positive and negative expectations; the prospect of lust or pain, liberation or traumatisation, success or failure, safety or danger. Since risk and danger are inherent to the state of arousal (Stoller 1979: 19), in addition to lustful anticipation, it can also give rise to a sense of powerlessness, which can then manifest in feelings such as fear and shame (Wurmser 2007).

COPING STRATEGIES

Assuming we actually possess the freedom to choose between lustfully succumbing to a state of arousal or using aggressive coping or passive avoidance strategies to avoid the risks and fears associated with it, then the psychoanalytical drive theory indicates that this freedom to choose is severely limited by the fact that "desire, drive as a limit constant between the physical and the psychological, as a psychosomatic unit [...] blocks the expectations and desires of consciousness" (Küchenhoff 2000: 56). The theory of the "inaccessibility of physical desire" (ibid.) derived from this understanding becomes problematic at the latest when used to justify a subject that cannot be held accountable for its actions because those actions resulted from a sense of being overpowered. Here we can identify one of the interfaces at which states of arousal triggered by sexual desire or the desire to use violence are biologistically interpreted as overpowering. Arising from a strategy described as a coping mechanism, the argument goes that transforming fear into lust, "replacing danger with pleasure" (Stoller 1979: 4) essentially becomes an affect the individual is helpless to resist. Robert Stoller's theory that sexual arousal is always accompanied by a certain level of hostility, the biographically specific approach to dealing with the sense of threat triggered by arousal, seems more plausible:

> My theory is as follows: In the absence of special physiological factors (such as a sudden androgen increase in either sex), and putting aside the obvious effects that result from direct stimulation of erotic body parts, it is hostility—the desire, overt or hidden, to harm another person—that generates and enhances sexual excitement. The absence of hostility leads to sexual indifference and boredom. The hostility of eroticism is an attempt, repeated over and over, to undo childhood traumas and frustrations that threatened the development of one's masculinity or femininity. The same dynamics, though in different mixes and degrees, are found in almost everyone, those labelled perverse and those not so labelled. (Stoller 1979: 6)

Simon and Gagnon counter Stoller's thesis by asserting that the reverse conclusion is just as plausible, namely that

> in many people, sexual arousal is what initially gives rise to hostility. In this context, hostility could be seen as a moral masquerade that sexual desire sometimes employs in the attempt to confound the preventative measures of the autonomous inner eye to allow the expression of worrisome feelings or self-constructions. The hostility the script directs against the other, or that it encourages from the other against the self, cannot be the source of desire, and instead serves merely to legitimise such desires by making them both socially acceptable and plausible. (Simon/Gagnon 2000: 84)

They take a different approach to accentuating the individual coping strategy of using hostility to ward off looming frustrations.

CORRESPONDING POTENTIALS

Sexual and violent interactions incorporate interdependent potentials: The potential to arouse can only develop if it encounters excitability in some form. When enacting sexual violence, the perpetrator fantacises that he has the ability to arouse the victim against her/his will, forcing a physical reaction though physical stimulation or transforming sexual lust into a lust for violence (Zipfel 2004). The ability to feel lustful desire is predicated on the experience of being desired (Quindeau 2005). If this sense of being desired, defined here as a positive experience, is absent, then sexual desire can be experienced as a threat, as subjugation to another, which is then deflected via an act of sexual violence against this other.

The power to inflict injury can only be realised in the presence of a counterpart vulnerable to injury (Popitz 1986).

> Human beings are victims of violence because we are bodies. And because we have a body, we can transform others into victims. This physical dual-existence defines our relationship to violence. We use our bodies to act, while as bodies we are doomed to suffer. We are capable of violence, and subject to violence. The body can inflict injury and is also open to receiving injury. (Sofsky 1996: 31)

The fragility of this assigned position arises from the fact that the power to inflict injury and the vulnerability to receiving injury are equally inherent in every individual. Accordingly, using our power to inflict injury could also be interpreted as an act that represents an attempt to nullify the actor's vulnerability to receiving injury.

The experience of pain and the experience of lust are both bound to the body. The very thing the contemporary image of individual sexual love promises as the highest level of human joy, namely the lustful merging with another human being whose body and spirit are beloved, proves, through the experience of inflicted pain, to be a fundamentally destructive attack on the self: "The body is not an element of a human being, but rather its constitutional centre. As such, the injury also affects soul and spirit, the self and the social form of existence" (Sofsky 1996: 66). So violently coerced sexuality counteracts the expectation of pleasure linked with the potential of one's own body. Inger Agger and Søren Buus Jensen note that the sexual imprinting of both the victim and the perpetrator are tied up in the psychodynamics of this interaction.

> The victim experiences the assault as an attack on her/his sexual perception of the body aimed at destroying her/his sexual identity. A key component of this traumatising and identity-destroying attack is the feeling of being made an accomplice in an ambiguous situation that confusingly comingles aggressive and libidinous elements (Agger/Jensen 1993, as cited in Skjelsbæk 2001: 220).

LIMITATIONS

The narrative and experiential links between sexuality and violence oscillate between the opposing abilities to reproduce and to kill on the one hand, and the understanding that we are always vulnerable and must ultimately die on the other. The inevitability of death as the ultimate expression of our sense of subjugation and powerlessness is countered by the real potential housed in the ability to kill and the imagined virility of being able to achieve immortality through generativity (here reproduction).

In the eighteenth century, it was popular to circumscribe sexual ecstasy as 'dying' and orgasms as 'le petit mort' (Laqueur 1992: 14). In the twentieth century, soldiers, who must always be prepared to kill and to die, have reported the 'sexual drive' experienced in the extreme situations they are faced with. Their descriptions illustrate how anger, displeasure, hate and horror can stimulate violence, and how the practice of excessive violence can trigger sexual arousal (Bourke 1999). Reports from soldiers have described the "wild joy of borderless inhibition" (Sofsky 1996: 184) triggered by commanding power over life and death. This "wild joy" is not just elicited by the triumphant knowledge of having cheated death, for "the perpetrator experiences absolute sovereignty, absolute freedom from the burdens of morality and society in the suffering and death of the victim" (Sofsky 1996: 61).

THE NEED FOR REGULATION

The "burdens of morality and society" or the achievements of civilisation in the modern era that confront the modern human subject fixate on a re-positioning of violence and of sexuality. The eighteenth century saw the establishment of a new "order of knowledge" and a historically unique construction of reality with "the *human being* as a self-empowered, organising subject" (Sigusch 2008: 28) at its centre. "*Human beings* as such did not exist before the end of the eighteenth century" (Foucault 1993: 373, as cited by Sigusch 2008: 27). At the same time, a dichotomy developed between the public and the private sphere that would come to characterise the modern era. The public sphere is the locus for negotiating interpretations of reality, along with the normative rules derived from them that manifest in the 'order of knowledge'. In contrast, the private sphere promises an intimate space of individual freedom in which moral standards are a matter of choice and may or may not be followed. Once established, this 'order of knowledge' becomes self-perpetuating and professes to act as a guarantor of order, peace and security through self-evident practical constraints and a definition of normality.

SHIFT IN THE DISCOURSE ON VIOLENCE

A significant moment in this modernisation process was a fundamental shift in the discourse on violence from Machiavelli's opening question, "When is violence called for and to what degree?" to Thomas Hobbes' deliberation, "How can violence be limited?" Violence is problematised *in and of itself,* a process that generates the idea that violence can only be considered legitimate if it serves as protection from even worse violence. A special concept for sorting violence into that which is permitted, necessary or forbidden develops (Reemtsma 2008a: 190ff), in which the state is granted a monopoly on violence.

Closer inspection reveals that the normative standard of renouncing all violence—supposedly unanimous in public discourse—is only rudimentarily followed in day-to-day reality.

Instead, real world practices of violence are subjected to a range of legitimising and rationalising patterns seeking to bridge the gap between the normative standard and actual practice. A co-worker who brags over drinks that he beat a woman to a pulp will, in all likelihood, alienate his listeners. When that same person claims to have "screwed a woman so hard she couldn't take it anymore," he can realistically expect knowing nods of acceptance and recognition.

The use of violence legitimised as a means for creating social order and generating a sense of community and cohesion is not just limited to youth subcultures. Corporeal punishment of children was not outlawed until the year 2000, and rape within a marriage has only been a crime since 1997. Violence and an inclination towards aggression are expressions of dominance and superiority and as such have positive associations as resources that enable us to successfully assert ourselves. On closer inspection, behaviours that seem odd and contradictory at first glance demonstrate compliance with the implicit agreement that violence may be employed to establish a position of superiority. Such as when GI Cooper, part of a supply unit stationed in Great Britain during the Second World War, asks his rape victim: "Why don't you speak to me? All the other girls around here do", and threatens her, "If you don't let me get what I want, I'll strangle you". Before letting her go after the rape, he asks if she would like to go dancing with him the following week (Lilly 2007: 54).

Jan Philipp Reemtsma suggests that in phenomenological terms, violence can be divided into three groups: locative, raptive and autotelic (these categories can overlap in the actual practice of violence). Locative is intent on moving or removing a body standing in the way of achieving a goal (such as in a battle during a war), raptive seeks to overpower a body so it can be used (primarily sexually) and autotelic destroys purely for destruction's sake (Reemtsma 2008a: 58).

The first two forms of violence inflicted on a body are inherent in instrumental moments, and can be presumed to be based on a means-to-an-end strategy. They are underpinned by a logic of reaping benefit from an action that, while understandable because of its overriding goal, is to be condemned for the means chosen. With both locative and raptive violence, the perpetrator initiates an interaction with the victim that at least leaves vestigial scope for a reaction. Such acts of violence are not legitimised, but they are 'understood', which can include understanding the perpetrator and often assigning the victim part of the blame for the interaction, such as when a woman who has been raped is imputed to have goaded the perpetrator into committing the act, or someone standing in the way is accused of being careless or in the wrong place at the wrong time.

Autotelic violence does not submit as easily to such attempts to label violence an ultimately explicable act, a phenomenon that can be managed using penalties and ostracism. The debate surrounding the mysteriousness of the phenomenon in which "ordinary men" (Browning 1992) are capable of autotelic excesses of violence might be read as an attempt to escape from the horror and confusion this form of violence generates, the troublesome reality of having to accept that such events were not limited to the pre-Modern era and are indeed rampant in the twenty-first century despite the expectation of ostracism, and the fact that they could happen to anyone. Perhaps it was also fundamentally an attempt to retrieve the idea of the pathology of such acts. Jan Philipp Reemtsma (2008b) cites Alexander Mitscherlich's response to accusations that his criticism of the German medical community under National Socialism denounced an entire profession simply because of a few crazy sadists: "To understand a crime of this magnitude we cannot resort to the assumption that it was committed by a few crazy sadists—there are just not that many out there".

> Just as absolute political power manifests itself in the ability to not just kill the bodies of subjects, but to eviscerate and exhibit them as well, in which the modern limitation of political power found its actual and symbolic expression to withhold the right to autotelic power, *so too absolute individual power manifests itself in the possibility of exerting autotelic violence—unrestricted power that pursues no other end than itself.* (Reemtsma 2008a: 71, author's emphasis)

This ability to exercise unrestricted power seems to hold the promise of an absolutely fascinating advantage, such as the advantage of freedom for men, "who would no longer have to let a woman or the guilt of morality hold them back when it came time to make people quake with fear:" such as the romanticised reliving of the First World War in 1923: "Finally, beyond good and evil for once! Finally, for once a man, inhuman, and superman!" (cit. in Kühne 2004: 41).

In 'At the Mind's Limits', Jean Améry addresses this individual opportunity to exert unlimited power as violence enacted *on* a body *through* a body when he describes his experience of torture in Nazi prisons:

> The first blow brings home to the prisoner that he is helpless, and thus it already contains in the bud everything that is to come. [...] The other person, opposite whom I exist physically in the world and with whom I can exist only as long as he does not touch my skin surface as border, forces his own corporeality on me with the first blow. (Améry 1977: 56)

"He is on me and thereby destroys me", he continues, adding "It is like a rape". When Améry experiences the lust for violence that triggers the enacting of violence by the perpetrator as a rape, he hints at the close connotation between sexuality and violence that regularly and often explicitly manifests itself in acts of torture when the attack on the body, such as on the victim's genitals, thematises the victim's sexuality.

COLLECTIVE SINGULAR SEXUALITY

The term "collective singular sexuality" developed as part of the modernisation process in which violence, as described above, was also resituated (Sigusch 2008: 46). In displacing religion as normative and endowed with meaning, it combines bodily experiences and activities that previously led an 'undefined' coexistence, sexualising and socialising them. While the society of the Middle Ages was characterised by inconsistency in sensation and behaviour, the needs and reactions of people in the modern

era are increasingly normalised and adjusted to meet the demands
of new production methods: abnegation and adaptability,
austerity, discipline, reliability, serviceability and self-control all
comply with the desired social character that is to be created less
through external force than through self-regulation techniques the
individual can learn. To comply with the demands of the civil
community, the modern subject feels compelled to subject feelings,
affects and needs to supervisory self-observation with the objective
of controlling them so as not to be overwhelmed by them.

If Sigusch's description of the modern "objective of sexuality"
is true, "fixated on lust yet anti-erotic, simultaneously intimate and
public, a belief in science, petty, denunciatory, hypochondriac,
improving and corrective, both degradative and constructive,
procreative, chastening, encompassing and totalising" (Sigusch
2008: 40), it reveals the impositions the individual is subjected to
by the modern era's demand for control (demographic policies,
eugenics, medicine) and instrumentalisation (orientation of affects
and need to align with the new demands in working processes and
the military) and which encourage self-hate and an abnegation of
lust.

Sexuality becomes a product of learning, a subject to social
control throughout its entire genesis (Wrede 2000: 32) that brings
forth a new order. This new order focuses on the erotically
charged nuclear family now responsible for ensuring compliance
with the ban on sexual activity involving children, procreation
as the only legitimate goal of sexual activity, state regulated and
controlled child rearing and the militarisation of young men,
the rationalisation of as many areas of life as possible, and the
definitive power of medicine. Since then, the debate around
sexuality has been subject to a paradox that still exerts influence
to this day:

> On the one hand, the unremarkable, 'normal', 'psychological'
> activities were granted a level of importance and injected with
> a level of lust that exploded the old order, and the insistent
> and never-ending conversation about sexuality, the isolating,
> observing, investigating, recording, transgressing, sinning,
> confessing, admitting, systematising, analysing, training, advising,

treating, codifying etc. enlarged, puffed up sexuality over the course of the eighteenth, nineteenth and twentieth centuries. It has been massively overrated, imbued with a symbolic and real meaning and granted a power over human beings that can only compare to that of our material goods and money fetishes. On the other hand, everything erotic, arousing, sexual was suppressed and rendered taboo, forbidden and subject to punishment, never to be named. This paradox of simultaneous emphasis and suppression, of encouraging that which is frowned upon, propagating that which should disappear, the self-rendering in public what has been self-induced; this paradox is still in effect to this day, though in a much more refined form. This forbidding creation of appealing repressive obsession, this interweaving of obliterating prohibition and generating demand places the sexual sphere in a permanent spotlight, creating an insatiable potential for conflict. (Sigusch 2008: 32)

At the moment of its conception, the civil form of sexuality becomes a "monstrous construct of sodomy/delinquency/guilty pleasure/dysfunction/illness" (Sigusch 2008: 41).

The spectre of onanism dominated debate in the eighteenth century, then 'perversions', specifically homosexuality, took centre stage in the nineteenth century. 'Sexual dysfunction and gender identity disorders' became the focus in the twentieth century, and today concepts of de-gendering and gender blending have been called upon to take control of the potential for conflict inherent in the concept of sexuality through normative standards and not uncommonly through medically induced forcible violations of the body.

MALE PHANTASIES

The persistent hegemonic and naturalistically conveyed idea of the gender binary expressed in a female and a male body is, as Thomas Laqueur demonstrated, an idea born in the late eighteenth century that replaced its historic predecessors—the idea of a single sex—and generated a new definition of the sexual nature of human beings. The one-sex concept of the body was based on the idea of a completely developed, superior male and an incompletely developed female counterpart. Without relinquishing the theory of male dominance, this model was replaced by a concept of complementary gendered bodies equipped with correlative reproductive functions (Laqueur 1992).

Corresponding male and female gender *characteristics* are derived from the complementary gendered *bodies*. These characteristics preordained a gender to either labour in the public (men) or the private (women) sphere (Honegger 1991). The hierarchically ordered patriarchal pair is represented as the vulnerable, inferior, dependent woman and her cosmopolitan, autonomous, male protector with his capacity to inflict injury. But since neither the human individual imagined as female nor as male flourishes in this harmony of complementarity, in real life gender constructs can only be enforced via considerable investment in normative constraints, differentiations and de-realisations. The gender identities assigned qua biological sex must be laboriously acquired in a never-ending process and the 'qualities' associated with them (superior, independent, potent, desirable, accommodating) must be on constant display, while those desires and needs that run counter to the respective gender identity are repressed and suppressed.

In her *Philosophical Investigation of Rape*, Louise Du Toit (2009) vividly describes how comprehensively the construct of harmoniously complementary gender binary hides the violence and exclusion that must factually be employed to relegate the female gender to its position in the private sphere, thus reserving the public sphere with the prerogative of interpretation and political decision-making exclusively for the male gender.

The use of violence and sexuality to uphold this gender order is a matter of course in daily life, a fact revealed in not only the immense hesitation that preceded the legal sanctioning of rape within marriage, but also the continuing ambivalent interpretations sexual violence is subjected to in public discourse, an ambivalence reflected in the sexism of everyday communication and which, as hate speech, can initiate or legitimise violent acts (Trömel-Plötz 1984).

DECONSTRUCTIONS

The sexual revolution of the 1968 generation did not dissolve the gender dichotomy, as the celebrated sexual liberation it sought promoted promiscuity for male sexuality. At the same time, women began demanding self-determination over their own bodies in direct response to the unreasonable demand of availability placed on them, with lasting effectiveness. Male self-representations and self-heroisations were assessed for their level of violence propensity and the 'the private is political' slogan introduced a process that resulted in public debate on the practices of sexual abuse and violence, which had remained hidden in the private sphere, and on the fixation with the penis and virility in representations of male sexuality. Men, who "have at their disposal a highly significant sexual organ but not a sexual body that can be occupied" (Dannecker 2005: 87), were confronted with the extremely limited space they conceded to the desires of women—an indirect response to "the heterosexual man's fear of femininity and his difficulty in yielding as an object of desire" (Dannecker 2005: 93).

The debates that began in the 1980s around the possible deconstruction of socially, historically and culturally formulated sex/gender definitions disrupted the impact of the gender binary so consistently discriminatory towards the female gender. Nevertheless, it has become clear that the original radicalness of the concept of self-liberation through radical challenge was not necessarily effective: "though not currently the case, in theory 'sex' can be conceived of without 'gender'. The reverse, however, does not apply. An irreducible 'remainder' persists with its own materiality, which, though it can be imagined through thought, cannot be conjured up by thought" (Axeli-Knapp 1994: 277).

According to Gunter Schmidt (2000), the "self-determination discourse" of the 1980s rendered "normal" sexuality, heterosexuality, just one of many lifestyles, a group that included the former "perversions", with the exception of forms of sexual behaviour that retained the perversion label due to a power imbalance between partners. The deconstruction of traditions around sexual, romantic and family relationships led to a "home in plurality" (Schmidt 2000: 270), in which "sexual preferences and orientations, types of relationships, forms of child rearing and cohabitation, versions of masculinity and femininity" were no longer proscribed, but negotiated based on a "consensual morality" (ibid.).

CONCLUSIONS

Gunter Schmidt's optimistic conclusion,

> so sexuality at the end of the century has undergone a process of liberalisation, democratisation and the elimination of drama. We have largely uncluttered sex, freeing it from religion, from the patriarchy (almost) and from psychoanalysis. Not bad for a time period of not even 50 years. It is almost a success story, […]. (Schmidt 2000: 270)

Sounds a bit too good to be entirely true. Sigusch's conclusion serves to qualify it: The "autonomous citizen", he says, citing Hegel, remains "disunited with reality" and as such

> the 'sighing' continued, the misery of life did not disappear, people did not lose their sense of 'uneasiness in culture' that Sigmund Freund would later mention (1930). And so they dragged themselves from one sexual revolution to the next for more than one hundred years, always hoping that life would begin. (Sigusch 2008: 31)

The idea of fundamentally proscribing, banning and containing violence cannot be realised simply via proclamations and the suppression of its continual excessive use, just as this is not the way forward to a sexuality free of violence and domination.

Maud Ann Bracke (2018) recently recounted how the Women's Movement of the 1970s used its 'speaking out' strategy as a countermeasure against intractable ignorance regarding everyday and omnipresent forms of sexual violence. Speaking out encouraged women to talk about their experiences in public and from their perspectives and wrest back control of interpretative authority over these experiences. Considering all the difficulties associated with speaking out, which authors like Renée Heberle (1996) have critically assessed, the strategy proved effective by counteracting isolation, rendering the shared gender-political context of the respective individual experience visible, and effecting change in national and international law despite all its shortcomings.

Returning to a policy of "La Prise de Parole" (de Certeau 1968) as part of the #MeToo debate could counteract an excessively compliantly optimistic take on the current *zeitgeist*, as Gunter Schmidt's conclusion above, and prevent the experience of sexual violence from being marginalised as a problem to be solved in the private sphere. In response to the misgivings expressed, which seem bizarre in view of the 'cases' up for debate, that public shaming essentially tosses the baby out with the bathwater and threatens erotic banter between the sexes, one could argue there is more at stake here than just sanctioning intolerable violence. Fighting to end such practices goes hand in hand with the right to sexual self-determination, the right to take pleasure in one's own desires and in intimacy, rather than serving the external desire fixated on the link between sexuality and violence—even if the tale that 'she doth protest too much' proves exceptionally firmly entrenched.[2]

Translated from German by Sarah Smithson-Compton.

NOTES

1. This also applies to autoerotic or self-destructive acts, which are ultimately the manifestation of reactions to social and emotional experiences.
2. This is not to ignore or deny the fact that men and women can both desire an intertwining of sex and violence; however this in no way justifies the demoralising assumption that it must always be so.

REFERENCES

Améry, Jean. 1977. *Jenseits von Schuld und Sühne: Bewältigungsversuche eines Überwältigten*. Stuttgart: Klett-Cotta.

218
GABY ZIPFEL

Axeli-Knapp, Gudrun. 1994. 'Politik der Unterscheidung', in Institut für Sozialforschung Frankfurt (ed), *Geschlechterverhältnisse und Politik*, pp. 262–87. Frankfurt a. M.: Suhrkamp.

Bourke, Joanna. 1999. *An Intimate History of Killing: Face-to-Face Killing in Twentieth-Century Warfare*. London: Granta Books.

Bracke, Maud Anne. 2018. '"Women's 1968 is Not Yet Over": The Capture of Speech and the Gendering of 1968 in Europe', *The American Historical Review*, 123(3):753–7.

Browning, Christopher. 1992. *Ordinary Men: Reserve Police Battalion 101 and the Final Solution in Poland*. New York: Harper Collins.

Dannecker, Martin. 2005. 'Männliche und weibliche Sexualität', in Ilka Quindeau/Volkmar Sigusch (eds), *Freud und das Sexuelle: Neue psychoanalytische und sexualwissenschaftliche Perspektiven*, pp. 80–93. Frankfurt a. M./New York: Campus.

DeCerteau, Michel.1968. *La Prise de Parole: Pour une Nouvelle Culture*. Paris: Seuil.

Du Toit, Louise. 2009. *A Philosophical Investigation of Rape: The Making and Unmaking of the Feminine Self*. New York: Routledge.

Heberle, Renée. 1996. 'Deconstructive Strategies and the Movement against Sexual Violence', *Hypatia* 11(4):63–76.

Honegger, Claudia. 1991. *Die Ordnung der Geschlechter: Die Wissenschaften vom Menschen und das Weib 1750–1850*. Frankfurt a. M.: Campus.

Irigaray, Luce. 1980. *Speculum: Spiegel des anderen Geschlechts*. Frankfurt a. M.: Suhrkamp.

Küchenhoff, Joachim. 2002. 'Öffentlichkeit und Körpererfahrung', in Gunter Schmidt/Bernhard Strauß (eds), *Sexualität und Spätmoderne: Über den kulturellen Wandel der Sexualität*, pp. 53–70. Gießen: Psychosozial-Verlag.

Kühne, Thomas. 2004. 'Massen-Töten: Diskurse und Praktiken der kriegerischen und genozidalen Gewalt im 20. Jahrhundert', in Peter Gleichmann/Thomas Kühne (eds), *Massenhaftes Töten: Kriege und Genozide im 20. Jahrhundert*, pp. 11–52. Essen: Klartext.

Laqueur, Thomas. 1992. *Auf den Leib geschrieben: Die Inszenierung der Geschlechter von der Antike bis Freud*. Frankfurt a. M./New York: Campus.

Lilly, Robert. 2007. *Taken by Force: Rape and American GIs in Europe during World War II*. New York: Palgrave MacMillan.

Popitz, Heinrich. 1986. *Phänomene der Macht*. Tübingen: Mohr.

Quindeau, Ilka 2005. 'Braucht die Psychoanalyse eine Triebtheorie?' in: Ilka Quindeau/Volkmar Sigusch (eds), *Freud und das Sexuelle: Neue psychoanalytische und sexualwissenschaftliche Perspektiven*, pp. 193–208. Frankfurt a. M./New York: Campus.

Quindeau, Ilka/Sigusch, Volkmar (eds). 2005. *Freud und das Sexuelle: Neue psychoanalytische und sexualwissenschaftliche Perspektiven*. Frankfurt a. M./ New York: Campus.

Reemtsma, Jan Philipp. 2008a. *Trust and Violence: An Essay on a Modern Relationship*. Princeton/Oxford: Princeton University Press.

———. 2008b. 'Theorie der Gewalt: Hässliche Wirklichkeit', *Süddeutsche Zeitung* (Munich), 25 January.

Schmidt, Gunter. 2000. 'Spätmoderne Sexualitätsverhältnisse', in Christine Schmerl/Stefanie Soine/Marlene Stein-Hilbers/Birgitta Wrede (eds), *Sexuelle Szenen: Inszenierungen von Geschlecht und Sexualität in modernen Gesellschaften*, pp. 268–79. Opladen: Leske&Budrich.

Sigusch, Volkmar. 2008. *Geschichte der Sexualwissenschaft*, Frankfurt a.M./ New York: Campus.

———. 1996. 'Die Zerstreuung des Eros', *Der Spiegel* (Hamburg), 03 June.

Simon, William/Gagnon, John H. 2000. 'Wie funktionieren sexuelle Skripte?', in Christine Schmerl/Stefanie Soine/Marlene Stein-Hilbers/Birgitta Wrede (eds), *Sexuelle Szenen: Inszenierungen von Geschlecht und Sexualität in modernen Gesellschaften*, pp. 70–98. Opladen: Leske&Budrich.

Skjelsbæk, Inger. 2001. 'Sexual Violence and War: Mapping out a Complex Relationship', *European Journal of International Relations*, 7(2):211–37.

Sofsky, Wolfgang. 1996. *Traktat über die Gewalt*. Frankfurt a. M.: S. Fischer.

Stoller, Robert J. 1979. *Sexual Excitement: Dynamics of Erotic Life*. New York: Pantheon.

Trömel-Plötz, Senta. 1984. *Gewalt durch Sprache: Die Vergewaltigung von Frauen in Gesprächen*. Frankfurt a. M.: Fischer Taschenbuch.

Wrede, Brigitte. 2000. 'Was ist Sexualität? Sexualität als Natur, als Kultur und als Diskursprodukt', in Christine Schmerl/Stefanie Soine/Marlene Stein-Hilbers/Birgitta Wrede (eds), *Sexuelle Szenen: Inszenierungen von Geschlecht und Sexualität in modernen Gesellschaften*, pp. 25–43. Opladen: Leske&Budrich.

Wurmser, Léon. 2007. *Die Maske der Scham: Die Psychoanalyse von Schameffekten und Schamkonflikten*. Frankfurt a. M.: Klotz.

Zipfel, Gaby. 2004. 'Schlachtfeld Frauenkörper', in Peter Gleichmann/ Thomas Kühne (eds), *Massenhaftes Töten: Kriege und Genozide im 20. Jahrhundert*, pp. 244–64. Essen: Klartext.

GENDER/ENGENDERING

Ideas about gender and its structural underpinnings shape armed conflicts as well as patterns of sexual violence. During periods of military combat and occupation, gender relations are often extremely volatile. 'Engendering' is an intersectional process, operating in relation to ethnicity, race, sexual orientation and nation, as well as other social divisions such as caste or class. Military practices and strategies of gendering both combatants and civilian populations need to be explored. To what extent do these practices and strategies shape patterns of sexual violence in war?

Sexual violence in armed conflicts impacts upon post-war social orders. War time experiences and practices continue to influence social relations after war has ended. Do these processes duplicate or disrupt gender norms of masculinity and femininity? And how are these norms tied to ideas of community, ethnicity and nation?

Intersectionality: A Critical Intervention

DUBRAVKA ŽARKOV

The idea of the conflictual positioning of women within, and complex workings of, different sets of power relations and structures of oppression can be traced back to Sojourner Truth (1797–1883) and her 'Ain't I a woman' talk; to the mid-twentieth century women's participation in anti-colonial struggles in (what was then called) the Third World; and to the criticism of white, middle-class, universalising forms of second wave feminism in the West, by black, migrant, non-heteronormative women's/feminist groups.

The term intersectionality is coined by Kimberle Crenshaw in the late 1980s, to indicate ambiguities and the conflictual positioning of black feminists in the struggle against both racism (in feminist movements) and sexism (in civil rights, anti-racist movements). The concept grew out of political struggles, and initially was coined as a radical social critique and a contribution to the analysis of social relations of power, of structural, systemic forces of oppression, exploitation, exclusion and marginalisation as well as privileges that influence women's and men's lives and experiences, through their ontological and epistemological location within the specific socio-political context.

Within academia, however, and especially with the 'identity turn,' intersectionality very quickly became reduced to a tool for analysing identity and (to some extent) identity politics, rather than power relationships and structures. Contemporary criticism is that the concept of diversity all too often replaces the concept of power, hence undermining intersectionality's potential for radical social critique, especially in the domain of (geo-political)

structural, economic inequalities. Liberal feminism especially—
as a dominant form of feminism in the West—is currently being
critiqued for erasing the history of black, Third World/Southern
and marginalised women's social movements and political struggles
that birthed the concept in the first place, and for appropriating
and 'whitening' it (Bilge 2013; Carbin/Edenheim 2013; Cho/
Crenshaw/McCall 2013; Ferree 2011; Salem 2016).

Some of the practices exposed in this criticism can also be
seen in the trajectory of the concept of intersectionality within
feminist war and conflict studies. In feminist work on war and
conflict, the idea of intersectionality was implicit in some work
before the mid-1980s. For example, it was understood that
the rape of women by enemy soldiers in the First and Second
World Wars was perpetrated because the women belonged to a
particular social and national group (for example, the rape of
German women by Soviet soldiers, or the rape of French women
by German soldiers). However, much of this work did not take
those realities as theoretically consequential for either gender or
conflict studies, often because it was informed by the second wave
(radical feminist) political and theoretical assumption that—peace
or war—through rape "all men keep all women in a state of fear"
(Brownmiller 1976: 51).

Explicit attention to the relevance of social identities and
relations of power 'other than gender' comes, within Western
feminist thinking on war, in the late 1980s and early 1990s (when
intersectionality as a concept is already in existence) with analysis of
the Falklands war (1982) and the First Gulf war (1991), in the UK
and US. This is especially so within the analyses of media, cultural
and political representations of UK and US women soldiers (as
symbols of the nation, race, emancipation) and Kuwaiti and
Iraqi women (as proverbial multiply oppressed Muslim women).
This work is to a larger extent focused on (multiple, fractured,
conflicting and contradicting) social identities, but not always on
power relations through which those identities are produced.[1]

The real qualitative turn in the explicit use of intersectionality
comes with the wars in ex-Yugoslavia and the Rwandan genocide,
and feminist attention to the intersections of gender and ethnicity.

With rare exceptions,[2] however, this was highly problematic, as the focus on identities has turned an intersectional analysis of 'gender and ethnicity' into the ethnicization of gender. Many feminist scholars doing intersectional analysis of those two violent conflicts have taken for granted the concept of 'identity wars' and have started with a pre-conceived idea about what specific social identities—rather than power relations—are relevant for which groups of women. So, the idea about the Balkans and Africa, and currently the Middle East, as traditional, backward and violent, pre-modern societies with 'ethnic,' 'tribal' and 'religious identities' has made it 'natural' that those identities are selected as relevant. In such an approach other identities have been largely ignored, so few feminist scholars have asked: why ethnicity and not class? Why religion and not colour? More importantly, such an approach has meant that scholars have not inquired how certain identities became privileged in the first place. Instead of asking what power relations are part of the privileging of specific practices and discourses that produce ethnicity, many scholars have simply taken identities for granted, as an essentialised category, an ontological mode of being of a specific subject.

Those ontologies are especially relevant for the feminist analyses of sexual violence in war, contributing to the revival of old colonial-cum-civilizational tales of the West and the rest. Therein, the Balkans and Africa continuously appear as ethnicised: 'local men' as rapists and 'local women' as rape victims. The 'internationals' (read: the West) are absent from the specific narratives of ethnicity and sexual violence, from the broader narratives of ethnicity as violent and from the narratives of identity altogether.

Here intersectionality serves to create two different ontological subjects: on the one side stands the Western female/male subject of non-violence (neither the perpetrator nor the victim) and of justice (who will protect the 'local' female victim and bring 'local' male perpetrators to justice using 'international' justice mechanisms). On the other side are the 'locals' marked by sexually violent masculinity and feminine rapability. Only the 'locals' are marked by (ethnic or any other) collective identity; the Westerner is defined as simply too modern a subject to adhere to collective identities. The scholarly distinction between backward, ethnic nationalisms, and modern, state-building nationalisms, allows for the maintenance of the distinctions between 'primordialism' and 'proper politics' and the subjects who pursue them. It is this ontology that bothers me (Žarkov 2014). This is, in my view, a fundamental element of othering that endlessly re-confirms—rather than challenges—hegemonic practices and discourses of contemporary wars and violence.

Consequently, feminist production of knowledge about war and violence focused on identities rather than on power constellations that allow for the erasure of everything but identities has also led feminists to accept—or at least: not criticise—currently hegemonic mainstream theorising on 'new wars,' 'greed and grievance,' 'youth bulge,' '(African) war-lordism' and alike, where identities and identity politics are defined as the core causes of contemporary 'local' wars. At the same time, those theorisations skilfully utilise (unstated) assumptions about gender, race, age, sexuality, ethnicity and class to recreate the Western subject of peace and justice, and the Balkan/African/Middle Eastern subject-object of violence.

The focus on identities has also resulted in the almost complete absence of feminist studies on political economies of war and violence, and their gendered, sexualised and racialised underpinnings. Possibilities for critical feminist analyses of the globalisation of the neo-liberal economy and its nexus with militarism, violent conflicts and war have been largely erased in the West by the disappearance of economic injustice as a major topic of feminist research as well as by the dominance of liberal feminism and its endorsement of the neo-liberal worldview.[3]

Such uses of intersectionality—as a method for studying identity and diversity, rather than power relations—combined with the absence of attention to structural economic, social and geo-political inequalities consequently serve to create different epistemological positions, indicating who is the subject of whose knowledge. So the (neo-)liberal Western feminist knowledge producer about contemporary wars is not very different from the (neo)liberal Western mainstream knowledge producer: they both assume that the western scholar is a knowing subject, and the 'local' (raped) woman and local (rapist) man are the objects of knowledge. Equally important, thus produced knowledge is translated into policies and practices, and the Western subject—next to defining itself as a subject of peace, justice and knowledge—also becomes an intervening subject. Here, the absence of 'identity' (defined as the cause of 'local' conflict) serves as a measure of neutrality and objectivity of the West (as the proverbial 'third party').

One hugely important consequence of such ontologies and epistemologies is the erasure of the feminist production of knowledge as a site of feminist political solidarity, especially transnational solidarity. The absence of (geo-)political economy in much of feminist studies of war and violence, in combination with the construction of identity as a marker of difference, and acceptance of much of the contemporary mainstream, hegemonic theorising on war, remain major problems for building alliances between feminist groups and movements. Thus seen, intersectionality has been a double-edged sword.

What would be a way forward in such a constellation? One suggestion: instead of simply studying identities and identity politics, and especially—instead of studying them as given, fixed, essential properties of *some* (!) women and men, we should approach them as products of social histories and power relationships, and ask: What is hidden when identities become over-exposed? We should also return to the study of structural inequalities and social relations of power, and global-to-local, geo-political and socio-economic injustices. We should continue to ask how gender, race, class, sexuality and ethnicity become part of those inequalities and injustices, however, not simply as identities, but as social relations of power constitutive of, and constituted by, time and space specific practices of privilege and exploitation.

NOTES

1. From late 1980s on, with constructivism in full swing, feminists not only study current wars, but also return to some of the 'older' wars—such as WW I and WW II—especially in the fields of literature and cultural representations. In many of those studies the

idea of intersectionality is very much present even if the concept itself is not. See for example the impressive collections edited by Cooper/Munich/Squier 1989; Cooke/Woollacott 1993; Melman 1998.
2. Such as, for example, work of Copelon 1993; Seifert 1996; Cockburn 1998.
3. See criticism by Mohanty 2003; Fraser 2009; Wilson 2015.

REFERENCES

Bilge, Sirma. 2013. 'Intersectionality Undone', *Du Bois Review: Social Science Research on Race*, 10(2):405–24.

Brownmiller, Susan. 1976. *Against Our Will: Men, Women and Rape*. New York: Bantam Books.

Carbin, Maria/Edenheim, Sara. 2013. 'The Intersectional Turn in Feminist Theory: A Dream of a Common Language?' *European Journal of Women's Studies*, 20(3):233–48.

Cho, Sumi/Crenshaw, Kimberle/McCall, Leslie. 2013. 'Toward a Field of Intersectionality Studies: Theory, Applications, and Praxis', *Signs: Journal of Women in Culture and Society*, 38(4):785–810.

Cockburn, Cynthia. 1998. *The Space Between Us: Negotiating Gender and National Identities in Conflict*. London: Zed Books.

Cooke, Miriam/Woollacott, Angela. 1993. *Gendering War Talk*. Princeton: Princeton University Press.

Cooper, Helen Margaret/Auslander Munich, Adrienne/Merill Squier, Susan. 1989. *Arms and the Woman: War, Gender and Literary Representation*. Chapel Hill: University of North Carolina Press.

Copelon, Rhonda. 1993. 'Surfacing Gender: Reconceptualizing Crimes against Women in Time of War', in Alexandra Stiglmayer (ed), *Mass Rape: The War against Women in Bosnia-Herzegovina*, pp. 197–218. Lincoln: University of Nebraska Press.

Crenshaw, Kimberle. 1989. 'Demarginalizing the Intersection of Race and Sex: A Black Feminist Critique of Antidiscrimination Doctrine, Feminist Theory and Antiracist Politics', *University of Chicago Legal Forum*, 1(1):139–67.

Ferree, Myra Marx. 2011. 'The Discursive Politics of Feminist Intersectionality', in Helma Lutz/Maria Teresa Herrera Vivar/Linda Supik (eds), *Framing Intersectionality: Debates on a Multi-Faceted Concept in Gender Studies*, pp. 55–65. Farnham: Ashgate.

Fraser, Nancy. 2009. 'Feminism, Capitalism and the Cunning of History', *New Left Review*, 56:97–117.

Melman, Billie. 1998. *Borderlines: Genders and Identities in War and Peace: 1870–1930*. New York: Routledge.

Mohanty, Chandra Talpade. 2003. '"Under Western Eyes" Revisited: Feminist Solidarity through Anticapitalist Struggles', *Signs: Journal of Women in Culture and Society*, 28(2):499–535.

Salem, Sara. 2016. 'Intersectionality and its Discontents: Intersectionality as Traveling Theory', *European Journal of Women's Studies*, pp. 1–16. https://doi.org/10.1177/1350506816643999 (accessed 20 August 2018).

Seifert, Ruth. 1996. 'The Second Front: The Logic of Sexual Violence in Wars', *Women's Studies International Forum*, 19(1–2):35–43.

Wilson, Kalpana. 2015. 'Towards a Radical Re-appropriation: Gender, Development and Neoliberal Feminism', *Development and Change: FORUM 2015*, https://onlinelibrary.wiley.com/doi/abs/10.1111/dech.12176 (accessed 20 August 2018).

Žarkov, Dubravka. 2014. 'Ontologies of International Humanitarian and Criminal Law: "Locals" and "Internationals"', in Dubravka Žarkov/Marlies Glasius (eds), *Narratives of Justice in and out of the Courtroom: Former Yugoslavia and Beyond*, pp. 3–21. Cham: Springer.

The Gender of Justice? Current Problems and New Directions in the Field of Sexual Violence in Armed Conflict

KIRSTEN CAMPBELL

NEW FIELDS, NEW PROBLEMS

Sexual violence in armed conflict has emerged as a highly visible problem in the fields of international criminal law, transitional and post-conflict justice and international peace and security in the last two decades (Buss 2014; Aoláin 2016). However, the identification of sexual violence as a problem in the scholarship and practice of these fields also inevitably invokes normative questions of prevention, prohibition, punishment and peace-building. This is because these fields describe conflict-related sexual violence through normative ideas of wrongful harms and rightful redress. Two dominant articulations of these normative ideas have emerged within these debates. These are ideas of 'gender harms' and of 'gender justice.' These ideas have now become two fundamental problems in these fields.

PROBLEM ONE: SEXUAL VIOLENCE IN ARMED CONFLICT AS 'GENDER HARM'?

Sexual Violence as Gender-Based Violence

In current scholarship and policy, sexual violence in armed conflict is typically described as 'sexual and gender-based violence (SGBV).' The idea of 'gender-based violence' first emerged in the context of feminist campaigning around violence against women in domestic jurisdictions in the 1970s, and then at the international level in the 1980s. While the 1979 Convention on the Discrimination Against Women did not address violence against women, these issues became increasingly visible in international campaigning and policy in the 1980s (Chinkin 1995, Merry 2006: 21). The Committee on the Elimination of Discrimination against Women (CEDAW) explicitly addressed this absence through their adoption of General Recommendation No. 19 on violence against women in 1992 (CEDAW 1992). This defined gender-based violence in terms of two elements. The first characterised gender-based violence as a form of discrimination on the basis that it is "violence that is directed against a woman because she is a woman or that affects women disproportionately." The second described gender-based violence as a category of acts, including sexual violence, namely, "acts that inflict physical, mental or sexual harm or suffering, threats of such acts, coercion and other deprivations of liberty" (CEDAW 1992). This approach was adopted by the Declaration on the Elimination of Violence Against Women by the UN General Assembly in 1993 (United Nations 1993).[1] Both instruments noted the particular vulnerability of women in armed conflict to gender-based violence. These definitions have been widely taken up in the field and are now used as standard concepts in international policy and literature.

This concept of sexual violence as gender-based violence was then taken up in the context of armed conflict in the 'Women, Peace, and Security' agenda of the United Nations (UN) in the 2000s, beginning with UN Security Council Resolution 1325, which called on parties to "armed conflict to take special measures to protect women and girls from gender-based violence, particularly rape and other forms of sexual abuse, and all other forms of violence in situations of armed conflict" (United Nations 2000: para.10). This agenda included a focus on sexual violence in armed conflict, explicitly characterised as a threat to international peace and security. With this focus came the establishment of the UN Action Against Sexual Violence, a multi-agency international programme in 2007, the appointment of a Special Rapporteur on Sexual Violence in Conflict in 2010 and four Security Council resolutions on this topic in 2008, 2009, 2010 and 2013 (United Nations Security Council 2008, 2009, 2010, 2013).

In these thematic policies and programmes, Karen Engle
points out that there is a shift from ideas of gender-based violence
against women to a gender-neutral concept of sexual violence in
armed conflict (2014: 13).[2] As defined by United Nations reporting
mechanisms under UN Security Council Resolution 1960, the
concept of 'conflict-related sexual violence' focuses on sexual
violence as a category of acts prohibited under international
criminal law (adopting the acts listed as such by the Rome Statute),
when committed in the context of conflict or post-conflict settings
and "other situations of concern" (United Nations 2011). The
Office of the Prosecutor of the International Criminal Court
(ICC OTP) itself refers to "sexual and gender-based crimes"
(ICC OTP 2014), a terminology that is now widely used in the
field of international criminal law (Brammertz/Jarvis 2016: 10).
The ICC OTP policy treats sexual violence as a gender-based
crime, which it defines in ostensibly 'gender neutral' and terms
as crimes "committed against persons, whether male or female,
because of their sex and/or socially constructed gender roles"
(ibid.: 3). This gender-neutral definition of conflict-related sexual
violence as a prohibited category of acts defined by the Rome
Statute is increasingly used in scholarly and practitioner literature.
However, the idea that conflict-related sexual violence is a gender-
based crime that disproportionately affects women remains an
important frame for these and subsequent general women, peace
and security resolutions, which continue to use the language of
'sexual and gender-based violence' and to identify women as its
predominant target. Key UN agencies continue to treat 'sexual
and gender-based violence' as the standard description of
violence against women, including in the monitoring, analysis and
reporting arrangements on conflict-related sexual violence in the
UN (United Nations 2015: 322, 2016).

The Gender Harm of Sexual Violence?

In these fields, then, there are two dominant concepts of the harm
of sexual violence. The first concept is sexual violence as a gender-
based violence, which understands sexual violence as a sub-set

of the category of gendered violence. This is a 'discrimination' model, which derives from ideas of sexual violence as a form of discrimination that breaches the fundamental rights of women. In this model, sexual violence is a 'gender harm,' which conceives sexual violence as a harm that disproportionately affects a category of persons because of their gender, namely women. Sexual violence in armed conflict is characterised as a 'gender harm' because it is a form of armed violence that targets or disproportionately affects women.

The second concept of harm is the 'gender neutral' model of sexual violence against men or women in armed conflict. This approach understands the harm as a category of criminal acts prohibited under international law, most often those designated as such by the Rome Statute. This concept of harm has two components. At the level of the individual, this model focuses on the "sexual aspect of the violence," as Karen Engle describes (2014: 28). The harm against the individual consists of a set of acts belonging to the same class because of their sexual nature. At the level of the international community, the sexual act only becomes harmful when rising to the level of an international crime. The harm consists of the breach of the international legal order, characterised as an illegal act, and/or its connection to armed conflict, characterised as a threat to international peace and security. Accordingly, this approach characterises the harm as a breach of international order, whether understood as legality or security.

These two models of the harms of sexual violence in armed conflict both present considerable conceptual problems. The model of sexual violence in armed conflict as a gendered harm suffers significant slippage between the concepts of sex, gender and social group. Ideas of gendered harms have assumed that women are victims of the harm. In doing so, they collapse ideas of biological sex (bodies identified as biologically female), gender identity (social norms of femininity) and gendered social groups (socially structured categories of persons as women). This reduction of 'gender' to 'women' is now increasingly reversed with the substitution of 'men' as the targeted group of sexual violence as the object of scholarly and policy attention. Regardless of whether groups of women or men are targeted, they take place in wars that are "thoroughly gendered" (Buss 2014: 6). It is crucial, therefore, to recognise the importance of gender relations for understanding how war is fought, who fights and who is 'targeted' for which forms of sexual violence (Chinkin/Charlesworth 2006). These gender relations of conflict include the construction of bodies as male and female, identities as femininities and masculinities and men and women as social groups, in differential and hierarchical relations of power. The second issue with the model of sexual violence as a gender harm is that it also slips between sexual, gendered and gender harms. There are important distinctions between harms to sexed bodies, such as the targeting of specific reproductive capacities of women, the gendered shaping of harms, such as the social meaning given to those reproductive capacities and harms to social groups, such as the targeting of women as civilians. These important distinctions and connections between harms to sexed bodies, the gendered shaping of harms and harms to social groups remain underexplored.

The gender-neutral approach focuses not upon the gender of the victim or the gendered nature of the harm, but upon the category of sexual acts prohibited under international law. As commentators have noted, this approach appears to capture the harm of sexual violence against both men and women. Moreover, there is now an emerging body of scholarship on variations in patterns of sexual violence in war which claims that 'gender' is not a 'causal' factor in conflict-related violence. This work rejects feminist explanations of the construction of gender as mono-causal, but, instead reduces 'gender' to the ascribed sexual identity of a group that is, groups of male or female victims (see, for example, Wood 2014; Cohen/Hoover Green/Wood 2013). In this approach, 'gender' necessarily becomes a variable, that is, a social characteristic of a group. Such an approach not only neglects 'gender' as a variable to be explained, but also fails to understand gender as a relation of power. Importantly, the 'gender neutral' model of the harm of sexual violence fails to capture the gendered nature of who targets whom and how, that is, the different forms that sexual violence takes against men and women, and the different patterns of perpetration by men and women. It is puzzled by how gender shapes different forms and patterns of sexual violence and the variations and continuities of groups of perpetrators and victims (Sellers 2008). Given that sexual violence against men and women takes different forms and occurs in different settings in conflict, and women are more likely to be disproportionately affected by sexual violence, an explanation of the gendered shaping of this violence is necessary.

The second issue is that a gender-neutral approach fails to situate sexual violence in the broader context of conflict, both in terms of addressing the social causes of sexual violence and the broader social structuring of conflict itself. As Davies and True describe, what has been lacking is an approach that can "deepen our understanding of the relationship between structural gender discrimination and mass SGBV" (2015: 3). Recent feminist scholarship has powerfully explored this relationship between structural gender inequality and sexual violence in pre-conflict and conflict contexts (see, for example, Davies/True 2015; Meger 2016). Without engaging with this hierarchical ordering of bodies, subjects and groups in 'peace' and 'war,' it is not possible to explain sexual violence in armed conflict, or to understand the relationship between sexual violence and other gendered harms of war. For example, sexual violence most often occurs as an element of wider patterns of gendered harms in conflict. Understanding this connection is an integral part of addressing this harm.

While this model appears to be gender-neutral, nevertheless it still relies on notions of gendered bodies and actions to identify the sexual nature of the violence. Particular gendered understandings of bodies and sexuality give content to the harm of sexual violence. As Judith Butler points out, 'the sexual' is a particular representation of acts and bodies. It represents this act (but not that) as sexual; this body part (but not that) as sexed; this body as female, but that as male. As such, it relies upon 'regulatory ideals' or norms that delineate certain acts as sexual, certain body parts as sexual organs and certain bodies as male and female. These norms give meaning to the otherwise abstract notion of 'sexual violence' because they structure the imaginary content of those harms in relation to masculine and feminine bodies. Because these 'regulatory ideas' constitute bodies as masculine or feminine, they also structure sexuality in terms of a heterosexual norm, since sexual desire for the opposite sex defines ideas of masculine and feminine sexuality. Accordingly, the notion of the 'sexual' in crimes of sexual violence is always already gendered.

THE 'GENDER RELATIONS' MODEL: NEW CONCEPTUAL STRATEGIES FOR UNDERSTANDING SEXUAL VIOLENCE AS A GENDERED HARM

To reframe these impasses in current approaches to 'gender harm,' I suggest three strategies for building a new 'gender relations' model of sexual violence in armed conflict. These strategies focus on building the key conceptual elements of this model, namely, (1) 'gender'; (2) 'harm'; and (3) 'conflict'.

The first theoretical strategy is to understand sexual violence in armed conflict in terms of gender relations, rather than understanding gender as an individual or group characteristic. This approach reframes the concept of sexual violence in terms of Butler's (2004) theory of performative gender. This is the idea of the construction of gender norms over time through the repetition of acts, such that the category of 'gender' is continually made through the iteration of these norms (Butler 2010: 168). In Butler's terms, the "regulatory norms of 'sex' work in a performative fashion to constitute the materiality of bodies, and more specifically, to materialise the body's sex, to materialise sexual difference in the service of the consolidation of the heterosexual imperative" (Butler 1993: 2). The 'regulatory ideal' that structures sexuality in terms of sexual difference is in actuality a heterosexual norm, for these ideas of masculine and feminine sexuality are defined in terms of sexual desire for the opposite sex (Butler 1997: 138–40).

Building on this concept of gender, sexual violence can be better understood as an act that through performance or enactment constitutes norms of masculinity and femininity through violence. This act produces sexual difference through its repetition of those norms by force upon the bodies of both men and women. Inger Skjelsbæk suggests that sexual violence is "the forms of violence which most clearly communicate masculinisation and feminisation" (2001: 227). Following this suggestion, we can understand sexual violence as a performative act that instantiates these categories of gender. For Butler, a performative act is "one which brings into being or enacts that which it names, and so marks the constitutive power of discourse" (1995: 134). 'Sexual violence' materialises ideas of masculinity and femininity—ideas of what it is to be a man or a woman—through its repetition of norms of sexual practices—what sexual acts are appropriate to men or women—which in turn relies upon notions of 'biological' difference—what it is to have a male or female body. This approach enables an understanding of how sexual violence ties together 'biological' bodies and 'social' roles, such that it produces bodies as male or female, to which it inscribes masculine or feminine norms through violence. For example, it understands sexual violence as an act that constructs a male body as feminine or constitutes a female body as a site of (national) reproduction, which thereby reproduces "the ideal types of 'masculinity' and 'femininity' as they are constituted in a patriarchal society in the state of war" (Nikolić-Ristanović 2000: ix).

Sexual violence in armed conflict constructs bodies through force, making and marking categories of ethnicity, religion and nation through categories of sexual difference. These categories are themselves made through this violence in the context of conflicts in which those persons were often not previously ascribed those identities, and where those identities are at stake in the conflict itself (Campbell 2007). Sexual violence in armed conflict constitutes these identities, making persons into the social categories of the perpetrator—so that, for example, a Yugoslav citizen becomes a Muslim woman. In armed conflict, violence of a sexual nature instantiates and solidifies these categories. An integral part of the harm is to reduce persons to social identities defined by the violence of the perpetrator, and in particular to their sex in the case of sexual violence. These norms of gender are always already structured in other norms of social differentiation,

particularly those social norms of ethno-nationalist belonging that
are contested in conflict (see, for example, Anthias/Yuval-Davis
1989; Enloe 2004).

In this 'relational gender' model of conflict-related sexual
violence, masculinity and femininity are hegemonic norms that
are constituted in relation to each other. As such, they should
be understood as relational terms, in which each term is given
meaning in relation to the other. For example, male sexual assault
involves the feminisation of its victims—you are not a man—
while female sexual assault involves the reduction of women
to their non-masculine role of femininity—you are a woman.
Moreover, these relational terms are filled with imaginary content
according to hegemonic gender norms in specific social contexts,
such that in this particular context, this is what it is imagined to be
a man, with a male body and masculine sexuality, and this is what
it is imagined to be a woman, with a female body and feminine
sexuality. To identify the specific harms of sexual violence in
particular conflicts, it is therefore necessary to identify how
notions of sexual difference and violence are made meaningful in
that social context.

The second theoretical strategy is to rethink 'gender harm' as
social injury. This strategy builds on Adrian Howe's (Cain/Howe
2008) work on social injury, which reconceptualises violence
against women as socially created injuries (Howe 1990: 51),
which are group-based and gender specific (Howe 1987, 1990).
This approach emphasises the social and collective nature of the
harm of sexual violence in armed conflict and moves away from
common notions of these harms as individual (such as breaches of
rights) or metaphysical (such as transcendent evil). This concept of
sexual violence in armed conflict as a 'social injury' helps identify
three key elements of this harm.

The first element is that these harms are injuries to persons
as members of social groups. Sexual violence in armed conflict
constructs those groups as such. This is because the iterative
injuries of conflict-related sexual violence create these categories
of persons, linking the making of classes of persons with the
coercive circumstances of conflict. The experience of sexual

violence is also shared with other members of the group. This harm is not only individual, but is also a collective experience of other members of that group. In the context of national legal systems, this collective process is usually described in terms of how injuries to that group reflect and reproduce social inequalities (Howe 1987: 428). However, in the context of international crimes, there is also a distinctive use of collective violence to create and destroy that class of persons. The process of using armed forces to identify, segregate and commit acts of sexual violence upon groups of 'Muslim women' is an example of this distinctive use of collective violence. Accordingly, the harm of sexual violence involves injuries to persons as social as well as physical subjects. This is the harm to the social subjectivity of persons, in which that violence destroys their membership of social communities.

The third aspect is that the harm produces not only social groups of victims, but also social groups of perpetrators. In this understanding of sexual violence in armed conflict, symbolic and material structures of armed violence produce these group patterns of perpetration. For example, what are often called opportunistic rapes of an individual by another individual occurs in the context of collective violence against targeted ethnic groups, and with the expectation of impunity for this reason (Mischkowski/ Mlinarević 2009: 53). The so-called opportunistic rape is not simply the act of an individual, rather it is also a collective act. It draws on the collective organisation of violence and the collective meaning given to communal group belonging ("I am Serbian, not Yugoslav, they are not Yugoslav, they are Bosniak"). This collective organisation of violence activates symbolic and structural resources and incorporates multiple social actors. In this sense, sexual violence is both a symbolic and imaginary relation of the perpetrator to the victim. The exercise of collective violence instantiates or materialises that relation of perpetrator to victim, and, in that action, constructs social groups of perpetrators and collective modes of perpetration.

The third theoretical strategy reconceives sexual violence in armed conflict as a continuum: that as a continuum of harms in a continuum of conflict, which are connected to gender relations in peace. This approach situates violence "along a continuum both in terms of time and space, and the varied forms and manifestations [that] reflect this" (Manjoo 2012: 27). Approached in this way, sexual violence is situated in "a continuum that spans interpersonal and structural violence" (ibid.). This approach builds on contemporary arguments that capturing these continuums of gendered violence is crucial for understanding gendered harms in war (Cockburn 2004; Manjoo 2012), and links older debates about both sexual violence and armed conflict as continuums of violence. The concept of sexual violence as a continuum of gendered violence has three elements.

The first element is the continuum of sexual violence, which is a wide set of acts occurring in differentiated patterns. This idea of sexual violence builds upon the idea of sexual violence in "peace time as a part of a wide range of violence against women, in which the violence is structured through heteronormative gender norms and practices" (Moser/Clark 2001: 31). Under international criminal law, 'sexual violence' is a category that describes a wide range of acts that structure violence around gender norms, ranging from forced nudity to sexual penetration. However, the acts that fall in this category in particular conflicts will depend upon how notions of sexual difference are given meaning in a given social context (Campbell 2007). The idea of the continuum of sexual violence better captures the variation between these different acts, as well as their commonalities in the gendered continuum of violence (Cockburn 2004; Seifert 1996).

The second element is the continuum of gender violence, which situates sexual violence in the continuum of gendered violence in conflict. Understood in this way, sexual violence is a form of gender harm, which is connected to other gendered harms of conflict, and is part of wider gendered continuum of violence (political, economic, social) of war (Moser/Clark 2001: 31). It also connects sexual violence in armed conflict to gender relations in war and peace (see, for example, Cockburn 2004), positing a continuity between gendered norms and inequalities in peace and war.

The third element is the continuum of conflict, which consists of differentiated zones of actors and patterns of organised violence. This approach can also capture the differentiated patterns of violence in conflict zones. The notion of the 'continuum of violence' draws on the idea of the spectrum of conflict in Western military doctrine, which understands conflict as differentiated zones of action and actors, rather than a single homogenous conflict (Royal Military Academy 2004). Linking these ideas enables us to identify the differentiated forms and functions of sexual violence in conflict zones, and to understand their relation to the continuum of armed violence (Skjelsbæk 2010). It provides a strategy for identifying different patterns of sexual violence in armed conflict, and their relation to different forms of armed violence in the continuum of armed conflict.

PROBLEM TWO: GENDER JUSTICE FOR SEXUAL VIOLENCE IN ARMED CONFLICT?

Justice for Sexual Violence

Current policy and practice typically understand justice for conflict-related sexual violence as the provision of criminal and/or civil accountability for sexual violence against women, and/or transitional justice processes that involve women's protection from sexual violence and their participation in post-conflict reconstruction (Coomaraswamy 2015). This understanding has shaped the emergence of the 'women, peace, and security' framework at the international level, and continues to inform policy and practice at national and international levels (O'Reilly 2018). These ideas of formal legal accountability and transitional justice processes and mechanisms continue to operate as the dominant models of 'gender justice' for conflict-related sexual violence.

The idea of gender justice first emerges in the context of feminist engagements with violence against women in the 1980s and 1990s discussed above, where it first came to be formulated as participation in social and political life, absence of discrimination, and positive rights (Goetz 2007). These ideas of equality, equity and rights also framed the first discussions of justice for sexual violence against women in armed conflict in the 1990s. The context for these discussions was the highly visible sexual violence in conflicts in the former Yugoslavia and Rwanda from 1991 onwards, as well as the significant campaign to address the so-called 'comfort women' issue at the international level. For example, CEDAW Recommendation No. 19, 1992 addressed the right to equal protection according to international humanitarian norms, and Recommendation No. 23, 1997 (CEDAW 1997) emphasised the inclusion of women in peace and conflict processes and international criminal justice and peace processes (and was adopted from Beijing Fourth World Conference on Women in 1995).

At the international level, justice for sexual violence was initially understood in terms of non-discriminatory application of international humanitarian law, the law governing the conduct of armed conflict, and as criminal accountability for violations of its humanitarian norms. From 1992 onwards, the UN Security Council issued a series of resolutions describing systematic sexual violence against women in the Yugoslavian conflict as a breach of humanitarian law, and as a threat to international peace and security under the UN Charter. However, the process of 'surfacing gender' in international humanitarian law in the early 1990s made visible the difficulties of integrating these previously ignored crimes against women into this legal regime, as well as the broader gendered nature of the rules of warfare that recognised these crimes through concepts of honour and national belonging (Gardam/Jarvis 2001; Copelon 1994).

With the establishment of the International Criminal Tribunals for the former Yugoslavia (1993) and Rwanda (1994), which prosecuted serious violations of humanitarian law, these ideas of gender justice came to focus on international criminal justice as such. Building on key feminist initiatives, the Tribunals developed an important body of jurisprudence and procedural rules through the first successful prosecutions of sexual violence as a crime under international law (see Brammetz/Jarvis 2016). With the establishment of the International Criminal Court in 2002, this body of law, which includes the substantive international crimes of violations of the laws of war, crimes against humanity and genocide, has now come to be known as international criminal law. At the same time, feminist scholars and advocates have revealed critical gendered justice gaps in accountability for these crimes in formal legal rules, trial practices and redress (see Charlesworth/ Chinkin 2000 and Buss 2016). These gaps included insufficient recognition of different types and effects of the harms of war upon women and men, disadvantageous treatment of female victims and witnesses, and failure to provide appropriate forms of redress. This has led to broader critiques that international criminal law is not 'gender neutral' justice, but rather is a form of gendered justice that reproduces social norms concerning men and women, and the unequal power relations underlying them (see, for example, the important work of Doris Buss and Karen Engle).

The focus upon criminal justice for conflict-related sexual violence shifts to transitional justice in the 2000s (Bell/ O'Rourke 2007). The publication of the key UN Report (2004) on transitional justice marked the emergence of a new set of ideas about justice in countries in transition from war to peace (Campbell 2014). At the international level, there was an increasing and ongoing concern with the participation of women in post-conflict transitional justice processes, and gender equality outcomes in post-war reconstruction. These ideas of justice in transitional contexts were broadened to include not only criminal justice proceedings, but also truth telling processes, reparations or institutional reforms. By 2010, an increasing concern with non-criminal harms and non-legal redress in transitional contexts had emerged, which ranged from reparations and compensation to developing and enforcing social and economic rights of survivors (O'Rourke 2013, Porobić/Mlinarević 2016). This wider idea of transitional justice also included the development of alternative feminist justice mechanisms, such as the Women's International War Crimes Tribunal on Japan's Military Sexual Slavery in 2000 or, more recently, the Women's Court for the former Yugoslavia in 2015.

This shift in models of justice for sexual violence is first seen in ideas of "post-conflict gender justice" (Askin 2002), which characterise criminal accountability for sexual violence in conflict as an essential part of transitional justice. With the shift to a broader understanding of justice in transitional contexts from 2000 onwards, justice for conflict-related sexual violence was increasingly tied to women's participation in transitional processes and has been characterised as an element of providing justice for conflict-related sexual violence, as can be seen throughout the Women, Peace and Security resolutions and reports, and most recently, in the Global Study of the Implementation of UN Resolution 1325 (Coomaraswamy 2015). A crucial element of providing transitional justice was understood to be addressing sexual violence victims in transitional mechanisms, such as truth and reconciliation commissions and processes, such as post-conflict reparations and reconstruction.

Gender Justice?

In these fields, then, gender is an integral aspect of justice for conflict-related sexual violence. In these models of justice, 'gender' characterises both the harms for which justice is sought, and the forms of justice that address those harms. As such, 'gender justice' has two inter-related elements in these approaches. The first element is that justice should address the gendered harm of sexual violence against women, whether it is legal or non-legal, criminal or transitional. The second element is that justice is gendered, in that it is shaped by structured inequalities between men and women. However, the problematic nature of these approaches to 'gender justice' is now becoming increasingly evident.

The model of 'gender justice' for the gendered harms of sexual violence in armed conflict assumes that sexual violence in armed conflict targets or disproportionately affects women, and that civil and criminal justice must address this group. This approach presents an important empirical and political argument, given the ongoing discriminatory practices of civil and criminal justice systems, as well as the gendered nature of sexual violence in war.

However, this idea of justice for gendered harms also raises two problems. The first is that it repeats the same conceptual slippage between ideas of biological sex, social gender and women as a social group as already discussed above in relation to gender harm. As a result, this model also confronts the same explanatory and political limitations as the idea of 'gender harm.' The second problem is the liberal model of justice as equality that these approaches to gender justice presume. As Goetz points out, "gender justice is often used interchangeably with notions of gender equality, gender equity, women's empowerment and women's rights" (2007: 17). This is because ideas of the right to equality and, relatedly, to non-discrimination on the grounds of gender, are central to this model of justice. However, this liberal approach does not resolve the long-standing 'same-difference' debate that continues to plague this area (see Lacey 1998). This is the issue of whether gender justice is achieved by the same (equal) treatment of men and women, or by recognising the (social, biological) differences between them. In essence, the liberal legal model of justice generates the circular question of whether gender justice should treat men and women equally in war and law, or whether it should recognise how war harms men and women differently. This circularity has only become sharper with recent greater focus upon male victims of sexual violence in armed conflict. How, then, to keep sight of the injustice of the disproportionate effects of sexual violence in armed conflict upon women, while not reproducing in models of justice the very gender categories that this violence seeks to impose upon its victims?

The model of 'gender justice' for sexual violence in armed conflict also assumes that legal accountability and transitional processes can provide justice for these harms. Survivors and civil society activists continue to call for appropriate prosecutions and transitional justice processes. However, there is a new emphasis on the limitations—or failures—of criminal or civil accountability and transitional justice for sexual violence in armed conflict. Such critiques argue that at best, criminal prosecutions and transitional mechanisms only offer the most limited forms of justice to survivors of sexual violence, or at worst, that they reproduce existing social inequalities (Boeston/Wilding 2014: 2; Engle 2016). These concerns in part reflect the long-standing debate as to whether feminists should engage with legal and state systems, or whether such systems will inevitably reproduce existing unequal social orders (Chinkin/Charlesworth 2006; Aoláin 2014). However, they also reflect an increasingly prevalent view in feminist and wider scholarship and policy in these fields.

Most importantly, such models of gender justice are seen as failing to address the broader social structures underlying sexual violence in armed conflict, so that the society does not experience a transition in these gendered relations of violence. Reflecting broader shifts in the field, the Global Study describes this approach as 'transformative justice,' which reflects the current debate concerning "the nature and quality of justice in situations of armed conflict" (Coomaraswamy 2015: 102). This critique has argued for a more fundamental reframing of existing legal regimes and mechanisms in terms of gender relations within conflict and post-conflict societies (Bell/O'Rourke 2007). This new approach links post-conflict justice for gender harms to social transformation, in which justice does not sustain the power relations that produce the violence of war, but instead seeks to change them (Valji 2007). In their important analysis, Boeston and Wilding characterise "transformative gender justice" as "the potential for justice mechanisms, in the broadest sense, to have transformative outcomes upon gender relations" (2015: 75). This important re-orientation of 'gender justice' links post-conflict justice for gender harms to 'societal transformation' that does not sustain 'dependence and subordination' that exists prior to conflict, or which its violence produces (Harris Rimmer 2010). As Boesten and Wilding describe, these are emerging debates, and the challenge of building a new concept of transformative gender justice for sexual violence in conflict remains.

THE 'RELATIONAL' MODEL OF TRANSFORMATIVE GENDER JUSTICE: CONCEPTUAL STRATEGIES FOR UNDERSTANDING GENDER JUSTICE

To develop this important idea of transformative gender justice for sexual violence in armed conflict, I suggest two conceptual strategies for building a new model. Each strategy focuses on the key conceptual and methodological elements of such a model, namely, (1) social injury as injustice, and (2) relational gender justice. They aim to address the political and theoretical challenges of how to describe the gendered social injuries that war produces, and of how to link justice practices to the transformation of social relations of domination and subordination in conflict.

The first conceptual strategy is to understand social injury as injustice. This approach links ideas of justice to the concept of gender harm as social injury. Following Iris Marion Young's classic analysis of justice, this approach begins by building upon the proposition that a theory of justice should recognise the structural injustices that groups suffer (Marion Young 1990). For Marion Young, injustice consists of structural oppression and domination that "immobilise or diminish a group" (ibid.: 7). Building on this idea, it becomes important to understand social injury as injustice, in that structural oppression and domination produces social injury to groups. However, the social injury approach does not begin by identifying groups, but by recognising social injuries as aggregate harms that produce groups themselves. These aggregate harms reflect and reproduce social structures of oppression and domination.

This approach emphasises the social and collective nature of conflict-related sexual violence, recognising that sexual violence is a collective injury to a group of persons, as well as an individual injury. Sexual violence injures persons as members of social groups, which the gendered structures of oppression and domination of conflict produce. As such, sexual violence is reconceived as a collective social injury, rather than only as a violation of individual rights. If sexual violence is understood as a social injury that is produced by and through gendered social relations, then it becomes possible to see how the gendered social relations of conflict produce that aggregate harm. It provides a means of tracing how gendered structures of collective violence produce different patterns of sexual violence, and different groups of perpetrators and victims. This approach suggests researchers should aim to understand individual narratives and experiences as aggregate harms, and to capture the structural conditions that create these harms and groups of victims and perpetrators.

Using this conceptual strategy provides the foundation of developing a method for identifying and naming the social injuries of sexual violence in armed conflict. This 'gender harm' mapping involves four steps. The first step describes the patterns of the harms of sexual violence in the given armed conflict. These injuries may be physical, sexual, familial, economic and social. The second step analyses the aggregate experience of these injuries, so that it becomes possible to describe the social injuries of sexual violence. This moves sexual violence from individual to generalised harms. With this shift, it becomes possible to describe the collective or group dimensions of these injuries. The third step is to identify and name the different categories of harms in conflict. This is the description of the elements and types of harms. The fourth step is to link these patterns of harms to patterns of perpetration. This analysis connects patterns of sexual violence to the continuum of gender violence in the conflict, and to the continuum of conflict. This step permits the identification of groups of perpetrators, connecting individual and collective perpetration, thereby providing new ways of understanding accountability in its fullest social sense. This gender harm mapping thereby provides a fuller understanding of the injustice of sexual violence, and helps to undertake the next step of identifying appropriate forms of redress for these harms.

The second conceptual strategy is to build a new understanding of 'gender justice' as relational. This idea of relational gender justice consists of two elements. The first element of gender justice consists of a relationship between social injury and the provision of its redress and remedy. Gender justice must provide adequate remedy and redress for the injuries of gender-based harms. However, if gender injustice is social, then so too must be its redress and remedy. Accordingly, this concept moves past ideas of criminal retribution or transitional reconciliation. Instead, the second element of the concept of gender justice focuses on the relation between justice practices and the social transformation of gender relations. This is an idea of justice as having the potential for transforming social relations of domination and oppression, and not only providing redress for wrongs. Accordingly, a relational gender justice approach focuses upon how justice practices address gender-based harms of conflict, and whether they work to create more gender just societies. This approach aims to translate unrecognised claims of collective injustice into legal concerns, inscribe these injustices into legal rules symbolising harms, and construct fair processes for determining those claims. It unsettles conventional ideas of individual justice, because it asks what forms of justice can address gendered collective violence and injuries of conflict.

Using this conceptual strategy provides the foundation for developing a methodology to identify relational justice practices for conflict-related sexual violence. This 'relational justice review' involves comparing patterns of social injuries of conflict-related sexual violence to the formal and informal justice mechanisms and processes available to address them, with the aim of identifying 'justice gaps' and developing new justice practices. The first step of this process identifies the patterns of social injury, as outlined above in the gender harm mapping. The second step identifies existing justice practice, such as applicable laws, justice systems and access to justice. The third step identifies justice gaps by assessing whether these existing justice practices adequately address the patterns of social injuries and provide appropriate individual and collective remedies for these harms. The fourth and final step develops new justice practices that can address any gendered gaps in them. Importantly, this includes developing collective programmes addressing the structural conditions that create these patterns of social injury. By addressing these structural conditions, the development of such collective justice practices provides the means of linking justice for these social injuries and building transformative social change.

This relational justice review methodology describes existing feminist processes of building new justice practices. An important example of this process can be found in 'The Concept and Framework for the Development of a Gender-Sensitive Reparations Program for Civilian Victims of War in Bosnia and Herzegovina' (Porobić Isaković/Mlinarević 2016). This Framework was developed by Women Organising for Change in Syria and Bosnia Initiative, and aimed to build a transformative reparations programme. This Framework developed a new approach to reparations by identifying patterns of gendered harms, naming social injuries, identifying gaps in existing justice practices and building new forms of individual and collective reparations which aim to contribute to transformative social change.

This model of relational gender justice does not identify 'justice' as an *a priori* expression of abstract norms. Instead, it asks what new forms of claims and redress might need to be created to build new and more just forms of social relations. As such, it raises three challenges for building transformative forms of legal, social and alternative justice for sexual violence in armed conflict. The first set of challenges concern how to develop new legal forms of justice. These include how to develop new substantive offences that can better symbolise the different forms of sexual violence in conflict, and how to ensure that legal proceedings reflect the patterns of sexual violence in a particular armed conflict so that they reflect specific patterns of illegality. The second set of challenges concern how to build and provide new forms of social justice. These include how to build appropriate connections between legal and social justice, to identify the forms of social and economic justice that might be appropriate for victims of sexual violence, and how ensure their equitable implementation. The third set of challenges concern developing feminist models of alternative justice. These include how to generate better alternative narratives or knowledges, agency or empowerment in all feminist engagements with justice practices.

This model of relational gender justice also raises the profound and difficult question of how to define 'gender justice' itself. The axiological question of how to define, and who defines, the just and the good is always implicit, but insufficiently explicitly explored, in this field. To engage with ideas of 'gender justice' necessarily raises the political question of the collective project of feminist emancipatory politics. However, this question cannot be defined in the abstract and in advance, but is the outcome of political struggle. It is this question of the political dimension of conflict-related sexual violence that remains a fundamental challenge for scholarship and policy in the field.

NOTES

1. "'Violence against women' means any act of gender-based violence that results in, or is likely to result in, physical, sexual or psychological harm or suffering to women, including threats of such acts, coercion or arbitrary deprivation of liberty, whether occurring in public or in private life."
2. This in part reflects the context of these resolutions of the situation in the Democratic Republic of Congo, in which significant numbers of male sexual violence victims were reported. It also reflects the development of reporting criteria for sexual violence under UN Res 1960, which aimed to distinguish conflict-related sexual violence from non-conflict related gender-based violence, traditionally reported in the UN system under the wider categories of violence against women or gender-based violence, such as harmful traditional practices or domestic violence.

REFERENCES

Anthias, Floya/Yuval-Davis, Nira. 1989. *Woman–Nation–State*. Basingstoke: Palgrave.

Askin, Kelly. 2002. 'The Quest for Post-Conflict Gender Justice', *Columbia Journal Transnational Law*, 41:509–21.

Bell, Christine/O'Rourke, Catherine. 2007. 'Does Feminism Need A Theory of Transitional Justice? An Introductory Essay', *The International Journal of Transitional Justice*, 1(1): 23–44.

Boesten, Jelke/Wilding, Polly. 2015. 'Transformative Gender Justice: Setting an Agenda', *Women's Studies International Forum*, 51:75–80.

Brammertz, Serge/Jarvis, Michelle. 2016. *Prosecuting Conflict-Related Sexual Violence at the ICTY*. Oxford: Oxford University Press.

Buss, Doris. 2016. 'International Criminal Courts' in Jill Steans/Daniela Tepe-Belfrage (eds), *Handbook on Gender in World Politics*, pp. 162–70. Chelthenham/Northhampton: Edward Elgar.

———. 2014. 'Seeing Sexual Violence in Conflict and Post-Conflict

Societies' in Doris Buss/Joanne Lebert/Blair Rutherford/Donna Sharkey/Obijiofor Aginam (eds), *Sexual Violence in Conflict and Post-Conflict Societies*, pp. 3–27. New York: Routledge.

Butler, Judith. 2010. *Frames of War: When Is Life Grievable?* London: Verso Books.

———. 2004. *Undoing Gender*. New York: Routledge.

———. 1997. *The Psychic Life of Power: Theories of Subjection*. Stanford: Stanford University Press.

Butler, Judith. 1993. *Bodies That Matter*. London/New York: Routledge.

Cain, Maureen/Howe, Adrian. 2008. *Women, Crime and Social Harm*. London: Hart.

Campbell, Kirsten. 2014. 'Reassembling International Justice: The Making of "the Social" in International Criminal Law and Transitional Justice', *International Journal of Transitional Justice*, 8(1):53–74.

———. 2007. 'The Gender of Transitional Justice: Law, Sexual Violence and the International Criminal Tribune for the Former Yugoslavia', *International Journal of Transitional Justice*, 1(3):411–32.

Chinkin, Christine. 1995. 'Violence against Women: The International Legal Response', *Gender and Development*, 3(2):23–8.

Chinkin, Christine/Charlesworth, Hilary. 2006. 'Building Women into Peace', *Third World Quarterly*, 27(5):937.

———. 2000. *The Boundaries of International Law*. Manchester: Manchester University Press.

Cockburn, Cynthia. 2004. 'The Continuum of Violence', in Wenona Giles/Jennifer Hyndman (eds), *Sites of Violence: Gender and Conflict Zones*, pp. 24–44. Berkeley: University of California Press.

Cohen, Dara Kay/Hoover Green, Amelia/Wood, Elisabeth Jean. 2013. 'Wartime Sexual Violence: Misconceptions, Implications, and Ways Forward', *United States Institute for Peace Special Report*, 8 February. https://www.usip.org/publications/2013/02/wartime-sexual-violence-misconceptions-implications-and-ways-forward (accessed 26 September 2018).

Committee on the Elimination of Discrimination against Women (CEDAW). 1992. *General Recommendation No. 19. Violence against women*. N.D.: United Nations. http://www.un.org/womenwatch/daw/cedaw/recommendations/recomm.htm#recom19 (accessed 27 September 2018).

———. 1997. *General Recommendation No. 23. Article 7 (Political and Public Life)*. N.D.: United Nations. http://www.un.org/womenwatch/daw/cedaw/recommendations/recomm.htm#recom23 (accessed

THE GENDER OF JUSTICE? 253

253

4

27 September 2018).

Coomaraswamy, Rashida. 2015. *Preventing Conflict, Transforming Justice, Securing the Peace: A Global Study on the Implementation of United Nations Security Council Resolution 1325*. New York: UN Women. http://wps.unwomen.org/index.html (accessed 27 September 2018).

Copelon, Rhonda. 1994 'Surfacing Gender: Re-Engraving Crimes Against Women in Humanitarian Law', *Hastings Women's Law Journal*, 5:243–66.

Davies, Sara/True, Jacqui. 2015. 'Reframing Conflict-Related Sexual and Gender-Based Violence: Bringing Gender Analysis Back in', *Security Dialogue*, 46(6):495–512.

Engle, Karen. 2016. 'Feminist Legacies', *American Journal of International Law Unbound*, 110:220–26.

———. 2014. 'The Grip of Sexual Violence: Reading UN Security Council Resolutions on Human Security', in Gina Heathcote/Diane Otto (eds), *Rethinking Peacekeeping, Gender Equality and Collective Security*, pp. 23–47. London: Palgrave Macmillan.

Enloe, Cynthia. 2004. *The Curious Feminist: Searching for Women in a New Age of Empire*. Berkeley: University of California Press.

Gardam, Judith Gail/Jarvis, Michelle J. 2001. *Women, Armed Conflict and International Law*. The Hague/London/Boston: Kluwer Law International.

Goetz, Anne Marie. 2007. 'Gender Justice, Citizenship and Entitlements: Core Concepts, Central Debates and New Directions for Research', in Maitrayee Mukhopadhyay/Navsharan Singh (eds), *Gender Justice, Citizenship, and Development*, pp. 15–57. New Delhi: Zubaan.

Harris Rimmer, Susan. 2010. 'Sexing the Subject of Transitional Justice', *The Australian Feminist Law Journal*, 32(June):123–47.

Howe, Adrian. 1990. 'Sweet Dreams: Deinstitutionalising Young Women', in Regina Graycar (ed), *Dissenting Opinions: Feminist Explorations in Law and Society*, pp. 40–57. Sydney: Allen and Unwin.

———. 1987. '"Social Injury" Revisited: Towards a Feminist Theory of Social Justice', *International Journal of the Sociology of Law*, 15(14):423–38.

International Criminal Court, Office of the Prosecutor (ICC OTP). 2014. *Policy Paper on Sexual and Gender-Based Crimes*. The Hague: ICC. https://www.icc-cpi.int/iccdocs/otp/otp-policy-paper-on-sexual-and-gender-based-crimes--june-2014.pdf (accessed 26 September 2018).

Lacey, Nicola. 1998. *Unspeakable Subjects: Feminist Essays in Social and Legal*

Theory. Oxford: Hart Publishing.

Manjoo, Rashida. 2012. 'The Continuum of Violence against Women and the Challenges of Effective Redress', *International Human Rights Law Review,* 1(1):1–29.

Marion Young, Iris. 1990. *Justice and the Politics of Difference*. Princeton: Princeton University Press.

Meger, Sara. 2016. *Rape Loot Pillage: The Political Economy of Sexual Violence in Armed Conflict*. Oxford/New York: Oxford University Press.

Merry Engle, Sally. 2006. *Human Rights and Gender Violence*. London/ Chicago: University of Chicago Press.

Mischkowski, Gabriela/Mlinarević, Gorana. 2009. ... *And That It Does Not Happen to Anyone Anywhere in the World: The Trouble with Rape Trials*. Cologne: Medica Mondiale. https://www.medicamondiale. org/fileadmin/redaktion/5_Service/Mediathek/Dokumente/ English/Documentations_studies/medica_mondiale_and_that_it_ does_not_happen_to_anyone_anywhere_in_the_world_english_ complete_version_dec_2009.pdf (accessed 26 September 2018).

Moser, Caroline/Clark, Fiona. 2001. *Victims, Perpetrators or Actors? Gender, Armed Conflict and Political Violence*. London: Zed Books.

Ní Aoláin, Fionnuala. 2016. 'The Gender Politics of Fact-Finding in the Context of the Women, Peace and Security Agenda', in Philip Alston/Sarah Knuckey (eds), *The Transformation of Human Rights Fact-Finding*, pp. 89–106. New York: Oxford University Press.

———. 2014. 'Gendered Harms and Their Interface with International Criminal Law', *International Feminist Journal of Politics*, 16(4):622–46.

Nikolić-Ristanović, Vesna. 2000. *Women, Violence and War: Wartime Victimisation of Refugees in the Balkans.*, Budapest: Central European University Press.

O'Reilly, Maria. 2018. *Gendered Agency in War and Peace: Gender Justice and Women's Activism in Post-Conflict Bosnia-Herzegovina*. London: Palgrave Macmillan.

O'Rourke, Catherine. 2013. *Gender Politics in Transitional Justice*. London/ New York: Routledge.

Porobić Isaković, Nela/Mlinarević, Gorana. eds. 2016. *Concept and Framework for the Development of a Gender-Sensitive Reparations Program for Civilian Victims of War in Bosnia and Herzegovina*. Sarajevo: Women's International League for Peace and Freedom/Bosnia-Syria Initiative. https://wilpf.org/wp-content/uploads/2018/04/ Gender-Sensitive-Reparations-Program.pdf (accessed 27 September 2018).

Royal Military Academy. 2004. *War Studies: A Text Book for the 21st Century British Officer*. Sandhurst: Royal Military Academy.

Seifert, Ruth. 1996. 'The Second Front: The Logic of Sexual Violence in Wars', *Women's Studies International Forum*, 19(1–2):35–43.

Sellers, Patricia Viseur. 2008. *The Prosecution of Sexual Violence in Conflict: The Importance of Human Rights as Means of Interpretation*. Office of the High Commissioner for Human Rights. https://www.ohchr.org/_layouts/15/WopiFrame.aspx?sourcedoc=/Documents/Issues/Women/WRGS/Paper_Prosecution_of_Sexual_Violence.pdf&action=default&DefaultItemOpen=1 (accessed 26 September 2018).

Skjelsbæk, Inger. 2010. *The Elephant in the Room: An Overview of How Sexual Violence came to be seen as a Weapon of War*. Oslo: Norwegian Ministry of Foreign Affairs/Peace Research Institute Oslo.

———. 2001. 'Sexual Violence and War: Mapping Out a Complex Relationship', *European Journal of International Relations*, 7(2):211–27.

United Nations. 2016. *Provisional Guidance Note: Intersections between the Monitoring and Analysis Reporting Arrangements (MARA) & the Gender-Based Violence Information Management System (GBVIMS)*. http://www.gbvims.com/wp/wp-content/uploads/Provisional-Guidance-Note-on-Intersections-Between-GBVIMS-MARA.pdf (accessed 27 September 2018).

———. 2011. *Analytical and Conceptual Framing of Conflict-Related Sexual Violence and Provisional Guidance Note*. http://www.stoprapenow.org/uploads/advocacyresources/1321456915.pdf (accessed 26 September 2018).

———. 2004. *Report of the Secretary-General on the Rule of Law and Transitional Justice in Conflict and Post-conflict Societies*. UN Doc. S/2004/616, 23 August. https://undocs.org/S/2004/616 (accessed 27 September 2018).

United Nations. General Assembly. 1993. *Declaration on the Elimination of Violence against Women*. UN Doc. A/RES/48/104, 20 December. http://www.un.org/documents/ga/res/48/a48r104.htm (accessed 26 September 2018).

United Nations. Inter-Agency Standing Committee. 2015. *Guidelines for Integrating Gender-Based Violence Interventions in Humanitarian Action. Reducing risk, promoting resilience and aiding recovery*. https://gbvguidelines.org/wp/wp-content/uploads/2015/09/2015-IASC-Gender-based-Violence-Guidelines_lo-res.pdf (accessed 26 September 2018).

United Nations. Security Council. 2013. *Resolution 2106, UN Doc. S/ RES/2106*, 24 June. https://www.securitycouncilreport.org/atf/ cf/%7B65BFCF9B-6D27-4E9C-8CD3-CF6E4FF96FF9%7D/s_ res_2106.pdf (accessed 18 October 2018).
————. 2010. *Resolution 1960, UN Doc. S/RES/1960*, 16 December. https://www.securitycouncilreport.org/atf/cf/%7B65BFCF9B-6D27-4E9C-8CD3-CF6E4FF96FF9%7D/WPS%20SRES%20 1960.pdf (accessed 18 October 2018).
————. 2009. *Resolution 1888, UN Doc. S/RES/1888*, 30 September. http://www.un.org/womenwatch/daw/vaw/securitycouncil/S-RES-1888-(2009)-English.pdf (accessed 18 October 2018).
————. 2008. *Resolution 1820. UN Doc. S/RES/1820*, 19 June. https:// www.securitycouncilreport.org/atf/cf/%7B65BFCF9B-6D27-4E9C-8CD3-CF6E4FF96FF9%7D/CAC%20S%20RES%20 1820.pdf (accessed 18 October 2018).
————. 2000. *Resolution 1325. UN Doc S/RES/1325*, 31 October. https:// documents-dds-ny.un.org/doc/UNDOC/GEN/N00/720/18/ PDF/N0072018.pdf?OpenElement (accessed 26 September 2018).
Valji, Nahla. 2007. 'Gender Justice and Reconciliation', in Friedrich-Ebert-Stiftung (ed), *Dialogue on Globalization*, No. 35. Berlin: Friedrich-Ebert-Stiftung. http://library.fes.de/pdf-files/iez/05000. pdf (accessed 27 September 2018).
Wood, Elisabeth Jean. 2014. 'Conflict-Related Sexual Violence and the Policy Implications of Recent Research', *International Review of the Red Cross*, 96(894):457–78.

Vicissitudes of Gender as an Analytical Category: Sexual Violence in Armed Conflicts Revisited

RUTH SEIFERT

Interest in sexual violence in armed conflicts surged in political and academic debates in the 1990s following the atrocities in Bosnia-Herzegovina, Kosovo/a and Rwanda. The issue was widely and intensely discussed and researched, until enthusiasm began to wane after the turn of the century. In academic and academic-political fields, there has been a great deal of empirical activity during the last 15 years. Today we know considerably more about the occurrence of sexual violence in the context of armed conflicts, and policy initiatives have proliferated as well. Particularly in the political realm, however, the accumulation of empirical data has not been paralleled by an equally strong interest in theorizing. Instead, policy measures often seem to be based on an implicit assumption that violence in general and sexual violence in particular happen in spaces where order and civilisation break down and are part of the chaos that ensues. As a consequence, many attempts in the political and practical realm aim to 'restore order' and provide protection for women through policies and legal guidelines. Two things are notable here: first, war, violence and the injury of humans in war are implicitly understood as a deviation from a normal order that must be re-established. The focus therefore lies on possible measures for preventing or ending collective violence. These goals are pursued *before* a key question has been asked: why is systematic and institutionalised reciprocal physical harm considered an inherent content of war and not "an unfortunate or preventable consequence of war" (Scarry 1988: 67)? Second, when normal order crumbles and violence spreads, sexual violence is considered a particularly abominable break down of civilisation and deviation from the norm where women are the 'natural victims' and men the 'natural perpetrators.'[1]

While violence is a defining characteristic of armed conflict, and is in essence about injuring and killing human beings, *sexual* violence is considered a deviation that can and should be excluded from the socially accepted violence that constitutes warfare. The underlying assumption is that we have laws and rules regulating the conduct of war and the perpetration of violence, and that violence against civilians, and in particular sexual violence against women, is a severe deviation from these rules. Yet the wars of the twentieth century have defied this understanding of war, as military actors have increasingly embraced strategies that include, or even primarily target, civilian deaths. Despite an ongoing controversy about exact figures, it is generally assumed that the death toll in armed conflict is 80 to 90 percent among civilians by the end of the twentieth century (Lagrou 2009: 169; McDonald 2013: 138).

Despite this wholesale violence against civilians, many policy efforts aim only to prevent sexual violence against women. This is not to say that this phenomenon has been given more attention than it deserved. The issue at hand is whether it is theoretically possible—and practically effective—to define non-sexual violence largely as a normality of war while labelling sexual violence an aberration. The rationale behind this approach is that sexual violence is not legally endorsed as a means of warfare, so it is classified as undue and uncivilised violence, whereas other kinds of violence are state-sanctioned and therefore legitimate by definition and require no additional probing. This policy orientation is represented in the UN Security Council Resolution on Women, Peace and Security 1325 from the year 2000, and resolutions 1820 (2008), 1888 (2009), and 1960 (2010), which link the position of women in armed conflicts to the security agenda and recognise conflict-related sexual violence as a matter of security and international relations. Such policy suggests a dichotomy between acceptable and unacceptable acts of wartime violence and conceives of sexual violence as an act that is more atrocious than other violent acts,[2] and has served as the basis for legal initiatives and policy measures (Meger 2016).

As research has shown, however, the phenomenon of sexual violence is much more complicated. Identifying the sites, meanings and rationale of (sexual) violence is crucial to countering it. It will only be possible to instigate change once we have found satisfactory explanations.

A CURSORY OVERVIEW OF EXPLANATORY APPROACHES

One explanation that is seemingly impossible to eradicate and is of sustained political and cultural significance is that sexual violence originates from biological urges, or—as Eriksson Baaz and Stern call it—the "sexed" story that associates sexual violence with an ultimately uncontrollable sex drive that is ascribed to men and is said to make men pawns of biology and bodily urges (Eriksson Baaz/ Stern 2012: 17; Malesevic 2010: 51ff). After decades of research deconstructing this notion, it still cannot simply be dismissed, not least because it continues to be a basis of military sexual politics and because in certain contexts it is mobilised by the perpetrators themselves as legitimation for their acts. This is illustrated by interviews that Eriksson Baaz and Stern conducted with soldiers, who appealed to their "natural urges" as male individuals even when attempting to justify *collective* acts of sexual violence (Eriksson Baaz/Stern 2012: 17). In their attempts at justification, individual aggression is collapsed into organised violence, and all violence is reduced to aggressive impulses (whether it involves sexual domination, the enforcement of hierarchies within a social group, or lashing out against a perceived threat) (Malesevic 2010: 54).

Another line of thought suggests a connection between military masculinity and sexual violence in armed conflict. Since until very recently, the military was (and for the most part still is) constructed as an exclusively male institution, violence and masculinity are discursively closely linked. Gender has to be produced in cultural and social spaces of production, and institutions are one of the major sites of its construction. As Douglas convincingly argued, institutions are places where subjectivities are constructed. Institutions bestow sameness, encapsulate past experiences and thus shape future behaviour patterns, stabilise and naturalise classification, shape bodies and minds, produce divisions of labour and furnish justifications for these divisions. In institutions we observe a confluence of embodiments and symbolic constructions of gender that structure actions at individual, organisational, and state levels (Douglas 1986; Prügl 2004). Given that the military as an organisation has been deeply linked to notions of masculinity and gendered identities, it can be identified as one of the major sites for the production, perpetuation and reification of (hegemonic) masculinity. Armies are places where norms of masculinity have been produced and reproduced, and where masculinity could (and presumably still can) be lived, displayed and 'proven' on an individual level as well. Behaviour patterns typical for military organisations, such as bragging about heterosexual conquests, putting up pictures of nude female bodies, sexual language and so on, are taken as evidence of masculinist dynamics inside military groups. The use of violence is, however, at the centre of the institutional production of masculinity. In our culture, men have a monopoly on the use of violence, and all the institutions that actively encourage the use of violence are exclusively male or clearly male-dominated. Over the course of history, the practice of violence has been embedded in male institutions and has become constitutive of our understanding of masculinity.

Since military masculinity is also constructed as heterosexual, it not only links masculinity with violence, but also connects the two to heterosexuality. It has been postulated that military culture simultaneously breeds and exploits a particular construction of male sexuality that is aggressive and fundamentally misogynistic and supports these concepts of military masculinity. On that basis, the tacit or open permission to express an aggressive and violent sexuality is considered one of the spoils of war. In other words, sexual violence in armed conflict cannot be explained as the merging of primal sexual and aggressive impulses. Instead by implicitly or explicitly making sexual violence a permissive part of warfare, the military serves and makes use of the very constructions of masculinity it has helped to produce.[3]

The most influential and widely discussed explanation that has placed wartime rapes into the context of armed conflict in gendered societies and has cast light on the political significance of sexual violence is the 'rape as a weapon of war' theory developed in the wake of war rapes in the Yugoslav and Rwandan genocidal conflicts. Eriksson Baaz and Stern call this notion "revolutionary," (Eriksson Baaz/Stern 2010: 2) since up to that point sexual violence had been treated as a politically, militarily and culturally relative, uninteresting, inevitable by-product of war that deserved no further theoretical consideration. The attempt to explain sexual violence in armed conflicts as a 'weapon' opened up new avenues in understanding the dynamics of war and armed conflict.

In its earlier and simpler forms, wartime rape was considered a strategy used deliberately to further military and political aims (Seifert 1993).[4] Indeed, a number of recent empirical studies suggest that sexual violence can be ordered as a military instrument (Koo 2002: 528; Stefatos 2012). Nevertheless, the concept of sexual violence as a form of strategy has been problematic from the very beginning. In many cases when large scale sexual violence has occurred, there has been no proof of procedures that would comply with the military definition of strategy as a premeditated plan of action to achieve a defined result. From the start, the 'weapon of war' concept was useful for scandalizing, but not for analysing the phenomenon.

Later versions extended the weapon of war approach and questioned the notion of strategy to focus more on the outcomes of the use of sexual violence. This reasoning draws on the insight that gender is a social and cultural construction intertwined with other cultural constructions. These constructions unleash specific dynamics in the context of collective conflicts. In particular, constructions of the gendered body and of the nation are merged, and bodies—male and female—become nationalised (Scarry 1988: 67; Seifert 2002). As a consequence, attacks on the body are not individual acts, but highly collective acts that view the body as a national body and a representation of the collective. This works differently for the male and the female body. The male body can be understood as a representation of the state, and a soldierly body imbues the political positions and interests with the power of corporeal reality. In Scarry's words, ideas, positions and interests are substantiated with the power of the material (corporeal) world (Scarry 1988: 67). The female body, on the other hand, is in Barth's sense an ethno-marker demarcating the boundaries of a collective or nation (Barth 1969; cf. also Seifert 2002, 2003b). The female body is understood as social territory representing the materiality of the nation, so that gender-specific acts of violence serve to both mark the social Us and to bring about, defend and expand the territorial occupation of the social sphere. As gender and nationhood merge, sexual violence in armed conflicts is aimed not only at the individual, but is also apt to disrupt the cultural and social fabric of the community as a whole (Seifert 2002). While not a strategy in the military sense of the word, sexual violence can nevertheless be said to have war-strategic effects.

Barth's idea of symbolic boundary drawing has been particularly fruitful in this context. He conjectured that collectivities can only be formed and identified through the drawing of boundaries. While these boundaries need not be geographical, they are primarily symbolic in nature. In many cultural contexts, the female body seems to be constructed as the type of boundary described by Barth. Against this background, it makes sense that sexual violence is particularly prevalent in ethno-national conflicts and in conflicts associated with establishing a boundary between population groups. In a similar vein, Hayden offers an analysis of sexual violence that situates the atrocities in the context of conflicts between collectivities in his investigations of sexual violence in the Indian Punjab region in 1947, in Delhi in 1984, in Hyderabad in 1990 and in Yugoslavia in the 1990s. Hayden found an upsurge in sexual violence when groups came to perceive themselves "as distinct from each other [and] stake[d] competing claims to the control over territory" (Hayden 2000: 27, 33). According to Hayden, rape seems to be employed when collectivities aim to create new borders and social boundaries. This happens primarily when a state is liminal, and the question whose state it is and how the population will be defined has not been answered. In these types of armed conflicts, it is not exclusively femaleness that preordains women to be the victims of sexual violence; it is the "intersection of gender with the multiple and varied identities of religion, nationality and ethnicity that allows groups of women to be distinguished between 'ours' and 'theirs'" (Koo 2002). In other words, the targeting of women cannot be completely separated from their ascribed belonging to a certain social, cultural or religious group.[5]

THREE INTERVENTIONS

The attempted explanations briefly outlined above make gender a central category of analysis and place wartime rape within the context of a gendered military, a gendered nation, and the gendering of warfare and collective violence. Critics have contested this premise. Cohen, Hoover Green and Wood (2013) make a vehement plea for de-gendering sexual violence in armed conflicts. For one thing, they emphasise that, contrary to early feminist claims, sexual violence against women is not rampant in all conflicts. Indeed, more recent empirical evidence has shown that rape in armed conflicts is neither ubiquitous nor inevitable. The frequency, form and targets of sexual violence vary among civil wars, interstate wars, so-called ethnic wars and secessionist conflicts, as well as between state and non-state actors (Wood 2006). There are scenarios in which sexual violence is rampant and others in which little sexual violence occurs. When sexual violence occurs on a large scale, it is with the permission of political and military leaderships. When sexual violence is counterproductive to the causes and interests pursued in armed conflicts, however, political and military leaderships will take disciplinary measures. This indicates that a key element in explaining and predicting the occurrence of sexual violence has something to do with the aims and objectives of the parties to a conflict.

For Cohen, Hoover Green and Wood, the single most important variable for explaining sexual violence is the nature of the armed groups involved. They observe that many armed groups effectively limit the perpetration of rape by group members and conclude that commanders can build institutions to prevent sexual violence if they chose to do so (Cohen/Hoover Green/Wood 2013: 12). If this is the case, then the question becomes why they sometimes chose not to create these institutions.

Drawing on research from Sierra Leone, Cohen finds that groups that recruit by abduction are more likely to commit rape, especially gang rape, and concludes that the degree of cohesion of an armed group is closely linked to the prevalence of sexual violence. According to Cohen, highly cohesive groups are considerably less prone to rape than less cohesive groups—such as those created by abduction or other, from a military point of view, non-professional measures. She concludes that rape is a means of socializing new members into a group in order to enhance cohesion. Rape is used as a socialisation tool that bonds the group members (Cohen 2013; Cohen/Hoover Green/Wood 2013: 9).[6] It is therefore more likely to occur in groups that need to create cohesion and less likely in already strongly cohesive groups. If this is the case, we need to ask why this particular form of violence is seen as effective for group bonding processes.

Cohen also emphasises that the occurrence of rape of men and sexual violence against men has been grossly underestimated and that the cultural taboo of male rape needs to be addressed. Indeed, while the empirical evidence at our disposal shows that women bear the brunt of rape, it is becoming increasingly obvious that the rate of sexual violence against men has been underestimated. A 2008 United Nations Office for the Coordination of Humanitarian Affairs' report on sexual violence in armed conflicts pointed out that "there is an extremely limited awareness of, and knowledge about, sexual violence against men and boys in conflict."[7] Furthermore, Cohen finds that female perpetrators sometimes commit acts of sexual violence. From these observations, Cohen concludes that rape has little to do with gender.

Cohen's de-gendered approach opens up a number of questions. According to her reasoning, rape is not a *gendered violation* if it is perpetrated against female as well as male bodies. This implies that if a biologically male body suffers rape and sexual violation, the dynamics of gender are inoperative. This ignores the fact that 'woman' is not a fixed category inextricably linked to female biological bodies. The very volatility and negotiability of gender and the meanings attached to it is what allows us to make sense of and unravel the logic of sexual violence against men.

Violence, and particularly collective violence, has the capacity to attack and destroy identities. Suffering is a socially and politically mediated experience. Sexual violence in collective conflicts is one example of the merging of the physical and the social body, and reveals the intersections of experiences of the body and bodily pain, cultural representations and the making and unmaking of collectivities. Diken and Laustsen (2005) described the specifics of sexual violence compared to other forms of violence. Referring to Bataille and Kristeva, they emphasise the 'abject' or the shaming aspects of sexual violence. While a person who has been punched in the face or severely physically mistreated, suffers severely, he or she has not been made abject. Sexual violence, on the other hand, is associated with the defilement of an individual and a community, creates abjection, and is accompanied by shame—felt on an individual and social level. Diken and Laustsen see abjection as a social construction that is apt to destroy the social order. Abject objects or persons are culturally constructed as stigmatised, polluted, anxiety-provoking or threatening to our own identity because they endanger the 'normal order' and signify indistinction and formlessness. Most cultures depend on well-established distinctions that guarantee social and individual identity. The abject, on the other hand, is characterised for obliterating distinctions—between human and not human, interior and exterior and essentially male and female. The abject is the in-between, the neither-nor, both included and excluded (Diken/Laustsen 2005: 111). In many societies and cultural contexts, sexual violence has the capacity to invade our innermost intimacy as it penetrates parts of the body that are associated with gendered identities in an individual as well as a collective sense. It crosses the boundary between interior and body, gendered identity, the psyche and the collectivity because the community finds it difficult to deal with an abject person as he or she presents a challenge to the established symbolic order (Diken/Laustsen 2005: 125).

Male and female rape survivors frequently talk about feelings of shame, humiliation, defilement, estrangement from selfhood and their body, and of feeling like outcasts in their communities. Female and male rape victims have endured bodily harm; both their personal and collective identities have been attacked and they have been transformed into problems for their communities while being estranged from them. The community has to find (often symbolic) ways to re-include rape survivors of any gender (which does not happen in some cases). Male rape victims report being feminised and suffering a degradation of their masculinity, including verbal framing from—male and female—perpetrators that designate them as feminine during and after the abuse. Communities that become aware of male rape may question the victims' masculinity, and there have been reports of women leaving husbands who survived rape because they felt the act of rape robbed their spouses of their masculinity (Dolan 2014). The rape of a man is widely seen to amount to his feminisation. Femininity is attributed to the victim of sexual violence and "in the context of male sexual violence in armed conflict, power and dominance manifest themselves in the form of emasculation" (Sivakumaran 2007: 270). Sexual violence carries more messages than other forms of violence. It makes the victims abject, ostracizing them from their communities and robbing them of their social standing (thus disrupting the community as a whole). It is a symbol of dominance over femininity or the emasculated man and is thus the exertion of male dominance regardless of the gender of either the perpetrators or the victims (Couturier 2012).

The 2003 atrocities committed in Abu Ghraib, Iraq, provide another telling example of the fact that sexual violence against men is strongly tied to the gender category (and not merely instrumental for a certain objective), and that feminisation and masculinisation play roles in the abuses enacted and experienced differently than other forms of violence and torture. Sexual violence is employed because it violates the construction of the core of identity in most societies, our gendered identity, and robs the victims of the social space they occupied before the act. This background reveals the deeper meaning behind the photographing and filming of the sexual torture of male prisoners in Abu Ghraib, and the subsequent sharing of these images with a wider public including the prisoner community. In order to produce collective effects, the male subjects' abjection had to be communicated to their communities so the abuse not only violated their physical and psychological integrity, but also robbed them of their social existence and denigrated the community as a whole. As Beck and Brandt (2011) point out, violence exerted in a collective context needs a target, a performer, and an observer. The damage that is done to the body of the target, the fear and pain that is caused, symbolises the victim's inferiority, while the performer expresses his or her superiority and power, and the observer as third constitutive element serves as a means for translating the somatic events into social reality (Beck/Brandt 2011: 349ff).

The overriding silence and denial that surrounds male rape, however, is less immediately comprehensible. Apperly (2015: 92) calls males exposed to sexual violence in armed conflicts "hidden victims" and O'Mochain (2015: 99) speaks of them as "forgotten victims," citing empirical studies that found evidence of male rapes in almost all recent armed conflicts, most recently the ongoing conflict involving ISIS. These violations do not concern just a tiny minority of men, and in many cases have been large scale and can be called systematic. The silence surrounding male rape, which virtually all publications on sexual violence against men emphasise, raises questions about gender, bodies, and power, and about feminist research and theory that might have contributed to this silence (Vojdik 2014).

Another issue that Eriksson Baaz and Stern (2009) argue has been neglected is the perspective of the perpetrators. They analysed interviews conducted with State Army FARDC soldiers in the Democratic Republic of Congo, focusing on their representations of rape and the reasons soldiers gave as to why rapes occurred. In talking about the acts of sexual violence they committed, the men differentiated between 'recreational rape' and 'evil rape.' Recreational rapes were ascribed to the nature of male sexuality and perceived as 'somehow ok' and "morally defendable, ethically palatable and socially acceptable," because the perpetrators are seen as victims of their urges (Eriksson Baaz/ Stern 2009: 497). In their accounts, these rapes happened because male urges had to be satisfied and the special circumstances of war offered little other opportunity for sex outside of rape.

The soldiers also spoke of evil rapes, by which they meant rapes that were carried out with utmost violence, severely injuring and/or killing the victim. While they did not characterise these acts as acceptable, they offered some justification like negative past personal experiences, dire life circumstances, subjection to violence, witnessing the killing of family members, exposure to bad treatment by military superiors, having to put up with deplorable living conditions, neglect and continuous frustration. The men suggested that such experiences 'naturally' translated into a wish to inflict pain and harm on others and consequently into violent rapes. Eriksson Baaz and Stern present the narratives the men produced to legitimise their actions in the interview situation (Eriksson Baaz/Stern 2009: 504) and attach a great deal of importance to these accounts within their interpretative framework. Indeed, the explanations the men give are strikingly similar to the scarce material we have from other scenarios of sexual violence in armed conflict. Russian soldiers who served in the Berlin area in 1945, for example, produced what amounts to a discourse of recreational rape and—probably even more often—of rape out of anger and wrath as revenge for the crimes the German Wehrmacht committed in the Soviet Union (Eifler 1999). Similarly, interviews with Serbian fighters in the 1990s revealed that they legitimised their actions, including aggressive sexual attacks, by citing their anger, frustration and fear, and the need to defend 'their own' against a dangerous enemy who had to be ousted from their community (Bašić 2004). In all cases, the perpetrators of extreme violence further attributed the atrocities they committed to the 'insanity of war' and the 'loss of normalcy and decency' in combat situations.

But what do these perpetrators' accounts contribute to our knowledge of sexual violence in armed conflicts? To start with, the interview method poses a problem. This approach marks an individualised (Western) understanding of subjectivity in a perhaps not quite as individualised social and cultural setting in which personal accounts may not be meaningful in the same way. The questions 'what was your motive for acting in a certain way?' or 'what is your personal opinion on a certain issue?' might be interpreted quite differently in certain, more collectively oriented settings. As respondents' answers showed, the men reproduced explanatory patterns that were taken from what would be considered socially acceptable explanations within a certain time frame and against a specific knowledge background. Their answers tell us more about the social discourses available to them than about individual motives or personal perspectives, or, for that matter, the cultural patterns hidden behind individual acts. This presumably mitigates the significance of what, from an individualised perspective, may be considered personal standpoints on collective acts.[8] Indeed, even in individualised social and cultural settings, war and armed conflict are highly collective experiences and individual accounts may lose significance. Perpetrators of violence in a collective context are usually "part of a hierarchical structure whose association with the violence in question has a considerable influence on the latter's meaning for the individual rapist" (Branche et al. 2012: 8). Perpetrators of violence may indeed not be able to produce any explanation of the motives for their behaviour. The autonomous individual of the Enlightenment Era, capable of rational accountability, is cast in doubt when, as Veena Das (cit. in Hayden 2000: 30) noted, human actions of that kind are informed by "repositories of unconscious memories." The actors themselves are embedded in a highly collective symbolic realm, which gives them—and the victims—little conscious access to their motivations.[9] While it is interesting to see what discourses the perpetrators draw on to justify or excuse their acts, whether their accounts can provide a basis for understanding and, ultimately, combating this form of violence is doubtful.

Since the characteristics of violence appear to be very personal, however, analysis often focuses on the psychology of the individual perpetrators with a "tendency to isolate the personality of the actor, to examine his or her antecedents, trajectory and family background and in some cases to resort to psychiatry and consider the violence as a form of madness or pathology" (Wieviorka 2014: 53). But even though violence in armed conflicts occurs at a micro level between human beings and human bodies, it does not necessarily call for a purely micro approach. In collective conflicts, violent acts are also central to historical developments and the shaping and destroying of whole societies, so understanding these requires a macro approach (Wieviorka 2014: 52). Therefore, mediation between the macro and micro perspective, between cultural meaning and individual action, is called for. While individualised or psychological accounts can tell us something about the individual desires and emotional dynamics motivating the perpetrators, they tend to minimise the social and political dimensions of acts of collective violence. Explanations operating exclusively at the macro level, on the other hand, neglect the individual processes associated with acts of violence that are presumably relevant if we want to understand why people can be driven by the same motive, yet commit different acts of violence or even no violence at all (Nedelmann 1997: 59).

Another approach to the issue of wartime rape has emerged in international relations that shifts focus from the actual act to ask instead why sexual violence has become a political and academic issue. Proponents of this approach argue that sexual violence in armed conflicts has been 'securitised' and 'fetishised' as a speech act in recent decades (Hirschauer 2014; Meger 2016). Hirschauer's understanding of the academic and political debates following the scandalisation of sexual violence in the 1990s is based on the securitisation theory developed by Buzan and Weaver (Buzan/ Weaver/Wilde 1998). Buzan and Weaver base their arguments on constructivist reasoning and question concepts such as 'security' (or lack thereof) and 'threat', pointing out that these are subjectively perceived concepts that only become social realities through speech acts, or when they are spoken about in a certain context and manner. According to this interpretation, anything can become a referent object of security as long as it resonates for a politically relevant audience and—to use a Foucauldian term—as long as it becomes a dispositive that is translated into a relevant political practice.

While wartime rape has existed since time immemorial, Hirschauer argues that we should turn our attention to the process of 'unsilencing' at the end of the twentieth century when gendered and sexual violence was demarginalised to be included in a political narrative that moved the issue to the political fore. According to Hirschauer, academic and political elites developed this political narrative in the wake of the sexual violence in Bosnia-Herzegovina and Rwanda. This discourse has led to the institutionalised securitisation of rape, making it part of the security domain, and the deploying of extraordinary measures in international law (Hirschauer 2014: 55, 192).

In a similar vein, Meger contends that there has been a fetishisation of sexual violence (Meger 2016: 149). She characterises fetishisation as a de-contextualisation of sexual violence and cites the generally undertheorised descriptions of sexual violence that present it merely as 'abject acts' of an evil nature in varying contexts. In the securitisation discourse, Meger argues, the theorisation of the violent act itself does not play a role. Instead, the emphasis is on 'doing something about it.'

While Hirschauer's analysis allows for the possibility of male rape, the rape-securitisation approach is firmly embedded in an understanding of rape as a 'female fate'. While it has certainly been shown that the large majority of acts of sexual violence are directed against women, in the securitisation approach, which considers the speech act of primary importance, the focus on sexual violence—itself a speech act—is limited to sexual violence against women. This is clearly demonstrated in the documents issued by the 'securitisation actors' of political bodies such as the UN Security Council, governments, the media, NGOs, and so on which, over the last 20 or so years, have almost exclusively focused on rape as a crime directed against women. While this may be politically warranted, it nevertheless narrows the analytical focus (Hirschauer 2014: 197).

Moreover, this also seems to place heavy emphasis on the question of how sexual violence in wars is framed in political discourses and appears to serve a tendency to de-emphasise the need for an analysis of the significance of sexual war crimes as acts of violence. One could say that a policy-oriented and instrumental gaze is prioritised over an analysis of the acts of sexual violence. While this doubtless provides insight into political discourses, the question is whether it is possible to proceed to effective policies without an in-depth analysis of sexual violence itself. Can sexual violence be solved on a discursive level without also considering the discourses of the bodies involved and the discourses of the violence exerted on those bodies?

Attacks on the body obliterate everything beyond the actual perceptions of the body, such as pain, fear and terror. Violent assaults annihilate language and reduce humans to sheer corporeality, while also representing attacks on symbolic systems of meaning. Violence makes the body 'speak' and redefines the relationship between those who exert and those who suffer violence or, to return to Scarry's seminal study: violence unmakes the world of the victim and the victim's world disappears in her/his pain, whereas the absence of pain makes and enhances the world of the perpetrator who transforms the pain of the victim in the extension and uncontested reality of his/her world (Scarry 1988: 150; McDonald 2013: 142). The victim's pain is converted into the powerful reality of the perpetrator's world. The kind of reality created in acts of violence can only be identified through a detailed description of the violent act itself (Trotha 1997). Thus essential aspects of the making and unmaking of the world might escape our attention when we bypass the actual acts of violence to focus on purpose and instrumentality. Violence is an extreme and atrocious interaction between two bodies, the degradation and deprecation of one body that is exposed to the power of another (McDonald 2013: 139). Exploring what is happening to perpetrator and victim and what kind of relationship the violent act constitutes between the two is an essential part of understanding the act itself.

CONCLUDING REMARKS

In the introduction to their recapitulation of theories of sexual violence in armed conflict, Eriksson Baaz and Stern (2012) call their text somewhat 'unruly.' If the text is unruly, it is because the topic is unruly. When we attempt to pinpoint sites of contestation for sexual violence, we find ourselves in a minefield of diverse purposes and objectives as well as in a world of diverse symbolic meanings and grammars of violence that are historically and culturally specific. Explanations of wartime rape are so multifaceted and intricate because they are so deeply embedded in varying symbolic contexts and also pursue varying instrumental purposes. What is of major importance in one context may not be of central significance in others. Given the highly culturally charged significance of rape and the many functions it fulfils in collective conflicts, we are faced with symbolic overkill, or to follow Foucauldian conceptualisation: rape is hyper-saturated with meaning (cit. in Gordon 1980: 186).

Violence in general and violence in particular is not merely destructive; the real threat to the individual forced to experience torture, pain and destruction is that it re-orders social and political categories and re-arranges the socio-political order by making the body the material with which politics is translated into incontestable material reality. In other words: "the somatic character of violence reduces the ambiguity inherent in any communication" (Beck/Brandt 2011: 352) and produces an (almost) incontestable social asymmetry and reality. Given the increasing global contestation of power relations, social divides, and set 'truths' as well as increasing material and cultural conflicts, and given the symbolic overkill sexual violence encompasses, it seems that far from being an echo from the past, sexual violence is instead—according to Diken and Laustsen—"what lies ahead of us" (Diken/Laustsen 2005: 126). (Sexual) violence and the suffering of male and female bodies are the means for making and re-making, for unmaking and destructing the world. The suffering of bodies produces social orders and dominant and subordinated subjectivities, particularly as the violated body continues to testify to what has happened long after the act (Beck/Brandt 2011: 351). Given the overwhelming social power violence unleashes, policies will not suffice. We will have to embed our analyses (followed by actions) regarding (sexual) violence into broader concepts of the production and reproduction of (gendered) social orders and subjectivities.

NOTES

1. Žarkov (2007: 155ff) questions this approach.
2. This understanding also characterised the *Global Summit to End Sexual Violence in Conflict* that took place in London in June 2014. This 'Rape Crisis Conference' was hosted by Hollywood actress Angelina Jolie and British Foreign Minister William Hague. The aim of the conference was to strengthen prosecution of perpetrators, organise support for victims, facilitate implementation of legal and other proceedings to hold groups and individuals accountable, and to produce a "seismic shift in attitudes" about the prevalence and continuing practice of rape in armed conflicts (Westmarland 2014). It is remarkable that sexual atrocities against women were singled out and scandalised at a glamorous event with absolutely no attempt to explore any background information.
3. Cf. for example, Hinojosa 2010.
4. For a discussion see Eriksson Baaz/Stern; cf. also Meger 2016: 153f.
5. The emphasis here has to be on the word 'completely' as the volatility of all the categories of social belonging mentioned above makes them basically negotiable in any context.
6. Lifton also describes this function of extreme violence. In his psychological investigations of the Holocaust, he notes that shared violence was unifying, drawing men together and instilling a sense of self-preservation of the group (Lifton 1979: 333).
7. United Nations Office for the Coordination of Humanitarian Affairs 2008: 2. See also Stemple 2009.
8. In a study of wartime experiences in Kosovo, interviewees answered questions about how they thought the ethnic conflict had been handled by asserting, "that is just the way we do things here." Cf. Seifert 2003a.
9. While perpetrators may not have conscious access to their motives this is not tantamount to saying they bear no moral responsibility.

REFERENCES

Apperly, Harry. 2015. 'Hidden Victims: A Call to Action on Sexual Violence against Men in Conflict', *Medicine, Conflict and Survival*, 31(2):92–9.

Barth, Fredrik. 1969. 'Introduction', in Frederik Barth (ed), *Ethnic Groups and Boundaries: The Social Organisation of Difference*, pp. 9–38. London: Allen & Unwin.

Bašić, Natalija. 2004. 'Kampfsoldaten im ehemaligen Jugoslawien: Legitimationen des Kämpfens und des Tötens', in Ruth Seifert (ed), *Gender, Identität und kriegerischer Konflikt: Das Beispiel des ehemaligen Jugoslawiens*, pp. 89–111. Münster: Lit Verlag.

Beck, Teresa K./Brandt, Willy. 2011. 'The Eye of the Beholder: Violence as a Social Process', *International Journal of Conflict and Violence*, 5(2):345–56.

Branche, Raphaëlle/Delpa, Isabelle/Horne, John/Lagrou, Pieter/Palmieri, Daniel/Virgili, Fabrice. 2012. 'Writing the History of Wartime Rape', in Raphaëlle Branche/Fabrice Virgili (eds), *Rape in Wartime*, pp. 1–16. Basingstoke: Palgrave Macmillan.

Buzan, Barry/Weaver, Ole/Wilder, Jaap de. 1998. *Security—A New Framework for Analysis*. Boulder: Lynne Rienner Publishers.

Cohen, Dara Kay. 2013. 'Explaining Rape during Civil War: Cross-National Evidence (1980–2009)', *American Political Science Review*, 107(1):461–77.

Cohen, Dara Kay/Hoover Green, Amelia/Wood, Elisabeth Jean. 2013. *Wartime Sexual Violence: Misconceptions, Implications and Ways Forward*. Washington D.C.: Institute of Peace.

Couturier, Don. 2012. 'The Rape of Men: Eschewing Myths of Sexual Violence in War', *On Politics*, 6(2):1–14. http://journals.uvic/index.php/onpolitics/article/view/12770/5965 (accessed 6 July 2018).

Diken, Bülent/Laustsen, Carsten. 2005. 'Becoming Abject: Rape as a Weapon of War', *Body and Society*, 11(1):111–28.

Dolan, Chris. 2014. *Briefing Paper for the Workshop 'Into the Mainstream: Addressing Sexual Violence Against Men and Boys in Conflict'*. Presented at the Overseas Development Institute, London, 14 May.

Douglas, Mary. 1986. *How Institutions Think*. Syracuse: Syracuse University Press.

Eifler, Christine. 1999. 'Nachkrieg und weibliche Verletzbarkeit: Zur Rolle von Kriegen für die Konstruktion von Geschlecht', in Christine Eifler/Ruth Seifert (eds), *Soziale Konstruktionen: Militär und Geschlechterverhältnis*, pp. 155–86. Münster: Westfälisches Dampfboot.

Eriksson Baaz, Maria/Stern, Maria. 2009. 'Why Do Soldiers Rape? Masculinity, Violence, and Sexuality in the Armed Forces in the Congo (DR)', *International Studies Quarterly*, 52(2):495–518.

Gordon, Colin (ed.): *Power/Knowledge: Selected Interviews and Other Writings 1972–1977*. New York: Pantheon Books.

Hayden, Robert M. 2000. 'Rape and Rape Avoidance in Ethno-National Conflicts: Sexual Violence in Liminalized States', *American Anthropologist*, 102(1):27–41.

Hinojosa, Ramon. 2010. 'Doing Hegemony: Military, Men, and Constructing a Hegemonic Masculinity', *Journal of Men's Studies*, 18(2):179–94.

Hirschauer, Sabine. 2014. *The Securitization of Rape: Women, War and Sexual Violence*. Basingstoke: Palgrave Macmillan.

Koo, Katrina Lee. 2002. 'Confronting a Disciplinary Blindness: Women, War and Rape in the International Politics of Security', *Australian Journal of Political Science*, 37(3):525–36.

Lagrou, Pieter. 2009. 'Irregular Warfare and the Norms of Legitimate Violence in Twentieth Century Europe', in Jost Dülffer/ Robert Frank (eds), *Peace, War, and Gender from Antiquity to the Present: Cross-Cultural Perspectives*, pp. 169–80. Essen: Klartext Verlag.

Lifton, Robert J. 1979. *The Broken Connection: On Death and the Continuity of Life*. New York: Simon & Schuster.

Malesevic, Sinisa. 2010. *The Sociology of War and Violence*. Cambridge: Cambridge University Press.

McDonald, Kevin. 2013. 'Grammars of Violence, Modes of Embodiment and Frontiers of the Subject', in Kevin McSorley (ed), *War and the Body: Militarisation, Practice and Experience*, pp. 138–51. London: Routledge.

Meger, Sara. 2016. 'The Fetishization of Sexual Violence in International Security', *International Studies Quarterly*, 60(1):149–59.

Nedelmann, Birgitta. 1997. 'Gewaltsoziologie am Scheideweg: Die Auseinandersetzung in der gegenwärtigen und Wege der zukünftigen Gewaltforschung', in Trutz von Trotha (ed), *Soziologie der Gewalt*, pp. 59–85. Wiesbaden: Westdeutscher Verlag.

O'Mochain, Robert. 2015. 'Sexual Violence in Conflict: Forgotten Victims in Secondary Source Literature', *Ritsumeikan Annual Review of International Studies*, 14:103–19.

Prügl, Elisabeth. 2004. 'International Institutions and Feminist Politics', *Brown Journal of World Affairs*, 10(2):69–84.

Rittner, Carol/Roth, John K. (eds), 2012, *Rape: Weapon of War and Genocide*. St Paul: Paragon House.

Scarry, Elaine. 1988. *The Body in Pain: The Making and Unmaking of the World*. Oxford: Oxford University Press.

Seifert, Ruth. 2003a. *Kriegserfahrung, Identität und Geschlecht (War Experience, Identity and Gender): Final Report on a Research Project supported by the Austrian Ministry of Education, Science and Culture*. Vienna: Österreichisches Ministerium für Bildung, Wissenschaft und Kultur.

———. 2003b. 'Im Tod und Schmerz sind nicht all gleich: Männliche und weibliche Körper in der kulturellen Konstruktion von Krieg und Nation', in Steffen Martus/Werner Röcke/Marina Münkler (eds), *Schlachtfelder: Codierung von Gewalt im medialen Wandel*, pp. 235–64. Berlin: Akademie-Verlag.

———. 2002. 'Rape—the Female Body as a Symbol and a Sign: Gender-Specific Violence and the Cultural Construction of War', in Ilkka Taipale (ed), *War or Health? A Reader*, pp. 280–94. London: Zed Books.

———. 1993. *Krieg und Vergewaltigung: Ansätze zu einer Analyse*, Freiburg: Kore Verlag.

Sivakumaran, Sandesh. 2007. 'Sexual Violence against Men in Armed Conflict', *The European Journal of International Law*, 18(2):253–76.

Stefatos, Katherine. 2012. 'The Victimisation of the Body and the Body Politic during the Greek Civil War', in: Raphaëlle Branche/Fabrice Virgili (eds), *Rape in Wartime*, pp. 1046–49. London: Palgrave Macmillan.

Stemple, Lara. 2009. 'Male Rape and Human Rights', *Hastings Law Journal*, 60(3):605–46.

Trotha, Trutz von. 1997. 'Zur Soziologie der Gewalt', in Trutz von Trotha (ed), *Soziologie der Gewalt*, pp. 9–58. Wiesbaden: Westdeutscher Verlag.

United Nations Office for the Coordination of Humanitarian Affairs. 2008. *Discussion Paper 2: The Nature, Scope and Motivation for Sexual Violence Against Men and Boys in Armed Conflict*. New York.

Vojdik, Valorie V. 2014. 'Sexual Violence against Men and Women in War: A Masculinities Approach', *Nevada Law Journal*, 14:923–52.

Westmarland, Nicole. 2014. 'Comment and Opinion', *Durham University News*, 16 June. https://www.dur.ac.uk/news/allnews/thoughtleadership/?itemno=21476 (accessed 5 July 2018).

Wieviorka, Michel. 2014. 'The Sociological Analysis of Violence: New Perspectives', *Sociological Review Monograph Series*, 62(S2):50–64.

Wood, Elizabeth. 2006. 'Variations of Sexual Violence during War', *Politics and Society*, 34(3):307–42.

Žarkov, Dubravka. 2007. *The Body of War: Media, Ethnicity, and Gender in the Break-Up of Yugoslavia*. Durham: Duke University Press.

The Legal and Cultural Value
of Sexual Violence

PATRICIA VISEUR SELLERS

INTRODUCTION

In autumn 1998, the United Nations' ad hoc tribunals'[1] delivered three landmark judgments dealing with sexual violence under humanitarian law. In *Prosecutor v. Akayesu*,[2] a Trial Chamber of the International Criminal Tribunal for Rwanda (ICTR) convicted Jean Paul Akayesu for sexual violence committed during the 1994 Rwandan genocide, while two Trial Chambers of the International Criminal Tribunal for the former Yugoslavia (ICTY) separately pronounced guilty verdicts for sexual violence in the matters of *Prosecutor v. Delalić*[3] and *Prosecutor v. Furundžija*.[4] The judgments simultaneously interpreted the scope of sex crimes under the statutes of the ad hoc Tribunals and substantively advanced the jurisprudence of sexual violence under international law. Collectively, they hold that rape and other forms of sexual violence constitute acts of genocide, crimes against humanity, violations of the laws or customs of war, namely war crimes, and grave breaches of the Geneva Conventions.

The *Akayesu* decision is singularly significant. The Prosecutor originally indicted Jean Paul Akayesu for participating in the killings of male and female Tutsis. During the trial, the Trial Chamber granted leave to amend the indictment, so that the Prosecutor could charge the accused with rapes and other sexual abuses committed against female Tutsis. In the judgment, the Trial Chamber found that the acts of sexual violence satisfied the *actus reus* of "causing serious bodily or mental harm to members of the group," a provision of the Genocide Convention that is incorporated into Article 2(2)(b) of the ICTR Statute.[5] The judgment held that rape and sexual violence indeed "constitute[d] genocide in the same way as any other act, as long as they were committed with the specific intent to destroy in whole or part, a particular group targeted as such."[6]

Akayesu likewise upheld the Prosecution's allegation of crimes against humanity and convicted the accused of various forms of sexual violence, including acts that were interpreted to come within the meaning of Article 3 (g) [rape], of the ICTR Statute. As a result, for the first time an international tribunal pronounced the elements of the international crime of rape and defined the conduct as "a physical invasion of a sexual nature, committed on a person under circumstances that are coercive."[7] In the *Akayesu* decision, the accused was also convicted of authorizing conduct, including forced nudity and sexual humiliation, that the Prosecutor had properly characterized as inhumane acts as proscribed by Article 3(i).

In *Prosecutor v. Delalić,* commonly known as Čelebići decision, Bosnian Muslim soldiers stood accused of sexually assaulting Bosnian Serb prisoners. One of the accused, a military superior, allegedly had repeatedly raped female detainees to elicit information and to punish them. The Trial Chamber opined that such acts rose to the level of torture, as defined by the Torture Convention and as incorporated into the grave breaches provision of Article 2. The Trial Chamber also was of the opinion that such acts were violations of the laws and customs of war, under Article 3 of the ICTY Statute.[8] Another *Delalić* accused was pronounced guilty of forcing two Bosnian Serb male prisoners to perform fellatio on each other in front of the other male inmates. The Trial Chamber found such sexually humiliating conduct to be a "fundamental attack on [these prisoners'] human dignity,"[9] and convicted the accused of war crimes and grave breaches.

In *Prosecutor v. Furundžija,* a Bosnian Croat commander of the "Jokers," a special military police unit, was indicted for conducting an interrogation of a female Muslim while she was in a state of forced nudity and while she was incessantly raped in the presence of the unit's members. A Bosnian Croat soldier who was arrested and likewise interrogated by the "Jokers" was forced to watch the sexual abuse in anticipation that he too would "confess" to having collaborated with the woman. The Trial Chamber found the accused liable for torture and outrages on personal dignity, including rape, both considered violations of the laws and customs of war under Article 3 of the ICTY Statute. In addition, the Trial Chamber, in an extensive discussion of the law of torture, interpreted humiliation to be a purpose motivating the infliction of torture, similar to the purpose of intimidation or coercion. Under the facts of this case, the Trial Chamber concluded that the victim had been tortured for the purposes of humiliation and intimidation, and in order to extract information. The Trial Chamber further held that the accused committed torture, not only against the Bosnian Muslim female but against the Bosnian Croat prisoner who was made to witness the rapes and sexual abuse.

Lastly, for the second time within four months and, likewise, for the second time in the annals of international criminal jurisprudence, a definition of rape as an international crime was set forth. To determine the elements of rape, the Trial Chamber drew upon general principles of municipal and international law and arrived at the same elements that the Prosecutor had consistently proposed in her pleadings.[10] The Trial Chamber defined rape to include acts of forced oral sex, concluding that the fundamental principle of protecting human dignity favoured broadening the definition of rape.

Moreover, in the winter of 2001, an ICTY Trial Chamber, in the *Prosecutor v. Kunarac*,[11] held that enslavement, as a crime against humanity, was committed against Bosnian Muslim females detained in the town of Foča, in the former-Yugoslavia. The females, ranged in age from 13 to 25 years old, had been detained in several locations and eventually reduced to slavery by individual Bosnian Serb soldiers. The Trial Chamber convicted the defendants of enslavement and held that they had exercised powers of ownership over the females, including ownership over all sexual access to them. Deploying the definition of enslavement from the 1926 Slavery Convention,[12] *Kunarac* represented the first conviction for enslavement as a crime against humanity based upon acts of sexual violence.

The stunning jurisprudence of *Akayesu, Delalić, Furundžija* and *Kunarac* cemented the groundwork for the ensuing two decades of international criminal jurisprudence that addressed armed conflict-related sexual violence as well as sexual violence inflicted during periods of genocide and of crimes against humanity.[13] Nonetheless, this initial jurisprudence served a dual purpose— redress of criminal conduct and refutation of sceptics who, in the early days of the ad hoc Tribunals, belittled the prospects of sexual assault prosecutions. Critiques asserted that any trials would be forced to bow to 1990s—read feminist—political correctness and that any judgments would be fatally devoid of legal rigor. That has not been the case. The judgments entailing sex-based crimes were 'grounded' in settled, yet evolving principles of humanitarian law and international criminal law. I took issue with the narrow, uninformed premise of the critics and continue to posit that, historically, the condemnation of sexual violence under humanitarian law has always expounded and been driven, in part, by contemporaneous social values. Such values encompassed preservation or pacification of civil society, alternating stances on the primacy of military objectives or humanitarian goals, escalated protection of the armed forces, and, eventually, promotion of non-discriminatory respect for the sexual integrity of persons, irrespective of civil status. Political and social mores permeated both the initial legality and then increasing illegality of sexual violence during armed conflict. I proffer that this intricate dynamic determines the 'cultural' value of sexual violence within humanitarian law.

ENDEMIC WARS AND PRESERVATION OF CIVIL SOCIETY

War is not endogenous to Europe, nor is humanitarian law a purely Western development. Nevertheless, the military campaigns of

European societies contributed greatly to the chiselling of the law of armed conflict. Concepts found in modern humanitarian law can be traced through medieval law, canon law and codes of chivalry down to the twentieth century Hague Conventions and Geneva Conventions. In the 1300s to the 1500s, the medieval European societies that first shaped humanitarian law were chiefly composed of realms and city-states. Their political and social structures were extremely hierarchical. Their economies ranged from entrenched forms of feudalism to incipient forms of mercantilism. State religions were fundamentalist and intolerant institutions that displayed little sympathy for dissent from church doctrines whether it originated among royalty, nobility or serfs.

The Pope, other religious leaders, such as bishops or princes of the church together with kings, knights and other aristocrats wielded unyielding power over their subjects, yet their intra-actions, based on mutual respect and tempered by mutual distrust, were the precursors to state sovereignty. Most Western persons existed in non-individualised entities that functioned on behalf of the church or state. Any notion of citizenship, in the modern meaning of that term, was unfathomable. Patriarchal values unyieldingly determined women's lives: Females of all ages were the property of their landlords, fathers, husbands or brothers.

Another feature of medieval European society was its almost permanent state of war. Keen noted, "War did not mean an exceptional period of international strife; it was the endemic condition of Western European society" (Keen 1965: 64). War was endemic because it performed a necessary function. It presented an acceptable tactical exercise to resolve political, economic and religious disputes. It sanctioned the means to the proverbial end. War could be waged and prolonged indefinitely, conditioned only upon the requirements that it be 'just'. If a war were 'just', humanitarian law could accord legitimacy to certain bellicose acts of kings, knights, the church and eventually the state.

Precisely because medieval European societies were enveloped by armed conflict, the motivation to preserve one's own civil society by safeguarding it from the destruction of war theoretically motivated all European sovereigns. Attackers and defenders alike would rather preserve civil institutions, including the church, commerce, government, agriculture, trade routes and even diplomatic channels in the hope of either continuing to reign or of reaping an intact society from one's enemy.

Consequently, the law of armed conflict responded to the paradox of constant, destructive war and the need to preserve civil society. Medieval edicts of humanitarian law, such as the Ordinances of War, enunciated by Richard II in 1385 at Durham and by Henry Vat Mantes in 1419, condemned attacks on churches, and prohibited the confiscation of livestock and farming tools and the violation of women and priests, including their murder.[14] The logic behind such ideas was not new. Other societies had, considerably earlier, instructed their soldiers to spare civil institutions and to safeguard non-combatants from the destruction of war. Most noteworthy, the first Caliph AbuBaker, stipulated in A.D. 632 that "[t]he blood of women, children and old people shall not stain your victory. Do not destroy a palm tree, nor burn houses and cornfields with fire, and do not cut any fruitful tree" (Obote-Oddora 1997: 108). In 1339, the Emperor Codalago ordered commanders to restrict the killing of innocents and to absolutely forbid the torching of shrines and temples (ibid.: 12). This intermittently enforced norm held that property and the cultural and economic goods of civil society were to be considered beyond harm's way and war's reach.

Condemnation of rape under the early laws of war essentially acted to preserve civil society's status quo, much like the proscriptions against killing priests, burning fields and looting the church. Interdiction of sexual violence extended not just to women but to non-combatant men, who were to be spared because of their contribution to the larger society. Females were to be spared because of their economic value, rather than their personal or individual integrity. Such legal principles would only evolve centuries later. This medieval legal prohibition of sexual violence concedes, almost by admission, that wartime rapes unravelled and destabilised civil society.

However, the relationship between sexual violence and preservation of civil society during armed conflict was even more complex. If, as a general rule, sexual violence against non-combatants was illegal, then, conversely, rape and other forms of sexual violence were at times deemed legal and were tolerated for the sake of preserving broader European values.

Within the context of a 'just war', the legality of bellicose acts was to be further determined by their circumstances. The state of siege serves to illustrate. In a 'just war', a sovereign possessed the right to demand the capitulation of an enemy town or fortress. If, upon receipt of due warning, an enemy refused to accept terms of surrender, the attacking army could declare the enemy's town under siege. The rules of siege in medieval humanitarian law sanctioned rape, murder and looting of the persons and property of innocent non-combatants by suspending these acts' illegality whenever the enemy refused to surrender. During a siege, the principles of 'just war' allowed one civil society to destroy another society. As a consequence, sexual violence became a legal act of war used to force the capitulation of an enemy's town. This contextual view of sexual violence did not conflict with contemporaneous medieval political values anchored in the legal culture; rather, it upheld them.

Other 'just wars' that allowed an army to inflict sexual violence included the European military campaigns against non-Christian nations. The Crusades, colonial wars and military slave raids enabled European armies to perpetrate notorious but 'legal' rapes as they marched through foreign societies. Such actions were justified as necessary to defend religious beliefs, secure claims to new territory or advance economic expansion. Stated differently, these were military actions to protect the larger status quo against so-called infidels and to permit the exploitation of so-called primitive peoples.

Sexual violence was likewise considered legal when committed by state actors during an internal armed conflict. A ruler's absolute right to quash internal dissent rested on the principle that states would not interfere in the internal affairs of other states. Thus, to preserve their domains from insurrection, sovereigns could literally destroy their own society however they saw fit. Rulers could purposely unleash sexual violence to defend their kingdoms, and, in turn, they could intentionally ignore its use. Either stance conformed to international law and was tempered only by a sovereign's internal edicts or decrees that were in effect during war. According to these medieval norms, the state could and did sanction sexual violence for political, religious or economic reasons.

By the end of the eighteenth century, the surge of mercantilism began to strengthen its economic grasp on European and European-derived societies. As a result, international actors entered into various trade agreements. The newly independent United States and its European allies, namely Prussia, France and the Netherlands,[15] entered into Treaties of Amity, bilateral trade instruments that, in addition to regulating commerce, captured states' customary law expectations of each other in the eventuality of war. Interestingly, these treaties' terms proscribed infliction of sexual violence as a mutual safeguard to minimise the disruption of economic life during war. Article 23 of the Treaty of Amity between the United States and Prussia stipulates:

> *If war should arise between the two contracting parties,* the merchants of either country shall be allowed to remain nine months to collect their debts and settle their affairs and may depart freely, carrying off all their effects without molestation or hindrances. And *all women and children, scholars of every faculty, cultivators of the earth, artisans, manufacturers, and their fishermen, unarmed and inhabiting unfortified towns, villages or places, and in general all others working for the common substance and benefit of mankind,* shall be allowed to continue in their employment, and *shall not be molested in their person* nor shall their houses or goods be burnt or otherwise destroyed. [emphasis added] (Malloy 1910)

Several principles of medieval humanitarian law remain conspicuous in Article 23: Society was still structured along economic, social, religious, cultural and patriarchal, non-individualised lines. The preservation of economic cohesion continued to regulate the waging of war. States expected that contributors to the "common substance and benefit of mankind"—

scholars, manufacturers, farmers, that is, the components of civil society—were to be removed from harm. Prohibitions of molestation, a euphemism for physical and sexual violence, applied to men and women as a generally accepted norm.

RISE OF THE MILITARY DOCTRINES AND CITIZENSHIP

Toward the end of nineteenth century, the 1864 Geneva Convention, the 1899 Hague Conventions[16] and revised national military codes had started an era of nascent codification of humanitarian law. General Order No. 100, commonly referred to as the Lieber Code, governed the conduct of Union soldiers during the American Civil War and exemplified a national code that drew upon the then-contemporary understanding of customary international law.[17] The Lieber Code intoned that modern wars were guided by principles of justice, honour and humanity that bound each soldier's conduct (art. 4). The latter regard for humanity had little grounding in the Middle Ages. Under the Lieber Code, military necessity dictated that the enemy could legally be killed, transportation destroyed and communications cut. However lawful aggression was circumscribed and, "the protection of the inoffensive citizen of the hostile country was the rule" (art. 25), Article 22 of the Lieber Code stated that "[t]he principle has been more and more acknowledged that the unarmed citizen is to be spared in property, *and honor* as much as the exigencies of war will admit."

The Lieber Code illustrates states' changing view of persons within civil society in general and women in particular, and the effects that wartime sexual violence has on citizens. Even the Code's references to "inoffensive citizen" or "unarmed citizen" denotes a deepening of domestic political changes initiated in the 1700s with the establishment of national congresses, parliamentary and republican systems of government, albeit with the recognition of constitutional monarchies. Preservation of society in the nineteenth century had mutated into meaning protection of citizens or those persons endowed with a legal relationship to the state that is accompanied by certain rights. The Lieber Code's political language is important, notwithstanding that in 1863, when it was issued, US society did not grant citizenship to Native Americans or to slaves. Although women of European descent could hold citizenship, they exercised limited property rights and were universally disenfranchised.

However, the apparent spirit of the Lieber Code, despite the prevailing political doctrines, social mores and economic institutions, offered wide protection to all enemy persons from acts of war that were unjustified by military necessity,[18] regardless of political status, sex, religious affiliation, occupation, function or status as property.[19] According to Article 44 of the Lieber Code:

> *All* wanton violence committed against *persons* in the invaded country, all destruction of property not commanded by the authorized officer, all robbery, all pillage or sacking, even after taking a place by force, *all rape*, wounding or maiming or killing of such *inhabitants* are prohibited. [emphasis added] (Schindler/ Toman 1988: 10)

The Lieber Code interpreted customary international law as condemning rape during invasions, and, in contrast to medieval law, rape remained illegal during military sieges. The Lieber Code's nineteenth century interpretation probably confirmed that states of siege no longer sanctioned maiming, killing or raping of inhabitants for the sake of obtaining a decisive military victory, even if an enemy refused to surrender. This expanding coverage of inhabitants of conquered societies, and the nascent notion of personhood, is most evident in Article 37 of the Lieber Code, which reads: "The United States acknowledges and protects, in hostile countries occupied by them, religion and morality, strictly private property; *the persons of the inhabitants, especially those of women*; and the sacredness of domestic relationships." [emphasis added] (ibid.: 9)

Article 37 constitutes an incipient admission by a major nation that regardless of the existence of a state of war, individuals continue to possess societal cultural values and religious beliefs that merit respect and, subsequently, protection. Furthermore, inhabitants of the occupied territories, especially women, were 'protected' from sexual assaults by occupiers. Women's protection went beyond the guarantees that they received as family members and persons within domestic and marital relations. Sexual violence was no longer a legitimate means to revel in complete victory during a military occupation. The accession of the citizen into civil society by the mid-nineteenth century acted to broaden and specify protection from sexual violence during armed conflict.

The Hague Convention IV,[20] adopted early in the twentieth century, confirmed the condemnation of rapes committed by occupying forces and squarely justifies the prohibition as consonant with the military's duty to preserve the normal functioning of occupied areas. Section 3 of the Annex to The Hague Convention IV, aptly titled "Military Authority over the Territory of the Hostile State", dictated measures that occupying forces must undertake in order to reinstate civil society. Several provisions deemed the occupier responsible for the safeguarding of public buildings, real estate, forests and agricultural estates (art. 55, Annex), as well as institutions dedicated to arts, religion, charity, education and science (art 56, Annex), and required the imposition of taxes, duties or tolls to closely follow rules of assessment predating the occupation (art. 48, Annex). Furthermore, the occupiers were to "take all the measures in [their] power to restore, and ensure [...] public order and safety" (art. 43, Annex).

Military occupiers likewise were enjoined from killing the inhabitants or inflicting upon them all manners of physical assaults, including sexual violence, as well as attacks on their dignity or moral sense: "Family honor and rights, the lives of persons, and private as well as religious convictions and practice, must be respected" (art. 46, Annex).

Often cited as having proscribed wartime rape, Article 46 most importantly disallows rape and all forms of sexual violence during periods of occupation, using language now familiar from the Lieber Code. Read together with the other obligations and duties of the occupying forces, Article 46 connotes that sexual violence imposed upon inhabitants of occupied territories impedes pacification and subverts the restoration of civil society. Such illegality only reinforces the humanitarian law premise that rape, along with other sexual abuse, is assumed to destroy the cohesion of civil society.

Social transformation is discernible from the language adopted in Article 46. The focus on the protection of persons has shifted from their institutional or cultural role, or role based upon their economic contribution or specialized labour, to an emphasis that situates persons within their families, their religious beliefs and private convictions. This language edges closer to individuality as conceptualized by Western society and is a refrain of the Lieber Code's elevation of the family as a unit of society that should remain unadulterated by attacks of sexual violence. Patriarchal mores did not wither away amid these turn-of-the-century culture changes. Rather, these mores were reasserted as guardians of family honour.

SOCIETY PROTECTION IN THE MID-20TH CENTURY WORLD WARS

World War I produced destruction previously unseen and unimagined by Western society. The Treaty of Versailles officially concluded the war and provided for the eventual prosecution of the Prussian Kaiser Wilhelm II and his senior staff. Although international trials were not forthcoming, it remains significant that the designated Commission responsible for determining what charges to levy against potential accused explicitly proposed that war crimes of rape and abduction of women and girls for purposes of prostitution could be prosecuted (Bassiouni 1992: 554). The Commission was in full awareness of how these grave illicit sexual assault acts contributed to the horrors of the German campaign that had destabilized Western Europe.

The Geneva Convention of 1929, drafted in the aftermath of World War I, brought together former enemies and allies to devise an international instrument that would protect prisoners in future wars from inhumane treatment. During the drafting convention, the German delegate observed that women had participated as combatants in World War I, and that women, in the future, would continue to be incorporated into the national defence effort.[21] The admission of women into branches of the military further prompted the German delegate to propose that the convention provide for protection from sexual violence, especially for female combatants who were captured by the enemy. The subsequently adopted Article 3 reads: "Prisoners of war are entitled to respect for their person and honor. Women shall be treated with all consideration due to their sex."

The 1929 Geneva Convention addressed a fundamental societal change, women's entrance into the military, and noted the detrimental impact wartime sexual violence had on female combatants. In response to increasing, state-supported exposure of women to combat, often as military nurses, all signatory nations jointly condemned the subjecting of female prisoners of war to sexual violence and provided for its absolute prohibition. While Article 3 could be interpreted as affording women special protection during war because society still regarded them not as equals but as the weaker sex, a more enlightened reading of Article 3 assumes that the provision inherently affirms the standing prohibition against sexual assaults on male prisoners as well. Under this reading, women are the beneficiary of a norm, rather than of any extraordinary protection. So, on the eve of World War II, in part because society had changed, states distinctly condemned sexual attacks inflicted upon their imprisoned troops and pledged not to subject enemy prisoners to sexual assaults. Fifteen years later, Article 3 was invoked at the Nuremberg and Tokyo trials.

Contrary to the verdict of certain scholars, evidence of sexual violence was admitted in the International Military Tribunals for Nuremberg (IMT) and the Far East (IMTFE) (Askin 1997: 180). The final decisions hold up to a legal analysis that the judges deliberated upon evidence of sex-based crimes and that such evidence indeed shaped the judgment. The Tokyo decision, and to a lesser extent the Nuremberg decision, beget no other reasonable conclusion (Sellers 2000a; McDonald/Swaak-Goldman 2000; McDonald 1999; Askin 1997; see also Tokyo trial documents, reprinted in Pritchard/Zaide 1981: 1029, 1066). The indictments (ibid.; see also Sellers 2000a: 23) and the decisions are complete with proscriptions that capture mid-twentieth-century legal culture as applied to sexual violence. For example, each Tribunal resorted to the recently adopted Article 3 of the 1929 Geneva Convention as a legal basis for convictions for ill-treatment of military personnel (International Military Tribunal 1947: 83) and of military nurses who were raped while imprisoned (ibid.; Pritchard/Zaide 1981: 2, 595). Prosecution concerning the Japanese invasion of the Chinese city of Nanking and the German invasion of western Russia relied upon the centuries-old prohibition of rape as a core war crime, while the occupations of Vichy France, eastern Russia and Manila were legally grounded in Article 46 of Hague Convention IV, which condemns sex crimes perpetrated during military occupation. In conformity with accepted military doctrine, the Tokyo judges disallowed sexual violence as a legitimate form of retaliation (Askin 1997; Sellers 2000a: 180), and disregarded Judge Pal of India's dissent implying that the report of countless rapes committed in Nanking might have been an exaggeration of Japanese misconduct (ibid.: 181–4).

In addition to war crimes, the International Military Tribunals placed crimes against humanity within their jurisdiction. Under the rubric of crimes against humanity, military and political authorities could be held responsible for crimes committed against any civilian, including citizens of their own state during an international war.[22] Stipulation of this broad responsibility was a direct response to the Nazis' murder of large numbers of German nationals who were members of religious or racial minorities, homosexuals, mentally or physically disabled or political dissidents. Although crimes against humanity was disdained as an unacceptable basis for prosecution by the US and Japanese delegates to the treaty talks at the conclusion of World War I (Bassiouni 1992: 558f), some twenty years later it emerged as an international offense, constituting a break with the previously absolute purview sovereigns had held over their own citizens.[23] Rapes and other sexual assaults were prosecuted at Nuremberg as crimes against humanity, and together with other conduct were characterized as 'inhumane acts' committed against a broad category of civilians including citizens, inhabitants, residents, enemy nationals, persons living under occupation or in annexed countries and other non-combatants. International societal mores no longer permitted a sovereign to attack even his own country's civilians, or to sanction rapes as part of that attack, at least in an international war.

Western society, stunned by the scale and intensity of destruction wrought by World War II, joined with other nations to furiously produce new international instruments, including the UN Declaration of Human Rights,[24] the Genocide Convention,[25] and the Geneva Conventions of 1949.[26] The drafters, in reaction to the war, unabashedly turned to law as a means to deter human carnage and cruelty.

The Preliminary Remarks to the Geneva Conventions underscore that they are "inspired by respect for human personality and dignity" and aim to aid "all victims of war without discrimination," including those who are "no longer the enemy."[27] The language resonates with the emerging regime of international human rights law and its germane concern for respect for individuals, regardless of their social, political or physical status. Jointly, the Geneva Conventions reaffirmed the principle of humane treatment owed to prisoners of war, as had been adopted in the 1929 Geneva Conventions, and then extended the prerequisite that humane treatment is owed to all persons hors de combat, including the wounded, the shipwrecked and prisoners of war, and to civilians during armed conflict. The drafters leave no doubt that humane treatment inevitably entails legal protection from all forms of sexual violence (Sellers/Rosenthal 2015).

Each Geneva Convention openly acknowledges that women are invariably exposed to war and are due humane treatment. The increased participation of women as members of the armed forces or as humanitarian personnel is apparent from distinctive drafting language. The first three Geneva Conventions therefore adopted a common provision that borrows from Article 3 of the 1929 Geneva Convention. The common provision asserts that whether wounded, shipwrecked or under prisoner of war status, "[w]omen shall be treated with all consideration due to their sex."[28]

Women as civilians are innate to provisions in the Fourth

Convention. Article 27, the preeminent article of the Fourth Geneva Convention is found in Section I of Part III that is entitled "Provisions, Common to the Territories of the Parties to the Conflict and to the Occupied Territories." As a supplement to Article 46 of Hague IV, Article 27 concerns military occupation but also guarantees protection to civilians who fall into enemy hands even when no official occupation is in force. Article 27 of the Fourth Geneva Convention is principally cited by feminist scholars to analyse the legal basis for rape under international law, since the provision succinctly grants women protection from "rape, enforced prostitution and any form of indecent assault." However, Article 27 deserves to be situated in its broader context.

A virtual 'mini' civilian convention, Article 27 provides protection based on contemporary values and expectations within post-war civil society, even though in many instances the international norms supersede individual rights under municipal law. Paragraph I of Article 27 prohibits infringement of religious and cultural practices, and obliges parties to have respect for the person, honour and physical and mental integrity of the person. Even threats, insults and public curiosity are not in conformity with humane treatment. Paragraph 3 of Article 27 insists upon the non-discriminatory application of the provisions of the Convention, an emerging norm of Geneva law that demands that parties act without adverse distinction based on sex,[29] and further that parties provide equal or better treatment to the aged, the young, the infirm and women.

Paragraph 2 speaks to the egregious effect that sexual violence has upon female civilians. Explicitly proscribed for the first time within a humanitarian law instrument are rape, enforced prostitution and any form of indecent assault. This separate paragraph on sexual violence within Article 27 attests to the centrality of the prohibition of such violence to the providing of humane treatment. The prohibition is broad, covering any form of indecent assault, and existing as if by way of explanation of the respect for honour of the person as presented in Paragraph I and the requirement to refrain from adverse discrimination based on sex, contained in Paragraph 3.

By 1949, there had developed a post-war concept of human rights, as a birth right of men and women owed to them by their state, and the parallel duty of parties to an armed conflict to provide men and women humane treatment, without discrimination owed to conditions such as their sex. Article 27 concerns the latter, influenced by the former. As a whole, the Geneva Conventions present mid-century values that interdict sexual violence because it is inconsistent with the humane treatment of the individual. The conventions do not, however, explicitly adjudge rape to be a grave breach.

LATE TWENTIETH CENTURY'S COLLECTIVE AND INDIVIDUAL PROTECTION

The Additional Protocols to the Geneva Conventions[30] actually commenced the phase in the drafting of humanitarian law that closes the twentieth century.[31] It is worth noting that by 1977, when the Additional Protocols were adopted, participants and advocates in international civil society encompassed states, international organisations (including UN bodies), regional organisations, nongovernmental organisations and individuals. That the Additional Protocols supplemented and filled the lacuna of the Geneva law is well accepted. Persons are protected under the Additional Protocols as combatants and fighters, or as members of the non-combatant, civilian population, as well as in their individual capacity, in a coherent framework of group and individual protection.

Article 51 of Additional Protocol I asserts in several sub-provisions that protection is owed to the civilian population and individual civilians during hostilities and military operations. Article 13 of Additional Protocol II applies to internal wars and likewise refers to the civilian population and individual civilians when declaring that they should not be the object of any attacks or acts or threats of violence. Both protocols demonstrate that a dual respect for individual rights and a type of 'group rights' that safeguard society by protecting each member reside at the core of protection (Khushalani 1982: 59). The set of rights, at this stage of the twentieth century, only can be interpreted to afford protection from all forms of destruction, including sexual violence.[32]

Consistent with a human rights approach, humanitarian law's duality of protection of individuals and collectives also allows for the centrality of the individual. The Additional Protocols affix absolute, inalienable rights in an individual-oriented framework when providing protection from inhumane treatment, including sexual violence. Article 75 of Protocol I, the 'protocol in miniature', states that:

1. Each party shall respect the person, honour, convictions and religious practices of all such persons.
2. The following acts are and shall remain prohibited at any time and in any place whatsoever, whether committed by civilian or by military agents [...].
    (b) outrages upon personal dignity, in particular humiliating and degrading treatment, enforced prostitution and any forms of indecent assault.

Article 75 regards society from the perspective of a person's integrity, be it physical, moral, religious or sexual. To that end, concomitant human worth cannot be subjected to sexual violence regardless of the stage or circumstances of an international armed conflict. Article 76 inserts a refrain from the Geneva Conventions that protects women in particular against rape, enforced prostitution or indecent assault, thus bestowing a non-adverse distinction upon women and a reaffirmation of the norms found in Article 75. That does not ignore that the Additional Protocol, like their Geneva Convention predecessors, are infused with a patriarchal regard that emphasizes protection of females (Gardam/Charlesworth 2000; Gardam/Jarvis 2001).

Article 4 of Additional Protocol II resounds with a similar orientation toward the individual in regard to protection from inhumane treatment. Article 4, a virtual "charter of human rights for persons involved in armed conflict" (Kushalani 1982: 68), states *inter alia* that:

1. All persons [...] are entitled to respect for their person, honour, and convictions and religious practices. They shall in no circumstances be treated inhumanely, without any adverse distinction.

2. [...] [T]he following acts are and shall remain prohibited at any time and in any place whatsoever:

   (e) Outrages upon personal dignity, in particular humiliating and degrading treatment, rape, enforced prostitution and any form of indecent assault.

Moreover, the Additional Protocols explicitly recognize that *all* children, irrespective of their participation in armed conflict or of their capture by an opposing force, are to be safeguarded from any form of indecent assault, hence sexual violence. Article 77 of Additional Protocol I and Article 4 (3) of Additional Protocol II (1) intone the special respect and the special protection owed to boys and girls to be spared the infliction of sexual violence by any party or armed force connected to an armed conflict (Sellers 2018a).

Hence, under the Additional Protocols, protection against sex-based crimes has become quite individualized, that is committed against persons, including children, with moral and physical integrity. Their provisions subsume grounded principles of humanitarian law, yet they are infused with human rights precepts that must be seen as lending to their interpretation.[33] In the evolution of principles or values, women and children have become persons and thus human with rights. Their humanitarian protection is inseparable from the safety and integrity of entire groups. Simultaneously conflict-related sexual violence, inclusive of rapes and slavery, has continued to be considered as harmful and destructive to the individual and to society as a whole.

Political correctness aside, if a primary aim of humanitarian law, *inter alia*, is to protect the civilian population and individual civilians, an acknowledgment that women and girls constitute the majority of civilians during war, particularly when males are drafted into fighting, is overdue. Proportionately then, a significant or core protection that humanitarian law offers is to spare females from rape and other forms of sexual abuse.

THE LEGALITY OF 21ˢᵀ CENTURY PROTECTION
FROM SEXUAL VIOLENCE

Finally, to return to the ICTY and the ICTR judgments concerning sex-based crimes, the jurisprudence delivered by these four Trial Chambers is replete with the 'grounded' yet evolving, contemporary nature of humanitarian law that has informed and produced every custom, principle, international instrument, or jurisprudence of an international tribunal. Sexual violence jurisprudence has not resorted to a lower standard of evidence, nor a less rigorous legal analysis; rather, it derives from the normal process of deliberating upon facts and the law, as that law is interpreted by contemporary standards.

As such, the ICTY and ICTR Trial Chambers have construed acts of sexual violence as a means to destroy an ethnic group,[34] as an attack against the civilian population,[35] and as an attack against the fundamental dignity of the individual who has been in the hands of the enemy,[36] as well as evidence of adverse religious and gender discrimination.[37]

CODA: THE LEGAL AND CULTURAL VALUE OF RAPE

Rape, the most commonly committed act of sexual violence, "strikes at the very core of human dignity and physical integrity."[38] Twenty years ago I suggested that—contrary to the historical origins of sexual violence and armed conflict, which at times countenanced legality—now no cultural or societal value could be advanced by only partial proscription of rape. Neither a military siege nor the characterisation of the armed conflict or the status of the person assaulted justified the act of rape. International law—humanitarian law, international criminal law and human rights law—I averred, permitted no derogation. Rape's complete illegality best serves the interest of the international community when, in armed conflict, or the commission of crimes against humanity or genocide, an individual is attacked because of their membership in a protected group or a community.

Humanitarian law's prohibition of rapes drew a nonwavering

line between legitimate actions and wanton or criminal conduct, underscoring that rape, *per se*, violated guarantees of humane treatment. By the late 1990s the international criminalisation of rape had been reiterated under crimes against humanity and condemned under the dreaded moniker of genocidal acts by the ad hoc Tribunals. To my knowledge, then, no circumstances existed in which rape could be authorized or tolerated or escape penal sanction under customary international law or international treaty law. Even given, what now is an accepted customary law basis for individual criminal responsibility under Additional Protocol II, all reasoned interpretation seemed to preclude evading prosecution for the crime of rape.[39] No legal lacunae appeared to subsist for rape.

Khushalani (1982: 51) called for the recognition of the protection of the civilian population as a *jus cogens* or peremptory norm in 1982. I refined that call to summon the international community to recognise rape, as committed against women, men, girls and boys, soldiers and civilians, religious, racial, ethnic or national groups, during armed conflict or the commission of crimes against humanity, genocide or whenever human rights law is triggered, as a peremptory norm, a *jus cogens* value, within the present legal culture of international society (Sellers 2000b).

In 2017, an appeals chamber of the International Criminal Court delivered a judgment to the defence's challenge to the Court's jurisdiction over rape and sexual slavery in *Prosecutor v. Bosco Ntaganda.*[40] The defence alleged that same-side sexual violence—specifically, rapes and sexual slavery committed by members of an armed force against children who also were members of that very armed force—was not within the jurisdiction of the Court. In other words, war crimes must be committed against persons of the opposite side or against persons who are no longer partaking in combat, or against persons with recognized protected status. Child soldiers, the defence argued, could not be situated among these protected groups. As such, proscriptions of wartime inflicted rapes were non-existent between soldiers of the same militia, and particularly between adults and child soldiers. These rapes, arguably, remained legally and culturally sanctioned. The

Ntaganda appellate judgment disagreed. It ruled that there was no conceivable reason to justify rape and sexual violence, even if the person can be legally targeted in combat.[41] The appellate judgment upheld the Trial Chamber's decision that rape and sexual slavery, due to their *jus cogens* status, are impermissible under international law.[42] In 2019, the *Ntaganda* trial chamber's final judgment ruled that: "provided that there is a nexus to the armed conflict, rape and sexual slavery against *any* person is prohibited, and that therefore members of the same armed forces are not *per se* excluded as potential victims of war crimes of rape and sexual slavery [...]."[43]

Accordingly, *Ntaganda*'s proscription of war-related rapes against children, and specifically against child soldiers, intones a welcome cultural value. The trial chamber judgment seems to extend the protects from rape and sexual slavery to beyond children and to *any* person irrespective of their age as long as the acts have a nexus with an armed conflict.

Ntaganda's acknowledgment of the non-derogable *jus cogens* status of rape and sexual slavery bespeaks a more profound shift in cultural values. In response to my prior query, it answers that irrespective of group or individual membership and regardless of circumstances, rape is non-derogable. Culturally, the legal value of the *jus cogens* crimes of rape and sexual slavery provide no licit lacunae for their commission during war, under international law.

This article is a re-issued and updated version of Patricia Viseur Sellers, 'The Cultural Value of Sexual Violence', *Proceedings of the ASIL Annual Meeting*, (93), 2008, pp. 312–324. Reproduced with permission of Cambridge University Press in the format Book via Copyright Clearance Center. This article is submitted in the author's personal capacity and is not attributable to any institutional affiliation.

NOTES

1. United Nations Security Council (UNSC) Resolution 827 (25 May 1993) established the International Criminal Tribunal for the

former Yugoslavia; UNSC Res. 955 (8 Nov. 1994) established the International Criminal Tribunal for Rwanda.

2.   *Prosecutor v. Akayesu, Judgment and Opinion*, ICTR-96-4-T, 2 September 1998 [hereinafter Akayesu Judgment].

3.   *Prosecutor v. Delalić et al., Judgment*, IT-96-21-T, 16 November 1998 [hereinafter Delalić Judgment].

4.   *Prosecutor v. Furundžija, Judgment*, 1T-95-17/1-T, 10 December 1998 [hereinafter Furundžija Judgment].

5.   Article 2(2) reads in part: "Genocide means any of the following acts committed with intent to destroy, in whole or part a national, ethnical, racial or religious group, as such: (a) killing members of the group; (b) causing serious bodily or mental harm to members of the group; (c) deliberately inflicting on the group conditions of life calculated to bring about its physical destruction in whole or in part" (*Statute of the International Criminal Tribunal for Rwanda*, 8 Nov. 1994, reprinted in *International Legal Material* (ILM), 33: 1158).

6.   Akayesu Judgment, para. 731.

7.   Ibid., para. 598.

8.   *Statute of the International Criminal Tribunal for the Former Yugoslavia*, 25 May 1993, reprinted in *ILM*, 34: 1159.

9.   Delalić Judgment, para. 1066.

10. The Furundžija Trial Chamber set forth the elements of rape as follows: (i) sexual penetration, however slight: (a) of the vagina or anus of the victim by the penis of the perpetrator or any object used by the perpetrator; or (b) of the mouth of the victim by the penis of the perpetrator; (ii) by coercion or force or threat of force against the victim or a third person.

11. *Prosecutor v. Kunarac et al., Judgment*, IT-96-23-T & IT-96-23/1-T, 22 February 2001.

12. *The Convention to Suppress the Slave Trade and Slavery*, 25 September 1926 (entered into force 9 March 1927), art. 1(1), reprinted in *League of Nations Treaty Series* (LNTS), 60: 253.

13. For further discussion of this jurisprudence, see generally Sellers 2018a; on the ICTY, Brammetz/Jarvis 2016 and Sellers 2009; on the ICTR, Bianchi 2013; on the Special Court for Sierra Leone, Oosterveld 2011; on the Extraordinary Chambers in the Courts of Cambodia (ECCC), Sellers/Oosterveld 2016; and on the International Criminal Court (ICC) Sellers 2016.

14. *Monumenta Juridica: Introduction to the Book of Admirality*, App. 549, ed. by T. Twiss, 1871, cited in Meron 1992: note 32.

15. See *Treaty of Amity and Commerce, U.S.-Prussia*, 10 September 1785, reprinted in Malloy 1910.

16. See *Convention for the Amelioration of the Condition of the Wounded in Armies in the Field*, Geneva, 22 August 1864, 18 Martens 607, 22 Stat. 940, TS No. 377; *Convention with Respect to the Laws and Customs of War*, The Hague, 29 July 1899, 26 Martens (2n) 949, 32 Stat. 1803, TS No. 403, reprinted in *American Journal of International Law* (AJIL) 1907: 129–34; 1 Friedman 221; Schindler/Toman 1988: 63–100; *Laws and Customs of War on Land, Annex to the Convention Regulations Respecting the Laws and Customs of War* (Hague II), The Hague, 29 July 1899, 26 Martens (2d) 949, 32 Stat. 1803, TS No. 403, reprinted in *AJIL* 1907: 134–59; 1 Friedman 221; Schindler/Toman 1988: 63.

17. *Instructions for the Government of Armies of the United States in the Field by Order of the Secretary of War*, 24 April 1863 [hereinafter Lieber Code], reprinted in Schindler/Toman 1988: 3–24.

18. Article 16 of the Lieber Code states: "Military necessity does not admit of cruelty—that is the infliction of suffering for the sake of suffering or revenge [...] nor the wanton destruction of a district" (cit. in Schindler/Toman 1988: 6).

19. Article 42 of the Lieber Code states that "Slavery, that is complicating [...] the ideas of property (of a thing) and of personality (that is of humanity) exist [...] in local law only" and distinguishes between property and personality, stating that to hold persons as property is incompatible with the humanity. Article 43 of the Code does not permit an officer to enslave a person or return a person to a status of slavery, concluding that "a person so made free by the law of war is under the shield of the law of nations" (cit. in Schindler/Toman 1988: 9f).

20. *Convention Respecting the Laws and Customs of War on Land, and Annex to the Convention, Regulations Respecting the Laws and Customs of War on Land* (Hague IV), The Hague, 18 October 1907, 3 Martens (3d) 461, 36 Stat. 2277, TS No. 539, reprinted in *AJIL* 1908, 90(2) [hereinafter Hague IV].

21. See *Convention Relative to the Treatment of Prisoners of War*, 27 July 1929, 47 Stat. 2921, TS No. 846. Commentary to the 1929 Geneva Convention 20; Rasmussen 1931.

22. Charter of the International Military Tribunal, annexed to the London Agreement, 8 August 1945, *United Nations Treaty Series* (UNTS), 8: 279, 59 Stat. 1544, 8 AS No. 472 [hereinafter

Nuremberg Charter], reprinted in Bassiouni 1992: 582. The crimes against humanity provision in Article 6(b) of the Nuremberg Charter is substantively identical to the scope of its Nuremberg counterpart in 5(c) of the Tokyo Charter and reads in part: "Crimes Against Humanity: Namely, murder, extermination, enslavement, deportation, and other inhumane acts committed against any civilian population, before or during the war, or persecutions on political or racial grounds in execution of or in connection with any crime within the jurisdiction of the Tribunal, whether or not a violation of the domestic law of the country where perpetrated."

23. The Nuremberg Judgment discusses crimes that German political and military leaders committed against their own country's nationals, while the IMTFE prosecuted crimes against humanity that were directed at civilians of other countries, such as China and the Philippines.

24. *Universal Declaration of Human Rights*, G.A. Res. 217A, 3 UN GAOR at 71, UN Doc. N8 l0 Art. 5 (1948).

25. *Convention on the Prevention and Punishment of Genocide*, 9 December 1948, *UNTS*, 78: 277, entered into force 12 January 1951.

26. *The Geneva Convention for the Amelioration of the Conditions of the Wounded and Sick in Armed Forces in the Field* ('First Geneva Convention'), *UNTS*, 75: 31; *Geneva Convention for the Amelioration of the Conditions of the Wounded and Sick and Shipwrecked Members of Armed Forces at Sea* ('Second Geneva Convention'), *UNTS*, 75: 85; *Geneva Convention Relative to the Treatment of Prisoners of War* ('Third Geneva Convention'), *UNTS*, 75: 135; and *Geneva Convention Relative to the Protection of Civilian Persons in Time of War* ('Fourth Geneva Convention'), *UNTS*, 75: 287.

27. Preliminary Remarks to the Geneva Conventions, in *The Geneva Convention of August 12, 1949*, edited by the International Committee of the Red Cross. [N.D.; 1994], Geneva: ICRC.

28. Common Article 12 of First Geneva Convention and the Second Geneva Convention, and Article 14 of the Third Geneva Convention.

29. The principle is contained in Common Article 12 of the First Geneva Convention and the Second Geneva Convention as well as Common Article 3 to each of the Four Geneva Conventions.

30. *Protocol Additional to the Geneva Conventions of 12 August 1949, and Relating to the Protection of Victims of International Armed Conflict*, 8 June 1977 (entered into force 7 December 1978), *UNTS*, 1125: 3, reprinted in *ILM*, 16: 1391 ('Additional Protocol I'); *Protocol Additional to the Geneva*

Conventions of 12 August 1949, and Relating to the Protection of Victims of Non-international Armed Conflicts, 8 June 1977 (entered into force 7 December 1978), *UNTS* 1125: 609, reprinted in *ILM*, 16: 182 ('Additional Protocol II').

31. For a comprehensive review of the late-twentieth-century phase of the drafting of international instruments that anchor the rights of women in the international setting, see Askin 1997: 204–60. The final chapter of the later twentieth century is most likely the Statute of the ICC, adopted 17 July 1998, in Rome.

32   Additional Protocol I, art. 51(1), (2) and (6).

33   It is important to consider that the 1959 *UN Declaration on the Rights of the Child*, https://www.refworld.org/docid/3ae6b38e3.html (accessed 15 August 2019), was proclaimed by the General Assembly and became the precursor of the 1989 *Convention on the Rights of the Child*. https://www.ohchr.org/documents/professionalinterest/crc.pdf (accessed 15 August 2019). The drafters of the Additional Protocols were cognisant of the burgeoning international human rights of children. Article 38 (1) of the *Convention for the Rights of the Child* specifies that "State Parties undertake to respect and to ensure respect for rules of international humanitarian law applicable to them in armed conflicts which are relevant to the child."

In 1979, less than two years after the completion of the Additional Protocols to the Geneva Conventions, the General Assembly adopted the *Convention for the Elimination of Discrimination against Women*, https://www.ohchr.org/documents/professionalinterest/cedaw.pdf' (accessed 15 August 2019), the primary human rights instrument that underscores the non-discriminatory protections that must be afforded to women. Moreover, and most significantly, in 1995, the *Beijing Platform of Action*, Section E, reiterated that the protections of the Geneva legal regime and the Additional Protocols extended to females in periods of armed conflict.

34. Akayesu Judgment, para. 731.

35. Ibid.

36. Furundžija Judgment, paras. 183–184; Delalić Judgment, para. 1066.

37. Ibid., para. 941.

38. Ibid., para. 495.

39. Furundžija Judgment, para. 186.

40. *Prosecutor v. Bosco Ntaganda, Judgment on the appeal of Mr. Ntaganda against the "Second decision on the Defence's challenge to the jurisdiction of the Court*

in respect of Counts 6 and 9", ICC01/04-02/06 OA5, 15 June 2017 [hereinafter Ntaganda Appeal Judgment]. For an examination of the numerous *Ntaganda* submissions and decision on the jurisdiction over same-side sexual assaults, see Sellers 2018b.

41. Ibid.; Ntaganda Appeal Judgment, paras. 64–65.
42. Second decision on the Defense's challenge to the jurisdiction of the Court in respect of counts 6 and 9, ICC-01/04-02/06-1707, 4 January 2017, para. 51.
43. Prosecutor v. Bosco Ntaganda, Judgment, ICC-01/04-02/06, 8 July 2019, para 965.

REFERENCES

Askin, Kelly Dawn. 1997. *War Crimes Against Women: Prosecution in International War Crimes Tribunals*. The Hague/Cambridge: Martinus Nifhoff Publishers/Kluwer Law International.

Bassiouni, Mahmoud Cherif. 1992. *Crimes Against Humanity in International Criminal Law*. Dordrecht: Kluwer.

Bianchi, Linda. 2013. 'The Prosecution of Rape and Sexual Violence: Lessons from Prosecutions at the ICTR', in Anne-Marie de Brouwer/Charlotte Ku/Renée Römkens/Larissa van den Herik (eds), *Sexual Violence as an International Crime: Interdisciplinary Approaches*, pp. 123–149. Cambridge: Intersentia.

Brammertz, Serge/Jarvis, Michelle (eds). 2016. *Prosecuting Conflict-Related Sexual Violence at the ICTY*. Oxford: Oxford University Press.

Gardam, Judith/Charlesworth, Hilary. 2000. 'Protection of Women in Armed Conflict', *Human Rights Quarterly*, 22(1):148–66.

Gardam, Judith/Jarvis, Michelle. 2001. *Women, Armed Conflict and International Law*. The Hague: Kluwer Law International.

International Military Tribunal. 1947. *Trial of the Major War Criminals before the International Military Tribunal: Nuremberg: 14 November 1945–1 October 1946*. 42 Vol. Nuremberg: Secretariat of the International Military Tribunal.

Keen, Maurice Hugh. 1965. *The Laws of the War in the Late Middle Ages*. London: Routledge/Kegan Paul.

Khushalani, Yougindra. 1982. *Dignity and Honour of Women as Basic and Fundamental Human Rights*. The Hague/Bosten: Martinus Nijhoff Publishers/Kluwer International Law.

Malloy, William M. (ed). 1910. *Treaties, Conventions, International Acts, Protocols and Agreements between the United States of America and Other*

Powers 1776–1909. Vol. 2. Washington: Government Printing Office.

McDonald, Avril. 1999. 'Sex Crimes at the ad hoc Tribunals: The Decisions in the Cases of Akayesu, Čelebići and Furundžija', *Nemesis: Tijdschrift over vrouwen en recht*, 15(3):72–82.

McDonald, Gabrielle Kirk/Swaak-Goldman, Olivia (eds). 2000. *Substantive and Procedural Aspects on International Criminal Law: The Experience of International and National Courts*. The Hague: Kluwer Law International.

Meron, Theodor. 1992. 'Shakespeare's Henry the Fifth and the Law of War', *The American Journal of International Law*, 86(1):1–45.

Obote-Oddora, Alex. 1997. The Judging of War Criminals: Individual Criminal Responsibility under International Law. PhD thesis: University of Stockholm, Faculty of Law.

Oosterveld, Valerie. 2011. 'The Gender Jurisprudence of the Special Court for Sierra Leone: Progress in the Revolutionary United Front Judgments'. *Cornell International Law Journal*, 44(1):49–74.

Pritchard, R. John/Zaide, Sonia M. (eds). 1981. *The Tokyo War Criminals Trial: Complete Transcript of the Proceedings*. New York: Garland.

Rasmussen, Gustav. 1931. *Code des Prisonniers de Guerre: Commentaire de la Convention du 27 Julliet 1929: Relative au Traitement des Prisonniers de Guerre*. Copenhagen: Levin & Munksgaard.

Schindler, Dietrich/Toman, Jiri (eds). 1988. *The Laws of Armed Conflicts: A Collection of Conventions, Resolutions and Other Documents*. 3rd rev. ed. Dordrecht: Martinus Nijhoff Publishers.

Sellers, Patricia Viseur. 2018a. '(Re)Considering Gender Jurisprudence', in Fionnuala Ní Aoláin/Naomi Cahn/Dina Francesca Haynes/Nahla Valj (eds), *The Oxford Handbook of Gender and Armed Conflict*, pp. 211–24. Oxford: Oxford University Press.

———. 2018b. 'Ntaganda: Re-Alignment of a Paradigm', *Sanremo Roundtable International Institute of Humanitarian Law*. http://www.iihl.org/wp-content/uploads/2018/04/Ntaganda-VI.pdf (accessed 17 April 2019).

———. 2016. 'Sexual Violence and Commanders' Responsibilities during Conflict', *Just Security*. https://www.justsecurity.org/30329/sexual-violence-commanders-responsibilities-conflict/ (accessed 17 April 2019).

———. 2009. 'Gender Strategy is Not Luxury for International Courts Symposium: Prosecuting Sexual and Gender-Based Crimes before

International/ized Criminal Courts', *American University Journal of Gender, Social Policy & the Law*, 17(2):327–35.

———. 2000a. 'The Context of Sexual Violence: Sexual Violence as Violations of International Humanitarian Law', in Gabrielle Kirk McDonald/Olivia Swaak-Goldman (eds), *Substantive and Procedural Aspects on International Criminal Law: The Experience of International and National Courts*, Vol. 1, pp. 263–332. The Hague: Kluwer Law International.

———. 2000b, 'Sexual Violence and Peremptory Norms: The Legal Value of Rape', *Case Western Reserve Journal of International Law*, 4(3):287–303.

Sellers, Patricia Viseur/Oosterveld, Valerie. 2016. 'Issues of Sexual and Gender-Based Violence at the ECCC', in Simon Meisenberg/Ignaz Stegmiller (eds), *The Extraordinary Chambers in the Courts of Cambodia*, pp. 321–51. The Hague: T.M.C. Asser Press.

Sellers, Patricia Viseur/Rosenthal, Indira. 2015. 'Rape and Sexual Violence', in Andrew Clapham/Paola Gaeta/Marco Sassoli (eds), *The Geneva Conventions in Context: A Commentary*, pp. 343–68. Oxford: Oxford University Press.

Challenges and Gaps that Contribute to Conflict Related Sexual Violence

There is global recognition that violence against women is a pervasive and widespread human rights violation that exists across the world. It has been labelled as an epidemic by the World Health Organisation (WHO; 2013) and the indicators are that violence against women is the foremost cause of death and disability among women. UN Women notes that malaria, cancer, traffic accidents and war combined kill fewer women than violence against women, and this is most often at the hands of people they know (United Nations N.D.).

The principles of dignity, equality, freedom, justice and peace underpin the 1948 Universal Declaration of Human Rights (UDHR) (see United Nations 1948). Article 2 of the UDHR states: "Everyone is entitled to all the rights and freedoms set forth in this Declaration, without distinction of any kind, such as race, colour, sex, language, religion, political or other opinion, national or social origin, property, birth or other status." The UDHR also includes the right to life, liberty and security of the person in article 3, and the right not to be subjected to torture or to cruel, inhuman or degrading treatment or punishment in article 5. In linking articles 2, 3 and 5, it is clear that these rights apply to all women and girls, without distinction—which is crucial for a life free of all forms of violence.

The underlying premise of this essay is based on the understanding of violence against women as functioning on a continuum, and also the reality that existing forms of violence are exacerbated during times of conflict (United Nations General

Assembly (UNGA) 2011). Liz Kelly (1988) has been credited with conceptualizing the "continuum of violence" where she notes that all forms of violence are linked to form a continuum. She argues that violence against women is not necessarily deviant and episodic, but is rather normative and functional, and is an everyday reality for women and girls globally . Despite events of violence against women being different, commonalities exist in the form of coercion and abuse which are used to control, constrain and limit the lives, status, movement and opportunities of women— thereby protecting the privilege and entitlement of men. Thus, it is not useful to focus on individual manifestations in isolation of context and realities. Male violence functions on a spectrum with socially accepted male control and aggression, patriarchal norms and family/relationship structures, coercive behaviour, inequality and discrimination, which in turn functions to maintain a male dominated gender order. Kelly identifies some basic common characteristics that underlie different events, including the many forms of coercion, abuse and assault that are used to control women. The concept emphasizes a continuous series of elements or events that pass into one another and which cannot be readily distinguished and separated into discrete categories of individual factors that contribute to acts of violence against women.

This essay will highlight the gaps and challenges that continue to act as barriers to effective responses and remedies in times of non-conflict (United Nations Human Rights Council (UNHRC) 2014a), and which contribute to the causes and consequences of conflict related sexual violence. This analysis provides an opportunity to reflect on my work as the United Nations Special Rapporteur on Violence against Women, its causes and consequences (UNSRVAW) (United Nations Human Rights Office of the High Commissioner (OHCHR) N.D.b). During this time, I conducted thematic research, collected first-hand information through visiting a wide range of countries, including some in conflicts or emerging from conflicts, and evaluated the measures undertaken by governments to address violence against women and girls.

States responses have, to differing extents, focused on:

a) legislative measures, including the ratification of international human rights instruments, the harmonization of national legislation or the adoption of specific legislation on violence against women; b) institutional and policy measures, including the introduction of specialized mechanisms to investigate and prosecute violence against women, provide support and services to victims and enhance cooperation and information-sharing between authorities and service providers; and c) awareness raising and capacity-building activities, including gender-sensitive training for civil servants, campaigns aimed at raising awareness on violence against women and the integration of a gender equality perspective into the public sphere (OHCHR N.D.c). With diverse levels of commitment, resources and political will, most countries have put in place measures in attempts to curb the prevalence of violence against women. However, and despite these efforts, violence against women remains a pervasive and widespread phenomenon, and no single country can claim that there is progressive elimination occurring. In fact, civil society in general and women's rights activists in particular, argue that the problem is increasing and is reaching epidemic proportions. This has been acknowledged by the World Health Organization (WHO 2013).

As with all forms of violence against women, violence occurs both in the public and the private spheres, including in the family; the community; in State institutions and at the transnational level. It occurs in times of peace, transitions, displacement, conflict or post-conflict (UNHRC 2009a, 2009b, 2013b, 2013c, 2013d, 2014a, 2015b). It can result due to domestic or intimate partner violence, from harmful and degrading societal practices that are violent to and/or subordinate women, from abuse of power and authority in custodial settings and during times of conflict, when women are used as weapons/tools of war. Domestic or intimate partner violence commonly includes instances of sexual violence, such as marital rape or incest (UNHRC 2009b). Practices that are harmful and degrading undermine the rights and status of women and girls, whether they are justified on the basis of religious, customary or other societal laws and norms. Harmful practices may entail some sort of sexual violence, such as female genital mutilation, forced and early marriages or widowhood cleansing rites (ibid.).

Conflict-related sexual violence against women and girls includes rape, sexual slavery, sexual exploitation, forced marriage, forced prostitution, forced abortion, forced pregnancy, forced sterilisation and the sexual transmission of infections, including HIV and AIDS (United Nations Secretary-General 2006). Conflict and post-conflict situations often exacerbate an existing environment of discrimination, subordination and lack of control over bodily integrity and sexual rights. Women are not only abused due to a group's desire to humiliate and destroy their enemy, but also due to the inequality inherent with their own group's cultural ideologies of gender and women's bodies (Manjoo/McRaith 2011). Therefore, women who are already vulnerable to myriad forms of interpersonal and structural violence and discrimination, whether at the household, community, or even state level, are more likely to become victims of sexual violence during conflict. In times of conflict, existing forms of discrimination are exacerbated, and new forms of violence are generated against women who are already vulnerable (UNHRC 2011). These include rape by state and non-state actors, maiming, sexual mutilation, abduction, forced marriages to soldiers (enslavement), torture and other forms of inhuman, cruel or degrading treatment or punishment (United Nations Commission on Human Rights 2001).

With regard to violence against women in the community, rape/sexual assault, sexual harassment, forced prostitution and sexual violence against women migrant workers, are some of the most common manifestations of sexual violence. Stalking, sexual violence against lesbians, bisexuals and transgender persons and bride-kidnapping, are other phenomena that exist. Sexual violence against women may also be perpetrated or condoned by the state. This includes violence during conflict, custodial violence, violence within state institutions and sexual violence against women from indigenous and minority groups, as part of targeted attacks by the state, including in respect of human rights defenders (UNHCR 2009b; OHCHR N.D.a). Through country visits it was clear that violence remains widespread and affects women of all social strata (UNHRC 2014b; 2013c; 2013b).

GAPS AND CHALLENGES IN ADDRESSING VIOLENCE AGAINST WOMEN

Although progress has been achieved in advancing equality and other human rights of women, there are gaps and challenges that have been identified in the quest to achieve the realization of all human rights, including the right to a life free of violence. Continuing and new sets of challenges that hamper efforts to promote, protect and fulfil human rights can be linked to the lack of a holistic approach that addresses individual, communal, institutional and structural factors that are a cause and a consequence of violence against women (UNHRC 2014b). Moreover, a culture of offender impunity and a lack of victim safety persist, and this contributes to the impossibility of achieving the goal of a life free of violence for women. Furthermore, the intrinsic link between human rights, violence against women and the exercise of effective citizenship, demands more effective prevention and protection responses, so that states meet their obligation to eliminate gender-based violence (UNGA 2014).

The following section will focus broadly on the continuing and new challenges to effectively address violence against women as highlighted in a 2014 report to the Human Rights Council. These include among others: the shift to gender neutrality; the persisting public-private dichotomy in responses to violence against women; the failure of states to act with due diligence in eliminating violence against women; the lack of transformative remedies that address the root causes of violence against women, including individual, institutional and structural aspects; the financial crisis, austerity measures and cuts in social services spending; the shift in understanding of gendered responses and the move towards a focus on men and boys; and the lack of a legally binding instrument at the UN level to hold both states and non-state actors accountable for this human rights violation, as a violation in and of itself (UNHRC 2014b).

1) Shift to neutrality

Violence against women is a systemic, widespread and pervasive human rights violation, experienced largely by women because they are women. In challenging the shift to gender neutrality, it is argued that the shift is framed in a way that understands violence as a universal threat to which all are potentially vulnerable, and, that male victims of violence require comparable attention and resources as that afforded to female victims. This perspective ignores the reality that violence against men does not occur as a result of pervasive inequality and discrimination, and also that it is neither systemic nor pandemic in the way that violence against women indisputably is. Attempts to combine or synthesize all forms of violence into a 'gender-neutral' framework tend to result in a depoliticized or diluted discourse, which abandons the transformative agenda. Also, this approach compromises the resources available to women's groups for specific service provision and advocacy, for example through the prioritizing of men's groups, and undermines transformative change efforts. Thus, a separate and different set of normative and practical measures is required to respond to and prevent violence against women and importantly, to contribute to the realisation of international law obligation of substantive gender equality, as opposed to formal equality.

The Declaration on the Elimination of Violence against Women, the General Recommendations of the Committee on the Elimination of All Forms of Discrimination against Women (CEDAW) and various regional treaties explicitly articulate an understanding that reaffirms and acknowledges that violence against women is both a cause and a consequence of discrimination, patriarchal dominance and control; that it is structural in nature; and that it works as a social mechanism that forces women into a subordinate position, in both the public and private spheres. CEDAW has criticized states that have adopted the gender-neutral approach in respect of discrimination broadly, including violence against women (United Nations Committee on the Elimination of Discrimination against Women 2007a, 2007b, 2008a, 2008b).

In addition to gender specificity in legislation, policies and programmes, it is argued that "where possible, services should be run by independent and experienced women's non-governmental organizations providing gender-specific, empowering and comprehensive support to women survivors of violence, based on feminist principles" (United Nations Department of Economic and Social Affairs 2009: 3.6.1). Generally, specificity is also mandated in the relevant regional human rights instruments on women and violence (Organization of American States 1994, Council of Europe 2011, African Union 2003).

2) Persisting public-private dichotomy in responses to violence against women

The public-private dichotomy is another manifestation of inequality and discrimination in responses to violence against women (Binion 1995, Romany 1993). The belief that personal relationships are not a matter of public concern continues to affect responses in the prevention, reporting and prosecution of cases of violence against women. The relegation of women to the private sphere is reinforced by among others: the gender pay gap; the 'double burden' of production and reproduction, which often limits the autonomy of women; and systems of guardianship or legal instruments consciously designed to limit women's access to the public sphere (UNHRC 2009a). Even in societies in which women make sustained and significant contributions to the workforce, their roles in public life tend to be curtailed and issues considered to be of particular concern to women, including violence against women, are often assumed to be private (Sullivan 1994).

3) Failure of states to act with due diligence to eliminate violence against women

A 2013 report to the Human Rights Council reiterates that state responsibility to act with due diligence requires that there is a framework for discussing the responsibility of states through a

dual lens of individual due diligence and systemic due diligence
(UNHRC 2013a, Cook 1994: 125). Individual due diligence
refers to the obligations that states owe to particular individuals,
or groups of individuals, including to prevent, protect, punish
and provide effective remedies. Individual due diligence places an
obligation on the state to assist victims in rebuilding their lives and
moving forward, and also requires states to punish not just the
perpetrators, but also those who fail in their duty to respond to
the violation. Systemic due diligence refers to the obligations that
states have to ensure a holistic and sustained model of prevention,
protection, punishment and reparations for acts of violence
against women and girls. It also requires an effective system of
monitoring and evaluation to ensure that state authorities are held
accountable for failures to protect against and prevent harm, due
to their response or lack thereof.

On a practical level, one can assume that there is a
correlation between prevalence rates and effective and responsive
accountability measures. The exercise of due diligence
requires that states have a responsibility to: (a) conduct effective
investigations of the crime, and prosecute and sanction acts of
violence perpetrated by State or private actors; (b) guarantee *de
jure* and *de facto* access to adequate and effective judicial remedies;
(c) include in the obligation of access to justice, a requirement to
treat women victims and their relatives with respect and dignity
throughout the legal process; (d) ensure comprehensive and
transformative reparations for women victims of violence and
their relatives; (e) identify certain groups of women as being at
particular risk for acts of violence due to having been subjected to
discrimination based on more than one factor, including women
belonging to ethnic, racial and minority groups; and (f) modify the
social and cultural patterns of conduct of men and women and
eliminate prejudices, myths and stereotypes regarding the status
of women.

4) Lack of transformative remedies that address the root causes of violence against women, including individual, institutional and structural aspects

Transformative remedies require that the problem of violence against women is acknowledged as systemic and not individual; and that it requires specific measures to address it as a gender-specific human rights violation (UNHRC 2010b). A gender-specific and holistic framework, including protection, prevention and empowerment approaches must include responses in laws, policies and programmes that acknowledges the historical, current and future realities of the lives of women through a lens of indivisibility and interdependency of human rights.

A holistic approach to remedies requires states to recognize the existence of structural and institutional inequalities linked to violence and discrimination. Whether this is based on race, ethnicity, national origin, ability, socio-economic class, sexual orientation, gender identity, religion, culture, tradition or other realities—inequalities and discrimination often intensify acts of violence. Efforts to end all forms of violence must consider not only how individual lives are affected by the immediate impact of abuse, but also how structures of discrimination and inequality perpetuate and exacerbate a victim's experience. Interpersonal, institutional, communal and structural forms of violence perpetuate gender inequalities, but also racial hierarchies, religious orthodoxies, ethnic group exclusionary practices and resource allocation that benefit some groups of women at the expense of others. Interventions that seek to only address the individual harm, and which do not factor in women's realities, do not challenge the fundamental and root causes of this human rights violation. Adopting a holistic model with regards to gender-based violence requires an understanding of the ways in which inter- and intra-gender differences exist. In meeting their international legal obligations, states must bear in mind that discrimination affects women in different ways depending on how they are positioned within the social, economic and cultural hierarchies that prohibit or further compromise certain women's ability to enjoy universal human rights.

The creation of hierarchies of violence against women, especially through political and funding action is a source of concern (UNSC 2008, 2009, 2010, 2013a, 2013b, 2015 and the United Kingdom's PSVI 2012). This is particularly evident in the articulation of sexual violence in conflict situations as being different and exceptional, as opposed to it being a continuation of a pattern of discrimination and violence that is exacerbated in times of conflict. This has led to a focusing on the manifestation of violence against women in conflict situations, to the detriment and ignoring of the low-level 'warfare' that women and girls experience in their homes and communities on a daily basis. Transformative change requires addressing the root causes of violence against women, taking into account the continuum of violence approach. The prioritizing of sexual violence in conflict has led to numerous concerns, including a shift away from an understanding of violence against women as both gendered and as part of a continuum of violence; a shift in resources, despite the need to address all manifestations of violence, including at the national level; a shift in focus by some United Nations entities; and the negative effect of donor-driven priorities in this process. The perception of many women's rights defenders is that these shifts have led to 'privileging' the manifestation of violence against women in conflict situations, which has been detrimental in the broader violence against women sphere (UNHRC 2009a, 2009b, 2013b, 2013c, 2013d, 2014a, 2015b, OHCHR N.D.c).

5) Financial crisis, austerity measures and cuts in social services spending

The reality in recent years is one that is reflected in the weakening of the women's rights sector, due to the financial crisis, austerity measures and cuts in social services spending. This has resulted in donor funding cuts for core service provision, including legal, policy and advocacy work in the women's rights sector. Also, the cuts in allocation of funds by governments for social services, is a challenge facing women's rights service providers in many countries (UNHRC 2013d, 2015b). Furthermore, cuts in funding to non-governmental organizations, as a form of reprisal against the work of women human rights defenders, while justifying it in terms of austerity, is also of concern (UNHRC 2012, 2010a).

6) shift in understanding of gendered responses and the move towards a focus on men and boys

In the past few years, there has been a move away from the historical understanding of a gender focus, as articulated and understood in international normative frameworks and by women's groups. Even though the shift to the 'men and boys' agenda is fraught with difficulty, it appears to have attracted a great deal of funding, recognition and political support. As noted earlier, compromising the resources available to women's groups for specific service provision and advocacy, has been detrimental to the women's rights sector, and it has undermined transformative change efforts.

Shamin Meer aptly articulates the concerns and frustrations expressed by women's rights NGOs and by individuals as follows:

> Gender, stripped of ideas of male privilege and female subordination, came to mean that women and men suffered equally the costs of the existing gender order. Women's organizations were increasingly asked "if you are working on gender, then where are the men", and they were increasingly pressured [...] to include men. On the heels of this pressure, a new [...] actor came into focus—men's organizations. The existence of already-weakened women's organizations was now further threatened and feminist attempts at movement-building faced additional challenges. [...] The increasing focus on men and men's organizations [...] is seen by some as a new fad, the latest silver bullet to achieving gender equality, and a threat to women's organizations and women's movements. In this view, donor attention to men's organizations seems to signify a shift of support away from women's empowerment and women's leadership, and a handing over of the reins in the struggle for gender equality to men. Men are once more in charge—only this time, they are in charge of women's liberation struggles. (Meer 2011: 2,4)

A brief analysis of the mandates and principles of organizations associated with engaging men and boys in efforts to counter violence against women reveals a series of internal contradictions which compromise the understanding of the foundational principles linked to women's human rights. This is reflected in several ways, including the reaffirmation of patriarchal norms of men as 'protectors' and, by extension, women as 'victims'; reinstatement of the family as the principal referent for analysis; depoliticization of the understanding of both gender equality and gendered violence; reinforcement of the public/private dichotomy; instrumentalization of arguments for the elimination of violence against women; conceptual confusion over men, masculinity and gendered roles; and the justifications and contradictions in the shift to men and boys and its supposed link to binding international law obligations.

There are many ideologies about the role of men and boys in the elimination of violence against women. Responses and the discourse often reflect that the focus is not on women as autonomous beings, disproportionately affected by inequality, discrimination and violence; but rather, violence against women is conflated with the interests of men and boys. The argument is that, since both men and women are subject to gender stereotypes and since corrupting forms of power are as damaging to men and to women, both would benefit from the dismantling of gender stereotypes. This ignores the reality that gender stereotypes, powerlessness and violence disproportionately impact women and girls.

A strategy associated with the engagement of men and boys is to appeal to the idea that women deserve respect as mothers, sisters, wives and so on. Emphasizing personal relationships is said to make it easier to understand the consequences of violence against women. This is also seen as an effective strategy in overtly patriarchal societies, in which calls to consider women as human rights-bearing individuals, are considered too radical to attract support, even among women themselves. This distorts the idea of women as autonomous individuals deserving of respect, and renders regard for the rights of women contingent on their status in the private sphere, which further reinforces the public/private dichotomy. From a pragmatic point of view, if men constitute the vast majority of perpetrators of violence against women, then engaging them in discussions, educating them to resist and reject the nature and consequences of hyper-masculinity and misogyny—and to overcome patterns of violence—is an obvious step towards the elimination of violence against women. Unfortunately, the trend reflects the setting up of separate men's organisations, which then compete for scarce resources.

7) Lack of a legally binding instrument addressing violence against women under international human rights law

The thematic reports of the UNSRVAW and other sources, have highlighted that a normative gap exists at the international level (Manjoo/Jones 2018). The approach of the UN system is one of normativity without legality and this is reflected in the endorsement of principles by states, through declarations and resolutions, but without the development and adoption of specific binding legal commitments, in respect of violence against women (UNHRC 2013a). The normative gap raises crucial questions regarding the accountability of states in the absence of specific legally binding obligations. The gap impacts state responsibility to act with due diligence, that is the responsibility of the state, as the ultimate duty bearer, to protect against and to prevent acts of violence. The lack of a legally binding instrument on violence against women precludes the articulation of the issue as a human rights violation in and of itself. It also does not provide for the comprehensive addressing of all forms of violence against women or the clear articulation of the obligations of states to act with due diligence to eliminate violence against women. There are many 'soft law' documents that address the issue, including the Vienna Declaration and Programme of Action (UNGA 1993b), the Declaration on the Elimination of Violence against Women (UNGA 1993a), the Beijing Declaration and Platform for Action (UN 1995) and general comments and recommendations of treaty bodies. However, although soft laws may be influential in developing norms, their non-binding nature effectively means that states cannot be held responsible for violations (Manjoo/Jones 2018).

The text of the Convention on the Elimination of All Forms of Discrimination against Women (CEDAW) does not explicitly address violence against women. Article 2 of CEDAW refers to the obligation of states to pursue by all appropriate means and without delay a policy of eliminating discrimination against women. The only article linked to violence against women is article 6 which deals with sex trafficking and prostitution. The scope of the treaty is limited to discrimination and not to relevant substantive rights violations such as the rights to life, freedom from torture, privacy and dignity, among others. To address this shortcoming, the CEDAW Committee has issued interpretative guidelines in the form of General Recommendations 12, 19, 30 and 35, specifically linked to violence against women. Other general recommendations also make references to violence against women, where relevant.

In 2017 the CEDAW Committee adopted General Recommendation 35 on gender-based violence against women, to update General Recommendation 19 on violence against women. Among others, the changes in the updated document include: new language used to identify the issue; the clarification of both general and specific human rights obligations; the reinforcement of the interdependency of rights and also the links between articles of the CEDAW and violence against women; detailed guidance to states in respect of general legislative measures, prevention, protection, prosecution and punishment, reparation, coordination, monitoring, data collection and international cooperation. Paragraph 14 of the general recommendation reiterates manifestations, causes and consequences of violence against women, including due to new and emerging practices. In paragraph 2 the Committee asserts that the prohibition of gender-based violence against women has evolved into a principle of customary international law, and that General recommendation 19 has been a key catalyst for this process (CEDAW 2017: 2). However, despite this misleading assertion about customary international law, in paragraphs 6 and 7 the Committee acknowledges that violence against women remains pervasive in all countries of the world, with high levels of impunity and, that in many states, legislation on the issue remains non-existent, inadequate and/or poorly implemented.

In contrast, there is more specificity in three key regional human rights treaties that address violence against women, namely the 1994 Inter-American Convention on the Prevention, Punishment and Eradication of Violence against Women, the 2003 Protocol to the African Charter on Human and Peoples' Rights on the Rights of Women in Africa and the 2011 Council of Europe Convention on preventing and combating violence against women and domestic violence. The normative underpinnings of the obligations of states to eliminate violence against women have evolved since 1994, and the regional treaties reflect international standard-setting policy developments, but within legally binding regional instruments. Despite the specificity of these instruments, there are limitations with regard to, for example, definitions and the comprehensiveness of the coverage of persons and acts as reflected in the instruments. Such gaps, as well as the absence of specific regional instruments in other regions of the world, underscore the need for a universal legally binding instrument on violence against women at the United Nations level (Manjoo/ Jones 2018).

In terms of sexual violence in conflict, sexual violence, especially rape, has always been used in times of conflict as a military strategy. In situations of ancient warfare, women were viewed as bearers of the enemy's soldiers and thus were objects of attacks. History bears testimony to the widespread use of rape, forced prostitution, forced impregnation and other atrocities against women during the two World Wars, the Vietnam War, the conflicts in the former Yugoslavia, the Democratic Republic of Congo and Rwanda, among others. The patterns include the use of rape and sexual violence as part of the provision of sexual services for soldiers, by including it as part of the standard operating procedures; the setting up of prostitution rings and brothels within the military complex; the instrumental use of sexual violence to undermine efforts that were aimed at ending conflicts; and in some instances, the sexual abuse of women for achieving ethnic cleansing goals. Although entire communities suffer the consequences of armed conflict, women and girls are particularly vulnerable (Manjoo/ McRaith 2011).

From a normative perspective, in the Middle Ages women had some legal protections. Examples include the 1385 and 1419 Ordinances of War that prohibited rape during war and imposed the death penalty for violations. The 1863 Lieber Code, the military code for the US Union Army, also expressly prohibited rape and highlighted the severe gravity of the offence. Sexual violence was not explicitly acknowledged as a war crime in The Hague Conventions of 1899 and 1907, but there are provisions therein that provide protection against rape. With such protection being based on notions of family honour, dignity, morality and so on, however, rape was not seen as a crime of violence against the victim, but was defined as a crime against honour and dignity (Manjoo/McRaith 2011).

The Genocide Convention of 1948 includes language in Article 2 that can be used to prosecute rape as genocide, while the Geneva Convention of 1949 provides the clear articulation of norms that can be used to prohibit rape as a crime. Article 27 of the Fourth Geneva Convention expressly prohibits rape. It states that "women shall be especially protected against any attack on their honour, in particular against rape, enforced prostitution or any form of indecent assault." However, rape and other types of sexual violence were not mentioned as 'crimes against humanity' in the Nuremberg Charter nor in the London and Tokyo Charters—it was only mentioned as "other inhumane acts". The trial transcripts of the International Military Tribunal and the International Military Tribunal for the Far East reflect that evidence of rape existed, despite the non-articulation of this crime in the normative frameworks, and that rape charges were brought against some individuals, for example rapes committed by Japanese soldiers against the civilian population of Nanking (Askin/Koenig 2000).

Historically, international law has largely linked sexual violence to notions of morality, honour and inhumane acts—rather than as specific gendered crimes against women. Also, sexual violence was viewed as a violation of international humanitarian law during situations of armed conflict or occupation. The notion that such violence was a violation of women's human rights was not part of the recognition under international law. Rape and other forms of sexual violence are now included (to differing degrees) as a crime against humanity, war crimes and genocide in the statutes of the Rwandan and Former Yugoslavian International Tribunals and also the Rome Treaty governing the International Criminal Court. Awareness about sexual violence as genocide was raised following the conflicts in the former Yugoslavia and Rwanda. The first specific jurisprudence relating to sexual violence and genocide is reflected in the 1998 Akayesu case (*Prosecutor v. Jean-Paul Akayesu, 1998*), handed down by the International Criminal Tribunal for Rwanda (ICTR), which held that sexual violence might constitute genocide.

The Rome Treaty governing the International Criminal Court in its definitions of genocide, war crimes and crimes against humanity, does include a gendered approach to sexual violence crimes, including rape, sexual slavery, forced prostitution, forced pregnancy, enforced sterilisation, any other form of sexual violence of comparable gravity including indecent assault, strip searches and inappropriate medical examination. The Protocol on Women in Africa ('Maputo Protocol', see African Union 2003) article 1(j) is the only treaty that defines violence against women as "all acts perpetrated against women [...] in private or public life in peace time and during situations of armed conflicts or of war". Article 11(3) places obligations on states "to protect [...] against all forms of violence, rape and other forms of sexual exploitation, and to ensure that such acts are considered war crimes, genocide and/or crimes against humanity".

Current international standards addressing gender-based violence in conflict and post-conflict settings draw on provisions from various human rights instruments that protect women's equality and non-discrimination rights. Although violence against women, in its broadest sense, is not specifically addressed in the Convention on the Elimination of all forms of

Discrimination against Women (CEDAW), some provisions are
used to address sexual violence. For example, CEDAW General
Recommendation 28 (see United Nations Committee on the
Elimination of Discrimination against Women 2010) articulates
important guidelines for State parties including calling on states
to collect information on the impact of conflict on women, and
to ensure that adequate responses are implemented. Also, state
parties are obligated to evaluate the *de jure* and *de facto* situation
of armed conflicts and its impact on women and to take steps
to eliminate discrimination. In 2013, CEDAW adopted General
Recommendation 30 (see United Nations Committee on the
Elimination of Discrimination against Women 2013) wherein it
highlights concerns about the gendered impacts of conflicts and
women's exclusion from conflict prevention efforts, post-conflict
transition and reconstruction processes. The Declaration on the
Elimination of Violence against Women recognises women in
conflict situations as a vulnerable group and thus its definition
of violence against women would include cases arising in conflict
situations. The 1995 Beijing Platform of Action (see UN 1995)
includes women in conflict as one of its twelve areas of concern
and highlights the types of sexual violence that violate women's
rights in times of armed conflict.

The United Nations Security Council (UNSC) is charged
with the maintenance of international peace and security. Its
powers include the establishment of peacekeeping operations,
international sanctions and the authorization of military action
through the adoption of resolutions. The UNSC has adopted eight
resolutions under the theme of women, peace and security—with
a focus on women's human rights and gender equality in conflict
situations. The first resolution adopted in 2000 was SC resolution
1325 (UNSC 2000) and it was the first time that the Council
addressed the differential and unique impact of armed conflict on
women. It is a milestone for addressing violence against women in
armed conflict, as it applies both human rights and humanitarian
laws to address the issue. The Resolution recognises the need to
protect women and girls during and after armed conflict and
calls on State parties to take special measures to protect women

and girls from gender-based violence, particularly rape and other forms of sexual abuse. It also stresses the importance of women in peace-building processes and their equal participation and full involvement in peace and security efforts. Since 2000, the annual reports of the Secretary-General generally indicate that there continue to be gaps in the linkage between women, peace and security in conflict and post-conflict settings. The fifteen-year global study on the implementation of UNSC resolution 1325 reflects an increase in the number of allegations of sexual exploitation and abuse, including by armed groups, peacekeepers and state agents (United Nations Women 2015).

The seven subsequent Security Council resolutions contribute to addressing implementation, enforcement and oversight mechanisms for the realization of the women, peace and security agenda. They include resolutions 1820, 1888, 1889 1960, 2106, 2122 and 2242 (UNSC 2008, 2009, 2010, 2013a, 2013b, 2015). The resolutions specifically recognise that sexual violence is a threat to security (national, regional and international); and that it is viewed as a tactic of war and as an impediment to the process and restoration of international peace and security. They identify factors that contribute to sexual violence, including inadequate measures to prevent sexual violence and protect civilians; lack of addressing of impunity for sexual violence and inadequate addressing of continuing gender-based discrimination. The resolutions acknowledge the progress in standard setting that recognises sexual violence as a self-standing crime in international law (including in the two ad-hoc Tribunals and the ICC), and stress that rape and other forms of sexual violence can constitute a war crime, crime against humanity or a constitutive act with respect to the crime of genocide.

CONCLUSION

The UN General Assembly adopted the Declaration on the Elimination of Violence against Women (DEVAW) in 1993 (see United Nations General Assembly 1993a) where in the Preamble it recognizes:

> Violence against women is a manifestation of historically unequal power relations between men and women, which have led to domination over and discrimination against women by men and to the prevention of the full advancement of women, and that violence against women is one of the crucial social mechanisms by which women are forced into a subordinate position compared with men.

Furthermore, the Declaration expressed alarm that opportunities for women to achieve legal, social, political and economic equality in society are limited, inter alia, by continuing and endemic violence. Twenty-five years later, this situation continues.

Normative and implementation gaps need to be addressed in the quest to eliminate violence against women (UNHRC 2015a, 2015c). Gaps and challenges raise crucial questions about state responsibility to act with due diligence and the responsibility of the state as the ultimate duty bearer to protect women and girls from violence, its causes and consequences. A legally binding framework on violence against women and girls within the United Nations human rights system should ensure that states are held accountable to standards that are legally binding, should provide a clear normative framework for the protection of women and girls globally, and it should have a specific monitoring body to substantively provide in-depth analysis of both general and country-level developments.

In addition, a holistic approach is suggested in a thematic report submitted to the General Assembly in 2011. Such an approach requires:

1. treating human rights as universal, interdependent and indivisible, yet taking into consideration the specificities of violence against women and engaging at a local level to adequately recognize the diverse experiences faced by women;
2. situating violence on a continuum that spans interpersonal, communal, institutional and structural violence, acknowledges that violence occurs because discrimination, inequalities and impunity have been allowed to flourish;

3. accounting for individual, institutional and structural discrimination and inequalities, thus considering not only how individual lives are affected by the immediate impact of violence, but also how structures of discrimination and inequality perpetuate and exacerbate the situation; and

4. analyzing not only the social and/or economic hierarchies between women and men (inter-gender), but also among women (intra-gender), to identify how discrimination and inequalities affect women in different ways depending on how they are positioned within social, economic and cultural hierarchies, in developing remedies (UNHRC 2011).

The ultimate objective of states' efforts when investigating and punishing acts of violence against women, and when protecting and offering redress to victims, should be the prevention of re-victimization and future acts of violence, including by addressing structural factors and also ensuring the empowerment of women. Comprehensive remedial schemes for women victims of violence should consider measures of restitution and compensation, rehabilitation and reintegration, substantive recognition of the harms suffered, as well as guarantees of non-repetition.

The continuum of violence concept demands an acknowledgement that conflict-related sexual violence is underpinned by norms and practices that include gender inequality, discrimination, male domination, coercion, violence and so on, in times of non-conflict. Thus, comprehensive remedial measures to deal with sexual violence require addressing the underlying individual, communal, institutional and structural factors that contribute and exercebate experiences of violence against women in times of conflict.

REFERENCES

African Union. 2003. *Protocol to the African Charter on Human and Peoples' Rights on the Rights of Women in Africa*. Maputo: AU.

Askin, Kelly/Koenig, Dorean (eds). 2000. *Women and International Human Rights Law*. Volume 2. New York: Transnational Publishers.

Binion, Gayle. 1995. 'Human Rights: A Feminist Perspective', *Human Rights Quarterly*, 17(3):509–26.

Cook, Rebecca. 1994. 'State Responsibility for Violations of Women's Human Rights', *Harvard Human Rights Journal*, 7(Spring), 125–75.

Council of Europe. 2011. *The Council of Europe Convention on Preventing and Combating Violence against Women and Domestic Violence*. Istanbul: CoE.

International Committee of the Red Cross (ICRC). 1949. *Geneva Convention Relative to the Protection of Civilian Persons in Time of War (Fourth Geneva Convention)*. Geneva: N.D.

International Peace Conference. 1907. *The Hague conventions of 1899 and 1907 Respecting the Laws and Customs of War on Land*. The Hague: N.D.

Kelly, Liz. 1988. *Surviving Sexual Violence*. Minneapolis: University of Minnesota Press.

Manjoo, Rashida/Jones, Jackie (eds). 2018. *The Legal Protection of Women from Violence: Normative Gaps in International Law*. London: Routledge.

Manjoo, Rashida/McRaith, Calleigh. 2011. 'Gender-Based Violence and Justice in Conflict and Post-Conflict Areas', *Cornell International Law Journal*, 44(1): 11–31.

Meer, Shamim. 2011. *Struggles for Gender Equality: Reflections on the place of men and men's organisations*. Johannesburg: Open Society Initiative for Southern Africa. https://forum.cartercenter.org/sites/default/files/2018-01/Struggles%20for%20Gender%20Equality.pdf (accessed 9 October 2018).

Organization of American States (OAS). 1994. *Inter-American Convention on the Prevention, Punishment and Eradication of Violence against Women ("Convention of Belem do Para")*. Belem do Para: OAS.

Prosecutor v. Akayesu, Judgment and Opinion, ICTR-96-4-T, 2 September 1998

Romany, Celina. 1993. 'Women as Aliens: A Feminist Critique of the Public/Private Distinction in Human Rights Law', *Harvard Human Rights Journal*, 6:87–125.

Sullivan, Donna. 1994. 'Women's Human Rights and the 1993 World Conference on Human Rights', *The American Journal of International Law*, 88(1):152–67.

United Kingdom's Prevention of Sexual Violence Initiative (PSVI). https://www.gov.uk/psvi (accessed 9 August 2018).

United Nations. 1995. *Beijing Declaration and Platform of Action, adopted at the Fourth World Conference on Women, 27 October 1995*. Beijing: UN.

———. 1948. *Universal Declaration of Human Rights (resolution 217 A)*, adopted 10 December 1948.

————. N.D. *United Nations Secretary-General's Campaign UNiTE to End Violence against Women. Human Rights Violations.* http://www.un.org/en/women/endviolence/situation.shtml (accessed 9 August 2018).

United Nations Commission on Human Rights. 2001. *Report of the Special Rapporteur on violence against women, its causes and consequences, Radhika Coomaraswamy, E/CN.4/2001/73.* Geneva: OHCHR.

United Nations Committee on the Elimination of Discrimination Against Women. 2017. *General Recommendation No. 35 on Gender-Based Violence against Women, Updating General Recommendation No. 19, CEDAW/C/GC/35.* New York: UNCEDAW.

————. 2013. *General recommendation No. 30 on Women in Conflict Prevention, Conflict and Post-Conflict Situations, CEDAW/C/GC/30.* New York: UNCEDAW.

————. 2010. *General Recommendation No. 28 on the Core Obligations of States Parties under Article 2 of the Convention on the Elimination of All Forms of Discrimination against Women, CEDAW/C/GC/28.* New York: UNCEDAW.

————. 2008a. *Draft concluding Observations of the Committee on the Elimination of Discrimination against Women. Finland, CEDAW/C/FIN/CO/6.* New York: UNCEDAW.

————. 2008b. *Concluding Observations of the Committee on the Elimination of Discrimination against Women. United Kingdom of Great Britain and Northern Ireland, CEDAW/C/UK/CO/6.* New York: UNCEDAW.

————. 2007a. *Concluding Comments of the Committee on the Elimination of Discrimination against Women. Netherlands CEDAW/C/NLD/CO/4.* New York: UNCEDAW.

————. 2007b. *Concluding Comments of the Committee on the Elimination of Discrimination against Women. Poland, CEDAW/C/POL/CO/6.* New York: UNCEDAW.

United Nations Department of Economic and Social Affairs. Division for the Advancement of Women. 2009. *Handbook for Legislation on Violence against Women.* New York: UN DESA.

United Nations General Assembly. 2014. *Report of the Special Rapporteur on Violence against Women, its Causes and Consequences, Rashida Manjoo, A/69/368.* New York: UNGA.

————. 2011. *Report of the Special Rapporteur on Violence against Women, its Causes and Consequences, Rashida Manjoo, A/66/215.* New York: UNGA.

————. 1998. *Rome Statute of the International Criminal Court (last amended 2010), U.N. Doc. A/CONF.183/9*.* Rome: UNGA.

————. 1993a. *Declaration on the Elimination of Violence against Women, A/RES/48/104.* New York: UNGA.

————. 1993b. *Vienna Declaration and Programme of Action, 12 July 1993, A/CONF.157/23.* New York: UN.

————. 1979. *Convention on the Elimination of All Forms of Discrimination Against Women (CEDAW) 1979, (UNGA resolution 34/180).* New York: UN.

————. 1948. *Convention on the Prevention and Punishment of the Crime of Genocide, General Assembly Resolution 260.* Paris: N.D.

United Nations Human Rights Council (UNHRC). 2015a. *Report of the Special Rapporteur on Violence against Women, its Causes and Consequences, Rashida Manjoo, A/HRC/29/27.* Geneva: UNHRC.

————. 2015b. *Report of the Special Rapporteur on Violence against Women, its Causes and Consequences, Rashida Manjoo, Addendum, Mission to the United Kingdom of Great Britain and Northern Ireland, A/HRC/29/27/Add.2.* Geneva: UNHRC.

————. 2015c. *Addendum to the Human Rights Council Thematic report of the Special Rapporteur on Violence, its Causes and Consequences, Rashida Manjoo (A/HRC/29/27), A/HRC/29/27.Add.4.* Geneva: UNHRC.

————. 2014a. *Report of the Special Rapporteur on Violence against Women, its Causes and Consequences, Rashida Manjoo, A/HRC/26/38/.* Geneva: UNHRC.

————. 2014b. *Report of the Special Rapporteur on Violence against Women, its Causes and Consequences, Rashida Manjoo, Addendum, Mission to India, A/HRC/26/38/Add.1.* Geneva: UNHRC.

————. 2013a. *Report of the Special Rapporteur on Violence against Women, its Causes and Consequences, Rashida Manjoo, A/HRC/23/49.* Geneva: UNHRC.

————. 2013b. *Report of the Special Rapporteur on Violence against Women, its Causes and Consequences, Rashida Manjoo, Addendum, Mission to Solomon Islands, A/HRC/23/49/Add.1.* Geneva: UNHRC.

————. 2013c. *Report of the Special Rapporteur on Violence against Women, its Causes and Consequences, Rashida Manjoo, Addendum, Mission to Papua New Guinea, A/HRC/23/49/Add.2.* Geneva: UNHRC.

————. 2013d. *Report of the Special Rapporteur on Violence against Women, its Causes and Consequences, Rashida Manjoo, Addendum, Mission to Croatia A/HRC/23/49/Add.4.* Geneva: UNHRC.

————. 2012. *Report of the Special Rapporteur on Violence against Women, its Causes and Consequences, Rashida Manjoo, Addendum, Mission to Italy, A/HRC/20/16/Add.2.* Geneva: UNHRC.

————. 2011. *Report of the Special Rapporteur on Violence against Women, its Causes and Consequences, Rashida Manjoo, A/HRC/17/26.* Geneva: UNHRC.

————. 2010a. *Report of the Special Rapporteur on the Situation of Human Rights Defenders, Margaret Sekaggya, A/HRC/16/44.* Geneva: UNHRC.

————. 2010b. *Report of the Special Rapporteur on Violence against Women, its Causes and Consequences, Rashida Manjoo, A/HRC/14/22.* Geneva: UNHRC.

————. 2009a. *Report of the Special Rapporteur on Violence against Women, its Causes and Consequences, Yakin Ertürk, Addendum Mission to Saudi Arabia, A/HRC/11/6/Add.3.* Geneva: UNHRC.

————. 2009b. *The United Nations Special Rapporteur on Violence against Women, Its Causes and Consequences, 15 Years of The United Nations Special Rapporteur on Violence Against Women (1994–2009) – A Critical Review, A/HRC/11/6/Add.5.* Geneva: UNHRC.

United Nations Human Rights Office of the High Commissioner (OHCHR). N.D.a. *Special Rapporteur on the Situation of Human Rights Defenders, Annual Reports.* https://www.ohchr.org/EN/Issues/ SRHR Defenders/Pages/AnnualReports.aspx (accessed 9 August 2018).

————. N.D.b. *Report of the Special Rapporteur on Violence against Women, its Causes and Consequences.* https://www.ohchr.org/en/issues/women/ srwomen/pages/srwomenindex.aspx (accessed 9 August 2018).

————. N.D.c. *Report of the Special Rapporteur on Violence against Women, its Causes and Consequences, Country Visits.* https://www.ohchr.org/EN/ Issues/Women/SRWomen/Pages/CountryVisits.aspx (accessed 9 August 2018).

United Nations Secretary-General. 2006. *In-Depth Study on all Forms of Violence against Women. Report of the Secretary-General, A/61/122/Add.1.* New York: UNGA.

United Nations Security Council (UNSC). 2015. *On Women and Peace and Security, S/RES/2242.* New York: UNSC.

————. 2013a. *On Sexual Violence in Armed Conflict, S/RES/2106.* New York: UNSC.

————. 2013b. *On Women and Peace and Security, S/RES/2122.* New York: UNSC.

————. 2010. *On Women and Peace and Security, S/RES/1960.* New York: UNSC.

————. 2009. *On Acts of Sexual Violence against Civilians in Armed Conflicts, S/RES/1888.* New York: UNSC.

————. 2008. *On Acts of Sexual Violence against Civilians in Armed Conflicts,* *S/RES/1820.* New York: UNSC.

————. 2000. *On Women and Peace and Security, S/RES/1325, 31 October.* New York: UNSC.

————. 1994. *Statute of the International Criminal Tribunal for Rwanda, (Resolution 955) S/RES/955.* New York: UNSC.

————. 1993. *Statute of the International Criminal Tribunal for the Former Yugoslavia, (Resolution 832) S/RES/837.* New York: UNSC.

United Nations Women. 2015. *Preventing Conflict Transforming Justice Securing the Peace: A Global Study on the Implementation of United Nations Security Council resolution 1325.* New York: UN Women.

United States of America. Adjutant General's Office. 1863. *Instructions for the Government of Armies of the United States in the Field (Lieber Code).* Washington: Government Printing Office.

World Health Organisation. 2013. *Research for Universal Health Coverage, The World Health Report.* Geneva: WHO.

"Stabbing, Slicing, Wounding": Urban Hindu Nationalism, Public Knife-Distribution and the Politics of Sexual Vulnerability in Mumbai, India

ATREYEE SEN

In January 2013, Shiv Sena, a highly militant Hindu nationalist organisation currently in power in Maharashtra, a state in western India, celebrated the birth anniversary of late Bal Thackeray, the extremist supreme leader of the political party who was its chief for almost forty years. On the occasion of his birthday, local party leaders of the Shiv Sena organised informal neighbourhood ceremonies, and most of these functions were held in open spaces or party-owned community centres in urban areas across the region. In many neighbourhoods in Mumbai, the economic capital of Maharashtra, these celebrations centred around the distribution of knives to women attendees, especially those from lower middle class and slum backgrounds. The party had placed an order for 100,000 Chinese retractable blades for this occasion and in a ceremony in South Mumbai itself, which I attended, almost 21,000 knives were distributed to poor women.

This spectacular gimmick, which was developed as a response to the 'India rape crisis' in December 2012, became very newsworthy. During the time of the rape (which I discuss below), Raj Thackeray, the leader of a Shiv Sena party faction, very openly stated that rural migrants from Bihar and Uttar Pradesh (states in north India stereotyped for its lack of development), were responsible for women's vulnerability in the city. While addressing journalists before the ceremony, the *vibhag pramukh* or chief of

South Mumbai, Ajay Chaudhuri, was asked to defend the knife
initiative. He stated that this was an apt tribute to Thackeray who
"used to say women should prefer a Rampuri [small knife] in their
purse rather than a lipstick." The political stalwart who won from
his constituency with a massive majority went on to state that the
knives were for "enhancing women's personal security" in the
backdrop of recent attacks against women, and they were directed
towards inspiring women to protect their bodies while negotiating
a terse urban terrain. He added that "the government has failed
to provide security to women, so we are distributing these knives
to help them defend themselves." During the meeting, various
male leaders who shared the platform with women receiving
knifes reassured female cadres that the law permitted ordinary
citizens to carry a knife below a six inch blade, and most of these
Chinese knives are extremely sharp but didn't have a blade above
three inches. They also carried small key chains with the photo of
Thackeray allegedly to mark this birthday.

Sudhatai, my informant in the field for 15 years, told me how
these knives were designed to debilitate sexual predators, and
not kill them. "Unless you use them on the throat in extreme
circumstances," she added in mirth. When the media descended
on the Shiv Sena party spokesman Rahul Narvekar about the
knife distribution scandal, he quickly stated: "This is a symbolic
gesture." He felt that a knife shorter than six inches in length did
not fit the definition of a dangerous weapon. "It's only to pass a
signal to eve-teasers [street molesters], anti-social elements and
perpetrators of crime against women that women are empowered
and they can take care of themselves", Narvekar said. However,
women attendees gossiped about how Chaudhuri, who played a
key role in launching the knife campaign, was far more assertive
than other Sena politicians and had used the platform of the
widely-read party newspaper, *Saamna*, to urge women to be bold
in public. "Don't be afraid of using this knife if someone attacks
you", said Chaudhari. "The way you cut vegetables, cut the hand
of the person who touches you the same way", he added. While the
Mumbai police claimed that they were examining the knives and
deliberating over the nature of legal action, Chaudhuri was quoted

addressing women in the party newspaper: "We have set up a team of nine advocates to protect you from any potential court cases that may arise." The Sena apparently planned to 'take care' of any legal cases brought against women who use the knife in self-defense.

The Shiv Sena top brass in its attempt to retain a moderate face while in office predictably denied any knowledge about the campaign. Bharat Raut, a member of parliament, told a top news channel that "this is something that's being done at a *shakha* [block] level." He was not aware if this campaign to authorise stabbing of sexually aggressive men had the support of Sena's supreme leadership. This dramatic attempt to openly arm (materially and symbolically) ordinary and at times impoverished urban women in Mumbai ignited a public debate on ethical and appropriate responses to tackle what is loosely defined as 'sex crimes'. In some of the celebrations, women were handed out small bags of chilli powder to throw into an attacker's eyes and temporarily blind him. "But that's for weaker women afraid to carry knives", said Sudhatai, establishing a clear hierarchy between women who carry knives and those who don't. "They [the ones inhibited to carry the Sena knife] are giving the wrong message to their daughters, encouraging them to remain unsafe in the city. I would say 'teach your girls to stab, not sing'". While the Mumbai Police stated that they have examined the knives and found them to be 'not dangerous', the local policemen authorised to manage crowds during the knife ceremonies were concerned about the sudden influx of small weapons in circulation.

This short case study reflects on Shiv Sena's initiative to publicly distribute modified kitchen knives to less affluent women leaders and cadres, who are compelled to negotiate public transport and urban street cultures, for seeking or sustaining employment in Mumbai's formal and informal economy. My brief analysis explores how this collective celebration of knife-carrying women by a right wing party is related to the weaponization of everyday objects intimately related to poor women's domestic/private spaces (knives, chilli powder). I argue that this form of symbolism around sexual violence, and covert public provocations of counter-violence endorsed by nationalist groups, have the potential to

further divide everyday street cultures along antagonistic gender
lines, and to re-inscribe stereotypes of male migrants, Muslims,
refugees, poor travellers and illegal encroachers into urban space
as the unwanted and disposable populations in the modern city.

SHIV SENA WOMEN WORKERS, URBAN POVERTY
AND CRUDE NATIONALISM

The increasing successes of a virulent variety of Hindu
fundamentalism in India gave birth to a cluster of 'rough' local
organisations, which fostered political, social and religious
insecurities in their regions for many years. One such organisation
was the Shiv Sena (Shivaji's Army), a regional political party
named after the martial Hindu king Shivaji. Even though
Maharashtra, the Indian state of which Mumbai is the capital,
has been a stronghold of the national, 'secular' Congress party
since Indian independence in 1947, a series of internal and
external socio-political challenges destabilised the Congress. The
Shiv Sena emerged in the 1960s as a small grassroots cultural
organisation, and it built a notorious reputation by building a
strong anti-migrant, anti-minority and anti-communist agenda,
and eventually orchestrating the collapse of the Congress
government (Katzenstein 1979). As the Sena grew in power and
popularity, the party was officially launched in 1966 in Bombay
under the charismatic leadership of Balasaheb Thackeray, who
emerged as the most controversial figure in Bombay's political and
cultural landscape (Eckert 2003). His party won several Municipal
Elections, and in 1995 joined forces with the Bharatiya Janata
Party (BJP), a pan-Indian Hindu fundamentalist organisation
currently in power at the Centre, to form the state government
(Heuze 1995). Thereafter, the Shiv Sena has been in and out of
office in several constituencies, eventually the alliance yet again
sweeping into power in the state in 2014. Since its inception as
an ethno-centric cultural organisation, Shiv Sena men have made
headlines because of their violent and murderous activities in
orchestrating Hindu-Muslim and Hindu-Christian communal
riots not just in Mumbai, but all over the state. Shiv Sena women

played an instrumental role in creating communal tension and orchestrating direct or indirect attacks on migrants and Muslims, well in keeping with the larger aims of an ethno-nationalist movement (Sen 2006, 2007). The Mahila Aghadi or the women's front was formally inaugurated in 1985, a year after the Shiv Sena formed an alliance with the BJP. By that time, most Sena women in the slums had developed an aggressive public image as picketers, as running abuse brigades (groups of women that embarrassed 'offenders' by shouting abuses in front of their homes/ offices for hours), and as violent demonstrators.

In December 1992 and January 1993, large-scale communal riots broke out in Mumbai, the commercial capital in western India, which left over a thousand people dead and several others injured. Following the organised destruction of the Babri Mosque by Hindu nationalists in the north Indian temple-town of Ayodhya, groups of angry Muslims held low intensity protests in Mumbai (in December 1992). The Shiv Sena led the ensuing violence, which involved both arson and indiscriminate attacks on people. The rioting dispersed from slum areas into apartment blocks, and in most localities entailed the systematic targeting of Muslims who comprised nearly 20 per cent of the city's population. The Mahila Aghadi took to the streets in droves, and their open participation in the riots disappointed secular movements in India. The women rioters on the other hand brought the marginalised Aghadi into the forefront of nationalist politics in Mumbai. In 1999, I initiated research among Aghadi members in a riot-affected Mumbai slum. Since that time, I have documented poor women's rationale for ideologically organising themselves around Hindu nationalism, and I explore how the Aghadi contributes towards sustaining a politically charged public life in Mumbai.

A significant part of the violent political rhetoric developed by the Shiv Sena women concerns the protection of ordinary Hindu women (against the lustful Muslim male in particular, and male aggressors in general). My broader research suggests that the Mahila Aghadi manipulated the nationalist discourse to address more localised gender interests (Sen 2007). The women's wing, which drew its primary membership from the expansive slums of Bombay. The Sena women loyalists were first- or second-generation migrants from the rural parts of Maharashtra and became engaged in a variety of legal and illegal economic activities to sustain their families in the slums. For example, several women were fruit and vegetable vendors during the day and covertly sold marijuana at night. Most of the women were married, yet faced various domestic uncertainties. A small section of slum women consisted of working widows (who found security and sisterhood within the Sena camp), and 'over-age' and unmarried women (whose life in the urban slums had prevented them from finding 'suitable' partners). Almost all slum women had experienced extreme poverty, displacement and class discrimination, evictions, familial and kin alienation, domestic neglect and sexual and financial vulnerabilities as workers within the informal/unskilled labour economy (Sen 2007; Bedi 2012).

The women cadres used their martial image and their notorious reputation within the politics of urban fear for certain social and economic benefits, which enabled them to survive everyday life within the exclusivist ethos of a commercial city. These 'benefits' ranged from securing material assets like illegal taps, electricity and cable connections by threatening local suppliers, to more intangible advantages like ensuring women's safety and mobility on the streets by thrashing male 'predators'. In the absence of direct communal violence in recent years, the Aghadi continues to mark urban public spaces as sites of women's vulnerability, the latter being heightened recently by the international hype around 'the India rape crisis'. Media attention directed towards rapes in Indian cities, including the assault on a young journalist in Mumbai, enabled the Aghadi to represent itself as protector, saviour and warrior for the vast majority of lower middle class and poor women negotiating public life in the city.

INDIA RAPE CRISIS, HINDU NATIONALISM AND URBAN WOMEN'S SELF-DEFENCE

On 16 December 2012, a 23-year-old physiotherapy student was raped and beaten on a moving bus before being thrown bleeding on an expressway in New Delhi, a city being dubbed by the international media as India's 'rape capital'. The attack and the student's death two weeks later caused public outrage at the failure of the government and police to protect women from rising sexual offences in a country, where one rape is reported approximately every 20 minutes. The sexual assault ignited unprecedented mass protests where women from various class, caste and political backgrounds came out into the streets in droves and demonstrated against the absence of women's rights in India. Numerous debates arose over the significance of these large-scale demonstrations in the cities when low caste poor women in rural areas have been raped, with little or no response from the state or upper caste communities.

The crisis reached breaking point when the now banned documentary 'India's daughter' showed how the rural migrant rapists, after having received a death sentence, blamed the victim for the rape. Some studies also showed how many urban women started to take up self-defence classes to contest their growing sexual vulnerability to poor, migrant rapists. Most of the women's wings of prominent Hindu nationalist organisations joined the demonstrations against the horrific rape. Eventually, a government commission set up to recommend revisions to India's sex crime laws stated that women who kill an attacker during an attempted rape should be able to plead self-defence. Which became another cause for the Shiv Sena to easily legitimise the carrying of knives by vulnerable women.

What becomes clear is how the incensed emotions around the sensitive issue around rape could be assessed as a strategic ploy by the Hindu nationalist political party to retain its long-term visibility as a supporter of rough and crude justice for the underprivileged local populations in Mumbai. The latter were identified as most susceptible to violence and rape from migrants and Muslims, who have been on the Sena 'hit list' since its inception. These politics are sustained by the increasing normalisation of the use of knives and daggers in communal violence—as items of attack, sexual assault and defence—and the increasing representation of the city as a war zone. These representations heighten the role of right-wing activists in retaining moral and physical integrity of its loyalists through territorial 'safekeeping'. The knives used during the Sena functions were stamped with images of the militant Bal Thackeray, which not only reassured women that the possession and use of knives was legitimised by a God-like male nationalist hero, but the active support of the party and the promise of a team of lawyers further absolved women of any moral responsibility towards the use of the knives. In this context of growing anxiety around crimes against women, the Shiv Sena women distributed kitchen knives and small packs of chilli powder to women in bus stops, as well as in informal knife distribution ceremonies in less affluent neighbourhoods. Thus the ordinary kitchen knife at home became extended into a sword in the world, blurring boundaries between the private and the public through the easy politicisation of gendered objects. I would like to question whether the representation of the kitchen as a domestic armoury, and the public space as a war zone, could suggest a subtle and covert militarisation of civil life in fraught urban centres.

Finally, I would suggest that the publicity that revolved around celebrating knife-carriers allowed ordinary women to feel temporarily mobile and assertive within a criminalising urban economy. While several women hailed the ceremony and loudly celebrated the party's policy to arm ordinary women, there were women who developed a critique (for example a small knife could not ward off gang-rape), though it was aired more informally in their local context.

This policy, even though it was criticized by the media as a cheap gimmick, created a controversial debate within slum areas about contesting women's vulnerability in the city. This was also related to a more global concern about the failures of various state and state-like agencies in protecting poor women who, through coercion or choice, enter the public sphere and want to retain control over their bodies.

REFERENCES

Bedi, Tarini. 2012. 'Motherhood, and its "Lack": Personal Loss and Political Community among Shiv Sena Women in Mumbai', *Women's Studies International Forum*, 35(6):478–86.

Eckert, Julia. 2003. *The Charisma of Direct Action: Power, Politics and the Shiv Sena*. Oxford: Oxford University Press.

Heuze, Gerard. 1995. 'Cultural Populism: The Appeal of the Shiv Sena', in Sujata Patel/Alice Thorner (eds), *Bombay: Metaphor for Modern India*, pp. 213–47. Mumbai: Oxford University Press.

Katzenstein, Mary Fainsod. 1979. *Ethnicity and Equality: The Shiv Sena Party and Preferential Policies in Bombay*. Ithaca: Cornell University Press.

Sen, Atreyee. 2012. 'Women's Vigilantism in India: A Case Study of the Pink Sari Brigade', in *Online Encyclopedia of Mass Violence*. Paris: Centre d'etudes et de Recherches Internationales.

———. 2007. *Shiv Sena Women: Violence and Communalism in a Bombay Slum*. Bloomington: Indiana University Press.

———. 2006. 'Reflecting on Resistance: Hindu Women "Soldiers" and the Birth of Female Militancy', *Indian Journal of Gender Studies*, 13(1):1–35.

✳ ✳ ✳

Nationalism and the Patriarchal Order

GORANA MLINAREVIĆ

In Atreyee's case study, a militant Hindu nationalist party, Shiv Sena, organises celebratory ceremonies during which they provide women with knives to defend themselves against male violence, in particular against rape. This happens at a time of heightened public awareness, during the so called 'rape crisis' in India. The organisers of the ceremonies allow only one group of women to be regarded as potential victims: the Hindu women from the poor and lower middle class living in the urban area. The attackers, in contrast, are perceived as men who are not only of other religious/ethnic backgrounds but who are also migrants from the rural area. So there is a particular construction here. A specific group of urban women, which appears to have little power in their own community, is armed to attack men from another particular group, that is, men who are perceived as others and characterised as generally violent (notably, the women from the rural area who belong to the community of these men remain largely invisible in this setting).

From my point of view, the empowerment of this first group, the lower middle class urban women stops here: They are not empowered to tackle any form of in-group violence or gendered power structures. They are not empowered to attack violent men from their own group. Instead, it seems that they are expected to preserve the existing gender dynamics and the patriarchal order within this specific urban area.

The knife distribution ceremonies are primarily put into practice by women who belong to the political cadre of the Shiv Sena organisation. It appears as if this group is also in charge of preserving the class order within this specific ethno-national group, as these cadre women appear to be superior to both lower class women and men. And the class order is again constructed in a patriarchal narrative. In order for the lower class women to be outside in public, they are encouraged to attack men, but apparently only enemy men from the lower classes.

It seems to me that Atreyee's case study can serve as an example for the general tendency to militarise women and their bodies, (ab)using women for the interests of a militant group. The empowerment of women in this context is not broadly expanding their scope for interpretation and action. Rather, women are merely allowed to be empowered within strict limits and to a restricted level—similar to the recruitment of women in private armies or private security firms, where they are only accepted at the 'front lines' as long as they do not question the gender order. Indeed, numerous examples evidence that women who enter private armies or security firms experience multiple forms of sexual and other exploitation by their male comrades, but have no possibilities of demanding their rights, last but not least due to the confidentiality agreements they signed before entering the organisation.

The men of the Shiv Sena organisation who are involved in the knife distribution ceremonies are, in contrast, presented as protectors, not just by handing out knives, but—in particular in the case of the chief of South Mumbai, Ajay Chaudhuri—also by promising to provide lawyers, preparing them to defend a woman in case she attacks an attacker. So the party organises the weapons, the legal support, the entire defence mechanism. Ultimately, it appears as if the men of Shiv Sena are safely securing their patriarchal roles whereas the women are exposed to violence, whether as passive victims or active participants.

"We are protecting *our* women"–this is a classical narrative of any ethno-nationalist conflict. In Atreyee's case study, however, there seems to be more, in the sense of: "We are using women not only in their role as victims, but also as potential attackers." For me, the most striking element in this case is this additional responsibility of women to defend themselves and, at the same time, to defend the nationalist patriarchal order.

Yet women's bodies are still victimised, they are still penetrable, it is still women's bodies that are attacked by others in order to damage other men. And even though women are not merely presented as passive victims, this whole ceremony of distributing knives is still there to confirm the same old nationalist patriarchal narrative.

From my point of view, we might even pose the question if these kinds of ceremonies actually serve to fuel the conflict. While the men did not yet take up arms themselves, because this is not a declared war, they are giving the arms to women, so that "you can do it instead of me". Women are recruited to participate in this conflict to help one group of men to overpower the other group of men. Of course this is hypothetical, but given the patriarchal dynamic it is always a plausible scenario.

I don't know enough about the socio-political context to understand why the men of Shiv Sena chose men they identify as Muslim immigrants as their enemies. I can only assume that they somehow felt threatened in their position in the public sphere.

In order to secure their power, it seems, Shiv Sena then used the technique of diversion. Since the focus on the 'rape crisis' in Indian cities already existed, they only needed to direct the story according to their wishes. It seems as if they navigated the existing narrative in such a way that they could use the already known male violence against women to proclaim war against a certain group of 'enemy men'.

Atreyee points out the militarisation of civil life in the urban sphere. I would also add the militarisation of the private sphere. What becomes clear is that the whole symbolism is attached to the kitchen. The two forms of arms that are given to women are kitchen knives and cooking ingredients, that is chilli powder. Furthermore, women are instructed to cut a man's hand like they "cut a vegetable". This whole set-up gives the impression as if it was important to Shiv Sena to keep the women close to the private sphere. In some ways this appears as a replica of the logic of recruitment of women in militaries: women are useful as workers and military personnel during a war, in particular when there is a shortage of able bodied men, but when the war is over they are expected to return to the private sphere.

This militarisation of the private is, however, ambivalent. On one hand the everyday kitchen appliances and activities are being charged with symbolisms of violence, attack and defence, in order to tackle men perceived as enemies. But at the same time, this militarisation reveals that women have arms within their reach in the private sphere and that they can use these against *any* perpetrator of violence, for example, also in cases of so-called 'domestic violence'.

Ultimately, however, Shiv Sena men remain on the 'safe side'. The women are apparently not empowered to kill, since the small retractable blade knives are not powerful enough. A woman cannot kill a man, maybe not even seriously injure him. She can merely sort of humiliate him and, in the best scenario, scare him off or buy time to flee.

Some women might have experienced the ritualistic celebration of the knife-distribution as empowering, feeling solidarity, in particular because they felt unprotected and left alone by the state, as Atreyee describes. However, from my knowledge of the situation during and after the wars in the former Yugoslavia, I would argue that solidarity between women is possible (and, indeed, not merely among women from the same group, but even amongst women who perceive themselves as belonging to opposing groups), but that this generally only happens when these women are raped by men of an 'enemy' group. For example, a 'Serb' woman who was raped by a 'Croat' man and a 'Croat' woman who was raped by a 'Serb' man can show solidarity to each other. This usually occurs within a mutual understanding of the experiences of war and rape and in the context of reconciliation and peace building. But if a woman was raped within 'her own' ethnic group, women's solidarity with her rarely exists within this group. In the parameter of the armed conflict, where the loyalty to your own group becomes the most important thing, a sort of solidarity within the patriarchal order is only possible when the enemy can be blamed. In this sense I would suspect that a woman in western India who attacks her attacker with a knife can only experience solidarity as long as she does not attack a man of her own ethnic/religious group.

Of course all the contexts are different. So, I think when researching we are obliged to look into the particular identitarian constructions whether they are nationalist, ethnic, religious or other. The problem is that these are never settled categories. Also, what is understood as ethno-nationalism/racism in Europe is perceived differently in America, Australia, Asia, Africa and so on. We need to understand the specific dynamics in a place in order to be able to recognise the ways gender dynamics develop.

However, I haven't seen any nationalistic project that has not been organised around patriarchal constructions. Even when taking the specificities into account, I thus think that we have to question if offering women a sense of belonging to a nationalist group affiliation might not always be a trap.

In recent years, we could observe in Bosnia, Croatia and Kosovo but also in Bangladesh that raped women in so-called 'ethno-nationalistic wars' are sometimes authorised to receive post-war compensation, even to the same level as the war veterans' pensions. In Bosnia, for example, women survivors of rape are one of the rare categories of civilian victims of war that receive a monthly compensation. This has been lauded as the result of a very significant post-war feminist intervention, and certainly it is an important one. However, what we also see is that in order to qualify to receive this compensation, a female survivor of rape has to declare that she belongs to one specific ethnic group and is a survivor of rape committed by a member of an 'enemy' group.

In the context of ethno-nationalism women have usually been considered the 'weakest link', and prone to transgressions such as marriage to the 'other', giving birth to the child that becomes the 'other', or simply refusing to identify as belonging to any ethno-national group. So it seems surprising that it is within the ethno-nationalist discourse that women survivors of wartime rape suddenly become visible. Indeed, in some contexts, they are even perceived as heroines who sacrificed their bodies, similar to war veterans, during the fight to protect a territory. In Kosovo for example, there is now a monument to women survivors of rape, which is called *Heroinat* (heroines). Or take the case of Bangladesh, where the women survivors of wartime rape were recognised as 'birangonas' (war heroines) (Mookherjee 2015: 129), and later—from 2015—even entitled to the status of freedom fighters, including all associated benefits and facilities (N.N. 2015). However, we are far from seeing that the status of women who survived wartime rape really significantly improved. In a patriarchal society, these women and the problems they face are still invisible. In Bosnia and Croatia, for example, they are authorised to enter the public space as victim-survivors only when a certain ethno-nationalistic group needs them for some form of mobilisation and establishment of power.

This new kind of politics of compensation and remembrance is generally regarded as progressive, because they are seen as a recognition of and reparation for women's specific experiences of war. Unfortunately, however, women's experiences are also obscured here, because women are only recognised as victims of rape, their other war experiences (as usually their war experiences are intersectional and multiple) remain invisible and unrecognised.

Thus, the question becomes: How much is this 'recognition' of violence against women, especially sexual violence, actually connected to the experiences of/in the war?

It seems that only certain patterns of wartime rape are accepted and authorised to enter public narrative—those perpetrated by the enemy. And who is regarded as enemy? The enemy is always the other, he is never within the so-called 'friendly army'. The negotiation is always along ethnic/religious lines, never along the line of gender determination. Any action that can be dismissed as non-wartime rape remains invisible.

Indeed, in identitarian conflicts, rape within one's own group is not understandable. Furthermore, there is no potential to recognise the rape of women who are seen as not belonging to any of the ethno-nationalist groups. In every group, there is the narrative of the male fighters and the responsibility of women to provide support, morally and materially, and this becomes the only acceptable understanding of the gender relations. In this sense, sexual violence within the same group is an 'indiscretion' that is not even perceived as a violation and as such it is invisible.

Ultimately, the question is: How do we understand violence against women in its totality rather than only in its' segments, in particular manifestations? In order to approach this question we have to, I believe, explore in much more detail how gender and gender dynamics are understood and used in ethno-nationalist patriarchal constructions.

REFERENCES

Mookherjee, Nayanika. 2015. *The Spectral Wound: Sexual Violence, Public Memories, and the Bangladesh War of 1971*. Durham: Duke University Press.

N.N. 2015. 'Bangladesh Gives 41 Women Freedom Fighter Status', *The Daily Star*, 13 October. https://www.thedailystar.net/frontpage/freedom-fighter-status-41-biranganas-156145 (accessed 02 January 2019).

* * *

The Ambiguous Role of Women in Self-Defence

ATREYEE SEN

Let me briefly return to Veena Das' (1998) understanding of the role of unfinished histories in creating public paranoia, and sustaining historical, cultural anxiety around sexual vulnerability of Hindu women in India. Charu Gupta (2001), for example, while exploring the incorporation of the female body in metaphors for nationalism in late colonial India, argues that the identity of the free nation was expressed in terms of devotion to the Bharat Mata or Mother India, who was inevitably a Hindu and a version of martial goddess Durga. While Mother India was represented in temples, anti-British songs and literature as a powerful mother goddess, she was also imagined as an enslaved, bodily bruised and all-suffering figure in chains while under colonial Christian rule. Without her physical dignity, she couldn't retain her divinity. The celebration of Mother India was primarily directed towards mobilising her children into political resistance, and she became emblematic of a bounded territory whose sexual honour needed to be protected by a male Hindu political citizenry. In postcolonial India, female celibate Hindu nationalist leaders, such as Uma Bharati and Sadhvi Rithambara, continued to use the iconography of Bharat Mata in their vituperative speeches to instigate men into violent action against 'the non-Hindu others', mainly Muslims and Christians, who had subjected the body of the nation mother to humiliation. According to Sikata Banerjee (2006), who studied Hindu masculinity and its relationship with female political participation in India, this sustained imagining of India as a woman's body fits into a more widely accepted discourse of nation as woman, which in turn links with ideas of female bodies being carriers of national honour. Gupta argues that this kind of lobbying against Muslims and Christians have roots in the 1920s, when Hindu nationalist groups gained currency by acting as vigilantes against the alleged kidnapping and rape of Hindu women by other women. First the Muslims raped us (during Mughal rule) then the Christians raped us (during colonial rule) and then the Muslims raped us again (during the Partition). Ritu Menon and Kamla Bhasin's (1996) critical narrative on the rape of women during Partition (in 1947) shows how the large numbers of violated Hindu women caught in the exodus between India and Pakistan contributed to this strong legacy of narratives of mass rape in the region, and generated a nationalist history around unfinished and on-going sexual assault from the other.

According to Tara Atluri (2013), who analysed the unprecedented levels of protest against the gang rape case, young men in urban India were demonised and blamed for the rise in sexual violence in the city. She argues that this form of vilification was related to global austerity and anxieties concerning migrant youth who do not physically, socially and economically belong to the city. The increased forms of economic precariousness have complicated cross-culturally the historical discursive construction of urban youth as deviant but politically progressive. She argues that newly expanding cities such as New Delhi and Mumbai are struck by the failures of agrarian economies, issues of rural male employability in the informal urban sector, the rise and visibility of female workers marrying at later ages, growing secular middle-classes, prominent queer communities, and intensified class divisions, amongst many others. Thus the fear of 'idle young men' or 'frustrated young men' is well integrated into this overall crisis of meaning in urban public life, especially since the Delhi rapists were young, unemployed rural migrant men in the modernising city. According to the author:

> Just as the image of the supposedly repressed 'Muslim woman' has been consistently used throughout the ongoing global 'war on terror' to justify war and occupation, the scripting of the migrant man as most likely to commit rape is another way in which feminism is appropriated to justify conservative political agendas. (Alturi 2013)

Many prominent Members of Parliament in India, including those affiliated with the lower caste-based Samajwadi Party, also criticised urban women; and responded to the brutal rape by saying that women needed to pay attention to their clothes to avoid being violated. In another news report, the Samajwadi Party chief, Mulayam Singh Yadav, said, "When boys and girls have differences, the girl gives a statement that 'the boy raped me', and that poor boy gets a death sentence. [...] Should rape cases lead to hanging? Boys are boys, they make mistakes." This was followed up by another press release by Samajwadi Party chief in Mumbai, Abu Azmi, who said women who get raped should also be punished. I suggest that these statements from 'backward India', by men from low caste, rural, northern or Muslim backgrounds, further solidified Shiv Sena's commitment to use the rape platform to promote its nationalist agenda, but still present itself as a progressive party devoted to safeguarding economic prosperity, cultural values and male chivalry, by safeguarding poor women employed in the modern city.

Gorana's discussion on using the kitchen as an armoury is significant. According to Carolyn Nordstrom (1998), who studied the war in Mozambique, one of the goals of terror warfare is to reproduce the hegemony of violence in the minutia of everyday life. The normal, the innocuous and the inescapable are infused with associations of lethal harm and control. According to the author,

> Perpetrators do this by using common everyday items to produce terror. Kitchen items, household goods, water sources, and tools become weapons of torture and murder. Public spaces are cast as strategic battlegrounds. [...] Places traditionally associated with safety and items traditionally used in the production of the ordinary are recast as inhumane and lethal. When a kitchen knife is used to mutilate a family member, or a post office becomes the site of a massacre, kitchen knives and post offices become attached to the production of violence in ways that last far beyond the conclusion of the war. (Nordstrom 1998)

Thus for the Sena women who participated in these knife distribution ceremonies, the 'fundamental ontological security' of domestic objects related to family, cooking and familial affect, transforms to create a far more complex and enduring understanding of a violent urban culture.

These kind of public celebrations of ordinary yet armed women, generate discourses on sexual vulnerability in which women can be celebrated as warriors and saviours, or they can be formulated as unnatural or murderous women in the city, consolidating the notion of women as a source of public nuisance instead of challenging it. Hence poor women's position within this politics of urban self-defence is ambiguous, and the contested historical discourses around rape and sexual vulnerability informs this aggressive feminine citizenship within an increasingly gendered and exclusionary urban economy.

REFERENCES

Atluri, Tara. 2013. 'The Young and the Restless: Gender, "Youth", and the Delhi Gang Rape Case of 2012', *Sikh Formations*, 9(3):361–79.

Banerjee, Sikata. 2006. 'Armed Masculinity, Hindu Nationalism and Female Political Participation in India', *International Feminist Journal of Politics*, 8(1):62–83.

Das, Veena. 1998. 'Specificities: Official Narratives, Rumour, and the Social Production of Hate', *Social Identities*, 4(1):109–30.

Gupta, Charu. 2001. 'The Icon of Mother in Late Colonial North India: "Bharat Mata", "Matri Bhasha" and "Gau Mata"', *Economic and Political Weekly*, 36(45):4291–9.

Nordstrom, Carolyn. 1998. 'Terror Warfare and the Medicine of Peace', *Medical Anthropology Quarterly: International Journal for the Analysis of Health*, 12(1):103–21.

Menon, Ritu/Bhasin, Kamla. 1996. 'Abducted Women, the State and Questions of Honour: Three Perspectives on the Recovery Operation in Post Partition India', in Kumari Jayawardena/Malathi de Alwis (eds), *Embodied Violence: Communalising Women's Sexuality in South Asia*, pp. 1–31. London: Zed books.

VISIBILITY/INVISIBILITY

Sexual violence frequently takes place in public spheres, and often requires purposeful and organisational labour. Nevertheless, it is also typically silenced or dealt with as an 'open secret'. Victim-survivors who are willing to speak are generally ignored or ridiculed. With these practices of dismissing or silencing, their testimony is obliterated from the public record. In other times and contexts, accounts of sexual violence become highly visible and politicised.

This tension between public visibility and practices of trivialising or silencing violence, provokes fundamental questions. What explains which of these different approaches prevail in specific temporal and geographical contexts? Who decides whether violence is a crime, transgression, or 'normal'? How are these responses shaped by international or global politics? How do societies deal with victims? And how do they evaluate the actions of perpetrators?

Bestialisation, Dehumanisation and Counter-Interstitial Voices: Representations of Congo (DRC) Conflicts and Rape

NGWARSUNGU CHIWENGO

> Congo wasn't a country and the Congolese weren't a people.
>
> Lieve Joris, *The Rebels' Hour*

> NGOs and activists enlist stories from victims as a way of alerting a broader public to situations of human rights violations. They also solicit and package stories to attract readerships. The kinds of stories they choose […] are sensationalized, sentimentalized, charged with affect-target privileged readers in anticipation that they will identify with, contribute to, and become advocates for the cause. The frames they impose on stories are designed to capture the interest, empathy, and political responsiveness of readers elsewhere, in ways they have learned will "sell" […]. NGOs harness their rights agendas to the market and its processes of commodification.
>
> Kay Schaffer and Sidonie Smith,
> *Human Rights and Narrated Lives*

The rapes of women in eastern Congo, which exceed those of Bosnia and Rwanda, and the massacres of the Congolese and Hutu populations in the Democratic Republic of Congo (DRC) have not been called genocide, have not elicited massive empathy, outrage, general public outcry and have failed to prompt a massive call to action as in the case of Invisible Children's global campaign against Joseph Kony. The women whose lips were cut off by the Kony militia, the rapes of babies, elder women, men, and the resulting fistulas did not result in a military presence to stop the atrocities. A tentative response to the international indifference to the Congolese drama resides in the powerlessness of the Congolese government to articulate the real nature of the crisis, the willingness of Congolese to be utilised in foreign political agendas and the lack of in-depth discussion of the ongoing rapes. Moreover, the crisis and the rapes have been downplayed by the international scripts presented in the United States media and literature, representing the Congolese as passive victims of their own nationally made disaster.

While Ted Koppel's report, *Still the Heart of Darkness* (2003), first broadcasted on 7 September 2001 (and pre-empted by the 11 September 2001 Al-Qaida attack of America), Eric Metzgar's *Reporter* (2009), aired on HBO in 2010, and Lisa F. Jackson's *The Greatest Silence: Rape in Congo* (2007; the documentary that finally raised awareness of the rapes of Congo women) have contributed much to the dissemination of the Congo (DRC) crises and fate of women, these works also reveal the dangers of representing the Other. These filmic narratives seek to elicit interest and the empathy of the international community, but familiar Congo tropes and the selection and deselection of information in the emplotment of the narrative have resulted in the naturalisation of violence. Moreover, the Congolese tragedy has been eclipsed by the Rwandan genocide. It is, therefore, important to listen to local interstitial voices because they disclose how narratives are informed by human rights activists' comprehension, personal and political understanding of events. Moreover, the marginalisation of Congolese intellectual voices from the international discursive space hinders a more in-depth understanding of the issues.

NARRATIVE FRAMES: CONRADIAN TROPES AND ETHNOLOGICAL GAZE

Understanding the Congo (DRC) conflict and war is no easy task. The Congolese crisis has frequently been referred to as a civil war (though it is unclear between which national factions) and the Mai-Mai resistance to the armies from neighbouring countries briefly dubbed génocidaires (the term did not stick). The conflict taking place in eastern Congo, moreover, appears to be taking place in another place, the Great Lakes region—a term that was used during the Belgian colonisation and refers to the "area lying between northern Lake Tanganyika, western Lake Victoria, and lakes Kivu, Edward and Albert. This comprises Burundi, Rwanda, northeastern Democratic Republic of Congo, Uganda, and northwestern Kenya and Tanzania" (The New World Encyclopedia 2008). Only a small part of Congo (DRC) is considered to be part of this compilation of different countries. Yet, numerous web articles discuss the rapes in Congo under the rubric 'Great Lakes'. There appears to be a conflation of Congo rapes with Rwandan rapes or a blurring of space in such articles 'Eleven DR Congo Soldiers Facing "Mobile Gender Court" on Mass Rape' (Great Lakes Voice 2011) or 'The Impact of HIV on the Rape Crisis in the African Great Lakes Region' (Hentz 2005).

A quick survey of documentaries and literature on Congo reveals the country is most often viewed through a colonial ethnological grid, which frames the Congolese disaster. It is frequently presented through images of primitivity and violence. This tendency to will Congo to its primal Conradian existence and to foreground its inability to break from the wild and to fend for itself is visible in the numerous titles of literature on Congo alluding to Joseph Conrad's *Heart of Darkness* (1981). Surely, Eric Metzgar's unedited HBO *Reporter: A Film about Nicholas Kristof* (2009) affirms the Congoleses' inability to govern themselves when the reporter Kristof asks a Congolese male if he is better off than his grandfather. Ironically, even when the young man responds his grandfather was better off than he because he did not endure a war, Kristof concludes at the end of the film that the Congolese are less well off than they were under the Belgians. This framing of the Congo that imagines it as chaos and the Congolese as incapable of fending for themselves produces, according to Kevin Dunn, a "'knowable' Congo that allows for Western non-intervention and isolation" (2003: 170) and imposes a meaning on events that elide the meanings victims attach "to the disaster." Because the war, the rapes and massacres are decentralised from the larger socio-political conditions in which they unfold, Western political and economic invasions are erased, and violence is naturalised. Trauma becomes, because of "environmental determinism and cultural essentialism," the natural condition of Congolese.

Ted Koppel's *Still the Heart of Darkness* (2003) is one such travel report highlighting, through the mobility and body of the camera, the Conradian starving, bestial Other inferred in its very title, which, according to Tom Bettag in an interview by Charles Cobb (2001), is the reference point conveying the continual "torment" and "agony" of Congo. As Ehud Ban Zve (2009: 269) contends, "linguistic choices are never free of connoted meanings." Koppel's desire to foreground this image is evinced in his repetitive use of 'heart of darkness,' echoing Conrad's primeval representation of Congo. In the report, post-colonial Congo, brought into modernity by colonisation, is progressively being reclaimed by the horror and madness of the jungle. The people strenuously push *chikudus* (rudimentary homemade scooters) up and down hills, and the women, no different from harnessed cattle, carry weights up to 500 pounds. The colonial Kisangani train station, immortalised by Hollywood in the 1950s film *The Nun's Story* and featured at the beginning of Koppel's report, is a far cry from the current abandoned infrastructure; the railroad has rusted to a standstill; the port, once full of life, is abandoned; the town of Kisangani is a mere ghost of its colonial beauty; and even the Congo River is devoid of life, except for a few dugout rudimentary canoes. Kisangani, according to Koppel, has "become a city of bicycles. Less a city, really, than the memory of a city. Tonight, Kisangani, Still the Heart of Darkness" (*Still the Heart of Darkness* 2003). As less "than a memory of a city," Kisangani has lost all characteristics susceptible of defining it as a modern urban space, and the very story of the country, as he later invites his viewers to think of what is happening, is "a mystery story, a murder mystery," which begs the question, committed by whom?

In addition to this Conradian travel trope, the Congolese conflict is obliterated by an ecological grid humanizing gorillas and dehumanizing the Congolese. Indeed, gorillas play a main

role in Congo conflict narratives as evinced in "Conflict in Congo
Threatens Bonobos and Rare Gorillas" (Vogel 2000), decrying
the increase in Bonobo orphans when Congolese orphans do
not appear to be an urgent concern, and specifically in Gillian
Whitlock's 'Remediating Gorilla Girl: Rape and Warfare and
the Limits of Humanitarian Storytelling' (2010), describing the
individualisation of Gorillas and the correlation between animal
rights and human rights narratives. Whether it is Anderson
Cooper from CNN or Koppel reporting, the gorillas eventually
appear on the screen. Congolese are definitely often in competition
with gorillas in victimisation narratives, for their fate is constantly
juxtaposed to theirs. The very plot of Koppel's report furthermore
alternates between Rwanda and Congo tragedies.

Despite the ethnological, ecological and Rwandan grids
through which Koppel reads the Congolese trauma, he
nonetheless provides information on the Leopoldian roots of the
conflict, the untold colonial genocide (equally wrapped in silence
even though, at the time, it was a cause célèbre of the proto-
human rights movement in England) and the economic reasons,
then and in our contemporary times, fuelling the genocide and
Congolese massacres. "Then it was rubber and ivory and today it
is diamonds," he claims. According to Koppel, the many diamonds
that change hands in Antwerp may originate in Kisangani, but
the "foreign dealers [...] find them these days in the Rwandan
capital of Kigali or the Ugandan capital of Kampala. [...] The
Rwandans, victims of the '94 genocide, are victims no more. They
control much of the diamond trade [in Congo]."

The report also features an interview with Martin Seemungal,
an ABC correspondent in Kisangani, who explains that United
Nations peacekeepers do not have access to certain areas and
contends, "We have reports from reliable sources that the rebel
group that controls this area is systematically killing people in
the jungle, that it's involved in another ethnic cleansing." While
the horror of the conflict needs to be disseminated, Seemungal
comments, "the colonel [second in command of the UN mission
in Kisangani] has concerns. The UN has concerns. The world
has concerns, but not much more" (*Still the Heart of Darkness* 2003).

With hindsight, Koppel's report provides an excellent in-depth analysis of the Congolese conflict, information on the direct (Mai-Mai and Interhamwe) and indirect (Uganda and Rwanda) actors and reveals significant information on the political and economic powers undergirding the conflict, later unravelled in the *Democratic Republic of Congo, 1993–2003 Mapping Report* (United Nations Human Rights Office of the Commissioner for Human Rights 2010).

VISIBILITY AND INVISIBILITY OF RAPE

If the trope of the Congo hinders true international understanding of the conflict, the atrocious war rapes of women in Congo have not been profoundly discussed nationally, for rape is veiled in murmurs and banned from the public space. Sex predators are often protected by societal silence, so women alone bear the traumatic consequences of being 'ruined' and spoiled. The unspeakable acts of sexual violence are suppressed from public spaces and the victims frequently hastily rewarded with husbands. The burden and shame of being "ruined," as Toni Morrison so well describes Maginot Line in *The Bluest Eye* (1972), are solely that of women, moral beings who should ward off their sexually-driven male predators. To speak of one's rape is, therefore, not a liberating act, for speaking results in the loss of one's reputation as Delphine's mother, in the Human Rights Watch report, *The War within the War*, suggests when she invites her daughter to be "brave" and "to conceal her ordeal" from other families, so "as to not lose her reputation" (2002: 53). Similarly, the telephone reports of the South-Kivu chapter of Congokazi: Congo Women Association[1] speak of concealment of raped women during International Women's Day marches, despite their liberation and affirmative discourse on rape because raped women are not prominently featured within the community. Socially marginalised raped women are provided structures and communities to heal and to integrate them within their societies, but the organisations, focusing on raped women, are called 'development associations' to avoid the stigmatisation of rape, and the women euphemistically referred to as 'vulnerable people,' hidden within the group of female marchers on International Women's Day.

Testimonials of women—subjected to vaginal penetrations with sticks, branches, bullets and knives and to razor blade vagina mutilations, as can be seen in Doctors without Borders reports, Lisa Jackson's film *The Greatest Silence* (2007) and Ted Koppel's report *Still the Heart of Darkness* (2003)—are hence courageous public acts in a country where rape is absent from the public forum and of which its president was unaware during Jeff Koinange's CNN interview on 31 May 2006 (Kabila 2006). And when rape does become part of the national dialogue (for example during the Parliamentarians Global Action conference on Justice and Peace (PGA) in 2009), the heinous rapes of eastern Congo are naturalised and trivialised as in the rhetoric of the Bandundu delegate who held rape occurs primarily in non-war zones or Gilbert Kalinda, reporter for the Provincial Assembly of North-Kivu, who stated that rape has accrued because excessive public discussions of rape have fostered ample curiosity and desire for rape. Likewise, Jaynet Kabila[2] fails to discern the distinctive viciousness of male and female rapes in eastern Congo by contextualizing them within the global war casualties of Germany, the Balkans and Uganda and assuming peace and stability would, alone, eradicate these violent assaults (Nzuzi 2009).

The Congolese government and communities are not alone in shrouding the rape of Congolese women and men and the massacres in silence. While rape and massacres have been addressed in American media, Congressional, United Nations and NGO reports on Congo crises, the majority of newspaper articles, activist movie stars, politicians, filmmakers and activists are dismayed and astonished that a war, in which more than 5.4 million people have died and more than 1.2 million people have been displaced (640,000 in the Kivu alone and 321,195 in neighbouring countries), could be veiled in silence since 2007. Ironically, even after the US Secretary of State Hillary Clinton visited the Congo in August of 2009 and promised much needed commitment to "banish sexual violence" and financial and medical assistance to survivors of rape, the trauma and rape

endured by the Congolese was disregarded for the muzzled
Congolese were invited to forget the past and to solely look towards
the future (Clinton 2009). While economic crimes, transgressions
of international laws and the looting of Congo are condoned,
the massacres (which should be labelled genocide) and the rapes
(femicide) do not elicit sanctions within the Security Council.
Conversely, the vicious and debilitating rapes of Congolese
women are characterised as self-inflicted as the Mai-Mai and the
Congolese army hold central positions in international reports.
This tendency to implicate some parties in the Congo conflict
and exonerate others is nowhere more apparent than in *Remedies
and Reparations for Victims of Sexual Violence in the Democratic Republic
of Congo*, which claims: "The violence is widely attributed by
victims and others to the influx of foreign forces from Rwanda
in the mid-1990s, and virtually every victim urged the panel to
help bring peace to the country and return these forces to their
own country" (United Nations High Commissioner for Human
Rights 2011: 11). Séverine Autesserre best clarifies the silence and
dismissal of Congolese trauma, which according to her, resides in
the international community's perception of the

> horrific violence in Ituri or the Kivus as further evidence of the
> "barbaric" character of the Congolese people. Therefore, the goal
> of their increased international involvement was merely to bring
> the situation back to "normal"–meaning, to a level of violence
> they considered normal for a peaceful Congo. (Autesserre 2010:
> 220)

Rapes of women during wars have been considered, as the
majority of texts on war rape expound, atrocities and by-products
of war. Yet the vicious female rapes in Congo are rationalised by
State Department and Human Rights reports, such as *The War
within the War*, as the by-product of the Congolese Family Codes
and retrograde traditions and customs that subordinate women
and relegate them to second-class citizens. Maria Mota of The
African Association for the Defense of Human Rights (AZADHO)
and Mariana Duarte of the World Organisation Against Torture
(OMCT) consequently contend "Violence against women in

DRC occurs in different forms and in a context widely influenced by socio-cultural factors, discriminatory laws, ethnic conflicts, wars, bad governance, etc. Violence against women is perceptible at various levels, in the family, in society and at the state level" (Mota/Duarte 2006: 18).

In a similar manner Eli Mechanic claims in the Partnership Africa Canada (PAC) Dialogue:

> In the DRC the connection between men and women is unfortunately usually one of sexualized power. According to HRW, UNIFEM and many others, women's position in Congolese society is totally subordinate to men—one example being that women cannot refuse sex in a marriage or demand a condom be used, even when their partner is known to be HIV positive and sleeping with other women. Polygamy, domestic abuse and marital rape are prevalent, with all considered acceptable and sometimes even normal. (Mechanic 2004)

These documents, as well as numerous other newspaper articles, comprehend monolithically the social status of Congolese women through Congolese family codes and political, economic and social structures. It would, indeed, be preposterous to dismiss the oppressive nature of the Congolese Family Code and other cultural practices, yet rape does not occur only in the Congo. Rape frequently takes place even in developed countries with more progressive laws such as the United States as Ruth Seifert (1992) and others have analysed. Rape, whether in rape-free and/or rape-prone societies, is predicated on male domination. All forms of rape, whether in times of peace or wars are based on male dominance and the need to re-establish or affirm male power. If we follow Seifert, the objective of rape is to degrade, humiliate and subjugate while inflicting physical pain, loss of identity and dignity. Indeed, all parties, rebels, militia groups, United Nations peacekeepers, soldiers and civilians are involved in rapes in the Congo.

To ignore this and to hold the vicious rapes of Congolese women as cultural-specific is to ignore Carole Pateman's contention, quoted by Josephine Donovan,

> in a patriarchy the laws reflect the basic patriarchal principle that males have sexual rights to women; this is the sexual contract. Thus marriage contracts and the law of coverture [...] guaranteed husband's control over their wives and the latter's subordination. Even today, some legal jurisdictions do not accept the concept of marital rape because of sexual contract premises. (Donovan 2008: 200)

Congolese traditions may be oppressive, but rapes are global occurrences; what is distinct about the rapes of DRC is their viciousness and genocidal nature.

HUMAN RIGHTS FILMIC DISCOURSES

Nicholas Kristof, in his desire to raise awareness and to elicit the empathy of American viewers, perpetually searches for individual stories, capable of conveying the collective Congolese trauma. During a quest for such an account of suffering in *Reporter* (2009), Kristof asks, in a dispassionate voice, traumatised groups of Congolese in refugee camps if they know someone who had been killed or had died the night before. Yet, he dismisses their reports of massacred people because they, according to him, cannot be trusted because people subjected to trauma tend to inflate the numbers. Finally, when he discovers the perfect subject for the story, the focus is not on the massacres but the poverty, the disease, the rags, the pain, and the emaciation of the subject. It is about the incapacity of the father to provide medical care for his spouse and daughter, the lack of medical infrastructures, and the infected wound incurred during a fall.

Yet, when one listens carefully to the conversation of the Congolese in Swahili and the film producer over voice comment on the woman, it is not the wound that is responsible for the victim's degeneration, but the rape that she incurred earlier, which derailed her from achieving her economic and social aspirations.[3] Kristof's story of the starvation and the lack of medical treatment of a single woman decentralises "the larger context in which the tragedy occurred" because the rape of the ailing woman is peripheral and the political context absent. Ironically, when

Kristof invokes starvation during an interview with another woman, the woman's response in Swahili suggests hunger is not the natural state of the people of Kivu, for if, as she claims, her husband could just *kuchiruza* (sell), as he did before, and if she could *lima* (cultivate), as she did before, they could both achieve their pre-war happier condition. Kristof's selection of events and emphasis on the starvation of the woman, who barely survives on bananas, ultimately obscures the social and political forces behind the Congolese tragedy and the rape, the primal cause of the woman's health degradation and dehumanisation.

Similarly, Jackson's moving and effective *The Greatest Silence: Rape in Congo* (2007), even as it highlights violence and the rape of Congolese women, also decentralises the larger socio-political conditions of the victims. Although the documentary foregrounds the existence of different militias, the rapes of Congolese women are ultimately committed by rapists within their own army. Other militias are mentioned in the documentary, but the rapists interviewed and boasting about their sexual exploits speak Congolese languages (Swahili and Lingala); the rapes of Congolese women, hence, become a natural cultural behaviour of Congolese soldiers. Indeed, *The Greatest Silence* unfolds with a red sun, a symbol of violence, at dawn. This violence is the result of Congolese soldiers whom Jackson asks to tell her what they did. "I slept with women," claims one of the soldiers and if it was not for the war, according to another, all this violence would not happen. Disguised, the camera focuses on the soldierly figures indicating the numbers of women they had raped. The second display of the soldiers focuses on Jackson's desire to understand the nature of rape. "Is it virility men seek? Is it a quest for power or a disease?" she queries. Following this interview, she fails to sleep for days having understood the nature of sexual terrorism. The third time the soldiers are featured, she wonders how the soldiers can have neither shame nor guilt.

During the last and fourth appearance of the soldiers in an abandoned building, the latter are Lingala speaking Mai-Mai. Interestingly, when one listens attentively to the statements of the Congolese soldiers, who should not be exonerated of their crime, referred to as "drunken," "extorting," "superstitious," the vicious actions are attributed to the Interhamwe, Rwandan soldiers or foreign rebels. Even René Lemarchand, after visiting eastern Congo, confirms that the raped women wearing "vacuous, haggard look[s]" are the result of the Forces Armées de la République Démocratique du Congo (FARDC), the remnants of Rwanda's Hutu génocidaires and their Congolese recruits, "the Forces Democratiques pour la Liberation du Rwanda (FDLR); Rwanda's proxy in North Kivu, General Laurent Nkundabatware (better known as Nkunda) and his Conseil National pour la Défense du Peuple (CNDP), to which must be added a flurry of local militias, the Mai-Mai" (Lemarchand 2008: 2f). These rapes, he contends, are inflicted to "shame the victim, to insult her honour and dignity and thus disqualify her from the sphere of civilized society" (ibid: 3). Moreover, the most brutal rapes, according to doctors interviewed by International Crisis Group (ICG), "appear to have been committed by FDLR, only surpassed in terms of numbers by FARDC soldiers, who are said to have perpetrated 40 per cent of all human rights violations during the second half of 2006" (ibid).

Congolese soldiers' irresponsibility is further highlighted in the film when Bernard Kalume, the interpreter, queries what kind of men could rape women they were supposed to protect. While the soldiers stress the context of war, their sexual desires and their patriotism to justify their rapes of war, which they describe as less heinous than that of Rwandan rebels, their humanity is questioned by the subjective voice-over of the film who repetitively wonders what kind of men would rape women and how these irresponsible soldiers can kill and kidnap their women rather than protect them. "How can one say this is a society of human beings?" asks Jackson, "it is a real jungle." This questioning of the humanity of Congolese men is later reiterated in Kalume's statements when he affirms his humanity and masculinity as protector. The references to rapes in Kabinda and question about Congolese lack of pride in the documentary normalise rape as a cultural-specific practice to Congo. Yet, a woman's comment *"Mulikuwa wa wili na ku chirurikiya batoto"* (You were two to worry about the kids) and the assertion of a woman towards the end of the film contending *"Mu inchi yetu atuna furaha ata banaume"* (In our country we are not happy, even men) confirm the victimisation of both men and women by a political situation they do not control.

Jackson bestows agency on Congolese women in allowing them to speak, yet the fact the rapists, prominently featured in the film four times and on the DVD cover, are Congolese (Mai-Mai, FARDC or Interhamwe, as in Koppel's report) diminishes the horror of these heinous rapes. Whether the rapes are committed by nationalist, sexist or lustful soldiers, the rapes are national-specific or committed by the sullied Interhamwes (those that stand/work/fight/kill together) and thus associated with Congolese culture and Hutu bestiality (affirmed in Metzgar's documentary through Kristof's representation of the young Hutus at Nkunda's as genocidaire). Indeed, Karen A. Ritzenhoff contends these male predators that concealed their identities are, according to Jackson, sexual terrorists that are framed "as animals motivated by instinctual needs" (2010: 135). Moreover, the conclusion of the film, featuring Jackson at her interpreter's home facing the Ruzizi river (separating Kivu from Rwanda), Jackson's evocation of his spouse's death during the Rwandan genocide, the Rwandan song of compassion sung by the interpreter and the latter's assertion he would rather die than see his daughter raped subsume Congolese rapes into the greater horror of the Rwandan genocide.

Congolese activists' and scholars' exclusion from international discursive spaces, producing the meaning of rape and massacres in the Congo, also hinders in-depth knowledge of the real motives and complexities of the war. The voices of Congolese scholars— such as Ambroise Katambu Bulambo (2001), Matabishi J. Ponga (2001), Gaspard Bagalwa Muheme (1999), Sando Kabuya-Lumuna (1997), Charles Djungu-Simba and Laetitia Nsimire Kalimberiro (2003)—never shape and determine the discourse on the Congo. While narratives on global genocides are warmly welcomed and encouraged, the proceedings of a Congolese colloquium organised in Brussels, 3 November 2001, was rejected, according to Djungu-Simba, because the collection used antipodal discourse, supposedly foregrounding a Congolese

hysteria about Congolese identity which is engendered by
eastern Congolese invasions or conflicts. The French publisher
L'Harmattan requested the editors should write two pages
forewarning the readers of their manipulation of the history of
Tutsis "*Pour discréditer le contenu du texte*"[4] (Djungu-Simba/Nsimire
Kalimbiriro 2003: 6f). Other Congolese scholars, who will remain
unnamed, have made similar claims about publishers suppressing
their analyses on the crisis of the Congo when their positions have
questioned accepted Rwandan master narratives. This control of
information in the media or Western discursive spaces is simply
a means to define reality in accordance with a favoured 'political
agenda.' As I contend, quoting Talal Asad, in *When Wounds and
Corpses Fail to Speak: Narratives of Rape and Violence in Congo*, human
rights discourse

> takes its force and meaning relative to structures of international
> policies, of nation states, and of totalizing narratives of
> emancipation in which the human being is redeemed. While it
> may provide useful instruments for mitigating harm (that's when
> we feel good about it) human rights discourse can also serve
> imperializing ventures. (Chiwengo 2008: 79)

COUNTER-INTERSTITIAL VOICES

To understand how political forces have stifled the horrific violence
the Congolese have endured since 1994, one needs to understand
the history of the Congo since the Rwandan genocide. In one
day 14 July 1994 Congo (DRC) welcomed more than one million
Rwandan refugees—and this, not for the first time. In order to
secure its borders and under the supposed threat of a possible
Banyamulenge (Congolese Tutsi) genocide, Rwanda dismantled
in 1997 the Hutu refugee camps in Congo and assisted, in the
name of a democratic revolution, Laurent-Désiré Kabila's Allied
Democratic Forces for the Liberation of Congo (AFDL) in toppling
an ailing Mobutu Sese Seko. To protect its borders, Rwanda
was allowed to occupy land more than a thousand kilometres
beyond its borders. The atrocities—rapes, displacements of
population, assassinations of eastern Congo intellectuals and

the Hutu genocide—remained veiled in silence. Subsequently, Laurent Kabila's Congo was, once again, invaded by discontented *Banyamulenge*. Since then the Congo has gone through numerous agreements (Lusaka, Sun City, Pretoria and Luanda Accords), and Nkundabatware, one of the main rebels to have committed atrocities in eastern Congo (protected by Rwanda), was arrested. Other unsuccessful joint activities—Kimia I and II and Amani Leo—subsequently followed. Women, girls and babies continue to be raped and the population in eastern Congo to be massacred and displaced in post-election Congo. Apparently, rapes of women and men have become the best means to accede to power, for they ensure the perpetrators' combat prowess, international political visibility, access to minerals and clout rather than shame and vilification.

Referring to the fact that rapes of women have been primarily attributed to Congolese males and army, Lisa Shannon (2010) is compelled to defend Congolese men and to contest the assumption that these rapes are of a cultural nature. Indeed, the non-specific cultural nature of the rapes of Congolese women is nowhere more apparent than in its perpetuation on the bodies of boys and men, which are only recently getting more coverage. Lisa Gambone states, in *A Terrible New Aspect of DRC War Crimes*,

> The increase of rape against men in a society where such traditional gender roles exist heavily underscores the fact that sexual violence in this context is not a random act—it is being used as a weapon of war by armed groups to force certain communities into submission. (Gambone 2009)

Jeffrey Gettleman (2009) also notes a spike in violence following Congo-Rwanda operations when ten per cent of male rapes occurred in June 2009. Because homosexuality is taboo in Congo, male rape has not been accurately reported; its very existence confirms, as male aid workers attest, "sexual violence against men is yet another way for armed groups to humiliate and demoralize Congolese communities into submission."

Careful examinations of the literature and reports on rapes in Congo reveal Congolese women's assertions about the identities of their rapists are not always believed. Among the numerous militias cited for committing rapes, Rwandan Tutsi soldiers, cited by Congolese women, are less likely to be mentioned until recently. But it is no longer a secret that Rwanda is heavily implicated in the conflict in Eastern Congo, as well as the Ugandan rebel group The Lord's Resistance Army in Upper-Uwele, where women have been literally silenced through the cutting of their lips. Moreover, the numerous integrations of rebel armies since 1997 into the national army has weakened and contaminated the Congolese army. This integration explains why the infiltrated and corrupt Congolese army refutes human rights accusations of Rwandan violence and rapes even when it is the accused Rwanda which should prove its innocence and this even when Dr. Denis Mukwege—the director of the General Hospital of reference/ médecin directeur de l'Hôpital Général de Référence/Panzi, quoted by Tshieke Bukasa—affirms, in the CEPAS report, that he has treated 30,000 rape victims. According to him, 80 per cent of women had been raped by armies speaking a foreign language, while only 5 per cent of women had been assaulted by speakers of local languages (Bukasa 2009: 6).

The discourse on the rapes of Congolese women can no longer be framed solely in terms of Congolese culture and laws. To have sustained peace and to protect the Congolese women, Rwanda, Uganda and all other international parties, such as Angola and Burundi, need to be made accountable. Peace has supposedly come to Congo, yet Congolese women continue to be the economic and political battlefield for minerals. They continue to die and to have their bodies defiled, yet Congolese are asked, by the international community, to forget while Rwanda, which advocates forgiveness, continues to avenge itself and spill blood on Congolese soil and import Congolese minerals. The Congolese that dare look to the past are marginalised and those that look towards the future are compensated and given the privilege to work with the international community. Would America, Paris or London forget the babies pounded in mortars, the mothers forced to sleep with their sons and eat their children? Would they forget the woman who had petrol poured in her vagina and set on fire?

Should the Congolese forget the women shot in their vaginas, stabbed with sticks, burned, women forced to sleep with their sons, sons forced to eat their mother's flesh, raped boys and babies, and fathers raped in front of their sons? Can Congolese forget when little children sing "*Naliya Congo Yetu*" (I cry for our Congo)? Should adults forget when little girls dream of becoming future presidents of the Congo, so they can inflict pain on those that have brought upon the Congolese so much suffering? Do they have the luxury to forget when even visionary African writers, such as Boris Diop suggest, in an interview with Lilyan Kesteloot-Fongang, the solution to the Rwandan ethnic crisis would be to "give Rwanda a part of Kivu where they could be settled" (Kesteloot-Fongang 2002: 731).

CONCLUDING REMARKS

If peace is to come to the Congo and if the Congo is to live in peace with its neighbours, if Congolese women are to regain their dignity and right to life, Congo must be given justice. It is good that Congo has a new zero tolerance law on rape; it's good that the international community is pressuring the Congo to punish perpetuators of war crimes and that the Hutu massacres have been acknowledged through *The DRC Mapping Report* (United Nations Human Right, Office of the Commissioner for Human Rights 2010), and the ICC in The Hague has found Thomas Lubanga guilty, but justice cannot be selective. The United Nations peacekeepers have not been brought to trial for raping girls, taking pornographic pictures of children and other crimes of paedophilia. So far, no hearings have been scheduled in their respective countries despite the promises made. The Congo and Congolese women's bodies can be cleansed and new inscriptions written on their bodies only when Nkudabatware and Bosco Ntaganda are also brought to trial and not respectively rewarded with a comfortable Rwanda arrest and promotion. Ethnic selectivity and international guilt about the Rwanda genocide must cease. Congo has numerous minority ethnic groups, which have not and do not have access to political and economic power.

Consequently, the genocidal framing of the Congolese crisis should not determine the welfare of a nation because Congo borders nine countries with ethnic groups overlapping on all these different borders; Kivu alone has a multiplicity of ethnic groups which intend to work and live together (Republique Democratique du Congo La Communauté Tutsi du Nord Kivu 2012).

Justice for women in the Congo and for Congo is possible when Congolese women and Congo become central, and not appendages of other nations' economic and political agendas. Congolese female bodies need not be mutilated, assaulted and violated so multinational companies, African and national greedy business people can exploit minerals without constrictions, and neighbouring countries can strengthen their economies and develop their countries. Congolese women, on whose bodies the international community's genocide guilt and Congolese and international communities' greed and will to power have inscribed their will to destroy the fabric of Congolese society and nation, must rewrite the future of the country because they are the backbone of the Congolese economy, family and nation. To do so, women and the Congo nation need integral national and international scholars and journalists willing to pursue the truth, and not certain truths, a national and an international community willing to invest in Congo with the understanding that Congolese minerals are foremost for its citizens and to be shared with other nations. The Congo, therefore, needs just regulations for mineral contracts, and not mere cosmetic agreements, and protection for children. It needs a national conversation on rape and, with the assistance of its international partners, a strong republican army to ensure the security and respect of its people, territorial integrity and sovereignty.

Congo also needs objective analyses of the situation in the 'Great Lake Region' and foremost a real International Criminal Tribunal on rape and other war atrocities, and not a special tribune within the Congolese judicial system. Perhaps, by doing so, it will become apparent Congolese female rape victims are not concocting stories and Interhamwes, Mai-Mais and the National Congolese army (FARDC) are not the only

COUNTER-INTERSTITIAL VOICES 373

militia groups inflicting vicious mutilations, but rather, as Lieve Joris notes in *The Rebel's Hour*, every time a Munyamulenge rebel passed away the rebels "held his story up to the light and appropriated whatever suited them," for they were people "engaged in mythology" (2006: xix).

The current rape of women in the Congo will have tragic results for decades. External help and compassion is good, needed and to be praised, yet for the trauma of the population to be healed, women in Congo must carry their burden, learn to engage in a national conversation, and educate themselves, men, boys and girls on the value of women and the evils of rape. Congolese women can heal not through temporary and occasional assistance, but through sustained and long-term projects that include women in rural sustained development and integrate, economically and politically, the Congolese female within her society. Feminism in the Congo—since the era of the fathers of Independence and the post-independence leaders, Lumumba, Mobutu and Kabila— has been a male project in their political agendas. Consequently, women in Congo must appropriate the feminist discourse of the country if they are to shape and name their future and identities. Women in Congo must learn to be participants and not mere receivers. The road is long and onerous, but the shattered Congo, once again whole, can place the Congolese female, full of dignity and pride, at the centre of the Congolese nation. The genocidal rapes of Congo—committed on female and male bodies, affirming the masculine militarisation of all groups and the sterilisation of Congo women through rapes, mutilations and fistulas, consequently maiming the national body through the destruction of the social fabric—must be recognised as war crimes, so Congolese women can write, on their bodies, new messages of hope, women's right to life and self-determination in an undivided Congo where there is liberty and justice for all.

The films and reports examined demonstrate the imperative for NGOs, human rights activists and reporters to become more aware of their racialised and politicised positions when telling the stories of victimisation of others and the Congo. They need to be more aware of their complicity in the dissemination of stereotypes, tropes and omissions, or their silence. All perpetrators of crimes and violence must be made accountable and not only specific groups of people.

The Congolese woman, on the other hand, needs to own the public discursive space. To become an agent, she needs to contest the numerous identities, constructed for her by the *évolués*,[5] the colonial state, the Mobutu era and the international community, through conversations about rape and her identity with other Congolese women and the society-at-large. The international community should, as in the case of *Fest'Africa Rwanda: Écrire par devoir de mémoire* (Writing out of duty towards memory)[6], give Congolese women and scholars access to the international discursive space. It is time for Congo women to speak and not always be spoken about and for, so it is time for the American media to give her access to its public forum, so she can speak, and not be represented or presenting pre-packaged scripts. It is time for the Congolese women to define their diverse identities, invented and refashioned since colonialism, and role within Congolese society, not only through internationally imposed gender programs and laws, but also through her appropriation of the public space through an educational reform that provides textbooks that cease to propagate negative and subservient images of women and the revision of high school and higher education curricula that integrates gender. It is time to educate women and create Women Studies departments and centres and not only postcolonial *'foyer sociaux.'* It is time for Congolese music and literature to project positive images of Congolese women by emphasizing less the body and reflecting the diverse status of and achievements of Congolese women. It is also time for the religious establishment, which has failed to fight strongly for Congo women, to cease propagating the subjection of women and their lack of control over their bodies. But foremost, it is time Congo is perceived as a sovereign nation without the trope of darkness and Congolese women as women and not backward others to be brought into modernity.

NOTES

1. *Congkazi*: Congo Women Association is an organisation that advocates against rape and seeks to develop Congolese women and children professionally, technologically and individually.
2. Jaynet spoke at the PGA conference as the president of the M'zee Laurent Desire Kabila Foundation and the Union of Women of Congo (DRC). This conference brought national and international parliamentarians together to find means to bring peace and justice to central Africa.
3. Indeed, she fell ill to wounds on her posterior, but the consequences of her illness are due the fact she lacked money. "She was raped by soldiers. Because she was raped no one wanted to marry her. She was a teacher in South Kivu, when she returned she had the money she had earned at the time. She hired people to cultivate her fields but soldiers pillaged her fields." Eric Metzgar is surprised to hear she did live in abject poverty, but "on the contrary, she had a plan. At one point her life had a direction."
4. Rene Lemarchand's much revised and updated article, 'Reflections on the Crisis in Eastern Congo' (2009), has omitted this information.
5. This term refers to the elite educated or supposedly 'civilised' Congolese during Belgian colonisation.
6. This project brought together established African writers after the 1994 Rwandan genocide in order to write about the genocide.

REFERENCES

Autesserre, Séverine. 2010. *The Trouble with the Congo*. New York: Cambridge University Press.

Bukasa, Tshieke. 2009. 'Le cri de cœur des "Shi"', *Le phare* (Kinshasa), 17 November.

Bulambo, Ambroise Katambu. 2001. *Mourir au Kivu: Du génocide tutsi aux massacres dans l'Est du Congo-RDC*. Paris/Kinshasa: L'Harmattan-Éditions du Trottoir.

Centre d'Etudes pour l'Action Sociale (CEPAS). 2009. *Rapport de la Conférence sur les Violences Sexuelles faites aux femmes et aux enfants à L'Est de RDC (Novembre 2009)*. Kinshasa: N.D.

Chiwengo, Ngwarsungu. 2008. 'When Wounds and Corpses Fail to Speak: Narratives of Violence and Rape in Congo (DRC)', *Comparative Studies of South Asia, Africa, and the Middle East*, 28(1):78–92.

Clinton, Hillary Rodham. 2009. 'Town Hall with Search for Common Ground and Congolese University Students', *U. S. Department of State,* 10 August. http://www.sfcg.org/articles/hillary-clinton-town-hall-with-sfcg.pdf (accessed 4 June 2018).

Cobb, Charles Jr. 2001. 'Central Africa: "Heart of Darkness"-Interview with Nightline's Executive Producer', *All Africa,* 9 September. http://allafrica.com/stories/200109090023.html (accessed 15 October 2018).

Conrad, Joseph. 1981. *The Heart of Darkness.* New York: Bantam Books.

Djungu-Simba K, Charles/Nsimire Kalimbiriro, Laetitia (eds). 2003. *Grands Lacs d'Afrique: Culture de paix vs Culture de violences.* Huy: Les Éditions du Pangolin.

Donovan, Josephine. 2008. *Feminist Theory.* New York: Continuum.

Dunn, Kevin. 2003. *Imaging the Congo: The International Relations of identity.* New York: Palgrave Macmillan.

Gambone, Lisa. 2009. 'A Terrible New Aspect of DRC War Crimes', *Foreign Policy Association,* 5 August. http://foreignpolicyblogs.com/2009/08/05/a-terrible-new-aspect-of-drc-war-crimes/ (accessed 15 Ocotber 2018).

Gettleman, Jeffrey. 2009. 'Symbol of Unhealed Congo: Male Rape Victims', *New York Times,* 4 August. http://www.nytimes.com/2009/08/05/world/africa/05congo.html (accessed 15 October 2018).

Great Lakes Voice. 2011. 'Eleven DR Congo Soldiers Facing "Mobile Gender Court" on Mass Rape'. http://greatlakesvoice.com/11-fardc-soldiers-facing-%E2%80%98gender-mobile-court%E2%80%99-on-mass-rape/ (accessed 8 October 2018).

The Greatest Silence: Rape in the Congo. 2007. [Documentary]. Lisa F. Jackson. dir. USA: Women for Women.

Hentz, Jennifer M. 2002. 'The Impact of HIV on the Rape Crisis in the African Great Lakes Region', *Human Rights Brief,* 12(2):12–5.

Human Rights Watch. 2002. *The War within the War: Sexual Violence against Women and Girls in Eastern Congo.* New York: Human Rights Watch.

Joris, Lieve. 2006. *The Rebels' Hour.* New York: Grove Press.

Kabila, Joseph. 2006. 'Congo President on Military Rapes: "Unforgivable" (interviewed by Jeff Coinage)', *CNN International,* 1 June. http://edition.cnn.com/2006/WORLD/africa/05/31/congo.rape/index.html (accessed 08 October 2018).

Kabuya-Lumuna, Sando. 1997. *Conflits de l'Est du Zaïre : Repères et Enjeux.* Kinshasa: Éditions SECCO.

Kesteloot-Fongang, Lilyan. 2002. 'Entretien avec Boubakar Boris Diop, Ecrivain Senegalais Marque par le Genocidaire Rwandais', in Marc Quaghebeur/ Jean-Claude Kangomba/Amélie Schmitz (eds), *Figures et Paradoxes de l'Histoire au Burundi et au Rwanda,* Vol 2, pp. 728–33. Paris: L'Harmattan.

Lemarchand, René. 2009. 'Reflections on the Crisis in Eastern Congo', *Brown Journal of World Affairs,* 16(1):119–32.

————. 2008. 'Reflections on the Crisis in Eastern Congo', *Wilson Center, University of Florida.* http://www.wilsoncenter.org/sites/default/files/lemarchand%20article.pdf (accessed 13 October 2018).

Mechanic, Eli. 2004. 'The Intersection between Men, Masculinities and Rape in the Democratic Republic of Congo', *Partnership Africa Canada Dialogue,* 1(2).

Morrison, Toni. 1972. *The Bluest Eye.* New York: Washington Square Press.

Mota, Maria Mossi/Duarte, Mariana. 2006. 'Violence against Women in the Democratic Republic of the Congo', *World Organization against Torture.* http://www.omct.org/files/2005/09/3072/cedaw36_ drc_en.pdf (accessed 15 October 2018).

Muheme, Gaspard Bagalwa. 1999. *Ces guerres imposées au Kivu: Intérêts économiques ou management social?* Louvain-la-Neuve: Bruylant-Academia.

The New World Encyclopedia [Online] 2008. *African Great Lakes.* http://www.newworldencyclopedia.org/entry/African_Great_Lakes (accessed 15 October 2018).

Nzuzi, Daniel. 2009. 'Jaynet Kabila partage son expertise de la tragédie des violences séxuelles à la conférence parlémenatire PGA sur la justice et la paix', *Parliamentarians for Global Action,* 12 December. http://www.pgaction.org/pdf/pre/Resultats%20PGA%20Conference%20Kinshasa%20FR.pdf (accessed 18 October 2018).

Ponga, Matabishi J. 2001. *Reflexe identitaire et ethnocentrisme tutsi en République Démocratique du Congo.* Lubumbashi: Éditions LEBE.

Reporter: A Film about Nicholas Kristof. 2009. [Report] Eric Metzgar. dir. USA: Merigold Moving Pictures.

Republique Democratique du Congo La Communauté Tutsi du Nord Kivu. 2012. 'Menaces de la communauté Tutsi si Bosco Ntaganda est conduit à la CPI', *Beni Lubero,* 15 March. http://benilubero.

378   NGWARSUNGU CHIWENGO

com/menaces-de-la-communaute-tutsi-si-bosco-ntaganda-est-
conduit-a-la-cpi/ (accessed 5 July 2018).
Ritzenhoff, Karen A. 2010. 'The Greatest Silence: Rape in Congo
(DRC). Directed by Lisa F. Jackson. Distributed by Women Make
Movies. 76 min, subtitled', *Film and History: An Interdisciplinary
Journal of Film and Television Studies*, 40(2):134–6.
Schaffer, Kay/Smith, Sidonie. 2004. *Human Rights and Narrated Lives:
The Ethics of Recognition*. New York: Palgrave MacMillan.
Seifert, Ruth. 1993. *War and Rape: Analytical Approaches*. Geneva: Women's
International League for Peace and Freedom (WILPF).
Shannon, Lisa. 2010. 'No, Sexual Violence is Not "Cultural"', *The
New York Times, The Opinion Pages*, 25 June. http://www.nytimes.
com/2010/06/26/opinion/26iht-edshannon.html (accessed 15
October 2018).
*Still the Heart of Darkness: The Killing in the Congo (Part 1, War in Congo: An
Overview, and Part 2, The Curse of Congo: A Story of Wealth, Exploitation,
and Ruin)*. 2003. [Report] Ted Koppel. prod. Princeton: Films for
the Humanities and Sciences.
United Nations High Commissioner for Human Rights. 2011. 'Report
of the Panel on Remedies and Reparations for Victims of Sexual
Violence in the Democratic Republic of the Congo', *United Nations
Human Rights Office of the High Commissioner for Human Rights*, 3 March.
United Nations Human Rights Office of the Commissioner for Human
Rights. 2010. *Democratic Republic of Congo, 1993–2003: Report of the
Mapping Exercise Documenting the Most Serious Violations of Human Rights
and International Humanitarian Law Committed within the Territory of the
Democratic Republic of the Congo between March 1993 and June 2003*.
New York: United Nations.
Vogel, Gretchen. 2000. 'Conflict in Congo Threatens Bonobos and Rare
Gorillas', *Science*, 287(5462):2386–87.
Whitlock, Gillian. 2010. 'Remediating Gorilla Girl: Rape Warfare and
the Limits of Storytelling', *Biography: An Interdisciplinary Quarterly*,
33(3):471–97.
Zve, Elud Ban. 2009. *A Palimpsest: Rhetoric, Ideology, Stylistics, and Language
Relating to Persian Israel*. Piscataway: Gorgias Press.

Finding the 'Map of Memory': Testimony of the Survivors of Military Sexual Slavery by Japan

HYUNAH YANG

In following postcolonial theorist Dipesh Chakrabarty (1992), I begin with a question: Who speaks for the Korean past?[1] In particular, who speaks for the Korean history of the Japanese military sexual slavery system? I raise these questions because certain positions seem to be absent in the writing of Asia's history during the period of colonialism and the Pacific war. The problem is not only that certain categorical positions are absent, such as those of a particular class, gender, nationality or sexuality, but also the absence of certain viewpoints and methods to represent them. In this essay, I try to address the subject of the women survivors of Japanese military sexual slavery through the representation of their testimony. If the 'comfort women' of Japanese sexual slavery has never attained a speaking subject on the history at both regional and global levels, searching for the methods of representing their testimony and voice will be the very issues that matter. This essay is about the method, ethics and, ultimately, epistemology of representing the numerous and nameless subjects that have been called 'Japanese military comfort women' (hereafter, emphasis omitted).[2]

Relatively widely known as the Japanese military comfort women system, the Japanese sexual slavery system operated, for the most part, during the period of the Manchurian and Pacific wars, from 1932 to 1945. The system was planned and implemented for the sexual satiation of Japanese male soldiers through the enslavement of women from Korea, China, Japan, Taiwan, Indonesia, the Philippines and beyond. Enslaved comfort women were brought to comfort stations throughout the vast region in which the Japanese imperial army fought for the Greater East Asia Co-Prosperity Sphere, which spanned East and South Asia as well as the South Pacific islands.[3] In the case of Korean recruitment, enslaved women were mostly teenagers, drafted via force, fraud and other means of menace; their total numbers are estimated to have been between 100,000 and 200,000, making Koreans the most numerous victims. Once installed in the comfort stations, the women were raped by dozens of Japanese soldiers each day; in some cases, this continued for years.

It was not until the late 1980s that the truth about this unthinkable system and its horrific and yet unpunished crimes began to surface. Although since then even basic information about the comfort system has been contested, at the moment the first survivor spoke out to say and recognise that 'I am a former comfort woman,' a new epoch opened in writing colonial history and perhaps in realising justice for these women. When the first self-identified Korean survivor, Kim Hak Soon, said, "I have wanted to speak [about] this experience," it was a deconstructive moment in the functioning of comfort women as a trope of shame and secrecy in Korean history (Testimony Book 1: 44). Whose shame and secrecy have enveloped the subjectivity of this woman? How can we understand our unpreparedness for this revelation, the 'opaque' in our knowledge?[4]

If 'sati' designates a metaphor for physical and epistemic violence against women in India, the enslavement of comfort women symbol 'ises' the violence against women in colonial Asia that has been unspoken (Mani 1990; Spivak 1988). With the goal of constructing a counter discourse of nationalist historiography, the postcolonial theorists turned to the subaltern, a figure that was never subsumed into the symbols and imagination of the political elite (Guha 1982; Spivak 1985). Although the notion of the subaltern critically reveals the homogeneity and elite-centeredness of nationalist history, the desire to preserve subalternity could easily be trapped in a logic of objectification. Examining the notion of 'will' as an index of subaltern consciousness, Spivak contends that "the texts of counter-insurgency locate [...] a 'will' as the sovereign cause where it is no more than an effect of the subaltern subject-effect" (Spivak 1985: 335). In this light, the subaltern is neither a demographic category nor a designative social grouping. Rather, it is a sign of the impossibility of the colonial state's hegemonic domination, of representing its people in the imagination of nationalist history-telling.

As such, the implication of the subaltern is a theoretical as well as a methodological one. The method of 'speaking' with the subaltern could not but be from below, but it differs from dominant approaches that assume the existence of an unmediated, uncontaminated 'pure voice' as such. Indeed, the very notion of pure voice is a better fit with loaded expectations of the purity of third world women (Mohanty 1991). In the sections that follow, I engage with these methodological questions by detailing our research as a testimonial team to document the testimony of surviving comfort women.

BREAKING AMNESIA AND FRAMING THE ISSUE

Testimonial research on the victims of the former Japanese Military comfort women in South Korea began as early as 1993, when the first survivor-victim broke her silence. Testimony books have subsequently been compiled through the tenacious efforts of researchers and activists.[5] Largely thanks to this work, the issue of the sexual enslavement of comfort women has been made public in Korean civil society, as well as in international policy forums such as the U.N. Commission on Human Rights, the International Labour Organisation, the International Court of Justice and foreign legislatures.

As such, survivor-victims' testimony has been the main force in breaking the long silence surrounding this atrocity. The silence itself, in a sense, constitutes the very nature of this issue and reflects the multi-layered power relationships in East Asia. Massive violence against women in Asia was barely recognised at the military tribunal conducted by the Allied forces after World

War II. Nor was it acknowledged when diplomatic relations normalised between Korea and Japan with bilateral treaty after decolonisation in 1965. The Korean government and political leaders turned a blind eye to the issue and to individual survivors until well into the 1990s.

The Japanese government has denied responsibility in committing such violence against women.[6] The Japanese government kept the official military and government documents classified and concealed, even going so far as to intentionally destroy some of them; many of the personnel involved in the system of military sexual slavery have died. Additionally, the norms regarding women's chastity in South Korean patriarchal culture have made it difficult for survivor-victims to speak out. A vicious cycle is perpetuated, even accentuated: in the gaze of patriarchal society, the tendency is to blame and to stigmatise the victim herself in cases of sexual violence, wherein the perpetrator remains unidentified. The agony of comfort women has been intensified, as the women were regarded as the ones to be punished for being 'contaminated' by the foreign men.[7] As such, doing testimonial work around this issue was tantamount to a struggle with prevailing historical amnesia and stigma inscribed on the women.

This essay was not written during the time of silence, but rather at the stage of post-silence. If we take this 'post' to mean, as it often does, an overlapping, a postponing, and some discontinuation from the prior, then the method of how to hear—that is, how to intervene in and undo existing methods of representation—is critical. Survivors' testimonies were assumed within the collectivity known as the 'Korean people.' Their testimony has been cited as proof of the pain and agony of the Korean people rather than the victim herself.

The Korean nationalist appropriation of these women as if they were the cultural property of the nation-state has been criticised by feminist scholars who engage with this issue, especially the transnational feminist scholars who claim the need to move beyond the national imagination.[8] Can transnational feminist interpretation of the issue, however, be a precise prism for understanding the issue and the victims' subjectivity? Although the comfort women as a group do not fit neatly within the pre-existing boundary of national history (that itself is ultimately based on the nation-state as a political entity), this does not mean that the ethnic group Chonsenjin (meaning Korean, at that time) was irrelevant in the execution of the sexual slavery system; belonging to the Korean ethnic group has been highly relevant to the subjects' claims around this issue. Furthermore, since the nation-state of Korea that succeeded colonial rule (1910–45) based its sovereignty on ruling the people of the Korean ethnic group, the Korean state has both the responsibility and the right to represent the human rights violations of that ethnic group during colonial rule. In this context, sole reliance on transnational feminism could render the category of ethnicity obsolete and the responsibility of the Japanese state obscure. In this light, both nationalist and transnationalist discourse needs to be reconfigured in engagement with this complex terrain, including with such gender- and ethnicity-based atrocities.

THE '2000 TRIBUNAL' AND THE TESTIMONY TEAM

It was in April 1999 that we first gathered and named ourselves a 'testimony team'.[9] This team was formed in conjunction with 'The Women's International War Crimes Tribunal 2000 for the Trial of Japanese Military Sexual Slavery' (hereafter '2000 Tribunal') that was held in Tokyo, Japan, 08–12 December 2000. Seeking to end the cycle of impunity of violence against women that occurred as part of the Japanese sexual slavery system, activists, researchers and lawyers from various parts of Asia gathered in Tokyo for the tribunal.[10] Delegates from North and South Korea, China, Taiwan, Indonesia, the Philippines, Malaysia, Netherlands, East Timor and Japan represented the victims as well as their respective countries.[11] Though the tribunal did not have power to enforce its judgments, it nonetheless carried moral authority in demanding the acceptance and enforcement of its findings and recommendations by the international community.[12]

The tribunal was unprecedented in its scope, encompassing

the various Asian countries and regions that were colonised, ruled under military occupation or otherwise victimised by Japan before and during World War II. It extended and surpassed the International Military Tribunal for the Far East that had been conducted by the Allied forces following the end of the war, which scarcely prosecuted Japan's military sexual slavery and other cases of sexual violence as war crimes.[13] The '2000 tribunal' was prepared within a context of increasing international attention to the issue of violence against women, as evidenced by the U.N. adoption of the Declaration on the Elimination of Violence against Women in 1993 and the adoption of the Beijing Platform of Action at the Fourth World Conference on Women in 1995.[14] After one year's deliberation following the tribunal, the final judgment was made in December 2001 that many of the accused individuals, including Japanese emperor Hirohito, as well as the Japanese state were liable for criminal responsibility for crimes against humanity committed through the system of sexual slavery.[15]

The testimony team was originally asked to produce supporting material to prove the damages inflicted on the former military comfort women. The evidence that the testimony team gathered, however, went far beyond the requirements of the legal context, spilling over into the spaces of history, postcolonial Korean state, subaltern subjectivity and third world feminism. However, it was fortunate that the testimonial works could substantiate the crimes committed against the women, such that the tribunal and the law were the formative forces in shaping memory and history. The Korean prosecutors team at the '2000 tribunal', found that while valuable, preexisting human rights conventions and customs, their legal idioms and reasoning, were sometimes insufficient to represent the atrocities inflicted on the victims in the former Japanese colony. The goals of our testimonial work were thus twofold: provide data on the crimes with which the tribunal could prepare an indictment, and publish a book of testimony in which survivors' testimonies could be more fully represented. The question of method discussed in this essay is largely based on our work on the Testimony Book, volume 4.

SPACE OF SILENCE AND JUSTICE

I have questioned the positivist attitude in studying comfort women's testimony, wherein the position of the women was restricted to that of 'informant,' while 'experts,' such as historians and writers, set the framework in which the women's testimonies were distributed and decoded (Yang 1997). This attitude affected the methods of listening to the testimony. The gaze of scholars and writers fell on the subaltern women from the outside, while the women themselves were deprived of any authorship regarding terms and concepts in representing the sexual slavery system and were rendered passive recipients of the final text. Particularly in the context of politics and law, survivors' testimony has been a field of contested truth.[16]

Dori Laub argues that the victim's narrative begins with a speaker who testifies to an absence, to an event that has not yet occurred (Laub 1992). The listener, then, is party to the creation of knowledge de novo. Storytelling itself is an event, the result of a conversation. In the case of Korean comfort women, the formative nature of the testimonial process was even more so. Due to the passage of time as well as their own social position, most survivors were unable to offer exact details about their servitude. Regarding the person who recruited them, survivors often referred to 'a man with military clothing' or 'a local officer' (yijang), for example, rather than detailing precise rank, status or name. Likewise, they have only vague information regarding the place where they were taken, such as 'somewhere in Manchuria' or 'a Chinese area adjacent to Russia,' typically offering only the name of the region and country at best. Inconsistent memory raised other problems. Once a survivor-victim testified that she had been mobilised as a comfort woman, she might, for example, later say that she had worked at a textile factory. Although such inconsistency could be corrected through follow-up studies, survivors' fragmented memory perplexed the researchers.

Although memory is not perfect, we found that the real flaws lay with the doubtful reception of the listeners and the wider society. A survivor's absent or unclear memory springs not so much from their weak memory or under-education as from an inability to access certain information. Survivor-victims had never been in a position to look at the context, system or map of the institution of sexual slavery, nor had they been privy to the knowledge that had been generated about it. Most had been drafted into the sexual slavery system through fraud, lies and threats, and had never been informed where they were going. Rather, the victims existed in a state of surveillance and control, as their conditions of confinement and secrecy became even harsher after they arrived at the comfort station. It is therefore the very situation in which a captive is asked to identify the facts of the circumstances under which she was enslaved, and this very information control constitute a critical element of the crime of enslavement.

Of course, passage of time was also a hindrance in recollection, because the survivors were being asked to remember details from events that had occurred some sixty or seventy years ago; most of them had been mobilised between 1932 and 1945. Forgetting detail is a destiny of human memory, although certain critical experiences are stamped on memory with surprising sharpness. A more important aspect of survivors' ability to recall events was the total absence of opportunities to speak about the experience and express themselves during the past fifty years. Most survivors were drafted into sexual slavery in their teens, usually between the ages of thirteen and sixteen. Since that time, they had never been asked to talk openly about the experience or encouraged to inquire about it, and no one had explained to them the reasons for what they had been through.

Without any public recognition, the nature of what had happened to them, the experiences became obscure even to the survivors. Was it rape or forced prostitution or enforced collaboration that the comfort women experienced?[17] Under which system exactly had they been drafted? Toward whom should the women justly feel anger? I interpret that this impasse precisely marks the postcolonial knowledge condition in conjunction with that of impunity of the grave violation of the human rights. It is an amnesia, but one that does not exactly mean forgetting; rather, it signifies the collective condition of a group that does not know what has been forgotten. Given that this amnesia was encouraged, it is a wonder that survivors have retained any memory of it at all. The testimony that survivor-victims were able to give was indeed the light that shone on this amnesic terrain.

EXPRESSING THE INEXPRESSIBLE

In most existing interviews, the details of a survivor-victim's experience of rape at the comfort station—for instance, how many soldiers came to her each day, how they treated her and how she resisted them—seemed to be located at the centre of her testimony. These details formed a kind of narrative apex, such that someone reading the testimony might get the impression that the survivor's voice sounds louder at this point, as if she is accusing the rapists. The most perplexing site of silence during interviews that our team conducted also surrounded the same experience. Most survivors that we interviewed chose a narrative style that I call mixed silence, in which silence and verbal expression alternate, producing meaning through their synthesis. Here I introduce some of these testimonies. They have been translated into English, so readers must bear in mind the distance of written English from oral and vernacular Korean.[18] The following is testimony from Han Oksun.[19]

> Until I left Taewon (a region in China), I had not allowed my body to be used sexually, so I was battered a lot. When I left there, I began to ... there was no way other than, I could no more stand the battering, with no reason, in the soil where three thousand miles away from home, there was no one to listen to me, no way other than that. I began to receive ... *with force really, with force really, with battering*. I had no way, my body was stolen, but I do not put the number, how many [of the soldiers] in my head. ... Now I forget these things that happened such a long time ago. Then, I moved to another place. (Bursts into tears.) (Testimony Book 4: 78; emphasis mine)

In Han's testimony, the experience of rape was both expressed and unexpressed. In between the incomplete sentences and underneath the language, unexpressed and inexpressible feeling and memory permeated. Rather than listening literally to this survivor-victim's vague memory and shame, the testimony team sensed the message it carried. In the language we listened to the sound of silence, and in the silence we heard the unspoken story.

I found that the survivors' stories overlapped with the realm of the 'unpresentable,' so that the very framing of the event had to be built from the stories, not from the pre-existing legal and discursive framing (Lyotard 1994). The notion of unpresentability extended our imagination and pushed us beyond the sphere of the already existing schema of truth. Lynn Huffer, for instance, in discussing Lyotard's *differend* and its connotation with law, problematises the limits of the law's idioms in light of linguistic incommensurability (Huffer 2006; Lyotard 1988). Pointing to the feeling and emotion that permeated the words of a sexual violence victim, who was unable to defend herself in front of a jury, Huffer reminds us of Lyotard's notion of the affect phrase (Huffer 2006: 18).

The attention to affect led us to be aware of the variety and richness (yet separateness) of verbal as well as nonverbal expressions in the testimony of former comfort women—facial and bodily expressions such as sighs and tears—as well as signs of alarm, thrill and laughter. Even the linguistic expression was often not grammatically easy to follow; inversion, interjection and unknown vernacular were frequently used, along with foreign words in Japanese and Chinese. Our team did not discard such expressions but tried to remember and record every sign of orality and physicality: non-verbal expressions, strange expressions and the rhythm, tone and style of each woman's narrative. We did this not to preserve a so-called pure and vivid voice but because it was through such expressions that readers of the testimony, including our own team members, could feel each narrator's spirit, her subjectivity so that sympathy and dialogue could begin in the witnessing community.

In her testimony, Ahn Bopsoon used evasion as a strategy for expressing the inexpressible:

> Yes, I was bold and strong [at that time, but] even to me, I was scared and intimidated, how could it not be intimidating, ah?

[Eating a peach with listener-interviewers.] Oh, this is sweet, very delicious. I think, is it a thing that a human being could not stand, a human being? When one marries a man, [he can] be scary [to the bride], even to a woman in her twenties or thirties. ... I was seventeen [at the comfort station], I was a child, what else? Have this (offers the peach), these are so sweet! (Testimony Book 4: 244)

This was the only moment, though it was very brief, when Ahn touched on the experience of being raped. We could not use the word rape in our discussions, however, since rape was not and still is not a word that survivor-victims use to describe their experience. This evasion of the word rape reflects the terrain of (women's) sexuality in Korea, in which women's passivity in sexual relations is the norm, though ironically any legally sanctioned intercourse also presupposes the woman's cooperation. Thus women's only and utmost agency in sexuality would be resistance to a man with whom she does not want to have a sexual relation, expressed through extreme passivity and not wanting.

Interestingly, both victims and listeners relied on and used a discursive layer of affect when discussing these events. The listener-interviewers would ask a purposely vague question such as 'what happened at the comfort station?' or 'how did you feel about/remember what happened?' In response, the women often used the expression of 'receiving [*padatta*] the soldiers' or would state, 'I was attacked [*danghetta*] by the soldiers.' In neither case do the words specifically point to rape. The concept of receiving is especially important, since this verb can also be used in the case of receiving a guest, for example, as if the woman were a sexual 'servant'. While *danghetta* is a more active expression to make the sexual inflection more explicit, this word is not equivalent to rape.

The lack of proper words for rape—the very core of the sexual slavery system's crime—coincided with the lack of historical acknowledgement of this issue for half a century. The word 'receiving' strangely made women feel guilty, and this unexplained guilty feeling is the very site around which justice ought to be brought. In the testimonies presented above, the alternating spaces of silence and sound mark an affect phrase that can be linked to certain messages and perhaps converted into a reasonable story of what occurred. The mission of our testimonial work is to establish some linkage between many unmediated gaps: between law and history; factual proof and the affect; the history of the elite and that of the subaltern; global and local feminism; trauma and the spirit. Experimentally and dangerously, we pursued the balance between them; in a word, between Asian women's voices and the justice.

SURVIVORS' SELF-REPRESENTATION: THE MAP OF MEMORY

In our testimonial work, we also had to pay attention to the personal life story telling. Although there was endless variety in the experiences of survivors, there was also a strong commonality to them. To make this process tangible, I describe the basic steps of our research.

The testimony research consisted of two levels of representation: listening to and recording the testimony, and making this record accessible to readers who were not present at the interview. While the first was about the dialogue between survivor-victims and researchers, the second was about the interaction between the researchers and potential publics who will read testimonies. In the first level, the researcher assumes the position of a potential reader of the testimony. This work involves devising and organising questions for the interview, meeting with and interviewing survivors, and transcribing the sound to written text (we called this the original text). In the second level, the researcher, as witness to the survivor-victim, occupies the position of the survivor in speaking to the world-audience. This involves some imagination about the eventual audience of the testimony. For this purpose, different members of the research team read the testimony carefully many times, editing the strange expressions, abrupt endings, and long and mundane stories in the transcribed text. Throughout the work of both levels of representation, there was constant discussion about the recording and editorial processes. The end result, including the final testimony book, represents a communal work in the fullest sense.

Editing was the final and the most painful process through which we attempted to render the story sensible to the public without discarding the testifier's affect and subjectivity. In this process, we maintained a firm principle of 'not' rewriting or adding anything to the text to make the testimony easy to follow. Instead, we used many parentheses and footnotes to help readers understand nonverbal expressions, specific styles of talking and the context of interviews.[20] Even with such contextualisation, however, we feel that the greater effort in making the testimony sensible must lie with the audience rather than with survivor-victims. Seen in this way, there were always three subject positions imaginarily present in the testimonial works: the testifier (that is, the survivor-victim), the researcher and the various audiences. Representational work involves managing the relationship within this triangle. We saw ourselves as an interpreter, or a link between the other two parties, allowing testifier and audience to encounter one another.

We often faced the question of whether any particular testimonial story ought to be included in the final testimony book. But the deeper question would be whether each story was 'relevant' enough to the experience of being a comfort woman. This question is not about the women's testimony but about the dominant image of what constitutes or can even be judged valid experiences of being a comfort woman. In the following testimony by Han Oksun, for example, Han talks about her experience of giving birth to her first child. Unlike her memory about rape at the comfort station represented earlier in this essay, this was a memory to which Han joyfully returned with lively vividness:

> [I said] "Oh, something was broken" (meaning that her amniotic water had broken). [A neighbor responded] "Oh my, then the baby is about to be out." So I pushed and rolled the blanket I used. I lay on my stomach and squatted on the floor. I also unfolded the yellowish thick papers in the room that a landlord lady had brought. It was like a cloth sack for flour. There were paper tissues as well [...]. The baby came out there, with the sound "took" (Sound of Han's laughter). (Testimony Book 4: 8)

She gave birth to two daughters, with one of whom she lived in Korea. The girl's father was a Japanese medical officer at the military comfort station, and Han's relationship with him was complex: he raped her like other soldiers, but they came to live together as if a de facto couple. Owing to him, Han was safe from further sexual exploitation at the station, and eventually he fathered her two daughters. The man even promised to bring Han to Japan after the war was over, but he died on the battlefield before he was able to do so. In her testimony, this man, to whom Han did not put any proper naming, occupies an ambiguous but important position, as does Han's daughters. The father of Han's daughters had to be kept a secret on her return to Korea, while her daughter, Han's only beloved family (since the second daughter was adopted by a Chinese couple and Han has never seen her), is the legacy of an agonising past; it is owing to this daughter's presence that Han can never be separated from that past for even a single moment. Her daughters are a site of secrets and of connection between past and present (Testimony Book 4: 72–94).

In the nationalist historical imagination, this story of self-contradictory affection for a Japanese soldier would transgress one's sensibility. Or it might seem too personal to be included in the historical record of a comfort woman. But we published this story in our testimony book because we understood this experience as a source of pain as well as energy that sustained this survivor-victim. Furthermore, Han's affection for the father (of her daughters) and daughter does not so much deny as reveal what it means to be a comfort woman during and after the colonial period.

As seen in this way, each survivor's testimony is a narrative of self-representation in which each woman looked at herself and her experiences reflectively with her own powers of interpretation. This self-representation raises questions about the authorship of history, a point I made earlier. We found that testimonies were not merely information that could be conveniently inserted into an already existing framework of history or the law (that would, in turn, judge the truthfulness and even meaning of the words) but that the testimonies themselves constituted the frames and codes. Thus our principle of representation was to design the testimony according to each survivor-victim's own framework of memory, such that it was the researchers and audience who had to follow her logics of representation. In this journey for testimony, we found the map of memory that each survivor has carried.

'MAP OF MEMORY': THE DEEP INSCRIPTION

After two members of the testimony team had met with each survivor on average three times (and sometimes as many as ten times) over a period of three to six months, the researchers became familiar with each survivor's memory mode. This mode revealed to us the uniqueness and individuality of each survivor. A critical element of this process was our political choice, as feminists and friends of subalternity, to give the initiative to the survivor for speaking. The researchers, as listeners, through interviews and transcription of the taped record, came to share the memory with the narrator as if the researchers had also been present at the time of the events. As time went on and the listener's own memory of the events became more detailed, so did the narrator's. Survivors became energised, as if they were meeting someone for the first time who treated their story as something that deserved to be listened to and remembered.

In the following, Ahn Bopsoon and a researcher, Lee Sun Hyung, talked about the place where the survivor-victim had been drafted; this conversation was transcribed in our original text.

> Lee: Wasn't the Siyoko club close to the downtown? And the Shonan hotel was nearby?
> Ahn: Yes, it was, yes.
> Lee: When many soldiers came to you [for sexual gratification], did you stay there?
> Ahn: (Gesturing with both arms as if drawing the location of each building) At the far left side, there were Daito and Geizo (the place where she was in which was the name of capital Seoul during the colonial Korea). (Lee 2002: 63)

Researcher and survivor-victim engaged in a descriptive dialogue, as if the researcher were in the location of the comfort station alongside Ahn and shared the memory with her.

In this process, we found that survivors recalled the past

following a precise order, with a consistent logic and sequence. This challenges the popular belief that survivors' testimony is arbitrary in nature. We found that most survivors used recognisable ways and modes of remembering. With their power of self-representation, each survivor repeatedly told the stories of their most significant experiences, using very similar words to describe them and a similar sequence of association. These experiences included the threat of dying, severe hunger and encounters with dramatic life-saving forces. From these central episodes, other smaller episodes were relayed, until the constellation of stories evolved into the narrative of an entire life. We called this order of memory and its structural features 'the map of memory' of each survivor.

For one survivor-victim, Kim Changyon, the experience of drowning in the sea was the central episode. When a torpedo wrecked the ship that was taking her to the South Sea Islands, Kim was thrown into the sea. This event seemed inscribed more vividly and intensely on Kim's memory than even the experience of forcible drafting or sexual exploitation as a comfort woman. The interviewer noted that, without interruption, Kim testified to this experience at a length of more than two transcribed pages, with a literal description that was amazingly rich compared with her usual reticence. Her testimony about this incident was detailed and passionate, as if she were projecting and watching her own film. She describes the situation: "We were like ants, with only heads being above the water. We shouted, 'Please save us,' and the soldiers in the helicopter [shouted to us], 'Be strong!'" (Testimony Book 4: 70) This memory was not only personal and ironical in which a captive were eager to survive but also historical and legal, in that it illustrated the inhumane conditions of forced mobilisation and the fatal possibilities it could have entailed. The message, however, is not confined to history or legality, since it also carries a much more affective texture.

For another survivor, the reason she was mobilised as a comfort woman was more important than recalling the person by whom she was taken. Choi Kapsoon described the context of her drafting when she was 15 years old:

Poorly, very poorly [did we live], without eating white rice once. Our family did tenant farming. After paying [the farm rent], no advance could be taken in the lifetime. In this [situation], one day a Japanese officer came to our house to capture my father and draft him as a soldier in the *kukukdae* (the corps for saving the nation), but my mother hid him. If he had been taken, [my mother said,] our family would have died from hunger. (Testimony Book 4: 121)

The daughter of a poor tenant farmer in colonial Korea, Choi was enslaved as a comfort woman in China in 1933 and remained there in a state of sexual slavery until 1945. She returned home to Korea, without finding any family, in 1948 after three years of walking on foot from China, selling beans and other things to make a living. In her life story, the central axes of Choi's memory seemed to lie in her mother and in hunger, and these concretised her memory of being a comfort woman. This does not mean that the sexual exploitation and forced mobilisation were not important but that these experiences had substantial meaning only within the context of these central axes. Between hunger and a mother who wanted to reduce the number of mouths to feed, Choi could not but 'choose' to go to the place where she would allegedly have rice and clothing. This was not a story about a cruel mother and child abuse but a report on the social and economic situation of colonial Korea in the 1930s, when agricultural exploitation, poverty and extreme hunger and famine were widespread across the peninsula.

Although the map of memory was less structured for some survivors than for others, we could see that each survivor recalled one central episode that in turn brought others into the discussion, as if they were threads intertwined with each other in memory. In other words, memory is structured as a system in which many small and large episodes are organically related, ultimately built into a tree of memory. Thus in the second phase of our testimonial work, we tried to reconstruct and edit the stories in the original text to follow each survivor's map of memory. This had several implications for our methods and philosophy of representation of the testimonies.

First, representing the map of memory allowed us to appreciate how each survivor constructed her own life and experiences, such that readers (including ourselves) could witness the survivor-victim's uniqueness, individuality and mode of interpretation. In this representation, readers not only encounter the agency of the survivors but also the inexpressible pain and cruelty that survivors endured.

Second, each map of memory was constructed after interviews and constant discussion between the two interviewers, as well as among the rest of the research team. As a result, it carried the memories that seemed mostly deeply inscribed and understandable to our team. In the final testimony book and indictment of the '2000 tribunal,' we quoted from the stories that were told repeatedly but also from the stories that seemed more difficult to tell, such as those of exploitation and rape.

In this regard, finding a map of memory as a principle of representation was our strategy in balancing between the commonality of the victims' experiences and the individuality of them, the law and story-telling. Survivors' memories were neither dreamlike and subjective stories nor a coherent construction of facts. Layers of cognition and emotion never seemed separate for survivor-victims, and we sought to convey both.

SURVIVORS AND VICTIMHOOD

Attention to self-representation in each map of memory deconstructed the typical image of comfort women as victims. It was difficult not to see the energy and agency that survivors carried in their expressions of hope, yearning for survival, compassion, anger and resistance. There were many survivors who expressed deep and fresh anger toward the Japanese military soldiers and government. This did not seem to be the result of the imposition of nationalist ideology, but of how survivors remembered the pain that colonial rule inflicted on them. Survivor-victim Kim Whasun expresses this sentiment:

> Sometimes I think, how can I kill the Japanese into pieces? How can I? It is useless to just think by myself. … The cruelest guy, I would like to kill. I came to think without consciousness, spontaneously. I want revenge. Just an apology would not possibly

> lighten my cloaked heart, no, it cannot. I would like to batter
> them until they die. ... I have been living so poorly, without being
> married once, and becoming this old. (Testimony Book 4: 42)

In another instance, Kim criticised the Korean government, too: "There were also many wrongdoings by the Korean government. We became comfort women due to the lost nation. Since there was no nation [of Korea], we were forcibly drafted. Thus, the Korean nation did harmful things, too" (Testimony Book 4: 43f).

Memory has multiple truths, so to judge a memory by only limited criteria amounts to cutting entangled threads with scissors. If we do this, we will lose the threads of the memory. Let us return to Choi Kapsoon. This is how Choi recalled her childhood and mother:

> How much my mother's heart was aching, when she (meaning the
> neighbor) demanded repayment for the rice [that I ate secretly].
> Where was the rice for us? I have lived in such a world, beaten by
> my mother so hard after having three spoons of warm rice [from
> that neighbor]. I was only six years old. (Testimony Book 4: 145)

It seems that Choi's heart was broken. Her mother is not the site of contempt and blame, the force that drove her to the comfort station, but rather someone Choi had missed for her entire life, someone who, Choi likes to believe, loved her enough to send her to a place where she would have a full stomach. Her mother is indeed a complex signifier who, I believe, eventually signified Choi's own identity. In other words, forgiveness and love of her mother seemed eventually to define her life. Choi worked ceaselessly throughout her life—farming, weaving textiles and performing housework—and took care of many people: her husband, her adopted son and her neighbour, even to the extent of repaying debts for them. This is the strength that the daughters of the subaltern have carried until today.

CONCLUSION: COLLECTIVE PAIN AND HEALING

Survivors' testimonies, while not a national voice, were undoubtedly a collective voice, and their narratives testified to the experiences of other comfort women and the imperial soldiers. The survivor-victims were witnesses to unspeakable atrocity, including the torture, disease and death of other victims. Over 90 percent of Korean comfort women are presumed to have died before they could return home, due to disease, miscarriage, drug use, torture, bombing or other attacks in the battlefield, and hardships encountered during travel back to the homeland. In this light, survivors' testimonies carry stories of the deceased women and men and represent the collective experiences of the subaltern in East Asia during World War II. Through their words, the numerous nameless dead women and men can be remembered.

Whether in the form of book, film or indictment, survivors' testimonies are the product of inter-subjectivity, of dialogue and empathy between survivors and the listeners/interpreters/witnesses. As memory has been collective, so too has been the experience of historical trauma (Halbach 1967; Caruth 1995). As we listened to survivors' memories, the trauma was transferred to us as listeners.[21] The acts of listening to and recording survivors' narratives are part of the process of building a community of such collective memory about the war, colonialism and postcolonial society. When the subaltern women's testimony becomes 'our story,' our cultural and historical identity can be constantly reconstituted.

In the '2000 tribunal' in Tokyo, the North and South Korea prosecutor's team drafted the indictment largely based on the sequence of survivors' collective stories of forced mobilisation, rape at the comfort stations, survival immediately after the end of the war and life in North and South Korea today. At each stage, discrete crimes were constructed through quotations taken from the testimony. Through our efforts to listen to these stories and incorporate them into the law, new concepts in human rights and women's rights could emerge.[22]

Throughout our testimonial work and during the '2000 tribunal,' we felt that the truth was already with us, and the language and affect in the testimony revealed the energy that the community needs to know and share. Linguistic incommensurability in the testimony is not a fixed destiny but reflects an ever-changing political state. For the subaltern women in Korea, the affect phrase-vernacular, nonverbal expression, but consistent memory was where their reasoning had been contained, and where it awaited further decoding with a dialogue of contemporaries like 'us.'

This article is a shortened version of Hyunah Yang, 'Finding the "Map of Memory"': Testimony of the Japanese Military Sexual Slavery Survivors', *positions*, 16(1), 2008, pp. 79-107. Reproduced with permission of Duke University Press.

NOTES

1. Between 1992 and 2004 the testimonies of Korean women who had been forcefully drafted for military sexual slavery by Japan were compiled in a series of six volumes, published in Korean (Seoul: Pulbit); hereafter cited as Testimony Book. Most of the testimonies in this essay are quoted from those given to the Testimony Team, which were published in volume 4 (2001) of the series. All of the survivors represented in this essay had passed away by the time this article was prepared for publication.

2. The victims under the system of Japanese Military Sexual Slavery were far from engaging in the 'comforting' activities. However, this essay employs the terminology of 'comfort women' or 'comfort woman,' since it carries the historical context where the term was used, and the political implication which evaded the aspects of massive violence and power imbalance involved in the 'comforting' act.

3. For a detailed discussion of the system, see Choi 1997; Yoshiaki 2000; Stetz/Oh 2001.

4. 'We' or 'us' used in this essay mostly refer to the research team of the testimonies of former comfort women. But they also designate the potential readers of this essay who may share the common state of unpreparedness to listen to the testimonies. Ultimately, this essay searches for a notion of a collective 'we' that does not simply gaze at subaltern comfort women but rather a 'we' that embraces the former comfort women as constituents of 'us'.

5. As indicated above, seven volumes of survivors' testimony were

published from 1993 to 2004 in South Korea. Volumes 1–6 deal with Korean comfort women, and an additional volume addresses survivor in China.

6. In the early 1990s, the Japanese government denied any official engagement in the comfort women system, but it has changed its attitude somewhat since 1992 by Minister Kono's statement which acknowledged Japanese military's involvement in mobilising the women against their will. The current Prime Minister Abe government, however, tended to deny the Kono Statement. Regarding the problems in the '2015 Korea-Japan Agreement,' see Yang 2017.

7. Elsewhere I have examined the discourse of the body that has been contaminated by a foreigner. See Yang 1998.

8. On the cultural appropriation of comfort women, see Youngae 1999. On transnational feminist critiques of the nation, see, for instance, Chizuko 2004.

9. The testimony team members (twenty to thirty persons in total, all of them volunteers) were mostly female graduate students, whose diverse areas of specialisation included history, women's studies, film and theology. I served as a director of the team until volume 4 of the Testimony Book was published in 2001.

10. For an introduction of this tribunal, see Puja 2001; Chinkin 2001.

11. Each country was supposed to send a prosecutor (or prosecutors' team) to represent the victims and their people. I played a part in this event as a country prosecutor for the North and South Korea joint team.

12. See the preamble to the charter for the Tokyo Women's Tribunal. http://www.iccwomen.org/wigjdraft1/Archives/oldWCGJ/tokyo/charter.html (accessed 26 October 2018).

13. The International Military Tribunal for the Far East took place between April 1946 and November 1948 in Tokyo.

14. The International War Crimes Tribunals for the former Yugoslavia (ICTY) and Rwanda (ICTR), established by the United Nations in the early 1990s, elicited an international awareness of violence against women in the context of war and other mass atrocities and prompted further elaboration of the appropriate legal measures for these crimes.

15. See the Final Judgment (2001) of the Tokyo Women's Tribunal and other aspects of the 2000 Tribunal, available at: http://vawwrac.org/war_crimes_tribunal (accessed 17 August 2018).

16. Whereas Japanese government has not recognised testimonies of the victims as the evidence of the facts, they were accepted as the evidence in the '2000 tribunal'.

17. Gay J. McDougall, special rapporteur of the U.N. Commission on Human Rights, defined the nature of crimes involved in the Japanese military's comfort women system in terms of sexual slavery and systematic rape, for which both the state and individuals are liable under the international conventions and customary international law.

18. English translations of cited testimonies in this essay are my own.

19. We used brackets for inserting the omitted words and parentheses for explaining nonverbal expressions, including gesture and context of narration.

20. As a result, the final testimony book contains diverse stories and styles. A frequent comment about the book is that it is difficult to read but, strangely enough, very moving.

21. For an in-depth look at the nature of trauma, physical and psychological, suffered by Korean comfort women, see Appendix II of the Korean Indictment of the Tokyo Women's Tribunal.

22. For an exemplary work of beautiful and thoughtful mediation between victim's testimony and refiguration of justice, see Minow 1998.

REFERENCES

Caruth, Cathy. 1995. *Trauma: Explorations in Memory*. Baltimore: Johns Hopkins University Press.

Chakrabarty, Dipesh. 1992. 'Postcoloniality and the Artifice of History: Who Speaks for Indian Past?' *Representations*, 37:1–26.

Chinkin, Christine. 2001. 'Editorial Comments: Women's International Tribunal on Japanese Military Sexual Slavery', *The American Journal of International Law*, 95(2):335.

Chizuko, Ueno. 2004. *Gender and Nationalism*. Melbourne: Transpacific.

Choi, Chungmoo. ed. 1997. 'The Comfort Women: Colonialism, War, and Sex', *positions: east asia culture critiques*, 16(1).

Guha, Ranajit. 1982. 'On Some Aspects of the Historiography of Colonial India', in Ranajit Guha (ed). *Writings on South Asian History and Society: Subaltern Studies*, Vol. I, pp. 37–43. Delhi: Oxford University Press.

Halbach, Maurice. 1967. *Collective Memory*. New York: Harper and Row.

Huffer, Lynn. 2006. 'Toward a Differend Idiom: Legal Storytelling and the Differend', paper presented at 'Storytelling and the Law: A Retrospective on Narrative, Ethics and Legal Change,' Feminism and Legal Theory Project, Emory School of Law, 27–28 October, Atlanta.

Laub, Dori. 1992. 'Bearing Witness, or the Vicissitudes of Listening', in Shoshana Felman/Dori Laub (eds), *Testimony: Crisis in Witnessing in Literature, Psychoanalysis, and History*, pp. 57–74. New York: Routledge.

Lee, Sun Hyung. 2002. *Ilponkun wianpu sengchoncha chungoˇn ui bangpopnon jok kochʼal* (Methodological Study on the Survivors' Testimony of Japanese Military Comfort Women), MA thesis. Seoul: Seoul National University.

Lyotard, Jean-François. 1994. *Postmodern Condition: A Report on Knowledge*. Minneapolis: University of Minnesota Press.

―――. 1988. *The Differend: Phrases in Dispute*. Minneapolis: University of Minneapolis Press.

Mani, Lata. 1990. 'Contentious Traditions: The Debate on Sati on Colonial India', in Kumkum Sangari/Sudesh Vaid (eds). *Recasting Women: Essays in Indian Colonial History*, pp. 88–126. New Brunswick: Rutgers University Press.

Minow, Martha. 1998. *Between Vengeance and Forgiveness: Facing History after Genocide and Mass Violence*. Boston: Beacon.

Mohanty, Chandra Talpade. 1991. 'Under Western Eyes: Feminist Scholarship and Colonial Dis-courses', in Chandra Talpade Mohanty/Ann Russo/Lourdes Torres (eds), *Third World Women and the Politics of Feminism*, pp. 51–80. Indianapolis: Indiana University Press.

Puja, Kim. 2001. 'Global Civil Society Remakes History', *positions: east asia cultures critique*, 9(3):611–20.

Spivak, Gayatri Chakravorty. 1988. 'Can the Subaltern Speak?' in Cary Nelson/Lawrence Grossberg (eds), *Marxism and the Interpretation of Culture*, pp. 271–316. Chicago: University of Illinois Press.

―――. 1985. 'Subaltern Studies: Deconstructing Historiography', in Ranajit Guha (ed). *Writings on South Asian History and Society*, *Subaltern Studies*, Vol IV, pp. 330–63. Delhi: Oxford University Press.

Stetz, Margaret/Oh, Bonni B. C. (eds). 2001. *Legacies of the Comfort Women of World War II*. London: M. E. Sharp.

Yang, Hyunah. 2017. 'Justice Yet to Come: The Korea-Japan Foreign Ministers' Agreement of 2015 regarding the "Japanese Military Sexual Slavery"', *L'Homme: Europäische Zeitschrift für feministische*

Geschichtswissenschaft, 28(2):115–25.

―――. 2008. 'Finding the "Map of Memory": Testimony of the Japanese Military Sexual Slavery Survivors', *positions: east asia cultures critiques,* 16(1):79–107.

―――. 1998. 'Re-membering the Korean Military Comfort Women: Nationalism, Sexuality, and Silence', in Elaine H. Kim/Chungmoon Choi (eds), *Dangerous Women: Gender and Korean Nationalism,* pp. 123–40. New York: Routledge.

―――. 1997. 'Revisiting the Issue of Korean Military Comfort Women: Questions of Truth and Positionality', *positions: east asia cultures critique,* 5(1):51–72.

Yoshimi, Yoshiaki. 2002. *Comfort Women: Sexual Slavery in the Japanese Military during World War II.* New York: Columbia University Press.

Youngae, Yamashida. 1999. 'Hankuk ae wianpu munjae ui haekyul undong ui kwaje' ('Tasks for Social Movements in Korea around the Issue of Comfort Women'), in Kang Duk Sang/Chin Sung Chung (eds), *Kunhyo˘ndae hanil kwankae wa cheil dongp'o (Korea-Japan Relations in the Modern Era and Korean Japanese in Japan),* pp. 248–82. Seoul: Seoul National University Press.

Narrating Rape as Collective Event: Sexual Violence by Red Army Soldiers in Berlin 1945

ATINA GROSSMANN

"Enjoy the war, because the peace will be terrible," the mordant Berlin wags had warned even as the Red Army drew nearer and the bombings and casualties, both civilian and military, mounted. Allies and liberated victims of the Nazis may have approached the 'whining' of the vanquished with jaundiced scepticism, but for many Germans the uneasy peace that relatively quickly emerged was haunted by the chaos, fear and violence produced, not by the regime that had catapulted them into war, but its defeat. Both that *Zusammenbruch* (collapse) and the moves toward reconstruction that would bring 'after a fashion, peace' were experienced in gendered terms. On the home front of unconditional surrender, the effects were inscribed directly and publicly on the bodies of women, whether they figured as victims of mass rape (most visibly in the Soviet zone and Berlin), as willing or pragmatic fraternisers (most visibly with American troops) or as mothers struggling to feed and keep alive their children (in all zones and sectors).

The defeated Reich that the victors encountered in spring 1945 wore a predominantly female face. German men had been killed, wounded or taken prisoner, leaving women to clean the ruins, scrounge for food and serve the occupiers, often as sexual partners and victims. As the Red Army fought its way westward, the retreating Wehrmacht put up an embittered defence, forcing exhausted and in part disbelieving Soviet commanders to continue hard fighting right into the centre of destroyed Berlin.

By February, the Red Army was only 35 miles east of Berlin, and still the Germans would not surrender as they tried to carve out escape routes for themselves to the west and north. Fortified by huge caches of alcohol conveniently left behind by the retreating Germans, reinforced by brutalised Soviet prisoners of war liberated along the way, and enraged by the street-to-street, house-to-house German defence loyally carried out by young boys and old men as well as regular soldiers, the Red Army pushed through East Prussia toward Berlin in what the military historian John Erickson has called "a veritable passion of destructiveness." In a remarkably infelicitous sentence, Erickson concluded: "The fighting drained both sides, though Russian lustiness won through" (Bartov 1986; Erickson 1983: 512, 603; Evans 1989).

After years of remarkable inattention since the 1950s, Red Army rapes became in the early 1990s the subject of vigorous scholarly and feminist debates on German women's role in the Third Reich. The sixtieth anniversary of war's end with its new emphasis on public recognition of German suffering, combined with a growing global awareness of rape as a war crime in civil and ethnic conflicts, brought renewed public attention, albeit in a less carefully contextualised manner, to the story of German women's victimisation.[1]

The numbers reported for these rapes vary wildly, from as few as 20,000 to almost one million or even two million altogether, as the Red Army pounded westward. A conservative estimate might be about 110,000 women raped, many more than once, of whom up to 10,000 died in the aftermath; others suggest that perhaps one out of every three of about 1.5 million women in Berlin fell victim to Soviet rapes.[2] Whatever the figures, it is unquestionably the case that mass rapes of civilian German women signalled the end of the war and the defeat of Nazi Germany. Sexual violence was an integral part of the final bitter battle for Berlin from 24 April to 8 May 1945.

In particular, the perpetration of sexual violence by Red Army troops, had been massively prefigured in Nazi propaganda. Terrifying images of invading Mongol barbarians raping German women were a vital part of the Nazi war machine's feverish (and

successful) efforts to bolster morale on the eastern front and keep
the home front intact. Nazi propaganda had been relentless in
characterizing the Russians as subhuman and animalistic. The
threat of a surging Asian flood and marauding 'Red Beast'
tearing through what was supposedly still a pacific and ordinary
German land was used to incite desperate resistance even long
after it was clear that the war was fundamentally lost. By the
end of the war, most German women had already seen graphic
newsreel footage of the bodies of "violated women, battered old
people and murdered children." Indeed, the very last newsreel
released in 1945 showed a white fence with the desperate message
scrawled on it, "Protect our women and children from the Red
Beast" (Deutsche Wochenschau 1945). Moreover, Germans
knew enough of Wehrmacht and SS crimes in the East to have
reason to believe that vengeful Russians would commit atrocities
and to make plausible the often repeated (and explicitly denied)
account of Soviet Jewish writer Ilya Ehrenburg's infamous call
for Soviet soldiers to seek retribution by raping "flaxen-haired"
German women—"they are your prey" (Ehrenburg 1964: 32).[3]
Whatever the level of ordinary Germans' detailed knowledge of
the systematic extermination of European Jewry, it was no secret
that Wehrmacht actions on the eastern (in contrast to the western)
front went well beyond the standards of ordinary brutal warfare.
German soldiers had been explicitly commanded to liquidate all
putative 'bolsheviks', and during their 'scorched earth' retreat
they laid waste as a matter of policy (not of indiscipline) to huge
territories with civilian populations and massacred entire villages.
Again and again in German recollections about what Russian
occupiers told them, the vengeful memory the victors summoned
was not a parallel violation, that of Germans raping Russian
women, but a horror of a different order; it was the image of a
German soldier swinging a baby, torn from its mother's arms,
against a wall—the mother screams, the baby's brain splatters
against the wall, the soldier laughs.[4]

Soviet rapes secured a particularly potent place in post-
war memories of victimisation, because they represented the
one instance in which Goebbels's spectacular anti-Bolshevik

propaganda turned out to be substantially correct. Millions of Germans were trekking westward in flight from the Red Army, and millions of German soldiers were marched eastward as POWs, but as Berliners—primarily women, children and the elderly— emerged from their cellars during the piercingly beautiful spring of 1945, the Soviets did not kill everyone on sight, deport them to Siberia or burn down the city. The musician Karla Höcker reported with genuine surprise, in one of the many diaries composed by women at war's end, that "the Russians, who must hate and fear us, leave the majority of the German civilian population entirely alone—that they don't transport us off in droves!"[5]

In fact, the Soviet Military Administration (SMA) moved quickly and efficiently to organise municipal government, restore basic services and nurture a lively political and cultural life. At the same time, official Soviet policy obstinately refused to acknowledge that soldiers who had sworn to be "honorable, brave, disciplined, and alert" and to defend the "motherland manfully, ably, with dignity and honor," would engage in atrocities on anything more than the level of "isolated excesses" (Berman/Kerner 1955: 48). Ilya Ehrenburg (1964:175), having quickly assimilated Stalin's new, more conciliatory line toward compliant Germans, insisted that "the Soviet soldier will not molest a German woman. [...] It is not for booty, not for loot, not for women that he has come to Germany."[6] Clearly, however, that new message did not impress the troops engaged in a costly final battle who had been told that "every farm on the road to Berlin was the den of a fascist beast" (cit. in Deutscher 1980: 130). Shocked at the continuing affluence of the society they had so determinedly defeated, and at Germany's contrast to their own decimated country, Russian soldiers told their victims, "Russia—my home. Germany—my paradise" (Vallentin 1955: 37).

NARRATING RAPE

For German women in 1945—certainly in Berlin and to its east— rape was experienced as a collective event in a situation of general crisis, part of the apocalyptic days of Berlin's fall. Rape confirmed their expectations and reinforced preexisting convictions of cultural superiority; it came as just one more (sometimes the worst, but sometimes not) in a series of horrible deprivations and humiliations of war and defeat: hunger, homelessness, expulsion and displacement, plunder and dismantling of factories, the harsh treatment of German prisoners of war in the Soviet Union, the death or maiming of menfolk, watching one's children die or sicken of disease and malnutrition. The story of rape was told as part of the narrative of survival in ruined Germany. "Rape had," many noted, "become routine" (Wieck 1990: 261). A certain matter-of-factness (Sachlichkeit), in some ways still reminiscent of the pre-Nazi Weimar 'new woman,' pervades many of these Berlin accounts. Margret Boveri, a journalist who had continued working throughout the Nazi years, was laconic about the Soviet "liberators" in her "Survival Diary" for 6–8 May 1945:

> Rode [on her bicycle] a ways with a nice bedraggled girl … imprisoned by Russians for 14 days, had been raped but well fed. … May 8, 1945. The usual rapes—a neighbor who resisted was shot. … Mrs Krauss was not raped. She insists that Russians don't touch women who wear glasses. Like to know if that is true … the troops were pretty drunk but did distinguish between old and young which is already progress. (Boveri 1945: 121f, 126)

Others accepted their fate as an inevitable, to-be-expected consequence of defeat, almost like a natural disaster that could not be changed and must simply be survived: "In those days I endured the Russians as I would a thunderstorm."[7]

Anne-Marie Durand-Wever, the physician who feared the revenge that would descend on "poor Germany" as its crimes were uncovered, also kept her diary notes on rape stoic and pragmatic. After "gruesome" nights in her cellar she returned to work in a first aid station; she hastened to test women and girls for venereal disease and to ferret out gynaecological instruments, since "I guess we'll have to do abortions," Durand-Wever was sure that "our" soldiers had comported themselves no differently, but on 23 May she made a sad note about her own daughter: "This afternoon Annemie was here with her child. Four Russians.

Swab inconclusive. In any case, sulfa medication (Albucid). For this one tends one's child!" Still in February 1946, she portrayed a "loathsome" situation of continuing rapes, venereal disease, unwanted pregnancies and mass abortions (Durand-Wever, unpublished diary).

During these 'dark times' of conquest and occupation, women, so often seen by both Germans and occupiers as innocent victims (of rape and war in general) or villains (as manipulative fraternisers), also presented themselves as resourceful agents. Some unknown but not insignificant number committed suicide to escape, or in reaction to, such violations. Many more, now "standing alone," as historian Elizabeth Heineman has described them, prioritised survival and their role as caretakers and providers. They scrounged and bartered for food and shelter and negotiated protection for their children and themselves with occupation soldiers (Heineman 1999; see also Meyer/Schulze 1985). In diaries composed at the time as well as in reworked diaries, memoirs and oral histories recorded years later, women reported extremely diverse experiences of what they variously named as rape, coercion, violation, prostitution or abuse. Some women and young girls were brutally gang-raped in public with a line of soldiers waiting for their turn. In some cases, women's bodies were slit open from stomach to anus, or they were killed afterward. Others were forced to have sex alone in a room with a lonely young soldier for whom they occasionally even developed ambivalent feelings of hate, pity and warmth. Some consciously offered themselves in exchange for protecting a daughter or made deliberate decisions to take up with an occupier, preferably an officer with power, to shield themselves from others and to garner privileges. And of course, there were also moments of genuine affection and desire. Women recorded brutality but also, at times, their own sense of confusion about the fine lines between rape, prostitution and consensual (albeit generally instrumental) sex.

Indeed, the more one looks at the diaries, memoirs and novels of the post-war years, rape stories are omnipresent, told matter-of-factly, told as tragedy, told with ironic humour and flourish. In a recurring trope, women are gathered at water pumps in bombed-out streets, exchanging 'war stories' with a certain bravado. Almost gleefully they reveal their stratagems to trick Russians as gullible as they were brutal: masquerading as men or ugly old women disguised by layers of clothing or faces smeared with dirt and ash, pretending to have typhus or venereal disease. But they also marvel at soldiers' apparently indiscriminate 'taste' in women, the fact that they seemed to prefer fat ladies, or their astounding sexual prowess even when utterly inebriated. In both official affidavits and more private accounts, women mobilised a wide range of direct and indirect vocabulary—Schändung (violation), *Vergewaltigung* (rape), *Übergriff* (encroachment), *Überfall* (attack)—to denote the 'it' (*es*) that had been endured (Nieden 1993: esp. 74, 95f). Sometimes they recounted stories of surprising escape or reprieve; often they resorted to generalities and passive voice (the awful scenes went on all night, we all had to submit), or referred specifically to the ghastly experiences of neighbours, mothers, and sisters that they themselves had supposedly been spared.

In a compelling diary edited and published by a popular German writer in the 1950s, an anonymous 'woman in Berlin'— recently identified as Marta Hillers, another young journalist who had continued to work in the Third Reich, occasionally composing minor propaganda texts for the Nazis—explained her reaction after a series of brutal rapes during the first chaotic weeks of April-May 1945:

> Then I say loudly damn it! and make a decision. It is perfectly clear. I need a wolf here who will keep the wolves away from me. An officer, as high as possible, Kommandant, General, whatever I can get. For what do I have my spirit and my little knowledge of foreign languages? As soon as I could walk again I took my pail and crept on to the street. Wandered up and down ... practiced the sentences with which I could approach an officer; wondered if I didn't look too green and wretched to be attractive. Felt physically better again now that I was doing something, planning and wanting, no longer just dumb booty. (*Eine Frau in Berlin* 2003: 78)[8]

Such unsentimental directness in reporting and dealing with sexual

assaults or efforts to elude them was quite typical. Curt Riess, a
Berlin Jew who had come back with deeply "mixed feelings" was
both horrified and cynical: "But it was strange, when the horrific
had happened five or six times, it was no longer so horrific. That
which one had thought one could not survive, was survived by
many twenty—or thirty times" (Riess 1953: 23, 26, 19). Another
younger Berlin Jew, who had returned from Auschwitz, recorded
with bittersweet amusement an exchange between two women in
the familiar rough (and quite untranslatable) Berlin dialect that,
almost despite himself, he was happy to hear again. Justifying her
usurpation of a space on the impossibly overcrowded train they
were riding into the city, one loudly announced,

> We Berliners had to let the bombs whip around our heads. I sat
> in a bunker for almost two weeks, was bombed out four times,
> and the Russians didn't exactly treat me with kidgloves either;
> in fact they raped me three times if you really want to know.
> (Winterfeldt N.D.: 438)

Which pronouncement provoked her equally loud mouthed
competitor to an often-reported retort: "She actually seems to be
proud that at her age the Russians would still take her."[9]

In a peculiar way, women's apparent sangfroid in the face
of mass sexual assault became part of the story (and myth) of
'Berlin kommt wieder,' of the city's irrepressible irreverent
spirit. Their self-preserving sexual cynicism can be attributed,
at least in part, both to the modernist *Sachlichkeit* of Weimar
culture and to the loosened mores of the Nazis' war, including
women's experience of fraternisation with foreign labourers
either recruited or forced into the war economy. Ironically, as
Heineman has observed, a "regime obsessed with racial purity
had become the catalyst of an unprecedented number of
relationships between Germans and foreigners" (Heinemann
1999: 58). Even more broadly, the fraying of bourgeois morality
that had alarmed cultural conservatives at least since World War
I and the Weimar Republic clearly continued into the Third
Reich and the Second World War, albeit in complex and selective
ways—a process delineated by Dagmar Herzog in her provocative

study of sexuality during and "after fascism" (Herzog 2005). The
Nazis' war had inevitably and paradoxically led to a loosening
of domestic bonds and an eroticisation of public life, unevenly
prosecuted, sometimes denounced and sometimes accepted by
the populace. Indeed, as Annemarie Tröger already argued in an
important 1986 essay, the disassociative endurance with which
women survived rape as well as their instrumental fraternising
affairs bore an uncanny resemblance to the *sachliche* encounters
in the Weimar 'new woman' novels of an Irmgard Keun or
Marieluise Fleisser. German women, Tröger contended, had been
trained into a sexual cynicism "freed from love," which served
them well during the war and its aftermath (Tröger 1986: 113).
In the post-war novel *Westend*, the main character narrates her
rape with precisely the cool, distant tone associated with 'new
woman' writers: "he carried out the act which he perhaps saw as
a kind of self-imposed duty coldly and without interest. She felt
sorry for the man on top of her" (Weber 1966: 104).

The *Russe*, whose arrival had been so desperately anticipated
by victims and opponents of Nazism and so dreaded by most
Germans, became, in Berlin, an object not only of terror but
of intense fascination and bewilderment for fellow occupiers
and occupied alike. In keeping with the images provided by
Nazi propaganda, there was the drunken, primitive "Mongol"
who descended on Germany like a vengeful "hungry locust" in
an "orgy of revenge" (cit. in Deutscher 1980: 122–4, 129f). He
was accompanied, however, by the cultivated officer who spoke
German, recited Dostoyevsky and Tolstoy, deplored the excesses
of his comrades, and could be relied on for protection even as
he eloquently described German war crimes. Germans frequently
counterposed these 'cultivated' Soviets from European Russia to
the equally if differently fascinating American occupiers, who—in
keeping with the images of American POWs in Nazi newsreels—
were categorised as vulgar, gum-chewing primitives.

The Soviets baffled their conquests with their seemingly strange
behaviour. They assaulted women but were tender and protective
toward children and babies. They would brazenly rip a watch off
someone's arm, grab a bicycle and then offer a big bear hug, two

kisses on the cheeks and a friendly farewell. Women reported that their attackers could be distracted or even cowed, like a child or puppy, by firm commands, or seemed genuinely convinced that looting was not a crime but proper restitution, and that rape too was merely part of their due. These contradictory impressions reflected the generally schizoid quality of the Soviet occupation: "By day they put the Germans, both men and women, to work in dismantling commandos, clearing up rubble, removing tank barricades; and by night they terrorized the city," even as some of their own officers were moved to shoot offending soldiers on the spot (Davidson 1959: 74).

In the end, perhaps, such negative but also confused interpretations of the Russians helped women to distance the horror of their own experience. The narrative of the Russian primitive or exotic curiously absolved him of guilt, as it also absolved women themselves. Such uncivilised, animal-like creatures could not be expected to control themselves, especially when tanked up with alcohol. Nor could women be expected to defend themselves against an elemental force, backed up of course in most cases by rifle or revolver. As one woman remembered, after the initial panic about a fate worse than death, "It became clear to me that a rape, as awful as it might be, had nothing to do with loss of honour" (Pausewang 1985: 62). Not a few women favourably compared Russian officers to contemptible, defeated German men who either abetted the women's humiliation or sought to punish them for it, sometimes to the point of killing victims to preserve that honour (*Eine Frau in Berlin* 2003: 138).

MANAGING RAPE

The communist and Soviet-dominated *Magistrat* quickly recognised the situation and particularly its public health consequences by authorizing a moratorium on the long-standing and controversial antiabortion § 218 of the penal code (as well as by instituting stringent venereal disease surveillance and treatment). Already on 23 May 1945, Ferdinand Sauerbruch, the famed surgeon installed as head of the Berlin Health Department (after the Soviet offer of a bottle of vodka had persuaded the suspicious and politically compromised doctor to accept the position), summoned public health doctors (*Amtsärzte*) to a meeting discussing the provision of abortions. The recorded minutes are more abbreviated than the obviously contentious discussion in which "the opinions of the doctors present were very polarised," but the result of several sessions that summer was the introduction of a medical indication for abortion that clearly included "social" and "ethical" (the shorthand for rape) considerations. In September, abortion was still the first item on the agenda of Health Department meetings.[10] The quick turn to discussions of abortion conveniently shifted the crisis of mass rape from one of violent sexual assault by a 'liberating' army into a public social and health problem. Yet it was in the context of this medicalised response that women were able to document their experience as well as receive safe abortions and treatment for venereal disease.

The Physicians' ad hoc decision to suspend § 218 and perform abortions on raped women was quickly institutionalised by a highly organised medical and social hygiene system that had never really broken down, at least in the cities. Indeed, despite the strict restrictions on voluntary abortions, secret wartime Nazi directives had permitted—or coerced—abortions on female foreign workers and women defined as prostitutes and non-'Aryans,' as well as on the growing number of German women who became pregnant, via consensual sex or rape, by foreign workers or prisoners of war. Ministry of Interior plans already in place for the establishment "in large cities [of] special wards for the care of such women" and for the elimination of their unwanted Mongol or Slav offspring were in fact sanctioned by all the occupiers after the German defeat.

Drawing on a mixed legacy of Weimar and National Socialist maternalist population policy, as well as Nazi racial discourses and the legal protection of occupation policy, women by the thousands related their rape stories in very specific terms to medical commissions attached to district health offices, which then sanctioned abortions right up to the very last months of pregnancy.[11] Matter-of-factly and pragmatically they asserted their right to terminate pregnancies that were not socially, economically or medically viable—in the name of saving the family or themselves and because, as another woman later recalled, "[i]t was irresponsible that in this terrible time of need I would put another child into the world."[12] Invoking this Weimar-inflected discourse of social (not moral or racial) emergency, one woman wrote to the Neukölln district health office, "I am pregnant due to rape by a Russian on April 27, 1945. I request removal of the foetus since I already have an illegitimate child and live with my parents who themselves still have small children." A woman who had been robbed of her bicycle and raped wrote on 9 November 1945, "Since I am single, my mother dead for 15 years, my father a half-Jew from whom I have had no sign of life for six years, it is impossible for me to set a child into the world under these conditions." Another affidavit, submitted on 6 August 1945, simply stated,

I have three children aged five to eleven years. My husband as a former soldier is not yet back. I have been bombed out twice, fled here in January from West Prussia and now request most cordially that I be helped in preventing this latest disaster for me and my family. (LAB Rep. 240/2651)

Along with the conviction of social necessity, women also deployed the vocabulary of Nazi racial hygiene, so ingrained into public discourse over the past twelve years. They frequently identified perpetrators among the western victors as Negro if American or North African if French. And since the vast majority of accusations in Berlin were directed against Soviets, women availed themselves of the rich store of Nazi racial imagery of the barbarian from the East. In a typical petition from 24 July 1945, a woman wrote, "I hereby certify that at the end of April this year during the Russian march into Berlin I was raped in a loathsome way by two Red Army soldiers of Mongol/Asiatic type."

Many petitions freely mixed the social-necessity discourse (familiar from Weimar debates over abortion reform) and the racial stereotypes (popularised by the Nazis) with threats of suicide or descriptions of serious physical ailments that might

have legitimated a medical indication under any regime. A letter
from 20 August 1945:

> On the way to work on the second Easter holiday I was raped
> by a Mongol. The abuse can be seen on my body. Despite strong
> resistance, my strength failed me and I had to let everything evil
> come over me.
>
> Now I am pregnant by this person, can only think about this
> with disgust and ask that I be helped. Since I would not even
> consider carrying this child to term, both my children would lose
> their mother. With kind greetings. (LAB Rep. 214/2814)

The frequent references to the need to care for existing children
testify to the linking of sex, sexual violence and motherhood
in stories of victimisation and survival. In sociologist Hilde
Thurnwald's detailed 1946 survey of family life in immediate
post-war Berlin, all the women in her core sample of two hundred
families insisted that this was not the moment to bear children,
although five women in the group were (unhappily) pregnant. This
maternal pessimism was, Thurnwald stressed, quite a turnaround,
even from the war years under National Socialism, when men on
the home front earned well and women whose husbands were
at the front received generous allowances and were exempted
from wage labour (Thurnwald 1948: 13). Victor Gollancz, the
maverick British-Jewish publisher so sympathetic to Germans'
plight, spoke for many when he foregrounded the reluctance to
reproduce as a symptom of the misery in *Darkest Germany*: "The
wish to have a child is waning. Instead of desiring a new child,
many women are now succumbing to a new despondency, thus
the diagnosis of a new pregnancy often arouses fits of despair."[13]

The desire to avoid childbirth, regardless of whether pregnancy
had resulted from rape, reflected the shocked confusion and
depression that gripped many Germans after a defeat that they
knew was coming and yet had still not fully expected. It was also
part of women's efforts, during a period of extreme shock and
privation, to save the children they already had, even at the price
of submitting to sexual violation and exploitation: "My heart was

pounding but I believe my soul was dead. He ripped open the door, placed the revolver on the night table, and lay down beside me in bed. The anxiety about my sleeping child let me endure everything."[14]

Women reported offering themselves in order to protect their young daughters: "They wanted to take my then 10 year old girl. What mother would have done such a thing? So I could only sacrifice (*opfern*) myself instead."[15] Such tales clearly expressed the double meaning of the term *Opfer*, so pervasive a reference in German wartime and post-war rhetoric, by claiming the negative connotation of 'victim' but also a more positive, redeeming, and even heroic sense of sacrifice.

CONTAINING RAPE AS POLITICAL PROBLEM

Given the realities of mass rape, German communists and SMA authorities could not impose a total silence around Red Army actions. They sought instead to find ways of talking about and containing the massive incidence of rapes. They denied, minimised, justified and shifted responsibility. They freely admitted violations, excesses, abuses and unfortunate incidents and vowed to get them under control. But they also trivialised rape as an inevitable part of normal warfare and as understandable if not entirely excusable in view of the atrocities perpetrated on the Russians by the Germans. In the words of a *Kommunistische Partei Deutschland* (KPD) newsletter, "We cannot and will not try to provide justifications, even if we do have explanations and could answer the question by referring to all the havoc that Hitler wreaked in the Soviet Union."[16]

In a common pattern of simultaneous acknowledgment and denial, Party memos and press reports referred frequently and openly to rumours of rape by Red Army soldiers, thereby reproducing and disseminating stories that, their coding as rumours or pernicious anti-Soviet propaganda notwithstanding, everyone presumably knew to be true. The *Berliner Zeitung* even ran a cartoon strip satirizing women's fears while encouraging their labour as Trümmerfrauen. Under the headline "Mongols in Berlin, the Latest Rumor," the sensible Frau Piesepampel informs her hysterical neighbour Frau Schwabbel that she has "no time for such nonsense" and no intention of worrying about "Mongols" now that the war is finally over. There is clean up work to be done, and she will not be distracted (N.N. 1945: 2). Thus, the official Soviet-licensed press, while formally denying stories of rape or passing the blame to "bandits," may have actually contributed to circulating and confirming them (Berman/Kerner 1955: 48).

Despite all efforts at containment, rapes figured prominently as public relations and political control problems. They provoked anti-Soviet sentiment, especially among German women, youth and dedicated anti-Nazis, precisely those groups considered most likely to support a new socialist and democratic peace-loving Germany. It was generally if not explicitly acknowledged that the communist-dominated Socialist Unity (SED) Party's embarrassing loss to the Social Democrats (SPD) in Berlin's first open elections in October 1946 was due in no small part to a heavily female electorate remembering and responding to the actions of the Soviet 'friends.'[17] The Soviets had worked hard to present themselves as liberators, organizing city services, licensing newspapers and political parties and promoting cultural revival, but in many ways their efforts came too late; the damage of the first few weeks could not be undone. In his report to the London paper *The Observer*, Issac Deutscher predicted that "next Sunday the women of Berlin will take their revenge against the humiliations that were forced upon them during the first weeks of occupation." The election results indicated that he was right (cit. in Deutscher 1980: 187).

For their part, German communist leaders and the SMA continually griped that discussions of guilt, complicity and responsibility or calls for *Wiedergutmachung* (referring to reparations to the Soviet Union) were met with "icy silence."[18] Germans, they clearly implied, should be grateful to have gotten off as easily as they did. Even in regard to rape, both Soviet occupiers and German communists contended that women would have had more of a right to protest if only, rather than senselessly battling the Red Army to the bitter end, right into the centre of Berlin, the German working class had fought fascism for even a day or two, thereby preserving some German honour and credibility vis-a-vis the Soviets. One communist intellectual petulantly remarked that those who had supported the war and the attack on the Soviet Union could not later cry "Pfui"; war was not, after all, "a socializing tool."[19] But there was little popular sympathy for Ulbricht's perhaps irrefutable logic in an early leaflet promising swift punishment for 'excesses.' Had the Soviets "exacted revenge eye for an eye (*Gleiches mit Gleichem vergelten*)," he asked, "German Volk, what would have happened to you?"[20] And while Soviet officers did sometimes exact summary punishment by shooting soldiers accused of rape, few worried as did the dissident Lev Kopelev in his memoirs of life as a political officer in the Red Army: "Why did so many of our soldiers turn out to be common bandits, raping women and girls one after another [*rudelweise*] on the side of the road, in the snow, in doorways? How did this all become possible?" His "bourgeois human[ist]" compunctions led to his arrest for being pro-German (Kopelev 1979: 19, 51, 137).

Even three years later, in 1948, when two overflowing meetings were held in the *Haus der Kultur der Sowjet Union* to discuss the ever sensitive subject "about the Russians and about us," the subject most on the predominantly female audience's mind was Soviet soldiers' violations. The SED argued that the memory of rape was whipped up and kept alive by Western propaganda.[21] The continuing prominence of rape in German narratives of victimisation in the period 1945–49 was not, however, due to propaganda by the western Allies. When Colonel Howley, who had served as the first US commander in Berlin, published his virulently anticommunist memoirs in 1950, he wrote at length about the horrors of the Soviet regime of rape, murder and looting (Howley 1950: 65f). But in his earlier official military reports from Berlin he had downplayed German anxieties about crime, disorder and hunger.[22] Even among the Americans, where such tales might have served as useful anticommunist propaganda, the discussion was restrained. In the early occupation years, US officials were far from seizing on rape stones to discredit their Soviet allies and competitors. This surely also had something to do with the fact that the US forces had their own problems, not only with fraternisation and prostitution, but also with sexual violence.

If German Communists worried about the effects of Red Army behaviour on support for the occupation, American officials and journalists certainly also debated the negative and corrupting effects—on both occupier and occupied—of servicemen's looting, brawling, raping and general "sexual antics" (Zink 1957: 138)

THE SILENCE THAT NEVER WAS

Public conversation, so common in the immediate post-war months and even years, was curtailed in both East and West once conditions had somewhat normalised. With the return of prisoners of war and the "remasculinisation"[23] of German society, the topic was suppressed as too humiliating for German men and too risky for women who feared—with much justification, given the reports of estrangement and even murder—the reactions of their menfolk.

German women, especially in the East and among refugees from the East in the West, were left with un-worked-through memories that had no easy public place even as they were repeatedly invoked or alluded to. There were no rituals of guilt and expiation as there were in commemorations of 'the victims of fascism,' no structures of compensation and memory such as those provided by veterans' organisations and benefits. In their privatised but pervasive discourse, women remembered and passed on to their daughters their experiences: of bombing raids, flight from the advancing Red Army, rapes and fear of rape. But they also transmitted memories of sturdy *Trümmerfrauen* tidying up the ruins of the bombed out cities. In an analogue to their heroic and pathetic brothers, fathers, husbands, lovers and sons on the eastern front—who also expressed no shame or guilt, because they perceived themselves as having had no choice—women too invented themselves as both victims and heroines. The memories remained raw, distorted and repressed but hardly completely silenced. They can be found abundantly in post-war literature, film and government documentation.

Women's stories were combined with men's more openly validated tribulations on the eastern front and as prisoners of war to construct a new national community of suffering that served not only to avoid confrontation with Nazi crimes but also as a strategy for reauthorizing and reestablishing the unity of the Volk, providing the basis for a 'sick' Germany to 'recover,' once again—a metaphor much used by post-war women's groups from all political camps. This sense of victimisation as well as women's pained pride in carrying on—often with children, and without men, at their side—entailed a considerable amount of nostalgia for the order and material comfort of life in the Third Reich.

The turn-of-the-millennium explosion of memory (and memory politics) about German suffering during and after the war relies in part on the nagging sense that this victimisation was never adequately expressed or recognised, and always overshadowed in both West and East Germany by the demand for a recognition of collective guilt for Germany's crimes. This insistence on what historians have called 'the silence that never was' certainly applies to popular perceptions that German women's massive and collective experience of sexual assault was quickly and profoundly silenced or tabooed. It is indeed the case that the ubiquitous stories of rape were not denied but rather downplayed or 'normalised' by virtually everyone, including the victims themselves. Depending on who was talking, rapes were presented as the inevitable by-product of a vicious war, or, in the 'antifascist' narrative, as understandable retribution or exaggerated anticommunist propaganda. Directly after the war, however, these framings did not mean that rape stories were denied or silenced.

This article is based on chapter 2 of Atina Grossmann, *Jews, Germans, and Allies: Close Encounters in Occupied Germany*, 2007. Reproduced with permission of Princeton University Press in the format Book via Copyright Clearance Center.

NOTES

1.   See the broad reception of the well-received but controversial publication of a revised and retranslated text about mass rapes in

Berlin which was originally published in 1954, *Eine Frau in Berlin* 2003; in English, *A Woman in Berlin* 2005. This interest was preceded by the positive response to Anthony Beevor's discussion of rape in Fall of Berlin (Beevor 2002). Research published in the 1990s includes Naimark 1995; Heimatmuseum Charlottenburg 1995; and the text accompanying Helke Sander's film on the topic (Sander/ Johr 1992). For earlier feminist analyses, see Ingrid Schmidt-Harzbach (1984); Erika M. Hoerning (1985) and Tröger (1986). For an even earlier feminist consideration of sexual violence in World War II, including attacks by Soviet liberators on German women, see Susan Brownmiller (1975: 48–79). On the thorny problems of historicizing rape at war's end and the controversy about Sander's film, see Grossmann (1995a).

2. Johr (1992: 48, 54f, 59). See also Kuby (1965: 312f), and especially Naimark (1995: 69–90).

3. Ilya Ehrenburg explicitly denied long-standing accusations that he, a Soviet Jew in the Red Army, had been "urging the Asiatic peoples to drink the blood of German women." See Brownmiller (1975: 70–3).

4. This terrifying image has a long lineage not limited to memories of World War II. For a specific reference in this context, see Ingrid Strobl's response to Sander's film, (1992: 55).

5. Höcker, 1984: 71, 25 May 1945 entry. For analysis of the outpouring of diary writing, see Nieden 1993.

6. See also Hoerning 1985: 327–46.

7. Interview with G. C., conducted in early 1990s, quoted in Heimatmuseum Charlottenburg 1995: 22.

8. My translation from *Eine Frau in Berlin* 2003. See also the controversies about the legitimacy of 'outing' the author's name and identity as a kind of Nazi 'new woman, as they played out on the feuilleton pages of major newspapers amongst male scholars and journalists. See especially Bisky 2003, for her 'outing' as the journalist Marta Hillers who had written propaganda texts for the NSDAP. For the enthusiastically received American edition, see *A Woman in Berlin* 2005. See discussion of controversy about the German republication in Heineman 2005: esp. 53–6.

9. "Die scheint ja och noch stolz druff ze sind, det se de Russen in ihrem Alter noch vorjenommen ham." Quoted in unpublished memoir by Winterfeldt N.D.: 438.

10. Minutes in Bundesarchiv Berlin (Sapmo), DFD BV (Bundesvorstand) 98, Sitzungen des Bundesvorstands des DFD. Meetings were held

on 23 May, 26 July and 23 August 1945; quote is from latter; Sauerbruch story from Mahle 1995: 65.

11. All depositions quoted from Landesarchiv Berlin (LAB) Rep. 214/2814/220. See also Rep. 214, 2814/221/1-2, 2740/156. For detailed discussion, including figures on timing of abortions, see Grossmann 1995b: 149–53, 193–9; and idib. 1995a.

12. Report by H. Gnädig, LAB Rep. 240/2651/98.3. All quotes from Rep. 240/2651 are from an essay contest sponsored by the Berlin Senate in 1976, 'Berlin 1945. Wie ich es erlebte', 812 contributors, most of them women, described their experiences from May 1945 to the end of the blockade in June 1949.

13. Quoting a Hamburg gynaecologist who also reports that "abortions are on the increase." Gollancz 1947: 46f.

14. Report by Gertrud Strubel, LAB 240/2651/131/1.

15. Report by Erna Kohnke, LAB 240/2651/655/1.

16. BAB (Sapmo) NL 182/856, 27. Der Funktionär, KPD Bezirk Thüringen, October 1945.

17. According to the West Berlin women's magazine *Sie* (13 October 1946: 3), the women outnumbered male voters.

18. BAB (Sapmo) NL 182/853, 39.

19. Harich 1948: 3. I am indebted to Norman Naimark for steering me to this source.

20. Aufruf der KPD, BAB (Sapmo) NL 182/853, 10.

21. Harich 1948: 3. See also Naimark 1995: 134–40.

22. US Army Military Government. Office of Military Government, Berlin Sector 1946: 8. New research shows that a considerable number of sexual assaults in Berlin were perpetrated by American soldiers. See Evans 2007.

23. I borrow the term "remasculinisation" from Robert Moeller who refers to Jeffords 1989.

REFERENCES

A Woman in Berlin: Eight Weeks in the Conquered City. 2005. New York: Metropolitan Books.

Bartov, Omer. 1986. *The Eastern Front, 1941–45: German Troops and the Barbarisation of Warfare.* New York: St. Martin's Press.

Beevor, Anthony. 2002. *The Fall of Berlin 1945.* New York: Viking Press.

Berman, Harold J./Kerner, Miroslav. 1955. *Soviet Military Law and Administration.* Cambridge: Harvard University Press.

Bisky, Jens. 2003. 'Wenn Jungen Weltgeschichte spielen, haben Mädchen stumme Rollen', *Süddeutsche Zeitung* (Munich), 24 September.

Boveri, Margret. 1945. *Tage des Überlebens: Berlin 1945*. Munich: Piper.

Brownmiller, Susan. 1975. *Against Our Will: Men, Women and Rape*. New York: Simon and Schuster.

Davidson, Eugene. 1959. *The Death and Life of Germany: An Account of the American Occupation*. New York: Alfred A. Knopf.

Deutsche Wochenschau. 22 March 1945 [news programme]. Nr. 755/10. Germany.

Deutscher, Isaac. 1980. *Reportagen aus Nachkriegsdeutschland*. Hamburg: Junius.

Durand-Wever, Anne-Marie. N.D. *Als die Russen kamen: Tagebuch einer Berliner Ärztin*, unpublished diary.

Ehrenburg, Ilya. 1964. *The War: 1941–45, Volume V of Men, Years-Life*. Cleveland: The World Publishing Company.

Eine Frau in Berlin: Tagebuchaufzeichnungen vom 20. April bis zum 22. Juni 1945. 2003. Frankfurt a. M: Eichborn.

Erickson, John. 1983. *The Road to Berlin: Stalin's War with Germany*, vol. 2. London: Weidenfeld and Nicolson.

Evans, Jennifer V. 2007. 'Protection from the Protector: Court Martial Cases and the Lawlessness of Occupation in American-Controlled Berlin, 1945–48' in Thomas Maulucci/Detlev Junker (eds), *GIs and Germans: The American Military Presence, 1945–1990*, pp. 212–34. London: Cambridge University Press.

Evans, Richard. 1989. *In Hitler's Shadow: West German Historians and the Attempt to Escape from the Nazi Past*. New York: Pantheon.

Gollancz, Victor. 1947. *In Darkest Germany*. London: V. Gollancz Ltd.

Grossmann, Atina. 2007. *Jews, Germans, and Allies: Close Encounters in Occupied Germany*. Princeton: Princeton University Press.

———. 1995a. 'A Question of Silence: The Rape of German Women by Occupation Soldiers', *October*, 72(Spring):42–63.

———. 1995b. *Reforming Sex: The German Movement for Birth Control and Abortion Reform, 1920–1950*. New York: Oxford.

Harich, Wolfgang. 1948. N.N., *Tägliche Rundschau* (Berlin), 12 December.

Heimatmuseum Charlottenburg. 1995. *Worüber kaum gesprochen wurde: Frauen und Alliierte Soldaten, Heimatmuseum Charlottenburg, 03. September–15. October 1995*. Berlin: Bezirksamt Charlottenburg.

Heineman, Elizabeth. 2005. 'Gender, Sexuality, and Coming to Terms with the Nazi Past', *Central European History*, 38(1):41–74.

————. 1999. *What Difference Does a Husband Make? Women and Marital Status in Nazi and Postwar Germany.* Berkeley: University of California Press.

Herzog, Dagmar. 2005. *Sex After Fascism: Memory and Morality in Twentieth Century Germany.* Princeton: Princeton University Press.

Hoerning, Erika M. 1985. 'Frauen als Kriegsbeute: Der Zwei-Fronten Krieg: Beispiele aus Berlin', in Lutz Niethammer/Alexander van Plato (eds), *'Wir kriegen jetzt andere Zeiten': Auf der Suche nach der Erfahrung des Volkes in nachfaschistischen Ländern*, pp. 327–46. Berlin: J.H.W. Dietz.

Höcker, Karla. 1984. *Beschreibung eines Jahres: Berliner Notizen 1945.* Berlin: arani.

Howley, Frank L. 1950. *Berlin Command.* New York: Putnam.

Jeffords, Susan. 1989. *The Remasculinization of America: Gender and the Vietnam War.* Bloomington: University of Indiana Press.

Johr, Barbara. 1992. 'Die Ereignisse in Zahlen', in Helke Sander/Barbara Johr (eds), *BeFreier und Befreite: Krieg, Vergewaltigung, Kinder*, pp. 46–73. Munich: Kunstmann.

Kopelev, Lev. 1979. *Aufbewahren für alle Zeit.* Munich: dtv.

Kuby, Erich. 1965. *Die Russen in Berlin 1945.* Bern/Munich: Scherz.

Mahle, Hans. 1995. 'Wie ich Prof. Dr. Sauerbruch und Dr. Hermes fand', in Christine Krauss/Daniel Küchenmeister (eds), *Das Jahr 1945: Brüche und Kontinuitäten*, pp. 65–77. Berlin: Dietz.

Meyer, Sibylle/Schulze, Eva (eds). 1985. *Wie wir das alles geschafft haben: Alleinstehende Frauen berichten über ihr Leben nach 1945.* Munich: Beck.

Naimark, Norman M. 1995. *Russians in Germany: A History of the Soviet Zone of Occupation, 1945-1949.* Cambridge: Harvard University Press.

Nieden, Susanne zur. 1993. *Alltag im Ausnahmezustand: Frauentagebücher im zerstörten Deutschland 1943–1945.* Berlin: Orlanda Frauenverlag.

N.N. 1945. 'Mongolen in Berlin! Die neueste Flüstergeschichte', *Berliner Zeitung*, 30 May.

Pausewang, Gudrun. 1985. 'Ein Maimontag', in Heinrich Böll/Peter O. Chotjewitz (eds), *NiemandsLand: Kindheitserinnerungen an die Jahre 1945 bis 1949*, pp. 59–65. Bronheim-Merten: Lamuv.

Riess, Curt. 1953. *Berlin Berlin: 1945–1953.* Berlin: Non-Stop Bücherei.

Sander, Helke/Johr, Barbara (eds). 1992. *BeFreier und Befreite: Krieg, Vergewaltigung, Kinder.* München: Kunstmann.

Schmidt-Harzbach, Ingrid. 1984. 'Eine Woche im April: Berlin 1945: Vergewaltigung als Massenschicksal', *Feministische Studien*, 3(2):51–65.

Strobl, Ingrid. 1992. 'Wann begann das Grauen?' *konkret*, 09:54–6.

Thurnwald, Hilde. 1948. *Gegenwartsprobleme Berliner Familien: Eine soziologische Untersuchung an 498 Familien.* Berlin: Weidmann.

Tröger, Annemarie. 1986. 'Between Rape and Prostitution: Survival Strategies and Chances of Emancipation for Berlin Women after World War II', in Judith Friedlander (ed), *Women in Culture and Politics: A Century of Change*, pp. 97–117. Bloomington: Indiana University Press.

US Army Military Government, Office of Military Government, Berlin Sector. 1946. *Report to the Commanding General US Headquarters Berlin District: 6 Month Report (4 January–3 July 1946).* Wilmington: Scholarly Resources.

Vallentin, Gabriele. 1955. *Die Einnahme von Berlin durch die Rote Armee vor zehn Jahren: Wie ich sie selbst erlebt habe: Geschrieben 1955.* Berlin State Archive: Acc. 2421.

Weber, Annemarie. 1966. *Westend.* Munich: Desch.

Wieck, Michael. 1990. *Zeugnis vom Untergang Königsbergs: Ein 'Geltungsjude' berichtet.* Heidelberg: Heidelberger Verlagsanstalt und Druckerei.

Winterfeld, Hans. N.D. *Deutschland: Ein Zeitbild 1926–1945: Leidensweg eines deutschen Juden in den ersten 19 Jahren seines Lebens.* Leo Baeck Institute Archives: ME 690.

Zink, Harold. 1957. *The United States in Germany 1944–1955.* Princeton: Van Nostrand.

Sexual Violence as Indictment, as Titillation, as Trope in *The Pawnbroker* (1961)

PASCALE R. BOS

When the American-Jewish author Edward Lewis Wallant published *The Pawnbroker* in 1961, it was the first novel in the English language to deal with the Holocaust from the perspective of a (Jewish) concentration camp survivor. Wallant, born in 1926, had served in the US Navy from 1944–1946 but had not seen the concentration camps himself and based parts of the novel that deal with the war trauma of his main protagonist on the limited descriptions he had come across in the media and on the conversations with a survivor whom he befriended after the war in New York.[1] The events of the Holocaust were still poorly understood in the US at the time, yet thanks to intuition or luck, much of what Wallant imagined about the experience of the Nazi camps he got right. In particular, his depiction of the protagonist's struggle with posttraumatic stress disorder with recurring nightmares is deemed exceptional for its time.

Not historically accurate, however, yet pivotal to its plot is the novel's representation of sexual violence; the sexual enslavement of the protagonist's wife in a concentration camp brothel. This event lies at the heart of the protagonist's trauma and its revelation constitutes the narrative's crucial turning point and is retained in the 1964 film adaptation by director Sidney Lumet (*The Pawnbroker* 1964). This depiction of organized prostitution of Jewish women in the service of Nazi (SS) officers was fictional in nature.[2] However, contemporary audiences would not have been aware of this. Indeed, this fictionalization was probably not intentional on the part of Wallant. As similar stories of Nazi sexual enslavement of Jewish women had circulated widely since the early 1940s (Bos 2014), he likely assumed that what he depicted was based on historical fact.

The consequences of having an inaccurate representation of sexual violence featured in an acclaimed work of literature and its film adaptation at a time when little is understood about the historical event it depicts outside of the community which survived it (and is therefore unlikely to be recognized as incorrect), are considerable. It silences victims from speaking out about the actual circumstances under which sexual violence transpired, and which in turn leads to a considerable delay in reconstructing such a history. The latter has certainly been the case with sexual violence during World War II and the Holocaust, the history of which has only began to be written over the past twenty years. Yet looking closely at such fictional representations can also prove insightful, granted one reads them with a critical eye and with the realization that depictions of sexual violence in war can serve several utilitarian functions for authors. Unpacking those functions in *The Pawnbroker*, this brief essay suggests that the trauma of sexual violence advances the plot and allows the author to illustrate something he deems essential about both the nature of the crimes and the criminals involved in the Holocaust and about the experience of the victims. With the critical distance of time and a feminist lens, we can reassess the representations to consider how they culturally reinscribe power and gender in discussions of war and sexual violence. Thus, a close reading of the particular scenes in question in *The Pawnbroker* novel and film makes visible how the representations fail to do justice to the experience of suffering of women.

THE NOVEL (1961): SEXUAL VIOLENCE AS TROPE, AS INDICTMENT

The Pawnbroker recounts a stretch of about two weeks in the summer of 1958 in the life of Polish-Jewish pawnbroker Sol Nazerman. Living in suburban New York with his assimilated American-Jewish sister's family while working in a pawnshop in impoverished black Harlem, he is an oddly emotionally stunted figure. He is pathologically stingy, unable to show compassion for his downtrodden customers who pawn their last possessions with him, and barely tolerates the enthusiasm of his young Puerto Rican assistant. Few, however, know of the details of Nazerman's past: a former professor from Warsaw, he has lost his children and wife to the Nazis and has survived the concentration camps Bergen-Belsen and Dachau. Coming up to the fifteenth anniversary of his and his family's deportation, he is experiencing increased psychological stress and nightmares. As the anniversary date nears, Nazerman's crisis reaches a crescendo when he comes to realize that the money of a local kingpin's criminal empire that he had been knowingly laundering through his pawnshop turns out to stem from the exploitation of local brothels. Nazerman unsuccessfully tries to confront the crime boss who threatens to kill him. This set of events triggers a long-repressed traumatic memory in Nazerman which reveals itself in the form of a nightmare set in a concentration camp.

After Nazerman repeatedly questions the whereabouts of his wife, a camp guard forces him to take a look into a barrack building where he witnesses the following scene:

> [T]he vast room [...] was broken into many cubicles. There were women in each one [...]. Wild laughter echoed from various parts [...] and, like the perverted echo of the laughter, the low crushed sound of moaning [...]. His wife, Ruth, sat on her bed with a sheet up over her nakedness [...] her own attention was riveted on the entrance of her cubicle with terrified anticipation [...]. A black-uniformed man entered [...]. He took off his clothes and for a few minutes just displayed his exposed body to the terrified woman on the bed. Finally he pulled the sheet from her nakedness. He seemed to be speaking to her [...]. Ruth began shuddering. Her face turned the colour of calcimine [...]. For a minute or two the SS man handled her breasts and loins vengefully. Her mouth stretched in soundless agony. As though he had been waiting for that, the SS man pulled her to her knees and forced her head down against his body. (Wallant 1961: 168–9)

Watching this scene unfold,

Sol began to moan. But just before tears could bring mercy to his
eyes, he saw her recognize him. And from that hideously obscene
position, pierced so vilely, she endured the zenith of her agony
and was able to pass through it. Until finally she was able to award
him the tears of forgiveness. But he was not worthy of her award
and took the infinitely meaner triumph of blindness, and though
he was reamed by cancerous, fiery torments, he was no longer
subject to the horrid view, no longer had to share the obscene
experience with her […]. And then he went a step further toward
the empty blackness of animal relief; he fainted and felt nothing
for a long time. (Wallant 1961: 169)

This pivotal scene through which Nazerman relives the moment
he inadvertently witnessed the forced prostitution of his wife Ruth
in a Nazi brothel years prior offers an explanation for Nazerman's
strange detached behaviour after the war, and it reveals the core of
the trauma from which he suffers. The novel traces the trauma's
profound effects as it shapes Nazerman's interactions with both
his customers in the pawnshop and his personal relationships, and
the further arc of the novel. Yet what precisely constitutes this
trauma? The nightmare has a confusing focal point. Whose gaze
is the narrator following? Who is subject, who is object? Whose
suffering are we witness to? And what or who is the suffering
caused or aggravated by?

The first part of the nightmare follows Nazerman's gaze as
he witnesses the makeshift Nazi brothel and recognizes his wife.
It describes Ruth's ordeal, and through Nazerman the reader
empathizes with his wife's suffering as caused by the (impending)
sexual violence. Yet the narration oddly shifts mid-way to describe
her as 'the terrified woman'. Then the narration shifts back to
Ruth's anguish as witnessed by Nazerman. The rest of the
nightmare focuses in on Nazerman, and now his suffering, rather
than his wife's, is at the centre. Even though it describes Ruth's
pain as it is aggravated by the realization that her husband is
witnessing her sexual violation (and her shame and powerlessness
are amplified by being observed by him), Nazerman's trauma
proves to be not about her sexual molestation, but rather about
his witnessing—of being forced by a Nazi guard to witness—his

wife's sexual violation. His inability to look away or to aid her and his interpretation of the sexual act as 'obscene, ' and his 'sharing' of the 'obscene experience' is deemed traumatic.

This particular scene with its odd focal shifts from victim to witness can be read as emblematic for how sexual violence functions emotionally and symbolically when read from a traditional (male) context. The shifts hint at the potentially shattering cultural effects acts of sexual violence can have on traditional communities. The harm extends well beyond the physical violation and damage to the (female) victim's sense of self, autonomy, and self-determination— about which we in fact learn nothing in this novel—as the injury is interpreted primarily as directed at the men and the community at large. Here, sexual violence is understood as an attack on a woman's 'purity' or chastity, and a failure to protect that purity because of a community's inability to defend itself becomes evidence of communal powerlessness. Thus, the attack on a woman's sexuality brings about collective shame and humiliation. In turn, the victim may be perceived as the agent of that shame, as responsible for bringing dishonour to her spouse, family, or community. This explains why it is not just the sexual assault that is harmful to the victim (Ruth), but why the sexual violence being witnessed is seen as adding to the victim's agony, and why the act of witnessing itself causes harm to the male witness (Nazerman).

The sense of obscenity and shame is moreover amplified by the brothel setting. The brothel carries associations of organized, consensual, contractual sex trade and suggests a complicity of the victims who can be seen as choosing to 'buy' their own survival at the expense of their own and the community's honour, as it interprets the sexual violence as sex, rather than as violence.

The rest of the novel confirms that Nazerman's crisis revolves around his having witnessed and abandoned his wife in her moment of greatest need. In the nightmare he relives that he is at once a voyeuristic observer to her pain and humiliation, and yet does not have the strength to properly bear witness to her suffering—he looks away, is blinded, and finally faints. Nazerman's looking away is an act of cowardice rather than an act of mercy. After all, he does not avert his gaze in order to shield his wife from his objectifying look, but rather to buffer himself from what is unfolding before him. It is *his* shame, *his* disgust, and his inability to endure his *own* humiliation and powerlessness that causes him to faint. He thus ceases to be a witness and gives up any pretence of resistance to her violation and in extension, to Nazi cruelty. This is thus the trauma from which the narrative suggests the protagonist suffers: his complicity in the pain of his wife's sexual violence. The resolution of the narrative hinges on Nazerman's refusal to continue to look away in the future by resisting further complicity with the exploitation of women in the present: at the risk of his life, he breaks off his profitable relationship with the criminal network whose prostitution money his pawnshop was whitewashing.

The scene's shifting gaze which never offers the point of view of the victim as a subject rather than mere object is typical for traditional narratives by male authors on sexual violence during war as it excludes actual victims from a discussion about sexual violence. In *The Pawnbroker*, sexual violence becomes a plot device to show its traumatic impact on the protagonist, and to illustrate what was imagined as a uniquely perverse tendency of Nazis to sexually enslave and abuse those whom they deemed racially inferior. Such depictions of sexual violence that suggest how uniquely cruel, immoral and criminal an enemy regime is can also lead to depictions of sexual violence that have the (in)advertent effect to titillate. This effect comes about when the audience of scenes of sexual violence is positioned voyeuristically—they neither identify with the perspective of the victim nor that of the perpetrator, but they are mere spectators. The same pivotal scene of Nazerman's traumatic remembering in *The Pawnbroker* as reimagined for the film adaptation illustrates this dilemma.

THE FILM (1964): SEXUAL VIOLENCE AS TITILLATION

In the film, this memory returns not in the form of a nightmare, but as a flashback in the present, triggered by the protagonist's encounter with a prostitute. Desperate to make some money, Mabel, a young African American woman (lover of Nazerman's assistant) rushes to the shop at closing time to pawn a gold pocket watch. Hoping for a better offer when Nazerman lowballs her, she reveals that the watch was hard-earned "for a private session" and that she can offer him the same: "I'm good pawnbroker, I'm real good, I do things you have never even think about before. Just $20 more, I make you happy, like you'd never know" (*The Pawnbroker* 1964). As she confides in Nazerman about her work, she mentions the name of her boss. At that moment, Nazerman recognizes the man for whom his pawnshop launders money, and he realizes his unwitting complicity with the Harlem sex trade. When Mabel proceeds to pull down the top of her dress to reveal her naked breasts and pleads with Nazerman to look at her, it sets off a set of flashbacks whereby his long repressed traumatic memory returns in full.

The screen images cut between Mabel, breasts bared in the present and her invitation to "look!" and memory images of the camp where Nazerman has returned from a work detail when a truck full of women arrives. The women are herded into a barrack and are followed by a large group of laughing German officers. A Nazi officer guarding Nazerman catches him observing the scene, grabs him and drags him to the barracks. He yells in German, "You want to see it, so I'll show it to you" and smashes Nazerman's head through the glass pane of the door and forces him to watch. We see two dressed Nazi officers scrub a naked woman in the shower, several naked women on beds in small partitioned rooms, another room where a naked woman is chatting with a uniformed Nazi officer, and finally Nazerman's wife, sitting on a bed, alone, naked but covered below her waist with a blanket, hands clasped tensely. A Nazi officer in riding crops walks into the room, hands on his hips. With his back to Nazerman and the audience he obscures the view of Ruth who is only partially visible through his legs. Now the scene cuts back to the present where Mabel, half-naked, asks Nazerman to look at her. As Nazerman's awareness returns to the present moment, he grabs Mabel's trench coat and covers her up, hands her money and sends her out. Not realizing what has just transpired, Mabel hurries off, humiliated. Nazerman, now fully conscious of how his present situation connects to the

past witnessing of the violation of his wife, erupts in anger. In the
next scene he attempts to confront his boss to liberate himself
from being implicated in his brothel enterprise in the future.

While it is sexual exploitation of women in the past and the
present that is ostensibly critiqued by way of the powerful scene,
the film's use of partial female frontal nudity to tell this story,
profoundly shocking for the time period and the very first time this
was shown in a regular film, suggests a more problematic reading.
While the filmmakers successfully challenged the Hays Production
Code in order to keep the nudity from being cut, arguing that it
was integral to the story, it can be argued that the scenes instead
somewhat deliberately invite a (male) voyeuristic gaze. For whereas
narratives such as *The Pawnbroker* which "dramatize the trauma
of being forced to watch sexual degradations and torture," do
so on the grounds "that it is incumbent on Americans to witness
such sexual spectacles because they constitute evidence of Nazi
perfidy [...]. [T]he consumption of explicit representation of sex
is transformed [...] from a crime into a responsibility" (Lambert
2013: 40), as Josh Lambert has suggested, and thus, "[...] as
distasteful as it is to witness forced prostitution and sexual abuse,"
in literature or film, doing so becomes "an ethical imperative [...]
when reckoning with the crimes of the Nazis" (Lambert 2013:
41),[3] this argument does not hold up well for *The Pawnbroker*.
Whilst this logic got the film through the censorship, and the
scenes in which the audience observes Nazerman looking at his
wife can perhaps be read as part of this ethical obligation to bear
witness to Nazi evil, pairing Nazerman's flashbacks of Ruth with
his and our watching of Mabel in the present complicates the
scene's reading. After all, while the context of Ruth's bearing of
her breasts is involuntary—she clearly suffers, and the scenes are
decidedly not erotic or seductive, and Nazerman is forced to look
at her yet wishes that he could look away—this is not the case for
the scenes with Mabel. Instead, she offers herself to Nazerman
and the audience's gaze voluntarily, and invites, even implores
them to look at her. While Nazerman does not respond to her
offer and tries to look away, we as an audience do not—the images
showing her naked last for over half a minute. Mabel's nudity is

moreover complicated by her blackness and Nazerman's and the audience's implied white gaze which carries a tainted history of slavery and the eroticization and violation of the female racial 'other.' Ironically then, while the film seems to critique the Nazi's erotic fascination with the Jewish female, this same exotic, erotic gaze risks being reinscribed to titillating effect through the viewer's lingering gaze on Mabel.

In closing, fictional narratives such as *The Pawnbroker*, in which the evil of the Nazis is imagined through the lens of sexual enslavement, are ostensibly important as they at least mention wartime sexual violence, and did so at a time when such topics were not yet openly discussed. However, in actuality they are problematic as their historically inaccurate, even titillating depictions of sexual violence focus on the suffering of men rather than women and obscure rather than elucidate the actual experiences of wartime sexual violence. Here, the sexual violence and sexual coercion is imagined as perpetrated predominantly by Nazi men in the context of the concentration camps and as taking the form of enforced prostitution or sexual slavery. This trope of Nazi perfidy obscures the broader fact that armed conflicts and war create situations of crisis, lawlessness and impunity that leave all whom are vulnerable open up to a wide range of opportunistic sexual predation by those with more power. Thus, the reality that (Jewish) women under Nazi invasion, occupation, or incarceration, were just as likely to be targeted by men other than Nazis, remains out of view.[4] Moreover, the trope of sexual slavery leaves female victims open to accusations of complicity. Thus implicated and exposed to the titillating gaze of a (male) audience, actual victims of sexual violence thought it better not to speak out about their experiences.

NOTES

1. The survivor whom Wallant befriended was the Polish-Jewish Morris Wyszogrod. They both started studying at the Pratt Art Institute in New York in 1947. While Wyszogrod spoke with Wallant privately about his experiences, he did not publish a memoir of his Holocaust experiences until 1999 (Wyszogrod 1999).

436　　　　　　　　　　　　　　PASCALE R. BOS

2. Robert Sommer's (2009; 2010) nuanced discussion of the evidence demonstrates that forced prostitution in concentration camps was rare and that the Nazis excluded Jewish women from the brothels they created for privileged prisoners. On sexual violence by Nazi soldiers and SS-men in different territories see also Mühlhäuser 2017.
3. "[T]he explicit representation of sexuality as part of the documentation of Nazi crimes" became justified in the US during and after the war as Nazis were seen as "sexually villainous" and "their crimes as partly sexual" (Lambert 2013: 38).
4. Much sexual violence that women in concentration camps experienced came at the hands of other incarcerated men in positions of relative power. See, for example, Hájková 2013.

REFERENCES

Bos, Pascale R. 2014. 'Her flesh is branded: "For Officers Only" Imagining/Imagined Sexual Violence against Jewish Women during the Holocaust', in Hilary Earl/ Karl A. Schleunes (eds), *Lessons and Legacies XI: Expanding Perspectives on the Holocaust in a Changing World*, pp. 59–85. Evanston: Northwestern University Press.
Hájková, Anna. 2013. 'Sexual Barter in Times of Genocide: Negotiating the Sexual Economy of the Theresienstadt Ghetto', *Signs: Journal of Women in Culture and Society*, 38(3):503–33.
Lambert, Josh. 2013. *Unclean Lips: Jews, Obscenity, and American Culture*. New York: New York University Press.
Mühlhäuser, Regina. 2017. 'Sexual Violence and the Holocaust', in Andrea Pető (ed), *Gender: War (Macmillan Interdisciplinary Handbook)*, pp. 101–16. Farmington Hills: Gale Cengage Learning.
The Pawnbroker. 1964. [Film]. Sidney Lumet. dir. USA: Landau Company.
Sommer, Robert. 2010. 'Sexual Exploitation of Women in Nazi Concentration Camp Brothels', in Sonja Hedgepeth/ Rochelle Saidel (eds), *Sexual Violence against Jewish Women during the Holocaust*, pp. 46–60. Hanover: University Press of New England.
———. 2009. *Das KZ-Bordell: Sexuelle Zwangsarbeit in nationalsozialistischen Konzentrationslagern*. Paderborn: Schöningh.
Wallant, Edward Lewis. 1961. *The Pawnbroker*. New York: Harcourt, Brace & World.
Wyszogrod, Morris. 1999. *A Brush With Death: An Artist In The Death Camps*. Albany: State University of New York Press.

What are we Talking about When we Talk about Wartime Rape?

JÚLIA GARRAIO

Pascale Bos' feminist analysis of Edward Lewis Wallant's novel *The Pawnbroker* (1961) and its 1964 film adaptation by director Sidney Lumet insightfully explores some cultural entanglements of depictions of sexual violence. Bos convincingly argues that the historical inaccuracies of Wallant's novel and Lumet's film depictions result not only from the author's and director's lack of personal experience and knowledge of the realities of sexual violence during the Holocaust, but foremost from the cultural imaginaries of rape which both artists navigated. Her case study elucidates the power of 'scripts' in the representation and perception of wartime rape. Far from being a taboo, rape has been used repeatedly as a device in war narratives to define the warring sides and the conflict itself. Short-term propaganda needs, but also politics of memory and cultural understandings of sexuality, structure the rhetoric of rape. The 'Nazi rapist', far from being a singular trope, resonates with a binary that is deeply entrenched in patriarchal war narratives: good soldiers (usually referring to 'us' or 'our side') protect women and children, while bad soldiers (normally 'the enemy') sexually assault women. In addition, the imaginary of war conquest has repeatedly conflated women's bodies, land and nation, thus sustaining and perpetuating the metaphor of rape as territorial invasion, foreign occupation and attack on a community. Since postwar US society remembered Nazi Germany as the invader/occupier of weaker European nations and increasingly as the persecutor of the Jewish people, Nazis *were expected* to have raped the women of the nations they attacked. Since in the 1960s concentration camps had already become an icon of Nazi atrocities, those spaces *could easily be imagined* to have been sites of sexual violence and debauchery.

Should we, as Bos does, examine critically works that, despite their historical inaccuracies, ultimately give visibility to wartime sexual violence? After all, Wallant and Lumet were right in assuming that Nazi racial laws did not prevent massive sexual abuse of Jewish women, and in holding the Nazi regime as responsible for those crimes. The problem is certainly not with whom the fingers are pointed at, but, on one hand, how the artistic representation reinforces male power over rape narratives and, on the other hand, how the understandings of rape that sustain the representation contribute to the silencing of certain forms of sexual violence. The implications of the imaginaries of rape as interpretative grids go beyond their potential in concealing the complexities and the broad spectrum of experiences and of perpetrators of wartime sexual violence. As Bos suggests, entrenched expectations can make victims refrain from speaking out as they realize that their experiences of sexual abuse do not correspond to what is expected as wartime rape, thus *making them unfit* for the role ascribed to rape victims.

Therefore, when addressing the aesthetics of rape, it is urgent to ask, as Bos does, 'who speaks?', 'under which circumstances?' and 'for what purpose?' Such approaches can bring awareness to the most pervasive cultural entanglement of wartime sexual violence: its functional character, that is, the tendency to condemn rape when it is verbalized and understood as a signal for something else and when it affirms the collective identity ascribed to victims and aggressors. Critically discussing these processes may bring us further along in understanding the apparent contradiction between the pervasiveness of practices of signifying wartime rape as atrocity ascribed to the enemy by societies that themselves harbour a vast spectrum of forms of sexual violence, which, in many cases, are not publicly articulated and may even be tolerated.

Scripts, Metaphors and the Evasiveness of Sexual Violence as an Individualized Gendered Experience

JÚLIA GARRAIO

When I attended *Retornar: Traços de Memória* [Return: Traces of Memory] (Peralta 2015)–probably the major exhibition so far on the issue of the 'returnees'[1]—I was struck by the presence of four photos of a Portuguese colonial soldier posing with black women. In the first photo, he holds a black child on one arm; with the other, he embraces a smiling woman dressed in local clothing while touching her naked breast. In the second photo, the soldier, with legs open, is holding from behind an almost naked woman by grabbing her breasts. In the third photo, he embraces a smiling girl in a white dress, his hand pointing at her genitals. In the fourth, surrounded by a large black family, the same soldier laughs carelessly while grabbing the breasts of a young woman sitting on his lap. They were part of *Atlas*, a composition of about 600 photos taken from private albums, which covered two opposing walls of the gallery.

I was perplexed not by the reality suggested by the four photos— the massive sexual exploitation and abuse of black women during the Portuguese colonial war[2]–but by their origin: a private album. Those photos might hint 'only' at sexual exploitation in a context of fighting and widespread poverty that led many women and girls to prostitution and intimate relationships with colonial soldiers. In the third photo, however, I might suspect something even more disturbing: After an attack on a village looking for rebel fighters and ammunition, some soldiers 'amuse' themselves with village women.

Private albums function as an archive of the moments and events that a person or a family considers worth remembering. They are the outcome of a process of selection, by which their author(s) frame and communicate the memories that are supposed to be shared with his/her/their family, friends and relatives. So how was someone's 'good history' compatible with photos suggesting normalized sexual abuse? And what were these photos supposed to signify in *Atlas*, a composition made mostly of photos of moments of happiness and leisure invoking a 'lost paradise' of white privilege in Africa?

The photos have to be examined in their different meanings and performativity though time and space from the moment they were produced in a private setting until their reception in a public memorialist context. Why did the soldier and his peers (one of them was most probably the photographer) want to immortalize those moments? What were those photos supposed to tell about the soldier in his album? Why did Joana Gonçalo Oliveira, the author of *Atlas*, choose them for her composition about the memories of the 'returnees'? Which meanings and narratives did they trigger in the public who attended the exhibition in 2015–2016? What kind of transformative processes took place as the photos made their way from their private origins to the public and cultural milieu? How deep was the gap between the original meanings and the later ones? And how far were the later meanings built upon a critical confrontation with the original ones?

I suspected that the tensions between the successive layers of meaning had prompted the author's decision to use the photos in Atlas in the expectation that they would trigger a dynamic process of connections and disruptions capable of generating meanings for the whole composition itself. To grasp these tensions, we have to retrace the pertinence of concepts such as 'porno-tropics' (McClintock 1995) and 'scientific pornography' (Stoler 1995) when addressing the role that the depiction of black women's bodies played in colonial photography. The case of 'Rosinha', a Bantu young woman whom the organizers of the 1934 Oporto Colonial Exhibition brought from Guiné to Portugal with a group of 'indigenous', reveals paradigmatically the sexual dimension of colonial rhetoric and the erotization of the Empire as a place of sexually available women for Portuguese men (see, for instance, Carvalho 2008, Lowndes 2013). The press was fascinated by her beauty and sensuality; photos and postcards of her almost naked body circulated widely in the conservative, Catholic and fiercely moralistic Portugal of the time.

While other European overseas empires display a similar iconography, in the Portuguese case one has to pay attention as well to the pervasiveness of lusotropicalism. Gilberto Freyre (1900–1987) had developed this problematic theory claiming that Portuguese Imperialism had a distinctive character due to its pro-miscegenation attitude: Portuguese were less racists and better colonizers who sexually mingled with local population. The historical background of slavery underlying the origins of the society that had inspired Freye's thesis, Brazil, as well as other emblematic spaces of Portuguese miscegenation (Angola's capital Luanda, for instance) were not articulated, nor were the racialised, economic and class inequalities and systemic racialized gender violence that persisted there beyond the abolition of slavery (e.g. Silva 2002). From the 1950s, official Portuguese propaganda as well as parts of society were all too eager to embrace lusotropicalism in a context of increasing international pressure to decolonize. The idea of lusotropicalism offered the regime a discourse to legitimize its grip over the colonies by claiming Portugal as a multicultural, multiracial and pluricontinental nation. Sexual contacts between Portuguese men and colonized women were hence normalized as part of the 'Overseas' gender and racial relations. Photos and postcards of black women were extremely popular both in the private and public spheres before and during the war. Though anti-colonial armed resistance had challenged the myth of the 'receptive savage', the sexualized body of black women continued to be an ideological locus that enabled the myth of Africa as a land of sexual abundance and availability to persist throughout the war.

Certainly, if we look at anti-colonial literature produced in the colonies at the same time we have a completely different understanding of sexual encounters between black women and white settlers and soldiers. The trope of rape and sexual exploitation is pervasive there as a symbol of colonial oppression and white violence. One of the most emblematic examples of Angolan anti-colonial literature is António Cardoso's *A Casa da Mãezinha*, written in 1962 while the author was imprisoned due to anti-colonial activities. It uses the setting of a brothel and explores experiences of sexual abuse and violence against black and *mestizo* women to denounce the colonial system. In its fictional representation, the sexually abused body becomes a symbol of the oppression of the colonized people and serves to encourage the emergence of a local anti-colonial masculinity that will rescue the abused women, and hence liberate the nation (Garraio 2016).

Portuguese writing critical of the colonial war also uses the trope of rape and sexual exploitation of black women to denounce colonialism. The most prominent example are the novels of the acclaimed author António Lobo Antunes (born 1942), who had served the Portuguese Army as a doctor in a military hospital in Angola (1971–3). His fictional depictions of the war are permeated with representations of rape, sexual abuse and labour exploitation of black women linked to independence fighters and black women working for the Portuguese (Ribeiro 2016).

More recently the controversial *Caderno de Memórias Coloniais* (2009), by Isabela Figueiredo (born 1963), herself a 'returnee' from Mozambique, confronted colonialism through a sexual prism by exploring the racialised gendered relations that shaped colonial society and exposing the sexual consumption of black women's bodies by white men. Figueiredo poignantly rebukes the essence of lusotropicalism as follows: "Black women fucked, they were the ones who did it, with everyone and with some more, with black men and with the husbands of white women, for a tip, certainly, for food, or out of fear" (Figueiredo 2009: 21). This brief sentence reveals not only the social context that made sexual exploitation of black women in the colonies pervasive as part of the colonial system and the economy of war, but also how the structural violence underlying those sexual encounters was made invisible.

Therefore, contemporary artists such as Vasco Araújo could exhibit photos suggesting sexual encounters between colonial soldiers and black women (Araújo 2014) assuming that the Portuguese public would regard them not in the terms of lusotropicalism, but as testimonies of colonial violence, as symbols of racialized sexual oppression. The success and public impact of writers such as Lobo Antunes and Figueiredo popularized this metaphor and made it available as a rhetorical device for younger artists and public consumption. Oliveira told me in an interview (22 August 2016) that she wanted the four mentioned photos to create a rupture in the nostalgic remembrance of the 'returnees'.

However, this strategy only works as long as the real viewer is similar to the 'imagined viewer'.[3] One has to keep in mind that the perceptions of the real viewer always underlie a variation of time-dependent social and cultural and politically influenced imaginations—and different views exist beside each other. Oliveira's imagined viewer then must be someone who is acquainted with Portuguese anti-colonial writing, interprets colonial photos of sexualized black women's bodies as signifiers of sexual exploitation and violence and understands rape of black women in the colonial system as a symbol of colonial oppression.

The transformative process that the colonial photos of black women undergo in their public representation stimulates a more sophisticated understanding of the phenomenon of sexual violence during the Portuguese colonial war as well as of the concept of wartime rape itself. The massacres of white settlers and their workers in Northern Angola in 1961—the events that, according to the Portuguese government, marked the official beginning of the war—were exhaustively photographed by embedded journalists and army officers. Photos of corpses of raped white women and dead babies circulated widely in Portugal to justify the war and abroad to delegitimize the anti-colonial movements and communism. The Portuguese ambassador at the UN used them in 1961 to denounce the "savagery of terrorists who cross the northern border of Angola to behead, rape and mutilate our women" (Ramos 2014). These images framed the perception and public memories of sexual violence during the colonial war as spectacular brutality and murder. Therefore, by making visible the pervasiveness of sexual exploitation of black women and by obliging the public to reconsider the systemic causes underlying sexual encounters between Portuguese men and black women, current practices of signifying photos of sexualized black women as sites of violence enable an enlargement of the public memory of sexual violence during the colonial war. More broadly, they contribute to a redefinition of the concept of wartime rape itself as they point at inevitable blind spots emerging from the reduction of sexual violence to categories as consent and the use of physical force and threats. They hence broaden the concept and situate it as part of the economy of war and a context marked by social racialized inequality, which made sexual violence possible, acceptable and invisible as prostitution and barter sex.

Nonetheless, throughout the journey of resignifications undertaken by this type of colonial photos—from the erasure of sexual violence and exploitation experienced by colonized women until the understanding of it as symbol of colonial oppression and violence—there is a persistent blind spot: the individualized experience of the subject. The sexually exploited body is transformed into a sign for social phenomena (that is it becomes a symbol for something else), hence functioning as a trigger for someone else's discourse and ideological agenda. Traditional rape narratives and their binary oppositions sustain the transformative process under which the portrayal of sexualized black women's bodies became a metaphor for colonialism. Rape is articulated as part of national and/or ideological narratives, and not as individualized memories and ways of dealing with the inflicted violence and resisting it. As an object to be signified, to be given a meaning, the sexually abused body does not exist as a voice expressing subjective experiences.

Inequality and violence shaped the colonial encounter, but the complexities of those power relations and structures of oppression risk being effaced in a 'script' where black women are represented homogenously as absolute and defenceless victims. Black women had an important active role in the resistance against Portuguese colonialism as both fighters and logistic supporters (in some cases that meant engaging in intimate encounters with colonial soldiers). Their experiences and sexual encounters attest to their agency in surviving and navigating an extreme hostile environment of racialized women's vulnerability, but also of ways of forging agency, that is black women were victims but they were also agents of their private lives and of the destiny of their countries towards national independence. A normative homogeneous understanding of the trope therefore risks erasing both the agency of black women and their forms of resistance in colonial times as well as sexual violence as a subjective experience.

The successive layers of meaning in the production and exhibition of the colonial photos of black sexualized bodies discussed here are hence a further case that highlights how sexual violence resists being communicated as a gendered subjective experience.

This research was produced in the context of MEMOIRS—Children of Empires and European Post-Memories, funded by the European Research Council (ERC) under the European Union's Horizon 2020 research and innovation programme (grant agreement no 648624).

NOTES

1. The concept 'returnee' refers to the circa 500,000 people holding Portuguese citizenship, who moved to Portugal after 1974 in the context of the independence of the former Portuguese colonies in Africa. The vast majority came from Angola and Mozambique. One third had been born there and many had never been in Portugal before.
2. The Portuguese Colonial war (1961–74) was fought in Angola, Mozambique and Guinea-Bissau, where it is remembered as the War of Liberation.
3. I use the concept 'imagined viewer' from the work of the Portuguese director and cinema theorist João Mário Grilo, who defined the 'imagined man' as the viewer created by the cinematic apparatus. See Grilo 2006.

REFERENCES

Araújo, Vasco. 2014. *Botânica* [exhibition]. At: Lisbon: Museu do Chiado.

Carvalho, Clara. 2008. '"Raça", género e imagem colonial: Representações de mulheres nos arquivos fotográficos', in José Machado Pais/Clara Carvalho/Neusa Mendes de Gusmão (eds), *O visual e o quotidiano*, pp. 145–74. Lisboa: Imprensa de Ciências Sociais.

Figueiredo, Isabela. 2009. *Cadernos de Memorias Coloniais.* Coimbra: Angelus Novus.

Garraio, Júlia. 2016. 'A Body to Make Luanda: The Black Woman from the Countryside in Angolan Literature', *Journal of Lusophone Studies*, 1(1):184–6.

Grilo, João Mário. 2006. *O Homem Imaginado.* Lisboa: Horizonte.

McClintock, Ann. 1995. *Imperial Leather: Race, Gender and Sexuality in the Colonial Conquest.* New York: Routledge.

Peralta, Elsa. 2015. *Retornar: Traços de Memória* [exhibition]. 4 November 2015–27 February 2016. At: Lisbon: Galeria da Avenida da Índia.

Ramos, Afonso. 2014. 'Angola 1961, o horror das imagens', in Filipa Lowndes Vicente (ed), *O Império da visão: A fotografia no contexto colonial português (1860–1960)*, pp. 399–434. Lisboa: Edições 70.

Ribeiro, Margarida Calafate. 2016. 'Lusos amores em corpos colonizados: As mulheres africanas na literatura portuguesa da guerra colonial', *Ellipsis*, 4:131–47.

Silva, Tony Simões. 2002. 'Raced Encounters, Sexed Transactions: "Luso-tropicalism" and the Portuguese Colonial Empire', *Pretexts: Literary and Cultural Studies*, 11(1):27–39.

Stoler, Ann Laura. 1995. *Race and the Education of Desire: Foucault's History of Sexuality and the Colonial Order of Things.* Durham: Duke University Press.

Vicente, Filipa Lowndes. 2013. 'Rosita e o império como objecto de desejo', *Público* (Lisbon), 25 August.

✳ ✳ ✳

Recognizing Sexual Violence as Violence

PASCALE R. BOS

Julia Garraio's essay analyses the cultural politics surrounding the inclusion and display of a set of photographs found within a 2015–2016 Portuguese exhibit on the public and hidden memory of that nation's recent colonial past. These were originally photographs held in private possession, preserved within a photo album, yet exhibited publicly they now become situated right at the intersection of the public and private gaze, and are suggestive of a national history of sexual violence that has always been visible rather than hidden. Her analysis calls forth questions, however, on how such violence is made visible *as violence*, where, and when, and on what remains unseen, unsaid, unspoken within the act of the photos' exhibition. She furthermore questions what the (un-) intended effects may be of putting such a history on public display by way of photographs which may call forth an uncritical reading.

The photos in the exhibit that attest to the sexual liberties some Portuguese occupation soldiers took with local women in Angola, Mozambique or Guinea-Bissau were originally found within a private photo album. While it seems surprising that the men who took such photos and those portrayed felt fine about being depicted in this fashion and saw no need to hide the images, this suggests both that what the photos revealed was initially not deemed problematic for them, and that they considered these memories worth preserving. Rather than thinking of their behaviour as unethical or criminal or even as violence at all and thus perceiving (and concealing) the photos as evidence of a crime, the men seem to have assumed that it would not offend anyone 'back home.' Indeed, the Portuguese soldiers' use of local women as erotic objects may very well have been read as harmless, Garraio argues, as an example of 'lusotropicalism'–a desire to (sexually) comingle with the local population which supposedly attested to the normalization of race relations in the colonies. Through their public display in an exhibit on Portugal's colonial past in Africa the photographs and the behaviour was put in an entirely different light, however. Garraio suggests that the curator may have included the photos without adding any further contextualization of gender and racial power relations in the colonies on the basis of the assumption that at this point in time, the Portuguese exhibit audience would be capable of critically deconstructing the images and see them for what they are: problematic, shameful reminders of the nation's colonial (war) past in which women of colour were objects to do with as the (male) coloniser pleased, rather than as subjects with their own agency, desires and agendas.

Yet Garraio asks what one risks by displaying such photos, without explicit explanation, and moreover, again with no consent given by the women portrayed in the photos, and furthermore, without us getting to know anything more about their experiences. Does such a display not in fact reinforce the (white, colonial) male gaze? Indeed, she argues, while the bodies of these women are now used in service of a progressive and culturally self-critical agenda, they still serve merely as a symbol or trope to recount histories of oppression and/or war. At the same time, such representations remain silent about the emotional and embodied experiences of sexual violence of (female) victims. That is, (female) victims are spoken about yet do not speak for themselves, and the sexual violence is meant to invoke histories of *other* kinds of violence. Such a presentation of the women moreover makes invisible their agency, even in matters of sexual exchange.

Nevertheless, Garraio seems to suggest that the exhibiting of such photos may represent progress in Portuguese society when she points to the figure of the 'imagined viewer'. The exhibit she discusses deals with photographs of violence that took place between 1961–1974, and within the span of the half century that has passed the audience has gained sufficient knowledge of its own colonial past and the eroticisation of (former) female colonial subjects that they can be assumed to be capable to unpack these images critically. One could thus read this exhibit as part of a discussion about sexual violence within the culture of a former colonial oppressor which has decided it can afford, as a wealthy Western European nation, to fess up and critique its racialised/sexualised past oppression of colonial subjects (and look enlightened in the process). A closer look reveals, however, that this more self-critical, progressive reading is by no means guaranteed. What comes into view, what is seen and how it is defined, depends on the specific socio-cultural setting at a given time. Indeed, to explore a greater variety of perceptions in more detail could provide us with deeper insights.

But let us remain with the intention of the exhibition organizers that the 'imagined viewers' indeed can critically position themselves towards the Portuguese colonial past. While such self-critique does not extend to making material or other reparations to the actual victims of this oppression and violence, it may prove to be a first step into that direction. While I share Garraio's concern that such a reading may be too optimistic and generous (for without proper contextualization the use of such photos still may function as spectacle rather than as critical intervention), I am not convinced that such representations are capable of enabling "an enlargement of the public memory of sexual violence during the colonial war" and a "redefinition of the concept of wartime rape." Or at least, not for this particular exhibit audience. Indeed, I fear that the exact opposite may occur: that the nature of these photos—stemming as they do from personal photo albums—manage to disguise the systemic violence at play. Sexual violence may be read again here either as merely a form of sex rather than violence, or as merely incidental violence—committed by these particular men in these particular photographs—rather than as structural and endemic. The question thus remains how we as artists and scholars can display such images without re-violating the women pictured, without activating within the viewer an objectifying, eroticising gaze, and while providing enough context to show that indeed, colonial scripts of racial subjugation, even if (or perhaps especially if) they include the eroticisation of the female colonial subject as exotic other, will inevitably lead to sexual objectification and sexual violence.

The Literature Database
www.warandgender.net: An Ongoing Project

LISA GABRIEL

A review of the research published on wartime rape and sexual violence in armed conflict reveals a steep rise in the number of publications in recent decades. In the early 1990s, the number of contributions was limited, and the wider scientific community was largely unaware of the publications that were available. Many of the works—anthologies and monographs as well as journals that published articles on the topic—were not included in the regular holdings of libraries. And indeed, the neglect, marginalisation and resistance to dealing with the issue of sexual violence in academia—remarkably congruent with the trivialisation of sexual violence in society and politics—was a crucial topic of research.

Ever since, there has been a significant development of the discussion in the field, in keeping with increasing interest and a comparatively high profile in politics and the media. A wide variety of publications from different disciplines have contributed to the academic debate, covering a range of theoretical and methodological approaches. Yet a disciplinary fragmentation of publications in the field persists. Furthermore, specific issues and disciplinary approaches draw more attention in public debate, such as questions of international politics and security, or the normative discussion on developments in international law. Findings from historical research and philosophy, in contrast, tend to arouse less interest.

The 'Literature Database www.warandgender.net' was developed to document the full breadth of work published in the field. Initial research for the bibliography dates back to the 'Women's Bodies as Battlefields' conference organised by the Working Group 'War and Gender' in Hamburg in 2001.[1] In the run-up to and follow-up after the conference, it became apparent that publications from this field of research were not easily accessible. A first bibliography was thus compiled and published in *Mittelweg 36* to make existing works more visible (Schwensen/ Mühlhäuser 2001). Research for the bibliography continued with a 2008 workshop on 'The Pervasiveness of Sexual Violence in Armed Conflict' which led to the founding of the 'International Research Group "Sexual Violence in Armed Conflict"' (SVAC) in 2010 (Schwensen 2009). Ever since, members of the Hamburg-based Working Group 'War and Gender' (the initiator of the SVAC network) and the library of the Hamburg Institute for Social Research cooperated to develop, improve and update the bibliography. Since 2015, it has been available to the public as an online database at www.warandgender.net/bibliography/.

Today, the collection provides an overview of literature on the historical and contemporary conflicts and wars that have been studied, as well as the spectrum of disciplinary, theoretical and methodological approaches, and research topics in the field. The search for, and selection of, publications is furthermore closely connected to topics and discussions in the SVAC group, and the foci of the selection mirror the network's ongoing work.[2]

While some topics draw attention from specific disciplines or at particular points in time, a number of questions surge up in the discussion again and again, and run through the history of the intellectual and academic exploration of wartime rape and sexual violence in armed conflict since its inception. In view of as yet unanswered questions like "what is sexual about sexual violence?" and "how is the sexual in sexual violence related to power and dominance?" it has been very instructive to combine the research for the bibliography with a re-reading of the history of feminist ideas and theories on rape and sexual violence. A historical and differentiated look at the work done so far on sexuality and sexual violence, including the earlier writings from the various women's movements of the twentieth century, results in a multi-layered understanding of theories, positions and political controversies that cannot be simplified into a two-dimensional cannon or a linear progression of paradigms.

In the current academic discussion seeking to understand and explain sexual violence in armed conflicts in its various forms and occurrences, there are many indications that a reflection of the state of the art of knowledge is underway—in reference to the existing empirical findings and research methods as well as in view of the theoretical debate. A revision of theorising and research thus far could not only be illuminating in terms of the insights and the limitations of past debates. It would also considerably raise awareness of the extent to which analyses, theories and controversies generally reflect overlapping contemporary and local developments and perspectives.

The bibliography provides an opportunity to retrace developments in research into sexual violence in armed conflicts through the years. This also involves charting fundamental problems associated with the subject over time. By documenting the scope of research papers, theoretical contributions, and controversies to date, the collection also serves as a foundation for extrapolating new research questions.

THE BIBLIOGRAPHY'S HOLDINGS

The 'Literature Database' archives academic publications from various disciplines on sexual violence in armed conflicts. The literature collected is concerned with the investigation, account and representation of the causes, the prevalence and the impact of sexual violence in armed conflicts, as well as the question of how sexual violence is dealt with individually and collectively in the aftermath of armed conflict. The collection contains essays from international journals and anthologies, monographs, and selected reports from NGOs and the media. A number of published memoirs from contemporary witnesses and 'grey literature', that is, articles of informal or self-edited periodicals and journals from the various women's movements of the twentieth century have been included as well. The bibliography lists research papers primarily from the fields of history, political science, sociology, anthropology, psychology, criminology, international law, literature, cultural studies, media studies, and interdisciplinary women's and gender studies.

The database represents a selection of literature from the field, published from 1945 to the present day. At the end of 2018, the bibliography roughly listed 2,500 titles, most in English, less in German. While the composition of the collection has developed in keeping with the thematic focal points and interdisciplinary discussions of the SVAC network, it also reflects what are perceived as significant developments in the field.

In researching the literature on sexual violence in armed conflicts, considerable effort is made to identify and account for scientific and feminist knowledge generated outside of the established Western, Anglo-American discourse and perspectives. Particular attention is also paid to the historical development of the academic field and the different origins of debates and ideas in military research, criminology, sociology as well as the feminist analyses and theories that emerged during the Women's Liberation Movement in the USA in the early 1970s.

The selection of works included in the bibliography is limited to publications in English and German, which narrows its scope. Only a limited selection of research published in French, Spanish and Portuguese is translated into English or German, and conversely research in English and German only covers some of the topical fields, especially regarding the landscape of research into wars and armed conflicts in the former European colonies. As such, the selected bibliography's linguistic profile also affects which regional and historical conflicts are covered.

Furthermore, there are studies and contributions available in other languages on topics the database covers fairly comprehensively. Even though the bibliography stores a wide collection of English and German language articles on 'comfort women'—women and girls sexually enslaved for the Japanese army during the Asian Pacific War, for example, these only allow for limited insights on current debates taking place (locally and internationally) in Korea, China, Japan and other Asian countries.

LISA GABRIEL

As a specialised database, the bibliography covers contributions that focus on the connection between sexual violence and armed conflicts. This raises the question of where to draw the line to related subjects—for example, sexual violence in non-war times—and where one field of study intersects with others outside the direct scope of the database. This can be a challenge, as the research on sex work around the military bases of UN peacekeeping forces illustrates. How can we differentiate between the issue of prostitution, human trafficking and sexual violence? To what extent do these phenomena share theoretical and analytical foundations and to what extent are we dealing with separate lines of research and debate? How did the respective discourses evolve historically? Indeed, deciding how to demarcate sexual violence in armed conflicts as a research area requires a continual process of discussion that also determines how the bibliography is compiled and developed.

Incorporating work on the bibliography into the research activities of the SVAC group also promotes exchange among experts and academics with expertise in different geographical and disciplinary areas, ultimately leading to a broader, more comprehensive representation of the existing academic literature in the database. As a result, for example, the literature we store on the history of rape and other forms of sexual violence during the Yugoslav Wars—including the international discussion of the same—is one of the most comprehensive collections in this area today.

USING THE ONLINE DATABASE FOR RESEARCH

As an online source, the database opens up a comprehensive overview of the history of research into and discourse on rape in war and sexual violence in armed conflicts. Along with the conventional research options, such as keyword and author searches, the bibliography's holdings can also be sorted according to specialised lists. The entire database can be sorted with regard to the 'person', 'corporate body', 'year of publication' and 'keyword' categories, which can provide insight into a range of interesting questions, such as: How has the number of annual publications developed over time? What topics are covered more frequently in a certain period of time? What keywords are still missing from the collection, possibly indicating a gap in the research?

The specific historical configurations of the early 1990s are regarded as instrumental in establishing rape in war and sexual violence in armed conflicts as a major topic of international research, law and security policy. The wars in former Yugoslavia and Rwanda were defining conflicts that shaped the understanding and theories developed about wartime sexual violence, and continue to impact ongoing developments in international case law. This does not, however, mean that research and publications were limited to just these conflicts during this time period. The titles listed in the database from that decade cover a much more multifaceted range of topics and regions, leading to questions like: What other historical and current conflicts play a central role in the international literature of the 1990s in expanding sexual violence in armed conflicts as a field of research? What issues were addressed and what problems explored? And how does this compare to research from other years, such as the mid-2000s?

By using the online database's search functions it is furthermore possible to retrace the discursive development of individual lines of inquiry in the field of sexual violence in armed conflicts over time, for example of research into men as victims: How has research and scientific discourse on male victims of sexual violence and rape in the context of militaries and war violence developed over the years? What keywords are listed, what search terms result in hits from the database, and how does this vary for different years of publication? In what contexts does the issue come up, which journals and anthologies cover it, and what conflicts and wars have been studied?

The database does not only provide a basis for new or more comprehensive analysis of a specific topic or a certain period of time, but the search results can also serve as an impetus for developing further research questions. As a whole, the bibliography presents a resource for inquiry into questions about the historical and global development of academic discourse on sexual violence in armed conflicts.

SOME FINAL REMARKS

The development of the database initially responded to the problem that the studies and other publications on this topic were not widely known and often difficult to access. Indeed, this lack of easily accessible information impacted what was (and is) known about the phenomenon of rape and other forms of sexual violence in wars and other armed conflicts, and impacted upon prevalent ideas on how it could be explained and understood, and what additional aspects and questions should be explored. Today, sexual violence in armed conflicts has developed into a broader and more heterogeneous field of research; there is also a better understanding that discourse on sexual violence in armed conflicts comprises a wide range of topics that deal with very different issues. Yet during my many years of research for the bibliography, it grew increasingly clear that some ideas and lines of debates were forgotten or generally ignored as the existing literature and knowledge were passed down. I repeatedly encountered sources and publications from very different years and origins that questioned the prevalent ideas about the current state of knowledge and its history.

This observation becomes clear, for example, when you consider how little research since the 1990s has taken up the history of ideas and literature on sexual violence and racism and integrated it into attempts to explain sexual violence in armed conflict. Yet writings of African-American authors were clearly seminal in the development of a theory of rape, dominance and war by feminist authors in the USA in the early 1970s.

The following intervention from the US-American discussions of the early 1980s is regaining topicality in view of the pending reflection of our body of knowledge on sexual violence in armed conflicts, and the repeatedly expressed intention to take a more differentiated approach to re-evaluating the history of feminist ideas of sexuality and violence. Referring to essays, reports and literary writings of African-American authors who explored the link between sexual violence and racism toward the end of the nineteenth century—Anna Julia Cooper, Ida B. Wells and Pauline Hopkins—Hazel Carby (1985) commented on the notoriously *white* perspective in the writing of the history of feminist ideas:

> Their analyses are dynamic and not limited to a parochial understanding of 'women's issues'; they have firmly established the dialectical relation between economic/political power and economic/sexual power in the battle for control of women's bodies. [...] As DuBois and Gordon have argued so cogently, we have "150 years of feminist theory and practice in the area of sexuality. This is a resource too precious to squander by not learning it, in all its complexity." But let us learn all of it, not only in its complexity but also its difference. (Carby 1985)[3]

Currently hundreds of scientific publications on rape and sexual violence in armed conflicts appear every year from a wide range of disciplines, making it nearly impossible to keep track of developments in this extensive landscape of research. At the same time, parts of the academic debate are revisiting very basic questions, stimulating a revision of the hitherto existing findings and theories. The unique configuration of the selected bibliography can serve as a helpful research tool here.

The 'Literature Database www.warandgender.net: An Ongoing Project' is the result of cooperation between Lisa Gabriel, Regina Mühlhäuser and Gaby Zipfel (Working Group "War and Gender" at the Hamburg Foundation for the Advancement of Research and Culture) and Gudrun Döllner, Christoph Fuchs and Ingwer Schwensen (Library of the Hamburg Institute for Social Research). The establishment and continuous update of the collection is kindly supported by the Hamburg Foundation for the Advancement of Research and Culture.

Translated from German by Sarah Smithson-Compton.

NOTES

1. *Women's Bodies as Battlefields—Sexual Violence against Women in Wartime*. International Conference, organised by Regina Mühlhäuser, Gudrun Schwarz and Gaby Zipfel, Working Group 'War and Gender', Hamburg Institute for Social Research, 7–9 June 2001.
2. For more details compare the objectives of the annual SVAC workshops http://warandgender.net/workshops/.
3. Citing Dubois/Gordon 1984. See also Higginbotham 1992.

REFERENCES

Carby, Hazel V. 1985. '"On the Threshold of Woman's Era": Lynching, Empire, and Sexuality in Black Feminist Theory', *Critical Inquiry*, 12(1):276–7.

Dubois, Ellen Carol/Gordon, Linda. 1984. 'Seeking Ecstasy on the Battlefield: Danger and Pleasure in Nineteenth-Century Feminist Sexual Thought', in Carole S. Vance (ed). *Pleasure and Danger: Exploring Female Sexuality*, pp. 31–49. Boston: Routledge.

Higginbotham, Evelyn Brooks. 1992. 'African-American Women's History and the Metalanguage of Race', *Signs: Journal of Women in Culture and Society*, 17(2):251–74.

Schwensen, Ingwer. 2009. 'Sexuelle Gewalt in kriegerischen Konflikten: Auswahlbibliographie für die Erscheinungsjahre 2002 bis 2008', *Mittelweg 36*, 18(1):67–90.

Schwensen, Ingwer/Mühlhäuser, Regina. 2001. 'Sexuelle Gewalt in Kriegen: Auswahlbibliographie', *Mittelweg 36*, 10(5):21–32.

Notes on Contributors

Aaron Belkin is a Professor in the Department of Political Science at San Francisco State University and Director of the Palm Center, California, USA. He designed and implemented much of the public education campaign that eroded popular support for LGBT discrimination in the American military, and summarised the lessons he learned about successful advocacy in 'How We Won: Progressive Lessons from the Repeal of "Don't Ask, Don't Tell"' (2011). Aaron is a co-founding editor of *Critical Military Studies* and he has written and edited more than thirty scholarly articles, chapters and books, among them 'Spam filter: gay rights and the normalisation of male-male rape in the US Military', in *Radical History Review* (2008). The conversation 'Militarized Masculinities and the Erasure of Violence' between Aaron and Terrell Carver was published in the *International Feminist Journal for Politics* (2012). In his book *Bring Me Men: Military Masculinity and the Benign Facade of American Empire, 1898–2001* (2012), Aaron explores the contradictory messages connected to military masculinity.

Debra Bergoffen is Professor Emerita of Philosophy at the George Mason University in Washington DC, USA, and a Bishop Hamilton Lecturer in Philosophy at the American University. Debra has published extensively in the area of continental and feminist theory. In addition to numerous articles in journals and anthologies, she is the author of *Contesting the Politics of Genocidal Rape: Affirming the Dignity of the Vulnerable Body* (2011) and *The Philosophy of Simone de Beauvoir: Gendered Phenomenologies, Erotic Generosities* (1996). She is the co-editor (with Paula Ruth Gilbert, Tamara Harvey and Connie L. Mc Neely) of *Confronting Global Gender Justice: Women's Lives, Human Rights* (2010) and co-editor (with

Gail Weiss) of *The Ethics of Embodiment: A special issue of Hypatia* (2011). Her essay '(Un)Gendering Vulnerability: Re-scripting the Meaning of Male-Male Rape' has been published in the *Canadian Journal of Continental Philosophy* (2014). In 'Antigone after Auschwitz' (2015), she reads Antigone in the context of the genocides of the twentieth and twenty-first centuries.

Pascale R. Bos is an Associate Professor in the Department of Germanic Studies at the University of Texas at Austin, USA. She is also associated with the Women's and Gender Studies, Comparative Literature, the European Studies Programs and the Schusterman Center for Jewish Studies. Pascale holds a PhD in Comparative Literature, and her research interests include twentieth century comparative Western European and US literature, gender studies, memory studies, and the history, culture and literature of the Holocaust. Her book explores *German-Jewish Literature in the Wake of the Holocaust: Grete Weil, Ruth Klüger, and the Politics of Address* (2005). Pascale has published 'Feminists Interpreting the Politics of Wartime Rape: Berlin 1945, Yugoslavia 1992–1993' in *Signs* (2006) and a first part of her ongoing work on 'Imagining and Imagined Sexual Violence against Jewish Women during the Holocaust' in *Lessons and Legacies XI* (2014). Her article on 'Sexual Violence in Ka-Tzetnik's House of Dolls' appeared in *Holocaust History and the Readings of Ka-Tzetnik* (2018).

Joanna Bourke is a Professor of History in the Department of History, Classics and Archaeology at Birkbeck College, University of London, UK, where she has taught since 1992. She is a Fellow of the British Academy. Over the years, her books have ranged from the social and economic history of Ireland in the late nineteenth and early twentieth centuries, to social histories of the British working classes between 1860 and 1960, to cultural histories of military conflict between the Anglo-Boer war and the present. She has worked on the history of emotions, particularly fear and hatred, and the history of sexual violence. Her book *Rape: A History from 1860s to the Present* (2007) has been translated into Italian, Spanish, Czech, Russian, and Greek. Other relevant works include *The Story of Pain* (2017); 'Wartime Rape: The Politics of Making Visible' in *Liberal Democracies at War* (2013); 'The Threshold of the Human: Sexual Violence and Terror in the "War on Terror"' in *The Oxford Amnesty Lectures* (2009); *Fear: A Cultural History* (2005) and *An Intimate History of Killing: Face-to-Face Killing in the Twentieth Century* (1999).

Kirsten Campbell is a Reader in the Department of Sociology at Goldsmiths College, University of London, UK, where she teaches sociology of law and social theory. She is also a member of the Research Unit for Global Justice, and the principal investigator of 'The Gender of Justice' project which examines the prosecution of sexual violence in armed conflict under international criminal law, focusing upon the International Criminal Tribunal for the former Yugoslavia. Kirsten has published extensively in this area, including articles in the *Leiden Journal of International Law, Journal of International Humanitarian Studies, The International Journal of Transitional Justice, Social and Legal Studies, Signs,* and *The Journal of Human Rights.* Kirsten's research builds upon a number of funded empirical projects, including the ESRC project 'The Legal Regulation of Armed Conflict', and her international collaborative work on transitional justice mechanisms and the legal shaping of memory.

Nwarasungu Chiwengo is an Associate Professor, Department of English Studies, University of Creighton, USA, and a Member of Faculty at the University of Lubumbashi, DRC. She teaches courses at Creighton in World Literature and African Literature, and is the faculty moderator of the 'African Students Association' and the faculty coordinator of Creighton's Black Studies Program. She is author of the book *Understanding 'Cry, the Beloved Country': A Student Casebook to Issues, Sources, and Historical Documents* (2007). Much of Nwarasungu's work deals with questions of narratives of violence, trauma, and embodiment, mainly in the context of the Democratic Republic of Congo. Her articles in English include 'When Wounds and Corpses Fail to Speak: Narratives of Violence and Rape in Congo (DRC)', which was published in *Comparative Studies of South Asia, Africa and the Middle East* (2008) as well as 'Making Visible and Eradicating Congo's History of Violence: Maiming the Female/National Body', which appeared in the volume *Violence in/and the Great Lakes. The Thought of V. Y. Mudimbe and Beyond* (2014).

Louise du Toit is a Professor in the Department of Philosophy at the University of Stellenbosch near Cape Town in South Africa. She is a rated researcher under the scheme of the National Research Foundation of South Africa and receives regular funding from that body. Louise is a board member of the International Association of Women Philosophers and was guest editor for a special edition of the *Philosophical Papers* on 'The Meaning/s of Rape' (2009). She has written on sexual violence from various perspectives, including philosophy of law, post-colonial studies, feminist philosophy of religion, and theories of meaning and the body. Louise is the author of *A Philosophical Investigation of Rape: The Making and Unmaking of the Feminine Self* (2009); 'The Equivalent Valuation of Sexual Specificities: The Parchment for Inscribing Gender Justice to Come' in *Tijdschrift voor Filosofie 77* (2015); 'Shifting Meanings of Postconflict Sexual Violence in South Africa' in *Signs* (2014); 'From Consent to Coercive Circumstances: Rape Law Reform on Trial' in *South African Journal on Human Rights* (2012) and 'Feminism and the Ethics of Reconciliation' in *Eurozine*, 16 March 2007.

Lisa Gabriel is a Researcher for the Working Group 'War and Gender' at the Hamburg Foundation for the Advancement for Research and Culture in Germany. She received her MA in Sociology, Military Studies and National Economics in 2010 at the Department of Sociology, University of Potsdam. In her MA thesis 'Gewalt und sexuelle Differenz: Zur Struktur der Debatte Allgemeiner Soziologie und Feministischer Kritik' she investigated theoretical concepts of violence in New German Sociological Thought as well as the intersection of the categories of gender and violence in Military Studies. As a member of a Research Group on the Former Nazi Concentration Camp for Girls and Young

Women, Uckermark, Lisa has studied the conditions that frame the commemoration of sexualised prosecution and sexualised violence in World War II. Her article 'Über die Bedingungen des Sprechens vom Überleben und das Zuhören' was published in *Unwegsames Gelände* (2013). Until 2016, Lisa worked at the open youth-center 'Manege' in Berlin. She freelances at 'Cultures', where she is a trainer for violence prevention and political education.

Júlia Garraio is a Researcher at the Center for Social Studies at the University of Coimbra in Portugal. Currently she is working on the FEDER-funded project 'Deconstructing Risk and Otherness: hegemonic scripts and counter-narratives on migrants/refugees and "internal Others" in Portuguese and European mediascapes'. Julia is a specialist in German literature and has analysed literary and cinematographic representations of the rape of German women in World War II. She has published extensively in this field, including 'Den Erinnerungsort "Deutsche vergewaltigte Frau" umformulieren' in *Literarisierungen der Gewalt* (2018); and 'Vergewaltigung als Schlüsselbegriff einer misslungenen Vergangenheitsbewältigung' in *Mittelweg 36* (2010). Her English publications include '"The Western Way is the German Way"' in *Filologia, Memória e Esquecimento* (2010); '"Arresting Gaddafi will be the most effective way to stop these rapes": Sexual Violence in the Western Media's Coverage of the War in Libya' in *E-cadernos* (2012) and 'Porn, Rape, and the Fall of the Third Reich: On Thor Kunkel's Novel "Endstufe"' in *Plots of War* (2012).

Atina Grossman is a Professor of History at Cooper Union in New York City, USA. She teaches Modern European and German History, Women's and Gender Studies. She has held fellowships from the National Endowment for the Humanities, German Marshall Fund, American Council of Learned Societies, Institute for Advanced Study in Princeton, and the American Academy in Berlin as well as Guest Professorships at the Humboldt University Berlin and the Friedrich Schiller University in Jena. Atina has published extensively on women's and Jewish history in Germany, with a special focus on questions of the politics of gender and sexuality in German society throughout the Weimar Republic and World War II as well as on issues of the memorialisation of post-World War II sexual violence in the German women's movement. Most of her work has been translated into German. Atina is author of *Jews, Germans, and Allies: Close Encounters in Occupied Germany* (2007) and *Reforming Sex: The German Movement for Birth Control and Abortion Reform, 1920–1950* (1995). Her numerous articles include: 'A Question of Silence: The Rape of German Women by Occupation Soldiers' in *October* (1995).

Renée Heberle is a Professor in the Department of Political Science and Public Administration at the University of Toledo, Ohio, USA. She serves as co-director of the MA Program in Law and Social Thought and as the Interim Director of the School for Interdisciplinary Studies. Situated in the fields of critical and feminist theory, Renée works on issues of political violence, sexual violence, prisons and the politics of incarceration. She coordinates the 'Inside/Out Prison Exchange' project and activities related to prison education. Renée published extensively on the subject of theorising sexual violence. Her first article 'Deconstructive Strategies and the Movement Against Sexual Violence', published in *Hypatia: A Journal of Feminist Philosophy* (1996), has been reprinted several times. Other works include the edited volume *Theorising Sexual Violence: Subjectivity and Politics in Late Modernity* (with Victoria Grace, 2009) and her chapter 'Sexual Violence' in *The Oxford Handbook of Gender, Sex, and Crime* (2014).

Elissa Mailänder is an Associate Professor at the Department of History at Sciences Po Paris, France. She earned her PhD at the École des Hautes Études en Sciences Sociales (EHESS) in France and the University of Erfurt in Germany in 2007. Her teaching and research focus on the everyday and gender history of Nazism, as well as violence and sexuality. Her book *Gewalt im Dienstalltag* (2009) was translated into English in 2015 (*Workday Violence: Female Guards at Lublin-Majdanek, 1942–1944*). Elissa has published extensively on the history of Nazi perpetrators and the structures, mechanisms and dynamics of violence in German concentration and extermination camps. Her publications include 'Making Sense of a Rape Photograph: Sexual Violence as Social Performance on the Eastern Front, 1939–1944' in: *Journal of the History of Sexuality* (2017); 'Meshes of Power: The Concentration Camp as Pulp or Art House in Liliana Cavani's The Night Porter' in *Nazisploitation* (2012) and 'Everyday life in Nazi Germany. A Forum' in *German History* (2009).

Rashida Manjoo is a Professor in the Department of Public Law at the University of Cape Town, South Africa, as well as a co-convener of the Human Rights Program of the Law Faculty. She is also the former United Nations Special Rapporteur on Violence against Women. Her research interests include human rights broadly with a particular focus on women's human rights. She has authored a number of journal articles, book chapters and reports on women's human rights, violence against women, transitional justice, and also the impact for women of the recognition of Muslim Personal Laws in South Africa. Her publications include *Women's Charters and Declarations: Building Another World* (2014); 'State Responsibility to Act with Due Diligence in the Elimination of Violence Against Women' in *International Human Rights Law Review* (2013); and 'Sexual Violence and the Law: Comparative Legislative Experiences in Selected Southern African Countries' in *Criminal Law Reform and Transitional Justice: Human Rights Perspectives for Sudan* (2011). Rashida's article 'Violence against Women as a Barrier to the Realisation of Human Rights', published in *Feminist Review* (2016), explores the impact of gender discrimination on the status of women and their access to human rights mechanisms.

Gabriela Mischkowski studied history and philosophy. In 1992, she was a co-founder of the women's rights and aid organisation medica mondiale in Cologne, Germany, and since then she is engaged in researching, combatting and prosecuting sexual violence in armed conflict. Since 1998, Gabriela freelances as medica mondiale's Program Advisor on Gender Justice and thus became a member of the 'Women's Caucus for Gender

Justice', an international feminist group of experts that took part in the negotiations for the International Criminal Court. Gabriela participated in several international fact-finding missions on sexual violence during armed conflicts in Gujarat/India, Aceh/ Indonesia and Northern Uganda. She is co-author of the study 'The Trouble with Rape Trials—Views of Witnesses, Prosecutors and Judges on Prosecuting Sexualised Violence during the War of Bosnia and Herzegovina' (with Gorana Mlinarević, 2009) and published numerous articles on questions of victim advocacy and social and legal response to wartime rape, among them 'Die andere Sicht "zur Sache": Elvire aus Süd-Kivu und das deutsche Völkerstrafgesetzbuch' in *Völkerstrafrechtspolitik: Praxis des Völkerstrafrechts* (2014).

Gorana Mlinarević is a Researcher in 'The Gender of Justice'- project which examines the prosecution of sexual violence in armed conflict under international criminal law, focusing upon the International Criminal Tribunal for the former Yugoslavia. She is also a feminist activist and researcher on post-war issues and experiences affecting women, primarily in Bosnia and Herzegovina and the region of the former Yugoslavia. She teaches in the areas of gender and transitional justice, feminist critique of nationalism and the Balkans in the Gender Studies Program at the Centre for Interdisciplinary Postgraduate Studies, University of Sarajevo. Gorana's interdisciplinary research explores intersections and tensions between identity politics and economic and social realities of the post-war societies and societies in so called transitions. She co-authored the study 'The Trouble with Rape Trial—Views of Witnesses, Prosecutors and Judges on Prosecuting Sexualised Violence during the War of Bosnia and Herzegovina' (with Gabriela Mischkowski, 2009). Her contribution 'Women's Movements and Gender Studies in Bosnia and Herzegovina' appeared in *Aspasia 5* (2011).

Regina Mühlhäuser is a Senior Researcher at the Hamburg Foundation for the Advancement of Research and Culture and an Associate Researcher at the Hamburg Institute for Social Research in Germany. She is a co-coordinator of the Working Group 'War and Gender' and a co-founder of the International Research Group 'Sexual Violence in Armed Conflict' (SVAC). Regina has worked at the concentration camp memorial sites in Neuengamme and Ravensbrück, and specialises in twentieth century history, in particular National Socialism and the Holocaust. Regina has published extensively in the field. Her book *Eroberungen* (2010) explores sexual violence and intimate encounters of German soldiers during the war in the Soviet Union, 1941–1945. It has been translated into Japanese (2015) and is forthcoming in English (2020). Regina has conducted field work in Korea, interviewing survivors of Japanese military sexual slavery. In her current project, she compares sexual violence by German, Japanese and Allied Forces during World War II. Her article on 'Sexual Violence and the Holocaust' appeared in the *Handbook Gender: War* (2017).

Ruth Seifert is a Professor in the Department of Applied Social and Health Care at the Technical University of Applied Sciences in Regensburg, Germany. Her research focuses on gender and the military, sexual violence in armed conflict, as well as social work in the context of armed conflict. As the head of the department's international office, Ruth organises student—as well as research exchange programmes, in collaboration with the Department of Social Work, University of Prishtina, Kosova. Ruth's publications in English include 'The Second Front: The Logic of Sexual Violence in Wars' in *Women's Studies International Forum* (1996); 'The Female Body as a Symbol and Sign: Gender-specific violence and the cultural construction of war' in *War or Health? A Reader* (2002); 'Sexual Violence in Armed Conflicts: A Debate Revisited' in *Reader on Gender* (2015) and two chapters on 'Causes' and 'Expertise', which are published in the *Handbook Teaching on Sexual Violence in Armed Conflicts* (2016).

Patricia Viseur Sellers is an International Criminal Attorney and the Special Advisor for Gender to the Office of the Prosecutor of the International Criminal Court. She is also a Visiting Fellow at Kellogg College of Oxford University and a Practicing Professor at the London School of Economics and Political Science. Patricia has served as a Legal Advisor and a Trial Attorney at the International Criminal Tribunals for the Former Yugoslavia and Rwanda. She has also been a Special Legal Consultant to UN Women, the Gender and Women's Rights Division of the United Nations High Commissioner for Human Rights, and the UN Secretary-General's Special Representative to Children in Armed Conflict. At the International Women's Tribunal Against Military Sexual Slavery by Japan in December 2000 in Tokyo, Patricia participated as Chief Co-Prosecutor. She has published numerous articles on gender and sexual violence in international criminal law. Her recent contributions include: 'Rape and Sexual Violence', in *A New Commentary to the Geneva Conventions* (2015); and '(Re)Considering the Gender Jurisprudence' in *The Oxford Handbook of Gender and Armed Conflict* (2018).

Atreyee Sen is an Associate Professor in the Department of Anthropology at the University of Copenhagen in Denmark. She is an urban anthropologist of violence and conflict, with a regional focus on South Asia. Between 2004 and 2015, Atreyee held senior academic positions at the University of Sussex and the University of Manchester in the UK. Her interdisciplinary research interests focus on the historical trajectories of religio-political conflict and how the latter generate sub-cultures of violence among marginalised urban communities. Atreyee has published the monograph *Shiv Sena Women: Violence and Communalism in a Bombay Slum* (2007) as well as several other articles on criminalised women who affiliate themselves with an extremist political movement. Another part of her research centres around the phenomenon of urban male child soldiering in Hyderabad, about which she has written in *Ethnography* and the *Journal of South Asian Studies*. Currently, Atreyee conducts research amongst city-based networks of former Indian Maoist guerrillas, investigating their journeys from empowerment (as politically motivated guerrillas) to victimhood (capture, torture, beatings, prison rapes).

Yuki Tanaka is a Research Professor of History, Emeritus at the Hiroshima Peace Institute, Hiroshima City University, Japan. In 2008, he was a visiting professor at Birkbeck College, London University, UK, and the Sir Ninian Stephen Visiting Scholar at the Law School, Melbourne University, Australia. Yuki specialises in the history of Japanese war crimes during World War II as well as the aerial bombing of Japanese cities conducted by the US. His publications include *Japan's Comfort Women: Sexual Slavery and Prostitution During World War II and the US Occupation* (2002); *Hidden Horrors: Japanese War Crimes in World War II* (1996); and the co-edited collection *Beyond Victor's Justice? The Tokyo War Crimes Trial Revisited* (with Tim McCormack and Gerry Simpson, 2011). In 2016, he published the second edition of Maria Rosa Henson's memoir *Comfort Women: A Filipina's Story of Prostitution and Slavery under the Japanese Military*, which includes his introductory article on the politics of denial by the Japanese government.

Meredeth Turshen is a Professor in the Edward J. Bloustein School of Planning and Public Policy at Rutgers University, New Jersey, USA. She has served on the boards of the Association of Concerned Africa Scholars, the Committee for Health in Southern Africa, and the *Review of African Political Economy*, and is on the editorial board of the *Journal of Public Health Policy*. Meredeth's research interests include international health and she specialises in public health policy. She has written *Gender and the Political Economy of Conflict in Africa: The Persistence of Violence* (2016), *Women's Health Movements: A Global Force for Change* (2007), and edited *Women and Health in Africa* (1991), *What Women Do in Wartime: Gender and Conflict in Africa* (1998) and *The Aftermath: Women in Postconflict Transformation* (2002). Meredeth has also written numerous articles on the political economy of gender, conflict, and sexual violence, including 'The Political Economy of Rape: An analysis of systematic rape and sexual abuse of women during armed conflict in Africa' in *Victims, Perpetrators or Actors? Gender, Armed Conflict, and Political Violence* (2005); and 'The Political Economy of War: What Women Need to Know' in *Sexual Violence in Conflict and Post-Conflict Societies: International Agendas and African Contexts* (2014).

Fabrice Virgili is the Research Director of the joint research unit Identity, International Relations, and European Civilizations at the National Center for Scientific Research at Paris I University, Panthéon-Sorbonne, in France. His research interests include sexual identity and war in the twentieth century; borders, confrontations, and intimacy; the children of Franco-German couples during World War II as well as war, violence and society. Fabrice has co-organised the exhibition 'Amours, guerres et sexualité 1914–1945' (with François Rouquet and Danièle Voldman), which opened in Paris 2007, and the conference 'Rape in Wartime: A History to Be Written' in 2009 (with Raphaëlle Branche, which was published in French in 2011 and in English in 2013). He published several books on gender and violence in the twentieth century, among them *La France "virile": Des femmes tondues à la Libération* (2000), which was translated into English (*Shorn Women: Gender and Punishment in Liberation France*, 2003) and *Naître ennemi: Les enfants nés de couplecolor: franco-allemands pendant la Seconde Guerre mondiale* (2009).

Hyunah Yang is a Professor at the School of Law at Seoul National University, South-Korea, where she teaches feminist jurisprudence and sociology of law. She is currently serving as a Commissioner at the National Human Rights Commission of Korea, and she was a President of the Korean Academic Association of Gender and Law (2008–2010). During the Women's International War Crimes Tribunal against Military Sexual Slavery by Japan, which was conducted in 2000 in Tokyo, Hyunah was one of the country prosecutors of the North and South Korea Joint prosecution team and represented survivors' testimonies. Her research and teaching interests have been various in social theory, feminist jurisprudence, human rights, postcolonialism, and representing victim's voices, in particular in the context of war, colonialism, and public atrocities. Her publications in English include 'Justice Yet to Come: the Korea-Japan Foreign Ministers' Agreement of 2015 Regarding the Japanese Military Sexual Slavery' in *L'Homme* (2017); 'Revisiting the Issue of Korean "Military Comfort Women": The Question of Truth and Positionality' in *positions: asia critique* (1997); and 'Remembering the Korean Military Comfort Women: Nationalism,

Sexuality, and Silencing' in *Dangerous Women: Gender and Korean Nationalism* (1998).

Dubravka Žarkov is an Associate Professor of Gender, Conflict and Development at the International Institute of Social Studies, Erasmus University of Rotterdam, Netherlands. Dubravka teaches on feminist epistemologies, conflict theories and media representations of war and violence. She is a co-editor of the *European Journal of Women's Studies*. Her main fields of research are gender, sexuality and ethnicity in the context of war and violence and their media representations, with specific focus on masculinities and sexual violence against men. She published widely on those issues, including *The Body of War: Media, Ethnicity and Gender in the Break-up of Yugoslavia* (2007) as well as the co-edited collections *Conflict, Peace, Security and Development* (with Helen Hintjens, 2015); *Gender, Conflict, Development* (2008) about the global dimensions of contemporary wars and *The Postwar Moment: Militaries, Masculinities and International Peacekeeping* (with Cynthia Cockburn, 2002). In 'The Body of the Other Man: Sexual Violence and the Construction of Masculinity, Sexuality and Ethnicity in Croatian Media', published in *Victims, Perpetrators or Actors?* (2001), Dubravka explored the visibility/invisibility of sexual violence against men.

Gaby Zipfel is a Senior Researcher at the Hamburg Foundation for the Advancement of Research and Culture and an Associate Researcher at the Hamburg Institute for Social Research in Germany. She is a co-coordinator of the Working Group 'War and Gender' and a co-founder of the International Research Group 'Sexual Violence in Armed Conflict' (SVAC). Between 1992 and 2012 Gaby was an editor of the Institute's magazine *Mittelweg 36*. She is also a member of the Editorial Board of *Eurozine*. Gaby's publications include 'Liberté, Egalité, Sexualité' in *Mittelweg 36* (2018); 'Sexuelle Gewalt–eine Einführung' in *L'Homme* (2016); '"Beyond good and evil for once!" Authorised transgressions and women in wartime' in *Eurozine* (2014); '"Let us have a little fun": the relationship between gender, violence and sexuality in armed conflict situations' in *Revista Crítica de Ciências Sociais—Annual Review* (2013); '"Wir werden fein den Mund halten müssen..." Anmerkungen zur Wirkungsmacht des Beschweigens', in *Mittelweg 36* (2010); 'Ausnahmezustand Krieg? Anmerkungen zu soldatischer Männlichkeit, sexueller Gewalt und militärischer Einhegung' in *Krieg und Geschlecht* (2008) and 'Blood, sperm and tears: Sexuelle Gewalt in Kriegen' in *Mittelweg 36* (2001).